M000296720

MUSEUMS WITHOUT BORDERS

Drawing together nearly 40 years of experience, *Museums without Borders* presents the key works of one of the most respected practitioners and scholars in the field. Through these selected writings, Robert R. Janes demonstrates that museums have a broader role to play in society than is conventionally assumed. He approaches the fundamental questions of why museums exist and what they mean in terms of identity, community, and the future of civil life.

This book consists of four parts: Indigenous Peoples; Managing Change; Social Responsibility; and Activism and Ethics. Ordered chronologically, each begins with an introduction which situates the ensuing papers in their historical and cultural contexts. Using an interdisciplinary approach that combines anthropology, ethnography, museum studies, and management theory, Janes both questions and supports mainstream museum practice in a constructive and self-reflective manner, offering readers alternative viewpoints on important issues.

Considering concepts not generally recognized in museum practice, such as the Roman leadership model of *primus inter pares* and the Buddhist concept of mindfulness, Janes argues that the global museum community must examine how they can meet the needs of the planet and its inhabitants. *Museums without Borders* charts the evolving role of the contemporary museum in the face of environmental, societal and ethical challenges, and explores issues that have, and will, continue to shape the museum sector for decades to come.

Robert R. Janes is currently an independent scholar who has worked in and around museums for 39 years as an executive, consultant, editor, author, board member, archaeologist, instructor, volunteer, and philanthropist. He lives in Canmore, Alberta, Canada.

PRAISE FOR THIS BOOK

"Janes is an unafraid original who writes organically from deep in his ethical soul. He energizes us to create museums in their purest, most consequential form, so that they will contribute to the survival of the planet. After reading this book, his urgency will become yours."

Elaine Heumann Gurian, *The Museum Group, USA*

"This compilation alerts the museum sector to new horizons in its collective conscience. With the blurring of traditional boundaries and the rise of a 'glocal' mindset, innovative attention to pressing societal and environmental challenges has become vital. Here, Janes draws on four decades as a scholar-practitioner to deliver a wake-up call for our sector to unleash its toolkit as a force for good in the Anthropocene."

Emlyn Koster, *Director, North Carolina Museum of Natural Sciences, USA*

"Janes' stock-in-trade in his long and varied museum career has been upending the field's sacred cows and entrenched practices with that rare combination of persistence, rigor, courage and elegance. This collection of his writings over his many years as a scholar-practitioner show the evolution of his own journey and provides an ethical framework that guides those who aspire to take positive action in the world."

Marjorie Schwarzer, *University of San Francisco, USA*

MUSEUMS WITHOUT BORDERS

Selected writings of Robert R. Janes

Robert R. Janes

Routledge
Taylor & Francis Group

LONDON AND NEW YORK

First published 2016
by Routledge
2 Park Square, Milton Park, Abingdon, Oxon OX14 4RN

and by Routledge
711 Third Avenue, New York, NY 10017

Routledge is an imprint of the Taylor & Francis Group, an informa business

© 2016 Robert R. Janes

The right of Robert R. Janes to be identified as author of this work
has been asserted by him in accordance with sections 77 and 78 of the
Copyright, Designs and Patents Act 1988.

All rights reserved. No part of this book may be reprinted or reproduced
or utilised in any form or by any electronic, mechanical, or other
means, now known or hereafter invented, including photocopying and
recording, or in any information storage or retrieval system, without
permission in writing from the publishers.

Trademark notice: Product or corporate names may be trademarks or
registered trademarks, and are used only for identification and explanation
without intent to infringe.

British Library Cataloguing-in-Publication Data
A catalogue record for this book is available from the British Library

Library of Congress Cataloging-in-Publication Data
Names: Janes, Robert R., 1948–
Title: Museums without borders : selected writings of Robert R. Janes /
    Robert R. Janes.
Description: Milton Park, Abingdon, Oxon : Routledge, 2016. |
    Includes bibliographical references and index.
Identifiers: LCCN 2015021325| ISBN 9781138906365 (hardback :
    alkaline paper) | ISBN 9781138906372 (paperback : alkaline paper)
    | ISBN 9781315695532 (e-book)
Subjects: LCSH: Museums—Social aspects. | Museums—Political
    aspects. | Museums—Moral and ethical aspects. | Museums—
    Canada. | Indians of North America—Museums. | Social change.
Classification: LCC AM7 .J365 2016 | DDC 069—dc23
LC record available at http://lccn.loc.gov/2015021325

ISBN: 978-1-138-90636-5 (hbk)
ISBN: 978-1-138-90637-2 (pbk)
ISBN: 978-1-315-69553-2 (ebk)

Typeset in Bembo Std
by Swales & Willis Ltd, Exeter, Devon, UK

Printed and bound in the United States of America by
Edwards Brothers Malloy on sustainably sourced paper

To our ancestors, descendants, and the more-than-human world –
with the hope and intention that we will not fail you.

A museum, then, must be an argument with its society. And more than that, it must be a timely argument. A good museum always will direct attention to what is difficult and even painful to contemplate. Therefore, those who strive to create such museums must proceed without assurances that what they do will be appreciated.

Neil Postman
"Museum as Dialogue" Museum News, (69), 5, September/October, 1990, p. 58

So what difference did it make that your museum was there? So what would have been the difference had it not been?

Stephen E. Weil
"Creampuffs and Hardball: Are You Really Worth the Cost?"
Museum News, *September/October, 1994, p. 43*

Sentiment without action is the ruin of the soul.

Edward Abbey
A Voice Crying in the Wilderness: Notes from a Secret Journal
(Vox Clamantis in Deserto) *(1989). New York: St. Martin's Press, p. 40*

CONTENTS

List of figures   *x*
Foreword by Richard Sandell   *xi*
Acknowledgements   *xiv*
Permissions   *xvi*

Introduction   1

PART 1
Other voices: Indigenous peoples   **15**

Introduction   17

1 Northern museum development: a view from the North   21

2 Museum ideology and practice in Canada's third world   29

3 First Nations: policy and practice at the Glenbow Museum   40

4 Personal, academic and institutional perspectives on museums
   and First Nations   48

5 Issues of repatriation: a Canadian view (with the late
   Gerald T. Conaty)   57

PART 2
Creative destruction: managing change   **73**

   Introduction   75

  6 Sober reflections: an undisguised view of change at Glenbow   80

  7 Beyond strategic planning: the Glenbow example   93

  8 Don't lose your nerve: museums and organizational change   105

  9 Museums and change: some thoughts on creativity,
     destruction and self-organization   124

10 Complexity and creativity in contemporary museum
     management (with Richard Sandell)   134

11 The mindful museum   149

12 Museum management revisited   162

PART 3
Museums without borders: social responsibility   **185**

   Introduction   187

13 What will communities need and want from museums
     in the future?   191

14 Exploring stewardship   198

15 Introduction to *Looking Reality in the Eye: Museums and
     Social Responsibility* (with the late Gerald T. Conaty)   210

16 Museums, corporatism and the civil society   222

17 Museums: stewards or spectators?   241

18 What are museums for? Revisiting *Museums in a
     Troubled World* (with Morten Karnøe Søndergaard)   255

PART 4
Dangerous times: activism and ethics   **271**

   Introduction   273

19 Experimenting with leadership: *primus inter pares*   278

20 Persistent paradoxes – 1997 and 2012   283

21 Debunking the marketplace   310

22 Museums and the new reality   339

23 Museum management and the ethical imperative   347

24 Museums in a dangerous time   375

    Epilogue   387

Bibliography of Robert R. Janes   *394*
Index   *401*

FIGURES

1 Map of the Northwest Territories, Canada 22
2 The Prince of Wales Northern Heritage Centre, Yellowknife,
  Northwest Territories, Canada 31
3 The author working with Dene elders 50
4 The challenge of organizational change 77
5 "What if we don't change at all . . . and something magical
  just happens?" 96
6 A prehistoric stone tool and a computer mouse 146
7 Liberate Tate stages a protest at Tate Britain (2011) 188
8 Robert R. Janes Award for Social Responsibility 251
9 Asian megacities are at risk from climate change 274
10 The Voltaire poster 344
11 The four scenarios 348
12 A polar bear jumps between ice floes 377
13 The Phipps Conservatory and Botanical Garden (Pittsburgh, US) 388
14 The Natural History Museum's mobile museum 390

FOREWORD

Richard Sandell[1]

It was during the late 1990s, carrying out research for a course I was to deliver on museum management at the University of Leicester, that I first came across Robert Janes' work. Over the two decades since that first encounter, Bob (as I have come to know him) – through his books, articles and talks; through opportunities to exchange ideas and to collaborate – has exerted a considerable influence on my own thinking, research and practice. The ideas expressed within his writings, whilst firmly rooted in the particularities of his Canadian experience, have proved to have a remarkably universal appeal – perhaps more so than those of any other writer on museums that I know – and to resonate with my students from all over the world, whatever their professional, cultural, political or disciplinary background. As result of this capacity to engage and challenge, Bob has become a familiar protagonist in innumerable lively classroom debates in Leicester and beyond around the unique role that museums can play in contemporary society.

Given the prominent position that his scholarly output has occupied in much of my professional life, I must admit that I approached this collection of selected writings with the expectation that I would be largely revisiting the familiar. It has been both surprising and rewarding, therefore, to find myself challenged in new ways by *Museums without Borders*, partly by encountering new (previously unpublished) material but, more significantly, by the opportunities afforded by reading across (and drawing out connections within) a remarkably varied body of work that spans nearly four decades.

Despite the variation in theme and content – and the different times in which these arguments were developed – the writings share a quality that makes the reader very aware that they originate from the same mind. This quality stems in part from the author's distinctive writing style (more on this in a moment) but more fundamentally, I would argue, from the influence of an enduring set of values that have undoubtedly shaped a very particular understanding of the museum.

Throughout the writings included here, the values which Bob holds dear – and evidently include a deeply felt concern for the natural world, a profound respect for cultural diversity and an almost intuitive belief in fairness and justice – are ever present and constant, but continually reanimated and brought to bear on the shifting circumstances which museums in a rapidly changing world must engage with and respond to. This values–driven approach produces challenging, but undeniably authentic and credible, ways of understanding the role and purpose of museums that, I would argue, begin to account for the wide appeal of Bob's writings and his capacity to speak to museum practitioners working in very diverse settings.

The writings presented here explore big issues – some of the most important of our time, ranging from the rights of Indigenous peoples to climate change – and encourage the reader to step back from the detail of everyday museum work (for example, the technical concerns of managing, researching and presenting collections) that can often obscure the bigger picture. Despite this unusually ambitious and outward-looking frame, the writings presented here are also imbued with pragmatism; they begin to suggest ways forward that have inspired many in the museum world to think and act differently. The content in these diverse writings, then, is challenging. The tenacious critique of conservatism, the unpacking of entrenched museum practices that are steeped in colonial thinking, places considerable demands on any reader who is open to reflecting on the tough questions that follow. At the same time, however, Bob's work is undeniably readable – accessible and generous (a style I have always envied since first reading the extraordinary prologue to *Museums in a Troubled World* [Janes 2009: 1-12], which remains in my mind as amongst the most memorable openings to any book).

That the writings included here have provoked fierce debate (and will continue to do so) is something of an understatement. As a thinker, writer and practitioner with an extraordinarily uncompromising and compelling – if sometimes disconcerting – vision for museums (how they should be run; their purposes and priorities; their obligations to communities, to society at large and to future generations; and their unique value), Bob is viewed by many as a source of inspiration and guidance in a collective effort to make museums more vital, relevant, ethical and socially purposeful organisations. At the same time, his persistent highlighting of the unethical implications that stem from museums' actions (and inaction) across the world (including an unquestioning adherence to market-led thinking; an unwillingness to acknowledge and respect the rights of Indigenous people and the pernicious effects of the *Declaration on the Importance and Value of Universal Museums*; the biases generated by undue corporate influence and poor governance; and the consequences of continued denial of climate change) has been a cause for consternation and discomfort for others. (Interestingly, I noted on a recent visit to Canada that whilst Janes' many supporters openly express their genuine admiration for his position in conference debates and acknowledge his considerable influence in publications, the minority who are uncomfortable with his insistence on accountability and self-reflection generally voice their discomfort privately.)

The opening remarks in his introduction to this volume hint at Bob's awareness that he has been viewed, at least by some, as unhelpfully pessimistic and critical of the field within which he has worked for many years. Indeed, his frustration with many aspects of orthodox museum thinking and his unrelenting critique of those who resist the notion that museums have an ethical responsibility to engage with both community needs and the broader challenges facing our planet can be plainly seen throughout the book. The writings included in this book, then, are undoubtedly provocative. The ideas and arguments that are threaded through them – which span nearly four decades of reflective practice – serve to unsettle and challenge their reader. Yet, it would be misleading to portray Bob Janes as a *provocateur* – as someone who deliberately courts controversy for its own sake. Indeed, those who know him well remark upon his modest, unassuming and collegial manner. Rather, this remarkable body of work is best characterised as a call to action, driven by the author's enduring optimism coupled with an unwavering belief in (and first-hand experience of) the unique capacity for museums to accomplish good work. Read the arguments presented here with care, question and interrogate the bold claims they make but, above all, consider how engaging with the difficult questions they pose might enrich your own understanding of the purposes of museums.

Note

1 Richard Sandell is Professor of Museum Studies at the School of Museum Studies, University of Leicester, United Kingdom. His recent books include *Museums, Equality and Social Justice* (with Eithne Nightingale) and *Re-Presenting Disability: Activism and Agency in the Museum* (with Jocelyn Dodd and Rosemarie Garland-Thompson). He has a deep concern for social justice and a belief that museums have a vital role to play in advancing equality for all.

Reference

Janes, R. R. (2009) *Museums in a Troubled World: Renewal, Irrelevance or Collapse?* London and New York: Routledge.

ACKNOWLEDGEMENTS

The acknowledgements for this book span thirty-three years of writing – a worrisome consideration if one hopes to be inclusive and fair minded. A number of the chapters in this book contain acknowledgements, as do all of the original sources of these chapters. The acknowledgements that follow are intended to express my gratitude to those individuals who have recently offered me assistance, support, and guidance in innumerable ways.

Costis Dallas, Edward M. Luby and Richard Sandell deserve special mention for reading my initial proposal and providing their unstinting support and encouragement when this book was only an idea. I am indebted to Joy Davis, Kris Morrissey, and Darren Peacock for reviewing the introductions and epilogue, and providing a wealth of comments that have improved this book far beyond what I was capable of achieving on my own. I particularly want to thank Darren Peacock for his stimulating observations on the many meanings of "without borders." Pamela Holway and Peter Welsh also provided insightful comments and invaluable encouragement.

I am honoured to have Richard Sandell's Foreword, and I thank him for his generous words and all his efforts on my behalf. I am also privileged to have a cover image created by the Canadian artist Lyndal Osborne and I thank her for her interest and support. I thank Gwyn Langemann (on behalf of the late Gerald Conaty), Richard Sandell, and Morten Karnøe Søndergaard for their permission to include our co-authored chapters in this book.

There are many people who have provided assistance and inspiration over the past several years while this book was taking shape – each in their inimitable way. This network of colleagues and friends forms part of the interconnectedness that is essential to work, life, and this book. I thank Gail Anderson, Leah Best, Carol Bossert, Fiona Cameron, Jennifer Carter, Mary Case, Kevin Coffee,

Nika Collison, Michele Corbeil, Peter Davis, Jocelyn Dodd, Victoria Dickenson, Joanne DiCosimo, Beka Economopoulos, John Eberhard, Peter Faid, Amareswar Galla, Michele Gallant, Patrick Greene, Viviane Gosselin, Elaine Heumann Gurian, Alexandra Hatcher, Hilde Hein, Mary Humphries, Sharilyn Ingram, Erica Janes, David Jensen, Emlyn Koster, Claudette Leclerc, Bernadette Lynch, Patrick McCloskey, Jerry McGrath, Bridget Mckenzie, Elizabeth Merritt, Andrea Michelbach, Meaghan Patterson, Richard V. Piacentini, Anita Price, Scott and Kitty Raymond, Rene Rivard, Bart Robinson, Mike Robinson, Lenore Sarasan, Marjorie Schwarzer, Marsha Semmel, Lois H. Silverman, Lynn Teather, and Douglas Worts.

I thank Elaine Heumann Gurian, Emlyn Koster and Marjorie Schwarzer for their generous endorsements of this book.

This is my fourth museum book done in collaboration with my editor at Routledge, Matthew Gibbons, and I am grateful for his unwavering support and guidance. His editorial assistant, Lola Harre, has set a new standard for author support and I cannot thank her enough for all her assistance in seeing this book through to publication. I also wish to thank Judith Oppenheimer for her copy editing, as well as Colin Morgan and Laura Christopher for managing the many production details. I acknowledge and thank Yosef Wosk, the Canadian Academy of Independent Scholars, and Simon Fraser University for awarding me an Independent Scholar Grant in support of this book. Their support of independent scholarship in Canada is pioneering.

Finally, I thank Priscilla Janes for her grace and mindfulness in all things.

PERMISSIONS

(Source information for the individual chapters can be found as a footnote at the start of each chapter.)

p. vi
Neil Postman, "Museum as Dialogue," *Museum News*, Vol. 69, No. 5, September/ October, 1990, p. 58. Reprinted by permission of the American Alliance of Museums.

Stephen E. Weil, "Creampuffs and Hardball: Are You Really Worth the Cost?" *Museum News*, September/October, 1994, p. 43. Reprinted by permission of the American Alliance of Museums.

Edward Abbey, *A Voice Crying in the Wilderness: Notes from a Secret Journal (Vox Clamantis in Deserto)*. New York: St. Martin's Press, 1989, p. 40. Copyright 1989 by Edward Abbey. Reprinted by permission of Don Congdon Associates, Inc.

p. 15
Terrence Heath, "Comments from Afar." In Robert R. Janes, *Museums and the Paradox of Change: A Case Study in Urgent Adaptation*. Calgary, Canada: Glenbow Museum and the University of Calgary Press, 1997, p. 156. Reprinted by permission of the University of Calgary Press/Glenbow Museum.

p. 48
William W. Lowrance, *Modern Science and Human Values*. London: Oxford University Press. Copyright 1986 by W. W. Lowrance. Reprinted with permission of Oxford University Press.

p. 73

Peter Block, *Stewardship*. San Francisco: Berrett-Koehler Publishers Inc., 1993, p. 43. Copyright 1993 by P. Block. Reprinted with permission of Berrett-Koehler Publishers.

p. 93

J. K. Galbraith, quoted in *The Scotsman*, November 25, 1992. Copyright 1992 by J. K. Galbraith, from *The Wealth of Nature*. Reprinted with permission of *The Scotsman*.

p. 185

Wendell Berry, *Life Is a Miracle: An Essay against Modern Superstition*. Berkeley, CA: Counterpoint, 2001, p. 84. Copyright 2000 by Wendell Berry. Reprinted by permission of Counterpoint.

p. 198

Joseph Epes Brown, *The Spiritual Legacy of the American Indian*. Copyright 1989 by J. E. Brown. Reprinted with permission of World Wisdom Publishing.

p. 210

Peter Block, *The Answer to How Is Yes*. San Francisco: Berrett-Koehler Publishers. Copyright 2002 by P. Block. Reprinted with permission of Berrett-Koehler Publishers.

p. 222

Arnold J. Toynbee, *A Study of History*. Copyright 1988 by A. Toynbee. Reprinted with permission of Oxford University Press.

p. 271

Jon Michael Greer, *The Wealth of Nature: Economics as if Survival Mattered*. Garbriola Island, Canada: New Society Publishers, 2011, p. 240. Copyright 2011 by J. M. Greer. Reprinted with permission of New Society Publishers.

p. 283

Michael Ames, *Cannibal Tours and Glass Boxes: The Anthropology of Museums*. Vancouver, Canada: University of British Columbia Press, 1992, p. 5. Reprinted with permission of the publisher. Copyright by the University of British Columbia Press 1992. All rights reserved by the publisher.

p. 290

Frank Conroy, "Think about It – Ways We Know and Don't," *Harper's Magazine* (277/1662), 1988. Copyright 1988 *Harper's Magazine*. All Rights reserved. Reproduced from the November issue by special permission.

p. 307

Peter Block, *Stewardship*. San Francisco: Berrett-Koehler Publishers. Copyright 1993 by P. Block. Reprinted with permission of Berrett-Koehler Publishers.

INTRODUCTION

This book is a body of work spanning my 39 years in the museum field. As a scholar-practitioner, my experience is multifaceted and includes serving as a museum director, chief curator, board member, archaeologist, author, editor, consultant, instructor, volunteer, and philanthropist. In incorporating these perspectives, this collection forms an evolutionary time capsule of the many issues that have shaped and will continue to shape the museum sector for decades to come. In exploring and addressing these issues, I have often used an interdisciplinary approach, combining anthropology, ethnography, museum studies, and management theory. I am indeed grateful for nearly four decades of intimate involvement in the continuity and change of museum practice.

As a scholar-practitioner, I have consistently questioned the conventional wisdom of mainstream museum practice. I have made every effort to do this constructively, with admitted lapses of patience, and with a degree of candour and self-reflection that has been noted in the museum literature. Every discipline and profession needs internal critics – those with sufficient knowledge and grounding in the work to be able to assess and question the many assumptions, beliefs, and habitual practices that dog all of human activity. Adopting a critical perspective also means that one cannot hide behind a discipline or a profession to remain immune from scrutiny.

In seeking to enhance the value of museums as social institutions, I have chosen to confront the political reality that surrounds museum work, and thus become an activist. I do not shy away from that term, as Part 4 of this book demonstrates. By activism I mean those activities that are undertaken for a purpose bigger than personal or institutional gain (Macy and Johnstone 2012: 217; Sandell and Dodd 2010). Although I have used "critic" and "activist" to describe my perspective, one of my colleagues prefers to see me as a "guide" for some of the difficult and intractable challenges of museum life (Peacock 2015). This observation is equally as valid, as I do wish to share dialogue and reflections with all those who are passionate about what museums could become. Regrettably, questioning and criticising are too often equated in our culture, and I ask the reader to consider my questioning more as an open-ended inquiry rather than as sitting in judgement.

The title of this book was inspired by Médecins Sans Frontières (MSF), or Doctors Without Borders, the medical relief organization that responds to public health emergencies. Working in 70 countries with national offices in 19 countries, MSF operates with complete independence from political, economic, and religious influences. The ultimate context of its work is the world and the relief of human suffering, and I find MSF to be an exemplar of the mindfulness that museums are capable of assuming. I am not, of course, referring to the provision of medical services, but rather to the ability of museums to assist in the creation of a new, caring, and more conscious future for themselves and their communities. This can be done only through authentic engagement with contemporary issues and aspirations.

The idea of "borders" is also a useful metaphor for this book for another reason, as borders are simultaneously "about limitation and restraint, but also offer the lure and possibility of discovery, change, and transcendence" (Peacock 2015). Borders are about the limits we impose on our thinking, such as habitual thought patterns. Borders also define the limitations inherent in professional practice, assumptions, and traditions. Borders are the boundaries of fear and inertia that prevent change; yet they also define the frontier of reflection and innovation – ripe for experimentation. Borders can restrict; borders can liberate. In the writing that follows, borders will be ever present and I invite the reader to reflect upon their many manifestations in the complex world of museums. The idea that museums have a broader role to play in society is the premise of this book – a notion that is not necessarily well served by assuming that mental borders are only the result of thinking and reasoning. In the words of Mary Case, who reviewed an earlier book of mine, "he [Janes] approaches his work from a spiritual perspective – the deep place of why museums exist and what they mean in terms of identity, community and the future of civil life" (Case 2010: 22).

In retrospect

Having the opportunity to assemble one's published and unpublished writing is a singular privilege, as collections of writings by a single author in the museum field are rare (Gurian 2006; Weil 1990, 1995, 2002). This is especially valuable, as it affords the opportunity for a retrospective survey of my learning that reveals patterns, themes, mistakes, and omissions – all attributes of a body of work. Bringing theory, research, and experimentation into the workplace has been a habit of mine, and is a result of my life experience and academic training, as well as personal values, political awareness, and, of late, a nagging sense of the ethical.

I now know that applying the method and theory of scholarship to the demands of the workplace is known as the scholar-practitioner model, although I only became aware of this much later in my career. The scholar-practitioner draws together the practical challenges of acting in the world with the reflective detachment born of theory, research, and experimental knowledge. Scholar-practitioners are also driven by values and ethical conduct, and add a problem-solving approach to scholarly practice – recognizing problems, examining them, and searching for productive solutions (Millar 2013). Ideally, the scholar-practitioner perspective also exemplifies mindfulness (Peacock 2015). Having weathered the pleasure and pain of the PhD endurance test, I remain comfortable with reading and writing as everyday tools. I have never questioned the value of searching far and wide for ideas and insights, and then assessing their fit with the often puzzling and stubborn challenges of the museum workplace and life in general.

There are two experiences that are deeply embedded in this collection of writings, and a brief summary of them reveals how events assume meaning in unanticipated ways and become formative in hindsight. In the course of obtaining a graduate degree in archaeology, my wife, Priscilla, and I spent six months living among a group of Dene hunters near the Arctic Circle in the western Northwest Territories (NWT) of Canada.[1] I had become convinced, as a result of doing summer fieldwork, that an exclusive concern with archaeology and artifacts was overlooking the richness of a living culture. Adopting the roles of novice, apprentice and helper, we lived with this egalitarian hunting band for six months and obtained all of our food, except for staples like tea, coffee, and rice, from hunting and fishing (Janes 1983).

Dene life in the bush was based on a profound knowledge of the environment, flexible task groups that worked around the clock when the fish were running or the waterfowl were migrating, and a concept of leadership based on competence and adding value, not authority or privilege. These qualities have resounded with meaning throughout my career, as I encountered the complexities of individual, small-group, and large-group behaviour in museums. These northern hunters provided an elegant model of competence and adaptation that inspires my ongoing search for organizational effectiveness and adaptability.

My second experience was becoming the founding director and first employee of the Prince of Wales Northern Heritage Centre in Yellowknife, Northwest Territories, Canada (1976–86). No one was more surprised than I to get this position, having never worked in a museum. It was a member of my Thesis Committee who had encouraged me to apply. Thus began my accidental apprenticeship in the museum field, as the building, staff, and exhibitions were to be ready for a public opening by the Prince of Wales in 1979, less than three years from my starting date. The centrepiece was an environmentally controlled building of 4,180.6 square metres housing a museum, library, archives, and art gallery in one of the most severe environments in the world – the Canadian Subarctic. The average temperature in Yellowknife (the capital) in January is around −26 °C (−15 °F), with temperatures dropping as low as −51.2 °C (−60 °F).[2]

Assembling the best staff I could find was my first step. With a core team of six people we solidified our purpose, divided up the tasks, worked either individually or as a group, and met the deadline and budget. None of us had any training in interpersonal communication or team dynamics – we each possessed particular kinds of knowledge, had an explicit understanding of our collective purpose, and were respectful of time and money. We valued self-managing work teams as a means of integrating diverse specialists for a common purpose. I must also mention that we had a supportive government that provided adequate funding, and lots of good luck.

Both of these experiences – living in the bush with one of the world's greatest hunting cultures, and developing a museum from idea to reality in a purported cultural backwater – became inextricable parts of my perspective as a museum worker. Both of these apprenticeships are reflected directly or tangentially in all the writing that follows. As a result, this book is partly autobiographical. In short, I "cut my professional teeth" in the culturally diverse, often self-organized, and interconnected world of Canada's distant North, where naïvety was accepted, risk taking assumed, and mistakes were permitted. Perhaps this initial experience in the NWT made me less adaptable, and more sensitive, to mainstream museum work.

I have come to realize after 39 years in the museum field that it is difficult to disguise one's personhood, irrespective of the conventions of scholarly writing. Nonetheless, my aim has always been to address the interpretation and explanation of empirical data (Kaplan 1964: 332–334). In pursuing explanation, my intention has been to discover and establish relations, however seemingly obscure. This is more a statement about method than a claim for objectivity, however. Inevitably, my writing is a subjective process shaped by my worldview and experiences.

Thinking retrospectively, some discussion of the New Museology is also in order. Although I have never claimed any allegiance to this perspective, it is clear that my experiences as a scholar-practitioner align with this school of thought. My understanding of the New Museology is that it involves a redefinition of the relationships that museums have with people and their communities. This is in contrast to the original idea of museums as collections focussed and building based, with the public understanding that museums are authorities that uphold and communicate truth (Harrison 1994: 160–176; McCall and Gray 2014: 20).

I note that much of the writing in this book is indeed a challenge to mainstream museum practice, including the role of museums in society. I do not know if my early resistance to mainstream museum practice constitutes a nascent expression of the New Museology, as my work has never been identified with a particular theoretical framework. I mention it here, as my work is either a precursor or descendant of the New Museology, and I wish to acknowledge this theoretical context for those readers who deem this important.

Overarching ideas

Wendell Berry (1987), the American poet and farmer, published a collection of essays entitled *Home Economics*, wherein he returned to the idea that the root of economics is stewardship. In a similar vein, my writing and public speaking have sought to explore and nurture the broader connections between museums and their communities, in keeping with the original meaning of economics. The word *economics* comes from an ancient Greek word (*oikonomia*), which meant the "management of a household."[3] Berry's understanding of home economics embraces all of existence and includes the household, the community, and the planet. Applying the home economics concept of stewardship to museums allows one to think more broadly about the roles and responsibilities of these unique institutions, including promoting and protecting the sustainability and well-being of individuals, families, and communities.[4] I believe that the long-term sustainability of museums will be achieved only when museums forge broader connections to community needs and aspirations, as the home economists are now doing.

As noted above, I have tried to establish relationships among seemingly uncon-nected things in the museum world, such as equating collections to biological seed banks, introducing the Roman leadership model of *primus inter pares* as an alternative to the lone CEO, and linking the Buddhist concept of mindfulness to museum practice. I have also sought to explore the important relationships between museums and the biosphere – the cultural and natural environments of our planet. By considering various concepts, imperatives, and beliefs that are not commonly considered in museum practice, I find myself constantly challenging the museum field – questioning and examining the museum's mission, professional practices, dominant traditions, and normative values.

Some of my writing has been described as "insurgent" and "confrontational" but it wasn't always that way (Wood 2011: 134). My early writing was respectful, albeit increasingly curious about museum traditions and practices, and it was not long before the questioning set in. As time passed, the complacency of museum workers in the face of enormous societal issues has caused me to become an icono-clast of sorts; to question the received wisdom of museums, and to ask the museum community why it is not responding more readily to the issues and aspirations of the communities it serves.

Museum complacency is rooted in a variety of sacred cows, unquestioned assumptions, and habitual behaviours, all of which have contributed to a danger-ously narrow sense of the museum's purpose in the twenty-first century. Many of these obstacles and internal challenges are examined in this book. It borders on hubris for any museum worker to assume or perpetuate the myth that all is well. In fact, the urgent task for the global museum community is to examine how far it is able to meet the expectations and needs of our planet and its inhabitants, ranging from climate disruption to human rights. A new breed of museums grounded in consciousness of the world around them is urgently needed, in order for museums to fulfill their latent potential as community organizations of the highest order. It is within the grasp of all museum workers to embrace greater consciousness in all that they do, and I submit that this mindfulness is the only realistic foundation for a sustainable future.

The experiences underlying these writings are diverse in character and content, and encapsulate the naïve, the traditional, and the experimental. As noted earlier, I have often combined perspectives from anthropology, ethnography, museum studies, and management theory – all in an effort to ask questions and redefine problems beyond the boundaries of routine thought, and to seek solutions based on a new or different understanding of commonplace and complex situations. There are numerous themes and variations in this book as a result, all of which have emerged from the application of the scholar–practitioner model to the richly complex, organizational life of museums.

Persistent themes

Emerging from the overarching ideas described above – the real meaning of economics, the role of museums in civil society, and the tyranny of tradition – are numerous themes and patterns that reappear throughout this collection. These reflect and amplify the larger ideas, such as my acknowledgement of interrelatedness or my respect for different cosmologies. I also discovered the magic of self-organization among museum staff in Yellowknife – a natural consequence of little or no organizational hierarchy. This discovery was complemented by repeated encounters with concepts such as chaos, complexity, emergence, non-linearity, paradox, and loss of control – apparently commonplace phenomena in the world of science, but unrecognized in the museum literature until my experiences at the Prince of Wales Northern Heritage Centre and the Glenbow Museum (Calgary, Alberta, Canada) prompted me to reflect on their relevance to museum practice (Peacock 2013: 235–245). Complexity theory in organizations is about how they adapt to their environments and deal with uncertainty, including individual and collective behaviour (Wikipedia 2015).

Again, it was the perspective of the scholar–practitioner that enabled me to recognize these phenomena, and motivated me to share them through writing. Paradoxically, it is only by challenging contemporary museum practices that museums will be able to assume their purpose as stewards of the biosphere, and sustain themselves as socially valued institutions – above and beyond the dictates of the marketplace, the tyranny of the expert, and a preoccupation with popularity. All of these seeming imperatives are too often obstacles to change, new thinking, and experimentation, and are currently rationalized as economic necessities. A return to purpose, as socially relevant and trusted organizations, is more important than ever for museums as they prepare for an unknown future – hopefully in full partnership with the individuals and communities they purport to serve. The collected works presented here are installments on the journey toward that end, and they constitute a trajectory whose endpoint is not yet known.

My earliest preoccupation with community involvement in the remote North sits in stark contrast to the unavoidably internal focus we adopted at Glenbow, as we confronted a brittle organization and the rapid withdrawal of public funding during the "nasty nineties." Dealing with this organizational crisis eventually created a different sensibility in me as a museum director – that museums have paramount social responsibilities as key agents of civil society. If organizational well-being was to be the only result of the angst and suffering of organizational change, I could not help but ask – Is that all there is?

The organizational crisis at Glenbow unwittingly opened a Pandora's Box of unquestioned assumptions and traditional practices, the consequences of which forced my colleagues and me to ultimately question the very purpose of museums. We were no longer able to afford the distractions of an outdated reputation, time-honoured procedures, and internal agendas. These luxuries of organizational life have always served as obstacles to genuine self-reflection, and when they are finally disassembled a rare opportunity arises to address a first principle – namely, if museums didn't exist, would we reinvent them and what would they look like? This is the question that we were forced to ask at Glenbow, and answering it inevitably led to a consideration of the social responsibilities of museums. This, in turn, eventually led to the activism that is chronicled in Part 4 of this book.

The chapters in this book have an inadvertent trajectory of their own. It began in the late 1970s with my novice anxiety about serving isolated communities in a remote region; then to internal preoccupations entangled in a formidable change process, and now back again to the broader responsibilities of museums – this time as agents of civil society and the biosphere. I have the benefit of a museum director's perspective for roughly half of these writings, and the vantage point of an author, editor, and consultant for the other half.

My hope has always been that museums will seek to serve a broader purpose, above and beyond the programs and activities driven by internal concerns and traditional practices. All of the articles, book chapters, and keynote presentations in this book embody this hope and intention, and all of them are ultimately interrelated. Although each chapters stands on its own, all sit on a continuum of thought and action that is inadvertently cumulative in meaning and intent. The reader will note these reoccurring ideas and perspectives, as thoughts, themes, and experiences accumulate and flow along the arrow of time.

Writing has allowed me to make sense of things in retrospect, as opportunities for reflection and synthesis are an uncommon luxury and easily ignored when the pressures of work are unrelenting. I am grateful for the opportunity to assemble this book and I hope that the questions, concerns, and issues herein will motivate other museum workers to do the same. I also hope to continue to wrestle with the large questions that confront us both as human beings and as museum workers, questions such as: 1) How can museums and museum workers be well used? 2) What is this good use? 3) What is good work? 4) Can museums really be "neutral"? and 5) How can we truly honour the public trust in museums?[5] These questions may be more or less imponderable for many museum workers, but there is some comfort to be had in an observation that has remained with me for decades. Frank Conroy (1988: 70), the American author and jazz pianist, once wrote:

understanding does not always mean resolution. Indeed, in our intellectual lives, our creative lives, it is perhaps those problems that we will never resolve that rightly claim the lion's share of our energies. The physical body exists in a constant state of tension as it maintains homeostasis, and so too does the active mind embrace the tension of never being certain, never being absolutely sure, never being done, as it engages the world. That is our special fate, our inexpressibly valuable condition.

Assumptions about the museum world

I have been guided by various assumptions throughout my museum career and they pervade all of the writing in this book. Because I accept these assumptions as being true without conclusive proof, it is best to make them known. My first assumption is that museums are potentially one of the most free and creative work environments on the planet, and the scope for creativity and initiative should be just about limitless in a well-run museum. There are very few other workplaces which offer more opportunities for thinking, choosing, and acting in ways that can blend personal satisfaction and growth with organizational goals. Unlike the private sector, museums are still relatively immune to the tyranny of production and sales quotas that marks the private sector. I note this with some hesitation, however, as attendance figures may well have become the museum equivalent of widget production.

In contrast to the public sector, museums are not normally forced to administer unpopular government policies. If one mentally combines this notion of organizational freedom with the assumption that we, as human beings, are the co-creators of our lives and our organizations if we accept the responsibility to do so – the result is the powerful force called personal agency, albeit rarely acknowledged in the organizational life of museums.

By personal agency, I mean the capacity of individual museum workers, not just their leaders and managers, to take action in the world (Davis 2011: 459–479). Personal agency has become essential to the well-being of the biosphere, as myopic politicians, self-serving bureaucracies, and malfeasant corporations pursue their self-interests. Museum workers are as insightful and motivated by concerns beyond the workplace as are any other human beings, yet they more often than not shy away from expressing their values and assuming their personal agency in the museum – likely for fear of losing their job or their friends.

This is not unique to museums and is undoubtedly true of other work environments. This fear is exaggerated, however, especially by those in authority, and the reader will note throughout this collection that personal agency is something to be celebrated and nurtured. Its potential will remain unfulfilled, however, as long as individual museum workers fail to ponder and make explicit "why" they do what they do. Answering this question is a prerequisite to installing personal agency as a vital organizational resource and a force for good.

My second assumption is that learning is essential to intelligent and caring change, and learning requires that we ask difficult and uncomfortable questions of ourselves, others, and museums as social institutions. This assumption underlies the purpose of this book. Self-critical and courageous leadership has always been the hallmark of effective organizations, irrespective of the sector, and this leadership is now essential for museums if they are to define a path to a sustainable future. With this challenge in mind, I ask a variety of uncomfortable, perhaps annoying, questions in this book about the what, how, and why of museum work.

I invite the reader to share these questions, with the hope that this book will be seen as a variation on Socratic questioning – to open up issues and problems, to uncover assumptions, to analyse concepts, and to distinguish what we know from what we don't know (Wikipedia 2015). I have never intended my writing to be a gratuitous attack on the value of museum work.

My third assumption follows directly from the previous one about learning – the future is not knowable. Irrespective of all the futurists and the pundits, the future is not knowable because the links between cause and effect in organizations are complex and mostly lost in the detail of what actually happens in between (Stacey 1992: 11). If museum staff and boards cannot know where their museums are going because the future is unknowable, then they should not all believe in the same things. They should question everything, and generate new perspectives and new options for action through discussion, debate, and dialogue.

Tradition and orthodoxy continue to dominate the museum world and there is no doubt that both of them are essential in providing the stability and knowledge that are essential to routine functioning. Yet, it is only through confronting convention that museums will be able to create, invent, and discover a new future for themselves and their communities. Habitual commitment to comfortable assumptions and traditions is not helpful in doing so. Museums can at least help to create an image of a desirable future for their communities in the midst of all of the global challenges. The tension between orthodoxy and change is a creative one and must be nurtured, and it can be managed for a greater purpose.

My fourth assumption is that museums have no equivalent in society. Neil Postman (1990: 55–58), the cultural critic and author, observed that the purpose of all competent museums is to provide answers to a fundamental question, "What does it mean to be a human being?" Governments are not equipped to do this; business is committed to homogenization and efficiency in the name of profit, and most universities are still grappling with their real and perceived separation from their communities. Museums are distinct from all of these institutions, and uniquely qualified to probe our humanness free of the agendas noted above. Herein lies their great strength and their great worth. In short, museums are unique and valuable social institutions that have no suitable replacement, irrespective of their shortcomings.

My fifth assumption is that museums should not hold themselves static – a stubborn liability for the majority of museums that stems from various causes, including insularity, the fiduciary responsibility for collections, and the museum's privileged position in society. To hold a museum static, however, while the values of the community and stakeholders are changing, is to doom the museum.

I do not intend or wish to condemn any museum, as I have spent far too long getting to know them and their capabilities. Global, national, and community values are in great flux at this time, however, as the world confronts intractable socio-environmental issues. All museums must be intensely mindful of stasis or change – or assume the attendant risks of decline, irrelevance, or collapse.

My sixth and final assumption is that everything that is required to fulfill the true potential of museums is here – now. There is nothing lacking. From the beginning of my career, there has been incessant talk of shortage in the museum world – be it money, staff, technology, or public support – and this self-limiting idea continues unabated. I, too, was once heavily influenced by this pervasive concept of limited good (money), and it was one of the catalysts that initiated the organizational change at Glenbow.[6] I struggle to understand this now, as perceived shortages of all kinds have become the museum mantra for maintaining the status quo.

Museums already have a boundless capacity to act with intelligence and sensitivity – money is not required to do this. There are abundant examples of socially responsible, outstanding museum projects that used existing resources or required only a modest investment. Museum workers also know intuitively that money is not the measure of their worth, irrespective of our collective enslavement to materialism. When will museums recognize that they are a privileged caste, whose purpose is their meaning (Handy 1994: 183)?

If this special advantage is not readily apparent to museum practitioners, trustees, and academics, then it can be revealed through workplace experimentation of all kinds – not in self-fulfilling prophecies about the need to remain neutral and refusing to "take sides" on societal issues that are value laden. If museums, as agents of civil society, do not assume responsibility, who will do so with any less bias – the politicians, the corporatists, or the ideologues of all persuasions? The answer is self-evident (Janes 2014: 403–411).

What follows

This book consists of four parts: "Other Voices: Indigenous Peoples," "Creative Destruction: Managing Change," "Museums without Borders: Social Responsibility," and "Dangerous Times: Activism and Ethics." The parts are ordered chronologically and each begins with an introduction and an overview of the ensuing chapters. Part 1, Other Voices: Indigenous Peoples, examines the evolving relationships between First Nations and museums in Canada, with particular reference to the Dene, the Inuit, and the Blackfoot Confederacy. These chapters chronicle concrete actions taken to nurture these relationships, above and beyond rhetoric and sentiment. The reader will note a concern with active community participation and the recognition of Aboriginal peoples as sources of expert advice for museums. Traditional museum practices are also continually questioned and museum authority is seen as something to be shared. Part 1 demonstrates that challenges and difficulties can also be opportunities, not constraints.

Part 2, Creative Destruction: Managing Change, is concerned with organizational change in museums with a focus on the efforts to reinvent the Glenbow Museum – complete with the stressors, failures, and successes. The reader will observe the importance of rethinking the museum's future and not waiting around for external forces to dictate the outcome – in part through strategic planning. The value of self-organization is also explored, in contrast to hierarchy, as are the merits of shared leadership and participatory management – with all of their ensuing complexities. The self-imposed challenges stemming from professional practice and assumptions are examined as barriers to sustainability, as is the pernicious influence of marketplace values and business tribalism in museum work. Individual and organizational mindfulness are paramount in addressing these challenges.

The role and responsibilities of museums in civil society are the focus of Part 3, Museums without Borders: Social Responsibility. I introduce the concept of social responsibility, in combination with the need for heightened stewardship for the world beyond the museum. Both social responsibility and stewardship are motivated by values, such as idealism and interconnectedness, and these values are identified and discussed. Overall, a broad sense of stewardship, in combination with socially responsible work, are sources of renewal and relevance for all museums. The continuing rise of corporatism in museum affairs, with its emphasis on popularity, money, and consumption is a constant concern in Part 3.

Part 4, Dangerous Times: Activism and Ethics, is a culmination of all of the previous chapters, in that confronting the "dangerous times" ahead will require an expanded organizational consciousness that is grounded in the recognition of other voices, an appetite for change and experimentation, and a heightened mindfulness of the needs and aspirations of the broader world. Without fail, this awareness will lead the thoughtful museum into the realm of social responsibility and beyond. The ideas and themes in Part 4 include the societal risks confronting museums, the unavoidable paradoxes of museum work, the ethical responsibilities of museums, and the need for activism to ensure a sustainable future. All of these chapters are intended to prepare museums for an uncertain and dangerous future.

Overall, the reader will note that various ideas and observations reappear in chapters throughout this book. I ask the reader's indulgence, as this repetition serves as the thematic underpinning in my writing, and allows me to address a variety of issues with some consistency. Some of this repetition is also due to the necessity of setting the stage, as in the introductory discussions of Glenbow's organizational change that reappear in various chapters in Part 2.

The book concludes with an Epilogue wherein I take Postman's idea of "museums as an argument with society" to an obvious and contemporary conclusion, including a discussion of the role of museums in addressing the consequences of climate change and disruption. My intent here is to link the writing in this book to this most urgent and vexing issue, and what role museums might play in mitigating the causes and consequences. Human society is in need of a new story to replace the one centred on continuous economic growth, and changing the narrative of unlimited growth is fundamental to addressing the reality of climate change and the role of museums in doing so. Last, the reader will find my complete bibliography, including my work as an archaeologist and anthropologist.

In conclusion, and as noted earlier, every discipline and profession needs internal critics – those with sufficient knowledge and grounding in the work to be able to assess and question the many assumptions, beliefs, and habitual practices that frame their work. My motivation for doing so is that museums are part of my community; they are part of my life. I view them as realistically as I can, but also with a sense of imagination and possibility. Both my imagination and current reality give rise to my belief that museums are vital instruments of social responsibility and intellectual self-defence, above and beyond their visual, tactile, emotional, and intellectual prowess.

Any vision of museums, however, must be tempered with the realities of museum practice, or it be may be unrealistic, misguided, or threatening. I hope that this collection of writing demonstrates that fearing these outcomes is groundless, and that it is both reasonable and essential to expand the purpose of museums at this point in history – both tangibly and imaginatively. I admit to an overarching belief in the unique characteristics of museums and their potential value to society, and I do so out of respect and admiration for the rich and deep legacy of the world's museums.

Having had this opportunity and privilege to express my apprehensions and my active hope for museums within this book, I also want to express my gratitude for 39 years of collegiality, learning, experimentation, and fun among a collection of remarkable museum people far too large to name individually. I have sometimes felt like a long-distance runner, but I clearly would not have persisted in this vocation were it not for this astounding array of dedicated, passionate, and creative individuals whom I have come to know and admire. I include those with whom I have crossed swords, as they have also been essential to learning. I am the beneficiary of this collective and distributed intelligence, and it is the foundation of my work, my reflections, and my active hope. This book is written in gratitude to all of you – your thinking, actions, writing, and inspiration are embedded in all that is written here.

This aggregation of writings may be likened to the overall structure of a piece of music. This is obviously not because of any pretension to the beauty, form, and harmony of music, but solely because musical form is defined as "a series of strategies designed to find a successful mean between the opposite extremes of unrelieved repetition and unrelieved alteration."[7] For my part, I have made every effort to ensure that the repetition in this collection is relieved and that there is sufficient alteration to merit the reader's time and interest.

Notes

1 The Dene people (DEN-ay) are an aboriginal group of First Nations who live in the northern boreal and subarctic regions of Canada. The Dene speak the various dialects of the Athapaskan language. Dene is an Athapaskan word meaning "man" or "person." The Athapaskans of the Northwest Territories have indicated a preference for the use of Dene to describe themselves and this term is used throughout this book.

2 Geography and Climate – Yellowknife. Available online: http://en.wikipedia.org/wiki/Yellowknife.

3 Economics. In Wikipedia, The Free Encyclopedia. Available online: http://en.wikipedia.org/wiki/Economics.

4 Home Economics. In Wikipedia, The Free Encyclopedia. Available online: http://en.wikipedia.org/wiki/Home_economics.

5 I am indebted to Wendell Berry for his thinking and writing about the "important questions" in our lives. See his book *Life Is a Miracle: An Essay against Modern Superstition*. Berkeley: Counterpoint, 2001.

6 Wikipedia. "Limited Good." http://en.wikipedia.org/wiki/Limited_good, 2014.

7 Musical Form. In Wikipedia, The Free Encyclopaedia. Available online: http://en.wikipedia.org/wiki/Musical_form#cite_note-3.

References

Berry, W. (1987) *Home Economics*, San Francisco: North Point Press.

Case, M. (2010) Review of *Museums in a Troubled World: Renewal, Irrelevance or Collapse?* Robert R. Janes, New York and London: Routledge, 2009. In *Museum*, May/June, 2010, 22–23.

Conroy, F. (1988) "Think about It: Ways We Know and Don't." *Harper's* (227/1662), November, 70.

Davis, J.A. (2011) "Putting Museum Studies to Work." *Museum Management and Curatorship*, (26) 5, December, 459–479.

Gurian, E.H. (2006) *Civilizing the Museum: The Collected Writings of Elaine Heumann Gurian*. London and New York: Routledge.

Handy, C. (1994) *The Age of Paradox*. Boston: Harvard Business School Press, p. 183.

Harrison, J. (1994) "Ideas of Museums in the 1990s." *Museum Management and Curatorship*, (13) 2, 160–176.

Janes, R.R. (1983) *Archaeological Ethnography among Mackenzie Basin Dene, Canada*. The Arctic Institute of North America Technical Paper No. 28, Calgary, Canada: The Arctic Institute of North America and the University of Calgary.

Janes, R.R. (2014) "Museums for All Seasons." *Museum Management and Curatorship*, (29) 5, December, 403–411.

Kaplan, A. (1964) *The Conduct of Inquiry*. San Francisco: Chandler Publishing Company.

Macy, J. and Johnstone, C. (2012) *Active Hope: How to Face the Mess We're in without Going Crazy*. Novato, CA: New World Library.

McCall, V. and Gray, C. (2014) "Museums and the 'New Museology': Theory, Practice and Organisational Change." *Museum Management and Curatorship*, (29) 1, February, 19–35.

Millar, J. (2013) "Theory to Practice or Becoming a Scholar-Practitioner." February 10. Available online: http://sites.psu.edu/joancsa/2013/02/10/theory-to-practice-or-becoming-a-scholar-practitioner/.

Peacock, D. (2013) "Complexity, Conservation and Change: Learning How Museum Organizations Change." In *Museums and the Paradox of Change* (3rd edition) by R.R. Janes. London and New York: Routledge, pp. 235–245.

Peacock, D. (2015) "Museums without Borders." Email communication (9 March).

Postman, N. (1990) "Museum as Dialogue." *Museum News* (69): 55–58.

Sandell, R. and Dodd, J. (2010) "Activist Practice." In R. Sandell, J. Dodd and R. Garland Thompson (eds), *Re-Presenting Disability: Activism and Agency in the Museum*. London and New York: Routledge, pp. 3–22.

Stacey, R.D. (1992) *Managing the Unknowable: Strategic Boundaries Between Order and Chaos in Organizations*. San Francisco: Jossey-Bass Inc., p. 11.

Weil, S.E. (1990) *Rethinking the Museum and Other Meditations*. Washington, DC: Smithsonian Institution Press.

Weil, S.E. (1995) *A Cabinet of Curiosities: Inquiries into Museums and Their Prospects*. Washington, DC: Smithsonian Institution Press.

Weil, S.E. (2002) *Making Museums Matter*. Washington, DC: Smithsonian Institution Press.

Wikipedia, The Free Encyclopaedia (2015) "Complexity Theory and Organizations," 25 January. Available online: http://en.wikipedia.org/wiki/Complexity_theory_and_organizations.

Wikipedia, The Free Encyclopaedia (2015) "Socratic Questioning," 5 March. Available online: http://en.wikipedia.org/wiki/Socratic_questioning.

Wood, E. (2011) "Introduction to Social Relevance Circa 2012." *Museums and Social Issues*, (6) 2, Fall, 134.

PART 1

Other voices

Indigenous peoples

We are not a materialistic people; we live by muscle, mind and spirit.

Eric Anoee, Inuk Elder, Arviat, Northwest Territories,
Canada (Heath 1997: 156)

INTRODUCTION

I encountered the "other voices" immediately upon arriving in Yellowknife, Northwest Territories, Canada (NWT) in 1976, as a museum director with no prior experience and fresh from graduate school. These voices came not only from the diverse peoples of the NWT, but also from the land itself. It was then that I sensed for the first time the meaning of social ecology – that social and environmental issues are intertwined and both must be considered simultaneously (Barnhill 2010: 91). The intertwining of society and the environment is no more pronounced than it is in the Northwest Territories of Canada, an immense wilderness region with a population that was two-thirds Native born – Inuit, Dene or Metis. Dualistic thinking is a liability here, in the home of the world's greatest hunting cultures.

This cultural diversity, coupled with the severe climate and isolation, posed a number of surprising challenges to me as a newly minted custodian of mainstream museum traditions. Reality immediately intervened with a barrage of complexities. How do you address the stated perception among northern Aboriginal peoples that museums are a colonial legacy and do not address the needs of living cultures? How do you involve Aboriginal peoples in the development of a museum in their homeland, at a time when their political aspirations were demanding acknowledgement and redress? Are environmentally controlled museums in remote Subarctic and Arctic communities necessary, achievable, or preposterous? What is the best organizational design to unleash individual talent and commitment? Should a museum have a single focus or be multidisciplinary? The questions multiplied daily, intensified by the absence of any museum precedents or experimentation in this remote region that could show the way. It was both disconcerting and motivating, and it demanded study, reflection, and action. In retrospect, it was a rare opportunity to move beyond the shadow of orthodoxy, think anew, and develop alternatives.

The obvious remedy was to rely on the received wisdom of traditional practice, but I was a novice and not yet immersed in the constraints of professionalism. My tenure as the founding director of the Prince of Wales Northern Heritage Centre (PWNHC) was one of merging professional standards with the realities of time and place – while always hoping to achieve a standard of excellence and quality in the work at hand. Living beyond the establishment aura allowed our staff and me the naiveté and freedom to learn, experiment, make mistakes, and grow.

The heart of the museum, the collection, is a case in point. Many of the 65 NWT communities wanted a museum to preserve and highlight their cultural traditions, but not in a manner that conformed to professional museum practice – that is, not in a permanent collection in an environmentally controlled building. The preservation and celebration of intangible cultural heritage – music, dance, and storytelling – were often the focus of concern, not the preservation of objects. Mainstream museum practice dictated, however, that a professional, publicly funded museum had to have environmental controls because without them the collections would deteriorate.

It was both my duty and my belief to convey this tenet to northern communities, and this I did until I began to listen more deeply. It soon became clear that the majority of people in the NWT's remote communities were not interested in adhering to professional museum practice; not out of any disrespect or hostility, but primarily because of their particular world-view in combination with the consequences of geographic isolation. As a result of listening and learning together, we developed alternative approaches to museum work, while also respecting museum traditions and professionalism. I cannot over-emphasize the inclusivity I experienced in the NWT, especially among the Dene, the Inuit, and the Metis. This was the nature of their societies – open, sharing, and respectful. I absorbed this inclusivity and brought it to the conduct of our work, as did my colleagues.

My directorship at the PWNHC was also an inadvertent exercise in social justice – another observation that has only become apparent to me in retrospect. At that time, the NWT was unable, legally or practically, to keep its cultural property in the territory. All material culture, including archaeological remains and archival documents, was sent to Canada's national museums in Ottawa, Ontario.[1] Rarely, if ever, were any of the objects shared or returned to the NWT. Northerners were decidedly unhappy with this arrangement and sought to keep their material heritage in their homeland.

The first strategy in undoing this colonial legacy was the development of a fully professional museum, a project that had the support of the NWT's political leaders and citizens. In retrospect, this was akin to a large-scale repatriation effort and was made possible by some of those same professional standards, such as environmentally controlled buildings, that I also criticize in the chapters that follow. This was my initial foray into the paradoxical world of museums.

The first two chapters below represent 10 years of individual and collective effort to make sense of the many questions noted above, as we worked to develop museum services in one-third of Canada's landmass. The chapter on "Northern Museum Development: A View from the North" lays out the challenges of museum development in a remote region, with an inquiry into alternative approaches to heritage preservation with the involvement of Indigenous peoples. The second chapter, "Museum Ideology and Practice in Canada's Third World," is a retrospective assessment of our work at the PWNHC, including an analysis of the ideas, values, and beliefs that guided our work. These considerations are rarely made explicit in the museum literature and I hope that a discussion of ideology helps to clarify the politics of culture that are still unfolding throughout the world. There are many lessons to be learned here for application elsewhere, but I doubt that there has ever been a more open and creative environment for growing museums than in the NWT 40 years ago.

The experience of living and working in the NWT was uppermost in my mind when I became the Director of the Glenbow Museum in 1989. I was highly motivated by what I had learned in the North and energized by the possibilities of furthering this work at Glenbow – a large, multidisciplinary institution with an international reputation and significant resources. I was surprised and dismayed to see the marginalization of First Nations peoples in the province of Alberta (Canada), unlike the NWT, where Aboriginal peoples held positions of authority throughout society and constituted the majority in the NWT Legislative Assembly. The Glenbow Museum was in the homeland of the Blackfoot Confederacy, although the Blackfoot's needs and aspirations were largely unheeded by the museum.[2] This was more a result of benign neglect and disinterest than any intentional ill-will or conflict.

Thus began a decade-long process of discovery and learning, eventually culminating in the largest, unconditional repatriation of First Nations sacred objects in the history of Canadian museums, in 2000 (Janes 2015: 241–262).). Although this repatriation was a highly visible and public event, the chapters that follow describe the modest, incremental growth in our evolving relationship with the Blackfoot – a process of reciprocity, deepening understanding, and mutual appreciation. The chapter on "First Nations: Policy and Practice at the Glenbow Museum" chronicles our attempt to improve relationships with First Nations through the development of both policy and practice. In "Personal, Academic and Institutional Perspectives on Museums and First Nations," I draw together what I had learned by 1994. These three perspectives are ultimately seamless, with each informing the other. Personal agency underlies these perspectives, as does risk taking. The last chapter in Part 1 is "Issues of Repatriation: A Canadian View," wherein the late Gerald Conaty and I challenge the European opposition to the return of sacred objects to North American museums.

I was recently told that addressing historical injustices (including repatriation) among museums, First Nations, Inuit and Metis in Canada is actually about human rights. I have never thought of this work in that way – my motivation was born of respect for diversity, a predilection for activism, and the undeniable presence of moral considerations – all of which the reader will note in the following chapters. Whether or not it is a human rights issue is not as important as the need to continue to address these unresolved issues. The progress is decidedly uneven across Canada, as it is among those museums worldwide that hold Aboriginal collections.

In addition, the museum community must now contend with the "Declaration on the Importance and Value of Universal Museums."[3] Signed by numerous luminaries of the museum world, the Declaration rejects repatriation on the grounds that "universal museums," with their encyclopaedic collections, are best positioned to act on behalf of the world. Despite this arrogant and retrogressive manifesto, I am hopeful that the next generation of museum workers will ensure that museums and Aboriginal peoples continue to collaborate and flourish, in a manner that will confirm the human rights of all Indigenous peoples in museums. The chapters in Part 1 embody this ambition.

Notes

1 Because of its status as a territory, rather than a province, Canada's Federal Government retained significant authority over territorial affairs. The devolution of political and administrative powers from the federal government to the NWT continues to unfold.
2 The Blackfoot Confederacy consists of four First Nations; the Kainai (or Blood), Siksika (Blackfoot; Northern Blackfoot), Apatohsipiikani (Piikuni, Peigan), and Ammskaapipiikani (Piegan, Blackfeet).
3 The full text of the "Declaration of the Importance and Value of Universal Museums" is contained in the International Council of Museums Thematic Files. See: http://icom. museum/fileadmin/user_upload/pdf/ICOM_News/2004–1/ENG/p4_2004–1.pdf.

References

Barnhill, D. L. (2010) "Gary Snyder's Ecosocial Buddhism." In R. K. Payne (editor), *How Much Is Enough? Buddhism, Consumerism, and the Human Environment.* Somerville, MA: Wisdom Publications.
Heath, T. (1997) "Comments from Afar." In R. R. Janes, *Museums and the Paradox of Change: A Case Study in Urgent Adaptation.* Calgary, Canada: Glenbow Museum and the University of Calgary Press.
Janes, R. R. (2015) "The Blackfoot Repatriation: A Personal Epilogue." In G. T. Conaty (ed.) *We Are Coming Home: Repatriation and the Restoration of Blackfoot Cultural Confidence.* Edmonton, Canada: The Athabasca University Press, pp. 241–262.

1

NORTHERN MUSEUM DEVELOPMENT*

A view from the North

Introduction

It is a recognized fact that Canadian museum development is centered in the southern tier of the country, where various common factors have contributed to the shaping of philosophical and pragmatic approaches to museums in Canada. These common factors include the numerical dominance of Euro-Canadians and their perceptions of museums, physical environments that fall within a certain range, and established communication and supply networks, to mention only a few.

When museums are extended into the Canadian North, however, they become part of a context that is qualitatively and quantitatively different than that of southern Canada, particularly with respect to environmental, societal, economic and political factors. These differences are so significant that those who are concerned with planning and implementing policies for museums and related activities in northern Canada must be prepared to meet the challenge of this new context. Others who are less directly involved in northern museum affairs should also be aware of potentially new dimensions in thinking about Canadian museums.

I would like to make some observations on northern museum development from my perspective as the Director of the Prince of Wales Northern Heritage Centre (PWNHC) in Yellowknife, Northwest Territories, Canada. Our experiences in creating what was at first a rather traditional museum in a northern setting are useful in elucidating some of the unique features of the northern context referred to earlier. In addition, our adjustment to various northern realities, as well as some

*Source: Robert R. Janes, Gazette [former journal of the Canadian Museums Association], Vol. 15, No. 1, Winter (1982): 14–23. An earlier version of this paper was presented at the annual meeting of the Canadian Museums Association, Ottawa, Canada. May, 1981.

thoughts about future directions for northern museums, are discussed. Although my comments refer specifically to the Northwest Territories, I am hopeful that at least some of them are applicable to other northern regions of the country.

The land and the people

The Northwest Territories occupies a total area of 3,376,689 square kilometers of forest, lakes and tundra north of the 60th parallel, or one third of the landmass of Canada [in 1999 the Northwest Territories was divided to form the Nunavut Territory]. The climate is semi-arid and severe, with temperatures ranging from 35°C to −56°C. The population of this entire region is a mere 46,398, resulting in an astoundingly low population density.

Over two-thirds of the population is native born, and consists of Inuit, Dene, and Metis peoples.[1] The remaining portion includes Euro-Canadians and those of other ethnic origins. At least eight different languages are spoken and residents live in and around 64 communities. Less than one quarter of these communities can be reached by road from southern Canada. The remainder depends upon aircraft and boat, as well as ice roads which are open in the winter only. As a result, transportation and communication problems are significant.

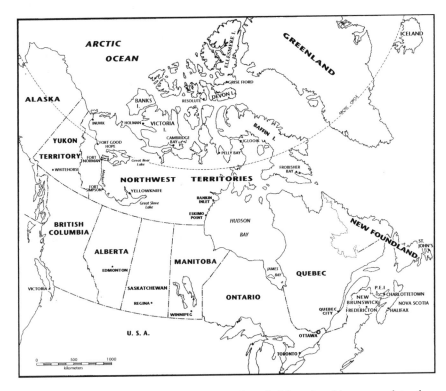

FIGURE 1　Map of the Northwest Territories, Canada. Note that this map predates the establishment of the Nunavut Territory in 1999. Courtesy of Priscilla B. Janes.

As a result of many factors, not the least of which is isolation, with its mental and physical costs, a significant portion of the Euro-Canadian population is transient. Many people come for one or two years and leave never to be seen again. In addition to the cynicism which these recurrent migrations provoke among the permanent residents, there are frustrating results for the operation of local museums. I have seen communities develop excellent boards with highly motivated staff, only to have these organizations dissolve after a brief period. The key to overcoming this is to foster the same degree of interest among the permanent residents, the majority of whom are Inuit, Dene or Metis. Only then will there be stability in community museum affairs.

The political setting

Unrecognized by many who work in the museum field, the concept of a museum is alien to the aboriginal peoples of the Northwest Territories. There was no equivalent to it in their cultures prior to the arrival of Euro-Canadians. Although certain objects were undoubtedly curated by successive generations, the idea of collecting such objects for study and exhibition is a colonial legacy. This is not to say that museums are unimportant. Rather, it does mean that our cherished belief in the rightness of collecting, preserving and interpreting our own material heritage and that of other peoples is simply not an article of faith among the Indigenous peoples.

A museum is judged by its collection (Guthe 1959: 21), and developing collections in the North is governed by laws and regulations peculiar to the region. Because 99 percent of the Northwest Territories is Federal Crown land, all items of archaeological, ethnological and historical significance are legally the property of the Crown. As an example, all archaeological specimens found are deposited in Ottawa with federal agencies. Specimens and reproductions can be retained in the Northwest Territories on a loan basis for educational and exhibition purposes. Loans of original material are normally made only if the local institution can demonstrate an ability to meet professional standards in the care and handling of the artifacts. We presently have over 300 specimens of northern significance on permanent loan from the National Museums.

Another fundamental point is the fact that the Northwest Territories is not self-governing. Although there is a 22-member elected Assembly, the head of Government is a Commissioner appointed by the Federal Government. For this reason and the others mentioned earlier, the Northwest Territories may be aptly described as Canada's third world. Apart from any political considerations which may arise from such a comparison, these facts have enormous implications for museum activity of any kind.

Finally, one must recognize that the people of the Northwest Territories are experiencing rapid and intense change. The frenetic search for nonrenewable resources on the northern frontier threatens the environment, including heritage resources. As the Legislative Assembly of the Northwest Territories seeks political rights, Native organizations are demanding self-determination. The development of northern museums will probably never be more important than it is now, recognizing their potential roles as custodians of the past and harbingers of the future.

Maintaining environmental controls

It is common knowledge that museum collections require certain environmental conditions to ensure their well-being and longevity. Achieving these standards in a temperate climate is challenge enough. Having now had the experience of achieving these standards in a severe northern climate, I would like to make some observations on the advisability and cost of doing so. The specific technical objectives we sought in designing the PWNHC were the year-round delivery of 20 °C temperature and 50 percent relative humidity to all portions of the building where artifacts and collections are exhibited, stored or studied.

Every construction detail was evaluated and reevaluated to ensure that the building conformed to three rather simple principles. The first principle is that the supporting structure of the building (i.e., steel beams) should be entirely within the exterior covering of the building so as to remain warm at all times. The second principle is that the insulation outside the vapour barrier should be continuous and form an unpenetrated covering over the entire building. The third principle is that the exterior covering of the building should protect this insulation and allow any moisture or frost which builds up to evaporate to the outside.

In addition to these sound northern building practices, buffer wall construction was used at the PWNHC. A buffer wall is a wall surface within a room set a few inches in from the inside surface of the exterior walls. Radiation is set continuously below this buffer wall and during the heating season warm air is continuously passed up behind the buffer wall by convection. This ensures that all exterior walls within a room are maintained at a constant room temperature.

Although we are still having some minor problems, the overall result has been a building which meets conservation standards despite the subarctic climate, an apparently rare accomplishment in circumpolar museums. But I must emphasize that achieving these standards has been very costly, and there is no end in sight. Each electronic humidification generator, and we have four of them, uses CAN$300 of electricity per month. The humidifiers put in long hours because the Northwest Territories is virtually semi-arid, as a result of being dominated by an extremely cold, dry air mass throughout the winter. It behooves all of us involved in northern museum work, including southern institutions, to recognize and appreciate the severity of the northern climate.

It appears that in the realm of museum funding, few, if any, agencies are willing to support the costs of electricity and fuel oil. Although one can certainly appreciate the concern that museums should establish sufficiently broad-based community support to meet basic operating costs, this is more often that not impossible in remote communities in the Northwest Territories. Museums there are extremely expensive to design, build and operate, trained staff are in short supply, and most communities have little or no tax base with which to support a permanent facility.

As an example, 1981 construction costs for a museum in Yellowknife were CAN$171.46 per square foot and CAN$243.47 per square foot in Iqaluit [formerly Frobisher Bay]. It is interesting to compare these prices with those in Winnipeg (Canada) where museum construction in 1981 cost CAN$80.00 per square foot (Department of Public Work, Government of the Northwest Territories, 1981). To put cost in perspective, a 5,000 square foot museum in Iqaluit would have cost well over a million Canadian dollars for construction alone in 1981.

A message heard regularly is that if communities expect to collect and interpret their material culture, they must have a proper museum facility with environmental controls. It is now time to realize that in the foreseeable future fully controlled buildings in the North are impossible in most instances, even if they are desirable. To offer sophisticated physical plants as the solution to community museum development is not particularly useful. Alternatives to traditional museum development must be considered.

Some northern alternatives

In order to fully understand and appreciate some of these alternatives, it is necessary to either abandon the commonly accepted definition of a museum or to broaden it considerably. It is more useful to start thinking of community museums in the Northwest Territories as preservers and purveyors of culture in its broadest sense, rather than as the repositories and interpreters of material culture alone. The emphasis in the following examples is not on collections *per se*, but on reviving traditional values and technologies, sharing them with the community at large, and overcoming ethnocentrism. Because the cultures of the Indigenous peoples are perpetuated by oral traditions, it is the object, plus the knowledge and wisdom which brought it into being, that is worthy of preservation.

In a Dene community near Yellowknife there is a group of men and women who are replicating the material culture of their ancestors. All materials used are the products of the hunt, and even the manufacturing techniques, such as hide tanning, are traditional. Many of these pieces are on exhibition in our institution. This is of enormous benefit to us, as early Dene ethnological material is rare. We have assisted them in establishing contact with other museums in southern Canada, and they are now starting to produce museum-quality specimens for these institutions.

In another Dene community a similar, yet distinct, project is underway. In this case, young and old women have joined together to revive and preserve various forms of decorative art, ranging from porcupine quill embroidery to bead sewing. Most importantly, the group has become a way of transmitting these skills to succeeding generations. We worked together to create a successful exhibition of their work at the PWNHC, at their request.

In both instances it is important to note that the initiative and interest are local, and that elaborate facilities and high operating budgets are not required. One legitimate concern is what is to become of the many objects they are now producing, since there is no curation as we understand it. In fact, many of the pieces are now in museum collections. Others belong to each of the groups and still others are the property of private individuals. These objects and the values inherent in them are undoubtedly more accessible to people than would have been the case had they been part of the permanent collections of a local museum.

In many instances the most immediate need is simply visual access to the Northwest Territories' natural and cultural history, i.e., exhibitions. In one community, a portion of a school hallway was fitted with specially designed exhibit cases to house reproductions of traditional utensils made by community residents. New schools are now being designed with this in mind.

In an Inuit community, a cooperative effort between a local heritage society and various government agencies is underway to develop a park interpretive centre. There is no desire to retain and curate large collections. The need is for space within the interpretive centre to house exhibitions developed by local people or obtained elsewhere. Space is also being set aside for a workroom which will be accessible to all members of the community who are engaged in heritage-related activities, ranging from stone sculpting to skin processing. This is another example of community interest in active participation, in addition to the passive viewing of exhibitions.

It is not necessary, however, to construct an interpretive centre to allow visual access to the natural and cultural record of the North. Multi-functional community centres are being built throughout the region, with diverse offices, programmes and community services all under one roof. The purpose is to reduce capital and operating costs by sharing space. This is another opportunity to incorporate museum-related activities at considerably less cost than if a separate building were constructed.

Another approach we are now exploring is the use of the educational resource centres developed by the Department of Education [Government of the Northwest Territories]. These centres serve remote communities by distributing educational materials. By providing copies of our travelling exhibitions to this extant network, we avoid the problems of duplicating a whole new set of community contacts, while achieving the maximum distribution of our exhibitions. Schools, adult education centres, band offices and so forth become the venues, and the exhibitions are designed with this in mind. Access is achieved with minimal capital costs.

One of the most exciting prospects for museum development in the Northwest Territories today is the interest and initiatives that are emerging from Native organizations. As an example, the Inuit Cultural Institute in Arviat [formerly Eskimo Point] recently received a planning grant from the National Museums Corporation [Government of Canada] to assess the feasibility of developing a museum and archives in the Arctic.

As Inuit presenting Inuit culture, they would be less prone to the unintentional ethnocentrism which often characterizes attempts to explain a culture other than one's own. This in itself could contribute immeasurably to an increased awareness of the need for heritage preservation. There are significant benefits for the museum community at large, as well. Native museums could become resource centres and sources of expert advice for other museums engaged in the research and presentation of Native cultures. This is not to say that oral tradition would become a substitute for scholarly inquiry, but that an emic perspective would be more readily available for those engaged in research and interpretation.

If done properly from the beginning, Native museums in the Northwest Territories could take their place alongside other institutions as professional custodial agencies for collections of national significance. In this way, decentralization and access could become a reality without threatening the objects themselves. This will require a very wise use of existing resources and tireless commitment, but the prospects are bright.

To return to the PWNHC, another exciting possibility is the enhancement of our research capability. The Northwest Territories desperately needs scientists and humanists in all fields to pursue northern studies – not only as scholars, but also as northern residents. This in no way is meant to denigrate the northern research undertaken by southern-based individuals and institutions. The Northwest Territories now requires, however, both the tangible and the intangible benefits of a scholarly community.

Current discussions on northern science policy underscore this very real need. Northern residents often feel they are the hapless victims of insensitive research projects conceived and staffed in the South for southern consumption. This situation would undoubtedly improve if more research originated in the North. To achieve this requires qualified people and facilities, both of which are now in short supply in the Northwest Territories. In the absence of a university, the PWNHC has an even greater responsibility to assemble scholars who represent all museum-related disciplines, and to create the proper physical and intellectual environment for the pursuit of northern knowledge. Planning has already started with this in mind, and it will take decades to meet this responsibility.

If the past five years are any indication, one can only be optimistic about the future. Generous financial support from the Government of the Northwest Territories has clearly demonstrated that organization's commitment to heritage preservation. We have also sought professional and technical support from institutions across the nation. The National Museums Corporation, in particular the National Museum of Man [now the Canadian Museum of History], and the Canadian Conservation Institute, has done much on our behalf. The development of northern museums cannot be done in any other way. Regional parochialism, disciplinary boundaries and political rhetoric cannot be allowed to hinder the use of the expertise and assistance the Canadian museum community has to offer.

Conclusions

In considering museums in the Northwest Territories, I have attempted to point out various problems and prospects that are worthy of attention. There are many more. Isolation, a severe climate, a vast region and a small, scattered population are facts we cannot control. Our plans must creatively adapt to these facts, while meeting the needs of northern residents and visitors who come to learn about Canada's North. Certain other realities also exist which influence the museum landscape, such as the operation of an expensive, professional museum in Yellowknife which radiates services and support outward.

Northern residents are also experiencing a new cultural awareness, coupled with a renewed respect for the past and a desire to preserve this legacy for posterity. This awareness is being expressed in many ways, much of which departs from our traditional definitions and conceptions about museums. It is most important at this time not to dampen or erode local interest and initiative by rigid adherence to preconceived notions of how things should be done. If a creative and fostering environment can be achieved, I am convinced that many of the other concerns will be addressed in the process. Access versus preservation need not be an issue, as there is ample room for professional custodial agencies and local alternatives. The key is to assess the countless possibilities and work toward that which is most compatible with recognized needs and interests. This is best accomplished in a spirit of non-partisanship.

The multicultural environment is the real challenge for heritage preservation in the Northwest Territories today. The eminent anthropologist Sol Tax was said "to have had the respect not to decide for others what is in their best interest . . ." (Hinshaw 1971: vii). The PWNHC, in its role as the Territories' senior museum institution, can do no better than to aspire to this wisdom. As the Northwest Territories is truly multicultural, so should be the preservation and interpretation of Canada's northern legacy.

Acknowledgements

I am grateful to Jane H. Kelley for her insightful comments on an earlier draft of this chapter. Many other people have contributed to this chapter through discussion, comments and criticisms over the past several years. These people include Ellen Bielawski, Duncan Cameron, Victoria Dickenson, Brian Eldred, Jose Kusugak, Thomas Kutluk, Gino Pin, Scott Raymond, William E. Taylor, Jr., Barbara Tyler and Marilyn Walker. The Prince of Wales Northern Heritage Centre, the Government of the Northwest Territories and the Arctic Institute of North America deserve special thanks for their many services and valuable support.

Note

1 Inuit are the Aboriginal people of Arctic Canada; the Dene people (DEN–ay) are an Aboriginal group of First Nations who live in the northern boreal and subarctic regions of Canada, and the Metis are descendants of people born of relations between First Nations women and European men.

References

Guthe, C. E. (1959) *The Management of Small History Museums*. Nashville: The American Association for State and Local History.
Hinshaw, R. (ed.) (1971) *Currents in Anthropology: Essays in Honor of Sol Tax*. The Hague: Mouton Publishers.

2

MUSEUM IDEOLOGY AND PRACTICE IN CANADA'S THIRD WORLD*

Author's note: This issue of *MUSE*, the journal of the Canadian Museums Association (CMA), was devoted to the proceedings of the 1986 CMA Conference session "The Politics of Culture and the Politics of Government: Conflict in Paradise." This conference session featured a paper by Jeanne Canizzo, an anthropologist and research associate at the Royal Ontario Museum in Toronto, Canada. I presented this paper in response to her presentation – hence the references to Dr. Canizzo's paper in the text below.

Introduction

> In the NWT, it is still possible for individuals and organizations to influence the course of events in very immediate ways.

Although I recently resigned as director of the Prince of Wales Northern Heritage Centre (PWNHC), I would like to discuss a number of considerations which have been of great interest to me over the past decade and, in particular, to explain conditions that are peculiar to the Northwest Territories (NWT). However, there is one qualification: I have no intention of speaking on behalf of the Aboriginal peoples of the NWT. My perspective is that of a white, middle-class professional who was given the responsibility of developing the NWT's first public heritage facility. As my remarks are clearly those of an insider, they cannot be considered to be a proper evaluation of the work that has been done.

*Source: Robert R. Janes, *MUSE*, Vol. IV, No. 4 (1987): 33–39.

In her paper on the transformation of the Barbados Museum, Dr. Cannizzo raises several fundamental questions which I will use to structure my own observations on the Northwest Territories. But before I do this, it is necessary to provide certain facts about the NWT and its peoples.

The Northwest Territories

The NWT consists of nearly three and one-half million kilometres of forests, lakes and tundra north of the 60th parallel. The population numbers only about 50,000 Inuit, Dene, Metis, and Euro-Canadians, resulting in an astoundingly low population density.[1] In comparison, the subcontinent of India, which is similar in size to the NWT, has a population approaching 550 million. Northern residents live in and around 62 communities, less than one quarter of which can be reached by road from southern Canada.[2]

It might sound strange to refer to Canada below the 60th parallel as being "southern," but I can assure you that "southern Canada" is a common expression throughout the Canadian North, and forms an important part of the northern ideology. Seven Aboriginal languages are spoken daily throughout the NWT, in addition to English, French and a variety of other European and Asian languages. Nowhere is this more dramatically visible than in the NWT Legislative Assembly, where seven different Aboriginal languages are available on the simultaneous translation equipment.

Another fundamental consideration is the fact that the NWT has not yet achieved the political self-determination that is taken for granted in Canadian provinces. In the NWT, nearly 98% of the landmass is currently the property of the federal government, and is administered by a federal department headquartered in Ottawa, Ontario.[3] However, great progress has been made in the recent past with respect to the NWT's relationship with the central government and the NWT now has a native northerner as its elected leader presiding over a 25-member elected Assembly with a majority of Native peoples. Nevertheless, many decisions which affect all northern peoples are still made in Ottawa, sometimes by people who have never even set foot in the NWT. This ongoing struggle for self-determination has been, and will continue to be, a passionate preoccupation of northern government, Native organizations and northerners in general. The proposed division of the NWT is one of the major issues which has received considerable publicity in southern Canada. The result is intense activity, plenty of confusion, and the undeniable fact that, in the NWT, it is still possible for individuals and organizations to influence the course of events in immediate ways. These are also important ingredients in a northern ideology.

Taken together, these considerations of a sparse, multicultural population, vast distances, underdeveloped transportation and communication networks, plus a political legacy which is only now turning its back on colonialism, are sufficient cause to describe the NWT as a third world. I have acquired all my professional museum experience within this third world, as a member of the so-called dominant culture living and working within a Native majority. In Dr. Cannizzo's apt description of the Barbados

FIGURE 2 The Prince of Wales Northern Heritage Centre, Yellowknife, Northwest
Territories, Canada. Courtesy of the NWT Archives/© Dept. of
Education, Culture and Employment/G-2007-030: 0046.

Museum before its transformation, we who have come north to do museum work are
the expatriates. I will explore the meaning of this by providing summary observations
on the institution where I have worked, as it is the principal source of my perspective.

The Prince of Wales Northern Heritage Centre

There are several factors which help to explain the history and role of the Prince
of Wales Northern Heritage Centre (PWNHC):

- *A clear political mandate.* As a result of the Territorial Museum Policy which
  received legislative approval in 1972, the PWNHC was given a clear political
  mandate. Residents of the NWT had expressed deep concern over the loss of
  northern artifacts to "southern" individuals and agencies and, as a result, the
  Territorial Museum Policy called for a professional facility in Yellowknife to
  curate a territorial collection, as well as to radiate museum and archival services
  throughout the NWT in support of local heritage development.
- *Financial commitment from the Government of the NWT.* When I was hired as
  the first director in 1976, the budget was set at CAN$70,000. Ten years later
  there are 20 full-time staff and an annual budget of CAN$1.6 million. The
  PWNHC is a division of the Territorial Government's Department of Culture
  and Communications.
- *The concept of a heritage centre.* The Prince of Wales Northern Heritage Centre
  differs from most other heritage institutions and museums because of the variety of activities housed under one roof, one administration, and one director.
  The PWNHC's current responsibilities include: collections management;

conservation; exhibitions; education/extension; the NWT archives; the NWT archeology program (both the administration of legislation and research), and heritage advisory services.

- *Commitment to decentralization.* Despite its rather large presence in Yellowknife, the PWNHC is a territorial institution with territorial responsibilities. All sections engage in territorial-wide programs and services, and these community responsibilities are specified in the staffs' position descriptions.
- *Internal organization of the PWNHC.* This can be characterized as "flat," in that the staff in charge of the seven organizational units mentioned above report directly to the director. The administrative structure is lean and simple, which is essential in promoting coordination and cooperation among the many specializations at the PWNHC. Cooperation and team work are highly valued.

Dr. Cannizzo's questions

Dr. Cannizzo raises three questions which I believe are fundamental to the conduct of museum work anywhere in Canada, and I would like to address these from a northern perspective. At the beginning of her conference paper, Dr. Cannizzo defines museums as "carefully created, artificially constructed repositories, or negotiated realities." Her first question is what is the ideology, or system of ideas, values and beliefs, that guides the policies and work of northern Canada's largest heritage institution?

Assessing the ideology

To begin with, this ideology is heterogeneous and defies simplistic labelling. As the PWNHC's first director, I must assume responsibility for much of this ideology, which is grounded to a significant extent in my advanced anthropological training in subarctic cultures. There are also several other aspects of this ideology which are best summarized as follows:

- The belief that Aboriginal cultural history is of paramount importance;
- The recognition that northern Native cultures are in process – meaning that they are adapting and evolving in the late twentieth century. They cannot be relegated to a prehistoric past of skin tents, bows, and arrows;
- The belief that Western methods of scientific investigation and scholarship and are essential in fulfilling the PWNHC's responsibilities. [Research was valued and supported in a variety of ways, including the publication of an *Occasional Paper* series, providing travel funds for professional meetings, providing secretarial services for scholarly papers, and arranging for special forms of staff leave to allow study and writing];
- The recognition that there is a wealth of traditional knowledge that underlies 7,000 years of Aboriginal occupation in the NWT, and that this knowledge is fundamental to all of the work that is done in the heritage field;

- The belief that heritage work is best served by decentralization and local initiatives. This means individuals, organizations and communities participating in terms of their own needs and aspirations, and not on the basis of the assumptions of a central heritage agency;
- The recognition that the concept of a museum is alien to the NWT's Native majority – the idea of collecting objects for study and exhibition is a colonial legacy. Because of this, non-traditional museum approaches must be nurtured to ensure that northern residents can preserve and celebrate their cultures in the broadest sense;
- The belief that excellence, professionalism and service go hand in hand, and that there is no substitute for the hard work and attention to detail that these demand;
- Finally, the recognition that the NWT is a little-known region with only a minor voice in national affairs. It has taken 10 years, for example, to get the National Museums of Canada to include the word "territorial" in their official documents. This is more than mere semantics, for the absence of the word "territorial" signals not only that the policy makers are overlooking the museum work in the NWT, but that they are also ignoring the special relationship which exists between the federal government and the NWT. The fact that the NWT is consistently overlooked and misunderstood means that we try harder, and that we have a unique perspective to offer Canada and the world.

The institutional ideology summarized above may appear to be anything but coherent. Embracing the scientific method along with traditional knowledge, for example, might be considered contradictory. Yet, when this ideology is translated into practice, these seeming contradictions dissolve, or at least become manageable.

Meaningful exhibitions

Nowhere is this varied combination of ideological beliefs and values more important than in a museum's responsibility to portray history as a process. Dr. Cannizzo expresses her concern about this when she asks, "will the displays be able to show us how the past and the present are linked; can the objects illustrate and tell us about relationships between races, classes and cultures?" This is the second question I will endeavor to answer.

Exhibitions are a time-honored approach to portraying the past. The question, as Dr. Cannizzo indicates, is whether or not the observer senses a link with that past. In the NWT, the past is very much a part of the present, as two of the world's great hunting cultures, the Dene and Inuit of the NWT, still maintain close and unyielding ties to the land. Because of this, the exhibition scripts for the main galleries were reviewed by members of the cultures that were being portrayed. This led to the use of the first person in all the exhibition labels, as well as the use of the NWT's major cultural groupings as an organizing principle in the exhibitions, rather than relying solely on a linear succession of historical developments.

Efforts have also been made to provide additional views of human history in the NWT by pointing out Indigenous contributions. For example, it is commonly believed that the Dene of the Mackenzie Basin were quick to reject their past and immediately adopt all the trappings of Western civilization when these were introduced by the fur traders. This is simply not true. On the contrary, the Euro-Canadian traders succeeded because the Dene maintained the adaptive patterns of their ancestors throughout the nineteenth century (Janes 1991). Scholarship is critical to this sort of rethinking and museums must assume this responsibility.

Undoubtedly the most fruitful attempts to link the past and the present in a meaningful way have occurred through the direct involvement of Indigenous cultures in what, for want of a better term, we call living heritage. The moose-skin boat project is one example of this and represents the revival of a moribund technology by a group of Mountain Dene. This 13 metre boat, made of untanned moose skins and spruce wood, is perhaps the most elegant and dramatic testimony of subarctic ingenuity in existence. It was built and sailed by Dene men, women and children of the late twentieth century, based on the knowledge and skills that have survived the passage of centuries. The boat is on permanent exhibition at the PWNHC, but this is somewhat incidental to the more enduring process which saw a group of people return to the northern mountains to build the boat and bring it home on violent mountain streams, in tune with the collective memory of their culture. An exhibition such as this one is the link to which Dr. Cannizzo refers, as it represents the expression of a cultural legacy by contemporary people.

The Centre's main exhibition galleries, however, are heavily dependent upon text which is not translated into the Aboriginal languages of the NWT, with the exception of several brief introductory statements. The use of Aboriginal languages was not of critical concern in the mid-1970s when these exhibitions were developed. Aboriginal languages are now a priority for the territorial government, however, and the PWNHC must also accept the responsibility to serve Aboriginal northerners in their languages. This will require the complete rethinking of the exhibitions and programs, a task that is now underway.

Indigenous representation

The third and final question posed by Dr. Canizzo is concerned with how the Indigenous peoples of Canada are presented and represented in museums. Having provided at least a cursory overview of how northern Aboriginal peoples are presented in the PWNHC'S exhibitions, the following discussion will consider how they are represented. That is, in what ways are Indigenous peoples involved in the management, programs and activities of the institution?

The majority of the PWNHC's staff is well-educated people from white, middle-class backgrounds who have moved north from southern Canada. In fact, only 10% of the staff is northern Native. This situation can be traced to the beginning of the museum, when the urgency attached to its development and opening precluded a long-term training plan and ultimate takeover by Indigenous peoples. Such an approach would also have been unorthodox in the mid-1970s.

The underrepresentation of northern Aboriginal peoples in all aspects of government, business and the professions is a major concern of the current territorial government and, as a result, an affirmative action program has been established within the public service. For the PWNHC, this means that by 1991, 33% of the staff should be Dene, Inuit or Metis. It must be emphasized, however, that this plan is not dependent upon dismissing current staff, and that it is contingent upon the availability of appropriate educational and training opportunities. Most importantly, the PWNHC's staff is committed to providing the opportunities that are essential to an effective, affirmative action program.

Despite the cultural homogeneity of the staff, the PWNHC is committed to Native involvement in a number of other less obvious ways outside of Yellowknife. This is only common sense, as Yellowknife is not the centre of the universe and few Aboriginal residents from remote communities have any interest in living and working there. Because the PWNHC can never presume to speak on behalf of all cultures in the NWT, even with a multicultural staff, efforts are directed toward supporting or assisting those who are in a position to do so. In short, we are attempting to contribute to the cultural empowerment of northern Native cultures.

Working with communities

For example, the PWNHC operates an archeological field school for young northerners, designed to enhance their awareness of Aboriginal cultural history and to give them practical training in field techniques. This is not a make-work project, but an integral part of an archeological research and rescue program – the rescue efforts being directed at sites that are threatened by human activity. Concerted efforts are also made to employ local people on archeological field projects in their regions. In this way, the PWNHC is slowly building up a group of trained and sensitive field workers who not only contribute their own skills and knowledge, but also develop an abiding commitment to the care of these heritage resources. Brief, nontechnical summaries of archeological work in the NWT are compiled annually, translated into the appropriate Aboriginal languages, and widely distributed throughout the NWT. The benefits of this open communication are numerous.

Through its Heritage Advisory Services, the PWNHC offers a full range of professional and technical services, advice and assistance, in addition to providing over CAN$200,000 annually in support of community heritage work. This funding covers, among other things, the salaries of full-time museum staff in Fort Smith and Iqaluit [formerly Frobisher Bay], and the heating bills for a group of elderly Inuit who get together to sew, carve and replicate traditional Inuit technology in a remote Arctic community. The PWNHC plays a supporting role, as all these community groups are independent entities.

An increasingly important role of the Heritage Advisory Services lies in the provision of training and technical assistance to communities. PWNHC staff are sent to communities, such as the librarian to assist a local history and language project in a Dene community above the Arctic Circle with training in cataloguing. Individuals also come to Yellowknife for more comprehensive orientation and training within PWNHC. In attempting to empower the Aboriginal peoples of the NWT in a heritage sense, the PWNHC can be seen as a broker. Because it is a fully professional facility, it has the necessary credibility to secure funding and donations, be fully consulted by national organizations and gradually assume responsibility for northern heritage matters. As a result, PWNHC has been able to act on behalf of local heritage interests, especially with respect to the seats of power which are located far from northern communities.

In search of empowerment

There are, however, certain disadvantages to a professional, centralized facility. First among these is the persistent tendency to look inward. It takes a great deal of time and money to operate such a facility, and it is easy to inadvertently overlook the needs of distant communities. Radiating services from Yellowknife throughout the NWT also results in astronomical transportation costs. For example, a return air ticket from Yellowknife to Iqaluit, the eastern seat of the territorial government, is about CAN$1500. Finally, a great deal of energy and commitment are required from all staff members to balance the diverse needs and interests of highly trained professionals engaged in a variety of activities with the needs and aspirations of the communities. It would be less than honest to conceal the recurring tension that results.

This process of cultural empowerment will only be complete when the Aboriginal peoples of the NWT have assumed a full and equal role in the preservation and interpretation of their cultural traditions. Unprecedented opportunities to do so loom on the horizon and preparations are now underway by at least one organization, the Inuit Cultural Institute (ICI), to ensure the successful assumption of such responsibilities. The ICI is developing the Inuit Silittuqsarvingat (IS) project, consisting of a traditional museum component combined with a distance education program based on the preservation and dissemination of traditional Inuit knowledge using Inuit Elders. The result will be an innovative approach to northern heritage work, owned and operated by Inuit. The IS project is destined to become the Inuit Heritage Trust when land claims are finalized and an Inuit government is formed in the eastern part of the NWT. At that time, the trust will assume responsibility for the preservation, care and study of Inuit heritage.[4]

A major responsibility of the PWNHC is to invest in the future by Providing whatever support is necessary to prepare the Inuit for this work. As the director of the PWNHC, I also provide professional advice and assistance as a member of the IS Development Committee – the membership of which is two-thirds Inuit. In addition, the PWNHC is currently training a young Inuk to assume the museum responsibilities.

Assisting individuals and organizations to assume responsibility for their own heritage affairs requires the capability to deliver a wide range of services and support. This is the enormous advantage of an integrated heritage institution like the PWNHC, as a number of specialists can be brought together quickly and easily to solve a problem or provide advice to a community. It is commonplace to find an archeologist, a conservator, the museum advisor and a curator working together on a common problem. For the vast majority of the population who are untutored in the learned complexities that distinguish archives from archeology, for example, the PWNHC is mostly able to deal directly with their interests and concerns, without having to tell them to go elsewhere. One community may need a travelling exhibit for school use, while another needs an archeologist to study a site which will be included in a local tourist brochure. This ability to respond to a wide range of interests and needs is particularly important in a multicultural environment, where diverse perceptions are the norm and there will never be any one way to do things. By nurturing creativity and flexibility in heritage work, the PWNHC hopes to ensure full and active participation by all northern residents.

Conclusions

What does all of this mean for the politics of culture, and the politics of government, in Canada's NWT? In short, it means that the Government of the NWT, with its Native leader and Native majority, is seeking expanded political rights as a foundation for self-determination. Increasingly, the NWT will be doing things on its own terms. Northern residents are experiencing a new cultural awareness and a renewed respect for their past, both of which are in part attributable to this current political ferment. In this context, the PWNHC, as a publicly funded institution, has a key responsibility to portray Northern Aboriginal cultures to all visitors, to Canada and to the world. It must also enable all Aboriginal residents to define and assume their rightful roles in the preservation and interpretation of their cultures.

In addition, the PWNHC must strive to achieve a balance, recognizing that one-third of the population is not Aboriginal. The results of this balancing act defy categorization, and can be both visible and invisible. A visitor to the PWNHC enters a sophisticated, environmentally controlled building costing CAN$10 million (see Figure 2), and immediately sees a 19.5 square metre painting of the Prince of Wales.[5] Unseen by the same visitor, however, is the Mountain Dene archeological crew chief unearthing artifacts in his homeland side by side with the PWNHC's subarctic archeologist. It is a complex world, and museums above all must strive to recognize this and strike a balance between diverse interests. We must not only react to change, but also help to define and initiate it when it is in our best interests, as well as in the interests of those we serve. In all these ways, the PWNHC is attempting to include and celebrate all segments of the NWT's truly multicultural population.

The successes achieved to date have been modest when compared to what needs to be done. The examples described above should not be seen as solutions, but as experiments, and each situation will call for new and creative approaches. Irrespective of what has been done or what is currently proposed, the PWNHC's programs and activities have imposed Western intellectual traditions and linear concepts of time on the Aboriginal cultures of the NWT. Mistrust does exist, as evidenced by a widely respected Dene leader who fears putting contemporary Dene tools, such as hide scrapers, in a museum exhibit case for fear that these tools will be relegated to the past in the minds of his people. Efforts are directed at overcoming this mistrust and extension programs are one way of doing this.

In the end, I cannot say what native perceptions of heritage and museums actually are. There is no doubt, however, that if the PWNHC were owned and operated by Dene or Inuit, it would not be the same institution that I have been describing. In short, their worldviews are radically different from ours. I personally value this cultural heterogeneity and believe that it is a key to the survival of our species. In contrast, it is apparent that the proponents of the animal rights movement have never considered this. Knowingly or unknowingly, this movement is attempting to dehumanize Canada's northern hunters, and it serves as a stark reminder that the work of museums is never finished. The PWNHC is currently making plans to present a more balanced and intelligent view of the anti-trapping and animal rights controversy – within the context of two of the world's greatest hunting cultures. The politics of culture will always be with us.

Acknowledgements

I am grateful to Lynette Harper, Chuck Arnold and Chris Hanks for their valuable comments on an earlier draft of this chapter. I also want to thank Lynne Stone of the Science Institute for her assistance with the typing, proofreading and illustrations.

Notes

1 The Inuit are the Aboriginal people of Arctic Canada. Inuit is a plural noun and means "the people." The singular noun is Inuk and means "the person." The Dene people (DEN-ay) are an Aboriginal group of First Nations who live in the northern boreal and subarctic regions of Canada, and the Metis are descendants of people born of relations between First Nations women and European men. At the time this chapter was written, two-thirds of the NWT's population was Native born – Dene, Inuit or Metis.

2 This description of the NWT dates to 1987 and there was a significant change in 1999, when Nunavut officially separated from the NWT. Nunavut is the largest, northernmost and newest territory in Canada and covers 1,877,787 km^2 (725,018 sq mi) of land and 160,935 km^2 (62,137 sq mi) of water in northern Canada. One of the most remote, sparsely settled regions in the world, Nunavut has a population of 31,906 of mostly Inuit, spread over a land area the size of Western Europe. See Nunavut, in Wikipedia, *The Free Encyclopedia*, for more details. Available online at: http://en.wikipedia.org/wiki/Nunavut.

3 The devolution of political and administrative powers from Canada's federal government to the Government of the Northwest Territories is currently in process, and a final Devolution Agreement is pending.

4 The Inuit Heritage Trust (IHT) was established and receives its mandate from the Nunavut Land Claims Agreement, the largest Aboriginal land claim settlement in Canadian history, signed in 1993. In Nunavut, IHT represents Inuit interests in issues relating to heritage, archaeology, ethnographic resources, traditional place names and spiritual places. For more details, see: http://www.ihti.ca/eng/home-english.html.
5 On April 16, 1979, HRH the Prince of Wales officiated at the opening of the facility that bears his title. See: https://www.pwnhc.ca/programs/about.asp.

Reference

Janes, R.R. (1991) *Preserving Diversity: Ethnoarchaeological Perspectives on Culture Change in the Western Canadian Subarctic.* New York: Garland Publishing Inc.

3

FIRST NATIONS*

Policy and practice at the Glenbow Museum

Introduction

Various disciplines within the human sciences are becoming increasingly aware of the importance of involving Aboriginal peoples in their work. With few exceptions, these peoples have been the subjects of anthropological and archaeological inquiry, rather than active participants. Recently, however, there is growing awareness of the need to involve Aboriginal peoples more actively in the policies and practices which govern the interpretation and presentation of their cultures. Because museums, as institutions, have fundamental responsibilities for this work, many of these recent developments are occurring there, rather than in university departments or government agencies.

Perhaps the most significant recent initiative in this regard is the 1989 establishment of the National Museum of the American Indian as part of the Smithsonian Institution in Washington, D.C. (Jacobsen 1989: 1). This new museum is a result of an agreement between the Smithsonian Institution and the Museum of the American Indian (M.A.I.) of the Heye Foundation (New York, US) to transfer the Heye collection to the Smithsonian. This collection includes approximately one million artifacts, a library with over 40,000 volumes, and a photo archives with 86,000 negatives and prints. The new National Museum of the American Indian will be situated on the mall at the foot of the U.S. Capitol, in conjunction with a facility in New York City – the original home of the Heye Foundation.

Of particular interest to archaeologists, anthropologists, and museum professionals is the legislation authorizing the establishment of the National Museum of the American Indian, as it also incorporates an agreement on the repatriation of human remains. The Smithsonian has in its collections the skeletal remains of

* *Source*: Robert R. Janes. This paper was presented at the Annual Meeting of the Canadian Archaeological Association, Whitehorse, Yukon, Canada. May 12, 1990.

about 18,000 Indians and Eskimos, and it recently reached formal agreement with Indian representatives to provide a process for the inventory, identification, and repatriation of these remains, when appropriate.[1]

Under the terms of this legislation, the US Secretary of the Interior is authorized to make grants to Indian tribes for the repatriation of these remains, as well as funerary objects. One million dollars US is expected to be appropriated in 1991 as a first step in carrying out the inventory (Jacobsen 1989: 14). Secretary Adams of the Smithsonian Institution called the new museum a "new kind of partnership in community outreach that will involve the whole of the Indian people in carrying forward to the world community their history, culture, experience, and world view" (Jacobsen 1989: 14).

I have provided these details on the American initiative, as it could likely set the standard for Aboriginal involvement in museum work in the early twenty-first century. If, as the recent advertisement for the first director of the National Museum of the American Indian indicates – that a Native person is the preferred candidate – we can expect even more interesting developments.

With no national museum of the Canadian Indian and Inuit in sight, what is happening in Canada to foster a renewed sense of harmony between Canada's original peoples and museum professionals? In the remainder of this chapter, I will review what the Glenbow Museum is doing, including some reflections on important considerations and future possibilities. I also want to take advantage of my involvement with the recently established Assembly of First Nations/Canadian Museums Association Task Force on Museums and First Peoples, and summarize our recent attempts to address these issues on the national level.[2]

Policy and practice at Glenbow

Although I am a newcomer to the Glenbow, it is fair to say that this museum has enjoyed a positive working relationship with the Indian peoples of the region, despite the controversy surrounding the Lubicon protest and the "Spirit Sings" exhibition.[3] This positive relationship has been strengthened immeasurably through the work of Glenbow's associate director, Dr. Hugh Dempsey, a prolific ethnohistorian who has done much to popularize the contributions of Aboriginal peoples to Canadian history.

In addition, Glenbow has been assiduous in gathering all types of materials pertaining to Aboriginal peoples in western Canada. Collected from a multidisciplinary perspective, these materials include documents, photographs, and artifacts, including abundant files from the offices of various Indian agencies which otherwise would have been destroyed. These diverse, but integrated, collections have become a focus of research on Aboriginal cultures by Native peoples, including recent work on Native land claims, histories of leading chiefs, and the preparation of course materials for Native studies programs in universities.

Not surprisingly, Glenbow has a policy in place to address Aboriginal concerns, at a time when many museums are just beginning to realize the importance of such policies. This policy is particularly relevant to this symposium, as it represents a commitment on the part of Glenbow to honour specific Aboriginal concerns. In the interests of time, I have selected several examples of these commitments as I will not be discussing the complete policy today. To quote from the policy:

1. If an Indian society or organized group – whose beliefs and practices have been performed continuously and without interruption for generations – requests the Glenbow not to exhibit their religious artifacts, such a request will be seriously considered.[4] Decisions will be based upon the particular circumstances surrounding each request.
2. If the Glenbow holds religious objects which are essential to the well-being of a society or group described above, every reasonable effort will be made to make these objects available to those groups, through loan or other means.
3. The Glenbow will not knowingly exhibit human remains from archaeological sites.
4. If a claim is made to the Glenbow that an Indian artifact was obtained by the museum, knowingly or unknowingly, through illegal means, and if clear evidence can be provided to support such a claim, every effort will be made to return the artifact in question to its rightful owner or heirs.

In fact, Glenbow has loaned religious paraphernalia to the Blackfoot Horn society, a secret, religious men's society on the Blood reserve in southern Alberta.[5] We have also agreed to return a medicine bundle to a secret, religious women's society on the same reserve. Both of these groups are based on traditions and practices that have been performed continuously for millennia.

Repatriation

Understandably, these rather explicit guidelines cannot necessarily encompass the variety of situations which can and do arise in the matter of repatriation. For example, since coming to Glenbow in September of 1989, I have been involved in numerous discussions resulting from requests to repatriate various objects. I have been struck with both the complexity and uniqueness of each request, which taken together underscore the need for broad, flexible, and magnanimous guidelines to deal with these situations. "Playing it by the book" is as foolhardy in this situation as it is in any other context involving peoples' needs, values, and aspirations.

Several of the complexities associated with repatriation that I have recently encountered include:

1. The difficulty in determining whether a request to return an artifact stems solely from the interests of a particular individual, or reflects the collective interests of a group of people, such as a band or a group of Elders. In these cases, we seek the advice of the Elders from the appropriate locale.

2. The difficulty in determining the motivation for the repatriation. Is it for spiritual reasons, educational purposes, or is it purely political in the sense that it represents undoing the wrong that the dominant society has done? All of these claims are potentially legitimate, depending upon the object and the situation.

3. The awkwardness and embarrassment which can result when it is learned that the object in question was given to the museum by an Aboriginal person in order to give it a home and to protect it from friends or relatives who intended to sell it. In some cases, this is actually recorded on the museum catalogue card.

4. The misunderstandings that arise when the interested parties view the repatriation solely in terms of late twentieth-century values and experience. Times have changed, and cultures are always in process, so that it is often difficult for Aboriginal peoples today to understand or appreciate decisions that were made by their relatives 25 or 50 years ago. Some individuals cannot believe that a relative would have donated or sold an object, not realizing that it was done at a time when commitment to the use of Aboriginal material culture was rapidly disappearing.

These complexities are indeed challenging, but they cannot be used as reasons for ignoring Aboriginal interests in repatriation. These complexities must be recognized and considered as essential to an equitable solution, irrespective of what the outcome may be. It is because of these complexities that Glenbow's policy on Aboriginal concerns contains two important considerations:

1. Aboriginal cultures change through time, values do not remain constant, and sensitivities change. What is unimportant to one generation may become vital to the next. It is important to be flexible and reasonable in any policy dealing with Aboriginal concerns so that these changing conditions and perceptions are taken into consideration.

2. Glenbow also appreciates the fact that religion has been an integral part of Aboriginal life for countless generations and that it is sometimes difficult to separate the religious from the secular. We recognize that some Aboriginal societies and groups are entirely religious in nature, while others are social. These factors, too, must always be taken into consideration.

In summary, the dilemmas and complexities of repatriation can be explained in part by the fact that Aboriginal cultures are dynamic and diverse. Neither of the two considerations noted above is intended to be a simplistic prescription for successful negotiating. What they do provide is the flexibility necessary to deal with these matters intelligently and openly. Glenbow's repatriation policy recognizes the importance of flexibility and unique circumstances, in an effort to achieve a balance between legitimate Aboriginal interests and the public trust. Continuous evaluation of any repatriation policy is essential to ensure that it remains sensible and productive.

Future possibilities

Repatriation is only one issue concerning the role of Aboriginal peoples in museum work. More important for the long term is a consideration of the broader context. This was formally recognized in Canada on a national level in 1988, when one hundred and fifty delegates from across the country met in Ottawa to discuss issues of importance to the museum and Native communities, including repatriation, human remains, stereotyping, and interpretation. This initial conference, co-hosted by the Assembly of First Nations and the Canadian Museums Association, was a result of the controversy surrounding the Lubicon Lake band's boycott of the Glenbow Museum's "Spirit Sings" exhibition during the 1988 Calgary Olympics (see note 2).

This sensitive situation was the final impetus for the 1988 meeting, although most of these issues and concerns were not new to the Canadian museum community. What was important was the willingness to sit down collectively and discuss these issues. Numerous recommendations resulted from the 1988 meeting (Assembly of First Nations, 1988: 1–4), including the following:

1. Seeking more firm commitments from museums and related institutions for funding and other resources for First Nations work;
2. Developing appropriate policies on access to museum holdings and information for First Nations;
3. Attacking and correcting stereotypes that are still perpetuated by, and inherent in, the history depicted by settler governments and institutions;
4. Defining, in contemporary First Nations cultural terms, what constitutes sacred and significant objects and materials in museum collections;
5. Recognizing the need for First Nation peoples to assume responsibility to preserve and present their histories and cultures;
6. Taking the knowledge and history of First Nations into Canadian classrooms and university lecture halls, as well as to First Nations students.

There was also consensus in 1988 to establish a Task Force on Museums and First Peoples to carry on the work that had been identified. This Task Force has now been established under the co-chairmanship of Tom Hill (Woodlands Cultural Centre, Brantford, Ontario, Canada) and Trudi Nicks (Royal Ontario Museum, Toronto, Ontario, Canada), and it met for the first time last February, 1990, in Brantford and Toronto.

It is important to note that this Task Force is not a body of political representatives, who would be required to report back to governing authorities at every stage of the discussions. Rather, it is a group of 18 experienced and willing individuals who will carry out the research and writing necessary to make recommendations for a second national symposium tentatively scheduled for early in 1991.

The February meeting of the Task Force produced a mission statement, or purpose, which is "to develop an ethical framework and strategies for Aboriginal

nations to represent their histories and cultures in concert with cultural institutions"
(Assembly of First Nations and the Canadian Museums Association 1992: viii). I
draw your attention to the words "in concert." These words were deliberately
chosen to emphasize the importance of working together and being in agreement,
as opposed to the much-abused process of consultation.

It was also agreed, in the interests of economy and efficiency, that the Task
Force should be broken down into three regional working groups in Canada
representing the east (Ontario, Quebec, Maritimes), central (Manitoba, Saskatchewan, Alberta, N.W.T.), and west (B.C. and Yukon). Each of these groups is
responsible for addressing the issues of repatriation, access, and interpretation in
whatever manner they see fit, bearing in mind the overall purpose of the Task
Force. A steering committee has been formed consisting of Tom Hill, Trudi
Nicks, Gerald McMaster, Bill Byrne, and Gloria Cranmer Webster, to oversee
the work of the working groups. It is expected that there will be tangible results
for discussion and action by the fall of 1990. This cooperative approach will hopefully eliminate the need for lawyers and judges to settle our differences of opinion
and perspectives, as has been the case in the United States. This alone makes the
work of the Task Force potentially invaluable.

Concluding remarks

In the meantime, staff at the Glenbow Museum are continuing to consider various
possibilities for increased collaboration with Alberta's Aboriginal peoples. We are
currently finalizing the terms of reference for a Native Advisory Committee, with
the intention of establishing it by early summer. This committee will have three
major responsibilities:

1. To advise Glenbow on matters relating to the research, collection, presentation,
    and interpretation of Aboriginal cultures in Alberta.
2. To advise on the planning, development, and evaluation of various activities,
    such as exhibitions, publications, public programs, and curatorial policies, as
    well as access to information and collections.
3. To serve as a link between Glenbow and the Aboriginal peoples of the region.

This committee will consist of one person from each of the Blackfoot, Blood,
Piegan, Sarcee, Stoney, and Cree First Nations, and will meet at least two times
a year. Although the Native Advisory Committee is advisory to the Board
of Governors of Glenbow, it is hoped that it will serve as the context within
which decisions can be made concerning Glenbow's involvement in a variety
of activities concerning museums and Aboriginal peoples – ranging from Native
internships to the repatriation of specific objects. Without such a forum, we risk
making decisions that are out of touch with current needs and aspirations.

In conclusion, I want to mention one difficulty that continues to concern me
since I first began working in museums in the Northwest Territories 14 years ago.

The concern is this – mainstream museums are prepared to loan artifacts to Aboriginal peoples if they maintain facilities with trained staff, acceptable environmental conditions, and security. This, of course, ignores the question of where the funding is to come from to develop these facilities, especially at a time when even established museums are finding it increasingly difficult or impossible to make ends meet. Deficit spending on the part of provincial and federal governments allows only one inescapable conclusion – there will be less and less money for cultural organizations until such time as those in power realize that such organizations are central to the quality of life, not peripheral to it.

My experience in northern Canada led me to conclude that climate-controlled facilities are not the solution to community museum development (Janes 1982: 18). The same is true of Alberta and the rest of Canada, so that alternatives to traditional museum development must be considered. Such alternatives are too numerous to mention here, but must reflect the Aboriginal worldview and the traditional and local knowledge upon which it is based. Because this worldview is so different from that of the dominant society, any attempts at reconciliation may be fraught with anxiety, misunderstandings, and potential conflict for all involved. This need not deter us, however, if we pay heed to the example set by the eminent anthropologist, Sol Tax. He was said to "have had the respect not to decide for others what is in their best interests . . ." (Hinshaw 1971: vii). As archaeologists, anthropologists, and museologists, it is important that our thinking and our behaviour reflect this fundamental tenet.

Acknowledgements

I wish to thank Hugh Dempsey, Ann Stevenson, Beth Carter, Dennis Slater, and Bill Byrne for their comments on an earlier draft of this chapter. I would also like to thank Deb Green for typing and proofreading the original paper.

Notes

1 The terms "Indian" and "Eskimo" were commonly used at the time this paper was written. At present, Eskimo is still used in the US as compared to Canada, where the word has been replaced with Inuit. In the US, the terms Natives use to refer to themselves vary regionally and generationally. Many older Natives in the US call themselves "Indians," while younger Natives often identify themselves as "Indigenous." Indian peoples in Canada are now known as First Nations. See: "Native Americans in the United States." Available online at: http://en.wikipedia.org/wiki/Native_Americans_in_the_United_States.
2 The Assembly of First Nations and the Canadian Museums Association formed the Task Force on Museums and First Peoples in 1989. Over the next three years, representatives of various First Nations communities and organizations, along with representatives of select museums, met nationally and in regional working groups to find a way of bridging what seemed to be an expanding chasm between museums and First Nations. While the Task Force's final report makes numerous recommendations for ways in which museums and First Nations can work together, it was left up to each institution to develop its own repatriation protocols and processes. See: Tom Hill and Trudy Nicks (editors), *Turning the Page: Task Force Report on Museums and First Peoples*. Ottawa: Canadian Museums Association and the Assembly of First Nations, 1992.

3 In 1988, the Glenbow Museum faced public demonstrations when it hosted "The Spirit Sings: Artistic Traditions of Canada's First Peoples." This exhibition was developed for the 1988 Winter Olympic Games and brought together items from Canada's Aboriginal peoples that had been dispersed around the world over the past several centuries. The controversy arose when the Lubicon Cree, a non-treaty band from northern Alberta, targeted the exhibition as a means of drawing attention to the lack of progress in their treaty negotiations with the Government of Canada. Although the Glenbow had no role in those discussions, Shell Canada Ltd. was the primary sponsor of the exhibition and was exploring for oil and gas in the contested area. Glenbow was criticized for acting in collusion with an industry portrayed as more interested in profits than social justice [I am indebted to the late Gerald Conaty for this succinct summary of this complex affair].

4 Indian peoples in Canada are now known as First Nations.

5 The Kainai (or Blood) reserve is the largest among the Blackfoot Confederacy and is located west and south of the city of Lethbridge, Alberta. The term "Blackfoot" is commonly used to refer to the four nations of the Blackfoot Confederacy: the Kainai (or Blood), Siksika (Blackfoot; Northern Blackfoot), Apatohsipiikuni (Piikuni, Peigan), and Ammskaapipiikuni (Piegan, Blackfeet).

References

Assembly of First Nations 1988 *Preserving Our Heritage: A Working Conference for Museums and First Peoples*. Executive Summary, pp. 1–4. Ottawa: Assembly of First Nations.

Assembly of First Nations and the Canadian Museums Association 1992 *Task Force Report on Museums and First Peoples*. A Report Jointly Sponsored by the Assembly of First Nations and the Canadian Museums Association. Ottawa, Canada.

Hinshaw, Robert (editor) 1971 *Currents in Anthropology: Essays in Honor of Sol Tax*. The Hague: Mouton Publishers.

Jacobsen, L. 1989 National Museum of the American Indian to Be Established on the Mall. *Anthropology Newsletter*, 30(9): 1, 14.

Janes, Robert R. 1982 Northern Museum Development: A View from the North. *Gazette*, 15(1): 14–23.

4

PERSONAL, ACADEMIC AND INSTITUTIONAL PERSPECTIVES ON MUSEUMS AND FIRST NATIONS*

Introduction

> The great challenge to our times is to harness research, invention, and professional practice to deliberately embraced human values . . . Experts . . . perform both center stage and in the wings. And all of us speak from the citizens' chorus. The fateful questions are how the specialists will interact with citizens, and whether the performance can be imbued with wisdom, courage and vision.
>
> *(Lowrance 1986: 209)*

Canada's Aboriginal peoples are now engaged in joining the "citizen's chorus," both as citizens and as experts. This is long overdue and there are many obstacles to overcome, but the relationships between mainstream museums and First Nations are changing and there is no turning back. Part of this change is challenging museum assumptions about how Aboriginal peoples think and act, and I wish to comment on this growing awareness from three perspectives – personal, academic, and institutional. One primary characteristic of the academic community is its relentless search for objective knowledge and, although I believe in the existence of such knowledge, it is important to understand that scholarship and professional practice cannot be divorced from our lives as individuals – our training, experience, aspirations, and values. Nowhere is this multiplicity of perspectives more important than in the realm of museums and First Nations.

As a result, this commentary incorporates both a personal and an academic perspective, as well as some observations from my position as the Executive Director of Glenbow (Calgary, Alberta, Canada), a multifaceted cultural institution with extensive

*Source: Robert R. Janes, *The Canadian Journal of Native Studies*, Vol. XIV, No. 1 (1994): 147–156. This commentary is a revised version of a presentation given at the Annual Meeting of the Alberta Museums Association in Medicine Hat, Alberta, Canada, October 30–November 1, 1992.

North American ethnological collections. These three perspectives – the personal, academic, and institutional – can be thought of as interlocking circles, as each perspective constantly influences the other. It is impossible to ignore any of these perspectives, if we are to forge new relationships between museums and First Nations.

A personal view

My first experience with Aboriginal people occurred in the Northwest Territories, and arose out of a need for archaeological field experience during my first year as a graduate student at the University of Calgary, Canada. In fact, I knew nothing of this vast wilderness north of the sixtieth parallel, having no recollection of even having studied it in school. Equipped with this benign ignorance, I joined an archaeological crew in the summer of 1971, bound for the central Barren Lands of the Northwest Territories, several hundred kilometres northeast of Yellowknife – one of the most remote regions in Canada and the world.

From the very beginning, the sense of adventure was enticing. It began with the equipment list issued by the Project Director, who advised that undershirts were mandatory, as mosquitoes bite through a shirt alone. The excitement was intensified when our float-equipped, de Havilland Otter aircraft delivered us and our field camp to the shores of the Thelon River, near a relic forest in the middle of the Thelon Game Sanctuary. In short, I had never imagined that such a region existed within North America, for it seemed so exotic to me that it deserved its own continent, or at least the isolation afforded by a gigantic sea. This is a land where ten thousand caribou walked by our camp on their way south and the black flies were so thick that they became mired in the contents of our sandwiches while we prepared them. My final amazement that summer was the onslaught of cold weather in the middle of August, and the urgency with which we struck camp while there was still time to land an aircraft on open water.

Mystified, excited, and firmly committed to doing archaeological fieldwork somewhere in the Canadian North, I participated in two more field projects in 1972 and 1973. On both field projects, I was part of a much larger effort to identify and record archaeological sites in advance of the proposed Mackenzie Valley Pipeline.[1] I had read about the skills and endurance of the Dene people who lived along the Mackenzie River and was intrigued by the prospects of meeting and working with them.[2]

This was not to be, however. Sensitivity to the value of the local and traditional knowledge of Indigenous peoples was not part of northern archaeological research design in the early 1970s. This was neither intentional nor conspiratorial, but simply a reflection of the apparent arrogance inherent in a Western scientific worldview. As we travelled the length of the Mackenzie River, we observed Dene going about their lives, met some of them, and even asked a Dene couple to assist us with the identification of some artifacts.

Yet, we never really involved these people in our work. The Dene and Métis residents must surely have wondered who we were – youths, fresh from southern

FIGURE 3 The author working with Dene elders, Elizabeth and Johnny Yakaleya, on the identification of artifacts recovered near Tulita, Northwest Territories during a survey of the Mackenzie River in 1973. Courtesy of Robert R. Janes

Canada, tramping through the bush in search of sites whose whereabouts were already firmly planted in the memories of various local inhabitants. But the excitement and newness of living and working in one of the world's greatest wildernesses was running high and, despite nagging doubts and private thoughts about the conduct of a human science (archaeology) that ignores living peoples, nothing was done to involve the Dene.

I gained more experience when I joined an archaeological survey of several interior lakes in the western Northwest Territories, not far from the Arctic Circle, in 1973. We worked well into October, when every night is below freezing and snow comes early and stays. We travelled fast – on foot, by canoe, and by prearranged charters using small, float-equipped aircraft. At one lake, we paid a visit to several families of Dene hunters who were busy catching fish for the winter's work in the bush, in order to introduce ourselves and tell them of our work. Several listened politely and then the Chief advised us that winter was approaching, and that sensible shelter consisted of a canvas-wall tent and a wood stove, both of which he then loaned to us for the duration of our stay. This was done without ridicule of our unheated nylon tent, or incriminating questions about what we were doing there. It was a simple act of polite generosity which left an indelible memory.

I spent the fall and winter engaged in graduate studies, excited by these field experiences and vaguely perplexed about what they had to do with getting a graduate degree in archaeology. I was also acutely aware of the distance that lay between my middle-class upbringing and the lives of these northern hunters. Although I had resolved to spend the next five years of my life studying Dene archaeology, I did not know any Dene people personally. This mixture of curiosity and unease led to the inevitable conclusion that I had to go north and live for a while.

An academic view

The time I spent living with the Willow Lake Dene in 1974–75 introduced me to the richness of a living culture, as compared to what one finds in the archaeological record. The vast majority of sites in the Subarctic are astonishingly meagre for a number of reasons. The soil is acidic, and perishable materials such as skin, bone and wood simply do not last very long in the ground. In addition, the Dene were highly mobile in the past and carried only minimal possessions. In other words, archaeologists need all the help they can get in trying to decipher the unrecorded history of these northern hunters, who have lived in the Northwest Territories for nearly 7,000 years. This led me to ethnoarchaeology, a type of research which is concerned with the study of a living society from an archaeological perspective.[3]

The reasoning behind this approach is quite simple. The contemporary setting can provide numerous clues to assist in identifying and recognizing what is found in the ground, in the absence of observable behaviour. I spent a good deal of time excavating a contemporary tipi in a hunting camp in an effort to define distinctive features of tipis which are observable in the ground (Janes 1989). These features, in the absence of surface tipi remains, are useful in detecting the presence of tipis in an archaeological site. By understanding what dwellings were used, archaeologists are able to piece together settlement patterns.

It is important, however, to counter any tendency to idealize these hunters and their way of life by noting that the years since this fieldwork in the 1970s and the 1980s have not necessarily been happy ones for the Willow Lakers. Alcohol abuse continues to take its toll, resulting in one intoxicated man dying in a snowmobile accident and another spending his early adulthood in jail for drinking-related offenses. Willow Lake elders have died of old age and hard lives, and a light plane accident took the life of a young Willow Lake woman. The Willow Lakers are not a pristine group of hunters frozen in time. They are individuals and families living through a time of profound cultural change, and the trauma cannot be separated from the joy.

An institutional view

Issues

The institutional perspective is perhaps the most important in the relationship between Aboriginal peoples and mainstream museums, as the latter are creatures of the dominant society and possess the larger share of power and authority.

If this relationship is to truly evolve, Canadian museums will have to assume a leadership role, and consider new approaches to what has always been an asymmetrical relationship. Ultimately, any constructive change will be influenced by the individual experiences and perspectives of those museum workers charged with this responsibility.

For example, as an individual and a researcher who has lived among Aboriginal peoples, I understand that their cultures are living ones and not frozen in time. As the Executive Director of a cultural institution, I must attempt to recognize and integrate all of these perspectives. There is no doubt that the personal and academic experiences of individual staff, such as the ones described earlier in this commentary, exert a profound influence on the direction of mainstream museums, despite claims of objectivity by museums.

Perhaps the most controversial institutional issue is the matter of fiduciary trust – Glenbow's obligation to hold its collections in perpetuity for the people of Alberta. When the question of whether to return or loan a ceremonial object arises, for example, the meaning of fiduciary responsibility is called into question. As a fundamental tenet of the museum profession, the idea of keeping collections forever understandably receives unswerving devotion from most museum workers. The real question, in my view, is whether such a commitment to posterity can be upheld within the context of unrelenting social change. With Aboriginal peoples throughout Canada striving for self-determination and social well-being, what responsibilities do museums have when they own materials that are crucial to fulfilling these aspirations?

We have decided, with the guidance of Glenbow's First Nations Advisory Council (consisting of representatives of the Blood, Peigan, Siksika, Stoney, Tsuut'ina, Plains Cree and northern Cree nations), that we have a major responsibility to support ceremonial activities with objects from our collections. We also recognize that the loans we have made may very well evolve into transfers of ownership. Museum workers always say that they are holding their collections for posterity. Perhaps, for Canada's First Nations, posterity has arrived.

The most common defense against any relaxation in the control of our collections is the "Camel's Nose" argument or the "Thin Edge of the Wedge." Recall Aesop's tale of the Camel's Nose. Once you compassionately let the camel stick his nose inside the tent, how can you refuse him further entrance? The inference for museum directors is that, having loaned or returned objects to First Nations, there would soon be a run on the collections and we would eventually lose everything to a variety of special-interest groups.

This argument should be rejected, for the abuse of a thing does not bar its use (Fletcher in Hardin, 1985: 63). In addition, those who use this argument act as if human beings are completely devoid of practical judgement. We must be willing to take some risks and draw some arbitrary lines in this uncharted territory of museums and First Nations. This is what the Assembly of First Nations/ Canadian Museums Association Task Force has asked museums to do (Hill and Nicks 1992: 8).

Trust

A fundamental ingredient in forging meaningful relationships with First Nations is trust – a firm belief in the honesty, integrity, and reliability of the other person. No amount of legal paperwork can create or ensure this trust. Rather, it requires time and openness to develop, which means a major commitment by both individuals and institutions. It is the ongoing personal involvement of key Glenbow staff which has forged the trust which underlies our growing involvement with Aboriginal peoples in southern Alberta.

But trust must be reciprocal or it means nothing, and we have learned this the hard way. We loaned a ceremonial object to one particular family, who then defaulted on the conditions of the loan and have subsequently ignored our appeals. This situation remains unresolved. Should we ban any further loans to anyone because of this particular family? We don't think so, as we have enshrined a management principle at Glenbow that says we will avoid practices and policies designed to protect the organization against making "mistakes." Such policies tend to force individuals and the organization to perform at the lowest level of competence.

Nonetheless, we have a loan agreement which is being ignored and some sort of action is required. Glenbow's First Nations Advisory Council has suggested that we work with local ceremonialists to resolve this dilemma through traditional means. To avoid similar situations in the future, they also suggested that we sanctify these loan agreements with a traditional pipe ceremony, in addition to the signing of legal documents. The First Nations Advisory Council reasons that traditional practices may exact a greater commitment to a loan agreement. The fact that these relationships are dynamic, and that we are learning as we go, is both disconcerting and salutary. In any event, there is nothing to be gained from rigid adherence to *a priori* assumptions and preconceived notions.

Professional standards

Another topic of real and potential conflict, as our relationships with First Nations evolve, has to do with professional standards. An enormous amount of time and money has been committed to ensuring that museum workers develop and adhere to a coherent body of method and theory, in order to sustain a high standard of professional practice. As we step outside the museum into the public arena, however, these standards of conduct may have little or no meaning to the majority of people who have an interest in what we do as institutions.

The tension arises when it is impossible or inappropriate to maintain professional standards as we respond to the needs of our various constituents. For example, it is unrealistic to demand that the borrower of a medicine bundle maintain 48% relative humidity in his home on the Reserve. Or, what of our requirement to fumigate or freeze incoming objects in order to avoid an infestation in our permanent collections? Should this apply to a medicine bundle which has been returned at the conclusion of a loan? The answer is no, and this has nothing to do with the validity of professional standards. Rather, we acknowledge that the application of various physical and chemical techniques is seen as disrespectful by those who possess special knowledge of the object. Neither should this bundle be readmitted to storage without undergoing inspection, as it could endanger other objects. It is not acceptable to simply reject the professional concerns in favour of increased service to a particular group. One of Glenbow's conservators suggested that the sacred objects be separated from the permanent collections, both physically and administratively, to allow for their special care.

As a result of these complexities, we have created a staff forum (the Native Affairs Group) at Glenbow for addressing these real and potential conflicts among our professional staff. It is a multidisciplinary team of staff whose purpose is to listen to each other, identify concerns, and design solutions that meet competing interests within the institution. Recognizing the parity of traditional and profes-sional knowledge is challenging the premises upon which many of our policies and practices are based, and we need to find the intelligent ground between pro-fessional standards and community needs. The Native Affairs Group is essential to thoughtfully fulfilling our obligations to First Nations, to balancing competing interests, and to undertaking initiatives in conjunction with our First Nations Advisory Council – all of which will serve us in the years to come.

Prospects

Collaboration with other museums with similar concerns and interests is also a necessity as our relationships with First Nations evolve. The Assembly of First Nations/Canadian Museums Association Task Force report has called for the co-management of collections by museums and First Nations, but what does this really mean in practical terms? It may or may not be realistic to think that Canadian museums could agree on a common approach to this new concept of co-management. It may not even be necessary, but it is important at this time to explore its meaning and ramifications. Our Senior Ethnologist, Gerald Conaty, is working with colleagues from Saskatchewan's Natural History Museum [now the Royal Saskatchewan Museum] and the Manitoba Museum of Man and Nature [now The Manitoba Museum], as well as with various Aboriginal groups and individuals, to develop a workable definition of co-management. The opportu-nity for these ethnologists to exchange ideas and concerns is in itself worthwhile, even if a generic model for co-management is ultimately unachievable.

It is important in all of this work that we take the time to reflect on the broader implications of what we are doing. Sacred bundles, for example, are powerful objects replete with implicit social status and power, in addition to their spiritual significance.[4] The return of bundles affects the balance of power in a community, and although this is really none of our business as museum workers, we must be sensitive to these complexities. Glenbow's First Nations Advisory Council has made this point very clearly. Such sensitivity requires a commitment to learning local and traditional knowledge, and to listening to community opinions and concerns surrounding these loans.

The benefits will also be greater for all of us if we make the effort to ensure that a meaningful dialogue occurs in conjunction with the transfer of these ceremonial objects. Reg Crowshoe, a Peigan ceremonialist, observes that this is not simply a matter of museums making objects available, as museums may also possess knowledge about the use, meaning, and context of the objects which has been lost to the memories of First Nations peoples. Reg Crowshoe is also calling for a deliberate process to ensure that relevant information is collected in Native communities. This documentation, along with the knowledge which the ceremonialists possess, will add immeasurably to what we know about our collections.

Concluding thoughts

It is not easy for me to summarize these issues and concerns, as they are complex and involve moral, professional, and political considerations which continually compete with each other for ascendancy. There are also broader implications which transcend the particular issues and situations. It is these broader implications which are probably responsible for much of the apprehension we feel as we reflect upon the irreversible course we have charted at Glenbow.

In the first place, releasing collections on other people's terms means giving up authority and responsibility, and sharing them with people whose background, education, and experience are radically different from our own. Furthermore, it is impossible to determine what the outcome of this sharing will be. It will undoubtedly result in challenges to the conventional wisdom of museum practice, such as our belief that replicas of objects are suitable for those who wish to possess objects which we consider too precious to share. Our recent experience indicates that Blackfoot Ceremonialists prefer to have authentic objects, not contemporary reproductions. If these concerns are not worrisome enough, what about the possibility that there could be further cultural decline among Aboriginal peoples and the objects we have loaned or returned will be neglected, destroyed, or otherwise lost? It is possible that this could happen, as it did before, but this degree of pessimism is stultifying, and could very well become the rationalization for inaction.

Museums which hold Aboriginal materials do so in part because they are committed to the fundamental tenets of anthropology, and one of these tenets is respect for cultural diversity. Canadian museums now have the opportunity to embrace this principle, albeit slowly and judiciously, as circumstances require. Sharing authority and collections is much more than a responsibility, however, as it is also an opportunity. To return to the quotation at the beginning of this commentary, museums now have a unique role to play in "imbuing the performance with wisdom, courage and vision," as they address the needs of the First Nations. Museums pride themselves on being the keepers of the collective memory, and they are now being approached by Aboriginal peoples who want their memories revitalized. To help make this happen is to vindicate the very purpose of museums.

Notes

1 The Mackenzie Valley Pipeline was intended to bring natural gas to North American energy markets. The Mackenzie Valley Pipeline Inquiry was commissioned by the Government of Canada in 1974 to investigate the social, environmental, and economic impact of the proposed gas pipeline that would run through the Yukon Territory and the Mackenzie River Valley of the Northwest Territories. This inquiry was notable for the voice it gave to the First Peoples whose traditional territory the pipeline would traverse ("Mackenzie Valley Pipeline." In Wikipedia. Available online: http://en.wikipedia.org/wiki/Mackenzie_Valley_Pipeline_Inquiry.

2 The languages spoken by the Indians of the western Canadian Subarctic belong to a language family known as Athapaskan. Those who speak the various dialects of the Athapaskan language are called Athapaskan or Dene (den'ay). Dene is an Athapaskan word meaning "man" or "person." The Athapaskans of the Northwest Territories have indicated a preference for the use of Dene to describe themselves, and this term is used throughout this commentary.

3 The term "ethno-archaeologist" was invented over a century ago, "to mean an archaeologist 'who can bring as preparation for his work an intensive knowledge of the present life' of the people whose prehistory is under investigation." See David, N. and Kramer, C. (2001) *Ethnoarchaeology in Action*. Cambridge: Cambridge University Press (page 6).

4 Sacred bundles contain items that were given to the Blackfoot by the Spirit Beings of their world. These bundles are used in ceremonies to renew connections with the Spirit Beings and Creator and to ask for help. They are accorded the care one would give to a child. See: The Blackfoot Gallery Committee (2001) *Nitsitapiisinni: The Story of the Blackfoot People*. Toronto: Key Porter Books Limited (page 13).

References

Hardin, G. (1985) *Filters Against Folly*. London: Penguin Books.

Hill, T. and Trudy Nicks, T. (eds) (1992) *Turning the Page: Task Force Report on Museums and First Peoples*. Ottawa: Canadian Museums Association and the Assembly of First Nations.

Janes, R. R. (1989) "An Ethnoarchaelogical Model for the Identification of Prehistoric Tepee Remains in the Boreal Forest," *ARCTIC* 42 (2): 128–138.

Lowrance, W. W. (1986) *Modern Science and Human Values*. London: Oxford University Press.

5

ISSUES OF REPATRIATION*

A Canadian View

Introduction

The repatriation of sacred materials from museums to First Nations peoples of the New World is arguably the most complex, perplexing, and politically charged issue currently confronting curators of ethnology and the institutions in which they work. Embedded within the arguments over the possession of the objects are concerns about identity, power (social and political), and history. Museums, as bastions of knowledge and keepers of society's material memory, often feel that their raison d'être is threatened by demands for repatriation. First Nations, as an underclass of society, find pride and meaning in these objects and the demands for repatriation can be read as demands for recognition as equal partners in society. While few curators, and fewer administrators, are at ease amid these discussions, it is unlikely that the debate will subside anytime soon. It is important that ideas and experiences be freely exchanged as the parameters continue to develop.

Christian F. Feest's (1995) article "'Repatriation': A European View on the Question of Restitution of Native American Artifacts" provides a thoughtful review of the history of international and intercultural disputes over the ownership of cultural property. He makes a useful distinction regarding the nature of the issues which arise among countries of the developed world, between the developed and the Third World, and between Indigenous Peoples and their colonizers. Disputes within each of these categories have been approached through different legal and extralegal channels with varied results. Feest then goes on to consider the legal and ethical considerations which he feels European museums face when considering

*Source: Gerald T. Conaty and Robert R. Janes, *European Review of Native American Studies,* Vol. 11, No.2 (1997): 31–37. The late Gerald Conaty was the Senior Ethnologist at the Glenbow Museum.

requests by First Nations for the return of holy objects.[1] He concludes that such requests are unsubstantiated on legal grounds and, while there may be ethical considerations, most requests are "hopeless, if not frivolous" (40).

Feest, like many other authors (e.g., West 1991; Carpenter 1991; Bernstein 1991; Sturtevant 1991; Thomas 1991; Merrill et al. 1993) focuses much of his discussion on the Native American Graves Protection and Repatriation Act (NAGPRA) and the effects of that legislation on American institutions. A very different course has been followed in Canada where, in 1989, a Task Force on Museums and First Peoples was convened jointly by the Assembly of First Nations (AFN) and the Canadian Museums Association (CMA) (Hill and Nicks 1992; Wilson et al. 1992; Nicks 1992).[2] Although individuals in the Canadian museum community had recognized the need for new relationships with First Nations (e.g., Janes 1982a, b, 1987, 1995; Brink 1992; Conaty 1989), the controversies surrounding the 1988 exhibition *The Spirit Sings* (Harrison et al. 1988; Vogel 1990) precipitated the establishment of a forum in which all parties could discuss the issues with candor.

The Task Force was organized into regional working groups which met twice each year along with an annual joint meeting. At the conclusion of its three-year mandate, the Task Force produced a report which urged the creation of equal partnerships among museums and First Nations. Under the headings of "Interpretation," "Access," "Repatriation," and "Training," the Task Force recommended that museum professionals actively find opportunities to include Aboriginal peoples in all aspects of their institutions, and that the accessibility be improved. As membership in the CMA is voluntary, the conclusions of the Task Force can serve only as recommendations against which we can benchmark the performance of ourselves and our institutions. The emphasis on discussion and negotiation as mechanisms of positive dispute resolution is in marked contrast to the legalistic and often confrontational approach brought on by NAGPRA. Our discussions with American colleagues indicate that the Canadian experience was, and continues to be, much more positive.

As one of Canada's preeminent museums, Glenbow is intimately involved with the issues surrounding not only repatriation, but also the representation of non-Western cultures in exhibitions and through programs. We feel that it is important for members of the European cultural community to hear how we are now dealing with these issues; issues which, perhaps, have a greater geographic and political immediacy for museums in the New World than for institutions in Europe.

We begin with an overview of First Nations–museums relationships and then discuss our present relationship with First Nations, including our ongoing practice of returning, on loan, holy objects and encouraging participation in our program and exhibition development. We will outline the benefits which have accrued to us over the past five years, including our gains in knowledge and understanding of First Nations cultures and worldview. Finally, we will address elements of Feest's article in light of our acquired perspective.

Museums and First Nations

The ways in which museums have collected, exhibited, and interpreted First Nations material culture have changed significantly throughout the history of museums–First Nations contact. The present overview, while far from comprehensive, outlines some general trends in this relationship. Essays in Ames (1992a) and Stocking (1985) offer more detailed discussions. By and large, the inequality of Aboriginal peoples vis-à-vis non-Aboriginal peoples in society has enabled non-Natives to assume a dominant role in shaping these relationships. Museums, as institutions of the dominant society, have remained aloof from, and largely irrelevant to, Native cultures.

We can identify three approaches in the development of collections and exhibitions about Native cultures. First, artifacts have been collected as strange memorabilia by explorers or as trophies taken by conquerors from defeated people. These articles, which filled the cabinets of curiosities in royal palaces, demonstrated the strangeness of these other cultures, thereby helping to justify Western domination – strange cultures are, somehow, less human. As exploration expanded, non-Western cultures were overwhelmed by European states. Scientists embarked on an effort to salvage whatever they could from the remnants of "vanishing" cultures. The analytical focus of this second approach represents a shift from the "strangeness" of the object to a comparative, evolutionary perspective. While these approaches encompass a broadly diachronic scheme, many of the developments occurred coevally. The development of semi-public and, subsequently, public museums, for example, can be traced to the cabinet of curiosities in the homes of royalty and the landed gentry (Ames 1992b). On the other hand, First Nations continue to be represented as both strange and vanishing in spite of the development of postmodern and post-colonial paradigms.

A third approach has emerged with the realization that First Nations cultures have neither disappeared nor been defeated. North American Aboriginal peoples are now demanding a greater role in museum work, and some museums, in turn, are beginning to see this involvement as essential. The nature of this contact is now being determined by both Native peoples and museums, rather than by museums alone.

The first two stages (conquest and vanishing cultures) developed within a modernist paradigm, with its emphasis on scientific and positivist understanding. Objects were removed from their utilitarian, social, and spiritual contexts to become part of an analytical system in which they were valued solely for their artistic and technological attributes.[3] The objects became artifacts. Their value was redefined as *objets d'art*, ethnographic objects, or merely as exotic. Their history of use and ownership, usually important in traditional societies, was often left unrecorded.

Two assumptions about the nature of knowledge lie behind these observations. Many researchers assumed that Native historical traditions ended at the time of European contact. The written chronicles of the newcomers provided the documentation of what really happened – how things really were. Oral traditions are often difficult to substantiate with empirical evidence – mostly because of scientific faith in written documents (McDonald et al. 1991; Ridington 1992; Cruikshank 1992; DeMallie 1994). As generations passed and the old people died, we assumed that traditional knowledge was lost. After all, if no one had written it down, how could it survive?

The other major assumption is that Native understanding of material culture is less relevant than scientific understanding. Native worldview is so fundamentally different from the scientific perspective that the two do not mesh. Usually, it is the Native knowledge that is relegated to quaint sidebars in an exhibition, while the museum remains the temple of knowledge as defined by the curators (see Clifford 1991 for contrasts between Native and non-Native museums).

We can see the results of these assumptions in the ways that artifacts are cata-logued and cared for, as well as in museum exhibitions and public programs. When artifacts are catalogued they are grouped into Western technological categories (e.g., clothing and adornment; hunting, fishing and warfare; cooking tools). Often these systems work well, providing an accessible guide to collections. Just as often, however, these categories obscure important cultural attitudes. A Peigan weasel-tail shirt is most certainly an article of clothing, but when worn by a ceremonial leader it also becomes an object of spiritual significance. Efforts at the Makah Cultural Centre Ozette, Washington (US), have been directed toward using Makah catego-ries, so that canoes, for example, are grouped with containers, not transportation devices. Alternative, non-Western systems of classification do provide insights into the diverse nature of culture.

Conservation research has made its important contributions to our understand-ing of the physical nature of objects. From this research, museums have come to understand how better to store and exhibit objects, thereby prolonging their existence. Many hours are spent ensuring that damage from improper storage, too much light, and fluctuating humidity is minimized. The focus on the physical aspect of objects reflects, again, a scientific understanding of the world and what is important in it – that which is observable and verifiable from a scientific point of view. Until recently, little thought was given to the spiritual needs of object – needs which must be defined by the originating cultures. For example smudging objects with smoke may alter the physical state while maintaining their spiritual condition (Clavir 1994; Conaty and Dumka 1996).

Exhibitions and public programs have, until recently, been the exclusive purview of non-Natives. Yet, as Ridington (1988: xi) has observed, anthro-pologists use as many metaphors based on unstated assumptions about the nature of reality as do Aboriginal peoples. Most exhibition stories have also been told in the third person, which is common to scientific discourse. Use of the third person suggests a dispassionate, uninvolved, and critical understanding of the subject. It leads the visitor to accept without qualification the veracity of what is presented. By admitting other voices to exhibitions, however, museums can highlight the importance of other ways of understanding and underscore the complexity of things.

Increased access by First Nations to the process of interpretation of their cultures by museums has brought Native peoples into closer contact with the museum culture. This contact, in turn, has fostered an expectation that they will have greater access to many other aspects of the museum world, including exhibition planning, collections management, and the overall administration. As access grows into partnerships, museums will be faced with the challenge of acknowledging the equality of traditional and academic knowledge. There are serious implications for admitting such parity – implications that will affect the way museums do research and, perhaps, the substance of the research. We may find that some of our usual academic freedoms are restricted.

For example, certain subjects and/or objects may not be available for study without Native permission. Scholarly and scientific papers may be subject to review by a Native audience prior to publication, and Native arguments and beliefs may have to be considered with equal measure alongside scientific research. Some of this has already begun under the guise of postmodernism (e.g., Leone et al. 1987; Hutcheon 1995; DeMallie 1994), wherein conventional interpretive approaches are being challenged as being culturally biased. It has been argued that traditional knowledge and scientific knowledge can coexist equally, but separately (McGhee 1989).

Glenbow and First Nations

The Glenbow Museum is setting a course which admits to the equality of the different knowledge bases, and is trying to bring them together rather than separate them. This strategy is reflected in our policies, our formal organization, our projects, and our general attitude toward the people with whom we work. In 1995, we prepared a *First Nations Policy* and a *Sacred Loans Policy* that formally acknowledge the unique relationship between Glenbow and First Nations. The *First Nations Policy* is based on the principles and recommendations of the CMA/ AFN Task Force on Museums and First Nations (Hill and Nicks 1992: 7–11). We are committed to ensuring that First Nations are included as equal partners in the process of planning, research, development, and maintenance of all exhibitions and programs that involve Aboriginal cultures.

We have also established guidelines for access to our collections. These guidelines not only assure that First Nations people will be able to review our collections, but they also address the issue of restricting access to some parts of our collections. This is discussed in further detail below. Our policy also commits Glenbow to respond positively to requests from First Nations for training. However, we have found that the needs of First Nations communities vary greatly and, consequently, our training program is flexible and the curricula are developed by both the trainer and the trainee on a case-by-case basis. Funding for this training is also on a partnership and case-by-case basis.

Our *First Nations Policy* was developed through extensive consultation with Glenbow's First Nations Advisory Council, as well as with Glenbow staff and management. Consensus was generally easy to achieve, although the issue of access to the collections remains problematic. In addition to artifacts, Glenbow houses the largest non-government archives in Canada. The First Nations Advisory Council wished to have restricted access imposed on material relating to First Nations. The archives staff, who are all dedicated to the principle of freedom of information, saw this as being counter to their professional ethics, although they did agree that information and photographs relating to sacred practices should be protected. We are now looking for ways to enable us to determine which documents should be restricted.

The issue of repatriation is addressed both in the general *First Nations Policy* and in a special *Sacred Loans Policy*. The latter acknowledges the special nature of parts of our collection. Accordingly, we have established loan guidelines which reflect the possibility that sacred material will return to communities for use in ceremonies. The conditions in which this material will be kept and used are far different from those of a mainstream museum. We also treat requests to study, exhibit, or photograph these objects differently than requests concerning other artifacts. We now require that such requests from researchers be accompanied by support from an appropriate ceremonialist (one who has the traditional, transferred rights to the type of item in question). Initially, the response to this was mixed. Now, more often than not, we have support and understanding from the researchers.

The critical issues arising from our program of lending sacred artifacts have led us to an inquiry concerning the meaning of these objects for First Nations. Most of our dialogue has been with members of the Blood, Peigan, and Siksika First Nations, and it is their perspective which we wish to discuss here.[4] Other First Nations may share all or part of this perspective. However, in keeping with First Nations protocol, we do not assume that a universal worldview encompasses all First Peoples. This emic analysis has helped us to better understand what is at stake when someone approaches the museum for the loan of a sacred bundle. It has also helped us understand some of the conflicting claims, statements, and advice we receive from First Nations peoples.

The meaning of sacred objects

To the Blackfoot, almost everything is considered animate.[5] This perception of animation has been developed over thousands of years of observing the world and taking notice of the constant change and flux which encompasses everything. The animals, the plants, the rivers, and even the rocks are always undergoing some kind of change. As things change physically, there is an accompanying change in their energy levels. This energy, or spirit as it is often referred to, is the unifying feature which defines most of creation as animate.

The Blackfoot understanding that everything has an inherent energy or spirit, together with the observation that there is continual change among all things, leads to the conclusion that there is a relational network among all of the animate beings. As something changes, it is activated in such a way as to affect the energy or spirit of other things. The constant change, which led initially to the understanding that almost everything is animate, is perpetuated by relational networks which encompass all beings.

In order to survive and prosper, it is important that all beings understand this relational network and contribute to the network's equilibrium and harmony. If any element changes too radically, chaos may ensue, with unpredictable and uncontrollable shifts in the networks. Clearly, these relational networks are very complex and may vary greatly from place to place. In recognition of this complexity and diversity, the Blackfoot do not consider that they are part of an expansive, global system. Rather, the universe of which they are part, and which they understand, is a prescribed geographical territory which defines the traditional Blackfoot homeland. Within this area, the Blackfoot are an integral part of the relational network of all of creation and they understand how to help maintain systemic balance. The networks beyond the boundaries may be strange or unknown, and balance (even survival) may be difficult to maintain.

The Blackfoot understand their universe as including three levels of beings, other than Issapaitapi, or the Supreme Being.[6] These are: the Above People (Ssponitapiisksi), the On Earth People (Ksaahkommitapiiksi), and the Underwater People (Sooyiitapiiksi). These people are the spirits of the various animals, plants, and other elements within the Blackfoot world, and they have given themselves to various sacred bundles or, sometimes, have given sacred bundles and ceremonies to the Blackfoot. Ssponitapiiksi include the sun, the moon, morningstar, other stars and planets, cranes, eagles, and other birds of the upper sky. Ksaahkommitapiiksi include birds of the lower sky, plants and animals of the earth. Sooyiitapiiksi are the fish and the underwater creatures, as well as beaver, marten, and others who live in the water and on land. Real People (Niitsitapi), human members of the Blackfoot culture, use the physical representations within the bundles as a means of connecting with the intangible (that is, the spirits and their power).

The Blackfoot contribute to the relational balance within their territory through ceremonies and songs given to the Niitsitapi by other living beings and by Creator. Parts of these ceremonies often record the occasion when the songs were transferred to the Real People and remind them of their obligation to maintain proper relationships. Often, the songs actively invoke the spirits of Other Beings and are aural expressions of the linkages between humans and all other Beings. The ceremonies and the songs are represented physically by the holy objects which are often referred to as bundles. A bundle may be as small as one item or as large as several hundred items.

The importance of these bundles for the Blackfoot people can be expressed in a number of different ways. They are, first of all, tangible evidence of the relational networks between the Blackfoot and the rest of Creation. Objects within a bundle were, most often, given to humans by the spirit of the class of items represented and remind the Blackfoot of the connection between humans and a particular class of objects (or species). As such evidence, these bundles entail the Blackfoot people's right to exist within the geographical space defined as traditional Blackfoot territory.

Songs, ceremonies, and bundles were given to the Blackfoot by the Other Beings as a sign that the Blackfoot were to be included within the relational network so that they might contribute to the harmonious balance and not be overcome by the continual change.

Sacred bundles also embody the norms, values, and protocols by which Blackfoot culture functions. The origins of songs, ceremonies, and bundles are recorded in Blackfoot oral tradition. These stories can describe appropriate behavior and can indicate the repercussions of inappropriate behavior. The traditional rights to tell these stories, and to reflect upon their meaning and applications, may be restricted to particular bundle owners. When disputes arise or issues of cultural norms are breached, it is these individuals who, through their bundles, evaluate the situation.[7] Since humans attain this authority only because of their bundle ownership, it is properly understood that the authority resides within the bundles, not with the humans.

This brief summary of our understanding of the Blackfoot worldview gives some indication of the vitality of sacred objects and their importance to the Blackfoot people. We have separated the theological principles and tried to explain how the physical objects (bundles) function within that framework. In reality (or rather, our etic understanding of reality), there is a much more holistic relationship: one cannot isolate songs from ceremonies from bundles, and one cannot think of the relational network without including bundles, Other Beings, ceremonies, etc. To speak of any one part in isolation is to risk making the whole incomprehensible. To remove any part (such as the holy objects) is to risk making the entire worldview dysfunctional and to risk unbalancing the relational network.

Regarding First Nations and repatriation

Feest's critique of the issues surrounding repatriation center on four main themes. First, the word "repatriation" has been erroneously substituted for "restitution" in the debate over the return of Native sacred objects. Second, the concept of sacredness cannot be clearly defined and, therefore, is subject to manipulation by First Nations. Third, Native conversion to Christianity in the late nineteenth and early twentieth centuries represents a break with tradition that current efforts at revival cannot surmount. Since there is no continuity between past ceremonialists and modern ones, the latter have no claim to the sacred objects of the former. Fourth, pluralism has confused the First Nations who now cannot present a cohesive front to museums. In the absence of a single, clear voice from First Nations communities, museums can be excused for inaction and an unwillingness to return sacred objects to the First Nations.

Feest begins his article by making a distinction between repatriation and restitution. He argues that repatriation, as defined by the *Oxford English Dictionary*, refers to the return or restoration of a person to one's country, while restitution is the return of something to its proper owner (Feest 1995: 33). The use of the term "repatriation" in the context of requests by First Nations for the return of material culture items imbues these objects with an emotional overtone, and confuses issues related to the reburial of skeletal remains with arguments over the ownership of artifacts. Feest implies that the choice of the term "repatriation" has been a politically motivated maneuver. This assumption of political motivation by First Nations, as opposed to the supposed apolitical curation by museums, underlies much of Feest's discussion and requires further scrutiny. It is, therefore, important to re-examine the terminology.

Following from our discussion of the Blackfoot worldview, it is clear that "repatriation" is, indeed, an appropriate term to use when discussing sacred bundles. To First Nations peoples, the bundles are not merely collections of physical objects. They are living entities which require the kind of vigilant care and attention that can only be undertaken within the context of a traditional lifestyle. When someone requests that a sacred bundle be repatriated, they truly wish to bring home a living member of their community. It is our experience that bundles are welcomed back with all the emotion of a long-absent relative who has returned home.

The cynicism with which Feest addresses the use of the term "repatriation" is disheartening. It establishes a dismissive tone and indicates, from the start, that he challenges not only First Nations' claims for sacred objects, but also their motives. Upon reflection, it is clear that the term is entirely appropriate for "objects" which are such an intricate part of First Nations cultures.

A second terminological problem raised by Feest centers on the application of the term "sacred." He quite properly notes the legal difficulties in defining sacredness within the Native American Graves Protection and Repatriation Act of the United States, as well as the difficulty inherent in a cross-cultural translation of the concept. However, his conclusion that "there seems to be no compelling reason why materials regarded as sacred should be more readily returned than others, *especially when there is evidence that the sacredness may be an attribution by a present population to something that was not considered sacred by their ancestors*" (37; emphasis added) is patronizing. This represents the sort of attitude that has earned museums the distrust of First Nations and the scorn of those anthropologists who understand that cultures do change.

We are not proposing that changing definitions of sacredness are not problematic. At Glenbow, we have frequently become involved in discussions about what is, and what is not, sacred. Disagreements can occur in many configurations – between communities; within communities; across generations; within generations; etc. Each request for repatriation brings its own proponents with their own understanding of sacredness. We are resigned to the reality that the definition may always be problematic and difficult for our organization to understand. However, by remaining open to the debate, we are improving our understanding of sacredness (Conaty 1994). Powers (1995) discusses the complexity of this issue within the Lakota context. Not to acknowledge this complexity is to stereotype First Nations and to expect them to be other than human.

But what of the instances where sacred objects were willingly and legally sold to museums? Feest (1995: 38) raises the concern that First Nations people who converted to Christianity represent a break in cultural tradition. Should the articles sold be returned to "born again pagans"? In our experience, the issue is, again, very complex. Not all religious conversions were voluntary, as First Nations were often given the option of Christianity or starvation. In other cases, the convert continued to practice both the new and the traditional beliefs. The continuation of traditions is clear in these circumstances. The proper course of action is not so clear when a traditionalist has sold or given his or sacred things to a museum because they felt that no one was interested or capable of continuing the ceremony. The museum seems to have been viewed as a death lodge where the bundles would remain, untouched by First Nations. We are finding that now, after thirty or forty years, the ceremonies have not become extinct and that requests are being made for the holy objects. Yet, both museum personnel and First Nations feel bound to honor the wishes of the elders, who are now deceased. More often than not, the precise wishes of the elders were never recorded. We are hoping that open dialogue will lead to an enlightened solution.

Feest (1995: 38) also points out that First Nations now exist as part of a pluralistic society and are, indeed, themselves very pluralistic. While many First Nations people might argue that they are less than full members of the larger society, we have found that most are also candid about the variety of opinions within their own communities. When those opinions concern the disposition of sacred objects, there are often prescribed protocols by which a decision-making process can be undertaken. These protocols may not always be immediately evident to someone who is not a member of a given community, and they may not always constitute a process which affords non-Native museum workers a great deal of comfort.

For example, we are continually advised by people of many different First Nations that we should seek advice regarding sacred objects only from people who have had rights to similar objects transferred to them through a traditional ceremony. That is, medicine pipe owners can only speak about medicine pipes, beaver bundle owners can speak only of beaver bundles, etc. If we have questions about such objects (including the possibility of lending one), we should bring the appropriate people together to discuss the matter. This means additional work with further stress for the museum worker. However, it has been our experience that these protocols do legitimize the decision-making process and give community sanction to the actions that result. Not everyone may agree with the decision, but they will recognize its legitimacy. Unfortunately for museums, undertaking this protocol often involves extensive research and a shift in paradigm, such that the First Nations worldview and justice are both acknowledged and respected.

Discussion

Throughout his article, Feest makes the argument that current demands by First Nations for the repatriation of their sacred things are more a political act than a religious one. He is right. The definition of sacred is profoundly political, especially if we accept the *Oxford English Dictionary*'s definition of political as "relating to a person's or organization's status or influence." Insofar as the sacred articles of the First Nations encapsulate a definition of who they are as a cultural entity within their universe, these items can be read as political texts. The retrieval of them from Western museums is a reclamation of a cultural identity which, in many cases, was nearly eradicated by European, American, and Canadian imperialism over the past five hundred years.

The retention of these objects within museums does not constitute an apolitical act. If we do not accept First Nations' claims to items which are so important to their self-identity, then we impose our own worldview on their culture and, worse, we impose upon them our own definition of what it means to be a Native. If we accept the pluralism which encompasses Western society, we must acknowledge peoples' rights to define their own culture. This is not to argue for the outright return of all objects upon demand. Feest quite properly outlines the complexity that faces conscientious museums. We wholeheartedly agree that museums must be judicious in returning sacred objects. Not only is posterity at risk, but sacred objects that are misused or ill-treated can harm people in many different ways. Museums should recognize this potential and undertake precautions appropriate to our status as responsible keepers of culture.

The conclusion that European museums are neither legally nor ethically bound to return sacred objects to First Nations reflects a colonialist policy which has less and less credibility in today's shrinking world. In his critique of Orientalism, Edward Said observed that:

> Perhaps the most important task of all would be to undertake studies in contemporary alternatives to Orientalism, to ask how one can study other cultures and peoples from a libertarian, or a nonrepressive and nonmanipulative, perspective. But then one would have to rethink the whole complex problem of knowledge and power.
>
> *(Said 1978: 24)*

Rethinking the structures of knowledge and power means that museums will have to relearn what they are and why they exist, for in the final analysis, all our efforts at change are about learning. But, while we may speak of the learning organization for convenience, it is the individuals within the organization who really do the learning.

Charles Handy (1989: 56) predicts that those individuals who are willing to learn, and to adapt to the habit of learning, will be best able to adapt to change and to benefit from it. Learning organizations, as is also true of individuals, are those which are skilled at creating, acquiring, and sharing knowledge, and using this knowledge to modify their behavior (Garvin 1993). A good museum is, by its very nature, a knowledge-based organization, but much or all of this knowledge and learning has been typically directed inward, and very little toward finding new and innovative ways of meeting societal expectations. This reluctance to adapt our behavior can be understood in terms of a "performer/ learner" model of human behavior, as well as through an examination of how professionals think.

At the risk of perpetuating a large generalization, the world can be divided into two types of people – the performer and the learner (Fritz 1991: 74–77). Performers adopt the strategy of staying within the confines of their current level of competence. They never attempt to accomplish anything that might fail, and thus limit their experience of growing beyond their current capacities. Learners, on the other hand, develop an ability to grow beyond their present abilities. To learners, perfect performance is not an issue – final results are. In Robert Fritz's (1991: 76) words, "if something is worth doing it's worth doing poorly until you can do it well." Learners use moments of failure, disappointment, and embarrassment as a basis for learning which, in turn, helps them become more competent.

Clearly, any time the world is divided into two categories it will be a superficial classification. Although the performer/learner model is useful, it is worth noting that most people undoubtedly express a combination of these two traits, in differing degrees. The expression of these traits may also be context specific – conservative in response to some issues, while risk taking in others (Ames 1995, personal communication).

A second explanation for the absence of learning in organizations has to do with how professionals think. One writer (Argyris 1991: 100) argues that it is the most well-educated and highly committed professionals who find it the hardest to learn. Because many professionals are almost always successful at what they do, they rarely experience failure. Because they have rarely failed, they have never learned how to learn from failure. When things go wrong in their view, their tendency is to become defensive, screen out criticism, and put the blame on everyone but themselves. In short, their ability to learn shuts down precisely at the moment they need it the most (Argyris 1991: 100).

Repatriation brings into focus issues of knowledge and power. As museum professionals, we have learned that we hold the knowledge about our collections and that their physical preservation in our vaults is a desirable objective that serves all of humanity. We are now being challenged by First Nations who point out that our knowledge is flawed, if not erroneous, and who decry the sterile environment in which their living connections with all of creation are kept. Furthermore, these challenges are finding support throughout the larger society.[8]

In North America, the problem of knowledge and power is being rethought by museums and First Nations: sometimes willingly; often with reluctance. But as Haas (1996: 51) suggests: "In relinquishing power and authority in representing cultural diversity, museums can become common meeting grounds for all cultures and forums for bringing cross-cultural understanding to a wider public audience." The first step toward power sharing is the acknowledgement of a people's right to self-definition and the right to access objects that are fundamental to that definition.

Epilogue

Among the Blackfoot peoples, the Brave Dog Society serves as a police force during the large summer Ok'an [Sun Dance] camp. The Brave Dogs hold nightly meetings, after which they often dance throughout the camp, stopping in front of tipis and demanding food and other gifts which they redistribute to the elders and less-fortunate. A story is told of the time the Brave Dogs stopped in front of the tipi of a well-respected elderly couple who owned several bundles. The tipi owner looked out, greeted the Brave Dogs, and returned inside for some gifts. When he returned, he presented the leader of the Brave Dog Society with a Beaver Bundle. The old man is reputed to have explained that he and his wife were old and too tired to provide proper care for the bundle. The couple's reputation did not suffer from their actions, and people continued to respect their knowledge and spiritual authority. Knowledge, it seems, can be transferred, but it does not necessarily have to be lost.

Notes

1 In Canada, the term First Nations refers to people of Aboriginal descent who, in the past, would have been called "Indians." It does not include either the Metis or the Inuit.
2 The Assembly of First Nations (AFN) is a political organization which represents the majority of Status Indians (that is, people whom the Government of Canada recognizes as of "Indian" descent) in Canada. The Canadian Museums Association (CMA) is the professional organization which represents museums and museum workers in Canada.
3 Franz Boas's dioramas at the American Museum of Natural History were an important exception to this approach. However, as Jacknis (1985) explains, Boas's vision and insights were not shared by his colleagues.
4 In particular, we wish to acknowledge the help and support of the late Dan Weasel Moccasin Sr., Daniel Weasel Moccasin, Jr., Rosaline Weasel Moccasin, Pat Provost, Jenny Bruised Head, Morris Little Wolf, Betty Anne Little Wolf, Reg Crow Shoe, Rose Crow Shoe, Joe Crow Shoe, Josephine Crow Shoe, Leonard Bastien, Willard Yellow Face, Allan Pard, Jerry Potts, Jr., Frank Weasel Head, Paul Raczka, Florence Scout, Beverly Hungry Wolf, Adolph Hungry Wolf, and Cliff Crane Bear.
5 "Blackfoot" is a Euro-American term that includes the Blood (Kainai), Siksika, Peigan (Pikuni), and South Peigan (Blackfeet) people who share a common language (with significant dialect differences) and other cultural practices. Each group has a unique identity and there is no word in their language for the general term "Blackfoot."
6 This discussion is taken from Conaty (1995).
7 We have used the present tense here, although the authority of traditionalists has changed greatly over the past century. The system is still functional and, although in the sphere of justice the non-Native legal system has taken precedence, a Native sense of justice is often considered in sentencing offenders.
8 As part of a recent Agreement in Principle to a land claim settlement, the governments of Canada, British Columbia, and the Nis'gaa First Nation agreed that artifacts would be returned to the Nis'gaa from the Canadian Museum of Civilization [now the Canadian Museum of History] and the Royal British Columbia Museum. The willingness of the government negotiators to relinquish Crown ownership of cultural objects reflects a fundamental change in the ways in which museums are being regarded by society.

References

Ames, M. M. 1992a (ed.) *Cannibal Tours and Glass Boxes: The Anthropology of Museums*. Vancouver, BC: University of British Columbia Press.

——— 1992b The Development of Museums in the Western World: Tensions between Democratization and Professionalization. In Ames 1992a: 15–24.

Argyris, C. 1991 Teaching Smart People How to Learn. *Harvard Business Review* 69(3): 99–109.

Bernstein, B. 1991 Repatriation and Collaboration: The Museum of New Mexico. *Museum Anthropology* 15(3): 19–21.

Brink, J. 1992 Blackfoot and Buffalo Jumps: Native People and the Head-Smashed-In Project. In: J. Foster, D. Harrison, and I. S. MacLaren (eds.), *Buffalo* (Edmonton, AB: Alberta Nature and Culture Series, University of Alberta Press), 19–44.

Carpenter, E. 1991 Repatriation Policy and the Heye Collection. *Museum Anthropology* 15(3): 15–18.

Clavir, M. 1994 The Conceptual Integrity of Conservation in Museums. *Muse* 12(3): 30–34.

Clifford, J. 1991 Four Northwest Coast Museums: Travel and Reflections. In: I. Karp and S. D. Lavine (eds.), *Exhibiting Cultures: The Poetics and Politics of Museum Display* (Washington: Smithsonian Institution Press), 212–254.

Conaty, G. T. 1989 Canada's First Nations and Museums: A Saskatchewan Experience. *The International Journal of Museum Management and Curatorship* 8: 407–413.

——— 1994 Relationships, Power and Sacred Objects. Paper presented at *Organizing the Past. The 12th International Conference on Organizational Symbolism*. Calgary, Canada.

——— 1995 Economic Models and Blackfoot Ideology. *American Ethnologist* 22(2): 403–412.

Conaty, G. T. and Dumka, H. 1996 Care of First Nations Sacred Material – Glenbow Museum. *ICOM Ethnographic Conservation Newsletter* 12: 4–5.

Cruikshank, J. 1992 Invention of Anthropology in British Columbia's Supreme Court: Oral Tradition as Evidence in *Delgamuukw v B.C. B.C. Studies* 95 (Autumn): 25–42.

DeMaille, R. 1994 "These Have No Ears": Narrative and the Ethnohistoric Method. *Ethnohistory* 40(4): 515–538.

Feest, C. F. 1995 "Repatriation": A European View on the Question of Restitution of Native American Artifacts. *European Review of Native American Studies* 9(2): 33–42.

Fritz, R. 1991 *Creating*. New York, NY: Ballantine Books.

Garvin, D. A. 1993 Building a Learning Organization. *Harvard Business Review* 71(4): 78–91.

Haas, J. 1996 Power, Objects, and a Voice for Anthropology. *Current Anthropology* 37 (Supplement): S1–S22.

Handy, C. 1989 *The Age of Unreason*. Boston, MA: Harvard Business School Press.

Harrison, J., Ames. M. and Trigger, B. 1988 "The Spirit Sings" and the Lubicon Boycott. *Muse* 6(3): 12–16.

Hill, Y. and Nicks, T. (co-chairs) 1992 *Turning the Page: Forging New Partnerships Between Museums and First Peoples*. Task Force Report on Museums and First Peoples. Ottawa, ON: The Assembly of First Nations and the Canadian Museums Association.

Hutcheon, L. 1995 The Post Always Rings Twice: The Postmodern and the Postcolonial. *Material History Review* 41 (Spring): 4–23.

Jacknis, I. 1985 Franz Boas and Exhibits: On the Limitations of the Museum Method of Anthropology. In: G. Stocking (ed.), *Objects and Others. Essays on Museums and Material Culture* (Madison, WI: University of Wisconsin Press), 75–111.

Janes, R. R. 1982a Archaeology in the Northwest Territories: The Social Context. *Northern Perspectives* 10(6): 5–10.

——— 1982b Northern Museum Development: A View from the North. *Gazette* (former *Journal of the Canadian Museums Association*) 15(1): 14–23.

—— 1987 Museum Ideology and Practice in Canada's Third World. *Muse* 4(4): 33–39.

—— 1995 *Museums and the Paradox of Change*. Calgary, AB: Glenbow Museum.

Leone, M., Parker, P., Potter, B. and Shackel, P. A. 1987 Toward a Critical Archaeology. *Current Anthropology* 28: 283–302.

McDonald, J., Douglas J., Zimmerman, L. J., McDonald, A. L., Tall Bull, W., and Rising Sun, T. 1991 The Northern Cheyenne Outbreak of 1879: Using Oral History and Archaeology as Tools of Resistance. In: R. H. McGuire and R. Paynter (eds.), *The Archaeology of Inequality* (Oxford: Blackwell), 64–78.

McGhee, R. 1989 Who Owns Prehistory? The Bering Land Bridge Dilemma. *Canadian Journal of Archaeology* 13: 13–20.

Merrill, W. J., Ladd, E. J. and Ferguson, T. J. 1993 The Return of the Ahayu:da: Lessons for Repatriation from Zuni Peublo and the Smithsonian Institution. *Current Anthropology* 34(5): 523–567.

Nicks, T. 1992 Partnerships in Developing Cultural Resources: Lessons from the Task Force on Museums and First Peoples. *Culture* 12(1): 87–94.

Powers, W. K. 1995 Innovating the Sacred: Creating Tradition in Lakota Religion. *European Review of Native American Studies* 9(2): 21–24.

Ridington, R. 1988 *Trail to Heaven: Knowledge and Narrative in a Northern Native Community*. Vancouver, BC: Douglas and McIntyre.

—— 1992 Fieldwork in Courtroom 53: A Witness to *Delgamuukw v B.C.. B.C. Studies* 95 (Autumn): 12–24.

Said, E. 1978 *Orientalism*. New York: Pantheon Books.

Stocking, G. W., Jr. 1985 *Objects and Others: Essays on Museums and Material Culture*. Madison, WI: University of Wisconsin Press.

Sturtevant, W. C. 1991 The New National Museum of the American Indian Collection Policy Statement: A Critical Analysis. *Museum Anthropology* 15(2): 29–30.

Thomas, D. H. 1991 Repatriation: The Bitter End or a Fresh Beginning. *Museum Anthropology* 15(1): 10–11.

Vogel, M. L. Vanessa 1990 The Glenbow Controversy and Exhibition of North American Art. *Museum Anthropology* 14(4): 7–12. [Originally published in the *European Review* of *Native American Studies* 4(1): 43–46 (1990).]

West, W. R., Jr. 1991 The National Museum of the American Indian Repatriation Policy: Reply to Sturtevant. *Museum Anthropology* 15(3): 13–14.

Wilson, T. H., Erasmus, G. and Penney, D. W. 1992 Museums and First Peoples in Canada. *Museum Anthropology* 16(2): 6–11.

PART 2
Creative destruction
Managing change

Our humaneness is defined more by our vulnerability than our strengths.
(Peter Block 1993: 43)

INTRODUCTION

Arriving as the Director of the Glenbow Museum in Calgary, Alberta in 1989, I encountered a variety of stark contrasts: from the northern frontier to a big city; from a medium-sized museum to one of the ten largest in Canada; from a staff with high morale and motivation to an unhappy, demoralized one; from a place where Aboriginal peoples were societal leaders and made many of the decisions governing their lives, to a city where they were ignored or marginalized; and from a supportive and generous government to a fierce, marketplace mentality.[1] All of these contrasts were alien to my limited experience and it was once again necessary to begin learning anew – with urgency.

Unknown to me, the Glenbow's funding agreement with the provincial government had expired just prior to my arrival, and a series of severe budget reductions rapidly followed. The museum had also been drifting without a director for a year or more prior to my arrival. Staff were cynical, the organizational structure was severely hierarchical and brittle, and there was widespread staff dissatisfaction with the status quo. In short, the Glenbow Museum, Art Gallery, Archives and Library, at the young age of 26, was facing bankruptcy and closure within the next five years – unless radical action was taken to address the future.

The writings that follow are about the work that was done to address the museum's uncertain future in the early 1990s, a task that was still underway when I resigned as CEO in 2000. The change process began with a strategic plan – Glenbow was the first among Canadian museums to have quantitative and qualitative performance measures. This strategic plan, as a blueprint for the future, touched off a process of experimentation and new ways of working that are described in detail in Part 2. The mistakes, missteps and failures are also discussed, and they are numerous. Nina Simon (2013: xvi) wrote, "The result was a participatory process enacted decades before 'participation' became a museum buzzword."

This process of organizational self-discovery led to the questioning and discarding of various museum assumptions and practices, similar to my previous experience in the Northwest Territories. There had been no crisis to provoke this re-examination in the NWT – unlike the Glenbow, where the future of the organization was in question as a result of the dire financial situation. There is nothing like a crisis to mobilize thinking and action, as long as the crisis is thoroughly explained and transparently shared throughout the organization.

In the course of considering a wide range of options to address this crisis, questions once again proliferated. For example, why was the permanent collection sacred and immune to deaccessioning? Why was the corporate hierarchy assumed to be the best organizational design? How do you streamline work processes in a complex organization like a museum? What are the most effective ways to ensure staff autonomy and initiative? What is the role and balance of earned revenues and the marketplace in a public museum?

These and various other questions are addressed in the articles that follow, writing that records both the creative and destructive results of organizational change, along with the anxiety, distress, and paradoxes that inexorably accompany it. Perhaps the greatest lesson in Part 2 is that the internal organization of a museum – its management and work design – is not merely an administrative nicety. How a museum is organized is directly related to the quality, relevance, and effectiveness of the work it does. Unrelieved hierarchy, for example, commonly spells the lack of personal agency, the absence of risk taking, and a preoccupation with internal agendas.

The relationship between organizational design and the nature of the ensuing work is rarely discussed either in the museum literature or at professional conferences. I am heartened by the work of one scholar-practitioner, Julia Harrison, who has observed this close relationship in her work and writing. She noted that "a more organically organized institution such as Glenbow [in contrast to a hierarchical one]," along with its institutional culture, were important factors in the museum's collaboration with the Blackfoot (Harrison 2005: 206–210).

An examination of organizational change at Glenbow also demonstrates its highly complex nature. With reference to Glenbow, Darren Peacock, a researcher in cultural informatics, noted that, "These change processes follow the principle of complexity – they are emergent, self-organizing and unpredictable, and take shape in conversations among organizational participants and stakeholders" (Peacock 2013: 243; Janes 2013: 1–191). He also suggested that the current anxiety and excitement caused by the advent of digital technologies in museums is "simply the latest demonstration of our difficulties in handling the perpetual problem of change" (Peacock 2013: 235).

Overall, the decade of the 1990s was a difficult one for museums in Canada, as it was for most North American museums. In contrast to the nearly unbridled growth of museums in the 1960s and 1970s, the 1990s was an era of budget cuts and financial restraint. Museums became forcibly aware of their own vulnerability, amidst the strident calls for increased accountability and financial self-sufficiency.

FIGURE 4   The challenge of organizational change © mike_expert / Shutterstock.

Earned revenues were touted as the universal salvation and the dictates of the marketplace arrived with a vengeance. The chapters in Part 2 are thus in contrast to those in Part 1, where my prevailing concern was with the social and environmental context of museum work – with particular reference to its value and meaning for Northern communities.

Although there is a steady concern with the fundamentals of mission and community, the preoccupation in Part 2 is essentially internal. Glenbow's Board of Governors, management, and staff concluded that there was no alternative but to dismantle and rebuild an organization that could withstand a 40 percent loss in operating money, while rebuilding simultaneously for resilience and enhanced public service. These incompatible imperatives required an obsessive examination of all aspects of Glenbow's internal workings, including organizational design, reporting relationships, work design, policies, work processes, procedures, internal communication, and individual roles and responsibilities – the list goes on.

The reader will note that this work was not done in a vacuum, and much effort was made to learn from other people's experiences, as well as from the literature. The museum literature, however, was decidedly lacking in academic research on museums as organizations. It is still lacking. This required that we develop our own coherent framework of method and theory based on the wider organizational and management literature, and this has been noted by the international museum community as a salutary benefit of our efforts (Moore 1997: 291).

Because the difficulties of change in museums are enduring and intensifying, it is sensible to learn as much about change as possible by sharing our collective experiences. In her Foreword to the third edition of my book *Museums and the Paradox of Change*, Nina Simon wrote "This book shows you what change looks like, what it takes, and what rewards exist when you try" (Simon 2013: xvi). I have selected the various writings for Part 2 with the intention of sharing these experiences once again. The first chapter, "Sober Reflections: An Undisguised View of Change at Glenbow," is an update on the many complexities, paradoxes, and ambiguities that were emerging from the organizational changes at Glenbow. These details are not normally published in the museum literature, and include frank observations from staff on the change process. The next chapter, "Beyond Strategic Planning: The Glenbow Example," is a sequel of sorts, in that it discusses the reinvention of Glenbow after the strategic plan was rejected by the Museum's principal funder.

The three chapters that follow, including "Don't Lose Your Nerve: Museums and Organizational Change," "Museums and Change: Some Thoughts on Creativity, Destruction and Self-organization," and "Complexity and Creativity in Contemporary Museum Management," are all attempts at unravelling the complexities, hazards, and opportunities of change management. Ideas and themes in these chapters include limits to growth, the importance of self-organization and project-based work design, participatory and reflexive management, the need for collective leadership, the paradoxes in museum work, and the impending dangers of marketplace ideology. As a staff, we found sources of comfort amidst all the stress of organizational change, and these are also discussed.

The penultimate chapter, "The Mindful Museum," introduces the idea of mindfulness in museum practice – meaning purposefully paying attention to what is important. Characteristics of museum mindfulness are discussed along with opportunities for museums to raise their consciousness of the world around them in an effort to become more responsible and relevant to their communities. The final chapter in Part 2, "Museum Management Revisited," is in part a critique of self-serving museum behaviours and beliefs that are enfeebling museums and diverting them from realizing their unique strengths. The latter half of this chapter is devoted to strengthening museum management in the face of these internal challenges.

The intent of all of these chapters is to motivate museums to think carefully and creatively about organizational change – not only its complexities and challenges, but also its undeniable opportunities. Intelligent and empathetic change is essential in transforming the museum's culture/industry business model into one of a locally embedded problem solver, in tune with the challenges and aspirations of their communities. All of these chapters demonstrate that uncertainty is the constant partner in doing so, which makes experimentation, proaction, and challenging tradition mandatory.

Note

1 Because of its status as a territory, rather than a province, the federal government retained significant authority over territorial affairs. The devolution of political and administrative powers from the federal government to the Northwest Territories continues to unfold.

References

Block, P. (1993) *Stewardship*, San Francisco: Berrett-Koehler Publishers Inc., p. 43.

Harrison, J. (2005) "Shaping Collaboration: Considering Institutional Culture," *Museum Management and Curatorship*, 20 (3): 206–210.

Janes, R. R. (2013) *Museums and the Paradox of Change: A Case Study in Urgent Adaptation* (3rd Edition), London and New York: Routledge.

Moore, K. (ed.) (1997) *Museum Management*, London and New York: Routledge, p. 291.

Peacock, D. (2013) "Complexity, Conversation and Change: Learning How Museum Organizations Change." In R. R. Janes, *Museums and the Paradox of Change: A Case Study in Urgent Adaptation* (3rd Edition), London and New York: Routledge, p. 243, p. 235.

Simon, N. (2013) Foreword. In R. R. Janes, *Museums and the Paradox of Change: A Case Study in Urgent Adaptation* (3rd Edition), London and New York: Routledge, pp. xv–xviii.

6

SOBER REFLECTIONS*

An undisguised view of change at Glenbow

Author's note: The Glenbow Museum was heavily reliant upon the Provincial Government of Alberta for funding when I arrived as the new director in 1989. In 1990, the provincial grant was reduced by about 14%, which translated into the loss of 19 positions or 13.5% of Glenbow's staff. We developed a corporate and strategic plan in 1990/1991, complete with performance measures, as a basis for negotiating a five-year funding agreement with the Province – to avoid the crisis management inherent in annual funding arrangements.[1] We invested 12 months in the planning process, only to have the Province reject the plan and our bid for multi-year funding in 1992. This, in turn, touched off a major change effort to avoid bankruptcy and this chapter is an update a year later on the organizational changes that ensued.

This chapter was originally prepared as a report for a meeting of the Museum Directors' Group.[2] It is included here because it contains a variety of organizational details that are not normally published in the museum literature, including frank observations from staff on the change process. The reader will also note the many complexities, paradoxes, and ambiguities surrounding organizational change.

Introduction

What follows is an overview of the change process at Glenbow, as of April, 1993. Overall, we reduced our expenditures by 20%; reduced 19 departments to six integrated and multidisciplinary work units; reduced 11 positions to part-time and eliminated 31 full-time staff through layoffs, and reduced the managerial staff from

*Source: Robert R. Janes, unpublished paper presented at the meeting of the Museum Directors' Group, Sudbury, Ontario, Canada, October 2–3, 1993. This paper was reorganized and edited for inclusion in this book.

24 to 14. In addition to providing a personal perspective on these changes, I have also included extensive comments from the staff. The axiom that best underlies the reasoning in undertaking this major organizational change is – "the best way to predict the future is to actually create it" (Bernard 1989: 16). The purpose of this chapter is to provide a candid overview of what has transpired to date with that aim in mind.

In search of reflection

As part of our organizational change, we are in the process of examining our assumptions and collective thought processes. This also means that we must increase our tolerance of apparent contradictions and see them not as contradictions, but as opposites that need to be balanced. For example, we can no longer assume that collections take precedence over public service, or that accessibility to the collections means compromising our conservation standards. Nor can we accept the dichotomy of entertainment vs. education. Rather, we intend to embrace the reality of complex and competing aims, in an effort to harness this creative tension in the best interests of the institution. Although the coexistence of rival interests is never peaceful, we intend to make this tension more effective. To what extent this rethinking has been embraced by staff is unknown at this time, but this critical reflection will continue to be fostered as the change process unfolds.

We will strive to be more vigilant about the way of thinking known as the "slippery slope," which assumes that any deviation from the so-called "normal" or habitual way of doing things will result in the entire institution collapsing into disorder and chaos. People who use this argument act as though they think human beings are completely devoid of practical judgement or act unreasonably (Hardin 1985: 62–64), and this is an obstacle to learning and change. A good example of slippery slope thinking is the argument for not loaning or returning artifacts from our collections to First Nations, because it is assumed that they will demand that all of our First Nations collections be relinquished.

We are also attempting to develop an organization that encourages staff learning and growth by promoting experimentation and risk taking. We cannot avoid taking risks because the outcome may be negative. If one way of doing things, or a new idea, or a solution to a problem does not work, we must try something else. Fear of failure stifles or prevents innovation, and it is essential that we learn from our mistakes. During the second year of implementing our strategic plan, for example, we discovered that all the planning in the world would not help us if we did not make a realistic assessment of our financial situation.

Update from the executive director[3]

What follows is a listing of projects, activities, and innovations that have emerged as a result of the organizational change and staff participation in it.

Physical move – Glenbow's multidisciplinary work units are now located together. We had some difficulty in achieving this because the collections and the laboratories cannot be moved. It's not ideal, but it's definitely an improvement.

Glenbow Museum Acquisition Society (GMAS) – This voluntary organization has now been transformed into the Glenbow Society. The Glenbow Society can now raise funds for general operating expenses at Glenbow, rather than solely for the purchase of collection items.

The archives and library – They are now open on Saturday, as a result of the client satisfaction survey results. Researchers and users made it clear that they desire to work on the weekends, so we responded.

Glenbow Magazine – The cost of producing the quarterly *Glenbow Magazine* has now been reduced by about 50%. This is a classic example of creative staff simply deciding to do things differently.

Financial information system – We are in the process of developing a financial information system through our computer network that will provide real-time financial data for all staff who require it.

Board of Governors – There is now a Union representative on the Glenbow's Board of Governors. This individual was selected by the Union membership and will be a non-voting member in the short-term. Both the Union and Glenbow's Board will undertake an evaluation of this arrangement in six months and determine the feasibility of continuing it.

Staff training – We have embarked on a series of training courses in conjunction with the University of Calgary, which are mandatory for all staff. The first course, now completed, was devoted to interpersonal communication and listening skills. The second course, scheduled for November, will be devoted to team problem solving and decision making and will also be mandatory for all staff.

As part of the communication course, all of the staff completed the *Personal Profile System* – an inventory designed to help individuals understand themselves and others in the work environment. It classifies people according to four general types – dominant (D), cautious/compliant (C), influences (I), and steady (S). In discussing the results of this inventory with the course instructor, I learned that the C and S types predominate at Glenbow. The S type desires security of the situation, the status quo, and traditional procedures. The C type desires standard operating procedures, a sheltered environment, and the status quo. It is thus no surprise that change at Glenbow has been, and will be, difficult. Simply put, the bulk of Glenbow staff do not like change.

Secretaries – The roles of various secretaries at Glenbow will soon be redefined. More and more staff are becoming increasingly independent as a result of doing their own word processing and administration. This is an opportunity to redirect the skills and energies of many of our secretaries into a variety of other areas. It is apparent that many of our secretaries would welcome this expansion of their responsibilities.

Staff involvement in hiring – We recently experimented with staff involvement in the hiring of our new Human Resources Manager. Staff were elected by their peers in each work unit to form an informal interviewing group that met with the short list of candidates for the Human Resources position. This group then prepared a report containing their recommendations, which was extremely useful as we made our final selection. I intend to incorporate this approach in the hiring of positions that serve the entire organization.

Joy Harvie Maclaren Scholarship – We continue to offer this scholarship to our staff, which is based on a CAN$100,000 endowment from the Harvie family (Glenbow's founders). This year the scholarship will allow one of our staff to complete a book manuscript, and two others to take part-time courses towards degrees at the University of Calgary.

Volunteer Coordinator – The reorganization at Glenbow made possible the creation of this position, which has had an immediate and positive effect on the morale of our volunteers. All of our volunteers were inadvertently neglected over the past couple of years of intense organizational change, and the Volunteer Coordinator is now addressing these deficiencies.

Alberta Lotteries – Glenbow will now be receiving its government contribution from the Alberta Lotteries Corporation. This may be a good thing in the long term, as Lotteries is the only agency which will negotiate multi-year funding agreements.

The Transition Management Team (TMT) – The President of our Union now participates in weekly senior management meetings at Glenbow, and we have renamed this group the Transition Management Team. This group is designed to head off issues surrounding the organizational changes before they become problems.

Deaccessioning – This process is now well under way, with minimal public concern, judging by the press and the telephone calls to Glenbow. In fact, public reception to this initiative has been overwhelmingly positive, with numerous people commenting that it is a practical way to assume responsibility for our future. It is museum colleagues who are the most critical – fearing the "slippery slope," yet again.

Senior management – Four of Glenbow's seven senior managers are new. Two of these individuals were hired from within Glenbow. Two of the senior managers, the General Manager of Glenbow Enterprises and the Director of Programs, Exhibitions and Special Loans, were hired from outside Glenbow. At my request, I was assisted by Joanne DiCosimo, the Director of the Manitoba Museum (Canada), and a human resources consultant in the selection process for these four positions. Joanne, as a senior museum director, provided an external perspective on these competitions and her involvement was a distinct advantage in the decision making.

Board retreat – There has been one board retreat to begin the process of reinventing the Board of Governors. The museum, as an organization, has changed dramatically and so must the Board in terms of its expectations and work processes. Is this ultimately possible?

Glenbow Enterprises – A general manager has now been hired to manage Glenbow's new business unit – Glenbow Enterprises. He brings a completely new perspective to this work, as he is from the private sector. We have combined the Development Department, the Shop, and our Facilities Rentals into Glenbow Enterprises and are currently considering a host of business initiatives to generate earned revenue.

My contract renewal – I understand in the course of considering the renewal of my employment contract, that the Director's Review Committee (a committee of the Board of Governors) consulted museum directors across the country with respect to my performance and their perceptions of Glenbow. Six museum directors received letters from Glenbow's Chairman concerning these questions. This external performance review by peers is a departure from the common approach in the museum community, and I think it is a valuable one.

Staff perspectives

The following excerpts are direct quotations from staff. They were gathered (in confidence) in an effort to gain insight and understanding into how the change process was affecting staff throughout the museum. These comments are qualitative and lack methodological rigour, but they do reveal certain patterns and regularities that were most helpful in gauging the successes and failures of the organizational changes to date. Overall, there are encouraging comments about the new, self-managed and multidisciplinary teams. At the same time, there is notable criticism of the lack of communication between staff and senior executives.

Encouraging comments

"Moving from the Interpretation Department into a new work unit was a change that I was looking forward to. It has been very positive for me to work with a new group of people, who come from different areas of the museum. I think it has made me more sympathetic to the work and professional concerns of other people in the museum . . . something I think we can all benefit from. I don't think this would have happened if Glenbow had not been restructured."

"The most positive aspect of the change for me is the formal acceptance that it is correct to deal directly with the person or group of people that the situation deems most appropriate, rather than having to go through a (sometimes) useless chain-of-command."

"First of all, I find the entire concept of the change exciting and positive. One of the more positive aspects of the change is the opportunity to have more responsibility and accountability. The idea of empowerment is exciting for a person in my capacity. I have been allowed also to 'broaden my horizons', so to speak. I have always felt that I was getting a free education working at Glenbow, but it is even more interesting now because of the mix of disciplines in the work unit."

"The first obvious plus is that we met our objective of reducing operating costs by approximately CAN$1.2 million a year through the reorganization."

"Although the Union/Management relationship hardened somewhat during layoffs, the process of involving the Union in layoff decisions appears to have helped motivate the Union executive to look forward to new ways of cooperating with management, and perhaps even rethinking the negotiating process and the collective agreement itself."

"At last, the Library and Archives are given the recognition that they are different from the museum and art gallery. This used to be a common area of discontent when I was the Coordinator of Collections. We tried to make them operate like a museum, but they are just too different to be treated the same."

"The new teamwork-oriented approach makes it much easier to present ideas to the work unit for discussion – the notion of empowerment has made it easier to work on problem areas – everyone is more open to positive experimentation."

"Everyone I spoke with – from technical and support staff to senior managers – had a clear understanding of the strategic plan and the directions that Glenbow wants to go. Everyone seemed to understand the reasons for the reorganization and, for the most part, to accept them. I had expected to encounter some very angry 'survivors', but so far everyone I have spoken to has accepted the changes."

"Although the reorganization has meant reductions in the number of staff, and increased workloads for many, there is energy and excitement about the possibility of finding new and creative solutions. I sense a genuine enthusiasm for finding new strategies and solutions."

"Working with colleagues with a common focus (publications) is resulting in exciting new ideas and perspectives; new links are being made with existing knowledge and experience. For example, the curatorial proposal for 'Artifiction' will invite Alberta writers to write something on an object or work of art of their choice. This will encourage a more evocative experience of the collections than the traditional curatorial view."

"Since we have implemented the concepts of empowerment and working within a self-managed team, I feel that I am able to accomplish a great deal more. I am able to set my own priorities and define my objectives within the overall goals of my unit, and I am solely responsible for seeing that the work is done. Because we have reassigned some of the workload within our unit, I can better allocate my time, and I have access to some of the resources in the unit's budget to help me accomplish my objectives."

"Since taking a team-oriented approach to accomplishing our goals, each person's knowledge, areas of expertise and strengths are recognized and encouraged.

At the same time, because the team is made up of a diverse group of people, any one individual's lack of knowledge or weaknesses in certain areas can be compensated for by another member of the team."

"A flattening of hierarchy improves relationships between individuals; innovation and creativity are increased, and there are greater opportunities to learn from mistakes (a valuable learning experience)."

"Ultimately, there will probably be less bureaucracy, as various processes are being streamlined. Staff at more junior levels are growing enormously through the broadening of their jobs."

Critical comments

"One of the negative aspects is that certain things haven't changed. I don't think that our commitment to public service is any stronger than it was a year ago. To me, this was a crucial part of the organizational change. Those people who I believe have a poor attitude toward visitor needs, haven't changed those attitudes. I don't know that they ever will. Although the organization was flattened during the reorganization, some people still adhere to old professional hierarchies."

"I think we need more face-to-face communication. I would like to see more of the floor-by-floor meetings that we were having a few months ago. I think it's important for people to feel like you [Robert Janes] are hearing their concerns directly. I also think more informal communication between you and the rest of the staff would be an asset. Perhaps you could visit a floor once a week, unannounced, and just talk with people who are working there."

"The turmoil and upset caused by the change has gone on longer than I expected and this makes getting the work done a slow, difficult and sometimes frustrating experience. Somehow we have to get over this and get on with life."

"Glenbow forced me into a position of 'bumping' one of my close friends out of his job. This was very hard to deal with, and it took me between two to three months to finally feel comfortable about it."[4]

"To ensure that Glenbow emerges stronger and better, there must be more consultation and communication with other staff members from the senior executive down. And I don't mean more meetings! If staff just talked personally with each other a little more, I believe it would alleviate some of the problems that have occurred in our area, at least. I believe that some people have taken the idea of empowerment a little too far and are now 'doing their own thing' without any involvement from the other staff members."

"I am concerned about the reluctance and hesitation on the part of curatorial and conservation staff to allow public and rental events in the galleries and on the lobby floors. They come up with a worst case scenario to justify their position, and don't respond to what would it take to allow these events to take place."

"The organization lost some excellent, technically skilled people through lay-offs and through attrition because they couldn't adapt to the new ways of working and the Museum's new directions."

"I think it is also very important to remember that not all Glenbow staff are or want to be trailblazers, leaping into the changes and initiating things on their own. The Interpersonal Communication course probably illuminated this the best. For the C's and S's of us at Glenbow, order, control, careful planning and the weighing of all the options are needed before we can embrace a change."

"There is still a great deal of uncertainty among the staff – will any of us be working next year? We cannot get a definite agreement from the government (which is no-one's fault except the people who voted Conservative in the last election), so we are all very aware that all the changes to slim down the operation may just be the beginning of many cuts."

"The people who were middle managers [department heads] in the former organizational structure are experiencing a real sense of loss about their status. They are not sure of how to assume new roles in the organization; they are not sure about the kind of work they should now do."

"The task of work redesign is daunting. There is enormous complexity within the Glenbow, and sorting out what we can do, how we should do it, and who should do it – while at the same time maintaining a semblance of order and continuity – is difficult. While the staff are generally excited about the 'new organization', some are having difficulty in giving up control of former responsibility areas."

"Empowerment is still confusing a lot of people. There seem to be many interpretations: 'I can do whatever I bloody well want.' 'I'm not going to do that any more.' 'That's somebody else's job.' 'I wish someone would just tell me what to do.' 'I used to be responsible for that, but I'm not sure any more.'"

"Within my unit, fewer staff means having to eliminate some services and lengthen the time it takes to provide others. We have also had to significantly raise the cost of providing some services to the public. This negatively affects our primary goal which is to increase the public's use of our collections."

"Morale is very low; I find it is worse now than six months ago. Part of it is because of recalled staff [laid off staff who were called back for temporary assignments] coming back with negative attitudes. Part of it is seeing more colleagues leave of their own choice."

Managing change

The stresses and strains of organizational change cannot be denied, and they are aptly described in the staff comments above. As a result, I want to summarize some of our plans to better manage the continuous change process we have created for ourselves:

1. I have reduced the time I spend meeting individually with the 11 people who report to me by about 50%. This additional time will be spent meeting with Work Units and having informal visits with staff throughout the building.

2. I have made a commitment to a formal evaluation of the change process in order to gauge progress and identify problem areas. I believe, however, that it is too early in the process and I think that the spring or summer would provide a more realistic assessment. This assessment will be an organizational ethnography.

3. Glenbow's Strategy Group (senior managers) will undergo a formal team-building exercise. It is a new group of people and we must get consensus on where we want to be three years from now, how we are going to get there, and how we are going to treat each other in the process. We must also determine how we are going to creatively balance the competing interests that are represented by Glenbow's senior managers.

4. Part of this team-building work for the senior management will be a visioning process. We must articulate a short, powerful vision statement to focus the commitment of board, staff, and volunteers. The building blocks of this vision are sustainability, the pursuit of knowledge, public service, and staff/volunteer satisfaction.

5. There will continue to be mandatory, staff-wide training.

6. We will review and revise our five-year Corporate and Strategic plan to ensure that it keeps pace with current realities and new issues. The goals remain the same, but various measures and objectives must be reconsidered in light of our smaller organization.

7. New position descriptions, as well as role and responsibility statements, will be prepared to reflect our new work design.

8. We will design and install a staff-wide, performance management system that rewards performance. Glenbow has never had one – only a salary increment system in the Collective Agreement.

9. We will design a professional development policy for all staff that lays out both opportunities and obligations. For example, staff are interested in a program where you earn 80% of your salary for four years, and then receive a one-year paid sabbatical in the fifth year.

10. A management/union retreat will be organized to begin the process of replacing our Collective Agreement with Glenbow's Union. This might take the form of a philosophical statement, based on organizational values and principles. I sense that our Union is sincerely interested in reinventing itself, but this does not necessarily mean doing away with the Union.

11. Every effort will be made to continue to alleviate staff stress whenever possible, through workshops, ongoing yoga classes, and taking the time to socialize and celebrate successes.

12. The staff satisfaction survey will be redesigned in accordance with our new organization and administered as soon as possible and on a regular basis. We have not had one for a year and I am most interested in how staff will react. Will it be used to punish the change agents or express genuine concerns?

Finally, I have no reason to believe that we are stalled as an organization, despite the existence of varying levels of anxiety and frustration. We continue to produce, as evidenced by a variety of projects in 1992/93:

- We are currently producing three new publications, including a video of installation artist Rita McKeough, as well as two books on Alberta graveyards and a pictorial history of Calgary. The latter two are commercial co-ventures.
- The redevelopment of the exhibitions on the 4th floor (1,115 square metres) is on schedule, and will open in April of 1994. It will consist of three cross-cultural, topical, and multidisciplinary exhibitions devoted to Africa, warriors in society, and personal adornment.
- Glenbow staff gave 82 professional lectures.
- Glenbow staff published 30 articles in journals and periodicals across the country.
- The Rural Loans Program toured 24 exhibitions to 23 sites around the province, reaching more than 500,000 Albertans.
- We welcomed 270 new donors and Friends to Glenbow, adding to our base of 5,000 supporting Friends of Glenbow.

Issues and concerns

Irrespective of the above summary, I do have an episodic fear that we may be stalled (to an unknown extent) in some areas of the organization, especially in Programs, Exhibition and Special Loans. This is more understandable, because this is the most complex collection of specialists within Glenbow, as it includes programmers, designers, curators, technicians, and marketers. It may also be that I simply have to become more patient with the change process.

I am also concerned with the conventional wisdom at Glenbow that everyone is going flat out and working sixty to eighty hours per week. I know that this is not true, and that those who are working hard now were working hard before the change began.

Third, I am concerned about the difficulty in getting a reasonably objective evaluation of where we stand as an organization, with respect to all the change since our initial strategic planning. What progress have we made? Have staff actually changed their attitudes towards their work? Is Glenbow beginning to fundamentally change as an organization or is everything we are doing simply window dressing? I am often haunted by these questions and it is time to design some sort of evaluative mechanism to analyze them, as previously mentioned.

My fourth concern is that the notion of public service continues to mean, in the eyes of an unknown number of our staff, the diminishment of professional standards. This is dualism again – either it's public service or the collection, rather than attempting to achieve some sort of integration. Last, I continue to be concerned about the lack of time to provide the care and the attention that individual staff members require during this anxious and difficult time. I know that face-to-face interaction is essential, but it is often impossible to leave my office because of the press of daily responsibilities.

Considerations, speculation, and unsolicited advice

The following observations stem from the work I have done since the beginning of our organizational transformation on February 22, 1993, when the staff reductions were announced. The most powerful and difficult notion for me is that there is no place where we ever "arrive." There are only temporary periods of stabilization. I firmly believe, however, that organizations must go through a period of intense self-examination to understand the dysfunctional patterns that have been built up over time. However, this self-examination cannot go on forever and we must get on with the reorganization.

What are our responsibilities as executives and managers to move beyond the trauma of change and to create the attitudes and practices that will foster learning in our organizations? There are many opinions, but some of the more important practices include: fostering a climate of observation, debate and feedback; getting comfortable in using conflict creatively; and making risk taking and learning from mistakes normal practices (Hart 1993; Hart and Quinn 1993; Hout and Carter 1995): We are also advised *not* to do the following:

- Reward only current practices and behaviour
- Fail to create forums for reaction, feedback and reflection
- Fail to link changes to a broad-based blueprint for change
- Treat each change as a brief aberration from the norm – an event rather than a process
- Back down and leave the sacred cows alone whenever people get uncomfortable.

That being said, I cannot help but speculate about the change process in general at Glenbow. It seems that reorganization and transformation will succeed to the extent that Boards of Directors, leaders, and managers care about individual staff and demonstrate that caring. Staff also need to understand the "big picture" and the inherent complexities, including an understanding of their role in contributing to the situation as a whole. This really means reassurance. A major difficulty we face as senior managers is identifying the time to provide this critical support on a daily basis, as the staff comments noted above testify.

My last attempt at speculation has to do with the effects of change and transformation on an organization's reputation. I have been advised by various staff that Glenbow's reputation has been severely tarnished in the museum community, as a result of having reduced the staff and resources devoted to the maintenance of professional standards, such as conservation. I speculate, however, that in the long term a tarnished image is less important than the overall prosperity of the institution. Is this view legitimate? Am I being cynical? It may be that organizational transformation will simply not succeed until there has been a generational change, and there are new staff in place who have no ties to the past. This may, in fact, be the case for our society in general – as people are so reluctant to embrace change.

I will complete this update with some unsolicited advice. To begin with, I have serious reservations about bringing back laid-off employees for temporary work at Glenbow, which can include periods of two weeks up to twelve months. This arrangement was negotiated with our Union prior to the layoffs, but it is now clear that some of these people are emotionally stuck as a result of the layoffs. They continue to reintroduce their anger and resentment to the core staff who are trying to move ahead. In addition, I have been told that one of these employees is deliberately slowing down project work in the hopes of further employment. I would not agree to this arrangement again.

Second, do not underestimate the effects of change on middle managers, or department heads, as they were called at Glenbow. We eliminated their titles, and hence the most visible signs of their status, rank, and authority. Several are still reeling from these changes and seem unable to function in a positive and productive manner. I assume responsibility for these difficulties, as I underestimated their reaction to change and failed to deal effectively with their concerns early on in the change process. I had attempted to do this, but grew impatient when I concluded that they, as middle managers, represented one of the biggest obstacles to change.

Last, I suggest that a future agenda item for the Museum Directors' Group be the topic of museum and art gallery consortia, such as the Museums West consortium that Glenbow helped to establish. We met recently in Oklahoma City (US) and a representative from the American Federation of the Arts (AFA) requested to be on the agenda. The AFA is a non-profit umbrella organization of 500 institutional members that organizes and circulates exhibitions of fine arts and media art. The AFA believes that consortia are the wave of the future, and they see this type of organization as key to effective travelling exhibitions at a time of increasing complexity and diminishing resources. Maybe the time has come for a formal Canadian consortium of some sort.

Conclusions

Although there is no "right" way to plan or undertake institutional change, it is vital that museums create their own future through serious reflection and subsequent action. There are some major benefits to be gained from planning, as it makes explicit the core values of an institution and, as a result, helps create a sense of common purpose. This common purpose does much to reduce the fragmentation and isolation that often characterize the components of large, complex organizations like Glenbow. Planning, however, contrary to conventional wisdom, is not an end itself. It is a process that holds significant potential for enhancing an institution's sense of itself and providing a context for innovation. A sense of collective purpose, innovation, and consensus building are essential ingredients in defining and achieving high levels of performance, irrespective of the size of the organization.

Stepping away from the demands of the moment through planning creates many opportunities for new ideas and new ways of doing things. Planning for the future also allows one to question what is important and what is no longer relevant or appropriate. This, in turn, lays the foundation for staff involvement and commitment, because the consensus building inherent in competent planning allows staff to be involved in those decisions which can, and will, affect their work.

Most importantly, corporate and strategic planning create an ongoing opportunity to tap the intellectual and emotional richness of museum workers, while at the same time emphasizing the importance of *why* and *what* people do, not *how* they do it. It is common knowledge that the majority of museum workers are unusually dedicated and motivated, and are not driven by the hope or promise of material gain. This very fact is a priceless asset, and means that all museum staff deserve the very best that competent leadership and management can provide – including full and continuous communication, the clear definition of responsibilities, the clear definition of the results to be achieved, and a supportive and nurturing work environment. In short, the role of leadership and management is to create conditions that enable those who do the work to do it more effectively and with maximum satisfaction.

Notes

1 *A New Decade of Distinction: Glenbow's Corporate and Strategic Plan 1992–1997* is available on file at the Glenbow Museum, Calgary, Alberta, Canada. It is also discussed in detail in Janes, R. R. (2013) *Museums and the Paradox of Change: A Case Study in Urgent Adaptation* (3rd Edition), London and New York: Routledge (pages 8–28).
2 I co-founded this formal network of Canadian Museum Directors with the late Barbara Tyler – the Executive Director of the McMichael Canadian Collection. We concluded that we needed a more formal network of museum directors to provide emotional and intellectual support to assist us in our efforts at major institutional change. She and I invited a dozen or so museum, gallery, and science centre directors to the Glenbow Museum for an inaugural meeting of the Museum Directors Group (MDG) in June of 1992. This group has taken on a life of its own and continues to meet two to three times a year at a member's institution. It is now called Museums Anonymous. Each director or CEO is required to report on his or her organization at each meeting, as well as to suggest special agenda items for analysis and discussion – often involving external resource people.
3 My title changed several times during my tenure at Glenbow – from director, to executive director, to president and CEO. The last title reflects the growing imposition of business terminology in museum affairs.
4 "Bumping" is the reassignment of jobs on the basis of seniority in unionized organizations in the private or public sector.

References

Bernard, E. (1989) "Collaboration with the Wider Community," *MUSE*, VII(3): 16–18.
Hardin, G. (1985) *Filters Against Folly*. London: Penguin Books.
Hart, T. (1993) "Human Resource Management – Time to Exorcize the Militant Tendency," *Employee Relations*, 15(3): 29–36.
Hart, S. and Quinn, R. (1993) "Roles Executives Play: CEO Behavioral Complexity and Firm Performance," *Human Relations*, 46: 543–574.
Hout, T. M. and Carter, J. C. (1995) "Getting It Done: New Roles for Senior Executives," *Harvard Business Review*, November–December: 113–145.

7

BEYOND STRATEGIC PLANNING*

The Glenbow example

> Ours is not an age of broad theory. It is an age of pragmatic thought and action . . .
> *(John Kenneth Galbraith 1992)*

Introduction

In reviewing the events of the past three years which have led to radical changes at Glenbow, I wish to provide more of a personal view than may be customary. Emotions run extremely high in periods of relentless change, and believe it or not, museum directors are also personally affected by the stress of change. Dealing with these emotions, one's own and those of colleagues, is one of the most difficult aspects of the change process. The simple fact is that the vast majority of people react emotionally *and* negatively to change and new ideas, irrespective of their training, intelligence and experience. I have grown to accept this as a universal law, akin to Newton's Third Law, which says that "to every force, there is an equal and opposing force." As the Executive Director and the initiator of Glenbow's changes, I am bound to feel more positive about them than an employee whose job has been reduced to half-time.

I write from the perspective of the Executive Director. Such a perspective suffers from limitations, in that I am mostly isolated from the daily work routines of Glenbow staff. At the same time, I have both the privilege and responsibility to view the institution holistically. It is important that the reader be aware of this, in order to balance what follows with the knowledge that none of us can claim objectivity in anything we do. In short, transforming an organization the size and

*Source: Robert R. Janes, MUSE, Vol. XI, No. 4, Winter (1994): 12–16. This chapter is based on a presentation made at the Annual Conference of the Canadian Museums Association in Regina, Saskatchewan, Canada, June 10–13, 1993.

complexity of Glenbow is a messy and chaotic process. There will be numerous outcomes and eventualities which are not even apparent at this time.

Prelude to change

When I arrived as the new Director in 1989, it was clear that major changes were in the offing. Although Glenbow is remarkably self-sufficient for a Canadian museum (we raise about 50% of our annual operation budget ourselves), we still require a major contribution annually from the Provincial Government of Alberta in fulfilment of their legal obligation to maintain and exhibit our collections. The agreement to provide this funding came to an end, coincidental with my arrival as Director, and there was nothing in place to ensure ongoing provincial support.

The corporate and strategic plans

My first priority as Director was the development of a corporate plan and a strategic plan, as a basis for negotiating a multi-year funding agreement with the Province of Alberta. Our two-part planning process began with a corporate plan. This was an exercise in defining Glenbow's institutional identity and purpose, and included achieving a common understanding among staff about values, management principles, and critical issues facing the organization, as well as an environmental scan. The strategic plan followed from this and was concerned with organizational operations – including goals, strategies, measures, standards, and objectives.[1] I want to emphasize the importance of achieving a common understanding among all staff about a variety of issues, such as organizational values, principles, and goals. It is critically important that this groundwork be done as a prelude to organizational change. Without such closure, there is often perpetual disagreement among participants on these and other fundamental topics.

A brisk touch with reality

Our first major setback occurred early in 1992, when we learned that the Provincial Government was either unwilling or unable to accept Glenbow's corporate and strategic plans as a basis for a multi-year funding agreement. I cannot overemphasize our collective disappointment at the Provincial Department of Culture's failure to provide any substantive comment on the plan. This was particularly frustrating to both staff and Glenbow's Board of Governors, as we had involved three members of the Legislative Assembly and a senior cultural official in all aspects of the planning work.

When it became clear that the corporate and strategic plans were not going to secure our future, I was forced to admit that our strategic thinking (what we wanted to do and how we were going to do it) had outstripped our organizational capability. Without the modest but incremental funding increases laid out in the strategic plan, we did not have the staff and resources to do what we intended to do. What next?

Glenbow's Executive Group (consisting of the Assistant Directors and me) did a financial forecast to assess the implications of declining public and private funding over the next five years. By the summer of 1992, the Provincial payment to Glenbow had declined 26% since 1988–89. At the same time, our fundraising efforts in the private sector were down by $150,000 and falling. Based on some conservative estimates about income and expenditures, the forecast showed a cumulative deficit of CAN$7.7 million by 1997, if we continued at our current rate of expenditures. This meant bankruptcy and closure for Glenbow within the next five years unless radical action was taken to address the future.

Our decision to look organizational change right in the eye was not simply a matter of less money, although this was the major catalyst in prompting our transformation. There were also deeper, underlying considerations that we had started to address during our earlier strategic planning, including the need to reflect on what we were doing, how we were doing it, and who we were doing it for. In short, we were confronted with the opportunity and responsibility to renew Glenbow by increasing our capacity for change. I want to dispel any direct comparison with the Art Gallery of Ontario (AGO – Toronto, Canada), having heard that our actions have been called "AGO-West." We were not waiting for the Province to deliver the funds to balance our budget. In fact, our work began in earnest nearly a year before such action would have been necessary. We did this in order to give ourselves deliberate, systematic planning time.

The six strategies

With this foreknowledge of an inevitable crisis by March of 1993, our Executive Group selected six major strategies designed to do three critically important things – reduce expenditures, increase revenues, and enhance Glenbow's overall effectiveness. These strategies are: deaccessioning; developing commercial alliances; revitalizing our commitment to public service; forging cooperative partnerships with related organizations; simplifying our work processes; and designing a new form of organization. I cannot review all of this work here, so I will focus on one area – designing a new form of organization.

Having concluded that a 20% reduction in expenditures (about CAN$1.1 million dollars) was required, we could not pretend that a reduction of this magnitude could simply be absorbed by stripping away staff and programs, and that Glenbow would remain the same. It was imperative that we examine the way we were organized, including all of the associated practices and assumptions. Many of us also knew, as a result of staff discussions, that our corporate hierarchical structure, which had served Glenbow so ably in the past, was becoming brittle and vulnerable as the pace of change accelerated.

"What if we don't change at all ...
and something magical just happens?"

FIGURE 5 "What if we don't change at all . . . and something magical just happens?"
© cartoonresource / Fotolia.

Creating a new organization

The underlying premise of our new organization is that managers can no longer hope to have all the information and skills necessary to make consistently adequate decisions in an increasingly complex world. The New Forms of Organization (NFO) team reviewed and evaluated various organizational models derived from the management literature and from numerous interviews.[2] One team member also visited the San Diego Zoo (California, US) to study their celebrated approach to team-based work; their successes and failures provided invaluable instruction to the NFO team. I want to emphasize that the museum literature was silent on this subject, apparently because the vast majority of museums have simply borrowed the corporate, hierarchical design from the private sector, with little or no recognition that we are knowledge workers, not manufacturers. This lack of appropriate models, coupled with the fact that we were facing a significant reduction in expenditures, led us to the conclusion that we had to start from scratch.

It was not a complete vacuum, however, because we were heartened by the organization theory which recommends more trust and less control, more diversity and less uniformity, and more differentiation and less systemization

(Handy 1976: 332). At the same time, managerial accountability will be more important than ever, and managers will have a much greater role to play in providing advice, guidance, and support to staff.

About the time the NFO team was finishing its work, I read a book which later proved useful for making sense of the task we faced and the information we had accumulated. This book, *The Age of Unreason* by Charles Handy (1989), argues that discontinuous change is all around us, as compared with continuous change, which says that the past is the guide to the future. The author argues that less than half of the work force in the industrial world will have "proper" full-time jobs in organizations by the beginning of the twenty-first century, because of the change from mass-manufacturing and mass-employment organizations to more knowledge-based organizations – those which create and add value through their knowledge and creativity (Handy 1989: 31–34; 51–52).

Handy then goes on to describe a conceptual model of a knowledge-based organization which consists of three parts – the so-called shamrock organization (Handy 1989: 87–115). The first leaf of the shamrock is the professional core, made up of the professionals, technicians, and managers who own the knowledge which distinguishes the organization from its counterparts. The second leaf consists of the contractors – those individuals and organizations that can perform work better and for less cost than the professionals. The third is the flexible labour force – all those part-time and temporary workers who are the fastest-growing part of the employment scene. Although the shamrock concept will be familiar to the private sector, with its emphasis on contracting out, it represents a refreshing departure from conventional thinking about museum organization. This conceptual model freed my thinking from the constraints of departments and divisions based on functional specializations.

In retrospect, I see that I made two mistakes at this point in our work. First, I allowed the NFO team to become moribund, by not involving them in the further conceptual developments which occurred after the team's report was completed. I did this mainly because the planning had evolved to the point of confidentiality (decisions about which positions would go and which would stay had to be the responsibility of senior management). This caused one of the NFO team members to feel that she was uninformed and unprepared to support the model when it became public. I had created certain expectations which were not met. This is perhaps the most difficult part of participative management – staff often expect or assume that their contributions will emerge intact at the end of a project.

My second mistake was innocent enough and took me off guard. I apparently erred in openly telling staff that I had been stimulated by Handy's book and that I felt it was a useful conceptual tool in our investigations. One staff member observed that "the Director had read a book and now he was going to turn the Glenbow upside down because of it." If the critics would take the time to read Handy, and then compare his observations with Glenbow's new design, they would readily see the difference between concept and reality. Perhaps I will be more circumspect in the future about my sources of ideas, although I will continue to uphold the critical importance of reading widely in areas which appear to be only peripherally related to museum work. I don't think that it is done enough, especially among senior museum and gallery managers.

ATTRIBUTES OF THE NEW ORGANIZATION

There are no textbook solutions to organizational design, and any alternative will be messy, incomplete and dependent upon the intelligence and good will of all staff. The following is an overview of some of the more important characteristics of our new organizational design.

- Eighteen departments and four divisions have been collapsed into six multidisciplinary work units, each headed by a Director (note the change in terminology from Assistant Director). We now have six Directors and one Executive Director.
- The number of managers has been reduced from 24 to 14.
- With the exception of Central Services, there are no departments based on professional specializations. For the most part, the internal organization of each work unit is flat, with staff reporting to a Director for routine work and to project leaders for project work.

  Membership in the work units will rotate (probably every two years) to allow staff opportunities to serve and learn in a variety of contexts. The boundaries between the work units are fluid, as staff at any given time will be involved in multiple projects which cross-cut the particular responsibilities of a work unit.
- We have taken the program staff of our former interpretation department and spread them throughout three of the work units, as part of our commitment to enhance public service. For example, the programmer in the collections management work unit will be essential in improving access to our collections in ways other than exhibitions. It is no longer sufficient for the public to see only the "tip of the iceberg." They must see much more of the iceberg if we expect to increase public understanding and support of our work.
- Some may say that this organizational design is an elaborate matrix. We have gone beyond the classic matrix, however, in that we no longer have specialized departments as the home bases. Our home bases are now permanent, multidisciplinary teams. Glenbow is probably best described as a project-based organization, as we have decided to tackle most of our core activities through project teams (Morgan 1989: 67) The functional departments that do exist, such as finance and security, play a supporting role. Otherwise, specialists belong to teams and make their main contributions through their teams. We hope to develop a network of interaction rather than a bureaucratic structure, where coordination is as informal as possible.

- Most importantly, we have structured our work so that each work unit is directly aligned with the major goals of the institution – to improve visitor satisfaction, to improve public knowledge and understanding, to improve new knowledge about our collections, and to improve accessibility to our collections.

- The Library and Archives have been combined and are under the management of a Director, who was elected by his peers for a two-year term. Our intention here is to initiate a process that will lead to a self-managed team in the Library/Archives, whereby the staff will do their own hiring, firing, performance appraisals, and so forth, without the need for a senior manager.

- Glenbow Enterprises is completely new for Glenbow, and will allow us both to fulfil our responsibilities as an employer and to generate additional income. Glenbow Enterprises will house a variety of commercial activities, including a satellite retail shop, consulting services in a variety of fields, and a facilities rental service. It will also allow half-time Glenbow employees the opportunity to use our reputation and infrastructure to increase their income when not working for the core organization. Glenbow will take a fee for this arrangement.

- We have also made a commitment to a full-time project manager for monitoring. This individual, using our Local Area Network of 86 personal computers, continuously monitors our performance toward achieving the objectives of our strategic plan, as well as overseeing program evaluation and satisfaction surveys for visitors, volunteers, the Board of Governors, and staff.

The staff satisfaction survey assesses staff satisfaction with respect to such topics as internal communication, degree of influence over one's work, and the quality of Glenbow's leadership. This staff survey is not without controversy. Some staff, for example, are frustrated because the survey does not measure their individual happiness, something which Glenbow could never assume responsibility for anyway. For me, this survey has partially replaced the rumour and innuendo which are characteristic of organizational life. Perhaps, most importantly, it allows the "silent majority" to register their opinions, as it is more often the negative and angry individuals who are most apt to express their views.

Despite the enormous reduction in our expenditures, we have made a major commitment to ongoing training. Our staff are not only being asked to produce results – they must also develop new ways of working together which emphasize cooperation, understanding, and shared perspectives (Hayward 1993: 27–30). The so-called "soft skills" required for this are not part of traditional training, and include such things as interpersonal communication, team building, and conflict resolution. We are now working with the University of Calgary to design and deliver training to Glenbow staff which recognizes our unique circumstances.

Managing change

I want to review our attempts at managing the human side of organizational change, including the events leading up to the laying-off of staff on February 22, 1993. Staff had been advised months in advance that February 22nd was layoff day. As you can imagine, the closer we came to that date, the higher the stress levels became. There were a number of ways we tried to help ease this tension, including stress-management workshops for all staff. These workshops were designed not only to give staff personal techniques for coping with stress, but also to give them the opportunity to suggest how to ease the stress throughout Glenbow.

All of our consultations with experts and the literature reinforced the importance of senior management being available and visible to staff, of getting out of our offices, and of demonstrating that we cared about what individuals were experiencing. It was also most important to listen to, respond to, and not deny peoples' feelings, irrespective of whether or not you agreed with them. At the request of staff, I changed the format of our staff meetings from one large meeting with all the staff to a series of much smaller ones.

Union–management collaboration

After much consultation, consideration, and preparation, the staff reductions were announced – first individually to those affected, then individually to all remaining employees, and finally, to the public. Long before that day, however, at the outset of the transformation process in June 1992, Glenbow's senior management had made a commitment to open communication. I invited the president of our union to join in discussions to anticipate issues stemming from this painful process – including layoffs, "bumping," part-time work, and job sharing.[3]

This informal and open approach between union and management began to change in January of 1993, primarily because the majority of staff had finally accepted the fact that changes, including staff reductions, were actually going to happen even though we had been openly discussing this since the previous July. Having accepted the inevitability of change, the union decided it was in its best interests to deal with it through formal negotiations. After six frustrating weeks of formal negotiations, all agreed that information and trust were more important than preconceived negotiating positions. As a result, we renewed our commitment to more openness and trust, and were able to agree on major items before the actual announcement of staff reductions.

This degree of union–management collaboration was unprecedented at Glenbow and was the key ingredient in working through these traumatic changes. A good example of this was the layoff process itself, which lasted for a week after the actual announcements. During this time, we adopted an issues-management approach, whereby the union and management dealt with individual employee issues, problems, and concerns as they arose. Despite these efforts, there was still confusion about severance packages, unemployment insurance benefits, and part-time employment – all of which contributed to staff stress. This underscores the need for exhaustive preparations and, even then, there will be surprises.

We were also mindful of the standard layoff procedure among corporations in Calgary, which involves surprise notification of dismissal, the provision of boxes for belongings, and then ushering laid-off staff out of the building within minutes or hours of the termination. We had tried this once in the past, and I can assure you that it was wrong, at least for Glenbow. Perhaps the security risks in the private sector justify this approach, but I still have my doubts.

The approach we adopted was much messier, and perhaps more traumatic in the short term, as it involved giving the terminated employees a number of options. For example, staff were given the choice of remaining at work until March 31, 1993, or leaving Glenbow with full pay. These options were in addition to a severance package that included psychological counselling. This meant that numerous staff who had lost their jobs were still with us, complete with their shock and anger. In fact, I found myself in a meeting with the 31 laid-off employees three days after the announcement, attempting to explain what we had done and why. I had to do everything in my power to keep my own emotions in control as I encountered their hurt and frustration. With one or two exceptions, they all behaved with honesty and dignity, and for this I will always applaud them. I also wish to publicly acknowledge our union for the above suggestions and many others, all of which contributed to a much more humane and sensitive outcome. We continue to work closely with our union on the management of change.

Survivor's syndrome

Of particular importance in all of this are the staff who kept their jobs – the so-called survivors. The combination of relief, guilt, and grief that they feel constitutes what is known as the survivor's syndrome, and it should not be underestimated. We continue to deal with this at Glenbow, having identified several staff that were emotionally trapped by the events of February 22, 1993 and continued to be influenced by them weeks or months later. These individuals have been given one-on-one counselling and several have benefitted enormously. The needs of the survivors also underscore the importance of a humane and sensitive layoff process. Those remaining in the organization are acutely aware of how their departing colleagues are treated, and if this treatment is seen to be shabby or arbitrary, there could very well be significant erosion in commitment and motivation among the remaining staff.

There is another item of unfinished business which continues to require our attention, and that is Glenbow's former department heads, or middle managers. Having never been a middle manager myself, I had underestimated their sense of loss when their positions were abolished, along with the inherent status and authority. I had assumed that they would see the change as liberating – relieving them of onerous administrative duties and procedural hassles. Some do see it this way, while others feel adrift. Many of them had assumed they would be laid off, in keeping with the thinning of middle-management ranks in the private sector. This was not to be, however, for the former department heads at Glenbow possess much of the knowledge and experience that make Glenbow what it is.

As anyone familiar with stress will know, the layoff process produces a cycle of emotions and reactions in people, and we have certainly experienced the classic grieving model at Glenbow. Staff first felt shock and a sort of numbness; then denial. This moved into anger, and then negotiating or bargaining. A good example of anger and denial is the anonymous letter sent to Glenbow's Board of Governors, which called for my resignation on the grounds of incompetent management. The author of this letter felt that all this change was my personal agenda, and that if I would only leave, Glenbow could get back to "normal." The next step is grieving for what has been lost, and eventually and hopefully, some sort of acceptance is achieved.

The neutral zone

We at Glenbow are now in the "neutral zone" (Bridges 1991: 5) This is the no man's land between the old reality and the new. In the words of William Bridges, the author of an important book entitled *Managing Transitions*, "It's the time and place when the old habits that are no longer adaptive to the situation are extinguished and new, better-adapted patterns of habit begin to take shape."

There are at least three things about the neutral zone that are critical to understanding effective organizational change (Bridges 1991: 5–6):

- You may mistakenly conclude that the confusion you feel is a sign that there's something wrong with you. People are assailed by self-doubt and misgivings about their leaders.
- You may be frightened in this no man's land and try to escape. This is apparently why there is an increased level of turnover during organizational change.
- Painful as it often is, the neutral zone is also a rare opportunity for creativity, renewal, and development. This is a time when innovation is most possible and when revitalization begins, as the restraints on innovation are at their weakest.

We are doing our best to work with these insights to ensure progress toward a new beginning, and we have adopted three working principles to assist us (Joiner 1986: 45–52). First, every staff member of the working units must have a clear understanding of their collective purpose, and purpose needs to be continually revisited to test its relevance to new conditions. Second, active experimentation must be encouraged. We simply must not try to analyze and design everything before taking action. We must take risks, learn from our mistakes and not punish. Third, we must foster a new kind of openness at Glenbow, and deal with conflicts and tensions openly, directly, and creatively. This requires a certain generosity of spirit from everyone involved, if we are to rise above pettiness.

A difficult apprenticeship

I will conclude with a simple listing of some of the highlights of my own education at Glenbow. Self-evident as these might appear, I assure you that my apprenticeship has often been difficult and painful:

- Full, open, and continuous communication throughout the organization is essential. It is the responsibility of each individual. Communication is a two-way process and you can't wait passively for it to be done to you;
- There can never be too much staff involvement in the design of change;
- All involved, especially management, must cultivate the ability to say "I don't know";
- Power sharing is the key to meaningful collaboration;
- Repetition is vital. If you've said something 25 times, say it 25 times more;
- Don't deny anyone's feelings throughout the change process – they are what they are. Accept them and deal with them constructively.

There are probably 100 more similar observations, but these particular ones have been some of the most difficult for me, and I am still learning. I suspect that, in the end, our efforts at change are all about learning. Finally, I want to publicly acknowledge all Glenbow staff for their vitality and commitment throughout what continues to be a difficult process. I know that there have been both personal and institutional injuries as a result, but I remain firmly convinced that all of this change has been, and will be, essential in charting a secure course for Glenbow.

Postscript

As I wrote this chapter, I learned that the Province of Alberta had reduced their contribution to Glenbow by another 5% for 1993–94. This means that we must now find CAN$169,000 to balance our budget. I am confident that there won't be any further layoffs this year in order to fund this shortfall. We now have a more sustainable Glenbow, with sufficient flexibility to meet this external threat. To what extent we will continue to be able to do so in the future will depend upon the severity of future funding reductions and our own efforts at achieving self-sufficiency. Only with self-sufficiency can we begin to truly manage our institutions.

Significant change requires a form of dying, and it is folly to expect that our organizational changes at Glenbow will not anger, disappoint, and frustrate people (DePree 1992: 35). The question is whether or not these emotions, and the energy they require, can be redirected toward the transformation of the organization. What we need to achieve at Glenbow is still beyond our capabilities. Confronted with this reality, we always have a choice. We can either learn by expanding our abilities and competencies, or we can quit (Fritz 1991: 22). I have Glenbow's distinguished history to convince me that quitting has never been an alternative.

Notes

1 *A New Decade of Distinction: Glenbow's Corporate and Strategic Plan 1992–1997* is available on file at the Glenbow Museum, Calgary, Alberta, Canada. It is also discussed in detail in Janes, R. R. (2013) *Museums and the Paradox of Change: A Case Study in Urgent Adaptation* (3rd Edition), London and New York: Routledge (pages 8–28).
2 The NFO team consisted of Anne Hayward (Cultural History Department), Barbara Burggraf (Development Department), Lisa Christensen (Art Department), Andrea Garnier (Archives), and Robert R. Janes (Executive Director).
3 "Bumping" is the reassignment of jobs on the basis of seniority in unionized organisations in the private or public sector.

References

Bridges, W. (1991) *Managing Transitions*, Reading, MA: Addison-Wesley Publishing Co., Inc.

De Pree, M. (1992) *Leadership Jazz*, New York: Dell Publishing.

Fritz, R. (1991) *Creating*, New York: Fawcett Columbine.

Galbraith, J.K. (1992). Quoted in *The Scotsman*, November 25, 1992.

Handy, C. (1976) *Understanding Organizations*, Harmondsworth, Middlesex, England: Penguin Books Ltd.

Handy, C. (1989) *The Age of Unreason*, Boston: Harvard Business School Press.

Hayward, A. (1993) "Notes for Museum Management: The Transition to Teams," *Alberta Museums Association's Review* 19(2): 27–30.

Joiner, W.B. (1986) "Leadership for Organizational Learning," in J.D. Adams (ed.), *Transforming Leadership*, Alexandria, VA: Miles River Press.

Morgan, G. (1989) *Creative Organization Theory: A Resource Book*, Newbury Park, CA: SAGE Publications, Inc.

8

DON'T LOSE YOUR NERVE*

Museums and organizational change

Author's note: This presentation was prepared for "Museums for the New Millennium: A Symposium for the Museum Community," September 5–7, 1996, at the Smithsonian Institution, Washington, D.C., US. This symposium was part of the celebrations for the 150th anniversary of the Smithsonian Institution and featured invited speakers and panelists from around the world.

The invited presentations were published in a commemorative volume by the Smithsonian and the American Association of Museums a year later. Each presentation in this volume is preceded by a moderator's introduction and concludes with questions from the audience.

Introduction by the Moderator, Spencer R. Crew – Saturday, Sept. 7, 1996[1]

Spencer R. Crew: Good morning. Our speaker this morning is Dr. Robert R. Janes. He is currently the executive director and CEO of the Glenbow Museum Art Gallery, Library and Archives in Calgary, Alberta, Canada. He has held that position since 1989. He has a Ph.D. in archaeology from the University of Calgary, and he is an adjunct professor there. I admire him for finding the time to balance these things in his life. Dr. Janes has written three books and numerous articles in the areas of archaeology, anthropology, and museology. We are here this morning in relation to his latest book, *Museums and the Paradox of Change* (Janes 1995), which examines the process of change in a major cultural organization. It is a book you really need to know about and to read. A recent review of the book began this way:

Source: Robert R. Janes (1997), "Don't Lose Your Nerve: Museums and Organizational Change." In *Museums for the New Millennium: A Symposium for the Museum Community,* Washington, D.C.: Center for Museum Studies, Smithsonian Institution and the American Association of Museums, pp. 81–96.

Bob Janes has written a dangerous book. Museum executives be warned: Reading this book may lead to heart palpitations, desert mouth, and shortness of breath. Janes, the director of the Glenbow Museum in Alberta, Canada, describes in detail the actions taken to transform an institution born in the 1960s, the age of endless potential, into a museum that would survive and perhaps even flourish in the nasty 1990s.

(Case 1996: 22)

All museum directors will recognize that scenario. I think we all find it useful to sit down and talk with others going down that same path. We are very fortunate today to have Dr. Janes with us to tell us more about his experiences and how we can profit from them, and we welcome his challenges. It is now my pleasure to introduce Dr. Janes.

Introduction

I am indeed honored to have been invited to speak to this important symposium, even more so because our host is none other than the Smithsonian Institution. Its work is legendary, even in Canada, where I have lived most of my adult life. With an American mother and a Canadian father, I have encountered the perennial enigma of Canadian identity that was so well described by one of your journalists, Richard Starnes (National Film Board of Canada 1976: 133). He observed that "Canadians are generally indistinguishable from the Americans, and the surest way of telling the two apart is to make the observation to a Canadian." Now, to begin.

Organizational change and adaptation occur with great difficulty in museums. My most vivid testimony to this is the death threat I received during the most painful of our organizational initiatives – the reduction of 25% of our staff. There could hardly be a more stark reminder of the impact of these events on individual human beings than such a threat. Nor is there a more cogent reminder of the responsibilities we have for the decisions we make and the actions we take to ensure the survival and prosperity of our museums. Significant change requires a form of dying (De Pree 1992: 35), and it is foolish to expect that organizational change will not anger, frustrate, and disappoint people. This is especially true when the changes go far beyond cosmetic tinkering. At Glenbow, we are insisting upon new ways of thinking and acting that will make us more responsive to the communities we serve. The real question is whether or not the emotions associated with change, be they rage or elation, and the energy these emotions require, can be redirected toward organizational change and improvement.

I also hope, perhaps naively, that change in museums will not have to be a zero-sum game, where progress can come only at the cost of dearly held values (Traub 1995: 60). The key to pushing, without the organization pushing back, is balanced inquiry and action. The indiscriminate use of trendy solutions is as destructive as a stubborn reverence for tradition. Because organizational change is chaotic, uncertain, and often mysterious, we have no choice but to try to be as intelligent and caring as we can. In a survey of 29 North American museums, conducted by Martha Morris (1995) of the National Museum of American History, fully 83% of the respondents said they had recently undergone some degree of organizational change. We should not be surprised by this, nor disturbed, as it is in the nature of complex adaptive systems to change. This is also true of our families and our other relationships (Flower 1995: 1).

Please note that I do not question why museums exist or whether they should be replaced by something else. My main interest is in museums as organizations, a subject that has received remarkably little attention in museum literature (Griffin 1987: 389). These concerns should not be dismissed as mere process, for the manner in which a museum does its work will either permit or preclude innovation, inclusive thinking, and the persistent questioning of the status quo, all of which are fundamental aspects of a museum's role. Museums will only thrive to the extent that traditional practices are continually questioned, improved, or done away with.

In preparing my remarks for today, I was continually reminded of John Kenneth Galbraith, who recently observed (April 27, 1995, University of Calgary, Alberta, Canada) that, in 60 years of teaching at Harvard, he has learned that you can take any idea, however simple, and extend it to 55 minutes. My task is just the opposite – summarizing our complex and lengthy change process in about the same time. I want to emphasize that most of what I will be talking about today is not particularly new or original. I ask that you consider my comments on Glenbow's change process as a summary of an experimental work-in-progress, which I hope will be useful to you in navigating the stormy seas between organizational realities and societal needs. We shall undoubtedly find it easier to change museums than to change the world (Phillips 1995: 3). My purpose in summarizing our work at Glenbow is to set the stage for the second half of my talk, which is a consideration of some of the opportunities and hazards facing museums as organizations in the late twentieth century.

Glenbow

It will help to know something about Glenbow at the outset, if only so that you can compare it to your own situation. Glenbow's uniqueness lies in the sum of its four parts – a museum, art gallery, library and archives – all under one roof and one administration. Glenbow's Western Canadian research library is the largest of its kind in Canada. The Glenbow Archives is the largest non-government archives in Canada, with two million photographs and manuscript collections occupying two shelf miles. Our art gallery, with a permanent collection of more than 28,000 works, attracts almost one-third of our annual visitors. Our museum includes the disciplines of ethnology, military history, cultural history, and mineralogy, for a permanent collection numbering 2.3 million objects.

Glenbow does not restrict its work to the city of Calgary. We also operate a rural and special loans program, which makes objects available to non-museum environments, including the Calgary International Airport. These programs served nearly 900,000 Albertans last year, as well as visitors from all parts of the globe.

To fulfill these responsibilities, we currently employ 86 full-time and 33 part-time staff. We are also deeply indebted to 260 active volunteers. In 1995, Frances Kaye, an historian at the University of Nebraska (US), provided a succinct description of Glenbow's role: "The Glenbow Museum, Art Collection, Archives and Library is quite simply the defining institution for prairie Canada, in much the same way that the Smithsonian Institution, in all its branches, is the defining institution for the United States" (Kaye 1995).

When I arrived as the new executive director in 1989, it was clear that major changes were in the offing. Although Glenbow is remarkably self-sufficient for a Canadian museum, we still require a major annual contribution from the Provincial Government of Alberta. An agreement to provide this funding had come to an end coincidentally with my arrival (at least, I hope that it was coincidental), and we decided to develop a corporate and strategic plan in 1990 as the basis for securing multi-year funding from the province. All of us were weary of the one-year-at-a-time, crisis management approach common to the funding of public agencies. Thus began our six years of continuous change, which is still unfolding.

Although financial concerns were a major stimulus for this initiative, there were other reasons that contributed to a perceptible, albeit largely unspoken, desire for change among the museum's staff. Glenbow had been without an executive director for a lengthy period prior to my arrival, and the institution was drifting. There was also a widespread belief among staff that Glenbow's management was simply top heavy. All these factors had created dissatisfaction with the status quo, so that even if stable funding from the province had been available, Glenbow would have needed a thoughtful overhaul.

Our corporate and strategic plans were a first for Glenbow, in that the planning process enabled all staff to become involved. It was also the first time a Canadian museum had incorporated explicit performance measures and standards, as well as a set of principles outlining how we would treat each other as individuals and as staff. Alas, the provincial government rejected both our plan and our request for multi-year funding out-of-hand, presumably because multi-year funding was a foreign concept to them and would also mean a loss of provincial control over Glenbow.

As infuriating as this was, in retrospect there was a hidden benefit to this impasse. It forced Glenbow's executive staff to confront the future with a vengeance, in the face of declining government support. We did some financial projections five years out, and glimpsed a huge deficit and eventual bankruptcy for Glenbow by 1998. A 20% reduction in operating expenses was required. With this kind of massive budgetary reduction, it is impossible simply to tinker with the organization chart. In short, we were confronted with the opportunity and responsibility to renew Glenbow by increasing our capacity for change.

The six strategies

This realization spawned another staff and board exercise, based on the assumption that people will become committed to that which they help create (Beer 1988: 4).

There is no doubt that openness to good ideas is the best assurance of organizational vigor (Boyd 1995: 175). This work resulted in the six strategies that continue to guide all our efforts at change. These strategies are designed to improve our overall effectiveness, increase revenues, and decrease expenditures. As I have discussed these strategies in detail in my recent book (Janes 1995), I will only summarize them today. They include:

1. *Developing non-commercial partnerships with other nonprofit organizations.* For example, our library/archives have developed an electronic database in partnership with nearly a dozen other archives in the province. This has greatly enhanced public access to our collections, in a cost-effective manner.

2. *A new form of organization.* We accept the need to reposition ourselves continuously, and this requires unprecedented organizational flexibility. To succeed at this, we must also cultivate a work environment that encourages staff involvement in organizational decisions at all levels. Organizations must embrace change, not just accommodate it.

    I realize that this is a far cry from current museum practice based on boundaries and control, but consider the paradox that "the more freedom in self-organization, the more order" (Jantsch 1980: 40). I will mention two attributes of our new organization, by way of example. We collapsed 22 functional departments and divisions into six multidisciplinary work units, and one of these units, the library/archives, now works as a self-managed team. The director of this unit is elected by his or her peers for a two-year term.

3. *Public service.* Canadian museologist Michael Ames observed that art galleries and museums "may not survive in any useful form if they do not become more commercial and popular" (1992: 160). The main purpose of this strategy is to develop new and creative ways of serving the public, and this has become our most challenging task. We need to become more market sensitive; not necessarily market driven.

4. *Business processes and cost reductions.* The purpose here is to continually examine how Glenbow can simplify and improve its work design and processes in order to reduce operating costs, bureaucracy, and the weight of tradition, without decreasing revenue. This work is never ending and requires constant vigilance, whatever the size of the organization.

5. *Deaccessioning,* or the removal of objects from our collections. Like good gardeners, we gather and tend our collections, but we must also prune. We openly designed and implemented a multi-year deaccessioning plan, in order to sell millions of dollars of high-value objects, which are irrelevant to our mandate. We did this both to refine our collections and to create a restricted endowment fund that would generate income to be used exclusively for the care of collections. Needless to say, this initiative has been controversial. It also has been successful.

6. *Commercial activities.* The focus of this strategy is developing business ventures to generate additional revenue. We developed a new business unit called

Glenbow Enterprises, which exists solely for this purpose. Its activities include consulting services, the Glenbow shop, a restaurant, and a variety of commercial ventures, ranging from product development to strategic partnerships, as well as our more traditional fund-raising activities.

Rethinking layoffs

But that is not all. In addition to adopting these strategies as our blueprint for change, we had to lay off 25% of our core staff (or 31 people) as part of our plan to become sustainable, with all of the attendant individual and organizational injury. Despite the corporate celebration of legendary layoff greats such as "Chainsaw Al" Dunlop of Scott Paper and "Neutron Jack" Welch of General Electric (his nickname apparently reflects the neutron bomb – people are eliminated but the buildings remain), laying off people is an unavoidably traumatic and hurtful undertaking. It has taken Glenbow staff well over two years to reconcile the pain and, even so, the experience has left an almost gun-shy quality in some otherwise healthy, competent staff.

Repeated layoffs are not a long-term solution for the difficulties that currently bedevil our organizations. Recent news from the corporate world bears this out. Although layoffs have apparently become a strategic business maneuver to be used in both good times and bad (Tough 1996: 37), recent research in the United States reveals that nine out of 10 firms that outperformed their industries over a 10-year period had stable structures, with no more than one reorganization and no change (or an orderly change) in the chief executive (*The Economist* 1996: 51).

There are some lessons in these revelations for museums. While downsizing may necessarily be thrust upon us, it must be part of a broader plan. Cuts must be made in the right places, so that the organization reinforces its most promising activities. When doing this, one must ask and answer the two most salient questions: What is the central purpose of the museum, and what resources are required to achieve it?

The critically important resources, of course, are people and their knowledge. Once again, there are lessons to be learned from the private sector, where middle managers have endured a highly disproportionate share of the layoffs. Apparently unknown to senior management in the firms engaged in these dismissals, middle managers often serve as the synapses and memory within an organization's brain (*The Economist* 1996: 51). Glenbow, thankfully, avoided this destructive behavior by studiously ignoring the corporate mania for eliminating middle managers. We adopted a different approach, by asking at the outset of our reorganization: Who are the people who own the knowledge that makes Glenbow unique? It turned out that most of these individuals were our department heads, the museum world's middle managers. I cannot imagine where Glenbow would be today without them. The lesson – pay particularly close attention to your knowledge-owners, especially if you are contemplating staff reductions as part of a reorganization. Avoid "dumbsizing" at all costs. This is a recently identified phenomenon wherein management does not realize a given job is necessary until it has been eliminated (Jackson 1996: 87).

Emergent complexities

The latest chapter in our process of continuous change is our disassociation from the Provincial Government of Alberta. Glenbow is now an autonomous, non-profit corporation and no longer a provincial crown agency. This has been called privatization, but the term is wrong, as Glenbow will never be privately controlled. Its collections belong to the people of Alberta, in perpetuity. In a country like the United States, where so many museums operate independently of any government, you might ask why I have chosen to mention this today. It's relevant because we are breaking some new ground, at least in Canada, and this work might be useful as some of you reconsider your relationships with your major funding partners. As part of our disassociation from government, we have developed a multi-year, fee-for-service contract with the province, which specifies the amount of money required to care for, and provide public access to, our collections.

We want to debunk the government's belief that it is doing Glenbow a favor each year by giving us taxpayers' money to care for the taxpayers' collections. We also wanted to be free of non-productive, government procedures and reporting requirements. We commissioned a third-party study of the costs of collections care and access at Glenbow in order to put these negotiations on a more empirical, business-like basis. It is already apparent that we will always want more money, while government will want to allocate less. Nevertheless, we have signed a contract, even though our lawyer has likened these negotiations to trying to remove a fishhook from your thumb!

Where have six years of continuous change at Glenbow left us? At first glance, the scorecard is not encouraging. For example, the provincial contribution to our operating budget has now decreased by 39% since 1989–90, the year I arrived as executive director. In addition, Glenbow's full-time, core staff has decreased from 137 in 1989–90 to 86 today, a decline of nearly 40%. There is no doubt that we have suffered some major setbacks.

It is also true that many museum employees throughout North America are feeling exhausted, and rightfully so. Six years ago, Glenbow staff and volunteers were thrust into what we believed was a temporary state of budgetary madness, from which we would emerge ready to return to business as usual. We have emerged – stronger, smarter, and much leaner – but now there appears to be no rest for the weary.

There is some instruction in this seeming disillusionment, however, which might help us to approach the twenty-first century more calmly and more productively. First, no matter how hard we might wish it, there will be no return to "normal," whatever that might be. To idealize the past is all too human, even when that "past" is largely responsible for the discontent that led to change in the first place. Second, we must learn to live with the notion that we will never find that mythical plateau where we can pause and say, "We've made it." This is most difficult for me to accept, simply because I am still not comfortable with the idea of organizational life as an endless home renovation. I long for the noise, dust, and confusion to be over, so that we can all spend some peaceful time in our new home. But I know deep down that this will never happen; there will never be a final, desirable state when the change is over and the house is finished.

There may be some comfort, albeit cold comfort, in noting that there are at least two kinds of tired (Chapin 1980). There's "good tired" and "bad tired." Bad tired occurs on the day you may have been successful, but you fought the wrong battles. Good tired happens on the day you lost every battle, but you fought the right ones. I would like to think that, when all of us feel tired in our museum jobs, it's the good kind of tired.

Opportunities and prospects

Setbacks and fatigue aside, the future is upon us and I want to spend the remainder of my time today outlining a sample of the opportunities awaiting any museum that is poised to seize them. Predictably, these opportunities exist in a world of chaos and ambiguity, alongside a variety of hazards, each with sufficient potential to damage, if not derail, the museum enterprise. I will also identify some of these hazards, before concluding with some brief reflections on what can be learned from all of this.

Opportunities abound for all museums to fulfill their purpose and to provide some answers to the fundamental question: What does it mean to be a human being? (Postman 1990: 50–58). Our visitors, indeed North American society, are searching for answers. Museums can help; perhaps even show the way. For example:

- A local child attended Glenbow's new and innovative museum school, the first of its kind in Canada. In an unsolicited letter from this child's parent, we learned that this family's dinner conversation had changed because of the daughter's new-found awe and excitement. The emotion is so palatable in this letter that I get a lump in my throat when I read it.
- At the conclusion of an exhibition commemorating the 50th anniversary of the Second World War, our exhibition team hosted a reception for the war veterans who had served as interpreters throughout the show. Unscheduled and unannounced, a frail, 80-year-old survivor of a Japanese prisoner-of-war camp rose and spoke. He said that, as a result of Glenbow's exhibition, he now felt recognized and valued as a citizen and a soldier for the first time in his life.

All museums must continually embrace the responsibility of providing meaning to people – for museums, in effect, are storehouses of individual and collective consciousness.

Sharing power

A second challenging opportunity lies in the notion of museums truly sharing power and responsibility with some of their primary constituents. For Glenbow, this includes the First Nations of the Blackfoot Confederacy (the Blood, Siksika, and Peigan Nations), as we house an extraordinary collection of their cultural patrimony. Several years ago, we started to lend sacred bundles to various ceremonialists for use and safekeeping.[2] Slowly and painstakingly, this has opened up an entirely new world for Glenbow staff – the world of Blackfoot culture. We, in turn, have hired an individual from the Siksika First Nation, lacking academic degrees but steeped in traditional knowledge. Mutual respect and understanding are increasing daily.

But all is not right. Our efforts to share these sacred objects have provoked anxiety among provincial government officials who are in a position to influence Glenbow's operating policies. They use the classic slippery-slope, or thin-edge-of-the-wedge, thinking. In short, because Glenbow has loaned or returned objects to the First Nations, these officials foresee a run on all our collections and the eventual loss of everything to a variety of special-interest groups. Furthermore, possession is nine-tenths of the law, and what if the Blackfoot do not return the loans?

Yes, both of these outcomes are possibilities, but they are the risks we must take if we truly respect the peoples whose cultures we so boldly interpret for public consumption. Consider this recent example. A Peigan woman, who served as the Holy Woman in the Ookaan ceremony this past summer, requested the loan of a particular sacred bundle to aid her son, who had recently undergone an unsuccessful operation that left him paralyzed.[3] The need for this sacred bundle came to her in a dream. Some public officials would have us decline this request, or insist that the bundle be immediately returned after the ceremony. But the Blackfoot people regard these bundles as living objects, which need all the care given to a young child. The ongoing presence of these sacred bundles in Blackfoot communities will have long-term benefits for many people. Museums are fond of saying that we keep our collections for posterity. I cannot help but think that posterity has arrived and is staring us in the face. What would you do? We loaned the bundle.

Knowledge and self-organization

My last two examples are best described as opportunities that have yet to be fully realized, and they have more to do with museums as organizations and how we do our work. The first of these opportunities requires that we manage our intellectual resources more effectively. Most people would agree that museums are knowledge-based organizations, and that the knowledge of our staff, along with our collections, are the most important assets. Although collections management has evolved its own body of method and theory, surprisingly little attention has been given to managing professional intellect (Quinn et al. 1996: 71). Some private sector organizations have become acutely aware of this and see the management of human intellect as the critical executive skill of the age. What does this mean for museums?

We recognize that a true professional commands a body of knowledge, and that he or she must keep current with that knowledge. Our challenge in museums is to maintain a self-motivated level of creativity among these professionals, without which we are unable to adapt to changing external conditions. There are various ways to nurture and sustain the creative professional, all of which are appropriate to museums. This obviously must begin with hiring the best people available, and then encouraging their development through repeated exposure to complex, real problems. Perhaps most importantly, leading organizations in various sectors are maximizing their intellectual capital by abandoning hierarchical structures, such as the departmental and divisional hierarchy that is still the hallmark of so many museums (Quinn et al. 1996: 76).

One alternative to hierarchy is the project-based organization, where professionals use self-organizing networks to do projects and solve problems, and then disband when the job is done. This approach underlies the meaning of interdisciplinary work, where the organization's capabilities exceed the sum of its parts. It is now time for more museums to begin to embrace these new ways of working. In an ideal world, the most effective organization would be one in which structure develops and changes as a natural expression of purpose (Owen 1992: 138).

We are not there yet, but Glenbow staff say that we are surprisingly close at times. In any event, this is the thinking behind our multidisciplinary work units. These work units are actually flexible pools of knowledge and experience, whose members work individually, collectively, and across the organization, depending upon the work to be done. There is a refreshing informality to all of this. Our challenge now is to develop a performance management and development system based on both collective and individual work.

Leadership

Last, I ask you to consider the nature of executive leadership in museums. My interest is in the idea of collective leadership, and I wonder if the time has come to experiment with this approach. There are basically two organizational traditions (Greenleaf 1977). In the hierarchical tradition, one person is the lone chief at the top of a pyramidal structure. We apparently see no other course, be it a museum, corporation, or university, than to hold one person responsible. All of us know, at least privately, that the "great man" model of leadership increasingly resembles the emperor with no clothes.

In my experience, there are museums where something different is actually happening. A group of people at the top of the organization, with shared responsibilities and clear accountabilities, are developing strategies together, reaching decisions by consensus, and coordinating implementation of these decisions. This is collective, executive leadership and most closely resembles the second organizational tradition, *primus inter pares*, or first among equals. This tradition apparently goes back to Roman times, although there is precious little mention of it in the voluminous leadership literature, nor virtually any references to its use in modern-day society. The principle is simple: There is still a "first," a leader, but that leader is not the chief executive officer. The difference may appear to be subtle, but it is important that the *primus* constantly test and prove leadership among a group of able peers (Greenleaf 1977: 61).

It would be worthwhile for our bolder colleagues to try out the *primus* model to test its utility. If one concedes that senior managers often act like self-interested, feudal barons (Hout and Carter 1995: 135), and that the chief responsibility of an effective CEO is to foster interaction and interdependence within the senior group, it may be that the *primus* model could move us one step closer to effective, collective leadership. In fact, why not extend this opportunity and responsibility for collective leadership to all staff, or at least senior staff, to give them the opportunity to provide fresh perspectives and to learn more about the overall operation?

Hazards

In addition to these and countless other opportunities yet to be realized, there are also numerous hazards for museums as the century comes to a close. I use the term hazard to denote risks and dangers, not insurmountable obstacles or lethal threats. Nonetheless, the hazards I will discuss are real enough, and they have already demonstrated their capacity to demoralize, demean, and otherwise divert museum workers from the task of arriving at the twenty-first century intact.

Paradoxes

The first of these hazards is the prevalence of paradox in contemporary museum work. Paradoxes are things that are simultaneously contradictory, unbelievable, and true or false in their meaning. The problem is that they can wear us out or, at best, leave us discouraged and frustrated. Consider the following paradoxes:

- At a time of diminishing resources, museums must provide new and creative ways of serving a growing and diverse public.
- At a time when a concerted effort must be made to identify new ways of enhancing the sustainability of museums, it is all most museums can do to keep the "wolf from the door." Designing and testing new ideas costs time, energy, and often money.
- At a time when far too many museums are preoccupied with their survival, it is also imperative that we accomplish our purposes. Survival does not necessarily equate with success (Weil 1994: 4).

The most useful thinking I've encountered in dealing with paradoxes is that of Charles Handy, who notes that paradoxes are like the weather, "something to be lived with, not solved, the worst aspects mitigated, the best enjoyed and used as clues to the way forward" (1994: 12–13). He also observes that "the secret of balance in a time of paradox is to allow the past and the future to co-exist in the present" (1994: 63). Museums can provide this unique perspective on behalf of society, but we are going to have to pay more than lip-service to the juxta-position of the past, present, and future in our programs and services if we are to fulfill this role.

Self-reference

Avoiding my second hazard requires that all museums cultivate their capacity for self-reference (Wheatley 1992: 95, 146–147). This is the ability to be guided by a strong sense of our particular competencies as an organization, so that as the organization changes, it does so by referring to itself – meaning the skills, tradi-tions, and values that have guided its operations. People in the business world call this "sticking to the knitting." This idea of self-reference is an important one, especially considering our current financial pressures. There is a growing belief among governments and the public that museums must become more commercial and embrace the notion that the customer is always right. Although we at Glen-bow are adamant about an absolute commitment to public service and maximum self-sufficiency, we must do this in a thoughtful and balanced way – as knowledge-based institutions, not as commercial enterprises.

For example, Glenbow hosts weddings to enhance earned revenues. However, if hosting profitable weddings means closing public galleries in order to do so, then we are losing sight of our purpose and are no longer engaging in self-reference. We do this at our own peril. The hazard here is a fuzzy sense of self-reference, which can destroy a museum just as surely as it has destroyed those many corporations that have strayed too far from their core business.

The importance of organizational self-reference leads me to my third hazard, which Canadian author John Ralston Saul has dubbed the "crisis of conformity," or more colorfully, "the great leap backwards." He is referring to North America's slavish adherence to the ideologies of corporatism and the marketplace, and to put-ting self-interest over public good (Saul 1995: 2). This trend is of potentially great concern in Canada, where the vast majority of the nation's foremost museums are highly dependent, if not totally reliant, on public funding.

What I hope to avoid altogether is the assumption that either business or the nonprofit sector holds the exclusive keys to the future. As we all know, business has never had a monopoly on virtue, effectiveness, or accountability. Business has everything to say about value in the marketplace, but often has less to say on the subject of responsibility, except to their shareholders. At the same time, business is rich in experience when it comes to organizing work, marketing, and adding value. Why would we ignore these lessons, especially when we can choose what is most germane to our particular needs?

The marketplace

Having said this, we must not ignore our responsibility to make known the inherent limitations of marketplace ideology for long-term, heritage preservation. I say this because all custodial institutions have enduring obligations to the dead and to the unborn, as well as to their visitors and users. Yet, the dead and the unborn neither vote nor buy; they have no voice in the dynamics of the marketplace. Collections care, for example, is not glamorous and it will probably never rank high on the private sector's sponsorship agenda. This means that there will always be a public responsibility to care for the collections bequeathed to our citizenry. We must make it known that museum collections are similar to other fundamental resources, such as the natural environment, in that they are collective property, essential to our identity and well-being, and unable to speak for themselves.

Museums must not rush to embrace marketplace ideology without first ensuring that there are long-term safeguards for our heritage resources, as these resources lie at the roots of our humanistic consciousness (Saul 1995). Unfortunately, these complexities of time and collective memory seem to have escaped the imagination of many politicians and officials, who are increasingly judging museums by the sole criterion of the number of people through the door. High attendance induced by blockbusters, like profits, are momentary. Both can quickly disappear. It is things like reputation, name recognition, and the trust of visitors, users, and supporters that will allow museums to stand the test of time (Flower 1995: 6). In the idiom of the marketplace, this means quality and market share.

Finding comfort

The fourth and final hazard concerns all of you as individuals, as it has to do with the cumulative stresses and strains of continuous change in our work. We must be aware of the inherent dangers and develop our own pain-management programs. I hope that your own situations are not as difficult as those of a colleague of mine, however. He is the president of a post-secondary educational institution and has described his efforts at organizational change as "similar to a Kamikaze pilot with a two-ship quota."

As you know, emotions run extremely high when we talk about change in museums, and dealing with emotions, one's own, and those of colleagues, is perhaps the most difficult part of the change process. I am always alert to ideas and concepts that provide some comfort and hope amid all the stress and I want to mention several of them. First of all, it is okay to make up solutions as you go along, because there is no "right way" waiting to reveal itself or be discovered. This cannot be overstated, as it is fundamental to the creative process. I suggest, however, that it is useful to pay attention to other peoples' experiences, as we are doing here today.

Second, don't fear ambiguity. Because the museum world has raised the practice of "no surprises" to a high art, few things make us more frantic than increasing complexity (Wheatley 1992: 109). We also have a hard time with questions that have no readily available answers. It is not necessary to fear ambiguity or complexity, however, if we can just give up our preoccupation with details and refocus our attention on the bigger picture. This also means that managers, executives, and board members don't have to control everything.

A third source of comfort to me is the realization that it is okay to stir things up. We must do this in order to provoke questions and create challenges. One writer observes that when things finally become so thoroughly jumbled, we will reorganize our work at a new level of effectiveness (Wheatley 1992: 116). I don't know if this is true, but I am willing to accept it as a possibility. My challenges as president and CEO continue to be balancing the needs of the organization with those of the staff, while determining how deeply I should listen to the negative people whose voices I tend to hear the loudest.

Finally, it is okay to admit the discomfort you're feeling. I see, in retrospect, how foolish I was in failing to recognize this during the low points of Glenbow's change process. I was too embarrassed to tell my colleagues that I was going to see a counselor to deal with the distress I was feeling. Stress becomes a hazard when you don't deal with it openly and constructively.

Concluding comments

Whether we face continuous change, opportunities, or hazards, the most important constant for all of us is our attitude towards learning. In the final analysis, all our efforts at change are about learning. This means learning from experience, learning from people, and learning from successes and failures. Learning organizations, like individuals, are those that are skilled at creating, acquiring, and sharing knowledge, and then using this knowledge to modify their behavior (Garvin 1993). Learning means collectively increasing your capacity to do something that you could not do before (Walmsley 1993: 40). We must consider the very real possibility that we, as individuals, are the predominant creative forces in our own lives, as well as the lives of the organizations within which we work. We also must try to ensure that this vast creative potential contributes to both individual and organizational betterment.

In addition, we must get comfortable with the fact that, despite all the work devoted to designing for the future, no one will be able to assess its value until it is over. While this doesn't mean that organizational change is a game of chance, it does mean that we will never know the outcome until it happens. This cannot be used as an excuse for inaction, however. The emphasis on the duties and performance of boards, managers, and executives has to be on the future and much of this performance cannot be assessed until after the fact (De Pree 1989: 114).

If reality is the pawn of ideas, and there are few, if any, assurances about the outcome, where does that leave us? Personally, I take heart in the words of Charlotte, the wonderful gray spider, in E. B. White's book, *Charlotte's Web* (White 1952: 64). Charlotte said:

> Never hurry, never worry, keep fit, and don't lose your nerve.

We at Glenbow can only aspire to Charlotte's advice, because we hurry all the time. We also worry a lot, and I have no idea how fit each of us is. But, we have not lost our nerve, and we have no intention of doing so. I sincerely hope that none of you do either. Thank you again for the honor of speaking here today and happy 150th birthday, Smithsonian!

Audience discussion – moderated by Spencer R. Crew – Saturday, Sept. 7, 1996

Crew: I want to thank Dr. Janes for sharing his experiences and his insights and his knowledge. We have some time left for questions from the audience. I would like to open the floor for comments or questions or an exchange of ideas.

Audience member: Is it possible to apply your concept of team leadership to include members of distinct communities that may be impacted? Are you having success in that area?

Janes: "We" is very important; a major ingredient in a collective approach to work that involves people external to the museum. A good example would be that we are opening a major show on breast cancer this fall. On the planning team there is one Glenbow staff member and nine community members. So community is an important term of reference.

Audience member: You mentioned that when you are doing staff reductions, you need to reduce the right staff, the staff that are no longer supportive of the mission of the institution as you now see it. And yet, when you are in a government environment, doing that kind of staff reduction is exceedingly difficult. We have just gone through a process in the federal government here in the United States where, essentially, whoever wanted to leave left. . . . How did you accomplish the targeted kind of staff reduction that you say was desirable?

Janes: We actually started with a blank sheet of paper and we redefined the purpose of the institution. As I said earlier, we determined the resources that we needed. For example, we were operating the largest conservation department west of Ontario. We had 11 conservators working at any particular time. We decided we could no longer afford that level of commitment to conservation, so that department was reduced from 11 to 3 people. I suppose the conservation standard dropped, but we are also being more effective by buying the conservation services of private conservators, rather than maintaining a very expensive and elaborate, in-house department.

The second key factor in the staff reductions is that we have a unionized staff. They are a local of the largest public service union in Canada. We took great pains to be totally open with our union about this layoff process. We actually formed a joint group, so that we had a mechanism to deal with layoffs and all the issues. We have a very progressive union. They could see the future of the institution was at stake, and they did unorthodox things in terms of a union, but they could see their efficacy. Is that the sort of thing you were thinking about?

Audience member: You didn't face civil service regulations that you had to work around, that were outside of your control?

Janes: No, we didn't, except for certain labor laws and the collective agreement we had with our union. We were able to bargain and negotiate to mutual benefit. It wasn't perfect and it was messy, but at least it allowed this outcome.

Mary Case, QM2 Consultants: We had a conversation at dinner last night about the difficulties directors face when they are walking around a museum, and they might make an off-hand comment. Or they need information and might ask a question. Fifteen minutes later there is this rumor that goes around the museum that says, "Oh, my God, he asked! Now, he wants to do this."

I wonder how you dealt with the difficulty of being the single person who is really at the top, no matter what changes you are trying to implement, and how other directors might get the information that they need? We know the hierarchical system is really good for getting information down, but not good for getting information up.

Janes: When I think back, one of the most important ways that we tried to deal with that was to change the way that I interacted with staff. For example, during two years of particularly intense change, I simply went around the building on a continuous basis and met with small groups of staff. . . . never more than eight people. Sometimes it would be 20 minutes; sometimes it would be two hours, but I simply took the time to sit down, to dispel rumors, to provide all the information that I knew at the time, and just communicate openly and directly.

We used to have large staff meetings, but we learned in several months that people were uncomfortable talking. Some didn't talk and some people dominated the conversation so we broke up into the small units. Admittedly, it took a great deal of my time but you simply have to do it, because process is everything in this difficult change. People have a need to know.

Robert Goler, National Museum of Health and Medicine: First of all, I would like to thank you for publishing your work. I think it is very important that more studies like this get out. I commend you for that. The question I have has to do with the for-profit arm that you established after reorganizing. I would like to ask how it seeks direction, how it decides what it is doing, and the extent to which the museum staff are involved in those decisions and implementation.

Janes: It is an integral part of the organization. We thought at first we would have to spin it off, to protect our nonprofit status, but we haven't had that problem yet. The vice president of that unit is part of what we call our strategy group; she is one of the six senior managers of the organization. The priorities are set for that unit, along with all the other work unit priorities, when we do our annual strategic plan update. For that particular unit, we actually specify numerical performance targets, whether they are for our shop, or whatever.

We also continuously engender the notion that Glenbow Enterprises will succeed to the extent that other staff become involved, because it is our unique knowledge and products that Enterprises will market. That has been problematical and it has taken time, because many staff don't see that their museum work needs to involve any commercial work. But we are slowly getting there. Curators, for example, are now advising on products that could be reproduced for sale in our shop or wholesale.

I think one of the most interesting things that we have done recently is building a corporate museum for Gulf Canada, the oil company. That corporation has a wonderful collection of ethnographic objects and the CEO is also a collector. He decided that all material should be shared with the staff and his business clients. We have a contract with Gulf Canada to basically conserve, curate, produce, and deliver a whole series of exhibitions throughout the corporation, and that has been very profitable for us. Gulf Canada doesn't mind paying for that, because they know they are getting the best service they can get. In doing so, we have had to draw upon 11 different Glenbow staff. Some have time to do it, others don't. What we have been able to do is go back to some of the people we laid off and to form a sort of subsidiary company, that is now doing that work under our supervision.

Audience member: I am an objects conservator. I was wondering if you could talk more about how you went about your deaccessioning campaign. Did you target objects in poor condition, or duplicates, or did you look at your collection and reassess the type of collection you needed to implement your mission? I think this is particularly applicable to general history museums. I think there are still a lot of poorly curated, unorganized collections, and it seems that to support all of these different mandates in the future, we need to go back and take a closer look at the collections and redefine what they really should be about.

Janes: Yes, that is an excellent point. We started with the duplicates; with the objects that were of inferior quality, and with the objects with little or no documentation. In addition, we were in a unique position because of the way Glenbow was founded. We had numerous high-value objects that were irrelevant to our mandate; we had a number of natural history works of art. We were also able to identify those things that had been in storage, but were never exhibited, never researched, and never used. These objects were also part of the deaccessioning program. We have been able to sell about CAN$5 million worth of material that doesn't affect our responsibility for our mandate at all.

Audience member: Was your mandate subject to provincial review and approval, since that is your touchstone?

Janes: Not really. The mandate enshrined in the Glenbow Alberta Institute Act (1966) is so general that we were able to put a finer focus on it. That is an interesting question, however, because some people in the government took issue with our deaccessioning program. They actually tried to shut it down with a court injunction. Rather than selling these objects, the government officials wanted us to give them to the provincial museums owned and operated by the government. We were able to negotiate our way out of that.

Crew: I have time for one last question, and I am going to ask it. That is the prerogative of the chair. You talked about the idea of moving to a more collective leadership approach. I am interested in how you convince your staff and your senior managers to accept that.

Janes: I don't know the answer to that. I am sorry. I think we have to just try the bold experiment and see what happens.

Acknowledgements

I wish to thank Gerry Conaty, Richard Forbis, Michael Fuller, Terrence Heath, Melanie Kjorlien, Mike Robinson, and Ron Wright for their invaluable comments on an earlier draft of this presentation. Evy Werner and Denise Savage-Hughes typed and proofread various drafts of this paper, as well as saw to the countless details inherent in this sort of work. I am indebted to both of them. I also wish to thank Glenbow's Board of Governors both for their ongoing support and their commitment to learning. Because this presentation is a continuation of my book, *Museums and the Paradox of Change*, I remain indebted to the many people who have contributed to this work, especially Glenbow staff. Finally, my thanks go to the Smithsonian Institution, especially Nancy Fuller and Rex Ellis, for the privilege of participating in this celebratory symposium.

Notes

1 Spencer R. Crew was the Director of the National Museum of American History, Smithsonian Institution, in 1996.
2 Sacred bundles contain items that were given to the Blackfoot by the Spirit Beings of their world. These bundles are used in ceremonies to renew connections with the Spirit Beings and Creator and to ask for help. They are accorded the care one would give to a child. See: The Blackfoot Gallery Committee (2001) *Nitsitapiisinni: The Story of the Blackfoot People*, Toronto: Key Porter Books Limited (page 13).
3 Ookaan is the collective reference to the whole Sun Dance ceremony and the associated activities. The Sun Dance is a distinctive ceremony that is central to the religious identity of the Indigenous peoples of the Great Plains, North America.

References

Ames, Michael M. *Cannibal Tours and Glass Boxes: The Anthropology of Museums*. Vancouver: UBC Press, 1992.

Beer, Michael A. *Leading Change*. Cambridge, Mass.: Harvard Business School, 1988.

Boyd, Willard L. "Wanted: An Effective Director." *Curator* no. 3 (1995): 171–184.

Case, M. "Tales of Change." Review of *Museums and the Paradox of Change: A Case Study in Urgent Adaption* by Robert R. Janes, 1995, Calgary, Canada: Glenbow Museum. In *Museum News*, September/October (1996): 22–23, 73.

Chapin, Harry. Conversation with the author, February 26, 1980. Available online: https://gartenberg.wordpress.com/2008/07/07/good-tired-and-bad-tired-which-are-you/.

De Pree, Max. *Leadership Is an Art*. New York: Bantam Doubleday Dell Publishing Group, 1989.

——. *Leadership Jazz*. New York: Bantam Doubleday Dell Publishing Group, Inc., 1992.

Flower, Joe. *The Change Codes*. Available online: http://www.well.com/user/bbear/change_codes.html, 1995.

Garvin, David A. "Building a Learning Organization." *Harvard Business Review*, July/August, 1993.

Greenleaf, Robert K. *Servant Leadership*. Mahwah, N.J.: Paulist Press, 1977.

Griffin, D.J.G. "Managing in the Museum Organization I: Leadership and Communication." *Museum Management and Curatorship* 6, no. 4 (1987): 387–398

Handy, Charles. *The Age of Paradox*. Boston: Harvard Business School Press, 1994.

Hout, T.M. and J.C. Carter. "Getting It Done: New Roles for Senior Executives." *Harvard Business Review*, November–December, 1995: 113–145.

Jackson, Tony. "Corporate America Is Dumbsizing," *The Financial Post*, May 25, 1996: 87.

Janes, Robert R. *Museums and the Paradox of Change*. Calgary, Alberta, Canada: Glenbow Museum, 1995.

Jantsch, Erich. *The Self-Organizing Universe*. Oxford: Pergamon Press, 1980.

Kaye, Francis. "If You Build It, They Will Come: History, Art, and Audience at the Glenbow." Calgary, Alberta, Canada: Glenbow Archives, 1995.

Morris, Martha. "Survey on Strategic Planning, Organizational Change and Quality Management." Deputy Director's Office, National Museum of American History, Smithsonian Institution, Washington, D.C., 1995.

National Film Board of Canada. *Between Friends/Entre Amis*. Toronto: McClelland and Stewart Ltd., 1976.

Owen, Harrison. *Riding the Tiger: Doing Business in a Transforming World*. Potomac, Md.: Abbott Publishing, 1992.

Phillips, Will. "Red Alert For Museums: A Crisis in Response Ability. Part I, Extended Version," 1995. Unpublished paper available from the author.

Postman, Neil. "Museum as Dialogue." *Museum News* 69 (September/October 1990): 55–58.

Quinn, J.B., P. Anderson, and S. Finkelstein. "Managing Professional Intellect: Making the Most of the Best." *Harvard Business Review*, March/April 1996: 71–80.

Saul, John Ralston. *The Unconscious Civilization*. Concord, Ontario, Canada: House of Anansi Press Ltd., 1995.

The Economist, "Fire and Forget?" April 20, 1996: 51–52.

Tough, Paul. "Does America Still Work?" *Harper's Magazine* 292, no. 1752 (May 1996): 35–47.

Traub, James. "Shake Them Bones." *The New Yorker*, March 13, 1995: 48–62.

Walmsley, Ann. "The Brain Game." *The Globe and Mail Report on Business Magazine*, April 1993: 36–45.

Weil, Stephen E. "Organization-Wide Quality Assessments of Museums: An Immodest Proposal." Paper presented at the International Council of Museums' International Committee on Management Meeting, London, September 1994.

Wheatley, Margaret J. *Leadership and the New Science*. San Francisco: Berrett-Koehler Publishers, Inc., 1992.

White, E.B. *Charlotte's Web*, New York: Scholastic Book Services, 1952.

9

MUSEUMS AND CHANGE*

Some thoughts on creativity, destruction and self-organization

Note by the Editor of *Museum International* in 1999: The Glenbow Museum, Art Gallery, Library and Archives in Calgary, Alberta, Canada, has become one of Canada's top cultural institutions with an international reputation for exhibitions, programmes and publications. Robert R. Janes, its President and Chief Executive Officer since 1989, is known as a leading voice in the changes taking place in Canada's cultural institutions. His most recent book, *Museums and the Paradox of Change* (1997), is a candid approach to controversial changes in a major cultural organization and speaks to the vital need for a shift in thinking as museums enter the twenty-first century. In this chapter he sets out some basic premises for change in today's museum context.

Introduction

When I arrived as the new Director of the Glenbow Museum, Art Gallery, Library and Archives in 1989, it was clear that major changes were in the offing. Although Glenbow is remarkably self-sufficient for a Canadian museum, about 25% of the annual operating budget comes from the Provincial Government of Alberta. An agreement to provide this funding had come to an end coinciding with my arrival, so we decided to develop both corporate and strategic plans in 1990 as the basis for securing multi-year funding from the province. Our corporate and strategic plans were a first for Glenbow, in that they enabled all staff to become involved. This planning was also a first for Canadian museums, in incorporating explicit performance

Source: Robert R. Janes, *Museum International*, Vol. 51, No. 2 (1999): 4–11. This article is a revised version of a keynote address presented at the Annual Meeting of the Museum Association of Arizona in Flagstaff, Arizona (US), April 29 to May 2, 1998. It has been further revised for this book to add text and references that were eliminated in the *Museum International* 1999 publication.

measures and standards, as well as a set of values and principles outlining how we would treat each other as individuals and as staff.

Unfortunately, the province rejected both our plan and our funding request, which forced Glenbow's staff to confront the future with a vengeance, in the face of declining government support. Five-year financial projections indicated a huge deficit and eventual bankruptcy for Glenbow by 1998. A 20% reduction in operating expenses was required in 1993, followed by another provincial cut of 25% in 1995. With this kind of massive budgetary reduction, it is impossible simply to tinker with the organizational chart. In short, we were confronted with the responsibility and opportunity to renew Glenbow by increasing our capacity for change.

The six strategies

This realization spawned another staff and board exercise, based on the assumption that people will become committed to that which they help create. There is no doubt that openness to good ideas is the best assurance of organizational vigour. This work resulted in six strategies which continue to guide Glenbow's efforts at change. These strategies are designed to improve our overall effectiveness, increase income and decrease expenditure, and include the following:

Developing non-commercial partnerships with other non-profit organizations. For example, our Library and Archives have developed an electronic database in partnership with twenty-four archives in the province. This has greatly enhanced public access to our collections, in a cost-effective manner.

A new form of organization. Organizational structure must embrace change, not just accommodate it. This requires unprecedented organizational flexibility and is a far cry from current museum practice based on boundaries and control, but reflects the paradox that "the more freedom in self-organization, the more order" (Jantsch 1980: 40). We condensed our hierarchical structure of twenty-two functional departments into six multidisciplinary work units, and one of these units, the Library/Archives, now works as a self-managed team. We are becoming increasingly comfortable with the idea of organizational asymmetry at Glenbow. An organization will include a variety of coherent groups within it, each of which is a unique entity with different requirements for learning and growing (Keating et al. 1996: 42). It seems sensible to recognize this.

Public service. The main purpose of this strategy is to develop new and creative ways of serving the public, and this has become our most challenging task. All museums must simply become more market sensitive. We struggle daily with the task of producing new and creative exhibitions, programmes, and services, and we now have staff dedicated to audience research and evaluation. They have recently convened a public advisory group consisting of people who do not visit or use Glenbow so that we can discover why they are not coming.

Streamlining business processes. The purpose here is to examine continually how we can simplify and improve our work in order to reduce operating costs, bureaucracy, and the weight of tradition, without decreasing revenue.

Deaccessioning, or the removal of objects from our collections. We designed and implemented a multi-year deaccessioning plan in order to sell millions of dollars of high-value objects which were irrelevant to our mandate, in order to create a restricted endowment fund that generates income which is used exclusively for the care of our core collections.

Commercial activities. The focus of this strategy is to generate additional revenue, and we developed a business unit called Glenbow Enterprises to promote this work. As an example, we have recently built a corporate museum for Gulf Canada Resources Ltd in Calgary.

None of these strategies is sufficient by itself, however. Their strength lies in their interaction, and in the balance they bring to our work.

Current realities

Many museum workers have the persistent feeling that, no matter what they do to ensure the survival, growth and prosperity of their organizations, it is never enough. Part of the answer to this lies in a number of issues and complexities, call them current realities, which envelop both our working and private lives. By either unwittingly or intentionally ignoring these things, we are at a disadvantage in fulfilling both our individual and organizational aspirations. It is worth while to explore some of these current realities, which if understood and embraced, might contribute to sustained organizational renewal, and also help to strengthen both individual responsibility and creativity.

The following description of the current realities of contemporary museum work is based on two assumptions: first, museum workers want some degree of self-actualization in their work (Morgan 1986: 43) – that is, they want jobs with some scope for achievement, autonomy, responsibility, and personal control, as well as work that enhances personal identity. Second, museums, both as organizations and as social institutions, are perhaps the most potentially free and creative work environments in the world. In contrast to the private sector, they do not have daily production quotas; in contrast to the public sector, they are not forced to administer unpopular government policies. In short, the museum is a truly privileged work environment, the most obvious drawback being the generally lower salaries. How many people in the late twentieth century are able to work in organizations whose purpose is their meaning? (Handy 1994: 183). All museum workers do.

The organization as metaphor

Admittedly, museum work is not only complex, but our organizations are also extremely ambiguous and paradoxical. The real challenge is to learn to deal with this complexity and this cannot be done by employing a single frame of reference (Morgan 1986: 17). Instead, metaphors may be used, which means attempting to understand one element of experience in terms of another. By using metaphors our view of reality is enriched, with the possibility that the more unexamined aspects of life and work will reveal themselves (Terry 1993: 163).

Organizational life is a case in point. Museums can be many different things at the same time (Morgan 1986: 37–321). They are:

- *Machines* – meaning that people and jobs fit together in some fixed design, based on functional rationality (think of large, bureaucratic museums).
- *Political systems* – a metaphor that sees loose networks of people with different interests, who gather together for the sake of self-interest, be it money, career, or influence. In fact, many of us are often critical of museums as being too political, assuming only a negative connotation of politics – ridden by manipulation and self-seeking. This is a limited view, however, because politics are often the means by which things get done, through argument, consensus, and commitment (Stacey 1992: 193). There are creative aspects of internal politics, as well.
- *Brains* – there are no museums in my experience that can truly claim this status. We have a long way to go before museums are as flexible, resilient, and inventive as the functioning of the human brain.

The "brain" metaphor is really about organizations learning how to learn (Morgan 1986: 87–95). Essential to this is double-loop thinking, which requires each of us to question and challenge all our basic museum norms, policies, and procedures (Argyris 1991). Museum people have not been very good at double-loop thinking, in part because of their love of "sacred cows," and the museum profession has many of them. Some of the more venerated sacred cows include an often hysterical prohibition against deaccessioning collections, or a belief that programmes and services with broad public appeal mean compromising museum professionalism.

This is "either/or" thinking, and will only be overcome when we are more open and reflective, and accept that error and uncertainty in our work are inevitable. Without encouraging the exploration of different viewpoints, we are condemned to our own internal perspective. It is wise to consider what Peter Drucker, one of the most influential thinkers on organizations and their management, has to say about this, which is that "all great change in business has come from outside the firm, not from inside" (in Lenzner and Johnson 1997: 125).

Metaphors not only help to understand the complex and paradoxical nature of organization life, but they also may help to stimulate much-needed change in the museum world. Bureaucracies, for example, impose goals and objectives without debate among the advocates of competing perspectives. Bureaucracy sees the executives and managers as the planners and visionaries – dictating brilliant strategies for everyone else to implement (Mintzberg 1987: 73). What is missing here is the deceptively simple point that strategies can *form*, as well as be *formulated*. Allowing this to happen constitutes the organizational shift from bureaucracy to brain, and requires developing a work environment that is flexible enough to allow a wide variety of strategies to *grow*.

For example, Glenbow recently opened *Healing Legacies: Art and Writing by Women with Breast Cancer* – an exhibition done in conjunction with nine community groups. The idea originated with one of our staff who is a breast cancer survivor, and there was nothing in the exhibition from our collections. Instead, the exhibition consisted of the paintings, quilts, sculpture, poetry and journal entries of 49 women from Alberta and the US. Our community was grateful and responded accordingly – 1,600 people attended the opening. Our collective learning began when we departed from the traditional assumption that one must use museum collections to create exhibitions.

The past is not the future

Moving from the organization as metaphor to the topic of change, one must also consider what change means in the museum business. There are two key points that need to be made about change and museums. First, the future is not knowable, despite the billion-dollar industry that says otherwise. This is because the links between cause and effect in organizations can be complex, distant in time and space, and very difficult to detect (Stacey 1992: 11). The technical term for this dynamic is non-linear feedback, and it means that the links between cause and effect are lost in the detail of what actually happens in between. No individual can foresee the future of any organization or control its journey to that future (Stacey 1992: 13).

If museum workers cannot know where the museum is going because the future is unknowable, then they should not all believe in the same things. They should question everything, and generate new perspectives through discussion and debate. Peter Drucker (1995: 32–33) calls this practice abandonment. He suggests that every three years organizations should challenge everything they think and do, so they will remain alert and adaptable and not be overtaken by events. In this way, they will create, invent, and discover their destination as they go, which is the true hallmark of an innovative organization (Drucker 1995: *passim*). Instead, the tendency is to build on our strengths and try to adapt to the existing environment, becoming better and better at what we are already doing well. We insist on repeating past and present behaviour, and thereby make incremental changes only.

Glenbow's Museum School is a case in point for the need to rethink how we work. Traditionally, schoolchildren visited Glenbow once a year on a field trip, for one or two hours. Although we still offer this service, one innovative staff member introduced a new strategy. We now have thirty classes of children who spend a minimum of five days per class at Glenbow. These classes, their teachers, and parent volunteers work with up to thirty-five Glenbow staff each week, based on a custom-designed curriculum that integrates the unique resources of Glenbow with the needs of the classroom teacher. This innovative approach to experiential learning has had a profound impact on students, teachers, and parents alike, and has resulted in a multi-year corporate sponsorship. Like successful organizations in the private sector, we have found innovative uses for our unique museum resources and in the process have created a demand for them which we have found a way to meet. No one asked us to develop a museum school.

My second point on museums and change is to recognize that we are now dealing with what is called open-ended change. This means that we do not know with any clarity what caused the change or what all of the consequences will be. Old ways of doing things do not necessarily work, and ambiguity and confusion abound. There is no doubt that many museums are now experiencing open-ended change. Nobody knows exactly what to do, so we must experiment. For example, I could never have predicted that in 1996 Glenbow, in an act of experimentation, would disassociate itself from the province and become an independent, non-profit corporation – no longer a provincial government agency.

Self-organization and shared responsibility

It is fashionable to talk of change, but we must move beyond the talk and seriously consider how we can best equip ourselves and our museums to deal with change constructively. One of the most promising developments in this regard is the idea of self-organization. This is a group phenomenon and it occurs spontaneously when members of a group produce coherent behaviour, in the absence of formal hierarchy within the group, or authority imposed from outside it (Stacey 1992: 6). People empower themselves, rather than being empowered by management.

What are the advantages of self-organization for museum work? Since no single individual can govern the organization's journey to the future, we must recognize that what happens to museums is created by, and emerges from, the self-organizing interactions among its people (Stacey 1992: 13). Despite all the conventional wisdom about management and control, senior managers cannot regulate this, even if they can powerfully influence it.

Instability and unpredictability, which occur in natural systems, also play a vital role in continuing creativity, and in doing things differently. One of the more extreme examples of intentionally provoking instability comes from the Honda Motor Company, where confrontation among employees is encouraged in order to break old patterns and foster creativity. Kawashima, the former president, has been quoted as saying, "I decided to step down as president because the employees began agreeing with me 70 per cent of the time" (quoted in Stacey 1992: 84).

Honda notwithstanding, it is not sensible for all museum chief executive officers to resign collectively. There are other alternatives for intentionally provoking instability and self-organization, as follows:

- Leaders should not impose solutions. Rather, solutions and strategies for change must be allowed to emerge from all parts of the organization, based on local initiative. For leaders, this means listening and understanding, but not abdicating authority to set the final course (Phillips 1997: 6).
- This requires that the museum know itself, and management must continuously promote this conversation. Who are we, and who do we want to be? This is

the idea of self-reference – the ability to be guided by a strong sense of your museum's particular competencies (Wheatley 1994: 95, 146–7).

- Organizational "messiness" must be tolerated throughout the museum, as the search for solutions is far from tidy. This kind of freedom creates a lot of diversity and disorder, so be prepared.
- Take action, for talking and planning cannot go on for ever. Experimentation is also critically important and it must be encouraged and supported. We have enshrined the need for experimentation at Glenbow as part of our operating philosophy.
- Prepare for the long term. Dealing with museum traditions, open-ended change, and self-organization is very challenging and requires enormous self-awareness, commitment, and time. One organizational specialist writes that meaningful change is a three-to-ten-year process (Wheatley 1997: 26). [In retrospect, I now believe that organizational change is never ending.]

The marketplace as cautionary tale

Any discussion of change in museums must consider the broader context within which we work in North America, specifically the marketplace economy. One of the prevailing truths about the marketplace is:

> In so far as there is a dominant belief in our society today, it is a belief in the magic of the marketplace. The doctrine of laissez-faire capitalism holds that the common good is best served by the uninhibited pursuit of self-interest.
>
> *(Soros 1997: 48)*

This observation comes as no surprise to the reader. What is surprising, though, is an emerging challenge to this belief in the marketplace. What are some of the iconoclasts saying? For George Soros (1997), perhaps the world's greatest financier, communism is no longer the threat to our open and democratic society – capitalism is, with its excessive individualism, competition, and lack of cooperation. Or consider Charles Handy, who writes that:

> The current system of capitalism is not going to be sustained. It is assumed that the company is owned by shareholders and it can be sold. But increasingly, the company is people's knowledge. People are going to resent being owned by other people. They will leave.
>
> *(Handy 1997: 15)*

These are vitally important messages for museums, and they affirm what we already know, which is that money is a crude measure of success. More importantly, what we are now seeing is a challenge to those who claim that the marketplace is in possession of the ultimate truth. Museums know deeply that nobody has a mono-poly on the truth, simply because all competent museums recognize and celebrate the diversity of thought and action. It is here that we encounter the profound potential of museums as truly public institutions, and museums must continue to expand their responsibility to celebrate diversity in all of its manifestations.

This is even more important if we agree with the observation that the market-place and its activities actually deplete trust (Rifkin 1997). It is the so-called "third sector" that contains the organizations upon which the marketplace depends, and these organizations are neither government nor business.[1] All the organizations in the third sector, including museums, are building and enriching the social capital upon which the marketplace is based. Neoconservatives appear to believe that markets create communities when, in fact, the opposite is true. Communities create the trust for the marketplace to unfold.

This challenge to the reigning marketplace ideology helps us to better understand some of the complexities of museum work, for museums are actually diversified portfolios. Many aspects of their work are subject to market forces, such as shops and restaurants, while other aspects (such as long-term collections care) have nothing to do with profit-making business, and probably never will. What must be avoided altogether is the simplistic assumption that either business or the non-profit sector holds the exclusive keys to the future. We must recognize the best of both of these value systems, and use them both, in an effort to achieve balanced sustainability for museums. In the final analysis: "The crucial dimensions of scarcity in human life are not economic, but existential. They are related to our needs for leisure and contem-plation, peace of mind, love, community, and self-realization" (T. E. Weisskopf in Capra 1982: 397).

Conclusions

The key to managing twenty-first century organizations will be maintaining an intelligent balance between theory and practice. Theory, to be valuable, must be practicable in the world of work, and the world of work must be informed by thought (Terry 1993: 7–8). My only hope is that this vital balance becomes the norm among all museum staff. Management, however, is only one ingre-dient in moving our organizations forward. All museum staff can do much to address contemporary issues and opportunities, and here are some possibilities to consider:

- Participate, both internally and externally. As one writer observed, "if you wait around to be told what to do, you'll be waiting a long time" (Handy 1994: 77).
- Weaken the control hierarchies in your museums, by engaging in self-organization.
- "Beware of people who make of change a cause of failure" (DePree 1992: 84).

It is also important to check continually the vital signs of your museum (Pascale et al. 1997: 84). The critical vital signs are:

> *Power* – Do staff believe that they have the power to make things happen?
> *Identity* – Do staff identify narrowly with their profession or department, or do they identify with the museum as a whole?
> *Conflict* – Are problems shoved under the rug, or do staff confront and resolve them. Listening is critically important to this and it is useful to remember that we have two ears and one mouth.
> *Learning* – Simply put, how does your museum deal with new ideas? Are they ignored or nurtured?

Collectively, these four vital signs tell a lot about the overall health and adaptability of any museum. If any of these vital signs are allowed to deteriorate too much, they can be highly destructive.

In this era of management hype and flavour-of-the-month techniques, one thing cannot be overstated. That is, outside experts do not necessarily know the answers that an organization needs to solve its problems or improve itself (Keating et al. 1996: 34). In fact, an organization's members are often the real experts on the organization, and on what is needed to improve it, the only difficulty being that much of this knowledge is tacit, or remains untested. At Glenbow, we are insisting on new ways of thinking and acting that will make us more responsive to the communities we serve. We have found that the key to pushing, without the organization pushing back, is balanced inquiry and action, because the indiscriminate use of trendy solutions is as destructive as a stubborn reverence for tradition. Because organizational change is chaotic, and often mysterious, we have no choice but to try to be as intelligent and caring as possible.

Acknowledgements

Glenbow's Board of Governors has consistently supported my efforts to record and share Glenbow's efforts at organizational change. I thank them for this, as well as their collective commitment to learning. I also acknowledge Richard Forbis, Doug Leonard, Abby Day, Ron Marsh, Melanie Kjorlien, and Barry Agnew for their valuable comments on an earlier draft. Because this chapter builds upon my recent book, *Museums and the Paradox of Change* (1997), I must also thank all the individuals who contributed to that work, most notably Glenbow staff. They have shaped my thinking and enriched my experience in ways too numerous to mention.

Note

1 The third sector refers to the not-for-profit sector, in contrast to the private and public sectors.

References

Argyris, C. (1991) "Teaching Smart People How to Learn," *Harvard Business Review* 69 (3): 99–109.

Capra, F. (1982) *The Turning Point*, New York: Bantam Books.

DePree, M. (1992) *Leadership Jazz*, New York: Bantam, Doubleday, Dell Publishing Group, Inc.

Drucker, P. F. (1995) *Managing in a Time of Great Change*, New York: Truman Talley Books/Plume.

Handy, C. (1994) *The Age of Paradox*, Boston: Harvard Business School Press.

—— (1997) "The Search for Meaning," *Leader to Leader*, No. 5, Summer, 14–20.

Janes, R.R. (1997) *Museums and the Paradox of Change: A Case Study in Urgent Adaptation* (Second Edition), Calgary, Canada: Glenbow Museum and the University of Calgary Press.

Jantsch, E. (1980) *The Self-Organizing Universe*, Oxford: Pergamon Press.

Keating, C., Robinson, T. and Clemson, B. (1996) "Reflective Inquiry: A Method for Organizational Learning," *The Learning Organization*, 3 (4): 35–43.

Lenzner, R. and Johnson, S.S. (1997) "Seeing Things as They Really Are," *Forbes*, 10 March, 122–128.

Mintzberg, H. (1987) "Crafting Strategy," *Harvard Business Review*, July–August, 66–75.

Morgan, G. (1986) *Images of Organization*, Newbury Park, CA: SAGE Publications.

Pascale, R., Millemann, M. and Gioja, L. (1997) "Changing the Way We Change," *Harvard Business Review*, November–December, 127–133.

Phillips, W. (1997) *Why Plans Fail*. San Diego, CA: Qm2: Quality Management for Museums. Unpublished museum briefing, 1–12.

Rifkin, J. (1997) "The End of Work." Public presentation on behalf of the Volunteer Centre of Calgary, Palliser Hotel, Calgary, Alberta, Canada, November 13, 1997.

Soros, G. (1997) "The Capitalist Threat," *The Atlantic Monthly*, 279 (2), February, 45–58.

Stacey, R. D. (1992) *Managing the Unknowable*, San Francisco: Jossey-Bass Inc.

Terry, R. W. (1993) *Authentic Leadership*, San Francisco: Jossey-Bass Inc.

Wheatley, M. J. (1994) *Leadership and the New Science*. San Francisco: Berrett-Koehler Publishers, Inc.

—— (1997) "Goodbye, Command and Control," *Leader to Leader*, No. 5, Summer, 21–28.

10

COMPLEXITY AND CREATIVITY IN CONTEMPORARY MUSEUM MANAGEMENT*

The complex world of museums

Museum workers often joke about the public perception of them and their work, noting the widespread belief that museums must be an ideal place to work – peaceful refuges, often elegant, usually clean and definitely not buffeted by the rude demands of a "real-life" workplace. The non-museum world is continually surprised, however, to learn of the complexities and demands of museum work. Much of this complexity stems from the very nature of the museum enterprise itself, and any discussion of the role of museum management must begin with an overview of some of these complexities. In short, the range of issues and pressures confronting museums in the twenty-first century is equal to that of any sector of organized life.

Consider that cultural administrators must operate complex organizations with inadequate resources and, unlike administrators in the private sector, are rarely able to accumulate budget deficits to undertake the research and development necessary to improve organizational effectiveness. At the same time, underpaid staff (often unionized) and volunteers must be motivated to perform to high professional standards. Both executives and staff alike must answer to governing bodies consisting of individuals or organizations whose experience and expertise have little or nothing to do with museum and gallery practice. This is in contrast to corporate boards, which seldom include anyone other than business people. At the same time, museums and galleries must also provide meaning and enjoyment to a diverse range of publics within the context of changing societal values. Museums,

Source: Robert R. Janes and Richard Sandell, pp. 1–14 in Richard Sandell and Robert R. Janes (eds.) (2007) *Museum Management and Marketing*, London and New York: Routledge.

Richard Sandell is Professor of Museum Studies, School of Museum Studies, The University of Leicester, United Kingdom.

in their role as custodial institutions of the world's material heritage, must also acknowledge and serve two unique communities – our ancestors and those who are not yet born. Neither of these museum constituencies vote nor consume, and thus have no visibility or involvement in the two dominant forces of contemporary society – commerce and politics.

Yet, these silent communities must be served. To add further complexity, most museums must somehow assume all these responsibilities in an era of declining or marginal public funding, while at the same time fostering individual and organizational change to ensure survival and sustainability. Simply making a profit might be seen to be a welcome relief from the potpourri of competing values and interests common to most museums. Museums, however, exist in a world of often baffling complexity and do not have the luxury of a simple profit and loss statement.

Managing these complexities within a rapidly changing world has necessitated substantial changes in mainstream museums, and many of these changes are discussed in this book. Embracing both management and marketing responsibilities, however, can still result in polarized thinking among museum professionals. There is often a tendency to see the adoption of business practices as a cure-all for the non-profit world or, conversely, a scourge to be ignored as fully as possible, although the latter view is far less common than it was a decade ago. It is understandable why polarized thinking emerges in the face of seemingly intractable management complexities, and it is instructive to have a closer look at a sample of these issues and their paradoxical relationships with this in mind. Nonetheless, it will be essential for museums to work through the tension between the dictates of the marketplace and traditional museum values, recognizing that this tension can stimulate creativity and new ways of thinking.

Management and marketing issues

The management and marketing issues discussed here are universally applicable to museums, irrespective of size and history, although larger museums perforce have a greater share. Most, if not all, of these issues are related to an increasing interest in the visitor experience, especially over the past decade. We hesitate to call this a shift from a focus on collections to a focus on visitors, as collections remain a preoccupation for most, if not all, museums. The growing concern with the visitor experience is more accurately seen as an add-on to existing museum responsibilities. This gradual change in perspective has been accompanied by a decline in public funding for museums, notably in North America and Western Europe, coupled with the increasing use of business solutions to address the challenges that beset museums.

For example, there has been a decline in museum attendance and the visitor base (Burton and Scott 2003; Martin 2002) that has prompted many museums to increase revenues through high-profile, blockbuster exhibitions and architectural sensationalism. The underlying theme in these initiatives is the conventional wisdom, "build it and they will come." Although the long-term success of this approach to business planning remains to be seen, it is generally recognized that these activities are so consumptive of staff time and resources that little of either are left over for other activities. At the same time, despite individual successes in audience development, there has been little change in the traditional visitor profile – those with post-secondary education and relatively high incomes are still the majority of museum goers (Cheney 2002).

These trends, in turn, have resulted in a preoccupation with revenues and attendance as the predominant measures of worth. Not surprisingly, many of the governing authorities responsible for these museums are also beginning to resemble corporate entities, with board members being chosen for their business experience and their fundraising skills. This tendency for business people to select other business people as governing colleagues is a sort of tribalism, and is characteristic of business in general. This tribalism is also embodied in the near absence of any non-profit executives on corporate boards of directors, and this limited perspective has noteworthy implications for both museum governance and operations.

Leadership

The increasing presence of the business model is also visible in contemporary searches for museum directors, or CEOs, as they are now called in deference to the corporate model. While an advanced degree in a related area or a professional designation may be required, the emphasis in these senior appointments is now clearly on fundraising, financial management, marketing, and public relations. Museum critics observe that the pendulum has swung too far, and museums are at risk of eroding their core missions under the leadership of well-intentioned business people whose knowledge and experience are limited to the dictates of the marketplace. This may also partly explain the increasing ennui among various museum executives, weary of the perpetual round of cocktail parties and events required to keep many museums solvent these days. This is not meant to demean the importance of these activities, but rather to highlight the importance of maintaining an intelligent balance between the core mission and economic realities.

There is relevant experience to be gleaned from the performing arts in this instance, as dance and theatre companies often have two positions – one for the managing director (read "business manager") and one for the creative director (read "scholar" or "scientist"). A clear protocol is essential in this instance to ensure both adherence to a common vision and effective communication. Museums would be wise to pay attention to the lessons of other sectors, if they are to manage these emerging complexities creatively.

Fortunately, the need for management and leadership training is clearly recognized by the museum sector, and there are a variety of well-established approaches for equipping museum professionals with the knowledge, skills, and experience to become leaders and managers. These include the Getty Leadership Institute (USA) and the Clore Leadership Programme (UK), as well as the inclusion of management and marketing training in museum studies programmes around the world.

It is important to note that leadership and management potential is not the exclusive domain of those with scholarly, scientific, and curatorial credentials. Other museum professionals, whether they are educators or marketers, also understand the museum context and can make effective leaders and managers. It is clear that contemporary management and marketing issues are broad and deep, difficult to avoid, and inextricably interconnected. It is this last characteristic, namely interconnectedness, that may have caught the museum community off guard in its rush to embrace business solutions.

Increasing complexity

It is not necessarily obvious that declining public revenues might ultimately create boards of directors lacking in cultural diversity and community connectedness, and museums are not alone in their confusion. This newfound complexity is reminiscent of the revelations that have emerged in the progression from Newtonian physics to quantum theory. Where scientists once saw the world as a great clock, with independent parts and well-defined edges, they now see a level of connectedness among seemingly discrete parts that are widely separated in time and space (Wheatley 1994: 39). A worldview marked by boundaries and reductionism no longer serves physics or museum management.

Museums are also of this world, and cannot expect to ignore or retreat from this mounting complexity. The challenge is to identify the knowledge and techniques that will best serve the well-being of museums in a manner that befits their particular role, while respecting the attendant ambiguity. It is important to note in this regard that museums are privileged work environments because they, like all non-profits, are organizations whose purpose is their meaning (Handy 1994: 183). This privilege is accompanied by the responsibility to take advantage of one of the most free and creative work environments on the planet through the application of thoughtful management and marketing.

For example, an important challenge for museum marketers is to build civic brands around ideas that are less tangible than customer service and efficiency (Demos 2005: 4). Such ideas could include community, shared ownership, and collective identity, and could be based on the use of marketing techniques to build brands that produce emotional identification and take credit for the public value that museums create. This is a creative alternative to using the language of the private sector, with its emphasis on individual, and often thoughtless, consumption.

Managing complexity

Surprisingly, and despite the growing body of management knowledge, a cloud seems to have settled and remained over leadership and management (Greenleaf 1996: 111). A partial answer lies in the observation that management is much more than a bundle of techniques, although many business schools still teach management with this approach. In the words of the late Peter Drucker (1995: 250),

"The essence of management is to make knowledge productive. Management, in other words, is a social function. And in its practice, management is a truly liberal art." The notion of management as a liberal art is an instructive one, and obligates us to now consider several ideas that encompass this broader view of management, including the need for intelligent change that the twenty-first century demands.

Self-organization

There is a burgeoning literature, and an enormous management consulting business, devoted to improving organizational efficiency and effectiveness in all sectors of society. A cursory search of the Internet using "business consulting" revealed 82 pages of text. Whether it is books sold in airport shops, or the ever-increasing number of business schools with MBA programmes, the task of helping both profit and non-profit organizations to manage better is a growth industry of extraordinary proportions. The demand is there, at least in the private sector, if a recent survey of UK business consulting fees is any indication. The average salary for a partner or director in a business consulting firm is 109,000 pounds sterling, accompanied by an average bonus of 76,000 pounds sterling, or a total of 375,550 in Canadian dollars (Woodhurst 2005). Yet, despite all the efforts of organizations and their management consultants to understand employees and to manage them more effectively, many employees remain stressed, poorly managed, and generally dissatisfied. According to the World Health Organization (Gait 2000: B15; Leka, Griffiths and Cox 2003), stress, anxiety, and depression will become the leading causes of disability in the workplace over the next 20 years.

One way of promoting the growth, development, and self-respect of museum workers is to abandon or minimize hierarchical structures – the preferred organizational model for the vast majority of museums. Various museums are learning, however, that creativity can be stimulated by organizing differently (Farson 1996: 102–105), while many small museums have known this all along. A promising development in this regard is the idea of self-organization, a group phenomenon that occurs spontaneously when members of a group produce coherent behaviour in the absence of formal hierarchy within the group, or authority imposed from outside it (Stacey 1992: 6). Decisions are made at the most local level in the organization where they can be made well, and this requires that managers respect and nurture the so-called informal leaders – those individuals who exercise influence and authority by virtue of their competence and commitment, and not because of any formal position in the hierarchy. Informal leaders exist at all levels in all museums and are essential ingredients in effective self-organization by fostering interaction and interdependence.

The key point is for management to focus on results, rather than insist upon any particular process or means for achieving the results. David Bohm (quoted in Jaworski 1998: 109), the physicist, writes that human beings have an innate capacity for collective intelligence, based on dialogue. Dialogue does not require that people agree with one another, but rather allows people to participate in a pool of shared meaning that can lead to aligned action. Simply put, hierarchical structures get in the way as staff attempt to navigate across and between organizational boundaries, be they departments, divisions, or the manager's office.

Responsible autonomy (Fairtlough 2005) is another alternative to hierarchy, and means a group deciding what to do, and being accountable for the outcome. Accountability is what makes responsible autonomy different from hierarchy. Zen Master Suzuki Roshi succinctly summarized this new thinking when he said, "to control your cow, give it a bigger pasture" (quoted in Locke 2000: 28). An instructive example of self-organization is the Museum of Anthropology in Vancouver, Canada (Krug, Fenger and Ames 1999: 254). The boundaries of their position descriptions are flexible, and the museum's informal organizational structure consists of democratic, non-hierarchical committees where the chairs rotate.

Of particular importance to museums is the increasing use of multidisciplinary, multifunctional, and cross-departmental teams that may include educators, marketers, and security staff, as well as curatorial and exhibition staff. In some instances, these teams also include individuals from outside the museum, who are given both the authority and responsibility for decision making, in full partnership with museum staff (Conaty and Carter 2005). Multifunctional teams are essential in cross-fertilizing the rich storehouse of knowledge, skills, and experience inherent in museums, not only to develop programmes and exhibitions, but also to enhance the general level of creativity, innovation, and problem solving.

Reflexive management

Management is about coping with complexity (Kotter 1990: 103), and a necessary ingredient in effective management is giving up certain unfounded beliefs, such as the belief in managerial control. This is essential because the future is not knowable, as the links between cause and effect in organizations are complex, distant in time and space, and very difficult to detect (Stacey 1992: 11). The technical term for this is non-linear feedback, and it means that the links between cause and effect are lost in the detail of what actually happens in between. Because no one can foresee the future of an organization, managers and staff should not all believe in the same things (Stacey 1992: 4), thereby avoiding the business tribalism mentioned earlier.

Museum workers should question everything and generate new perspectives through discussion and dialogue. This approach is much more conducive to creation, invention, and discovery, and all these are not only essential in addressing complexity, but they are also prerequisites for innovation and creativity. Typically, most museums continue to build on their strengths, becoming better and better at what they are already doing well. As counterintuitive as it may seem, there are more thoughtful approaches to management.

As the museum world becomes more complex, both managers and staff alike would benefit from greater tolerance of ambiguity, instability, and unpredictability, although this is much easier to write about than to do. We are now dealing with what is called open-ended change (Stacey 1992: 150–153), meaning that we do not know with certainty what is causing the changes we are experiencing in our organizations, or what the consequences will be. Old ways of doing things do not necessarily work, and there is abundant confusion and anxiety. Open-ended change is rampant in both our work and personal lives, and it is best addressed by identifying what the problems are, what the opportunities are, and then deciding what questions to ask. New mental models have to be developed and shared before the challenges of open-ended change can be addressed (Stacey 1992: 156).

For example, there is a technique used in business to assist with the creation of new mental models, known as scenario thinking or planning (De Geus 1997: 38–54; Schwartz 1996). Scenario planning is about thinking out loud and speculating, not making arguments requiring high burdens of proof (Scearce and Fulton 2004: 23). It is a simple, dynamic, and flexible process that results in powerful stories about how the future might unfold in ways relevant to a museum or a particular issue. An even more important result is a greater sense of the context in which an organization operates today, and the contexts in which it may operate in the future. Bearing in mind the growing complexity described in this introduction, museums ignore these reflexive management tools at their own peril.

The second curve

It is common for museum managers to use a variety of change programmes and processes to cope with this ever-increasing complexity. Many of these programmes are ephemeral, often abandoned, and quickly replaced by new and different approaches. Some tough lessons have been learned as a result of the quick-fix approach to management; the most important being that change in museums, as in all organizations, must evolve in a way that sustains commitment and individual capacity. This takes time, as change is a long march and needs ongoing leadership (Kanter 2000: 36). Museums may need continuous care, not interventionist cures, and it has been suggested that nursing should be the model for all management (Mintzberg 1996: 66–67). This model implies the importance of steady, consistent, caring and nurturing. More ominously, it has been noted (Galt 2000: B15) that it is only a matter of time before employers are held liable for the psychological harm caused to employees by poor management practices.

Whether it is interventionist change or gradual change, the real challenge of intelligent management lies in what is sometimes called second curve thinking. This is in reference to the S-shaped or sigmoid curve, which actually sums up the story of life itself (Handy 1994: 49–63). In effect, people, organizations, and civilizations start slowly, grow, prosper, and decline. Decline, however, is not inevitable if you adopt second curve thinking. This requires museum staff and leaders to challenge all the assumptions underlying current success, and this must begin with questions. Second curve thinking is admittedly a profound paradox, as it requires change, or scenario planning at least, at a time when all the messages coming through are that everything is fine. This is not as unrealistic as it may sound, if museums are willing to consult people outside of the museum community, as well as hire them, as they will bring in new ideas and fresh perspectives.

It is also important to pay particular attention to front-line staff, including marketers, as they are in direct contact with visitors and users, and are usually the first to know when something is lacking or not working. In the final analysis, each museum is unique and must find its way in this process. The fundamental requirement of second curve thinking is to be sceptical, curious, and inventive before you have to be. If you don't do this before you are forced to, chances are you are already in decline. In short, it requires profound courage to move to the second curve. For many museums, steeped in tradition and relatively privileged as a result of their widely recognized social status within society, second curve thinking may exceed their grasp.

More on leadership

Until now, no distinction has been made between management and leadership in this introduction. Although often considered to be one and the same, they are best described as two sides of the same coin. The challenge is to combine them, and use each to balance the other (Kotter 1990: 103). It was noted earlier that management is about coping with complexity. Leadership, on the other hand, is about coping with change (Kotter 1990: 104–107). This can mean a variety of things, but fundamentally it requires keeping people moving ahead, most often in directions they have never taken or are reluctant to consider. This is done, in part, by appealing to people's needs and emotions, including the need for achievement, providing a sense of control over one's life, and fostering the ability to live up to one's ideals. These are powerful considerations, and the study of leadership (like management consulting) is now a huge industry with an enormous literature, as well as an abundance of conferences and experts. This lucrative bandwagon does not diminish the fact that the thinking about leadership has become more intelligent and relevant.

For the longest time, charisma and style were seen to be all-important leadership characteristics. Fortunately, we are now beginning to see how important it is for leaders to motivate and inspire. This requires that leaders be clear about purpose and direction, be inclusive, model the appropriate behaviours, and recognize and reward success – in addition to the other requirements noted above. Not so obvious is the need to balance organizational and individual needs, sustain the energy required to do all of the above and, perhaps most importantly, determine how deeply to listen to the negative people whose voices are often the loudest. Along with these requirements is the necessity to acknowledge and support the so-called informal leaders mentioned earlier – those individuals who have no formal leadership designation, but whose competence and influence are widely recognized and respected.

Leaders must also not forget the "Principle of Systematic Neglect" (Greenleaf 1996: 302). For responsible people, there are always more things to be done, or that ought to be done, and this is especially acute in the world of museums. The "Principle of Systematic Neglect" requires that effective leaders decide on the important things that need doing, in order of priority, and neglect all the rest. Leaders are also increasingly required to be psychologically hardy (Kabat-Zinn 1990: 203), and those who have this hardiness have several things in common. They believe that they can make things happen; they are fully engaged in giving their best effort everyday, and, last, they see change as a natural part of life. They see new situations more as opportunities and less as threats. It is also important for museum leaders to cultivate awareness although, surprisingly, such awareness does not necessarily provide solace. On the contrary, it may disturb and awaken. As one management writer (Greenleaf 1996: 323) observed, "the able leaders I know are all awake and reasonably disturbed."

What are we learning?

Irrespective of the burgeoning complexities that buffet museums like a strong wind, it is clear that museum academics, practitioners, and educators are paying attention to these current realities in a variety of ways, as evidenced by the museum literature. It is not sufficient, however, to simply acknowledge management and leadership complexities without an effort to consider their origin and implications. There are two key protagonists in this rising complexity, the first being the rapid intervention of marketplace thinking in museum management. Standing opposite this economic view of the world is the other protagonist – a museum's capacity for self-reference, meaning the ability to be guided by a clear sense of purpose and values. This concept will be described in more detail shortly.

Tempting as it is to create a polemic and dismiss the economic view of the world as outdated, the situation confronting contemporary museum management is far more complex. It is not an exaggeration to note that creatively managing the tension between market forces and museum missions may turn out to be the most vital issue confronting museums in the twenty-first century. At stake might well be the identity of museums as unique social institutions or, conversely, their destiny as impresarios in the business of architectural sensationalism and culture as entertainment. This complexity has multiple origins, several threads of which will now be examined.

Complex portfolios

The first of these threads is the recognition that museums are complex portfolios. Museums have numerous assets that can be conceived and operated strictly as businesses, including food services, gift shops, and facility rentals. Other assets have nothing to do with the marketplace, such as the preservation and care of collections. It is essential for boards and managers to have a clear sense of which is which, and not to confuse the two. Using visitor statistics, for example, to assess the success of a museum, library, or archive is misguided as it ignores the impact of a single user who writes a book that is read by thousands of people. It is also not useful to bemoan the abandonment of traditional museum practices in the face of very real economic and social imperatives. To do this is as naïve as insisting that museums must become profit-driven enterprises if they are to survive in the contemporary world. In short, neither the business nor the non-profit sector holds the exclusive keys to a secure future. The world of museums is far too grounded in the uncertainties of everyday life.

Limits to growth

Part of this growing confusion, among managers and governing authorities alike, is based on the belief that continuous economic growth is essential to our well-being, and that the consumption of everything is an appropriate means to achieve unlimited growth. There is every reason to believe, however, that limitless economic growth is creating genuine and profound dilemmas, including the destruction of the natural environment and serious disillusionment with buying things as a means of personal fulfilment.

Much of this looming crisis, along with the attendant pressures on museums, is a result of a widespread misconception in Western society that markets create communities. The opposite is true, as the marketplace and its activities actually deplete trust (Rifkin 1997). It is the organizations of the non-profit sector, not government or business, which build and enrich the trusting, caring, and genuine relationships – namely, the social capital – upon which the marketplace is based. These organizations range from political parties, to Girl Scouts, to museums, and there would be no marketplace without this web of human relationships. Social capital is born of long-term associations that are not explicitly self-interested or coerced, and it typically diminishes if it is not regularly renewed or replaced (Bullock and Trombley 1999: 798).

The challenge for museum management is to help governing authorities, staff, and society to better understand these complexities and their implications, not the least of which is that the reigning economic growth model is an ideology that has profound implications for museums. This ideology is an integrated set of assertions, theories, and aims that constitute a socio-political programme. Its primary measure of worth is money, which is at best a crude measure of success when applied to museums. The application of strict economic criteria to museum management is obviously misleading when, for instance, one considers that good collection management is based on a 300 to 500 year business plan, not the quarterly results common to business. In contrast, the average life expectancy of a company in Japan and much of Europe is 12.5 years, while the average lifespan of a multinational corporation (Fortune 500 or its equivalent) is between 40 and 50 years (De Geus 1997: 1–2; 2005).

The message is vital – museum managers must be aware and thoughtful as they seek management solutions to a host of paradoxes and unanswered questions. Bigger is not necessarily better, and millions of dollars or pounds do not guarantee either market sensitivity or organizational competence. Reputation, name recognition, and the trust of visitors are not the property of bigness. These traits are about quality, and worthiness can be achieved by museums of any size. In fact, smallness is often a virtue when you consider the inherent inflexibility of most large museums. Small museums can "think big" through alliances, cost sharing, and creative collaboration, without all the inherent disadvantages of bigness (Ohmae 1998: 20).

A new direction

The other protagonist in the evolving story of management complexity, as mentioned earlier, is the concept of self-reference. This is a fundamental concept that aids in sensible change in a turbulent environment. For all organizations, museums included, self-reference means "a clear sense of identity – of the values, traditions, aspirations, competencies, and culture that guide the operation" (Wheatley 1994: 94). It can also mean letting go of past practices, and deciding what not to do any longer. Deciding what not to do is a key element of strategic planning. Self-reference can also be a source of independence from the external environment. As societal forces demand new responses from museums, a strong sense of self-reference provides the foundation for change.

This is particularly important in avoiding new ventures and unmindful solutions that underlie the limited lifespans of businesses and corporations noted above. This does not mean, however, that self-reference is a justification to remain beholden to tradition. On the contrary, intelligent self-reference can be a source of strength and stability in a turbulent environment, and allows a reconsideration of the role of museums in contemporary society. Such rethinking is now well underway, and one expression of this is an increasing interest in the social responsibilities of museums (Brown and Peers 2003; Janes and Conaty 2005; Sandell 2002). We will conclude this chapter with a discussion of the meaning and implications of socially responsible museum work.

Social responsibility

The idea of a socially responsible museum is grounded in a new sense of accountability, as well as in new approaches to achieving long-term sustainability. This work places a greater emphasis on values, both moral and societal, while also respecting the marketplace. Defining what socially responsible museum work means for museums is neither simple nor formulaic, as there are a multitude of possibilities and approaches. It is also important to realize that there are no fixed procedures or rules for engaging in socially responsible museum work, and all museums have the opportunity to explore and discover what is appropriate and useful for them. The underlying premise, however, is the time-honoured assumption that museums exist for the public good. Put another way, social responsibility might be considered the "will and capacity to solve public problems" (http://www.pew-partnership.org/resources.html). Broadly speaking, being socially responsible can also mean facilitating civic engagement, acting as an agent of social change, or moderating sensitive social issues (Smithsonian Institution 2002: 9).

A recent collection of case studies describing socially responsible museums (Janes and Conaty 2005: 8–10; Block 2002: 47–65) revealed that they had at least four values in common, including idealism, intimacy, depth, and interconnectedness. Idealism means thinking about the way things could be, and then taking action, rather than simply accepting the way things are. The second value is intimacy, which is about communication and the quality of the contact that is made. Quality communication lies in direct experience and there is no substitute for human relationships, and all the time, energy, and attention these relationships require. Depth is about being thorough, complete, and building relationships with particular groups of people, as well as about thinking, questioning, and reflecting. Finally, there is interconnectedness, reflected in the growing societal awareness of the deep connections between our own well-being and that of our families, organizations, the environment, and the whole of humanity. All these values are essential for museums that wish to understand what is important to their communities, and we are indebted to Peter Block for identifying these critically important values (2002: 47–65)

From a practical management perspective, museums also need to ensure that there is a sense of shared purpose, and that a commitment to socially responsible work is enshrined in the museum's mission. In addition, there is an ongoing need for active experimentation and risk taking. Most innovation occurs from hundreds of small changes and ideas which add up to enormous differences. Socially responsible work is also a shared responsibility, and museums must be prepared to reach out to their communities to acquire the expertise and experience they themselves lack. Last, is the vital importance of openness, as boards, staff, and volunteers must feel free to discuss their values and beliefs. This makes for a more authentic museum, and is the foundation for socially responsible work.

None of these things will guarantee success in this era of unanswered questions, if one accepts, as the late Peter Drucker noted, that management is a liberal art. Knowledge, flexibility, and passion are also essential ingredients in balancing the paradoxes of contemporary museum management. For museums to achieve balance, governing authorities and staff must get much better at defining strategic futures for their museums, while also ensuring that their boards are representative of community diversity and aspirations. One size does not fit all, and the marketplace is but one interpretation of reality. There is also no such thing as a single management approach, or a perfect organizational or leadership model. The key component of management is creativity, including imagination, intelligence, judgement, and common sense (Lapierre 2005: 8–9).

Gone are the days when one year of experience, repeated 20 times, is acceptable for museum managers and leaders. They must learn continuously, a notable challenge for those who are unwilling or unable to read the museum literature, not to mention the abundant knowledge outside of the museum field. Curators can no longer be content to claim authority on the basis of knowledge that is often exclusively theirs. Knowledge stemming from collections and their stories is a precious resource, and it must be shared in any number of ways. A curator is not only a keeper, but also a messenger of a museum's collective wisdom. Why can a curator not make explicit the successes and failures of our species in a manner that could inform and guide contemporary behaviour, whatever the particular society happens to be?

Even as museums seek to include and honour varied perspectives, marketers must come to understand that the customer is not always right, and that all museums have a leadership role in defining the value they add to communities. Together, marketers and curators could begin by simply asking if there are any deficiencies in their community that their museum could help to address. In summary, all these questions reach far beyond education and entertainment as the primary mission.

The real world of museums

It is helpful to consider socially responsible museum work as a purpose-filled experiment, whose intention is just as much about learning as it is about achieving (Block 2002: 3). In doing so, the choice of a worthy destination is more important than simply settling for what one knows will work. This, in turn, requires a willingness to address issues that have no easy answers, and these are legion – encompassing the need for greater intercultural understanding, our persistent failure to steward the natural environment, the growing plight of the disadvantaged, and the contested ground of consumerism versus the responsibilities of citizenship. The economic necessity of seeing people and communities as museum audiences needs no further explanation, but it is hoped that the exploration of museums as meaningful social institutions will continue to grow to inspire the next generation of museum workers. Understanding does not necessarily mean resolution, however, as it is those problems that we will never resolve that claim the lion's share of our energies (Conroy 1988: 70).

FIGURE 6   A prehistoric stone tool and a computer mouse. How much creative destruction has accompanied this transition? © Matt Ridley. From *The Rational Optimist: How Prosperity Evolves* by Matt Ridley, Fourth Estate, 2010. Reproduced with permission.

What is essential is the need to keep reflection and dialogue alive, and to avoid stagnation, complacency, and the tyranny of outmoded tradition. Management is the means to the end, not an end in itself, and it provides essential tools with which to address the endless stream of uncertainties, paradoxes, and questions that beset any thoughtful museum. The essential task of all sound leadership and management is to ensure both individual and organizational consciousness. Management, as is true of most of human thought and activity, will continue the ceaseless cycle of new theories, fads, and trends. Despite all of this activity, there are no silver bullets or panaceas, as the world of museums continually demonstrates. It is only through heightened self-awareness, both organizationally and individually, that museums will be able to fulfil the lofty triad of preservation, truth, and access (Weil 2004: 75).

References

Block, P. (2002) *The Answer to How Is Yes*, San Francisco: Berrett-Koehler.

Brown, A.K. and Peers, L. (eds) (2003) *Museums and Source Communities: A Routledge Reader*, Oxford: Routledge.

Bullock, A. and Trombley, S. (eds) (1999) *The New Fontana Dictionary of Modern Thought*, London: HarperCollins.

Burton, C. and Scott, C. (2003) "Museums: challenges for the 21st century," *International Journal of Arts Management*, 5: 56–68.

Cheney, T. (2002) "The presence of museums in the lives of Canadians, 1971–1998: what might have been and what has been," *Cultural Trends*, 48: 39–72.

Conaty, G.T. and Carter, B. (2005) "Our story in our words: diversity and equality in the Glenbow Museum," in R.R. Janes and G.T. Conaty (eds) *Looking Reality in the Eye: Museums and Social Responsibility*, 43–58, Calgary, Canada: The University of Calgary Press and the Museums Association of Saskatchewan.

Conroy, F. (1988) "Think about it – ways we know and don't," *Harper's*, vol. 277, no. 1, 662: 70.

De Geus, A. (1997) *The Living Company: Habits for Survival in a Turbulent Business Environment*, Boston: Harvard Business School Press.

De Geus, A. (2005) *Corporate Longevity*, Leigh Bureau-W. Colston Leigh, Inc. Online. Available http://www.leighbureau.com/keyword.asp?id=2055 (accessed 21 February 2006).

Demos (2005) *Civic Brands: Public Value and Public Services Marketing*. Online. Available http://www.demos.co.uk (accessed 23 February 2006).

Drucker, P. (1995) *Managing in a Time of Great Change*, New York: Truman Talley Books/ Plume.

Fairtlough, G. (2005) *The Three Ways of Getting Things Done: Hierarchy, Heterarchy and Responsible Autonomy in Organisations*, Triarchy Press. Online. Available http://www.triarchypress.co.uk/pages/the_book.htm (accessed 22 February 2006).

Farson, R. (1996) *Management of the Absurd*, New York: Simon and Schuster.

Galt, V. (2000) "Toxic stress posing major risks: study," *The Globe and Mail*, 25 October: B15.

Greenleaf, R.K. (1996) *On Becoming a Servant-Leader*, D.M. Frick and L.C. Spears (eds), San Francisco: Jossey-Bass Publishers.

Handy, C. (1994) *The Age of Paradox*, Boston: Harvard Business School Press.

Janes, R.R. and Conaty, G.T. (eds) (2005) *Looking Reality in the Eye: Museums and Social Responsibility*, Calgary, Canada: Museums Association of Saskatchewan and the University of Calgary Press.

Jaworski, J. (1998) *Synchronicity*, San Francisco: Berrett-Koehler.

Kabat-Zinn, J. (1990) *Full Catastrophe Living*, New York: Bantam, Doubleday, Dell Publishing Group, Inc.

Kanter, R.M. (2000) "Leaders with passion, conviction and confidence can use several techniques to take charge of change, rather than react to it," *Ivey Business Journal*, May/June: 32–36.

Kotter, J.P. (1990) "What leaders really do," *Harvard Business Review*, 68(3): 103–111.

Krug, K., Fenger, A.M. and Ames, M.M. (1999) 'The faces of MOA: a museum out of the ordinary', *Archiv fur Volkerkunde*, 50: 249–263.

Lapierre, L. (2005) "Managing as creating," *International Journal of Arts Management*, 7: 4–10.

Leka, S., Griffiths, A. and Cox, T. (2003) "Work organisation and stress: systematic problem approaches for employers, managers and trade union representatives," *Protecting Workers' Health Series No. 3*, Geneva: World Health Organization. Online. Available www.who.int/occupational_health/publications/en/oehstress.pdf (accessed 22 February 2006).

Locke, C. (2000) "Internet apocalypso," in *The Clue Train Manifesto: The End of Business as Usual*, Chapter one. Online. Available http//www.cluetrain.com/apocalypse, html (accessed 20 January 2002).

Martin, A. (2002) "The impact of free entry to museums," *Cultural Trends*, 47: 3–12.

Mintzberg, H. (1996) "Musings on management," *Harvard Business Review*, 74: 61–67.

Ohmae, K. (1998) "Strategy in a world without borders," *Leader to Leader*, 7: 17–23.

Rifkin, J. (1997) "The end of work," address on behalf of the Volunteer Centre of Calgary, Palliser Hotel, Calgary, Canada, 13 November.

Sandell, R. (ed.) (2002) *Museums, Society, Inequality*, Oxford: Routledge.

Scearce, D. and Fulton, K. (2004) "What If? The art of scenario thinking for non-profits." Global Business Network. Online. Available http://www.gbn.com/ (accessed 2 January 2006).

Schwartz, P. (1996) *The Art of the Long View: Paths to Strategic Insight for Yourself and Your Company*, New York: Doubleday.

Smithsonian Institution (2002) *21st Century Roles of National Museums: A Conversation in Progress*, Washington, D.C.: Office of Policy and Analysis.

Stacey, R.D. (1992) *Managing the Unknowable*, San Francisco: Jossey-Bass Publishers.

Weil, S.E. (2004) "Rethinking the museum: an emerging new paradigm," in Gail Anderson (ed.) *Reinventing the Museum*, 74–79, Walnut Creek, California: AltaMira Press.

Wheatley, M.J. (1994) *Leadership and the New Science*, San Francisco: Berrett-Koehler.

Woodhurst (2005) "The Woodhurst 2005 Salary Survey." Online. Available http:// www.woodhurst.com/ (accessed 2 January 2006).

11

THE MINDFUL MUSEUM*

Introduction

Are museums mindful of what is going on in the world around them? The planet Earth and global civilization now confront a constellation of issues that threaten the very existence of both. There is a burgeoning literature that offers dire warnings and solutions, but museums are rarely, if ever, mentioned.[1] Are not museums (with the possible exception of contemporary art museums) the self-proclaimed custodians of posterity, assuming that the responsibilities of today will be the gifts of the future? If so, there is an alarming disconnect between this belief and the trajectory that many museums are on, preoccupied as they are with the marketplace, quantitative measures of performance, and internally driven agendas devoted to collecting, exhibiting, ancillary education, and entertainment.

Rethinking the role of museums as social institutions will require no less than a reinvented museum – a mindful organization that incorporates the best of enduring museum values and business methodology with a sense of social responsibility heretofore unrecognized. Stewardship of the highest order will also be required, demanding active engagement and shared authority with those individuals and communities that museums purport to serve.

Museums have inadvertently arrived at a metaphorical watershed where it is now imperative to ask broader questions about why they do what they do, to confront a variety of admittedly unruly issues, and to propose some new choices. This metaphorical watershed is not unlike Peter Drucker's concept of a "divide." In his words, "Within a few short decades society rearranges itself – its worldview; its basic values; its social and political structure; its arts; its key institutions. Fifty years later, there is a new world" (Drucker 1994: 1).

*Source: Robert R. Janes, *Curator: The Museum Journal*, Vol. 53, No. 3 (2010): 325–338.

To assume that existing models of museum practice can somehow fulfill the requirements of the future is to invite the scorn and alienation of future generations. As E.O. Wilson noted, "We are creating a less stable and interesting place for our descendants to inherit. They will understand and love life more than we, and they will not be inclined to honor our memory" (Wilson 2006, 81). Recognizing the possibility of this disturbing outcome, how might we envision a mindful museum?

Mindfulness and the museum

The word "mindful" entered the museum vocabulary recently in an article titled "The Mindful Museum," by the American essayist Adam Gopnik. He wrote: "The mindful museum should first of all be mindful in being primarily about the objects it contains. Your first experience when entering the mindful museum should be of a work of art" (Gopnik 2007: 90). Although Gopnik notes that he uses "mindful" in the Buddhist sense – "of a museum that is aware of itself, conscious of its own functions, and living at this moment" – I submit that he has confused the self-absorbed behavior of museums, grounded in habit and traditional practice, with the real meaning and value of mindfulness. Ironically, the preoccupation with objects and collections is one of the primary obstacles preventing museums from becoming truly mindful. While I acknowledge that Gopnik is mainly concerned with art museums, this does not explain his use of "mindful," especially with respect to its Buddhist meaning. Now that the concept has entered the museum world, we could do with a clearer understanding of what "mindfulness" actually means.

The systematic cultivation of mindfulness has been called "the heart of Buddhist meditation." It is a particular way of paying attention, and one of its major strengths is that it is not based on any belief system or ideology. Its benefits are accessible to anyone (Kabat-Zinn 1990: 12–13). In essence, mindfulness is cultivated by purposefully paying attention to things we ordinarily ignore; it requires that we should always know what we are doing. Mindfulness actually helps us to be more aware of events in the outside world and our reactions to them (Fontana 1999: 112). Becoming more mindful is particularly important at this point in our evolution as a species, as global stresses and strains mount – all compounded by the endless distractions of the digital revolution.

Chaotic cascades

We need only consider the dramatic changes in new technology to appreciate the new and relentless pressures of the digital age on museum work. There are computers at home and work, fax machines, cell phones, pagers, laptops, smartphones, high speed connectivity, email, and the Internet, all of which are convenient, efficient, and useful, but at a cost to mindfulness. Jon Kabat-Zinn, a professor of medicine and a meditation teacher, describes the consequences:

> This new way of working and living has inundated us all of a sudden with endless options, endless opportunities for interruption, distraction, highly

enabled "response ability" . . . and a kind of free-floating urgency attached to even the most trivial of events. The to-do list grows ever longer, and we are always rushing through this moment to get to the next.

(Kabat-Zinn 2005: 148)

Added to these stresses and distractions is the chaotic thinking that marks much of our everyday lives, as our brains continue their ceaseless chatter. Much of our thinking is narrow and repetitive, and based on our personal history and our habits. Our minds are filled with anxieties about the future, how we're possibly going to get everything done that needs to be done, what people said or didn't say, are we successful, are we getting the recognition we deserve, will we ever get enough time for ourselves, about having no time, about needing more time, about having too much time, and so on and so on. Our thinking can be described as a waterfall – a continual cascade of thoughts (Kabat-Zinn 1994: 94).

Museum chatter

Understandably, museums also suffer from unavoidable distractions, cascading thoughts, and institutional chatter. There is the continuous preoccupation with the number of visitors, the building, security, education, food, merchandise, shopping, entertainment, technology, special exhibitions, and visitor demands – just a sampling of the front-of-the-house concerns. Then there is the internal chatter, beginning with the governing authority, which may or may not be performing adequately; may have an ineffective chair; may be exercising undue or conflicting influence on the work of the museum; or may be failing to raise the necessary funding to balance the fragile operating budget. Then there is the staff, from the most senior to the most junior, who are simply human beings living out the intricacies of their lives more or less effectively – a good portion of which is done in an institutional setting. Perhaps there are also leaders and managers with 25 years of experience – the same year repeated 25 times.

Organizational stress is another perpetual distraction, and an ever-increasing feature of organizational life that has not received the attention it deserves in the museum sector. Many museum staff are understandably weary and skeptical, given the penchant for lay-offs to balance the budget, the low pay, and the fact that there will be no mythical plateau where they can pause and say "We've made it" and return to business as usual. There is no business as usual, or an idealized past, for that matter, contrary to the wishful thinking of many museum workers. The resulting stress must be seen as an inherent danger, nonetheless, and be confronted organizationally with intelligence and caring.

Negative people

Stress is also a factor in the "negative people syndrome," another source of institutional chatter and perpetual ruminations. There is always a certain amount of negativism afloat in even the most exemplary museum, and it can be salutary in counteracting complacency and providing an inadvertent source of humility for those who are paying attention. Overall, however, staff negativity is a bane, and can translate into constant complaining, hostility, and a notable lack of generosity of spirit among colleagues. It can also lead to compliance and passivity, both deadly hurdles to creativity and action. Although the negative voices are usually the loudest, it is important to acknowledge that skepticism and questioning are integral parts of a well-functioning museum. The continuous task is to determine if the negativism is self-serving or of benefit to the organization. Which leads me to the last example of unrelenting chatter: the ambiguity that envelops all museums, whether or not they are mired in habit or becoming more mindful.

Ambiguity

Ambiguity should not be feared, however, contrary to the dictates of the marketplace. Marketplace disciples spend vast amounts of time and energy seeking control over their internal and external environments, in order to enhance the bottom line and profitability. Corporations, in general, succeed to the extent that they can exercise sovereignty over people's lives through marketing, hidden trade agreements, preferential government treatment, globalism, and so forth, all of which provide them with ostensible public support for their corporate self-interests. The museum world is far more complex, with few privileged connections and no history of influence peddling with which to bolster one's fortunes.

Museums have no choice but to confront the ambiguity, complexities, and paradoxes which make them what they are. Paradoxical questions and imperatives abound: Is the customer always right? Are museums sustainable without significant contributions of public funding? Are there too many museums? What is the purpose of a competent museum? What role should traditional practices play in an effective museum? In light of all this ambiguity, museum boards and staff have labored long and hard to avoid surprises. Admittedly, few things disturb them more than increasing complexity (Wheatley 1992: 109–110). Questions with no ready answers are also significant management challenges in museums, and leave anxiety and discouragement in their wake.

Becoming more mindful

The consequences of this preoccupation with complexity and control are nicely summed up by Margaret Wheatley, an organizational consultant and writer:

> We still believe that what holds a system together are point to point connections that must be laboriously woven together by us. Complexity only adds to our task, requiring us to keep track of more things, handle more pieces, make more connections. As things increase in number or detail, the

span of control stretches out elastically, and, suddenly, we are snapped into unmanageability.

(1992: 110)

And snapped into unmindfulness, as well. All of the museum chatter discussed above, be it about governance, management, morale, stress, or ambiguity, is equivalent to our cascading thoughts as individuals, and prevents museums from seeing what is actually going on in the world around them. These distractions also drown out the need for individual and organizational reflection, and the learning required to answer the crucial question of *why* museums do what they do. Unlike individuals, museums are obviously incapable of mindful meditation as organizations, but asking the question *why* is a workable alternative for enhancing organizational consciousness and mindfulness.

The crucial need is for the organization to recognize that much of the incessant internal chatter can be repetitive, inaccurate, disturbing, toxic, and unrelenting, and to not let it subvert vision, purpose, and the capacity of the museum to ponder the larger picture, clarify what is most important, and determine how it might be of real use in a troubled world. This could, in fact, be immensely liberating and assist museums in overcoming the inertia and self-interest that define much of the status quo within the museum community. Are museums, as social institutions in the civil society, capable of expanding their consciousness and recognizing their privileged position grounded in public trust, respect, and support? This does not require a radical forsaking of the values and traditions that sustain museums, since a mindful museum can exist in its own conventional consciousness, while at the same time bringing a much greater awareness to its work and its role in the broader community.

Some characteristics of mindfulness

Synthesis over process

Increasing a museum's mindfulness does not require the wholesale discarding of conventional practices. In fact, museums can become more mindful in the course of their habitual activities, as long as sufficient attention is paid to the mission. The mindful mission will favor synthesis over process and – instead of the typical museum commitment to "collecting, preserving and interpreting" – the mindful museum recognizes that processes are only the means to the end. It is also essential to realize that disparate voices are the stuff of insight and possibilities, and this is especially important now, when society suffers from dissonant voices speaking in isolation (Hawken et al. 2000: 310–313). The ongoing debate about the environment is a good example of the clash of dissonant voices: the free-market capitalists (rooted in conventional economics where growth is everything); the environmentalists (who see the world in terms of ecosystems and focus on depletion and damage), and the synthesizers.

All museums have the responsibility and the opportunity to become synthesizers, and foster an understanding of the interconnectedness of the problems we face, both environmental and social. The mindful museum rejects marketplace ideology and demonstrates that solutions will arise from place and culture "when local people are empowered and honored" (Hawken et al. 2000: 312). A mindful museum can empower and honor all people in the search for a sustainable and just world, by creating a mission that focuses on the interconnectedness of our world and its challenges, and promotes the integration of disparate perspectives (Janes 2008: 23).

Values

The mindful museum will also have a slate of well-considered values, but not those packaged and delivered by management consultants and branding gurus. Rather than self-serving values such as "excellence in peer recognition" and "professionalism," these values will reflect the commitment required for effective participation in the broader world. The list might include idealism, humility, interdisciplinarity, intimacy, interconnectedness, resourcefulness, transparency, durability, resilience, knowing your community, and knowing your environment.

Internal organization

The design of the internal organization must also reflect an increased awareness, if the promise of mindfulness is to be achieved. This will preclude the popular hierarchical organization, as it has proven categorically to restrict initiative and reward passivity. Instead, the mindful museum relies upon multifunctional work groups, not the homogeneous and silo-like departments and divisions common in museums today. These work groups will also persist through time, unlike temporary project teams, and all of them will benefit from the presence of writers, poets, artists, and performers, as well as *ad hoc* participants from the array of agencies and organizations that underpin the museum's role in the community. These non-traditional staff will be a key source of the emotion, imagination, intuition, and reflection that are essential to catalyze and sustain the museum's mindfulness.

Rapid response groups

The organizational chart will also include one or more rapid response groups (RRG), since museums are notoriously ineffective in altering their work plans to address unanticipated issues and opportunities. The RRGs will enable the mindful museum to respond more effectively to such contingencies. Sounds idealistic? It is, but without a change in how the work gets done, there can be little hope of changing what gets done. The way a museum does its work will either permit or preclude inclusive thinking, the questioning of the status quo, and heightened awareness of the external world.

More opportunities for consciousness

Branding

The above examples are only a glimpse of the many possibilities for enhancing mindfulness and more conscious museum work. There are many more, such as branding, which is now seen to be integral to a successful museum (Kotler et al. 2008). With few exceptions, however, most museums do not brand their values, ideas, mission, or substantive contributions. Instead, they brand "stuff" (exhibitions, dining, shops, and so on) and treat visitors and users as consumers and customers using the language of the marketplace: customer service, efficiency, entertainment, value for money, and so on (Janes and Conaty 2005: 1–17). All of this rhetoric is imported uncritically from the marketplace, even by those proponents who claim a special knowledge of museums. Most importantly, the majority of museums have failed to understand that branding is about differentiation – identifying what is unique and valuable about your museum, including what you do, why you're good at it, and why you're different.

Isn't it time for museums to move beyond the language of the marketplace to create civic brands around ideas and values that are based on the answers to key questions? These questions should consider why the museum exists, what changes it is trying to effect, what solutions it will generate, and what the museum's non-negotiable values are – such as collaboration, inclusiveness, diversity, consciousness, and so forth. Having answered these fundamental questions about the "why" and the "what," the task is then to develop a constellation of activities that both create and maintain the brand. Branding values and ideas is another means of heightening museum consciousness and moving beyond the reigning model of economic utility.

Collections

What about the cost of collections care? Why doesn't the global museum community have a current understanding of these costs that is analyzed and shared as a means of rationalization? They don't, and without such knowledge, it is impossible to allocate scarce resources intelligently in the face of new or competing priorities. Why are collection costs treated as fixed, when they are actually discretionary? The use of collections is still marked by little or no imagination and is hidebound by tradition.

Public programming

Moving from collections to public programming, where are the collaborative forums (including filmmakers, videographers, artists, poets, writers, storytellers, game creators, social activists, public agencies, and non-government organizations) working with museums to help them better understand the realm of experience design embedded in meaning, values, and relevance? These creative forums should involve recognized museum and non-museum innovators, thinkers, and experts in an annual think tank – or preferably a "think leak," where the results of the work are widely disseminated, thus sharing the fruits of their collaborative efforts with the broader community. The typical museum conference may offer several keynote addresses from outsiders, but the overall insularity remains a pronounced liability. It has been noted that all great change in business has come from outside the firm, not from inside, and there is no reason to assume that museums are any different (Lezner and Johnson 1997: 122–128).

In search of mindful museum practice

Although the concept of the mindful museum may suffer from a certain amount of abstraction, various museums and related organizations continue to move beyond the tyranny of the marketplace and traditional practices to demonstrate a greater awareness of their roles and responsibilities. One doesn't read or hear much about these examples in the mainstream media, or in the museum literature, because what they do lacks the sensationalism and celebrity appeal that drive our society's preoccupation with consumption and conformity. Many of these progressive practitioners are undoubtedly too busy to make their work more widely known. The following organizational examples have replaced passivity and compliance with creativity, altruism, and originality, and are defining new ways of being for museums as mindful social institutions. Additional examples of mindful museum practice, including Museum Victoria (Melbourne, Australia) and the Heifer Village Museum (Arkansas, US) are discussed in "Museums: Stewards or Spectators" (Chapter 17).

The Commonwealth Association of Museums – The first example of progressive thought and action is the Commonwealth Association of Museums (CAM), a professional association and international NGO (non-governmental organization) working toward the betterment of museums and their societies in the Commonwealth nations.[2] CAM is committed to fostering a strong role for museums in their societies and communities, with attention to the most urgent contemporary issues. Museums are encouraged to use their resources and their knowledge of their countries to ensure that the critical link between culture and development is used effectively for the betterment of society.

CAM's areas of concern are the safeguarding of both tangible and intangible heritage, biodiversity, and environmental sustainability. A review of the online mission statements of several national museum associations (in the United Kingdom, the United States, and Canada) revealed a focus on "enhancing the value of museums" or "advancing the museum sector." The expanded awareness demonstrated by the Commonwealth Association of Museums might well serve as a model for all museum associations as global issues become increasingly prominent.

The Canadian Conservation Institute – Museum conservators might be considered an unlikely source of innovation, but significant change is well underway among these specialists. The Canadian Conservation Institute (CCI), one of the world's distinguished conservation laboratories and service centers, is promoting a refreshing perspective that challenges conventional wisdom.[3] Contrary to the museum community's slavish worship of environmental controls, the CCI's website notes that certain types of artifacts are much more sensitive to relative humidity fluctuation than others, and it is neither economical nor environmentally acceptable to have tightly controlled conditions if they are not necessary.

During the author's recent correspondence with CCI, one of the senior scientists referred to the time-honored mantra of 50% relative humidity (RH) and 22 degrees Celsius (72 degrees Fahrenheit) as the presumed museum standard, and indicated his dismay over the pretense surrounding artifact loans. He noted that nearly every loaning museum specifies impossible levels of control, which they themselves cannot possibly maintain. By challenging these conventional beliefs, the CCI's conservators hope to remove some of the misinformation surrounding these issues. This willingness and ability to question time-honored assumptions are rare and laudable in the museum world, and also absolutely essential to learning, growth, and change. Now it is most important that this reinterpretation be disseminated throughout the museum world so that practitioners and their museums can benefit from this rethinking.

Museum Clusters – My third example of a notable museum innovation comes from Taiwan, and is based on the cluster concept first proposed by Michael Porter, professor at the Harvard Business School (Tien 2010: 69). This concept has come to be regarded as a strategic tool for local economic development. In Taiwan, museum clusters are geographic concentrations of interconnected museums which work closely with local suppliers, tourist attractions, and public sector entities. Cluster-based development is founded on the premise that a museum can realize higher levels of competence when it looks beyond its own limited capability to address challenges and solve problems.

A case study of the Danshui museum cluster indicates that the organizational structure is flat and emphasis is placed on the sharing of resources. In addition to the director in overall charge of the museum cluster, each museum has its own manager (Tien 2010: 80). The three museums share an administration team, an education team, and a day-to-day operations team. I am not aware of this degree of integration and cooperation among North America's fiercely independent museums, but as funding continues to decline, the museum cluster is an obvious solution.

Fortunately, we have these examples of thinking and doing to demonstrate the abundance of creative possibilities. They are heartening reminders that elite boards, big budgets, and quantitative measures are not the hallmarks of meaning and worth. On the contrary, the fruits of privilege are ultimately constraining, misleading, and maladaptive, as history has proven time and again. Many museums continue to revel in marketplace success, be it high attendance, shop sales, or burgeoning tax-receipted donations, but none of these things is resilient. Instead, they are brittle embodiments of an increasingly maladaptive past.

In addition to these organizational initiatives, there is also the work of various individuals who are mindful of the present, and I want to mention an outstanding example. The late Stephen Weil, scholar-practitioner, was articulate in his aversion to self-serving museums, and he left a legacy of articles and books that offered alternatives.[4] His thoughts and values are best summarized in one of his typically penetrating questions: "If our museums are *not* being operated with the ultimate goal of improving the quality of people's lives, on what other basis might we possibly ask for public support?" (Weil 1999: 242). This question continues to reverberate, with only marginal attention being paid to its contemporary implications. As highly regarded as Weil's work is, I detect no groundswell of approbation among practitioners to ensure that his questioning is constantly held in view.

The post-museum meets the mindful museum

Assuming that any or all of these progressive practices gain in popularity, the result will be more conscious and hence more effective museums. One organizational specialist, Margaret Wheatley, believes that some organizations are moving into the realm of increased consciousness anyway, because we inhabit "an intrinsically well-ordered universe" (Wheatley 1992: 117). Well-ordered or not – it is difficult to ignore the current human impact on the biosphere – and it's too early to know if museums will commit to this path. Any progress towards increased consciousness will require decreasing hierarchy, as well as inter- and intra-organizational interaction and exchange. Perhaps when these are achieved, along with some of the other attributes described earlier, the mindful museum and the post-museum will become one. Museum theorist Eilean Hooper-Greenhill argues that it is time to move beyond the idea of the museum as a locus of authority conveyed primarily through buildings and exhibitions, and adopt a new model which she calls the post-museum (2000: 151–162).

The post-museum is fundamentally different from the traditional museum and is intended to embrace a variety of societal perspectives and values, with the traditional museum perspective being only one voice among many. Perhaps most importantly, the post-museum involves intangible heritage, along with the emotions of visitors, since the post-museum is directly linked to the concerns and ambitions of communities (Hooper-Greenhill 2000: 152). The congruence between the post-museum and the mindful museum is significant, and hopefully liberating for those who might require a theoretical construct for altering the museum's traditional agenda.

The consequences of inaction

The need for heightened stewardship is obvious as the warning signs of our collective vulnerability continue to accumulate: population stress; the increasing scarcity of conventional oil; the degradation of our land, water, and forests; and the structural instabilities in the global economic system – not to mention climate change and global warming. All of these complexities can be distilled into a rather simple model of what could transpire if these events continue to unfold.

The economist Jeremy Rifkin notes that "our modern economy is a three-tiered system, with agriculture as the base, the industrial sector superimposed on top of it, and the service sector, in turn, perched on top of the industrial sector" (1980: 217–218). Each sector is totally dependent on more and more non-renewable energy – fossil fuels. Rifkin notes that as the availability of this energy diminishes, the public and private service areas will be the first to suffer, because services are "the least essential aspect of our survival." In short, an economy with limited energy sources will be one of necessities, not luxuries or inessentials, and will be centered on those things required to maintain life. Where do tourism, edutainment, museum shops, permanent collections, and blockbuster exhibitions fit in this looming scenario?

Although museums are unique and untapped resources in heightening societal stewardship, they are a public service, and the extent to which they will weather the future is difficult to predict. It's obvious that reducing energy consumption and avoiding large and consumptive building footprints are prerequisites, making the recent museum building boom even more inexplicable. Energy-efficient buildings, however, are only one ingredient in a meaningful future. Along with the willpower required to reduce consumption is the greater need to transform the museum's public service persona and culture-industry business agenda – defined by collections, ancillary education, and entertainment – into one of a locally embedded problem solver, in tune with the challenges and aspirations of communities.

An ecological metaphor

An ecological metaphor is useful here, since ecology is about the relationships between organisms and their environments – dependent, independent, and interdependent relationships. Museums have predicated their survival on being both dependent (for all forms of support) and independent, as exemplified by commonplace comments such as "give us the money; we know what to do" or "how dare you measure our performance." In the process of overlooking the meaning of interdependence, museums have contributed greatly to their own marginalization. It is time to consider the ecology of museums and recognize that the broad web of societal relationships is essential for successful adaptation in a complex and increasingly severe world.

The lack of interdependent relationships among most museums is a growing liability, and being valued for ancillary educational offerings and often ersatz entertainment is no longer sufficient to ensure intelligent sustainability. As some of the most conservative institutions in contemporary society, many museums will be unwilling or unable to grasp the import and necessity of rethinking their current successes and failures. This is not a bad thing, for the disappearance of myopic museums may well be beneficial, as the public and private resources allocated to museums diminish. There may, in fact, be too many museums, even now. However, this is not about the survival of the fittest, but about choosing renewal over decline.

Conclusions

The meaning and value of enhanced mindfulness have yet to be tapped by the museum community at large, and its potential might well be limitless. For those boards and museum workers who are disturbed at the thought of rethinking their traditional role and responsibilities, one question remains. How is it that museums, as social institutions, may remain aloof from the litany of socio-environmental issues that confront us, when many of these issues are intimately related to the purpose, mission, and capabilities of museums as we know them? This is not a call for museums to become social welfare agencies or Greenpeace activists, but rather to heighten their awareness and deliberately coalesce their capabilities and resources to bring about change, both internally and externally. Margaret Wheatley writes: "There is no power for change greater than a community discovering what it cares about."[5] Will communities continue to care about museums in their current guise? Will museums discover what they care about? Or are museums at risk?

Acknowledgements

This chapter is based on *Museums in a Troubled World: Renewal, Irrelevance or Collapse?* by Robert R. Janes (2009). The author wishes to thank Matthew Gibbons, editor for Classics, Archaeology and Museum Studies at Routledge, for permission to use this material. I am indebted to Richard Sandell, Joy Davis, James M. Bradburne and Elaine Heumann Gurian for their generous assistance and support throughout the preparation of the book on which this chapter is based.

Notes

1 For several powerful overviews of the world's challenges, the reader should see Homer-Dixon (2001; 2006); McKibben (2006) and Wilson (2003).
2 Commonwealth Association of Museums, accessed Feb. 11, 2010 at http://www.maltwood.uvic.ca/cam/about/index.html.
3 Canadian Conservation Institute, accessed Feb. 12, 2010 at http://www.cci-icc.gc.ca/crc/articles/enviro/index-eng.aspx.
4 A special issue devoted to Stephen Weil, in *Curator: The Museum Journal* vol. 50 no. 2, 2007, is a result of a conference held in honor of Stephen Weil at the University of Victoria, Cultural Resource Management Program, Victoria, British Columbia, Canada, Sept. 13–15, 2006.
5 Wheatley, M.J., quoted in *Wikipedia.* Accessed Aug. 22, 2008 at http://en.wikipedia.org/wiki/Margaret_Wheatley.

References

Drucker, P.F. 1994. *Post-Capitalist Society.* New York: HarperCollins.
Fontana, D. 1999. *Meditation: An Introductory Guide to Relaxation for Mind and Body.* Shaftesbury, Dorset, UK: Element Books Limited.
Gopnik, A. 2007. The mindful museum. *The Walrus* 4 (June): 87–91. Article adapted from the 2006 Holtby Lecture at the Royal Ontario Museum, Toronto, Canada.

Hawken, P., A. Lovins, and L.H. Lovins. 2000. *Natural Capitalism*. New York: Back Bay Books/Little, Brown and Company,

Homer-Dixon, T. 2001. *The Ingenuity Gap*. Toronto: Vintage Canada.

———. 2006. *The Upside of Down: Catastrophe, Creativity, and the Renewal of Civilization*. Toronto: Alfred A. Knopf.

Hooper-Greenhill, E. 2000. *Museums and the Interpretation of Visual Culture*. London and New York: Routledge.

Janes, R.R. 2008. Museums in a troubled world: Renewal, irrelevance or collapse? Address to the Committee on Audience Research and Evaluation (CARE), Annual Meeting of the American Association of Museums, Denver, Colorado.

———. 2009. *Museums in a Troubled World: Renewal, Irrelevance or Collapse?* London and New York: Routledge.

Janes, R.R. and G.T. Conaty, eds. 2005. *Looking Reality in the Eye: Museums and Social Responsibility*. Calgary: The University of Calgary Press and the Museums Association of Saskatchewan.

Kabat-Zinn, J. 1990. *Full Catastrophe Living: Using the Wisdom of Your Body and Mind to Face Stress, Pain, and Illness*. New York: Bantam, Doubleday, Dell Publishing Group, Inc.

———. 1994. *Wherever You Go, There You Are: Mindfulness Meditation in Everyday Life*. New York: Hyperion.

———. 2005. *Coming to Our Senses: Healing Ourselves and the World Through Mindfulness*. New York: Hyperion.

Kotler, N.G., P. Kotler, and W.I. Kotler. 2008. *Museum Marketing and Strategy: Designing Missions, Building Audiences, Generating Revenue and Resources*. Second edition. San Francisco: Jossey-Bass.

Lezner, R. and S.S. Johnson. 1997. Seeing things as they really are: An interview with Peter F. Drucker. *Forbes* 10 (March): 122–128.

McKibben, B. 2006. *The End of Nature*. New York: Random House.

Rifkin, J. 1980. *Entropy: A New World View*. New York: Viking Press.

Tien, C. 2010. The formation and impact of museum clusters: Two case studies from Taiwan. *Museum Management and Curatorship* 25(1): 69–85.

Weil, S. 1999. From being *about* something to being *for* somebody: The ongoing transformation of the American museum. *Daedalus: Journal of the American Academy of Arts and Sciences* (128): 229–258.

Wheatley, M.J. 1992. *Leadership and the New Science: Learning about Organization from an Orderly Universe*. San Francisco: Berrett-Koehler.

Wilson, E.O. 2003. *The Future of Life*. New York: Vintage Books.

———. 2006. *Creation: An Appeal to Save Life on Earth*. New York: W.W. Norton and Company.

12

MUSEUM MANAGEMENT REVISITED*

Towards a new paradigm

Stephen Weil, the renowned museum scholar-practitioner, was crystal clear about a fundamental point: there is no "essence of museum" that must be preserved at all costs.[1] Museums exist in, of, by, and for society and are obligated to continually ponder their work in an effort to be worthwhile and make a difference. In framing the following discussion, I have borrowed the concept of a "new paradigm" from Stephen Weil's article "Rethinking the Museum: An Emerging New Paradigm." According to Thomas Kuhn, the historian of science who popularized the word, replacing a paradigm is tantamount to a revolution.[2] Such an event has not yet occurred in the museum world and the prospects are limited, so I use the term advisedly. This new paradigm is about museums enhancing community well-being, with well-being broadly defined as "the contribution of the economic, social, cultural, and political components of a community in maintaining itself and fulfilling the various needs of local residents."[3]

Because I am interested in fostering substantive changes in the purpose and work of museums, the use of "new paradigm" underscores the extent of the change required. I will move beyond a concern with the method and theory of museum management and consider aspects of contemporary museum practice that are obstacles to change. It is noteworthy that museums have not been subjected to much public scrutiny or demands for accountability (other than by funders or the occasional culture or history wars) – unlike the education and the health care sectors. Some citizens are concerned about the moral complexities of museums, however, and have expressed themselves with honesty and verve.

*Source: Robert R. Janes, pp. 347–370 in Robert R. Janes (2013) *Museums and the Paradox of Change: A Case Study in Urgent Adaptation* (Third Edition), London and New York: Routledge.

One of the most refreshing and populist inquiries into the business of museums is the 2008 *YouTube* video entitled "The Creation of Value: Meditations on the Logic of Museums and Other Coercive Institutions."[4] Although this is a brilliant and truthful inquiry, I fear that the actors (two animated cats) are too appealing to generate real concern among museum practitioners. Nonetheless, the dialogue is an incisive and nasty commentary on contemporary museum practice. Interestingly, this video was produced by *The Pinky Show*, a nonprofit organization that focuses on information and ideas that have been misrepresented, suppressed, ignored, or otherwise excluded from mainstream discussion. *The Pinky Show* has discovered museums and portrayed them most unflatteringly – yet another signal that museums are distant and stereotypical in the minds of many.

Weil's call for a new paradigm from inside the profession, and *The Pinky Show*'s social media revelation that a certain socioeconomic class dominates museums, both illustrate from opposite perspectives that museums are in need of reform. This is also true of all contemporary social, government, and private sector institutions, as all of them are increasingly lacking in resilience and responsiveness, as well as failing to take action to have something new and better come into being. In short, they are failing to create a new future.[5] If this is too ambitious, museums could at least help create an *image* of a desirable future – the essential first step in its realization. Instead, the focus is on problem solving in contemporary social institutions, be it poverty or museum attendance. But problem solving does not create what is necessary or desirable.

By reform, I mean taking action so that museums and their staffs become more resilient and responsive, as well as embrace a broader social role. Museums may or may not be able to contribute to solving many of the global problems, but museums of all kinds are in a position to invent a new future for themselves and their communities. Admittedly, reform means change and there are countless obstacles to doing so, beginning with the many self-inflicted challenges that dog most museums. I have written at length about this elsewhere, but these difficulties persist and require updating. These self-inflicted challenges or internal limitations, call them what you will, are contributing to growing disaffection among current and future museum supporters, as well as undermining the invulnerability that museums have always enjoyed based on tradition and status. All of the topics below are management considerations, although some are also solidly coupled with governance issues. It is unrealistic to hope that all of these could be addressed by one museum, but even if one or several of these considerations were to be given attention, a new sense of realism could emerge.

Meditations on magical beliefs

In my earlier book, *Museums in a Troubled World*, I included a chapter on museums and their self-inflicted challenges in an effort to identify some of the unquestioned assumptions, groupthink, and sacred cows that influence or control much of what goes on in museums. I suggested that these habitual behaviours are enfeebling otherwise competent museums and diverting them from realizing their unique strengths and opportunities as stewards of the natural and cultural world.[6] The Museums Association (UK) is also grappling with similar idiosyncrasies and they hosted a session entitled "Great Lies to Tell about Museums" at their 2012 annual conference.[7] As I do not yet have the temerity to call them "lies," I will refer to them as magical beliefs. I see little or no attenuation in these liabilities with the exception of deaccessioning, which seems to be gaining more visibility and acceptance among museum workers. I will refresh my list of these self-inflicted challenges as a prelude to a discussion on strengthening museum management. All of these challenges, lies or not, are either mistaken beliefs or failures in reasoning, irrespective of their status as established practices and perspectives.

Neutrality

There is a widely held belief among museum boards and staff that they must protect their neutrality (with the exception of their expert pronouncements on quality and excellence), lest they fall prey to bias, trendiness, and special interest groups. The meaning of neutrality has changed over the past decade, however, as museums have increased their reliance on corporate, foundation, and private funding, and more and more business people are appointed to governing boards. The unspoken argument is that museums cannot risk doing anything that might alienate a private sector sponsor, real or potential. The simple truth, apparently unrecognized by the proponents of museum neutrality, is that corporations and the business community are themselves special interest groups, grounded in marketplace ideology. When will museums confront this elephant in the room? As the poet/farmer, Wendell Berry, succinctly notes, "Influence and consequence are inescapable. History continues."[8]

The sanctity of collections

There are so many adherents to the sanctity of museum collections that to question this at all is heretical. But heresy is now required, as the global museum world staggers under the weight of redundant, ignored, and inferior collections. The absolute number of stored objects in the world's museums continues to increase unabated, irrespective of the belief that museums have entered an era of visitor-centred activities that has replaced collecting. Museums are simply taking less care of the objects they acquire. I do note that deaccessioning is now an acceptable discussion topic on the Internet and at professional meetings, but the extent to which collections are actually being rationalized, shared, or downsized remains insignificant.

Collections remain the primary rationalization for maintaining the status quo, and are as likely to sink a museum in the future as to legitimize its status. When will museums confront the sanctity of collections, and work out regional, local, and national collaborations to reduce costs, reduce redundancy, and reduce their dependency on the rhetoric of collecting? There are some indications of real change in this regard, as described in a recent article on museum mergers in the United States. Martha Morris, Professor of Museum Studies, discusses the details of several successful museum mergers and notes their advantages and challenges.[9] There is no doubt that museum collections do have an irreplaceable role to play as the knowledge databases of our civilization, and to serve as a foundation for creative adaptation in a changing world.

The self-sacrificing museum worker

I honestly have no intention of demeaning the work and commitment of museum workers as I examine the perception of the "self-sacrificing museum worker," which is one that I regularly encounter working in and around museums. Its origin, to a great extent, stems from the notoriously low salaries paid to museum workers, although this is a perception that can defy generalization because of the country of employment, the type of museum, the position, one's qualifications, and so forth. In fact, some museum workers are well paid (most notably those in museums owned by provincial, state, and national governments), with generous benefit packages and salary scales controlled by collective agreements. Nonetheless, the perception of inadequate compensation persists and underlies the belief that to be left alone to pursue one's own interests is a form of compensation for the poor pay.

My observations are firsthand and my concern is real, as the "self-sacrificing museum worker" persona contributes to the internal, and often self-serving, agendas of many museums. The notion of self-sacrifice easily serves as an impediment or an excuse, and undermines the motivation and initiative required to embrace new ways of thinking and working. In fact, there are few workplaces which offer more opportunities for thinking, choosing, and acting in ways that can blend personal satisfaction and growth with organizational goals.[10] These opportunities constitute one of the privileges of museum work, and must be weighed against the burden of low pay.

Boards of directors work well

There is an abundant literature on the complexities of nonprofit governance, and many resource manuals on museum governance in particular. But the emperor is without clothes, as museums of all sizes and kinds continue to struggle daily with mediocre or failed governance. Bad museum governance is pervasive, from unbridled deficit spending, to a lack of operational policies, to bad hires, to individual board members acting alone on behalf of the board with no sense that governance is a collective responsibility. The result of this incompetence, exacerbated by good intentions, is a serious drain on the scarce resources of museums, not to mention the anxiety and tension resulting from a governing authority at odds with the best interests of the organization. This is especially damaging when the board are not even aware of the disjuncture and are acting unwittingly.

Two initiatives are required to improve this situation. First, professional training in governance principles and conduct, however abridged, must be mandatory for all board members, irrespective of the size of the museum. This training must also include the methods and resources for understanding and reflecting the needs, interests, and aspirations of the community, as well as nurturing the ability to rethink the museum's vision and mission in response to this enhanced mindfulness. Second, the director, CEO, or director/curator must be protected from the vicissitudes of incompetent governance by means of a director's review committee (call it what you wish). This committee would consist of several board members and would meet in-camera as required, to allow the director the complete freedom to discuss the work of the board without fear of reprisal for being candid. The relationship between the board and the director must be collegial and professional – not superior/subordinate – and the director's review committee provides a formal and confidential channel to steward this relationship.

Earned revenues are the answer

"Earned revenues are the answer" is the mantra of the marketplace ideology that now pervades North American museums and beyond. There is no doubt that museums in general have embraced this responsibility with dedication and competence, as earned revenues are now a key component of annual operating budgets. Canadian museums doubled their earned revenue in the decade from 1993 to 2002, when the serious erosion of public funding began. Of the earned revenue reported by Statistics Canada in 2002, admissions rose by 67%, but accounted for just under 32% of total earned revenue, in contrast to its 39% share in 1993. Sales in gift shops, cafeterias, and other earned revenue sources accounted for approximately 64% of earned revenue in 2002. In absolute terms, gift shop sales rose by more than double.[11] This strong trend continued with Statistics Canada reporting in 2009 that government revenues accounted for just over one-half of operating revenues (52%); earned revenues represented 37% of revenues, and private sector fundraising accounted for 11% of operating revenues.[12] The story is equally as robust for American museums, with the latest "Annual Condition of Museums and the Economy Report" for 2011 showing an average of 38% of operating revenue derived from earned income.[13] Philip Katz, the Assistant Director for Research at the American Association of Museums, suspects that the current "true" number for the field as a whole is around a third.[14]

These statistics demonstrate that museums have embraced the marketplace with great intensity and have succeeded in making earned revenues an integral part of their operating budgets. One could argue that these activities are related to the consumption of stuff and selling high-end services such as weddings, with little attention paid to exploring more creative and culturally relevant activities. Nonetheless, museums have successfully embraced this business model. This success, coupled with the increasing number of business people now serving on museum boards, has given rise to the unfortunate belief that increasing earned income is the answer to budgetary difficulties. The simple fact is that there are limits to earned income, and the idea that a museum could be economically self-sufficient has no basis in fact. Predictably, this belief has been uncritically embraced by governments at all levels, with the politicians knowing little or nothing about the actual state of museum finances.

At least two initiatives are required to redress this misperception. First, governing authorities must understand that museums are not businesses, although they are duty bound to be business literate. Second, all national museum associations must organize a multi-sectoral discussion among governments, funders, and museums to determine what constitutes a fair balance between public funding and earned revenues. Only then will museum staff be relieved of the relentless worry to do more with less, endure continuous cost cutting, and otherwise feel inadequate to the task. The task is to set reasonable targets for earned revenues in conjunction with all funders, design the museums to live within these means, and then get on with the work. Let the incessant criticism from marketplace ideologues and self-flagellation cease.

The lone director

I have written about the pitfalls of the lone CEO leadership model elsewhere, but with no take-up – not even any criticism.[15] Yet, the all-powerful, lone director or CEO continues to cause unnecessary difficulties and damage because of the excessive amount of authority inherent in this position. I will mention the magical belief in the lone CEO only briefly here, in order to underscore the need for change. I understand that this leadership model is the Western world's tradition, albeit uncritically borrowed from the corporate world. The notion that a single individual should be all powerful in an increasingly complex world is absurd, as effective leadership is less the property of a person than the property of a group.[16]

Alternative approaches to museum leadership must become a focus of museum studies departments, with a view to critically assessing different ways of leading. One alternative is the *primus inter pares*, or "first among equals" leadership model. This model is about collective, executive leadership and apparently goes back to Roman times as discussed in Chapter 8. The principle is simple: There is still a "first," a leader, but that leader is not the chief executive officer.

Boards of directors also have an opportunity to consider their options and experiment accordingly. It is important to reiterate that *how* work is organized is a major determinant in the nature and quality of the work being done. This intimate relationship is seldom acknowledged or discussed, and is a major obstacle to creative museum management. If the digital age is ushering in a new era of participation, then perhaps there will come a time when every museum worker is not subordinate to a single, other person. The well-being of museums and leaders would be enhanced with a greater emphasis on shared authority, especially at a time of unprecedented complexity, and the *primus inter pares* model is the means to that end.

Social responsibility is what we do

My understanding of a socially responsible museum is one that acts to benefit society, above and beyond education and entertainment. It implies a certain activism, which also includes the welfare of the biosphere. As someone who is interested in the broader role of museums in society, I am more than curious when colleagues note that museums, by their very nature, are socially responsible. After all, they have a fiduciary obligation for their collections that has no time limit and is intended to serve the past, present, and future. This is indeed true, and lies at the heart of museums as unique and irreplaceable institutions, but holding collections *per se* does not constitute social responsibility. Art galleries are even more confident in asserting that their traditional practices constitute social responsibility, noting that by just exhibiting contemporary art they are being socially responsible. The argument, so I'm told, is that contemporary artists probe societal consciousness – exposing and exploring societal issues and foibles, ranging from hypocrisy to war to poverty. Yes, but not always. As the art critic Julian Spalding asks of contemporary art:

> Why do we have to make do with a stack of bricks, a pickled shark and a filthy bed? Further, "*Real* art is the expression of elusive feelings and thoughts that can't be communicated by any other means. When these feelings and thoughts are profound, we are drawn to look at this work of art again and again and again."[17]

Collections and the exhibition of contemporary art do not in and of themselves make a museum any more or less relevant. It's what is done with these things that lends meaning, value, and relevance. In the absence of a conscious attempt to serve a purpose beyond internal concerns (building collections, the art market, exhibitions, etc.), it is insincere to claim that museums and galleries are socially responsible.

Museum conferences are good for learning

"The meeting was good for networking" is a typical response from many museum conference attendees these days. This may be damning with faint praise, because the weak or non-existent references to program content, to new learning, to inspiration, and to controversy, demonstrate that something is lacking in these annual rituals. There is no doubt that networking (establishing and renewing personal and professional relationships) is essential to professional work of any kind, but one would hope that the social function could be accompanied by substantive content on the "how" and "why" of museum work.[18] Instead, the focus remains on the "what" – exhibitions, programs, and collections – with virtually no discussion of innovation, experimentation, research and development, serious obstacles, and failed initiatives. Darren Peacock notes that "the same staid, stuck and sclerotic conversations that afflict organizations can also be a feature of the wider discourse within a field or profession."[19] There is little doubt that the discourse on organizational change at professional museum meetings suffers from all three of these afflictions.

As an example, I recently attended a session on "Leading Change" in museums at a national conference. The panel consisted of several senior museum leaders who gave anecdotal, and seemingly impromptu, remarks on their experiences with organizational change. There was no formal introduction to the topic, no critical or reflexive exploration into the method and theory of change, and no attempt to interrelate the observations of the various speakers – before, during, or after their remarks. Overall, it was uninformative, devoid of study and rigour, and basically a disservice to the audience. A critical perspective might have emerged from the audience, but the panelists only left 10 minutes for discussion.

This carelessness persisted to the end, as the panel unanimously concluded that the so-called "digital kids" (those who have grown up in the new digital landscape) will be the future decision-makers and that museums must accept and adapt to this inevitability. This is the sort of conventional thinking that demands disciplined inquiry and reflection, however. None of these panelists apparently knew that "digital kids" are highly complex, and their potential impact on museums is even more complex. Recent research reveals that "young people growing up in today's networked world, and counting on the Internet as their external brain, will be nimble analysts and decision-makers who will do well."[20]

The same experts also expect "that constantly connected teens and young adults will thirst for instant gratification and often make quick, shallow choices." Where will that leave museums in 2020? The survey respondents in this Pew Research Centre project (*The Future of the Internet*) urged major educational reform to emphasize new skills and literacy, including teaching the management of multiple information streams, and emphasizing the skills of filtering, analyzing, and synthesizing information. An appreciation for silence and focused contemplation were also mentioned.

These comments are indicative of several systemic problems that plague most, if not all, museum conferences. First, content development for these meetings is formulaic, with little or no attempt to break the mould and try something new. The conference format sees little or no change from year to year. The quality control of the presentations varies considerably, with program committees being so heterogeneous, and the membership so varied (from volunteer-run to national museums), that the "lowest common denominator" must of necessity prevail. Another major factor is cost, as many museum workers simply cannot afford to attend. With registration costs starting at several hundred Canadian or US dollars, exclusive of travel costs, meeting attendance has become a luxury for many. The 2011 Audited Financial Statements of the Canadian Museums Association (CMA) indicates earned revenue of CAN$206,057 from the annual conference. In 2010, the earned revenue from the annual conference was CAN$259,700.[21]

While this entrepreneurship is admirable, what has become of the annual professional meeting as a source of new learning, discussion, and debate with the full range of one's colleagues – not just those who can afford it? There needs to be a conference about the conference, to redesign and replace the conventional conference model with something of greater value. In Canada, for example, perhaps the provincial museum associations could collaborate and organize several regional meetings, with the advice and assistance of the CMA. There is no clear solution at the moment, but the status quo is no longer serving museums in Canada. I suspect that this may also be true in other countries.

We know what's best

As well-intentioned as they are, museums generally suffer from an inherent insularity, coupled with diffidence and arrogance. These paradoxical qualities, and most museums exhibit all three, underlie a predilection for deciding what is in someone else's best interests – the "we know what is best" syndrome. The most obvious explanation for this attitude is the self-respect associated with higher education and advanced degrees, although the American Association of Museums revealed some surprising information.[22] A 2009 survey noted that 27.1% of the US museum workforce had a Bachelor's degree and 11% had advanced degrees (1.7% with a doctorate or other professional degree and 9.3% with a Master's degree). That means that less than 40% of US museum workers (total of 402,924 museum workers) have university degrees.

If academic achievement is only a partial explanation for authoritative and insular thinking, one must consider the privileged position of museums in society – allowing them to stand on the sidelines and pursue agendas of their own making. While the pressures of the marketplace (admissions, earned revenues, the search for popularity, etc.) have certainly impinged upon this sanctity, most museums remain remarkably free to determine what to do with their time and money. The most glaring exceptions are government-owned museums, and this will be discussed shortly. Another explanation for the museum's inadvertent paternalism might be, ironically, the isolation that museums have enjoyed as social institutions. Museums are rarely, if ever, acknowledged in the global discussion of climate change, environmental degradation, the inevitability of depleted fossil fuels, and the myriad local issues concerning the well-being of particular communities.

Bad museum behaviours

Whether the explanation is academic snobbery, a privileged position, or benign irrelevance, the result is the same – a persistent tendency among museums to claim to know what's best for their audiences and their communities. This perspective continues to produce what Bridget McKenzie, a cultural consultant and activist, calls "bad museum behaviours," and I am indebted to her for this frank description. The following comments on bad behaviours are distilled from her writing, and include additions and modifications based on my own experience.[23]

- Spending too much money on iconic collections, hoping to attract more visitors to see them while neglecting more ordinary and contemporary collections.
- Spending too much money on vanity architecture and expensive exhibitions, hoping to attract more visitors while neglecting how people make meaning of collections. The imaginative use of collections seems to be an insurmountable challenge for museums.
- Maintaining work practices and traditions that bear little connection with the true meaning of stewardship, which is to care for things that do not belong to us.
- Failing to recognize that contemporary life is a time of extraordinary upheaval, requiring museums to place a much greater focus on contemporary issues and their meaning for individuals and communities.
- Resisting efforts to increase and measure the social impacts of museum work.
- Believing that when money gained from corporate malfeasance (which can include the destruction of the natural environment and violence) is given to a museum, it becomes morally pure and acceptable.
- Concealing, intentionally or not, a variety of performance indicators including the annual budget, membership revenues, endowment and endowment income, energy consumption, volunteer hours, fundraising, and so forth.
- Believing that museums may abstain from addressing societal issues and aspirations because they have complex histories and unique missions which absolve them from greater accountability.

In concluding this review of magical beliefs, there are two more that can be dealt with summarily but merit attention because of their pervasiveness. The axiom "that numbers are what counts" (admissions, shop sales, meals sold, etc.) is one of these. The preoccupation with quantitative performance measures is a liability for intelligent museum practice, and continues to dominate museum workers who should instead be concerned with purpose, meaning, and value. This oversimplified emphasis on quantitative measures is yet another instance of the uncritical borrowing of methods and techniques from the business sector – another magical belief common in the museum world. There are many uncritical borrowings, ranging from the silly (corporate terminology such as "CEO" and "human resources") to the harmful. Examples of the latter include the hierarchical organizational model and museum branding based on consumption rather than content and values. Why these business methods are so rarely scrutinized by museum boards and staff is puzzling, especially in museum studies programs. The academy is an ideal setting for critically assessing the appropriateness of using various business techniques and models.

Miscellaneous impositions

There are also factors that originate outside of museums that are gaining momentum as impositions on museum practice. The controversies they generate are familiar to many and are not likely to abate, but rather intensify, and managing them will require increasing attention from museum workers. The first is the perennial conversation about the perception that "museums are for the rich." This is not a new topic, and much interest was generated when the UK's national museums shifted to free admission in 2001. The norm is still paid admissions for most of the world, although there is some creative rethinking underway such as the application of exit prices. Instead of charging visitors when they enter the museum, exit fees are charged when visitors leave the museum. The longer they spend in the museum, the higher the exit price.[24]

The Detroit Institute of Arts (DIA) has done something completely different and persuaded regional voters in Michigan (US) to back a slight tax hike in property taxes to support the financially unstable DIA (it has lost all its state support over the past 20 years). In exchange for residents supplying US$23 million of public funding each year for the next decade (which will allow the museum to build up its operating endowment), the DIA will provide free admission to the residents of three counties. *The Chronicle of Philanthropy* calls this initiative an important lesson for leaders of arts institutions who "continue to rely on outdated revenue models or have simply slashed spending rather than explore innovative ways to operate in a changed economic world."[25]

It is noteworthy that the "museums are for the rich" debate is now being reinvigorated on social media, with a recent installment appearing on the *Museum Planning* blog and then unfolding on *MuseumLink*.[26] There is general agreement among those that commented that many museums have become too expensive and are charging exorbitant admission to offset the costs of vanity architecture and expensive exhibitions. This is offensive to many of the blog commentators because museums receive public funding. There are numerous frank observations on this blog, such as "given a choice between feeding a family or going to a museum, a family will choose to eat." To what extent these comments are reflective of society at large is unknown, and one could argue that those who have the time to blog and tweet are probably not worried about eating. Nonetheless, the negative sentiments about elitist museums persist and they have now made their way to social media.

I note that the Director of the Royal Ontario Museum (ROM) in Canada, Janet Carding, recently lowered their exorbitant admission fee – installed by her predecessor to pay for the costly overrun on a vanity architectural renovation. In addition, the ROM is faced with the challenge of financing a major reorganization to take the museum into its second century while being fiscally responsible – a significant imposition for any museum. Recognizing that there was no viable way to increase the operating budget to finance the change process as part of a new strategic plan, Carding did something unprecedented in my experience. In July of 2012, she informed the museum's 350 employees that they will reduce the museum's spending on salaries and benefits (currently CAN$30 million) by 10%. She started the process by introducing voluntary severance packages.[27]

Carding's initiative not only provides greater financial flexibility and long-term stability, but it also sets the stage for innovation, as we learned at Glenbow.

She laid out the unpleasant facts (ROM has to change), asked the hard question (where's the money coming from?), and in the process created a transparent sense of purpose. In an environment of trust, with tolerance for mistakes and failures, new ways of thinking and working are certain to emerge.

The last imposition of note is the steady presence of government intervention in the management of some museums, something that is not likely to go away. We have two recent instances in Canada, not to mention numerous examples in the United States, which have resulted in various national museums recanting and changing their exhibitions. The so-called culture and history wars are alive and well. My first example is an exhibition on the Allied campaign to strategically bomb Germany during the Second World War, wherein 600,000 German civilians were killed.[28] The Canadian veterans and their politicians objected to the curatorial implication that this campaign might have been immoral or unnecessary. The exhibition text was revised and the Director of the Canadian War Museum left his position.

A more recent example comes from the Canada Science and Technology Museum, whose recent travelling exhibition on human sexuality offended members of the public and ultimately the federal Minister of Culture.[29] One of the offending pieces was a video of a boy and girl masturbating. Both praised and condemned, the video was eliminated and the exhibition was restricted to those 16 years and older. The Minister intervened and prevailed. If museums are the new agora, as many of them now claim to be, they will have to be willing to go beyond the rhetoric and actually present alternative perspectives, especially those that run against mainstream opinion. Socrates was not condemned to death for supporting the status quo. When actions do not follow words, the absence of courage is close by. Granted, national museums are government property, but individuals are not. This is something that museums will have to ponder more often as societal issues intensify and governments, such as Canada's, become more ideologically entrenched. As public, knowledge-based institutions, museums have a role and responsibility to steward intellectual self-defence.[30]

In concluding this discussion, I note that the museum exhibition itself may be the heart of the problem. I have discussed the increasing obsolescence of museum exhibitions elsewhere, and I want to reiterate that they are not particularly helpful in building relationships with community, or in fostering meaningful dialogue and interaction between individuals and groups. Museum exhibitions are "stultifyingly the same," in the words of Kathleen McLean, and lacking in imagination.[31] Yet, they remain the central preoccupation of all museums – unadapted to a changing environment and becoming increasingly obsolete.

Strengthening museum management

My purpose in recounting some of these magical museum beliefs and impositions is to identify them as obstacles to more innovative management – management that might help, to quote Stephen Weil again, to "define what it is, ideally, that we envision the museum as doing in its third function" (dealing with the public). The responsibility for innovative management is not only the purview of managers and executives, but also extends throughout the museum at all levels of the organization. For too long, managers and executives have been the scapegoats for those who have been unwilling or unable to move beyond their job descriptions.

The following discussion is devoted to suggestions for moving beyond the superior/subordinate dichotomy, and embracing certain actions and attitudes that will embolden individual responsibility and strengthen the organization in admittedly untested ways. These ideas and approaches are explained below and include cultivating individual agency, the importance of scholar-practitioners, the value of "no people," and the three faces of sustainability. Used individually or collectively, these are a mix of familiar, new, and unorthodox approaches that have the potential to expand conventional museum management beyond its current limitations. The truth will lie in the doing.

Cultivating personal agency for museum workers

Joy Davis, a veteran museum educator and trainer, published an article recently that examines the influence of personal agency and workplace climate on the transfer of learning from a professional education program to museum settings.[32] By personal agency, I mean the capacity of individual museum workers (not only leaders and managers) to take action in the world. I will extend Davis's concept of personal agency beyond what is learned in professional development, and consider the meaning of personal agency as it applies to the existing knowledge, experience, and values of individual museum workers in the workplace. I have always been struck by a seeming paradox – the widespread disconnection between individuals who work in a museum and the manner in which the museum functions as an organization. Individual staff members are insightful, innovative, and motivated by concerns and values beyond the workplace, yet the relationship between workplace and personhood remains largely unrecognized and unexplored. Individual qualities and concerns that transcend the workplace are rarely translated into organizational reality.

Guidelines are therefore required for cultivating personal agency that will assist in strengthening the contemporary management of museums. The following guidelines are intended for individuals of all ranks and positions in the workplace, with the full understanding that some museums are more respectful of personal agency than others, and hence good judgement and common sense are essential in pursuing personal agency. If the hierarchy is pronounced, many of the recommendations below can be pursued by not drawing attention to one's self, or "flying under the radar" as the saying goes. The fear of losing one's job for deviation from convention is oversold, especially now. Any intelligent manager or leader will be on the lookout for courage and new ideas.

Governance

1. Ask to attend a board meeting and/or arrange a reception with your board of directors and the staff. Meet your board members – ask them about their lives and experiences and make sure that they know what you do at the museum.
2. Assist in ensuring that all board members are given a thorough tour and briefing on all aspects of the museum's work. Follow this up with questions and a discussion.

Leadership and management

1. Meet personally with your CEO or director at least once a year, and review what you have accomplished, the challenges you faced, and constructively discuss how things might be improved.
2. Meet privately with your supervisor at least quarterly, for review, discussion, and reflection.
3. Make every effort to ensure that your museum has clearly articulated strategic goals and that these are widely communicated.
4. Insist upon personal involvement in the strategic and operational planning.
5. Ask yourself, your colleagues, your supervisor, and your leaders "why" you are doing what you are doing? This questioning will help to move the museum beyond the "what" and the "how."

Work environment

1. If there is an intractable issue or situation that is adversely affecting your work, speak out. Advise your manager or CEO of the difficulty and ways to address it. Have the courage of your convictions to remedy the situation.
2. Beware of the myth of the "irreplaceable employee." This is common throughout museums and allows competent, but otherwise disruptive and toxic staff, to persist in their jobs despite the harmful effects of their behaviour. Deal with this forthrightly with your supervisor.
3. Every staff person should know what types of results he or she is responsible for.[33]
4. Every individual in the organization should have only one supervisor.[34]
5. No one should have the authority to direct or veto any decisions or actions where he or she is not accountable for the results. This applies to committee and group work, as well as to individuals.[35]
6. The museum should avoid rules, practices, and policies that are designed to protect the organization from making mistakes. These rules are designed with the least competent individuals in mind, and force all staff to perform at the lowest level of competence.[36]
7. Individuals who have similar positions need not have similar levels of authority, as authority can be delegated to match the abilities of the individual to handle responsibilities.[37]

Work design

1. Decision-making should be decentralized throughout the museum to the "lowest level" in the organization where the work can be done well. In short, staff should have as much responsibility as possible for decisions which affect their work.
2. Functional divisions, such as departments, impede work and decision-making and should be reduced to a minimum.
3. Teams, no matter how cooperative and multifunctional, are not the sole means of working, and the importance of individual work must be recognized by management. Team work and individual work must coexist.
4. Be continuously aware that in museums of all sizes there are generally multiple criteria, often conflicting, that need to be considered when making and carrying out decisions. This is the nature of museum work, and life itself, and should not be avoided.[38]

Finances

1. Insist on seeing a full and transparent annual budget summary. This should be the subject of an all-staff meeting, with questions and discussion. Equip yourself with sufficient business literacy to know how to read the budget and determine what it means.
2. Know where your work unit or activity sits within the overall budget and how much money is allocated to your work.
3. If money is being spent in mysterious ways, or if deficit spending has become commonplace, insist upon an explanation and full transparency. This is your responsibility as a steward of the organization.

Communication

1. Any person in the museum, irrespective of level or rank, must be free to go directly to any person in the museum for information or assistance needed to perform his or her job. Going through hierarchical channels is only applicable to situations involving directions, approvals, or vetoes.[39]
2. Insist on regular meetings with your work unit – the frequency can be determined.

Personal

1. When appropriate, share aspects of your non-work life, whether it be involvement in an environmental NGO or work as an artist. These seemingly unrelated skills, knowledge, and experience are essential as a museum broadens its awareness and engages in the interests, issues, and aspirations of its community.
2. Cultivate and nurture your skills and knowledge, even if the museum is unable to support this. Continuous learning is vital to individual growth and the benefits will become apparent.

I realize that there is a certain idealism in these actions, because many of them are concerned with values – those enduring beliefs that describe how we want to treat others and how we want to be treated ourselves. It is important to note that the greater the congruence between individual and organizational values, the stronger the organization. As mentioned above, some museums will be more respectful of personal agency than others, but testing even one of these guidelines is guaranteed to be liberating for the individual and the organization – nothing ventured; nothing gained.

Honouring the scholar-practitioner

The scholar-practitioner model is well established in various disciplines, especially in medicine, and merits serious attention in museum management and governance. Although it was once commonplace for curators to assume directorships, there was an eventual backlash to this trajectory on the grounds that curators were academic and scholarly, and out of touch with the real world of management and money. The museum world now abounds with directors who have no advanced education in any related discipline, including an increasing number with no museum experience at all. My concern with the devaluing of the scholar-practitioner is losing the advantages inherent in a scholarly mindset – advantages that can be of great value to the leadership of any complex organization.

The defining characteristic of a scholar is a penchant for learning and a hunger to know more, and these qualities would do much to alleviate an unfortunate tendency among senior museum administrators with many years of experience. That is, the stubborn inclination to repeat the same year over and over again with few, if any, new initiatives based on new learning. Marsha Semmel refers to the importance of an "action learning cycle" for leaders, which consists of "experiencing/ re-experiencing; inquiring and reflecting; learning; and acting."[40] Reflecting and learning are key attributes of a scholarly temperament and they will play an ever-increasing role in organizational leadership, change, and adaptation.

There are other qualities of a scholarly temperament that are of value to management, including open-mindedness to new and different ideas without which there can be no learning. Also embedded in learning with an open mind are a variety of other scholarly traits such as self-discipline, diligence, self-motivation, curiosity, reading, study, and contribution to community. Although a concern with community is not normally associated with scholarship, the world has actually been shaped by the work of scholars who have shared their dedication and creativity – ranging from Leonardo da Vinci to John Ralston Saul. These are also individuals who have chosen to act, equipped with their scholarly resources. Society at large is the benefactor of the scholar's deep thinking, learning, and action, and one can only hope that these gifts will persist alongside the conformity and shallowness demanded by our ever-growing dependency on the technological and corporatized world.

As the Editor-in-Chief of *Museum Management and Curatorship* (*MMC*), I see the regrettable lack of practitioner contributions daily. For example, the last seven volumes of *MMC* (through 2011) contained a total of 115 full-length, peer-reviewed articles, with a total of 28 of these articles authored by museum practitioners – people who actually work in museums. That is only 24% of the articles, with the remaining 76% of the articles written by academic museologists, consultants, educators, and graduate students. Recognizing the amount of experience and knowledge residing in the minds of the world's practitioners, their minimal presence in the museum literature is a profound shortcoming. The thousands of wise and accomplished practitioners are apparently too taxed by their work to devote the time and energy to the advancement of knowledge. As an editor of a museum journal, I ponder daily how to unlock this wealth of silent experience and wisdom in the minds of the world's museum workers, as both are needed now more than ever. What's to be done to overcome the practitioners' silence?

One solution is for museum studies departments to develop specific programs to encourage and support practitioners (at all levels) to share their knowledge and experience. Such programs could offer mentorships between students and practitioners, and break the perplexing silence between the working museum and the academy. Museums are the focus of much museum studies research, but is there a reciprocal exchange of advice and assistance? Do museum studies programs care about what is actually transpiring in contemporary museums, and do they use this intelligence to inform their teaching and research?

I submit that many museum studies departments are as insular as museums, constrained by university administrations driven by the bottom line, as well as heavy workloads. But if museum academics don't respond creatively and soon, who will bridge the divide between what museums actually require for trained staff and the learning required to provide it? The need for reading, studying, and learning will not diminish – only increase – because the real challenge for intelligent management lies in being skeptical, curious, and inventive before you have to be. This requires continuous reading, reflection, and dialogue with the benefit of disparate perspectives. There is no better opportunity than university-level museum studies to engage in this work.

I propose that scholarly training, commitment, and accomplishments be recognized and valued once again in the selection of museum leaders and managers, as well as for curators and other specialties. This must also include a focus on cross-disciplinary and interdisciplinary work, as the bounded understanding of a single discipline falls far short of the broad and deep perspective that museums require to fulfill their societal roles. I exclude connoisseurship in this recommendation, which is "expertise" in the matters of taste and cultural patterns of choice and preference. As fascinating and respectable as this expertise is, the future of museums does not hinge on the discernment of high aesthetic standards.

More important is the systemic obstacle to legitimizing scholarly work in the museum world. There are no external rewards there, in contrast to universities where scholarship is still the *sine qua non* of recognition and advancement. It may be cold comfort for the museum scholar-practitioner, but the reward is inherent in the work and lies in enhancing the power and substance of the vision and purpose, as well as the overall effectiveness of the museum. There may be no promotions and certainly no tenure, as in the academic world, but the result will be a sounder, more intelligent museum.

The "No People"

I wrote earlier about negative people and the inevitable negativity that is present in even the well-led museums.[41] As difficult as it feels, this negativity has its merits in counteracting complacency and challenging conventional wisdom. Although the negative voices are usually the loudest, it is important to acknowledge that skepticism and questioning are integral parts of a well-functioning museum. The essential task lies in continually determining whether the negativism is self-serving or of benefit to the organization.

The role and meaning of "No People" in organizations was examined in a recent book and the implications for the organizational culture of museums are salutary.[42] The No People are those individuals in organizations who know when leaders and managers need to hear "no," especially when they are most likely to ignore their advice. In short, No People have no interest in quiet compliance. They are not people who simply say "no"; rather they are adept at providing timely and critical guidance to leaders and managers. Bruce Avolio, the author of *The No People*, notes that it is incumbent upon all organizations to nurture No People to ensure that leaders are challenged, and that the best decisions are made in the best interests of the organization.[43]

The obvious question for any museum worker is "why would you tell your director what you really think and risk losing your job and perhaps career?" This risk explains why so many staff are what Avolio calls the "Yes People," those individuals who are comfortable telling their leaders how right they are about what they are doing, whether or not this is true. Overcoming this potentially lethal conformity requires that staff feel safe to identify problems and opportunities, and are recognized and rewarded for doing so. This kind of behaviour has been called "leading up" (as opposed to the top-down leadership culture) and is not what subordinates are supposed to do in a hierarchical structure.

Typically, it is the lone CEO and his or her close associates who are all-knowing. Nonetheless, both No People and leading up are key ingredients in organizational adaptation, resilience, and creativity. Research reveals that leaders who encourage their followers to become No People tended to lead the most productive research and development teams in terms of innovative outcomes.[44] In order to do this, museums must be made safe for challenging authority and leading up. There are ways to create this work environment and thereby strengthen the overall effectiveness of museum management.

One of the most important means of creating this work environment is for leaders and managers to model the appropriate behaviour – they have to model what they expect to develop in others. Leaders and managers at all levels must demonstrate their willingness to "take the no position when it is appropriate and when it serves the needs and goals of the organization."[45] In addition to this key requirement, a transparent and safe work environment requires some clear standards of moral and ethical conduct, similar to the management principles that Glenbow installed as part of its strategic plan.[46]

It is also most important that leaders do not prioritize their needs ahead of their staff, and that they listen deeply to what people are saying and encourage them to challenge orthodoxy. They must also be attuned to the needs and interests of their communities, which is a particular challenge for many museum directors who are often less connected with the public. Last, leaders must be as open and transparent as they can be and, when it is impossible to do so, explain why.[47]

Nurturing an organizational culture that allows No People may seem idealistic or impractical, but it is essential in unlocking the collective intelligence of the museum staff. David Bohm, the physicist, writes that human beings have an innate capacity for collective intelligence, based on dialogue.[48] Dialogue does not require that people agree with one another, but rather allows people to participate in a pool of shared meaning that can lead to aligned action. No People are essential to finding out what is really happening in a difficult or changing situation. Further, dissension and disobedience are essential to examining ideas, initiatives, and unresolved difficulties, although many leaders do not want to talk about these issues. Thus they reduce their collective ability to learn, adapt, and evolve.

Sustainability is multidimensional

Greening the museum

The question of sustainability is perhaps the most vexing management question for contemporary museum leaders and managers – will the organization survive and prosper over the long term? Initially, sustainability centred on "green" work practices – reducing utility costs, reducing wastage, building more efficient buildings, and generally "reducing, reusing and recycling." This sense of a greater responsibility for the environment now has a foothold in the museum world, as exemplified by the following definition in *Wikipedia*:

> Green museums strive to help people become more conscious of their world, its limitations, and how their actions affect it. The goal is to create positive change by encouraging people to make sustainable choices in their daily lives. They use their position as community-centered institutions to create a culture of sustainability.[49]

There is also the Green Museum Initiative, started by the California Association of Museums, USA.[50] They have initiated the Green Museums Accord, which consists of various principles, including assessing the environmental impact and sustainable alternatives to museum projects; measuring the museum's ecological footprint; undertaking programs to educate colleagues and visitors about sustainable museum practices, and publicly declaring participation in greening your museum as part of the Green Museums Accord. All museums, not just those in California, are invited to take the pledge, which requires the endorsement of the museum's CEO or executive director, or a board resolution.

The extent to which museums are embracing a greater sense of responsibility in their work practices is impossible to tally, but I suspect it is not unlike the bell curve that characterizes any kind of change. On one end is the small percentage of people who are still complaining that the Protestant Reformation happened; on the other end of the curve are those committed and inspired by change and new ways of working. In the middle of the curve are the majority of people who are the "show me's" – waiting to see what will happen.

Nonetheless, there appears to be a critical mass of environmental consciousness emerging, with the Association of Science and Technology Centers (600 members in over 40 countries) raising awareness about global warming and the importance of the Polar Regions. In addition, the American Association of Museums has established a Professional Committee for Green Museums for dialogue, data sharing, and networking; the Canadian Museums Association has developed *An Interactive Sustainable Development Guide for Canada's Museums*, and the United Kingdom's Museums Association has initiated an active dialogue and discussion to encourage museums to think about sustainability. All of these efforts are laudable and essential, and it is hoped that museum management, especially in profligate North America, will rapidly move to reduce the collective environmental impacts of museum work. The impact of changing exhibits and de-installation alone is severe, with an unconscionable amount of materials and supplies still ending up in landfills.

Beyond green

Greening the museum, however, is not sufficient, even if museums are able to reduce their consumption to sustainable levels. Museum sustainability is actually a multifaceted undertaking and this complexity was examined in an excellent article by Alan J. Friedman.[51] Some summary comments are in order here, as Friedman's clear analysis is of benefit for anyone seeking a deeper understanding of what sustainability actually means – it is not unidimensional. Friedman identifies three dimensions of sustainability: financial, intellectual, and social, with the financial being the most obvious threat to long-term well-being. I will not dwell on the financial here, both because the cause and effect is obvious and the unrelenting discussion of museums and money has already consumed enough print and conversation. Friedman's contribution lies in identifying both intellectual and social sustainability as being of equal importance, considerations that are persistently overlooked in the rush to pay the bills. Yet, all three of these dimensions are intimately related and success in one can create a virtuous circle for the benefit of all.

Intellectual sustainability "involves the institution's immersion in the field it treats."[52] Are the staff staying current in the field and contributing to its advancement, both museologically and with respect to related disciplines? This commitment has been under siege for decades in museums, with the loss of curatorial positions, the rapid growth of fundraising departments, low or no attendance at professional meetings, and the diminishment or demise of research. Without a commitment to the intellectual core of a museum (which is after all, a knowledge-based institution), museums are at risk and many have now become impresarios – handling exhibitions and events from elsewhere to generate revenues. Clearly this is necessary for both business and programming reasons, but not to the exclusion of the museum's own intellectual capital and unique resources. It is also important to note that a commitment to the intellectual core of a museum does not mean adherence to narrow, disciplinary allegiances, but rather a commitment to knowledge in the service of understanding, wisdom, and mindfulness. In short, a discipline-based focus must be a strategy in the service of societal well-being.[53]

Of particular interest to me is Friedman's idea of social sustainability, with its focus on the "perceptions of the broader community about the institution, and how strongly that community supports the organization, in good times and bad."[54] Friedman concedes that social sustainability is the most difficult to measure, because it involves the perceptions of the broader community about the museum. At the heart of social sustainability is the recognition of interdependence, and the lack of interdependent relationships among most museums and their communities is an increasing liability. Being valued for ancillary educational offerings and often ersatz entertainment is no longer sufficient to ensure social sustainability. There are now myriad opportunities for museums to more closely align with the issues and aspirations of their communities, and embed themselves as advocates, collaborators, and problem solvers. Achieving this heightened sense of interdependence is a brave new world for museums and it must become a strategic priority.

Notes

1 S.E. Weil, "Rethinking the Museum: An Emerging New Paradigm," in G. Anderson (ed.), *Reinventing the Museum*, Walnut Creek, CA: Altamira Press, 2004, pp. 74–79.

2 T.S. Kuhn, *The Structure of Scientific Revolutions*, Chicago and London: The University of Chicago Press, 1962.

3 J. Kusel and L.P. Fortmann, "What is Community Well-Being?" in J. Kusel and L. Fortman (eds), *Well-being in Forest-Dependent Communities* (Volume I), Berkeley, CA: Forest and Rangeland Resources Assessment Program and California Department of Forestry and Fire Protection, 1991, pp. 1–45.

4 The Pinky Show, *YouTube* video entitled "The Creation of Value: Meditations on the Logic of Museums and Other Coercive Institutions," 2008. Available online at: http://www.youtube.com/watch?v=gaFbmuEUdwI.

5 R. Fritz, *The Path of Least Resistance*, New York: Ballantine Books, 1989, pp. 31–46.

6 R.R. Janes, *Museums in a Troubled World: Renewal, Irrelevance or Collapse?* London and New York: Routledge, 2009, pp. 57–93.

7 "Great Lies to Tell about Museums," themed conference session, Museums Association Conference 2020, November 9, 2012. Available online at: http://www.museum sassociation. org/museums2020/conference-2012.

8 W. Berry, *Life Is a Miracle*, Berkeley, CA: Counterpoint, 2000, p. 127.
9 M. Morris, "A More Perfect Union: Museums Merge, Grow Stronger," *Museum Magazine*, July–August, 2012.
10 Janes, *Museums in a Troubled World*, pp. 15–16.
11 British Columbia Museums Association, *Revenue Generation (Creating Profit Centres)*, BCMA Best Practices Module, British Columbia Museums Association, Victoria, BC. Available online at: http://www.museumsassn.bc.ca/Images/Best%20Practices%20 Modules%202/ Revenue%20Generation%20FINAL.pdf.
12 Hill Strategies Research, Inc. "Heritage Institutions 2009," *Arts Research Monitor* (10/4), October, 2011. Available online at: http://www.artsresearchmonitor.com/article_ details. php?artUID=50706.
13 American Association of Museums, "Museums and the American Economy in 2011: A Report from the American Association of Museums (April 2012)," Washington, DC. Available online at: http://www.aam-us.org/upload/ACME12-final.pdf.
14 Philip Katz, email, June 15, 2012.
15 Janes, *Museums in a Troubled World*, pp. 62–66.
16 R. Farson, *Management of the Absurd: Paradoxes in Leadership*, New York: Simon & Schuster, 1996, p. 144.
17 J. Spalding, "Down with Con Art Bring Back Real Art." Available online at: http:// www. julianspalding.net.
18 W. Phillips, "The Three Agendas," *Management Briefing*. REX Roundtables for Executives 2012. See RexRoundtables.com.
19 D. Peacock, "Complexity, Conversation and Change: Learning How Organizations Change." In R.R. Janes, *Museums and the Paradox of Change: A Case Study in Urgent Adaptation*, London and New York: Routledge, 2013, pp. 235–245
20 J.Q. Anderson and L. Rainie, "Millennials Will Benefit *and* Suffer Due to Their Hyperconnected Lives," Pew Internet, Pew Research Center's Internet & American Life Project, Washington, DC, February 29, 2012, pp. 3–5. Available online at: http://pew internet.org/~/media//Files/Reports/2012/PIP_Future_of_Internet_2012_Young_ brains_PDF.pdf.
21 Canadian Museums Association, *Annual Report 2011*, "Audited Financial Statements for the Year Ended December 31, 2011," Ottawa, Canada: Canadian Museums Association, 2011, p. 27.
22 American Association of Museums, *The Museum Workforce in the United States (2009)*, report, Washington, DC. Available online at: http://futureofmuseums.org/reading/ loader.cfm?csModule=security/getfile&pageid=2313.
23 B. McKenzie, Next after MuseumNext, *The Learning Planet Blog*. Available online at: http:// the learningplanet.wordpress.com/2012/05/28/next-after-museumnext/ #commentsBridget McKenzie-Home blog.
24 B.S. Frey and L. Steiner, "Pay As You Go: A New Proposal for Museum Pricing," *Museum Management and Curatorship* (27/3), August, 2012.
25 "Opinion: Arts Managers Should Emulate Detroit Museum," *Philanthropy Today, The Chronicle of Philanthropy*, August 17, 2012, Available online at: http://philanthropy.com/ blogs/philanthropytoday/opinion-arts-managers-should-emulate-detroit-museum/52275.
26 M. Walhimer, "Museums Are for the Rich," MuseumPlanning blog. Available online at: http://museumplanner.org/museums-are-for-the rich/?goback=%2Egde_36036_ member_ 120583694.
27 M. Knelman, "How CEO Plans to Guide ROM into Its Second Century," August 2, 2012, *thestar.com*. Available online at: http://www.thestar.com/entertainment/onstage/ article/1236039-how-ceo-plans-to-guide-rom-into-its-second-century.

28 D. Dean, "Museums as Conflict Zones: The Canadian War Museum and Bomber Command," *Museum and Society* (7/1), March, 2009, 1–15.

29 Canada Science and Technology Museum, "Sex: A Tell-all Exhibition." Available online at: http://www.sciencetech.technomuses.ca/english/whatson/2012-sex-a-tell-all-exhibition. cfm. See also B. Kay: "Ottawa Sex Exhibition Is an Issue of Waste, Not Prudery." *National Post*, May 20, 2012. Available online at: http://fullcomment. nationalpost.com/2012/05/20/ barbara-kay-ottawa-sexhibition-is-an-issue-of-waste-not-prudery/.

30 As an example of this, see R. Sandell and E. Nightingale, *Museums, Equality and Social Justice*, London and New York: Routledge, 2012, for new research on the politics of identity and the potential of museums and galleries to contribute to more equitable, fair, and just societies.

31 Janes, *Museums in a Troubled World*, pp. 78–79.

32 J.A. Davis, "Putting Museum Studies to Work," *Museum Management and Curatorship* (26/5), December, 2011, 459–479.

33 "Principles," in *A New Decade of Distinction: Glenbow's Corporate and Strategic Plans 1992–1997*, Calgary: Glenbow Museum, p. 4 (compiled by R.R. Janes).

34 "Principles," p. 4.

35 "Principles," p. 4.

36 "Principles," p. 4.

37 "Principles," p. 4.

38 "Principles," p. 4.

39 "Principles," p. 4.

40 M.L. Semmel, "Reflections on Museums and Change, 2012." In R.R. Janes, *Museums and the Paradox of Change: A Case Study in Urgent Adaptation*, London and New York: Routledge, 2013, pp. 258–269.

41 Janes, *Museums in a Troubled World*, pp. 149–150.

42 B.J. Avolio, *The No People: Tribal Tales of Organizational Cliff Dwellers*, Charlotte, NC: Information Age Publishing, 2011.

43 Avolio, *The No People*, pp. 2–14.

44 Avolio, *The No People*, p. 21.

45 Avolio, *The No People*, p. 40.

46 Avolio, *The No People*, p. 66.

47 R.R. Janes, *Museums and the Paradox of Change: A Case Study in Urgent Adaptation*, London and New York: Routledge, 2013, 16–17

48 David Bohm in J. Jaworski, *Synchronicity*, San Francisco: Bennett-Koehler Publishers, 1998, pp. 109–112.

49 "Green Museums," in *Wikipedia*. Available online at: http://en.wikipedia.org/wiki/Green_museum.

50 The Green Museums Initiative. Available online at: http://www.calmuseums.info/gmi/AboutGMI.html.

51 A.J. Friedman, "The Great Sustainability Challenge: How Visitor Studies Can Save Cultural Institutions in the 21st Century," *Visitor Studies* (10/1), April, 2007, 3–12.

52 Friedman, "The Great Sustainability Challenge," 5.

53 I am indebted to Douglas Worts for his comments on the role of academic disciplines and museum missions. Personal communication, August 8, 2012.

54 Friedman, "The Great Sustainability Challenge," 8.

PART 3

Museums without borders
Social responsibility

Freedom in both science and art probably depends upon enlarging the context of our work, increasing (rather than decreasing) the number of considerations we allow to bear upon it. This is because the ultimate context of our work is the world, which is always larger than the context of our thought.

(Wendell Berry 2001: 84)

INTRODUCTION

The world's issues and challenges have changed dramatically since the organizational upheaval at Glenbow in the last decade of the twentieth century. The erosion of public funding was the overarching concern for Canadian museums in the 1990s and led to a preoccupation with visitor numbers, high-profile exhibitions, and burgeoning marketing departments to increase earned revenues. The pressures on all museums now reach far beyond money and popularity to include the recognition of societal needs and issues – ranging from the onset of climate change to social justice. In Wendell Berry's words on the previous page, this means "enlarging the context of our work" and "increasing the number of considerations we allow to bear upon it." As deeply trusted, social institutions in civil society, museums are essential in fostering public support for decisive action to address these topical issues. Among these pressing issues are climate change, water scarcity, overpopulation, habitat destruction, loss of topsoil, rising toxin levels, and increasing financial inequality.

The chapters in this part are concerned with the museum's unique role and potential in stewarding a more intelligent, altruistic, and conscious future for themselves and their communities. Although the germ of this awareness may have been with me from the outset of my museum work, "the light bulb may appear over your head . . . but it may be awhile before it actually goes on" (Conroy 1988: 68). It was the enormous investment of time, energy, and emotion required to rethink Glenbow that "turned on the light" for me. As this work increased in intensity and complexity, a persistent question haunted me – "to what end?"

Collections, exhibitions, education, and entertainment were no longer adequate reasons to justify the commitment to change. These activities were not the ends, but the means to the end. In short, *why* were we doing what we were doing?

FIGURE 7   Liberate Tate stages a protest at Tate Britain (2011). The group aims to end the Tate's corporate sponsorship with British Petroleum. © Amy Scaife/Corbis.

The question of *why* lies at the heart of Postman's argument with society (see the epigraph of this book). The question of *why* also lies at the heart of "museums without borders" – museums that have enlarged the context of their work to include a fine sense of their social responsibilities. The question of *why* must be asked relentlessly.

It is clear to me, in thinking about the uncertain future of museums in a world beset by imponderable challenges, that hope is an essential ingredient in any successful outcome for museums, yet it is insufficient on its own. Holding on to hope can rob one of the present moment and divert attention from what needs to be done (Steinberg 2008: 136). My interest is in hope and intention, rather than in hoping that the challenges will resolve themselves (Janes 2014: 408). This combination of hope and intention has been called Active Hope and it has been defined as a practice – it is something we *do* rather than *have* (Macy and Johnstone 2102: 3). In short, "we choose what we aim to bring about, act for, or express."

The pursuit of socially responsible museum work also has a moral dimension – a relatively new topic in the museum field (Marstine 2011). William James, the American philosopher and psychologist, wrote about the morally significant life and noted that such a life "is organized around a self-imposed, heroic ideal and is pursued through endurance, courage, fidelity and struggle" (Brooks 2014). Is it not possible, and desirable, for museums to adopt a perspective similar to that of the "morally significant life," in their quest to provide substantive and meaningful service above and beyond education and entertainment? Cannot museums also be "for all seasons," in the manner in which Sir Thomas More, the sixteenth-century Chancellor of England, was described. He was known as the ultimate man of conscience who "remained true to himself and his beliefs while adapting to all circumstances and times . . ." (Wikipedia 2014).

There is no doubt that moral considerations pervade much of museum work, although there has never been much pressure in the museum community to shoulder such weighty matters. The meaning of social ecology – that social and environmental issues are intertwined and both must be considered simultaneously – has never lost its meaning and relevance, however. This, too, is a moral issue. The ability of museums to link both nature and culture in their work, whether or not they are natural history or science museums, is an unheralded gift for museums. Citizens are crying out for enlightened leadership from public institutions to address the issues that are relevant to their lives, to their civic responsibilities, and to their place in the biosphere – in a manner that transcends ideology, political partisanship, and corporate malfeasance. Museums of all kinds are untapped and untested sources of ideas, knowledge, and memory, and are uniquely placed to foster individual and community participation in the quest for greater awareness and workable solutions to global problems.

The writings in this chapter are an exploration of what socially responsible engagement for museums means, as well as how it might be achieved, including its moral and pragmatic dimensions. I use the word "engagement" with some hesitation, however, as it has been appropriated by marketplace parlance and is synonymous in the minds of many practitioners with increasing audience size, popularity, and revenues. Engagement has suffered the same abuse as the word "sustainability" – it has lost its power of reference and precision, and is commonly used for narrower, materialistic purposes. Perhaps the same fate will befall "social responsibility," but so far it remains outside the circle of mainstream museum dialogue and has avoided becoming a slogan or abstraction. I hope that the study of socially responsible museums becomes as popular as visitor studies, as it may then receive sufficient attention to realize its potential.

The first chapter, "What Will Communities Need and Want from Museums in the Future?" was the result of a rare opportunity to return to Glenbow after my departure to address the senior staff and the Board of Governors. I identify various issues that were only dimly perceived by the museum community at that time – ranging from the threat of continuous economic growth to the newly identified "Cultural Creatives" demographic. In the next chapter, "Exploring Stewardship," the continuing assault on the biosphere is described and analyzed (from SUVs, or sport utility vehicles, to language loss), with the conclusion that museums have a fundamental role to play as planetary stewards. The seeds of my 2009 book, *Museums in a Troubled World*, germinated in this keynote address. The third chapter is the Introduction to our book *Looking Reality in the Eye* (co-edited with the late Gerald T. Conaty) wherein we assembled nine original case studies of socially responsible museum work and introduced a set of foundational values to guide progressive museum work. This book was seminal for me, as we concluded that socially responsible museum work is a prerequisite for long-term sustainability.

My continuing alarm with the intrusion of marketplace ideology is examined in the fourth chapter, "Museums, Corporatism and the Civil Society," and includes a critical overview of the consequences of corporatism for museum affairs. I also refine my earlier writing about museums as civil society organizations (Janes 1997: 232–233; 254–258), and discuss in detail the ability of museums to generate social capital. The next chapter, "Museums: Stewards or Spectators?," is a keynote address that builds on *Museums in a Troubled World* – noting that global challenges have worsened since 2009. I discuss the meaning and importance of organizational resilience as an antidote, and the need for experimentation to foster resilience in museums. Various inspiring examples of successful innovation from other sectors are included.

The last chapter is a collaboration with a Danish colleague who wished to consider the pressures of the marketplace on Nordic museums, and how my work might assist with the complexities of collaboration between museums and business. I have included "What Are Museums For? – Revisiting 'Museums in a Troubled World'" because it ponders museums from an international and informed business perspective. In summary, if social responsibility can be seen as the will and capacity to solve public problems, it is my hope that it will also serve as an inspired source of renewal and sustainability for all museums – especially as our local, national, and global challenges deepen.

References

Berry, W. (2001) *Life Is a Miracle: An Essay against Modern Superstition*, Berkeley, CA: Counterpoint, 2001.

Brooks, D. (2014) "Becoming a Real Person." *The New York Times*, September 8. http://www.nytimes.com/2014/09/09/opinion/david-brooks-becoming-a-real-person.html?rref=opinion&module=.

Conroy, F. (1988) "Think About It – Ways We Know and Don't," *Harper's Magazine*, 227 (1662): 68–70.

Janes, R. R. (1997) *Museums and the Paradox of Change: A Case Study in Urgent Adaptation*, Calgary, Canada: Glenbow Museum and the University of Calgary Press.

—— (2014) "Museums for all Seasons," Museum *Management and Curatorship*, 29 (5): 403–411. Available online: http://dx.doi.org/10.1080/09647775.2014.967109.

Macy, J. and Johnstone, C. (2012) *Active Hope: How to Face the Mess We're in without Going Crazy*, Novato, CA: New World Library.

Marstine, J. (2011) *The Routledge Companion to Museum Ethics: Redefining Ethics for the Twenty-First-Century Museum*, London and New York: Routledge.

Steinberg, E. (ed.) (2008) *The Pocket Pema Chodron*, Boston and London: Shambala Publications, Inc.

Wikipedia (2014) "Sir Thomas More – A Man for All Seasons." Available online: http://en.wikipedia.org/wiki/A_Man_for_All_Seasons.

13

WHAT WILL COMMUNITIES NEED AND WANT FROM MUSEUMS IN THE FUTURE?*

Introduction

I want to thank Glenbow's Strategy Group [senior management team] for inviting me to participate in this important discussion. I am mindful of my unusual position at this time, having just resigned as Glenbow's President and CEO for the past 10 years, and I feel privileged to be called back as a participant. I called this an important discussion for the simple fact that there is no time like the present to challenge all the assumptions underlying current success, and begin with new questions which can lead to ideas and possibilities (Handy 1994: 49–63). Admittedly, this is paradoxical, for it requires change at a time when most of the messages coming through are that everything is pretty good.

The other paradox is that boards and executives who are obsessed with change, or stability, will eventually harm or ruin their organizations (Mintzberg 1987: 75). The lesson here is to pay attention to how much change and when, because determining when your organization is ready for a strategic revolution defies any formula.

One of the biggest obstacles to organizational change is our inborn tendency to build on strengths and adapt to the existing environment, becoming better and better at what we are already doing well. My purpose today is to go beyond the existing environment, and attempt to identify some issues in our community that may be only dimly perceived by museum staff and boards. For my presentation today, I have defined community in its broadest sense to include museum workers, citizens, and consumers.

---

*Source: Robert R. Janes, presentation prepared for the Glenbow Museum's Roundtable Meeting on the Museum of the Future, The Banff Centre, Banff, Alberta, Canada, March 4–6, 2000. This meeting included the Chair of Glenbow's Board of Governors, Glenbow's new CEO, and Glenbow's senior managers (The Strategy Group). References have been updated.

Quality of life versus economic growth

My first issue is concerned with the quality of life versus economic growth – perhaps best summed up by the question, "can less mean more?" All of us understand that, as long as we base our economy on private, corporate enterprise, we need growth in order to have a healthy economy. There is good reason to believe, however, that limitless growth is creating some genuine and profound dilemmas, including the unthinking consumption of finite natural resources, damage to the natural environment, and growing disillusionment with buying "stuff" as the key to universal happiness.

Nonetheless, our recent experience has shown quite clearly and painfully that economic growth is an economic necessity. If there are limits to economic growth, and growth is in conflict with other aspects of the quality of life, we are in a genuine dilemma. We are faced with a poverty of thought, not to mention action (Robinson 1984: 58). What is the role of a major multidisciplinary museum like Glenbow in addressing this poverty of thought and action? When will our community demand some sort of forum for the exploration and understanding of these complex and potentially life-threatening issues? It is important to note that museums, unlike business and government, have no particular agenda to promote. Indeed, do museums have any right or responsibility at all to get involved in such matters? Deliberately deciding to act, or not to act, would seem to be preferable to indifference.

The Cultural Creatives

My second topic has to do with the identification of a new demographic group in the United States called the Cultural Creatives (Ray 1996). This group has been called something big and new in American history, and a reason to have faith in the future. Who are these people and what do they value? To begin with, they tend to be middle or upper middle class, and there are 50% more women than men among them. There are roughly 44 million of them in the United States, and generally speaking, the Cultural Creatives are readers and listeners, not TV watchers. They are aggressive consumers of culture and also producers of culture.

Of particular interest to the museum business is the fact that the Cultural Creatives apparently invented the term authenticity as consumers understand it, leading the rebellion against things that are fake, poorly made, or throwaway (Ray 1996: 33). Of equal interest is the Cultural Creative as the prototypical consumer of the experience industry, always in search of an intense and enlightening experience, rather than a thing. They are also deeply committed to sustainable ecology and favour limits to growth.

Assuming that there are direct parallels between the United States and Canada, I think we can safely assume that the Cultural Creatives are also among us. I also think that there are probably a number of them in this room. How will the mainstream museum address the needs and interests of this growing segment of our community, which rejects the hedonism, materialism, and cynicism of modern media, consumer, and business culture? Can the museum business ignore the Cultural Creatives, especially when they seem to embody what are best called transformational values on a large scale?

The museum and the community

My third issue stems from the thinking of Milenko Matanovic (1991) and centers on the role of the museum in the community. Matanovic, who is the president of a non-profit organization dedicated to exploring connections between art, culture, and nature, notes that churches once functioned as gathering places where people of different classes, backgrounds, and ideologies could come together in one place at one time. Much of this has been replaced by information technology, eliminating the need for face-to-face encounters. Matanovic sees this as a threat to democracy, for the success of democracy, in his view, rests on the relationship between individuals and their community.

He sees a need for community forums where basic questions can be raised; where people have the opportunity to speak about their identity as a community; about the unique character they wish to preserve; about the changes that ought to happen in their lives; and about the visions they wish to realize. Matanovic argues that a deliberate and conscious imaging of the future is vital for the health of a culture. In short, he believes that the future must be talked about. In our current social system, there is little patience for these questions. Do museums, as social institutions, have a responsibility and an opportunity to play an active role in the health of the civil society, by offering time, space, and resources to steward the wisdom of our citizens? How can this be done?

The topics I have just described – economic growth, the Cultural Creatives, and the role of the museum in community building – are decidedly important issues. I suppose that they are so large and complex that museums could safely ignore them. But that might mean a lost opportunity.

Fortunately, there are also issues of less dramatic scope, several of which I now want to mention. They differ from the previous ones in being more about the business of museums, and how that business is conducted. Although some might argue that these are internal concerns and best left out of a discussion about community, I have always believed that the manner in which a museum does its work – meaning how it is organized, the interplay of leadership and management, and the nature of its governing authority – is absolutely fundamental to its success or failure as a human enterprise.

Executive leadership

One of the key ingredients in how a museum does its work is leadership, and there is some surprising, new information about leadership in museums. In a recent doctoral study (Suchy 1999) of 75 museum directors in Australia, the United States, Canada, and Britain, Shereen Suchy discovered that emotional intelligence was the primary competency for museum leadership in the 1990s. Emotional intelligence includes self-awareness, mood management, motivation, empathy, and social skills. This doesn't mean that hard skills, such as budget analysis and organizational restructuring, are not important, but recent research suggests that rational/logical thought contributes about 20% of life success, and emotional intelligence makes up the other 80%.

This research also indicates that museums are potentially significant generators of social capital in a market economy (Suchy 2004: 10–11). Among other things, social capital consists of trust and respectful relationships. If museums are creators of social capital, and are one of the few remaining organizations to provide the public an opportunity as stakeholders in their cultural heritage, what can the public reasonably expect from museums in the future? There are at least four things they can expect, all of which concern leadership (Suchy 2004: xviii).

1. First, museum leaders must represent the organization both internally and externally.
2. Second, leaders must create a work context where people can give their best. This means an increasingly self-managed work environment.
3. Third, leaders must act as ethical entrepreneurs to ensure the organization's future.
4. Leaders must develop trusting relationships with internal stakeholders (staff, volunteers, and Boards), as well as external stakeholders including the public, sponsors, and supporters of every description.

Furthermore, I submit that these four requirements are also the responsibility of *all* senior executives, as well as the leadership of the boards of directors.

Business literacy

One of the hard skills that is becoming vitally important for museum executives is the ability to reframe the museum's role from a custodian of cultural property to more of a customer service role (Suchy 2004: 18). This is not an either/or proposition, however, as both responsibilities must be accommodated in some sort of intelligent balance. My fifth topic today is the need for business literacy within the museum culture, something which is no easy task under any circumstances.

In brief, business literacy in museums means the staff's ability to fully understand how the business operates (Morris 1998: 4). If staff understand the "big picture" of their museum (the situation as a whole), they will assume a greater investment in the outcome. For the internal community of museum workers, this means they will need full budget information and help on how to understand it, as well as full knowledge of all the strategic priorities. This so-called open book management will become increasingly important as the pressure to enhance financial self-sufficiency mounts. Business literacy is essential to both individual and organizational accountability.

This is where the broader community also has some legitimate interests and desires. There may come a time when the tax-paying public might legitimately ask why there are so many museums, with many of them collecting identical objects. Furthermore, they might ask why can't museums behave like many archives do that define their collecting territory, rationalize their collections among institutions, and avoid duplication? Why should the possessiveness and insularity of collecting museums be allowed to persist in the face of ever-increasing collection management costs?

I'm not suggesting that connoisseurship become the focus – where only the very best is collected. Rather than waiting for this to become a public issue, might it be useful to start thinking now about cooperative models and economies of scale with respect to collecting and collections? Any commitment to business literacy would seem to require this.

Branding, knowledge, and consumption

I will conclude my remarks with a sixth and final issue – this one about a Canadian museum that is currently redefining itself in terms of the needs and wants of its communities. Unfortunately, this museum cannot be named, as I have been privy to their planning documents on a confidential basis only. Their new plan begins with the observation that they are a traditional "brand" at a crossroads at which "without a fundamental, systemic branding discipline and process, it risks being swept into consumer irrelevance by high velocity change in the way that culture, information and entertainment are being demanded, supplied and consumed in the marketplace" (Anonymous 1999: 4).

To address this imminent crisis, this museum has employed an international marketing firm and the first step in their process is a "Consumer Opportunity Assessment." This assessment will be the foundation of their new master plan, which will articulate what needs to be done to get from the present to an ideal future. Their new focus is on "experience marketing." I'm not aware of any other museums, at least in Canada, which have adopted such a disciplined and focused approach to brand management. In fact, this museum is basing its future on the principles and best practices of branding, straight from the marketplace.

There is no doubt that many museum people will find both the intent and the language of this approach (jargon ridden as it is) to be alarming, offensive, and perhaps unacceptable. Why should a knowledge-based institution, committed to sophisti-cated learning, adopt the standards of a well-managed, commercial brand? Such a reaction is inappropriate, however, when you consider the purpose behind this initiative. Not only does this museum want to substantially increase its audiences and earned revenues, but they are also equally concerned with changing lives – including the provision of long-lasting memories and personal meaning for their audiences. They want to become a destination of joy and wonder, rather than a duty.

I have devoted more time to this topic than the other five, for the simple reason that it addresses the very purpose and meaning of museums. Museums can produce compelling experiences to the extent that they have access to outstanding collections and the knowledge that accompanies them. If museums are to retain and grow their special niche, they must also continue to provide the authenticity, integrity, quality, and value which the public expects. These expectations will undoubtedly increase, if the alienation with consumer culture moves beyond the Cultural Creatives into the broader society.

The challenge for museums is to ensure that there are sufficient material and intellectual resources within the organization to support the research and development required to create the compelling products and services. In fact, there appears to be an opposite trend. More and more museums and galleries seem to be adopting the role of impresario – borrowing and showing collections and blockbuster exhibitions from elsewhere. Although some of this is essential, the danger lies in it becoming the sole preoccupation. If so, it might be better to privatize the museum and make it a for-profit enterprise. Why spend money on public collections and infrastructure if they are not used?

Optimistically, it could be that museums, by both borrowing and producing, will develop a new kind of consumption that is more appropriate for the twenty-first century and much less impactful – that is, the consumption of knowledge and experience, rather than "stuff." Museums are unique in their ability to do this, and sophisticated marketing is essential. Our communities expect no less.

Conclusions

In conclusion, the six topics or issues that I have presented today range from the manageable to the imponderable and all of them are now embedded, to a greater or lesser extent, in the communities we serve. It is tempting to want to focus on one or two of these issues, when in fact all of them are intimately interrelated. They are like a continuous sequence in a light spectrum – not easily divided up.

The only real antidote to the unnerving effects of such complexity and incoherence is integrity (Wheatley and Kellner-Rogers 1996: 60), which means knowing who you are and having a fine sense of one's obligations. For museums, this means an ability to be guided by a strong sense of one's competencies as an organization, so that as the museum changes, it does so by referring to *itself* – meaning the skills, tradition, values, and aspirations that guide its operations (Wheatley 1994: 94, 145–147). Finally, it may be comforting to remember that it is "perhaps those problems that we will never resolve that rightly claim the lion's share of our energies . . ." (Conroy 1988: 70).

References

Conroy, Frank 1988 Think About It – Ways We Know and Don't. *Harper's Magazine*, Vol. 277, No. 1662, pp. 68–70.

Handy, Charles 1994 *The Age of Paradox*, Harvard Business School Press, Boston.

Matanovic, Milenko 1991 An Interview with Milenko Matanovic, by Greg Powell. In *Humanities Today*. See also: http://pomegranatecenter.org/milenko-matanovics-resume/.

Mintzberg, Henry 1987 Crafting Strategy. *Harvard Business Review*, July–August, pp. 66–75.

Morris, Martha 1998 Organizational Health. *NEW Standard*, Vol. 1, No. 3, pp. 1–5. American Association of Museums, Washington, D.C.

Ray, Paul H. 1996 The Integral Cultural Survey: A Study of the Emergence of Transformational Values in America. Institute of Noetic Sciences, Sausalito, California.

Robinson, Lukin 1984 Is Economic Growth an Economic Necessity? In *Quality of Life vs. Economic Growth: Can Less Mean More?*, pp. 43–70. Edited by John Yardley, Community Seminar No. 4, The Calgary Institute for Humanities, The University of Calgary, Alberta, Canada.

Suchy, Shereen 1999 Museum Directors: First with Passion. Commentary provided by the author via email, January, 2000.

—— 2004 *Leading with Passion: Change Management in the 21st-Century Museum*, AltaMira Press, Walnut Creek, California.

Wheatley, M.J. 1994 *Leadership and the New Science*, Berrett-Koehler Publishers, San Francisco.

Wheatley, M.J. and M. Kellnor-Rogers 1996 *A Simpler Way*, Berrett-Koehler Publishers, San Francisco.

14

EXPLORING STEWARDSHIP*

We are all related.

From a Lakota pipe ceremony (Brown 1989: xiii)

Introduction

The Heritage Forum Planning Committee has given me a significant challenge – to explore the meaning and value of stewardship from a broad perspective. Why the difficulty? To begin with, it seems that no one is writing about stewardship from a holistic perspective, especially in a manner which encompasses all the varied interests of this Heritage Forum. Those who do write about aspects of the subject, whether it be museum collections or nature, seldom, if ever, use the word stewardship. The dictionary definition (Mish 1986: 1157) is also inadequate, as it refers to "the individual's responsibility to manage his life and property with proper regard to the rights of others."

For all these reasons, I have developed my own working definition of stewardship for the purposes of this talk, which is to assume personal responsibility for the long-term care of public resources. Underlying my particular choice of words is Eric Hoffer's (in Postman 1996: 101) observation that "the test of a civilization is in its capacity for maintenance." Care and maintenance are interchangeable from this perspective. I am also aware that the idea of stewardship is not without controversy. The deep ecologists, for example (Woodhouse 1996: 433), reject the view that people should assume stewardship over other life forms and the earth, and they prefer to let nature take its course. That is all I'm going to say about deep ecology, as it makes the very idea of this talk irrelevant.

*Source: Robert R. Janes, keynote presentation for the SaskCulture's Spring Heritage Forum, Saskatoon, Saskatchewan, Canada, May 26, 2001.

To begin, I want to explore some examples of what I believe to be an assault on stewardship, followed by some observations on the strengths we already possess as a committed stewardship community. I will conclude with some thoughts on how we can sharpen our thinking for a more integrated approach to stewardship. I will attempt to do all of this in 35 minutes, being ever mindful of Franklin D. Roosevelt's advice to speakers, which was "Be sincere; be brief; be seated" (Kittrell 1996: 6).

The assault on stewardship

What price failure?

The Globe and Mail newspaper (McArthur 2001: B7) recently reported that the former President and Chief Executive Officer of Laidlaw Inc. received a severance package of CAN\$3.4 million. This was despite the fact that he was the same CEO who expanded the company into health care, and later admitted that this dual focus was a mistake. As a result, he was asked to resign by the Board of Directors and Laidlaw shares, which once traded as high as CAN\$23.40, closed in late April at 25.5 cents. The question is – does multi-million dollar compensation for leading a company astray constitute stewardship?

The most ridiculous vehicle ever

Ford Motor Company entered the "full-size" sport utility vehicle (SUV) market last year with the production of the Ford Excursion (Roberts 2001: 69–75). It is the largest passenger vehicle on the planet, at 5.7 metres long, 2.13 metres high, and weighing 3.63 metric tons. Fuel consumption ranges from 1.57 kilometres per litre on hills, to 3.36 kilometres per litre on the highway, as compared to the Toyota Prius – a gas/electric hybrid car which gets 28.48 kilometres per litre.

How does one account for what has been called "the most ridiculous vehicle ever" (Roberts 2001: 74)? To begin with, all SUVs are exempt from emission controls and fuel-economy requirements because they are considered to be low-production, light trucks, and intended mainly for working people. In fact, SUV gas mileage is so low that their popularity has now dragged the average fuel efficiency for new cars in North America to its lowest point since 1980.

The Excursion also produces 122 metric tons of carbon dioxide during its 199,500 kilometre lifespan, almost three times that of a Honda Civic automobile. By forcing a mere 15% improvement in SUV and light truck gas mileage, the United States could save more oil each year than the projected annual production of the Arctic National Wildlife Refuge (Roberts 2001: 75). This Refuge happens to be the calving ground for Canada's Porcupine Caribou Herd, and the Gwi'chin First Nation of northern Canada have relied on these animals for millennia. Does the production and sale of the Ford Excursion constitute stewardship?

Disappearing languages

Moving from animals to people, it has been estimated that between 10,000 and 15,000 languages once existed simultaneously in the world (Kane 1997: 130–131). Today, only about 6,000 survive, and only about half of these are being learned by children. As a result, about half of these languages are likely to become extinct within the next century.

In North America, children are learning only 38 of the surviving 187 Aboriginal languages. English is now the world's dominate language, with more non-native speakers than native ones. In addition, some 80% of the world's electronically stored information is also in English (Kane 1997: 131). Because languages embody the diversity of human experience, we have now constrained the range of our thinking through the loss of these languages. Does this ever-increasing trend towards linguistic homogenization constitute stewardship?

Loss of the built environment

My next example of the assault on stewardship concerns the built environment. The popular press has been lamenting the aging infrastructure of our National Park System in Canada, especially in Banff National Park – the flagship in the system. Hundreds of millions of dollars are apparently required to upgrade aging park buildings and equipment, and only a fraction of this money is available. In addition, 21% of Canada's built heritage has been lost in one generation, and Parks Canada has no system of monitoring or reporting on the National Historic Sites it does not own (Minister's Round Table 2001). There is no legislation to protect archaeological sites on federal crown land, or underwater. And so on and so on. Does this sound like stewardship to you?

Killing our relatives

My final example of the contemporary assault on stewardship might be considered to be more personal, as it has to do with how we treat our closest living relatives – the primates. This is the order of mammals which includes humans, apes, and monkeys. Nearly half of the 233 known species of non-human primates are now threatened with extinction (Tuxill 1997: 100–101). Our greatest impact on these animals is our practice of taking over their habitat for our own use, in addition to the fact that we are the only primates (with the exception of chimpanzees) who deliberately hunt other primates.

With respect to habitat loss, the negative trends continue to accelerate. Primates aside, the conversion, degradation, and fragmentation of ecosystems continues apace around the world. In many countries, more than half of the original territory has been converted from natural habitat to other uses, much of it irreversibly (Abramovitz 1997: 98–99). I ask my rhetorical question a final time – do these trends constitute stewardship?

Diagnosing the assault

At the risk of being repetitive, I hope that the foregoing pattern is clear. Stewardship, be it cultural heritage, the built environment, or nature, is continuously under siege. Unfortunately, there is no conspiracy on which to blame these alarming developments. The engineers at Ford, for example, did not set about to destroy the Arctic National Wildlife Refuge. No, the problem is much deeper and more insidious, because the problem is all of us and our society (Handy 1997: 28). Any thinking person is beginning to discover that working harder and buying more stuff are not necessarily leading to what we had hoped for. Many of us have now entered that deeply perplexing realm of being in conflict with our own sense of values and principles, and we are losing our sense of stewardship. I now want to speculate on how this might have come to pass.

Reductionism

Perhaps the most insidious factor in our muddled thinking is our propensity for reductionism. We come by this habit honestly, as reductionism was one of the Enlightenment's gifts to the development of science. At its best, reductionist thinking is the cutting edge of science – "the search strategy employed to find points of entry into otherwise impenetrably complex systems" (Wilson 1998: 54). At its worst, reductionism is oversimplification, grounded in the belief that "complex wholes and their properties are less real than their constituents, and that the simplest part of something is the most real." Put another way, "the whole is not greater than the sum of its parts" (Woodhouse 1996: 11).

This in turn leads to fragmented thinking and the assumption that things are understandable in isolation from their contexts (Woodhouse 1996: 15). Whether it's the Ford Excursion or the persistent loss of habitat, all are examples of reductionist thinking run amok.

Separating people and nature

Another liability that pervades all the previous examples of failed stewardship is best described as dualism – the belief that "alternatives to thought and endeavour are polarized, and guided by the law of the excluded middle" (Woodhouse 1996: 14). This is also called "either-or" thinking. More specifically, this kind of thinking finds expression in the view that nature exists to serve the interests of human beings, and that we, as humans, have dominion over the plants and animals. In the end, all aspects of our lives are embedded in nature, and to think that we can somehow separate ourselves, or opt out, is simply not possible without dire consequences. Having said this, it is also essential to recognize that nature does not belong to us – it is not "our" natural environment (Franklin 1999: 85). Nature is not infrastructure standing by to accommodate us. Rather, it is its own entity and people are but one part of it – it is high time that we learn to live with this essential truth.

Divisible versus indivisible benefits

In addition to the threats posed by reductionist and dualistic thinking, there is also the matter of divisible and indivisible benefits. I am indebted to the brilliant physicist and humanist, Ursula Franklin (1999: 65–67), for her clear thinking on this topic. In short, divisible benefits are those which accrue to the individual or organization because they earned them or created them. Indivisible benefits, on the other hand, are concerned with the "common good" – such things as justice and peace, clean air, drinkable water, and so forth. They belong to everyone. All of us give up our autonomy, and quite a lot of money, to our governments in order to protect and advance this common good.

As several of my earlier examples indicate, however, there appears to be a marked deterioration among all levels of government worldwide in safeguarding our indivisible benefits. Canada's built environment is a case in point, as mentioned earlier. We hold many of these heritage resources in common yet, often times, no one seems to be responsible. Whether it is historic sites or global environmental deterioration, it is essential that all levels of government be accountable for safeguarding the world's indivisible benefits. Multi-national corporations, second only to governments in their influence on public policy, have clearly demonstrated time and again that the common good can be an inexhaustible arena for private gain.

The tyranny of economists

I will conclude these comments on the underlying reasons for the assault on stewardship with some observations on economists. Most of the previous examples, ranging from the Ford Excursion to the demise of non-human primates, are grounded in an economic world view. In short, this world view states that continuous economic growth is essential to a healthy society. There is every reason to believe, however, that limitless growth is creating genuine and profound dilemmas, including damage to the natural environment and growing disillusionment with buying "stuff" as the key to happiness.

We are faced with a poverty of thought and action in this regard, and professional economists are one of the greatest obstacles to achieving some degree of understanding and realism (Wilson 1998: 290). For whatever reasons, economists largely ignore human behaviour and the environment in their analyses and pronouncements. Most importantly, they do not use full-cost accounting, which means that they fail, for example, to recognize the depletion of natural resources as a cost. Happily, there is a new subdiscipline called ecological economics, but it still is only marginally influential (Wilson 1998: 292).

The general failure of this academic discipline to acknowledge the real world is not going unnoticed. Economics has actually been called "a pseudoscience and a form of brain damage" (Henderson 1980: 22). On a lighter note, perhaps some insight into how economists see reality can be gleaned from the reputed epitaph of Allan Greenspan, the high priest of contemporary economics (Charlton 1993: 112). It reads:

"I am guardedly optimistic about the next world, but remain cognizant of the downside risks."

Stewardship: building on strengths

I am an optimistic person and I do not want to leave any of you with the impression of doom and gloom, as a result of the muddled thinking I have just described. I was attempting to set the stage for a more constructive discussion of the current state of stewardship. The examples I will now describe all demonstrate a very real and mature commitment to stewardship, and all of them exemplify three essential qualities of effective stewardship – a sense of interconnectedness, the recognition of diversity, and an appreciation for the depth of time.

Archaeology

I am aware that archaeologists and their various societies in Saskatchewan are involved in creating a new vision for Saskatchewan's heritage and, personally, I am delighted with this. I also think that all of us should be grateful. Other than the fact I was once an archaeologist, why am I saying this? In short, archaeology is a strong antidote to our society's increasing devaluation of the past. The late Christopher Lasch (1979: 5), the provocative American historian, wrote:

> To live for the moment is the prevailing passion. . . .
> We are fast losing the sense of historical continuity,
> the sense of belonging to a succession of generations,
> originating in the past and stretching into the future.
> It is the waning of the sense of historical time.

Not only does archaeology counteract this waning sense of historical time, it is also one of the best subjects we have for engendering an "awareness of the preciousness of the Earth – of its meaning as our home in the past, present and future" (Postman 1996: 104–106). Although archaeology provides both a meaningful sense of time and a sense of interconnectedness with the previous inhabitants of our planet, a cautionary note is in order. Because the method and theory of archaeology is grounded in the scientific method, it is always important to guard against the arrogance inherent in this perspective.

For better or for worse, science has become the model for describing reality when, in fact, it is actually only one way of describing things (Franklin 1999: 31). Much of archaeology, despite its scientific rigour, more often resembles a narrative more than it does definitive truth. Because of this, stewardship in archaeology will always require the recognition of competing and diverse narratives – including people's local and traditional knowledge – most notably that of the First Nations. This knowledge is both empirical and metaphorical, and is integral to the fabric of cultural history. I will conclude these comments on archaeology with a personal example of what I mean.

While doing an archaeological survey in the boreal forest of the western North-west Territories (Canada), I came across a piston rod from an outboard motor lying in the forest. It had apparently cracked and been repaired. First, the shaft had been shrink-wrapped in green (untanned) moose hide, and then meticulously bound with brass snare wire in a manner that can only be described as elegant. If only this object could speak. Was it ever used after being repaired? Did it work? Most importantly, this object symbolizes a completely different world view. When a piston rod breaks in our culture, it means the end of the machine's useful life, or an extremely expensive repair if possible. The northern hunters (the Dene) who created this object were apparently not intimidated by the gravity of their mechanical problem.[1] They had no machine shop, in any event. In the absence of high organization and technological dependency, they saw possibilities and acted.

Collections

Long-term collections care in museums is another model of effective steward-ship which exhibits the qualities of interconnectedness, time depth, and diversity. Most museums that I know of are committed to keeping their collections forever, and when I worked at the Glenbow Museum in Calgary we defined "forever" as 500 years. We did this in part to impress upon our Board of Governors that our obligation to these objects was long term and expensive, and that the typical business focus on the next quarter's results has no meaning in collections care. This means, of course, that staff and facilities must be in place, and as all museum workers know, this is a never-ending juggling act and underlain by a strong sense of moral responsibility.

This well-developed sense of stewardship might be strengthened even more, however, with some sober discussion throughout the museum community about redundancy and overlap in museum collections. Will all museums continue to grow their permanent collections, with no thought to duplication, the need for increased public access, and the long-term costs? Is keeping everything, forever, an intelligent and honest approach to stewardship when time and money are limited?

Leaders, boards, and organizations

A third focus of active stewardship is our heritage organizations themselves – their leaders, managers, Boards, staff, and volunteers. For leaders and managers, the most important task these days is bringing about intelligent organizational change to enhance both effectiveness and relevance. There are as many approaches to this task as there are leaders, and the results to date are equally as varied. There are successes and many failures. The failures are, in part, the result of our preoccupation with interventionist cures for our organizations, rather than continuous care. Henry Mintzberg (1996: 66–67), the management professor, has suggested that nursing should be the model for all management – steady, consistent, nurturing, and caring. This is stewardship personified, and it should begin in our own organizations.

Non-profit boards of directors are perhaps the essence of stewardship, in giving freely of their time to ensure the long-term well-being of every type of heritage organization. I mention this here by way of tribute to them, and also to suggest some ways to enhance governance, and hence, stewardship. For example, a formal orientation for each new board member is essential, as is a role and responsibility statement. It is also valuable for a board to develop a means of self-evaluation, in order to continually monitor its effectiveness.

Glenbow's board members, for example, complete a 60-second questionnaire after each meeting to determine whether they were given the necessary information by staff for effective decision making, and to determine to what extent the meeting was devoted to strategic direction or mired in operational details. Perhaps the most radical idea to enhance governance would be the annual hiring of a third party to interview staff, volunteers, and stakeholders about the board's strengths and weaknesses.

Staff and organizations

Moving from governance to organizations as a whole, many organizations in the heritage field are actually models of stewardship when you consider their longevity. In contrast, the average life expectancy for multinational corporations is between 40 and 50 years (de Geus 1997: 1–2). This discovery provoked such alarm that an inquiry was undertaken to determine why. The author of this work concluded that the exclusive focus on the production of goods and services has doomed the vast majorities of companies to rapid extinction.

De Geus (1997: 9) also discovered, however, four traits that characterized 30 companies which have been around for 100 to 700 years. These traits were financial conservatism; sensitivity to the world around them; employees who felt like they belonged to the organization and identified with its achievements; and last, considerable tolerance and encouragement for experiments and learning that promoted change.

Here we have a splendid description of what constitutes stewardship in the organizational world, and I am happy to report that heritage and non-profit organizations have considerable experience and success with all four of these traits. If there is any need for improvement, I suggest it is in the realm of flexibility and tolerance for change and new possibilities. Part of the difficulty lies in our stubborn commitment to rigid organizational models borrowed from the corporate world. Many organizations are learning that creativity can be stimulated by organizing differently (Farson 1996: 102–105; Janes 1997) – the idea of self-organization being one such possibility. Many small organizations have known this all along.

The gift of the First Nations

In addition to the ethic of stewardship inherent in archaeology, permanent collections, and the community of heritage organizations, we live in the midst of viable First Nations communities – if only we had the wisdom to truly appreciate their sense of the world. It is not necessary to argue that First Nations are innate conservationists and stewards in order to appreciate the extent to which these cultures have achieved a profound degree of interconnectedness with the biosphere.

I am obviously not a First Nations person, so to presume to speak on their behalf is inappropriate. I am also conscious of the fact that there is no singular First Nations perspective, as the diversity of their cultures can be seen simply in the number of languages they speak. Nonetheless, there are some general characteristics of Aboriginal cosmology which can help to enhance our understanding of what stewardship means.

One of the most quoted phrases from the American Indian wars was Crazy Horse's comment at a battle in which the Lakota were outnumbered. He said, "Today is a good day to die" (Lopez 1978: 5). Regrettably, no one pays much attention to the second part of his remark which was "for all the things of my life are here." To repeat, Crazy Horse actually said, "Today is a good day to die, for all the things of my life are here."

To me, this story expresses a remarkable sense of interconnectedness. Life for Aboriginal peoples is not a sequence of goals to be accomplished, but is complete when one enters adulthood. For Aboriginal peoples, one can only continue to grow in that state, fully enmeshed in family, relatives, friends, and the natural world. "With that continuous sense of a full life, no one was tyrannized by the prospect of death" (Lopez 1978: 5).

This refusal to fragment experience into mutually exclusive dichotomies is not only the basis of interrelatedness, but is also integral to the First Nations' concept of time as "living in the moment of the present" (Brown 1989: 117), rather than in the categories of the past, present, and future. Living in the present allows a continual and immediate interrelationship with the environment in which one lives, and this is the same state of awareness so many people are now seeking through formal meditation.

Out of this sense of interconnectedness and non-linear time comes the deep respect, and ultimate sacredness, with which First Nations peoples view the forms, beings, forces, and changes of the natural world (Brown 1989: 119). Need I say more about the relevance of the Aboriginal world view to the task at hand?

Sharpening our skills

I have never been happy with those speakers who breeze into town, raise momentous issues, and then leave town having failed to provide any practical suggestions on how to make things better, however modestly. Before I conclude, I want to make several suggestions which I think might enhance our approach to stewardship:

1. First, "restore the guardian" (Hawken 1993: 59). As mentioned earlier, our government, or guardian system, seems to be breaking down, in part because of the money, power, and influence exercised by business and corporations. We have to get business out of government and make sure government is accountable for our indivisible benefits.

2. Second, take note of the newly identified "green wave." The results of a recent Environics poll (Joanne DiCosimo: personal communication, November, 2000) indicate that Canadian youth from 14 to 24 years of age have expressed serious concern for the future health of the planet. We must build on this concern by connecting with youth in our work and in the schools.

3. Next, question the experts. With science having become the model of explaining reality, along with all of its experts, there is a marked decrease in the reliance of people on their own experience and senses (Franklin 1999: 31). We must simply trust ourselves more.

4. Fourth, beware of postmodernism. This is the school of thought based on the assumption that an "objective evaluation of competing points of view is impossible, since all points of view are to some extent biased by race, gender and culture" (Woodhouse 1996: 22). The biases are undoubtedly true, but the real danger in adopting this perspective is that we abandon passion and critical thought in the name of relativism. Postmodernism has been called the culture of no resistance (Zernan 2001: 88), and intelligent stewardship often requires resistance. Whether it is an exaggerated trust in the method of science, or postmodernism, I am suggesting that both are extremes. And extremes are usually not that useful (G. Conaty: personal communication, May, 2001).

5. Last, we must reduce our ecological footprint. The ecological footprint, which is the productive land needed to support each Canadian with existing technology, is 4.3 hectares (or 10.75 acres). In most developing countries it is less than half a hectare. To raise the whole world to the U.S. standard of living would require two more planet Earths (Wilson 1998: 282).

Conclusions

As I conclude my talk, I want to take this opportunity to congratulate all of you for your initiative this weekend. The very fact that you have brought together such a diverse and rich assembly of heritage interests is in itself a cause for acknowledgement. To then assume responsibility for building linkages within this complex community, based on the concept of stewardship, is to model the behaviour that all of us across the country must begin to emulate.

I say this because creating the opportunity to simply talk to each other is essential to creating our common future (Franklin 1999: 122–123). Whatever ills I have described today can only be addressed by what people, individually and collectively do, or refrain from doing. Talking together, beyond competing interests, is fundamental to overcoming the reductionism and dualism that underlie many of our current difficulties. I am quite certain that your commitment to integration and cooperation will have an impact far beyond the seeds sown here today.

It is not surprising to me to learn that the First Nations figured this out long ago. According to the Pawnee (Brown 1989: 124), a Great Council of all the Animals meets in perpetual session in a cave under a mountain. These animals monitor the affairs of humans wherever they may be on earth. If a man or a woman is in need or in trouble, and seeks aid with humility, the council will choose one of its appropriate members – whether winged, four-legged, or crawling – who will then appear and give something of its own power that should thereafter guide the person's life.

I think that the entire Western world could use the help of the Great Council of the Animals, but I sense that we will need to do a great deal more work on our sense of humility before this can happen. In the meantime, we can take heart that many people are beginning to reject technology and economics as the main determinants of our future (Eisler 1987: 195). Rather, our future must be shaped by human values, reciprocity, and stewardship in a manner similar to what you are doing here this weekend.

Note

1 The Dene people (DEN-ay) are an aboriginal group of First Nations who live in the northern boreal and subarctic regions of Canada.

References

Abramovitz, Janet N. 1997 Ecosystem Conversion Spreads. In *Vital Signs 1997*. Worldwatch Institute and W.W. Norton and Company, New York, pp. 98–99.

Brown, Joseph Epes 1989 *The Spiritual Legacy of the American Indian*. Crossroad Publishing Company, New York.

Charlton, James (Editor) 1993 *The Executive's Quotation Book* (revised edition). Reprinted with permission from St. Martin's Press, Inc., by CCH Canadian Ltd.

de Geus, Arie 1997 The Living Company. *Harvard Business Review*, Vol. 75, No. 2, March–April, pp. 51–59.

Eisler, Riane 1987 *The Chalice and the Blade*. HarperCollins Publishers, San Francisco.

Farson, Richard 1996 *Management of the Absurd*. Simon and Schuster, New York.

Franklin, Ursula M. 1999 *The Real World of Technology* (revised edition). House of Anansi Press Limited, Toronto.

Handy, Charles 1997 Finding Sense in Uncertainty. In *Rethinking the Future*, edited by Rowan Gibson. Nicholas Brealey Publishing Ltd., London, pp. 16–33.

Hawken, Paul 1993 A Declaration of Sustainability. *Utne Reader*, No. 59, September/October, pp. 54–61.

Henderson, Hazel 1980 Making a Living without Making Money. *East West Journal*, March, 1980, pp. 22–27.

Janes, Robert R. 1997 *Museums and the Paradox of Change: A Case Study in Urgent Adaptation* (second edition). The Glenbow Museum and the University of Calgary Press, Calgary.

Kane, Hal 1997 Half of Languages Becoming Extinct. In *Vital Signs 1997*. Worldwatch Institute and W.W. Norton and Company, New York, pp. 130–131.

Kittrell, Ed 1996 *Funny Business*, May, 1996. Georgetown Publishing House, Washington, D.C.

Lasch, Christopher 1979 *The Culture of Narcissism*. W.W. Norton and Company, Inc., New York.

Lopez, Barry (Editor) 1978 The American Indian Mind. *Potentials, Quest*, 78, pp. 1–16.

McArthur, Keith 2001 Laidlaw Paid Ex-CEO $2.1 million. In "Canadian Business," *The Globe and Mail*, April 26, p. B7.

Minister's Round Table 2001 Threats to Canada's National Historic Sites. Presentation at the Minister's Round Table on Parks Canada, Hamilton, Ontario, April 1–4, 2001.

Mintzberg, Henry 1996 Musings on Management. *Harvard Business Review*, Vol. 74, No. 4, July–August, pp. 61–67.

Mish, Frederick C. (Editor in Chief) 1986 *Webster's Ninth New Collegiate Dictionary*. Merriam-Webster Inc., Springfield, Massachusetts.

Postman, Neil 1996 *The End of Education*. Vintage Books, New York.

Roberts, Paul 2001 Bad Sports. *Harper's Magazine*, Vol. 302, No. 1811, April, pp. 69–75.

Tuxill, John 1997 Primate Diversity Dwindling Worldwide. In *Vital Signs 1997*. Worldwatch Institute and W.W. Norton and Company, New York, pp. 100–101.

Wilson, Edward O. 1998 *Consilience – The Unity of Knowledge*. Alfred A. Knopf Inc., New York.

Woodhouse, Mark B. 1996 *Paradigm Wars*. Frog, Ltd., Berkeley, California.

Zerzan, John 2001 Greasing the Rails to a Cyborg Future. *Adbusters*, May/June, No. 35, p. 88.

15

INTRODUCTION TO
LOOKING REALITY IN THE EYE:
MUSEUMS AND SOCIAL
*RESPONSIBILITY**

. . . for what worked yesterday becomes the gilded cage of today.

(Peter Block 2002: 31)

What was old is new again

The idea that museums should serve a social purpose is not a new concept. Modern museology has its roots in the "cabinets of curiosities" that were developed by the gentry during the Age of Discovery (fourteenth to sixteenth centuries) and those collections that were owned by the state were often used for larger, ideological purposes. Museums are the products of the society that supports them. Although the concept of a museum can be traced to ancient Greece, the philosophy and purpose of contemporary museums were shaped in eighteenth-century Europe. It is important to note these historical developments if we are to understand and appreciate the enduring role of museums as social institutions.

As the Age of Discovery made Europeans aware of the vastness and diversity of the world that lay beyond the continental boundaries, the explorers of these new worlds brought back samples of natural and human phenomena for those who had financed the expeditions. These collections were often housed in rooms filled with "cabinets of curiosities" where the gentry could reflect upon the strange wonders of the world.

This structure began to change near the end of the eighteenth century. With the French Revolution, collections that had belonged to the Crown, the Church,

---

Source: Robert R. Janes and Gerald T. Conaty, pp. 1–17 in Robert R. Janes and Gerald T. Conaty (eds.) (2005) *Looking Reality in the Eye: Museums and Social Responsibility*, Calgary, Canada: The University of Calgary Press and the Museums Association of Saskatchewan. The late Gerald Conaty was the Senior Ethnologist at the Glenbow Museum, Calgary, Canada.

and the aristocracy became the property of the State (Grasset 1996: 190) and were put on exhibit for all the people of France. The Decree of July 27, 1793, opened the Louvre and guaranteed that the people of France would have the right of access to the collections. Later, as Napoleon I (1804–15) conquered most of Europe and North Africa, his plunder was brought back to France and housed in museums throughout the country. Collections which initially served as mementos of the past and evidence of present wealth soon became objects of study, sources of patriotism, and a medium for post-Revolutionary propaganda.

In Britain, the creation of a national collection began earlier with the founding of the British Museum. But the real democratization of museums in Britain lagged behind developments elsewhere, as conservative opinion reacted to the revolutionary attitudes of the Continent. Access to the national collection continued to be restricted to those who were acceptable (i.e., aristocratic men). However, by the 1850s a new role of civic responsibility was emerging for museums in Britain (Bennett 1996). The gentry believed that if museums were opened for public access, labourers would eschew the local tavern for a chance to ponder the art and artifacts of Western civilizations. Time spent in such contemplation was thought to lead to character reformation and a general improvement in the nature of the working class.

Museums continue to have an important social role and their underlying message has come to reflect the value of progress. Often this message is conveyed most effectively through the use of the ethnological collections, where the inevitability of progress emerges from cross-cultural comparisons. As both Cameron (1971) and Ames (1992) observe, the creation of these public collections had a profound effect on the meaning embedded within them:

> the public . . . came to believe that they had the right to expect that the collections would present and interpret the world in some way consistent with the values they held to be good, with the collective representations they held to be appropriate, and with the view of social reality they held to be true.
>
> *(Ames 1992: 21)*

Museums, thus, became temples of the dominant society (Cameron 1971: 17), reifying its principles and beliefs. They became places where the individual could compare his or her private view of reality with the view held by society in general. It is important to remember, however, that this reality had been constructed by the educated classes of society and that the perceptions of more marginal groups were mostly excluded from this reality.

Purpose and sustainability

Just as today's societies are incredibly diverse and complex, museums are no longer the monolithic institutions of the past. Instead, many are focusing their efforts more narrowly, telling particular stories with larger meanings. Often, these stories reflect issues and people that have been marginalized by mainstream society – First Nations, immigrants, and chronic illness. This approach can also lead to an activism that embraces community issues and aspirations, in an effort to provide value and meaning.

The book (*Looking Reality in the Eye: Museums and Social Responsibility*) for which this Introduction was written is about the search for meaning among a group of museums, science centres, and art galleries, at a time when many of these institutions worldwide are struggling to maintain their stability in the face of the complex challenges of the non-profit world.[1] These challenges range from declining attendance to finding the appropriate balance between public funding and earned revenues, and none of them is easily overcome. At the same time, a growing number of museums are moving beyond the imperatives of the marketplace, with its preoccupation with money and efficiency, to embrace activities that are seemingly remote from the bottom line. Although the reasons for this are varied, there are several troublesome aspects of our contemporary world that help to make sense of this emerging search for significance in the museum world.

The contemporary search for meaning is in part a reaction to various scientific, technological, and societal developments, and it is useful to consider how these facts and events have converged over time to provoke the institutional responses chronicled in *Looking Reality in the Eye*. The story begins long ago, with one observer (McKibben 2003: 15) noting that meaning in human life has been in decline for a very long time, almost since the beginning of Western civilization. This is in contrast to our hunting and gathering ancestors, whose world and its inhabitants, be they plant, animal or mineral, were saturated with meaning. Consider the Pawnee account of the Great Council of Animals as an example (Brown 1989: 124). This Council meets in perpetual session in a cave under a round mountain, and monitors the affairs of humans wherever they may be on Earth. If a man or woman is in need or in trouble, and seeks aid with humility, the Council will choose one of its appropriate members – whether winged, four-legged, or crawling – who will then appear to the man or woman and give something of its own power, or present advice, that should thereafter guide the person's life.

Human wholeness, and hence meaning, thus depend on a receptiveness to the potentialities and mysteries of the natural world. Today, Western society looks on the same landscape and deems it deaf and dumb, or else sees a treasure trove of resources and feels little or no obligation for collective responsibility. The widespread belief that nature exists to serve the interests of people has eroded much of what our species once found meaningful.

This belief in humankind's dominion over plants and animals is also the rationale for extracting wealth at the expense of the environment, yet another expression of our preoccupation with money as the measure of worth. This sentiment is now fully installed in the boardrooms of many cultural institutions, with *The Toronto Star* (Hume 2000) reporting that "the gap between the haves and the have nots of the museum world will be greater than ever." The Director of the Museum of

Modern Art in New York is quoted as saying, "If you want to stay competitive in the cultural arena, you can only do it by investing large sums. That means you have to spend US$200 to US$300 million just to keep up with the next guy."

Is this another form of Darwinism, this time in cultural clothing, yet grounded in size, power, and money? Perhaps, but the authors assembled in *Looking Reality in the Eye* demonstrate that bigger is not necessarily better, and that millions of dollars do not guarantee either market sensitivity or institutional competence. The reader will also note that reputation, name recognition, and the trust of visitors are not the property of bigness, as worthiness can be achieved by organizations of any size. There is little danger that the spectacular will replace the speculative at the institutions described in *Looking Reality in the Eye*.

Of particular concern is that many museums now see no other way but to consume their way to survival or prosperity, failing to recognize that this is an outdated economic perspective. This is doubly puzzling in light of the discernment that should accompany the historical legacy of museums as knowledge-based institutions. Nevertheless, most of us remain seduced by the desire for more of everything, and marketplace economics continues to dominate our culture and worldview. This should, however, be a cause for concern among those many museums that have staked their future on attendance figures, earned revenues, and culture as entertainment.

Recent research indicates that the museum sector is struggling to maintain its audiences, and that the visitor base is declining (Burton and Scott 2003: 56–57). Nor has there been any diversification in the traditional visitor profile, which is still marked by high income and a high level of education. In addition, there is much anecdotal information which suggests that earned revenues are not infinitely expandable, which is further complicated by the complete failure of museum practitioners and funding agencies to thoughtfully consider what constitutes an appropriate balance between public funding, private funding, and earned revenues for public institutions.

Much of this looming crisis, along with the attendant pressures on management, is a result of a widespread misconception in Western society that markets create communities. In fact, the opposite is true, as the marketplace and its activities actually deplete trust (Rifkin 1997). It is the organizations of the non–profit sector, neither government nor business, which build and enrich the trust, caring, and genuine relationships – the social capital – upon which the marketplace is based. These organizations range from political parties, to museums, to Girl Guides, and there would be no markets without this web of human relationships. Social capital is born of long-term associations that are not explicitly self-interested or coerced, and typically diminishes if it is not regularly renewed or replaced (Bullock and Trombley 1999: 798). The contributors to *Looking Reality in the Eye* are fully aware of this, and they provide rich case studies in the creation of social capital and its vast potential as a source of meaning and inspiration.

What if our political and business leaders realized that business of all kinds can only be properly conducted in a society rich in social capital? This might result in non-profits, including museums, being measured in terms of the *social* capital they generate, and being compensated accordingly. Grants and handouts would become artifacts, and museums would be paid for the value they add to individuals and communities. All of the institutions described here would find themselves in enviable positions in such a world, as they have become highly skilled at creating the trust, empathy, and meaning that constitute social capital. Because none of this work is inspired by the marketplace, these organizations also serve to counteract the three thousand marketing messages each of us is now subjected to each day. As Mark Kingwell (1998: 45) notes, none of these messages has anything to do with thinking or knowledge, much less meaning: they are about buying stuff.

The relentless erosion of meaning in everyday life, and its replacement with culture as consumption, goes beyond our alienation from nature and the imperatives of the marketplace. Although not necessarily a cause, the emotional narcissism of the Baby Boomer generation is another factor to consider. It is not this generation's creative intelligence that is at issue, but rather its tendency towards extreme individualism. We introduce this notion here with some apprehension, recognizing that the bulk of current museum leaders in North America are of this generation, as are most of the contributors to this book. Because the influence of this generation on the organizational behaviour of museums is neither recognized nor debated, it invites speculation. It is important to note that narcissism is not only the overvaluing of self and one's abilities, but is also the undervaluing of others and their contributions. This is a normal trait of childhood and is mostly outgrown with age, although critics argue that the Boomer generation is characterized by a very high cognitive capacity coupled with persistent selfishness (Wilber 2001: 17–32).

In short, this narcissistic individualism can culminate in an inability to take other people, places, and things into account. Determining to what extent this trait can be extended to the contemporary management of museums is dangerous, but one question cannot be ignored: Is the current insularity and fragmentation of the museum community related to the emotional makeup of Baby Boomers, or is it merely a coincidence? There is nearly continuous rhetoric on the need for partnership and collaboration between museums, as well as with their communities, with only modest results to date. If meaning is to be found in the relationship of the individual to community, and the opportunity this provides to find out who one is (McKibben 2003: 18), it is axiomatic that museums have a primary role in facilitating this search. Perhaps only a generational change in leadership will fulfil this promise.

Setting aside any further speculation on the peculiarities of Baby Boomers, there is ample evidence to conclude that they have contributed to the erosion of meaning in another way. It is this generation that has significantly influenced academic studies and continues to "extend an egalitarian embrace to every stance, no matter how shallow or narcissistic," including deconstructive postmodernism (Wilber 2001: 26–28). Postmodernism is the school of thought based on the assumption that an objective evaluation of competing points of view is impossible, since all points of view are to some extent biased by race, gender, and culture (Woodhouse 1996: 22).

Although such biases are a fact of life and mostly unavoidable, the danger in adopting this postmodern perspective is that we abandon passion and critical thought, both of which are key ingredients in the search for meaning, in the name of relativism. The postmodern result is a mishmash of pluralistic relativism and fragmented pluralism, where everything is of equal weight and value, and everyone does their own thing. Thus emerges the paradoxical individual – empowered and enabled, but also isolated and disconnected (McKibben 2003: 16). Where once the church, the village, and the extended family reconciled this meaninglessness, we are now in need of alternatives.

Apart from postmodernism's contribution to fragmented thinking, it is important to note another inherent danger in this school of thought. Postmodernism has also been called the culture of no resistance, having abandoned the "arrogance" of trying to figure out the origins, logic, causality, and structure of the world we live in (Zerman 2001: 88). Forsaking the effort to understand our shared experience is perilous, especially in light of our relentless materialism. The socially responsible museum is capable of providing a different source of meaning for its community, politely oblivious to the narrow agendas of both the corporatists and the postmodernists.

There is nothing to be gained, however, by retreating from the status quo, as environmental destruction, postmodernism, capitalism, and "Boomeritis" are embedded in our lives. They have been slowly gathering force and substance, and are now so predominant in our society that they demand a response. These social, environmental, and technological pressures have, in effect, created a metaphorical fork in the road, not only for individuals, but also for museums. This fork is an opportunity to choose another path, especially for those who have pondered the outcome of North America's current trajectory.

Many museums have made a choice, knowingly or unknowingly, to pursue popularity and increased revenues through high-profile exhibitions and architectural sensationalism. This strategy is so consumptive of staff and money that there is often little left of either to pursue other activities. Yet, many museums are succeeding at this, especially the larger ones, although the long-term sustainability of this business plan is not yet known. Some of these museums have come to resemble corporate entities, even at this early stage, with revenues and attendance being the predominant measures of worth. Many of their boards of directors are also increasingly indistinguishable from their corporate counterparts, with the directors chosen for their business experience, corporate tribalism, or ostensible influence in fundraising. Although such qualifications are not new in the arts world, the danger lies in the growing tendency for these boards to self-select on the basis of these criteria, to the exclusion of other attributes reflecting gender, cultural diversity, and specialized knowledge unrelated to business.

Values

The museums portrayed in *Looking Reality in the Eye* have pondered the metaphorical fork in the road mentioned above and chosen a different path, with a new sensibility. It is important to note, however, that they are also continuing to engage in traditional museum work at the same time. Although embracing a socially responsible mission does not require forsaking either education or entertainment, it does require an intuitive appreciation of certain values that are largely absent or unspoken in contemporary museum work (Block 2002: 47–65). We are indebted to Peter Block, a leader in civic engagement, for identifying and exploring these values. To name or discuss some of these qualities might invite ridicule or embarrassment in the museum community, as they appear to bear little or no relationship to bottom-line thinking about revenues and expenditures. The truth is actually more complex, and socially responsible museums demonstrate that the values of idealism, intimacy, depth, and interconnectedness are not only the warp and weft of meaning, but are also the foundation for long-term sustainability.

All of the museums discussed in *Looking Reality in the Eye* are concerned with "why," and consistently illustrate that these four values, far from being New Age hype, are rather the touchstones for creating meaning in a community. Idealism, intimacy, depth, and interconnectedness are the tests of genuineness and quality in a socially responsible museum, in contrast to the current preoccupation with attendance figures and revenues. The premise is that attendance flows from significance, and significance flows from the provision of meaning and value to one's community. These are the true faces of sustainability. Blockbuster exhibitions have certainly demonstrated their ability to bring in crowds and revenue, but in ways much like an addictive substance. The impact is fast and undeniable, but quickly dissolves in the quest for more, and there is never enough. One senior museum director, highly successful at profit-making blockbusters, noted that these exhibitions were eroding his museum's brand (Bill Barkley, personal communication, 2001). Many people were only visiting when there was a blockbuster, none of which had anything to do with the museum's unique strengths and abilities.

It is clear that museums have choices to make that go beyond the role of impresario, if they are willing to grapple with the four values mentioned above. This task must begin with idealism, which means thinking about the way things could be, rather than simply accepting the way things are. All of the contributors to *Looking Reality in the Eye* are not only preoccupied with this, but they also have a penchant for action. There is little doubt that envisaging an ideal future is not a popularity contest, especially when it becomes the core of your institutional vision. But it is this idealism, this striving for constant improvement in the human condition, which separates the socially responsible from the socially aware.

Idealism does not count for much without intimacy, as intimacy is about communication and the quality of the contact which is made. Quality communication lies in direct experience, so it makes sense that electronic and virtual interaction are only part of the solution. Although they lack quality and intimacy, they do provide broad exposure, which is valuable in its own right. In the end, there is no substitute for human relationships, and all the time, energy, and consideration they require. All the museums discussed in *Looking Reality in the Eye* have made deep and enduring commitments to the maintenance of human relationships, which in turn have led unavoidably to depth, the third value so critical to the creation of meaning.

Depth is about being thorough and complete, even when this requires a tremendous investment of time and resources. Some of the museums in *Looking Reality in the Eye* have invested decades of staff time in building relationships with particular groups of people, all in an effort to try to understand what is important. Depth is about thinking, questioning, and reflecting, and taking the time to do this. Be warned that the obstacles to such a commitment are endemic, beginning with our society's addiction to speed and superficiality in our daily lives. "Speed is the antithesis of depth" (Block 2002: 51).

Finally, there is the matter of interconnectedness, a word which is sure to send the empirically minded running for the hills. In fact, there is more substance to this notion than one might assume, as there is a growing societal awareness of the interconnectedness of things, including families, organizations, the environment, and the whole of humanity. It is increasingly difficult to deny that our individual well-being is indissolubly linked to the health of society and our environment (Leonard and Murphy 1995: xi). Even science is searching for more comprehensive models that are truer to our understanding of the interconnectedness of space and time, and the body and the mind (Kabat-Zinn 1990: 151). It is no longer tenable to ignore the undesirable consequences of our apparently unthinking adherence to marketplace ideology, with its sole emphasis on individual and corporate autonomy. Make no mistake, it is an ideology. It is an integrated set of assumptions, theories, and aims that constitute a socio-political program and agenda. Worst of all, it is marked by the "truculence of certainty" (Whalley 1959: 69).

The museum stories in *Looking Reality in the Eye* are proof that there are alternatives, and that a sense of interconnectedness is an antidote to the inevitable uncertainty which pervades any attempt to learn and think in new ways. Moreover, making your institution vulnerable, and hence more responsive to your community, is neither a new nor a revolutionary idea. John Cotton Dana, the American library and museum director, believed that museums should grow out of the individual nature of their communities, and that they should be accountable to the public (Grove 1978: 33). Dana advised his contemporaries to "learn what aid the community needs, and fit the museum to those needs." He said this eighty-five years ago.

Courage and accountability

If the reader is annoyed with or threatened by the idea of moving beyond the museum as temple or forum (Cameron 1971), there is another, more constructive way to view the work described here. It is also about organizational renewal and all that means for enhancing long-term sustainability, and herein lies the true challenge of intelligent management. In effect, individuals, organizations, and societies start slowly, grow, prosper, and decline (Handy 1994: 49–63). Decline is not inevitable if you are willing to challenge all the assumptions underlying current success, and this must begin with questions, which then lead to ideas. This is paradoxical, because this must be done at a time when all the messages coming through are that everything is just fine. Each museum must find its own way in this process. The critical requirement is to begin the exploration by being skeptical, curious and inventive before you have to be. If you don't do this before you are forced to, chances are that you are already in decline.

To begin with, it is helpful to consider this work as purpose-filled experiments, whose intention is just as much about learning as it is about achieving (Block 2002: 3). In doing so, the choice of a worthy destination is much more important than simply settling for what we know will work. This, in turn, requires a willingness to address questions that have no answers. This is not as daunting or unrealistic as it may sound, recognizing that new knowledge comes when you simply bear in mind what you need to know (Wilber 2001: 39). Put another way, keep holding the problem in mind and it will yield; it is the will and the passion to do this that are most important. Time, patience, and commitment are also essential. You may also expect to feel a bit like an outsider as you confront these responsibilities, as there is good reason to believe that acting on what matters may mean living on the margins of our institutions and culture (Block 2002: 84–85), at least for awhile. Cultivating some detachment from the mainstream may mean lower attendance figures than a blockbuster exhibition could provide, or perhaps silence or rude skepticism from one's colleagues, but the museums discussed in *Looking Reality in the Eye* are proof that these issues eventually become less troublesome.

Such difficulties are to be expected if one is in search of genuine accountability, which is not the easiest sort of accountability, nor the obvious choice, for many museums. Genuine accountability is about purpose in the workplace, including questions of social responsibility, social equity, civic engagement, and the meaning the institution has for the community (Block 2002: 190). For all those museum practitioners wedded to traditional practices or current formulas of success, we reiterate that this kind of accountability is not mutually exclusive, and can be achieved while getting the other work of the organization done. Most importantly,

> There is nothing lacking. Nothing more is needed than what we already have. We require no remarkable, undiscovered technologies. We do not need heroic, larger-than-life leadership. The only requirement is that we, as individuals, choose a revitalizing future and then work in community with others to bring it to fruition.
>
> *(Elgin 1993: 193)*

If reluctance still lurks in the thought of assuming responsibility without authority, museums must ask themselves from whence they think their authority will come. Because museums will never be in control of society or communities, waiting around for the authority to act responsibly is as heedless as it is impossible. There is no barrier to social responsibility, and no one way to pursue it. Discontent will also be unavoidable – discontent from failed experiments, discontent from the keepers of the status quo, and discontent from never being certain. The contributors to *Looking Reality in the Eye* know all about this, but they also know it is "better to play the edge of discontent, the inevitable escort of transformation" (Leonard and Murphy 1995: 51).

Assumptions and biases

We are obligated to make known our most obvious assumptions and biases as we conclude this introduction. First, we assume that we can be the co-creators of our lives, both personal and professional, if we accept the responsibility to do so. Second, we assume that museums are among the most free and creative work environments on the planet. In contrast to the private sector, they do not have production or sales quotas, nor do they suffer the malaise of creating false needs. Unlike the public sector, museums are not forced to administer unpopular government policies. In short, museums are privileged work environments. How many people in the twenty-first century are able to work in organizations whose purpose is their meaning (Handy 1994: 183)? All museum workers share this privilege.

We also assume that learning is essential to the intelligent and caring change that our world requires, and learning requires that we ask difficult, and perhaps rude, questions of ourselves and others. Self-critical thought is rapidly becoming a survival skill, however reluctant the museum establishment is to concede this necessity. Encouraging some serious reflection on the nature of social responsibility in museums is, without question, the main motivation for creating *Looking Reality in the Eye*.

We also believe, as career museum workers, that much lies beyond both the ingrained acquisitiveness of museums and their ever-increasing commitment to entertainment. With respect to the former, we note with dismay the recent "Declaration on the Importance and Value of Universal Museums" (The Arts Business Exchange 2002: 14). In this document, the directors of eighteen of the world's most prominent art museums conceded that calls to repatriate objects in museum collections have become an important issue. They also declared that "to narrow the focus of museums whose collections are diverse and multifaceted would therefore be a disservice to all visitors." Cutting through the ambiguity of this statement, it means that repatriation is no longer an issue for the world's most elite cultural institutions, irrespective of the merits of the case. We cannot help but liken this perspective to the aging generals of the First World War, who, having been brought up on horses, simply assumed that the world would remain the same. The consequences of this inertia may not be as severe for the cultural elite as they were for the troops, but they will inevitably be just as humiliating.

As a society, we continue to amuse ourselves to death (Postman 1985), and museums appear to be increasingly compelled to do the same. Whether it is plastic replicas of Egyptian funerary objects, or the mummified remains of our Neolithic ancestors, many museums have joined the perpetual round of entertainments. We understand the short-term economic necessity of seeing people only as audiences, but we also hope that the search for meaning will survive to inspire the next generation of museum workers, perhaps less beholden to the tyranny of the marketplace or undisguised ethnocentrism. There is still inspiration to be had, such as that contained in the following account.

One of the most quoted phrases from the American Indian Wars was Crazy Horse's comment at a battle in which the Lakota were outnumbered. He is regularly quoted as having said, "Today is a good day to die" (Lopez 1978: 5), although no one pays much attention to the second part of his remark. What he actually said was, "Today is a good day to die, for all the things of my life are here." Without presuming any comparison between our worldview and that of the First Nations, we would like to think that museums have a role to play in helping to create that continuous sense of a full life that Crazy Horse was talking about.

Museums are uniquely placed to foster this sense of interrelatedness, along with the deep respect required for inter-cultural understanding, easing the plight of the disadvantaged, and stewarding the environment. We would also like to think that museums, as social institutions, might one day become integral to one's perception of life – a life that is both complete and fully at home in the community and in the natural world. This is a choice that any museum can make, and many are already doing so. For the others, we hope that our book, *Looking Reality in the Eye*, will help point the way.

Note

1 The word "museum" is meant to be inclusive and include all types of museums, art galleries, and science centres.

References

Ames, Michael M. 1992 De-schooling the museum: A proposal to increase public access to museums and their resources. In *Cannibal tours and glass boxes: The anthropology of museums*, Michael M. Ames, pp. 21, 88–97. Vancouver: University of British Columbia Press.

The Arts Business Exchange 2002 Museum directors issue statement on object repatriation. Electronic Newsletter, p. 14. Contact *editor@artsbusiness.com*.

Bennett, Tony 1996 The museum and citizen. In Tony Bennett, Robin Trotter and Donna McAlear (Eds.), *Museums and Citizenship: a resource book*. Queensland Museum Memoir Series, 39(1): 1–15.

Block, Peter 2002 *The answer to how is yes*. San Francisco: Berrett-Koehler.

Brown, Joseph Epes 1989 *The spiritual legacy of the American Indian*. New York: Crossroad.

Bullock, Alan and Trombley, Stephen (Eds.) 1999 *The new Fontana dictionary of modern thought*. London: HarperCollins.

Burton, Christine and Scott, Carol 2003 Museums: Challenges for the 21st century. *International Journal of Arts Management*, 5(2): 56–68.

Cameron, Duncan F. 1971 The museum, a temple or the forum. *Curator*, 14(1): 11–24.

Elgin, Duane 1993 *Voluntary simplicity*. Revised edition (first edition 1981). New York: Quill, William Morrow.

Grasset, Constance D. 1996 Museum fever in France. *Curator*, 39(3): 188–207.

Grove, Richard 1978 John Cotton Dana. *Museum News* (May/June), 33–39, 86–88.

Handy, Charles 1994 *The age of paradox*. Boston: Harvard Business School Press.

Hume, Christopher 2000 Arts story: Cultural vacuum. *The Toronto Star* (August 26), 1–5 (taken from thestar.com).

Kabat-Zinn, Jon 1990 *Full catastrophe living*. New York: Delta Trade Paperbacks, Bantam, Doubleday, Dell.

Kingwell, Mark 1998 Fast forward. *Harper's*, 296 (1776; May), 37–46.

Leonard, George and Murphy, Michael 1995 *The life we are given*. New York: G.P. Putnam's Sons.

Lopez, Barry (Ed.) 1978 The American Indian mind. *Potentials, Quest*, 78: 1–16.

McKibben, Bill 2003 The posthuman condition. *Harper's*, 396 (1835; April), 15–19.

Postman, Neil 1985 *Amusing ourselves to death*. New York: Penguin.

Rifkin, Jeremy 1997 The end of work. Address on behalf of the Volunteer Centre of Calgary (November 13). Palliser Hotel, Calgary, Alberta, Canada.

Whalley, George 1959 Address to the graduating class. *The Blue and White*, Rothesay College School, New Brunswick, pp. 64–71.

Wilber, Ken 2001 *A theory of everything*. Boston: Shambhala.

Woodhouse, Mark B. 1996 *Paradigm wars*. Berkeley: Frog.

Zerzan, John 2001 Greasing the rails to a cyborg future. *Adbusters* (May/June), 35, 88.

16

MUSEUMS, CORPORATISM AND THE CIVIL SOCIETY*

Introduction

> True growth is the ability of a society to transfer increasing amounts of attention and
> energy from the material side of life to the nonmaterial side, and thereby to advance
> its culture, capacity for compassion, sense of community, and strength of democracy.
>
> *(Arnold J. Toynbee 1947: 198)*

In 1990, the late Stephen Weil published an article in *Museum News* (Anderson 2004: 74–79) wherein he referred to "an emerging new paradigm" in the museum field that defined the essential functions of museums as preservation, study, and communication. Weil credits the Dutch museologist Peter Van Mensch with this three-function paradigm and then devotes the bulk of his 1990 article to seeking a sharper definition of what the third part – to communicate – actually means. Weil sums up his search for a fuller articulation of the range and consequences of museum communication in the following eloquent passage (2004: 79). It is quoted in full, since it serves as both the point of departure and the underlying reason for this chapter:

> We need to be able to define the purposes for which a museum deals with its public in far finer and more precise ways than we thus far have. Acknowledging how greatly the answers might differ from one museum to another, or even at different times within the history of any single museum, we must be able to say just what a museum would like the outcome of its public program to be. Should this outcome impact a visitor's life in some significant way? If so, in what dimensions, when, how greatly, and how

---

Source: Robert R. Janes, *Curator: The Museum Journal*, Vol. 50, No. 2 (2007): 219–237.

often? Do we believe that this outcome can come about wholly from our own exertions, or do we conceive of the visitor as a collaborator in this effort? Is the impact of the museum limited to its visitors or does its role – as an authority, as an arbiter – extend into the community generally? If so, in what ways, how far, and toward what ends?

The purpose of this chapter is to revisit these salient questions 17 years later, in an effort to determine if we are any closer to understanding the range and consequences of the third part of the paradigm – that of communicating – which also includes, in the spirit of Stephen Weil, a museum's relevance, accessibility, and value to its community. In so doing, I wish to broaden the discussion beyond the conventional context of arts and culture within which museums are normally examined, and to consider museums from a different perspective – as agents of the civil society. In an effort to underscore the importance of shifting one's perspective from arts and culture to a broader social one, it is necessary to consider some worrisome trends currently besetting museums and galleries of all sizes and shapes.

The rise of museum corporatism

The questions posed by Weil in 1990 are more relevant than ever, as contemporary museums and galleries search for meaning at a time when many of them worldwide are struggling to maintain their stability in the face of the complex challenges of the nonprofit world. These challenges range from declining attendance to finding the appropriate balance between earned revenues and public funding, and none of them is easily overcome. Many of these challenges are economic, and are grounded in a belief that continuous economic growth is essential to our well-being, and that the consumption of everything is an appropriate means to achieve unlimited growth. Indeed, capitalism has become inescapable. As philosopher Mark Kingwell notes, "every moment of waking and sleeping life is shot through with commitment to the goods and services of the global economy" (2000: 184). One result of this prevailing worldview in North America is the rise of museum corporatism, characterized by the primacy of economic interests in institutional decision making.

It comes as no surprise that museums are not immune to the imperatives of the economists and the marketplace, and that there is a growing preoccupation with money as the measure of worth (Kimmelman 2005; Levit and Levy 2006; Perl 2006; Grattan 2006: 10–11). This sentiment is now fully installed in the boardrooms of many cultural institutions. *The Toronto Star* reported (Hume 2000) that "the gap between the haves and the have-nots of the museum world will be greater than ever." The director of a prominent American art museum is quoted as saying, "If you want to stay competitive in the cultural arena, you can only do it by investing large sums. That means you have to spend 200 to 300 million [dollars] just to keep up with the next guy." Many museums now see no other way but to consume their way to survival or prosperity, failing to recognize that this is an outdated and increasingly vulnerable perspective, as the following discussion illustrates.

In pursuit of prosperity, many museums have made the choice to increase their popularity and revenues through high-profile exhibitions, and architectural sensationalism, or architectural conceit, depending upon one's perspective (Grattan 2006: 10–11; Hume 2005). This strategy is so consuming of staff and money that there is often little left of either to pursue other activities. Yet various museums are succeeding at this, especially the larger ones, although the long-term sustainability of this approach to business planning is not yet known (Hudson 2006: 38–41).

In a recent research paper prepared for the Getty Leadership Institute, Adrian Ellis concludes that this approach is not sustainable (2002). The problem with the expansion plan, or the galvanizing building initiative, as the context to raise funds, refinance, and move forward, is cogently summarized by Ellis (2002: 21):

> [T]his strategy . . . is a form of pyramid selling or Ponzi scheme. Eventually, after the noise has died down and the new building is completed, the logic of the weakening balance sheet kicks in again. Unless the scheme was so successful that it has generated a whole new set of contributed funding opportunities, then the systemic under-financing reappears, and in a heightened form, given the larger facility and the more ambitious programming on which the facility is premised. The museum stands faced, again, with the three options of crisis appeal, more populist programming, or obfuscatory expansion.

Many of the museums that have adopted the corporatist growth model have also come to resemble corporate entities, with revenues and attendance being the predominant measures of worth. Many of their boards are increasingly indistinguishable from their corporate counterparts, with too many directors being chosen for their business experience, corporate loyalty, or ostensible influence in fundraising. Although such qualifications are obviously important, the danger lies in the growing tendency for these boards to self-select on the basis of these criteria, to the exclusion of other attributes such as cultural diversity and community connectedness.

Beyond corporatism

All of this is puzzling, considering the critical thinking that should accompany the self-proclaimed role of museums as knowledge-based institutions. The belief in limitless growth should be a cause for serious concern among those many museums that have staked their future on attendance figures, architectural vanity, and culture as entertainment. Ironically, and despite all of these initiatives, research indicates that the museum sector is struggling to maintain its audiences, and that the visitor base is stagnant or declining. These trends will be discussed later in this chapter; it is sufficient to note at this point that the challenge for governing authorities, museum management, and staff is to understand that the reigning economic growth model is an ideology, and that it has profound implications for museums. The application of strict economic criteria to museum management is misleading when, for instance, one considers that sound collection management is based on a long-term business plan, not the quarterly results common to business. In contrast, the average lifespan of a multinational corporation (Fortune 500 or its equivalent) is between 40 and 50 years (de Geus 1997: vii, 1–2). Adopting the marketplace model, where growth and money are the primary measures of worth for a museum, is no less ideological than hosting a meeting of World Trade Organization culture jammers (social activists who oppose commercialism by identifying the contrasts between corporate image and the realities of the corporation).

Criticism of the reigning economic model could be considered gratuitous, however, from the perspective of the boards and executives who are responsible for the fiscal health of public museums in the face of declining or stagnant government funding, apathetic audiences, and strident labor unions. Many museum directors are vociferous in pointing out that they would not be pursuing a marketplace agenda if they were not forced to by financial circumstances. Considering the very real fiscal pressures confronting museums, the remainder of this paper is devoted to exploring the possibilities of an alternative approach to the marketplace model for achieving accountability and long-term sustainability. There is good reason to believe that the spread of marketplace ideology is not only enfeebling otherwise competent organizations in the name of so-called fiscal responsibility, but it is also serving to divert museums from realizing their unique strengths and opportunities as social institutions in the civil society.

Civil society

The concept of civil society is by no means new. Its definition is attributed to the nineteenth-century German philosopher G. W. F. Hegel, best known for his Idealist philosophical system in which dialectical logic sees contradictions as fruitful collisions of ideas from which a higher truth may be reached by way of synthesis (Bullock and Trombley 1999: 126, 222, 387). Simply put, "civil society" is the sphere of society lying between the private sphere of the family and the official sphere of the state, and refers to the array of voluntary and civic associations, such as trade unions, religious organizations, cultural and educational bodies, that are to be found in modern, liberal societies. In Hegel's words, "individuals can attain their ends only in so far as they themselves determine their knowing, willing, and acting in a universal way and make themselves links in this chain of social connexions [sic]" (1952: 65).

The Centre for Civil Society at the London School of Economics notes that "civil society" refers to the arena of uncoerced collective action around shared interests, purposes, and values.[1] In theory, its institutional forms are distinct from those of the state, family, and market, although in practice, the boundaries between state, civil society, family, and market are often complex, blurred, and negotiated. Civil society commonly embraces a diversity of spaces, actors, and institutional forms, varying in their degree of formality, autonomy, and power.

Of particular importance in considering museums as agents of civil society is the concept of social capital, since it is civil society organizations that generate the networks, norms, trust and shared values – the "social capital" – that is transferred into the social sphere and not only helps to hold society together, but is also instrumental in facilitating an understanding of the interconnectedness of society and the interests within it. Social capital is born of long-term associations that are not explicitly self-interested or coerced, and it typically diminishes if it is not regularly renewed or replaced (Bullock and Trombley 1999: 798). In short, the civil society enables individuals to participate in a variety of ways in the life of society without direction by the state.

Museums and civil society

In a country like Canada, where most professional museums are owned and operated by some level of government, the role of museums in civil society remains undiscovered and unexplored (Janes 1997: 232, 254–258). Whether a museum is government owned or not (the latter being more characteristic of U.S. museums), the concept of civil society provides a valuable context in which to clarify some persistent complexities that cause much hand-wringing in the search for a clearer understanding of the meaning and value of museums. This is particularly important for museums at this time, since the concept of civil society serves to explain how an increasingly economic view of museums can be both limiting and destructive, and can undermine the unique contributions that museums are capable of making.

An economic view of democratic society sees only individuals and government (Dahrendorf 1990: 24–32). This perspective, grounded in marketplace ideology, creates the space for autonomous activity, but then corrupts civil society by turning everything into commodities. This is best summed up by the eminent sociologist Sir Ralf Dahrendorf (1990: 26):

> If we allow an economic view of society to prevail, then the institutions that provide a buffer between the state and the individual will be left unprotected, leading to their disruption. In the end, universities will be places not of teaching and research, but appendixes of economic growth; the arts will be mediums not of human expression and enjoyment but of commerce, entertainment, or advertising.

Dahrendorf's observations of 17 years ago were prescient; the future has arrived. The pressures to buy, sell, and entertain are front and center. Whether the offerings consist of plastic replicas of Egyptian funerary objects or the mummified remains of our Neolithic ancestors, many museums have joined the perpetual round of entertainments, complete with the inevitable sameness inherent in contemporary consumerism. The short-term necessity of seeing people only as audiences is understandable, but it is only short-term and it is only bottom-line driven.

Museums, as constructions of civil society, are a necessary counterbalance to the rhetoric of the free market. As such, museums have a much more enduring role to play in society by clearly demonstrating that no one group or ideology possesses the sole truth about how society should develop. A competent museum is testimony to the fact that a healthy society is a multitude of competing interests, aspirations, plans, and proposals that cannot be ignored in favor of the rubric of economic utility. Recognizing this creative chaos is the only guarantee of an open society (Dahrendorf 1990: 24). Museums are the obvious caretakers and promoters of these complexities.

The concept of social capital is also relevant here, particularly as defined by Robert D. Putnam in his well-known study of the decline of civil society in the United States (2000). He identified two types of social capital – bonding and bridging – with "bonding social capital" referring to social networks between homogeneous groups of people (similar age, race, religion, and so on). "Bridging social capital" consists of social networks among heterogeneous groups who are dissimilar and diverse. Both of these types of social capital are essential to the civil society, with the bridging variant being critically important in multi-ethnic societies if they are to achieve some degree of stability and cohesion.

Putnam, in the article that led to the book cited above, also suggests the need for further research, including an inquiry into what types of organizations most effectively embody or generate social capital, including reciprocity and the broadening of social identities (1995: 65–78). Museums, although notably absent from the roster of civil society organizations, are already engaged in the creation of both kinds of social capital, as the following examples demonstrate.

Museums as creators of social capital

This discussion of museums as creators of social capital begins with collections, which are simultaneously the most celebrated and the most enigmatic dimension of what defines a museum. Although there is pronounced agreement among museum workers that collections are the *sine qua non* of their institutional identities, the use of museum collections is generally constrained by the weight of tradition and a decided lack of imagination. More often than not, the mere presence of collections is seen to be sufficient reason to maintain the status quo, which means continued collecting and storage with little or no effort to ask honest questions about their purpose, much less identifying creative ways of using them. As Keene quotes in her valuable book on the meaning and use of museum collections, "museums are organisms that ingest but do not excrete" (2005: 1–11).

Nonetheless, collections management has undergone a gradual change in museums over the past decade, most notably with a shift from preservation to access (Hayward 2001: 145–156). No longer is the task of preserving objects and records for posterity considered to be an appropriate end in itself. A redefinition of collections management is underway, with a new emphasis on public interest and audience needs (Keene 2005). If collections can be used to assist in redefining the role of museums as generators of social capital, as the following examples illustrate, this might well serve to disarm the traditionalists in both the marketplace and the museum – thereby introducing the possibility that many of the other resources found in a competent museum could be similarly employed.

Collections and social capital

The Memorandum of Understanding (MOU) between the Glenbow Museum in Calgary (Canada) and Mookaakin Society is one of the first of its kind in Canada. The MOU was signed in 1998 to promote and preserve the Kainai Nation's spiritual doctrines and observances that have existed since time immemorial, including the unique language and history of the Kainai (Mookaakin Cultural and Heritage Society and the Glenbow-Alberta Institute 1998: 1).[2] This agreement allows both parties to cooperatively address matters relating to the Kainai and other Blackfoot collections, which are housed in the Glenbow Museum. There are 17 clauses in this agreement that define, in practical terms, the mutual obligations and requirements. For example, the Glenbow Museum is obligated to develop a process to allow the Kainai access to spiritually sacred materials, cultural objects, and data, including full disclosure of the Kainai museum collections at the Glenbow. The Glenbow will also support the repatriation of Kainai sacred objects that are housed in museums outside of Canada, by participating in discussions with the International Council of Museums and other professional agencies.

The Royal British Columbia Museum (RBCM) in Victoria, British Columbia (Canada) has been a leader in nurturing meaningful relationships with First Nations for decades. In the 1970s, the RBCM had a program of loaning ceremonial regalia (masks, robes, rattles, and so on) from the permanent collection for family and community events. The Aboriginal Material Operating Policy (AMOP) is the latest expression of this relationship, and commits the museum to the "involvement of Aboriginal peoples in the interpretation of their cultures as represented in exhibits, education programs, and public programming developed by the museum" (Royal British Columbia Museum 2003: 1). This policy also commits the museum to continuous dialogue with Aboriginal communities in British Columbia with respect to collections, repatriation policies, and cooperative management efforts.

The Glasgow Museum Resource Centre (GMRC) [Scotland] is a publicly accessible museum storage facility that houses around 180,000 objects, and was designed from the outset to enable people to access their collections.[3] The key issue in the planning was the balance between accessibility and security, and it was decided that supervised tours provided the most affordable balance. The GMRC could not afford to invest the necessary money in glass-fronted shelving, so most of the objects are on open shelves or have grilles. This approach provides a genuine sense of intimate contact with the object.

The GMRC building is in an industrial area in a run-down part of Glasgow, chosen deliberately to help contribute to the revitalization of the area, and also because there is good access by public transport. The key concepts that underlie the current and future work of the GMRC are those of participation and active engagement (Glasgow Museum Resource Centre 2002: 2). The purpose is to create and promote opportunities for the public to actively engage with the heritage that the Glasgow Museums hold on their behalf. Overall, the GMRC believes that museums can be a catalyst for change in people's lives, and can contribute greatly to the quality of life for all residents and visitors by supporting the concept that every citizen has the right to both access and excellence in our diverse culture (Glasgow Museum Resource Centre 2002: 66).

The concept of the Museum of New Zealand Te Papa Tongarewa (Te Papa), located in Wellington, was developed through an extensive national consultative process (Te Papa 2005). Te Papa's conceptual framework incorporates several key dimensions, including unified collections, the narratives of culture and place, the idea of forum, bicultural partnerships between the dominant society and Indigenous peoples, and a multidisciplinary approach to delivering museum services for diverse audiences. Te Papa's conceptual framework recognizes three priority concerns: the earth on which we live, those who belong to the land by right of first discovery, and those who belong to the land by right of treaty.

These three concerns underlie Te Papa's mission, which is to serve as a forum for New Zealand "to present, explore and preserve the heritage of its cultures and the knowledge of the natural environment in order to better understand and treasure the past, enrich the present and meet the challenges of the future" (Te Papa 2005). Te Papa has embraced this mission with commitment and creativity, as exemplified by "A Guide to Guardians of Iwi Treasures," a document that outlines essential considerations in developing sustainable working relationships with Indigenous peoples (Te Papa 2001: 1–8). Te Papa's approach is based on the recognition that museums must increasingly accept that *iwi* (Indigenous tribes) must be involved in the interpretation, exhibition, and care of their artifacts, and that this involvement can only be achieved through strong and effective partnerships.

The other aspect of Te Papa's work which is of particular value is the museum's commitment to certain core concepts underlying the partnerships. These concepts are, in fact, spiritual in nature and are concerned with *tikanga*, or the correct way of doing things. The correct way of doing things is associated with *tapu* and *mana*. Everything has inherent *tapu* (power and influence of the gods) because everything was created by Matua (Supreme God). *Mana* has various meanings, including the power of the gods, the power of the ancestors, the power of the land, and the power of the individual. *Tikanga* is both custom and protocol, and it is instructive to note how Te Papa, a mainstream cultural institution, is integrating spiritual values and beliefs into what are normally seen as the secular activities of a museum. The Te Papa commitment to this is expansive and demonstrates the possibilities of rethinking conventional practices in museums – thereby enhancing intercultural understanding and social cohesion.

Art, healing, and social capital

In addition to these examples of generating social capital through the innovative use of collections, there are important initiatives in forging trust, networks, and shared values that have nothing to do with collections *per se*. One such initiative is the McMullen Art Gallery at the University of Alberta Hospital in Edmonton, Canada, a small gallery whose irrelevance had it destined for closure. This purpose-built gallery is located within the hospital and was founded with the belief that "art should be where there is hurt and healing" (Pointe 2005: 114). Yet, by 1999, only 4% of the 10,000 annual visitors were hospital patients, and only 15% were hospital staff.

All that has changed, as a result of self-critical analysis and the recognition of the gallery's potential as a creator of social capital. The gallery now employs visual artists, poets, writers, musicians, and a dancer, who work directly with patients and their families in the creative process. Patients paint the windows of their rooms, make murals on hospital walls, and create "The Poets' Walk," an installation of patients' writing. After his wife's death in the hospital, a man wrote a note to one of the gallery's poets (Pointe 2005: 120):

> I want to thank you for your great kindness to my Sofia during her long and horrible ordeal. . . . Your visits meant much to her. The words you have written give me solace, and were enormously appreciated by both Sofia and me. Thank-you, they are now treasured mementoes of a difficult end. . . .

Museums, bioregionalism, and social capital

The last example that demonstrates the key role that museums can play as agents of civil society involves neither collections nor visitors, but rather the watershed of one of North America's most important and heavily used rivers (Dallet 2006).[4] In 2001–2002, a variety of non-profit organizations from seven American states that share the Colorado River came together to organize and present *Moving Waters: The Colorado River and the West*. The purpose of the project was to generate a regional consciousness of the river, and to focus on the importance of the river to all its users in non-economic terms. This consortium of humanities councils, museums, libraries, and community councils wanted a public conversation about the river, including its historical, philosophical, and cultural dimensions. Traveling exhibitions, radio documentaries, public meetings, and the voices of scholars, poets, activists, scientists, and First Nations were all used to forge a bioregional consciousness that transcended the insular concerns of local jurisdictions and individuals. Cogent questions were posed for public discussion, such as "does a river have rights?" and "can you own flowing water?"

There is perhaps no better example of the value of civil society collaboration among museums and related organizations than the Colorado River Project, especially with its multidisciplinary focus on complex human issues within an elaborate ecosystem. Even if they were to express an interest in forging such a dialogue, it is highly unlikely that government, with its rigid bureaucracy and policy agenda, and business, with its profit agenda, would be capable of addressing these issues. Museums have unlimited potential to be an integral part of similar processes in a variety of societal sectors that are striving to nurture trust, cooperation, and deeper understanding.

Are museums communicating?

It is now time to return to the questions posed by Weil (2004: 79) in the introduction of this chapter, and to consider whether or not museums are moving in the direction he so ardently desired as a scholar-practitioner. Particularly:

> should this outcome impact a visitor's life in some significant way? If so, in what dimensions, when, how greatly, and how often? Do we believe that this outcome can come about wholly from our own exertions, or do we conceive of the visitor as a collaborator in this effort? Is the impact of the museum limited to its visitors or does its role – as an authority, as an arbiter – extend into the community generally? If so, in what ways, how far, and toward what ends?

There is now some cause for optimism in considering these questions, as illustrated by the foregoing examples of thoughtful collections management, meaningful visitor engagement, and multidisciplinary inquiry encompassing both culture and nature. Viewed from a broader perspective, however, the prognosis for museums is unsettling, as a number of disturbing trends continue to unfold. Despite all of the marketplace initiatives such as blockbuster exhibitions, architectural renewal, and culture as entertainment, research indicates that the museum sector is struggling to maintain its audiences, and that the visitor base in developed countries is stagnant, declining, or increasing disproportionately less than the number of new and renovated museums (Burton and Scott 2003: 56–57; Cheney 2002; Hill Strategies Research Inc. 2003). Statistics Canada (2004) reported in 2002 that the average attendance at Canadian museums remained the same as in 1999.

In addition, despite the significant progress that individual museums have made in broadening their audiences, there has been little or no diversification in the traditional visitor profile, which is still marked by high income and a high level of education (Cheney 2002; Martin 2002). There is also recent research that suggests that earned revenues are not infinitely expandable. In a study of museums and commercialization, Toepler and Kirchberg concluded that the business-like activities of museums "do not appear to generate net revenues that will allow museums to become more self-sustainable in fundamental ways" (2002: 19). Their data also suggest that museum merchandising in general has already reached the limits of future growth. While the funds generated from commercial sources have increased over time, as a general pattern, the share of total museum income accounted for by commercial revenue has not increased (Toepler and Dewees 2005: 143). All of these trends are further complicated by the failure of the museum community, at least in Canada, to ponder what constitutes an appropriate balance between public funding, private funding, and earned revenues for public museums.

At the same time, there are also societal forces at work which have consequences for museums. In a report on the impact of Canada's new funding regime, the Canadian Council on Social Development notes that nonprofit and voluntary organizations are constantly juggling their missions to suit the funding agenda, in response to a demand for greater accountability (Scott 2003). This demand is coming from governments, foundations, and private funders, and many of them want museums and galleries to demonstrate their value to their communities, to be more inclusive, and to help build stronger communities. In addition, the results of a 2003 survey of 2,400 Canadians indicate that 60% of the respondents believe that "museums can play a more significant role in Canadian society," although this role was not defined (Canadian Museums Association 2003). For those respondents who visited museums most often, this view rose to 82%.

It is difficult to ignore the growing disconnection between the market-driven search for meaning and relevance – as increasingly promulgated by boards of directors and museum executives – and the desires of governments, foundations, donors, and citizens that museums demonstrate their societal value and play a more significant role. Stephen Weil obviously sought the latter alternative in his relentless pursuit of museum relevance, but in the meantime the economic model of museum competence has now become commonplace. Irrespective of their demonstrated ability to generate social capital and be socially responsible, the value of museums is now measured in terms of consumption, including visitation, retail sales, food purchases, gallery rentals, and so forth (Keene 2005: 159). While these services clearly provide essential operating revenues, the current preoccupation with them obscures the fact that they are the means to the end, not the end in themselves. By confusing these fundamentally different realities, museums are forsaking the opportunity to creatively rethink their purpose, and are instead embracing an increasingly fragile and unsustainable economic model based on fickle consumerism and showmanship. To attempt to improve the current situation by adopting the same marketplace ideology that has reduced the level of public support for museums so dramatically over the past two decades could be ignored as wishful thinking, or perhaps solipsism, if the implications were not so apparent.

Accommodating corporatism

Broadly speaking, there are now at least two distinct trends, or perhaps worldviews, unfolding as museums continue to define their futures: one committed to the status quo and economic utility; the other in pursuit of a new and different accountability grounded more in societal interests and aspirations. These are not dialectical forces competing for supremacy, however, since neither has demonstrated any long-term survival power. As noted earlier, the long-term effectiveness of the "build it and they will come" perspective remains to be seen. There is also only a modicum of evidence that demonstrates the potential for financial sustainability inherent in adopting a socially responsible mission (Koster and Baumann 2005; Koster 2006; Pointe 2005). Nonetheless, with the growing popularity of museum corporatism, it is useful to consider what can be done to diminish its most negative aspects and hasten the development of museums as agents of civil society.

Reforming the marketplace

The first possibility is to strive to perfect the marketplace, not abolish it (Heath and Potter 2004: 334–335). In short, the current marketplace is flawed, hypo-critical, and far from ideal, and there needs to be more government, not less, to redefine equitable rules on behalf of citizens and communities. In the ideal market, there would be no monopolies, no barriers to entry in any industry, and competition would be based entirely on the price and quality of the goods being sold. In addition, there would be no advertising – a growing necessity in light of the 700 to 3,000 advertisements the average person must face every day (Heath and Potter 2004: 206).

In the ideal market there would be no windfall profits and, most importantly, all businesses and corporations would have to factor in the full social and envi-ronmental costs of their actions in every decision made. Reforming the market is not a short-term answer to the choices confronting museums, however, espe-cially considering the growing intimacy between corporate interests and national governments in economically developed countries. This is readily apparent in the arena of globalization, where problems that were once resolved by national gov-ernments re-emerge in an international context, where the rule of law is absent (Heath and Potter 2004: 335). Reforming the market in the foreseeable future is unrealistic – the vested interests weigh far too heavily and there is no apparent leadership to pursue this agenda.

Creating more autonomous museums

As noted earlier, the majority of the large public museums in Canada are government owned and operated, as is the case in the United Kingdom, Australia, and Western Europe, as well as with national museums everywhere. With government ownership, the status of the museum as a civil society organization is both ambiguous and variable, and depends upon the degree of government control. There are various government museums that enjoy a great deal of autonomy in their governance and operations, and thus are positioned to act more or less independently in the civil society space between the individual and government. There are also many government museums that are tightly controlled by legislation and cultural officials, the latter dutifully impeding organizational autonomy in the name of policy and procedure, while also conveying this timidity to museum boards and staff.

One of the more debilitating examples of this restricted autonomy is the appointment of the governing boards for Canada's national museums, although this situation appears to be improving with the federal government paying increasing attention to the recommendations of board-nominating committees.[5] These board appointments are political patronage and rarely include anyone who has any substantive knowledge of museum practice. This is by no means a reflection on those appointed, but rather demonstrates the workings of an archaic, self-serving political system that is oblivious to the complexities of nonprofit governance and management. The solution is obvious for those museums in this predicament: eliminate the dependent relationship by redesigning the legal relationship to achieve more organizational autonomy.

At least one museum has opted for this alternative (Janes 1997: 249–252), although doing so is admittedly fraught with risks, including the potential withdrawal or reduction of government financial support, as well as the pervasive and unnerving anxiety that accompanies a radical departure from the status quo. The conventional argument states that tight controls are essential to ensure a high level of accountability for the tax dollars spent on government museums. In fact, this is a disingenuous rationalization, as it is a matter of record that government museums are no more accountable than any other type of museum. The opposite is more likely to be true, as revealed by the research of Griffin and Abraham (1999: 45–92). In contrasting the prevalence of effective management practices across 30 government and non-government museums and science centers in four countries, they note that of the 10 worst organizations, 8 are government. Whether it is reforming the marketplace, or achieving more autonomy for government museums, neither appears to be achievable at this time, or practical enough to accomplish what needs to be done.

Branding the civil society

Branding is a course of action with significant potential to nurture the role of museums within civil society and, paradoxically, it is also instrumental to the success of the marketplace. A brand is an engineered perception made up of the name of an organization, its products, services, and perceived attributes (Scott 2000: 36). The purpose of the branding is to create an identity that comes to be associated with your brand and no other (Heath and Potter 2004: 210). There are three types of brands, including corporate brands, product brands, and values brands, with museums belonging in the category of values (Scott 2000: 36). A values brand, according to Scott, "has an enduring core purpose, which creates a long-term bond with those sectors of the market sharing the same values" (2000: 36). It is by no means apparent, however, that museums are aware of these distinctions, since museum branding and marketing strategies treat visitors and users as consumers and customers (Kotler and Kotler 2000: 273). Museums use the language of the marketplace in addressing their purported needs and aspirations.

With few exceptions, most museums do not brand values – they brand "stuff," and the language used is all about customer service, efficiency, entertainment, value for money, and consumption (Janes and Conaty 2005). The uncritical use of these private sector techniques has not gone unnoticed. There is now a growing interest in moving beyond the language of the marketplace to create civic brands around ideas that are less tangible, and intended to both build emotional identification and take credit for the public value (read social capital) that nonprofit organizations create (Demos 2005: 4; Ferguson 2006; Institute for Media, Policy and Civil Society 2004). Herein lies the most hopeful approach for nurturing a civil society identity for museums. There are several requirements for doing so, which are summarized below (Institute for Media, Policy and Civil Society 2004: 1–10).

The brand is central to the values and mission of a museum and well-funded marketing departments cannot be given the task of defining the brand. It cannot be manufactured, but must be based on the answers to several key questions, including why does your museum exist, what changes are you trying to effect, what solutions will you generate, and what are your non-negotiable values (collaborative, inclusive, diverse, empowering)? These questions are hauntingly similar to those posed by Weil 17 years ago. One can only conclude that the forces of the marketplace have diverted most museums from experimenting with the answers.

For a start, marketers might ask if there are any deficiencies, issues, or interests in their community that their museum could help to address. Having answered these fundamental questions about why and what, the museum then is tasked to develop a constellation of activities that both create and maintain the brand, as exemplified by the activities of innovative museums discussed earlier in this chapter. In short, branding is a powerful technique for allowing museums to move beyond the reigning model of economic utility and to create an alternative language to that of the private sector – a language more appropriate for museums as instruments of civil society.

Conclusions

This chapter has provided a critical overview of the growing dominance of marketplace thinking in museum affairs. Clearly, the extent and meaning of this phenomenon are highly variable, with the larger urban museums experiencing the most impact. It also bears repeating that nothing is to be gained by insisting that either business or the nonprofit sector holds the exclusive keys to the well-being of museums, irrespective of their size or governance structure. Museums are diversified portfolios, and some of their work (restaurants and product development, for example) is directly subjected to market forces (Janes 1999: 22). Other activities, such as intercultural collaboration and raising bioregional consciousness, have no obvious import for the market economy. It is important to note that a museum's mission can assume both the imperatives of the marketplace and the challenges of social responsibility. The essential requirement is the board and staff leadership to enable these disparate aims to coexist within the mission.

As a context for the paradoxical juxtaposition of market imperatives versus non-profit values, it would be desirable for museum boards, executives, and funders to acknowledge a more realistic understanding of museum finances, as aptly summarized below (Ellis 2002: 1):

> Museums are usually loss-making enterprises and red-ink businesses. We too easily forget that the implications of this fact permeate every aspect of the financial dynamic and culture of nonprofit organizations. There are many kinds of goods and services for which the market does not generate enough demand at a sufficiently high price to stimulate supply, given the marginal cost of producing those goods or services. Much of what we think of as the business of nonprofits fits this category, from lobbying for human rights . . . to providing live performances of symphonic music. . . . Left to the market, the costs of supply are either too high or the level of effective demand is too low for these activities to be priced in a way that is accessible to more than a very select band of consumers, if at all.

The cause for alarm lies in the growing imbalance in the metaphorical museum portfolio discussed above, with museums opting for the "bigger is better" mentality so ingrained in consumer society and so familiar to the increasing number of business people assuming governance roles on museum boards. The solution lies not in becoming more like businesses, but in differentiating the value of museums based on their unique resources and attributes (Falk and Sheppard 2006). Departing from the status quo of marketplace imperatives opens the door to more creative definitions of museums as social institutions in the civil society – institutions whose complexity and potential stem from a uniquely high level of passion and commitment. Rather than being overwhelmed by the dictates of unrelenting capitalism, and the uncertain future it is creating, museums must exploit their uniqueness, resist homogenization, and test alternative means of achieving meaning and sustainability.

The risk in not doing so lies in the domination of marketplace thinking – a phenomenon in the museum world that has diverse origins, including the economic necessity of balancing government budgets, the uncritical adoption of business methods by museum practitioners, and the tribalistic thinking that characterizes both business and its leaders. This tribalism refers to the strong in-group loyalty of the business community, as well as the exaltation of business leaders above those in other sectors of society. This perspective is best exemplified by a prominent Canadian business leader who referred to nonprofit management as an oxymoron. Righting this imbalance is a significant challenge, especially for museum leaders – recognizing the seduction of large capital spending and the ensuing public profile, as well as the rewards of keeping the peace between a "marketplace" board and management. It should be noted that the museum world also suffers from its own kind of tribalistic and group thinking, which limits experimentation and innovation.

One key to meeting this challenge was intuitively known to Stephen Weil, although he never identified it by name in his many publications. This is the concept of orthogonal thinking, which recognizes that the "conventional, consensus reality we call the human condition is itself inexorably and strongly conditioned in the Pavlonian sense" (Kabat-Zinn 2005: 347–352). Adopting an orthogonal perspective requires that conventional reality be seen from a different perspective, more spacious than that of individual and organizational self-interest, and more admitting of creativity, compassion, and wisdom. It is a matter of what one is willing to see or not see, and to what extent one is able to ignore perceptions and remain habitually inattentive to what is really going on. Weil was always committed to promoting awareness among museum people about their responsibilities to society; he warned against being inward looking.

Isn't this "orthogonal perspective" also Weil's habit of mind, and what he wished for when he spoke and wrote about museums? If individuals can change their consciousness, Kabat-Zinn argues, institutions can too, by moving beyond conditioned thinking and conventional reality, and by considering new possibilities, insights, and actions (2005: 353). Such thinking is what animates civil society, and is grounded in questions about what constitutes caring for the greater good, what this might entail, and then doing what needs to be done.

This level of organizational reflection and consciousness fits neatly within the concept of the post-museum, as defined by Eilean Hooper-Greenhill (2000). She argues that it is time to move beyond the idea of the museum as a locus of authority conveyed primarily through buildings and exhibitions, and adopt a new model: the post-museum. The post-museum is fundamentally different from the traditional museum and is intended to embrace a variety of societal perspectives and values, with the traditional museum perspective being only one voice among many. Perhaps most importantly, the post-museum involves intangible heritage. Along with the emotions of visitors, the post-museum is directly linked to the concerns and ambitions of communities (Hooper-Greenhill 2000: 152). The congruence between the post-museum and the role of museums in civil society is obvious and, hopefully, liberating for those who might require a theoretical construct for the thoughtful renewal of museums. At the very least, Hooper-Greenhill presents a cogent and convincing pathway for all museums that are committed to learning and growth.

Stephen Weil was crystal clear about this fundamental point: there is no "essence of museum" that must be preserved at all costs. Museums exist in, of, by, and for society and are obligated to continually ponder their work in an effort to be worthwhile and make a difference. What is essential in this process is the need to keep reflection and dialogue alive, and avoid complacency and the tyranny of outmoded tradition. Equally important is the need to remain vigilant and thoughtful in the face of the enormous pressures to conform to the prevailing imperatives of the marketplace. The essential task of all sound leadership and management is to ensure both individual and organizational consciousness. It is only through heightened self-awareness, both organizationally and individually, that museums will be able to fulfill the lofty triad of preservation, truth, and access described by Stephen Weil (2004: 75), and assume their role as key institutions in the civil society.

Acknowledgements

This chapter is an outgrowth of two public presentations, including the First Annual Stephen E. Weil Memorial Lecture at the Annual Meeting of the Mid-Atlantic Association of Museums (MAAM) in Baltimore, Maryland in October 2005, and a keynote address at "The Museum: A World Forum," University of Leicester, United Kingdom, in April 2006. I would like to thank Alexandra Badzak, the late Gerry Conaty, Robert Ferguson, Eilean Hooper-Greenhill, Suzanne Keene, and Richard Sandell for their valuable comments on an earlier draft of this chapter.

Notes

1 For the Centre for Civil Society at the London School of Economics, see http://www.lse. ac.uk/collections/CCS/what_is_civil_society.htm.
2 The Kainai (or Blood) Reserve is the largest among the Blackfoot Confederacy and is located west and south of the city of Lethbridge, Alberta, Canada. The term "Blackfoot" is commonly used to refer to the four nations of the Blackfoot Confederacy: the Kainai (or Blood), Siksika (Blackfoot; Northern Blackfoot), Apatohsipiikani (Piikuni, Peigan), and Ammskaapipiikani (Piegan, Blackfeet).
3 Mark O'Neill, Glasgow Museums, personal communication, March 30, 2005.
4 "Moving Waters: The Colorado River and the West." Available online: http://www.neh. gov/humanities/2001/septemberoctober/feature/watershed.
5 Joanne DiCosimo, Canadian Museum of Nature – personal communication, June 12, 1997.

References

Anderson, G. 2004. *Reinventing the Museum: Historical and Contemporary Perspectives on the Paradigm Shift*. Walnut Creek, CA: AltaMira Press.

Bullock, A. and S. Trombley, eds. 1999. *New Fontana Dictionary of Modern Thought*. London: HarperCollins.

Burton, C. and C. Scott. 2003. Museums: Challenges for the twenty-first century. *International Journal of Arts Management* 5(2) (Winter): 56–68.

Canadian Museums Association. 2003. Canadians and their museums: A survey of Canadians and their views about the country's museums. Accessed May 15, 2006 at http://www.museums.ca/Cma1/ReportsDownloads/surveyanalysis2003.pdf.

Cheney, T. 2002. The presence of museums in the lives of Canadians, 1971–1998: What might have been and what has been. *Cultural Trends* 48: 39–72.

Dahrendorf, Sir R. 1990. Threats to civil society, east and west. *Harper's* 281 (1682) (July): 24–26.

Dallet, N. 2006. Making connections: An exhibition along the Colorado River. Paper presented at The Museum: A World Forum, April 25–27. University of Leicester, United Kingdom.

De Geus, A. 1997. *The Living Company*. Boston: Harvard Business School Press.

Demos. 2005. Civic brands: Public value and public services marketing. Accessed February 23, 2006 at http://www.demos.co.uk.

Ellis, A. 2002. Planning in a cold climate. Unpublished research paper prepared for the Directors' Seminar: Leading Retrenchment, the Getty Leadership Institute, Los Angeles, California.

Falk, J. H. and B. K. Sheppard. 2006. *Thriving in the Knowledge Age: New Business Models for Museums and Other Cultural Institutions*. Lanham, MD: Altamira Press.

Ferguson, R. 2006. The non-profit imagination. Accessed June 5, 2006 at http://www. knowledgemarketinggroup.com/pages_index/jun082006_index.htm.

Glasgow Museum Resource Centre. 2002. Audience development plan. GMRC #2D-1. PDF file. Accessed April 10, 2005 at http://www.glasgowmuseums.com/venue/index. cfm?venueid=8.

Grattan, N., ed. 2006. New museums. *Muse* 24(3): 10–11.

Griffin, D. J. G. and M. Abraham. 1999. Management of museums in the 1990s: Governments and organizational reform. In *Management in Museums*, K. Moore, ed., 45–92. London: Athlone Press.

Hayward, A. 2001. *Standard Practices Handbook for Museums: Unit 3 – Collections. Museum Excellence Series: Book 1*. Edmonton, Alberta, Canada: Museums Alberta.

Heath, J. and A. Potter. 2004. *The Rebel Sell: Why the Culture Can't be Jammed*. Toronto: HarperCollins.

Hegel, G. W. F. 1952. *The Philosophy of Right*. Encyclopaedia Britannica Great Books 46. Originally published in 1821. Chicago: Encyclopaedia Britannica, Inc.

Hill Strategies Research Inc. 2003. Museums and art gallery attendance in Canada and the provinces. Accessed May 19, 2006, at http://www.hillstrategies.com/docs/Museums_ report.pdf.

Hooper-Greenhill, E. 2000. *Museums and the Interpretation of Visual Culture*. London and New York: Routledge.

Hudson, A. 2006. New! Improved! The rhetoric of relevancy in a construction boom. *Muse* 24(3): 38–41.

Hume, C. 2000. Arts story: Cultural vacuum. *The Toronto Star* (August 26).

——. 2005. A fragile renaissance: Toronto's big-name architecture is rising against perilous landscape. Once the fever subsides, how we will afford our culture? *The Toronto Star* (October 8).

Institute for Media, Policy and Civil Society. 2004. Not-for-profits: Brand superstars in the making? Accessed June 6, 2006 at http://www.impacs.org/files/CommCentre/ Brand%20Superstars.pdf.

Janes, R. R. 1997. *Museums and the Paradox of Change: A Case Study in Urgent Adaptation*. Calgary, Canada: University of Calgary Press.

——. 1999. Embracing organizational change in museums: A work in progress. In *Management in Museums*, K. Moore, ed., 7–27. London: Athlone Press.

Janes, R. R. and G. T. Conaty, eds. 2005. *Looking Reality in the Eye: Museums and Social Responsibility*. Calgary, Canada: University of Calgary Press and Museums Association of Saskatchewan.

Kabat-Zinn, J. 2005. *Coming to Our Senses: Healing Ourselves and the World Through Mindfulness*. New York: Hyperion.

Keene, S. 2005. *Fragments of the World: Uses of Museum Collections*. Oxford: Elsevier Butterworth-Heinemann.

Kimmelman, M. 2005. What price love? *New York Times* (July 17).

Kingwell, M. 2000. *The World We Want: Virtue, Vice, and the Good Citizen*. Toronto: Viking.

Koster, E. H. 2006. The relevant museum: A reflection on sustainability. *Museum News* 85(3): 67–70; 85–90.

Koster, E. H. and S. H. Baumann. 2005. Liberty Science Center in the United States: A mission focused on external relevance. In *Looking Reality in the Eye: Museums and Social*

Responsibility, R. R. Janes and G. T. Conaty, eds., 85–112. Calgary: University of Calgary Press and Museums Association of Saskatchewan.

Kotler, N. and P. Kotler. 2000. Can museums be all things to all people? Missions, goals, and marketing's role. *Museum Management and Curatorship* 18: 271–287.

Levit, R. and E. Levy. 2006. On cultural politics. *Harvard Design Magazine* (Spring/Summer): 86–93.

Martin, A. 2002. The impact of free entry to museums. *Cultural Trends* 47: 3–12.

Mookaakin Cultural and Heritage Society and the Glenbow Alberta Institute. 1998. Memorandum of Understanding between the Mookaakin Cultural and Heritage Society and the Glenbow Alberta Institute. Unpublished document on file at the Glenbow Alberta Institute (Glenbow Museum), Calgary, Alberta, Canada.

Perl, J. 2006. Arrivederci MOMA. *The New Republic*. Accessed February 1, 2006, at http://www.tnr.com/index.mhtml.

Pointe, S. 2005. Is art good for you? In *Looking Reality in the Eye: Museums and Social Responsibility*, R. R. Janes and G. T. Conaty, eds., 113–127. Calgary: University of Calgary Press and Museums Association of Saskatchewan.

Putnam, R. D. 1995. Boarding alone: America's declining social capital. *Journal of Democracy* 6(1): 65–78.

———. 2000. *Bowling Alone: The Collapse and Revival of American Community*. New York: Simon and Schuster.

Royal British Columbia Museum. 2003. Aboriginal material operating policy. Accessed April 6, 2005 at http://www.royalbcmuseum.bc.ca/corporateservices/aboriginal-material operatingpolicy-2.pdf.

Scott, C. 2000. Branding: Positioning museums in the twenty-first century. *International Journal of Arts Management* 2(3): 35–39.

Scott, K. 2003. Funding matters: The impact of Canada's new funding regime on nonprofit and voluntary organizations. The Canadian Council on Social Development, Ottawa, Canada. See also www.ccsd.ca.

Statistics Canada. 2004. Heritage institutions, 2002. Accessed June 12, 2006 at http://www.statcan.ca/Daily/English/041025/d041025a.htm.

Te Papa. 2001. A guide to guardians of Iwi treasures. *Te Papa National Services Resource Guides*, Issue No. 8. Accessed April 4, 2005 at http://www.tepapa.govt.nz.

———. 2005. About us/What we do – Our concept, act, mission and corporate principles. Accessed April 4, 2005 at http://www.tepapa.govt.nz.

Toepler, S. and V. Kirchberg. 2002. Museums, merchandising and nonprofit commercialization. *National Center for Nonprofit Enterprise Working Paper*. Accessed June 12, 2006 at www.nationalcne.org/papers/museum.htm.

Toepler, S. and S. Dewees. 2005. Are there limits to financing culture through the market? Evidence from the U.S. museum field. *Journal of Public Administration* 28: 131–146.

Toynbee, A.J. 1947. *A Study of History*, Volume I, New York: Oxford University Press.

Weil, S. E. 2004. Rethinking the museum: An emerging new paradigm. In *Reinventing the Museum*, G. Anderson, ed., 74–79. Walnut Creek, CA: AltaMira Press.

17

MUSEUMS*

Stewards or spectators?

Introduction

Exploring the value, purpose and priorities of museums at the start of the twenty-first century is a critically important initiative, and I am honoured to be speaking to you today by videoconference from the Banff Centre for the Arts in Banff, Alberta – located in the heart of Canada's Rocky Mountains. At a time of increasing pressure on our fragile biosphere, I believe it is important to minimize our personal impact on the planet, in part through decreasing the frequency of jet travel and the carbon footprint it creates (see Note 1). This videoconference keynote may be the first of its kind for an international museum conference, and I am hoping that more museum conferences will adopt this approach.

The 12 months since the publication of my book *Museums in a Troubled World: Renewal, Irrelevance or Collapse?* have left me both inspired and discouraged and I want to address both of these reactions.[1] I will set the stage for my remarks with several observations and questions from Ruben Nelson, a Canadian futurist. He notes:

> To date, every culture, including our own, has unconsciously assumed and planned for a future that is an essential continuation of the world as we know it – an essentially familiar future, even if it holds some surprises. Given our 200,000 years of experience as Homo sapiens, this assumption is

*Source: Robert R. Janes, keynote presentation for "The Museum 2010: An International Conference Exploring the Value, Purposes and Priorities of Museums at the Start of the 21st Century," May 17–19, 2010, National Taipei University of Education, Taipei, Taiwan. (This presentation was delivered by videoconference on May 17, 2010, from the Banff Centre for the Arts, Banff, Alberta, Canada.)

not unreasonable. It's not surprising that no culture, past or present, has yet developed the capacities – those habits of mind and institutional infrastructure – that would allow it, openly and consciously, to ask two fundamental questions, which are: Is it sound to assume that our future will be in essential continuity with our present; that we do not live in a rare time of essential deviation in the trajectory of history? Further, is it sensible to assume that globalizing, modern, industrial capitalism can be made sustainable – without undergoing a fundamental transformation?[2]

A troubled world

To explore these questions and their complexities, I can do no better than turn to Thomas Homer-Dixon, the Canadian political scientist, who has looked broadly and deeply at our civilization and identified various global pressures that he calls the "five tectonic stresses that are accumulating deep underneath the surface of our societies."[3] These include:

1. Population stress arising from differences in the population growth rates between rich and poor societies, including the spiraling growth of mega-cities in poor countries;
2. Energy stress – above all, from the increasing scarcity of conventional oil;
3. Environmental stress from worsening damage to our land, water, forests and fisheries;
4. Climate stress from changes in the makeup of our atmosphere; and
5. Economic stress resulting from instabilities in the global economic system and ever-widening income gaps between the rich and the poor.

I would also add another tectonic stress, and that is the erosion of cultural diversity, sometimes called the ethnosphere. Globalization is not merely a question of marginalization for Indigenous peoples – it is a multi-pronged attack on the very foundation of their existence and livelihoods. I cannot help but ask if curating permanent collections of the world's exotic patrimony is an adequate response to the increasing loss of cultural diversity, or should museums be advocates and defenders of its preservation? In short, what constitutes museum stewardship for those peoples on the margins of the modern world?

Internal obstacles

If these global stresses are not sufficient to make us rethink our individual and collective responsibilities, let's consider some internal stresses that are particular to museums as organizations. These are not only sources of stress, but they are also obstacles to learning and growth, and to moving beyond the status quo. There are many, so I will limit my discussion to several that are familiar:

- The first internal museum challenge is the persistence of what I call the "fallacy of authoritative neutrality." Most museums maintain that they are obligated to assume a so-called neutral stance in all of their public offerings, lest they be accused of espousing certain values or opinions. This is fuzzy thinking at its best, because to remain neutral is to maintain the status quo with all of its value-laden deficiencies.

- Second, museums continue to proclaim themselves as knowledge-based institutions, while research continues to decline or disappear, even in our flagship institutions. Why is this happening, why is information becoming more important than knowledge, and why cannot museums be more honest about their responsibilities?

- The third challenge is that of organizational hierarchy, as most museums have uncritically adopted the corporate hierarchical model, with its attendant rigidity, fragile morale, and the all-powerful director or CEO at the top of the hierarchy. Increasing complexity in our work lives is making hierarchy unworkable, and the alternative lies in self-organization.[4] In short, creativity can be enhanced by organizing and leading differently.

- The fourth internal obstacle is the museum's major preoccupation – the collections. Yet, the management of collections is still marked by little or no imagination and is hidebound by tradition. As one museum worker noted: "Museums are organisms that ingest but do not excrete."[5]

- The last obstacle is the stultifying sameness of museum exhibits.[6] The obsolescence of museum exhibitions is a result of various factors, including a lack of imagination about what exhibitions could be, as well as the traditional ways in which they are developed – requiring large amounts of time, people, and money. Nonetheless, the museum community mostly accepts these limitations and continues to produce more of the same, often at great cost.

The three agendas

Admittedly, museums are highly complex organizations – housing multiple professional allegiances, competing values and interests, and a range of diverse activities that would haunt the most seasoned corporate executive. To help simplify these complexities, I will use the concept of the "three agendas."[7] The first agenda focuses on the work and content of the museum (the "what"), including the mission, exhibitions, programs, and collections. This is where boards of directors and staff normally focus, as well as nearly all museum conference programs.

The second agenda is about "how" things are organized – the people and resources required to do the work, including strategic plans, organizational structure, staffing, training, communication, and resource allocation. In short, the second agenda is the all-pervasive culture of the organization, and the automatic pilot that keeps the museum moving along in its old and familiar track, even when changes are being made in the first agenda.

The third agenda is concerned with change – with a focus on the mental and emotional constructs in individuals that set the stage for how they interact within the organization. This agenda is about individual development, learning, and transformation, all of which museums must address if they are to answer the crucial question of *"why"* they do what they do. Too many museums are "stalled out" because of unresolved third agenda issues, and there is no doubt that these issues are daunting, unacknowledged, or intractable for many museums – which explains why they are not the subject of professional discussions and public forums. The third agenda is my primary focus here, as meaningful change will require that museums and museum workers rethink their roles and responsibilities at a time of unprecedented global challenges.

Whither museums?

Irrespective of the three agendas, are museums mindful of what is going on in the world around them, and inside their own organizations? Blockbuster exhibitions, museum shops, and internally driven agendas devoted to collecting, exhibiting, ancillary education, and edutainment are not actually the point, when one considers the urgent need for ingenuity and leadership required to address the litany of social, environmental, and organizational issues mentioned earlier. It is important to note, however, that the erosion of stewardship, in both the natural and cultural worlds, enjoys our collective denial because there is no individual, organization, or conspiracy to blame. The problem is actually much deeper and more difficult, because the problem is all of us.

Many of us, including museums as organizations, have entered that perplexing realm of being in conflict with our own sense of values and principles, and we are uncertain about what to do. As Gareth Morgan, the management scholar, noted, "Organizations end up being what they think and say, as their ideas and visions realize themselves."[8] Perhaps a more accurate observation is that "museums end up being what they do *not* think or say."

Will museums continue to believe that tradition and status will exempt them from increasing irrelevance, or will they seize the opportunity to assume responsibility as gifted and privileged social organizations? Museums of all shapes and sizes are untapped and untested sources of ideas, knowledge, and information, and are ideally placed to foster individual and community participation in the quest for greater awareness and workable solutions. Nonetheless, far too many museums have largely abstained from a broader commitment to the world in which they operate. Instead, they have allowed themselves to be held increasingly captive by the economic imperatives of the marketplace and their own internally driven agendas.

Myopia persists

Museums may not be any more inattentive than usual, but recent examples indicate that management myopia persists, while the challenges continue to accumulate.

For example, in discussing the future of museums and their seeming irrelevance with colleagues, I encounter at least three forms of denial.[9] These include *existential* denial, as in, "there's no problem, it's not happening"; or *consequential* denial, as in "it doesn't really matter – there are more important concerns"; or, third, *fatalistic* denial, as in "there's nothing I can do about it anyway." These reactions are neither adaptive nor useful, but they are commonplace and reassuring.

Other challenges for museums are emerging from the innovative work of the British think-tank Demos, which is investigating the role of culture, including museums and libraries, in democratic societies. In a report entitled *Cultural Value and the Crisis of Legitimacy: Why Culture Needs a Democratic Mandate*, the author notes:

> There is a nervousness about art and culture in our political discourse that results from a democratic deficit. Public approval of culture is hidden; politicians are scared off culture by the media; and cultural professionals have spent too much time in a closed conversation with their funders, feeding them with statistics and "good" stories. . . . As a result the relationships between the public, politicians and professionals have become dysfunctional.[10]

I suggest that this nervousness about culture and museums is just as pronounced in Canada and the US as it is in the UK, although I do not know about the situation in Taiwan.

Another example of museum myopia, this one from Portugal, is even more ominous in light of the celebrated claim that museums are unique spaces for civic engagement. In an article by Ana Delicado entitled "Scientific controversies in museums: notes from a semi-peripheral country," the author discovered that:

> Museums are seen not as forums for debate, let alone as sites for promoting public participation in decision-making, but merely as places to convey scientific truth and to persuade the lay public to accept and trust the decisions that are made on their behalf.[11]

My last example of museum myopia concerns the continuous and widespread lament among museum workers about the lack of public funding for collections care and management. One North American museum association recently called for strong graphic images of endangered collections for upcoming newspaper coverage. Is it sensible to think that the public will empathize with the consequences of uncontrolled collecting and the attendant lack of forethought? Will museums continue to collect when they cannot care for what they have?

The consequences of inattentiveness

These examples demonstrate the persistence of museum myopia and the question remains – why does this matter? As I discussed in *Museums and a Troubled World*, all of these complexities can be distilled into a rather simple model of what could happen if the social and environmental issues mentioned earlier continue to intensify. The economist Jeremy Rifkin wrote that "our modern economy is a three-tiered system, with agriculture as the base, the industrial sector superimposed on top of it, and the service sector, in turn, perched on top of the industrial sector."[12] Each sector is totally dependent on more and more non-renewable energy – fossil fuels.

Rifkin writes that as the availability of gas and oil diminishes (and oil reserves are expected to peak by 2020, according to the International Energy Agency), the public and private service areas will be the first to suffer, because services are "the least essential aspect of our survival."[13] In short, an economy with limited energy sources will be one of necessities, not luxuries or inessentials, and will be centered on those things required to maintain life. Where do tourism, edutainment, museum shops, permanent collections, and blockbuster exhibitions fit in this looming scenario?

Although museums *are* unique and untapped resources in heightening societal stewardship, they are a public service and the extent to which they will weather the future is difficult to predict. It is obvious that reducing energy consumption and avoiding large and consumptive buildings are prerequisites, making the recent museum building boom even more bizarre. I do note that more and more museums are committing to responsible work practices, but energy efficiency is only one ingredient in a meaningful future. Along with the willpower required to reduce consumption is the greater need to transform the museum's culture-industry business model into one of a locally embedded problem-solver, in tune with the challenges and aspirations of communities.

For museums, change has become discontinuous, and the past is no longer the guide to the future. Judging by the growing fragility of the global museum community, museums have little to lose by moving beyond the status quo and embracing a more mindful mission. As museologist Douglas Worts wrote, "Culture needs to be understood as to how we live our lives, and not what we do in our leisure time."[14] Putting it more bluntly, museum consultant Adrian Ellis noted that "We have too many museums with big bodies and small brains, whereas what a museum really needs is a big brain."[15]

Moving to the conscious world of the mindful museum will be marked by acute uncertainty and high-consequence risks – meaning those risks over which we have no obvious control, such as global warming.[16] This is all about the search for something better, something not yet, or in other words – hope. Hope is one of the deep components of human creativity and it will be an essential ingredient as museums become increasingly aware of their responsibilities to the world around them. In short, hope keeps possibility open. And as quoted in *Museums in a Troubled World* (page 185), James Knustler notes that hope is not a consumer product, and that we are going to have to generate our own hope by facing reality and dealing with the circumstances that it presents.

Still searching for resilience

I have mentioned the importance of hope as a prelude to the last half, or the happier half, of this address. Various individuals and organizations have adopted new ways of thinking and working, all of which embody the hopefulness I have just described. These examples are also indicative of resilience, and I must digress here for a moment to emphasize this quality – resilience is surely one of the keys to the continuation not only of museums, but also of the world as we know it.

Resilience means "the ability to recover from, or adjust easily, to misfortune or change."[17] Resilience also suggests a frame of mind that is not bound by deadening routine, habit, or traditional practices. Resilient organizations and systems are flexible, agile, and adaptable, and there's an important distinction between resilience and sustainability. Resilience emphasizes the need to increase our ability to withstand crises. Sustainability, on the other hand, can be a brittle state – unforeseen changes can cause its collapse. Resilience is all about being able to overcome the unexpected. Sustainability is about survival. The goal of resilience is to thrive.[18] So should be the goal of museums – to thrive.

To avoid catastrophe, it has been suggested that we should build "resilience" into our critical technological and social systems, so that they do not fall apart when hit by significant shocks. More importantly, Homer-Dixon notes that, as ecology replaces physics and becomes humanity's master science, and a complex-systems perspective begins to influence our way of seeing the world, our relationship with expertise will change. We will learn that we should not rely so much on "experts" to manipulate the systems around us, because these elites have little real understanding of how these systems work. As the twenty-first century progresses, ecology's best lesson may be that we need to take more responsibility for our own well-being – museums included.[19]

New thinking for a new vision

Change, renewal, and developing resilience are indeed weighty responsibilities and museums are going to need all the help they can get. I have continued my search for thinking and initiatives with the potential to assist museums in reinventing their future – ranging from the non-threatening to the radical. The first of these is as simple and challenging as acquainting ourselves with the idea of "catagenesis" – an awkward word, but a valuable concept, that means renewal through breakdown.[20] Most of us, at some point in our personal or professional lives, have suffered a crisis – loss of a job or the death of a loved one, for example. In response, we examined our assumptions, gathered our resources, and started again, more often in new and better ways. This is catagenesis – the everyday reinvention of our lives.

It would be helpful if museums, as organizations, adopted a similar perspective, for it is only through breakdown, reorganization, and renewal that museums can adapt to a changing environment. Denying what's going on around us, and making only incremental adjustments in our work and thinking are probably about the worst things we can do. Or, as the Head of the Rockefeller Foundation said – "a crisis is a terrible thing to waste."[21]

Museums might also consider experimenting with some innovative, yet no longer new, ideas from the digital world – I'm thinking particularly about crowdsourcing. An excellent example is the for-profit InnoCentive, which has linked together a network of about 150,000 engineers, scientists, and entrepreneurs around the world.[22] They use a Web-based platform to gather solutions to problems that have confounded people working in just one place. In short, hundreds or even thousands of people who have never met, and never will, compete to solve a problem. Happily, I note that the Institute of Museum and Library Services in the US has launched a wiki called "UpNext" – a forum for exchanging ideas and seeking solutions to the major challenges affecting museums and libraries.

Another remarkable approach to thinking differently is the concept of Positive Deviance, or PD.[23] Positive Deviance is based on the observation that in every community there are certain individuals or groups (the positive deviants) whose uncommon, but successful behaviours, enable them to find better solutions to a problem than their peers. These individuals or groups, however, have access to exactly the same resources and face the same or worse challenges as their peers. The PD process invites the community to identify and optimize existing and sustainable solutions from *within* the community, and not rely on external resources to solve problems.

In 1991, for example, more than 65% of all children living in Vietnamese villages were malnourished. Using the idea of PD, an NGO (non-governmental organization) and four communities discovered that certain families (the positive deviants) avoided malnutrition because they collected tiny shrimps and crabs from rice paddy fields and added these to their children's meals along with sweet potato greens.[24] The positive deviant families were also feeding their children three to four times a day, rather than twice a day, which was customary. Hence the positive deviants' children were much healthier. The museum community could also experiment with PD, in an effort to release the stranglehold of tradition and find out what is really working in everyday museum practice. I am thinking particularly of the demonstrated resilience of small and medium-size museums, which is more often than not overshadowed by the large and so-called elite museums.

Moving beyond tradition

In addition to these alternative ways of thinking, various museums have chosen to move beyond traditional practices. The examples I will now describe have replaced passivity and compliance with creativity, altruism, and originality, and are defining new ways of being for museums as social institutions. My first example is from Museum Victoria in Melbourne, Australia, which has a Senior Curator of Sustainable Futures who is responsible for an ongoing project called "Water Smart Home." Australia is the driest inhabited continent in the world, and yet one of the highest consumers of water per capita. A key to creating a sustainable water future is to change the way Australians think about and use water in their daily lives. The Museum's "Water Smart Home" is a community-based project that engages, educates, and inspires the public in how to reduce, reuse, and revalue water.[25]

The second example is the Heifer Village Museum and Foundation in Little Rock, Arkansas (US) – a hands-on, global education facility with interactive exhibitions that introduce visitors to the possibility of a world free of hunger and poverty, while caring for the earth.[26] The Heifer Foundation gives gifts of livestock and training to families to improve their nutrition and generate income in sustainable ways. The museum features an outdoor commons area and a state-of-the-art conference hall where international experts and thought leaders, staff, and visitors learn from each other, as well as directly from those who are achieving self-sufficiency around the world. This is a powerful reversal of traditional roles – a *museum* in the service of global philanthropy.

My last example of a notable museum innovation comes from Taiwan and is based on the cluster concept first proposed by Michael Porter, the Harvard Business School professor. In a recent article by Chieh-Ching Tien of the National Taiwan University of Arts, museum clusters are described as geographic concentrations of interconnected museums, founded on the premise that the cluster-based approach enhances best practice and innovation, as well as new market opportunities.[27] In the Danshui museum cluster, for example, the organizational structure is flat and emphasis is placed on the sharing of resources. In addition to the director in overall charge of the museum cluster, each museum has its own manager and the three museums share an administration team, an education team, and a day-to-day operations team.

I am not aware of this degree of integration and cooperation among North America's fiercely independent museums but, as funding continues to decline, the museum cluster is a creative solution. Fortunately, we have all of these examples of non-traditional thinking and doing to demonstrate the abundance of creative possibilities. They are heartening reminders that elite boards, big budgets, and quantitative measures are not the hallmarks of museum effectiveness.

In praise of museums

I hope that I have made it clear that there are many reasons why communities should care about their museums, albeit more for their unfulfilled potential than for their conventional practices. However, does the museum community itself actually care about its broader, non-museum relationships? It is important to note that, in the contemporary literature on global challenges, museums are seldom, if ever, mentioned – either as friend or foe. Perhaps anonymity is bliss, but it is akin to irrelevance as global issues intensify.

What are museums to do in light of their self-inflicted challenges, the tyranny of marketplace ideology, and all of the pressing global issues? I submit that renewal – rethinking, replacing, and rejuvenating – is the only alternative. There is much lip-service paid to the vital concept of renewal in organizations, but very little actual renewal. This is because authentic renewal is a tough and burdensome process, and is easily ignored in the face of other organizational pressures. Yet, global society is weighed down, perhaps paralyzed, by outdated institutions in all sectors. The fact that most museums think that everything is fine is the most important reason for widespread renewal. As uncertain as the future is, I now want to discuss four reasons why museums can, and must, transform.[28]

First, museums are seed banks, and are the repositories of the evidence of our adaptive failures and successes, as well as our creativity. In this sense, museums are akin to the biological seed banks that store seeds as a source for planting, in case seed reserves elsewhere are destroyed. Modernity has led to the loss of knowledge about sustainable-living practices that have guided our species for millennia, and the need to revisit this cumulative knowledge and wisdom may come sooner than expected, as the destruction of the biosphere makes industrial technology increasingly harmful. The record of material diversity contained in museums may have a value not unlike biodiversity, as we seek resilient solutions in an increasingly brittle world.

Second, museums are diversity personified. It is estimated that there more than 55,000 museums in 202 countries.[29] It is as if there is a global museum franchise, only it is self-organized, has no corporate head office, no global marketing budget, and is trusted and respected. This informal network exists by virtue of the apparently universal need for museums, and its inherent diversity is a critical antidote to the globalized, corporate homogenization that is eroding our world. With a global presence grounded in individual autonomy and diversity, yet united in purpose and tradition, this vast network of museums has untold potential for nurturing both museum and societal renewal.

My third reason underpinning museum renewal is that museums are keepers of locality. No one would dispute the fact that the majority of the world's museums are expressions of locality and community, and are spawned by communities of all sizes and shapes. Wendell Berry, the poet/farmer, writes that "the real work of planet-saving will be small, humble and humbling," and that problem solving will require individuals, families, and communities.[30] The ubiquity of museums and the familiarity they enjoy are the building blocks of renewal and planet-saving, especially as the need increases to seek ingenuity and solutions on a smaller scale – in communities.

Last, museums bear witness, and this is eloquently summed up by Wendell Berry again, who wrote:

> One thing worth defending, I suggest, is the imperative to imagine the lives of beings who are not ourselves and are not like ourselves: animals, plants, gods, spirits, people of other countries and other races, people of the other sex, places – and enemies.[31]

Are not museums founded on "imagining the lives of beings who are not ourselves?" All museums specialize in assembling evidence based on knowledge, experience, and belief, and in making things known – the meaning of bearing witness. The scope for bearing witness has expanded exponentially in recent times, and now includes our damaged biosphere, as well as a litany of human rights conflicts. It is puzzling that so fundamental a trait as bearing witness is languishing from disuse, obscured by the pressures of the marketplace and museums that are too timid to assert its value.

Conclusions

As I conclude my remarks, one question remains for all those who may be disturbed at the thought of rethinking the traditional role of museums as custodians of collections and purveyors of ancillary education and entertainment. That is – How is it that museums, as social institutions, may remain aloof from the litany of socio-environmental issues that confront us, when many of these issues are intimately related to the purpose, mission, and capabilities of museums as we know them? This is not a call for museums to become social welfare agencies or Greenpeace activists, but rather to heighten their awareness and deliberately align their capabilities and resources to bring about change – both internally and externally. It has been noted that "There is no power for change greater than a community discovering what it cares about."[32] Will communities continue to care about museums in their current guise? Will museums discover what *they* care about? Or are museums at risk?

ROBERT R. JANES AWARD FOR
SOCIAL RESPONSIBILITY

CHANGING THE WORLD...ONE COMMUNITY AT A TIME

Visit almost any Alberta community and at its heart you will find a museum. As integrated community institutions, and custodians of community identity, museums are uniquely positioned to explore innovative solutions that help their communities adapt to demographic shifts, economic changes, and influxes of new populations.

This Award is the vision of Dr. Robert R. Janes to support and further the work of museums that are solving community issues and promoting health and well-being. Together with the Alberta Museums Association, our ambitious goal is to create healthy, vibrant, and sustainable communities by investing in initiatives that effect real social and environmental change.

AWARD RECIPIENTS

• Each year, a $3,000 award will be provided to one Alberta museum that has worked with social service groups or community stakeholders to create positive change for a locally identified social or environmental issue.

• Funds are provided to support museums with proven track records in order to investigate what makes their programs work, scale up their activities, and create models that will allow their work to be replicated elsewhere.

Get Involved

Your donation to this Award will increase its ability to effect real change in Alberta's communities. Private individual donations received from Alberta residents may be eligible for matching funding.

For more information, or to donate online, visit **www.museums.ab.ca**.

Donations can be submitted to:

ALBERTA MUSEUMS ASSOCIATION
SUITE 404, 10408-124 STREET, EDMONTON AB, T5N 1R5
E: INFO@MUSEUMS.AB.CA
F: 780.425.1679 P: 780.424.2626

Be a Catalyst for Change

Use this card to submit your donation today! I would like to provide a tax deductible donation in the following amount to the Robert R. Janes Award for Social Responsibility:

☐ $10   ☐ $25   ☐ $100   ☐ _____

*First Name: _____   *Last Name: _____

*Address: _____

Email: _____   Phone: _____

* Indicates required field. Tax receipts will be issued for donations of $10 or more.

☐ I wish for my donation to be recognized anonymously.

☐ Visa   ☐ MasterCard   ☐ Cheque

Credit Card Number: _____   Expiry Date: _____

Signature _____

FIGURE 8   Robert R. Janes Award for Social Responsibility, announcement, Alberta Museums Association, Canada, 2013.

I remain haunted by the words of E.O. Wilson, the Pulitzer Prize-winning biologist, who wrote, "We are creating a less stable and interesting place for our descendants to inherit. They will understand and love life more than we, and they will not be inclined to honor our memory."[33] To assume that existing models of museum practice can somehow fulfill the requirements of the future is to invite the scorn and alienation of future generations. The world is also in need of intellectual self-defense as an antidote to the self-interest of corporatists, government passivity, and the belief in money as the measure of worth. Museums, as public institutions, are morally and intellectually obliged to question, challenge, or ignore the status quo and officialdom, whenever necessary. Resistance, independence of thought, and hope are essential to renewal, as is resilience.

With the exception of museums, there are few, if any, social institutions with the trust and credibility to fulfill this role. It is time to honour this trust and broaden the purpose of museums to encompass mindfulness and social responsibility. Human adaptation lies at the heart of current global challenges, and all museums can help. Not surprisingly, society is largely unaware of the museum's unique potential, much less demanding its fulfillment. This is ideal, for it permits museums to engage in deliberate renewal of their own design, but the time to do so grows short. Marketplace ideology, capitalist values, and corporatism are clearly not the way forward for museums, having conclusively demonstrated their toxic fragility and moral bankruptcy.

Museums have always been important to me because they are organizations whose purpose is their meaning – to borrow a phrase from Charles Handy, the British social philosopher.[34] The meaning and purpose of museums are now in need of urgent rethinking and redefinition, based on deep listening to the issues and challenges that confront our world. Judging by the state of the troubled world and the urgent need for community organizations of the highest order, museums are positioned to realize their potential in a manner that truly reflects their inherent worth.

In conclusion, it is my hope that each of you will help point the way to greater awareness in the troubled world of museums. The importance of your leadership in raising the consciousness of the museum community brings to mind a quote from the essayist Arthur Koestler, who wrote:

> It all looks beautifully obvious – in the rearview mirror . . . But, there are situations where one needs great imaginative power, combined with *disrespect* for the traditional current of thought, to discover the obvious.[35]

All of us are capable of discovering the obvious, and I wish each of you the best of success in both your museum work and your personal lives.

Note

1 A carbon footprint is the total amount of greenhouse gases produced to directly and indirectly support human activities, usually expressed in equivalent tons of carbon dioxide (CO_2). Carbon dioxide is a greenhouse gas that is causing global warming.

References

1 Janes, R. R. 2009. *Museums in a Troubled World: Renewal, Irrelevance or Collapse?* London and New York: Routledge.

2 Nelson, R. 2008. "One Way to Frame the Space for Our Dialogue." A Weekend Exploration of "A New Axial Age?" Delta Lodge at Kananaskis, Kananaskis, Alberta, Canada, May 2–5, 1–2. See also: http://www.internationalfuturesforum.com/s/213.

3 Homer-Dixon, T. 2006. *The Upside of Down: Catastrophe, Creativity, and the Renewal of Civilization,* Toronto: Alfred A. Knopf, pp. 11–12.

4 Janes, R.R. and R. Sandell. In Richard Sandell and Robert R. Janes (eds.) 2007. *Museum Management and Marketing,* London and New York: Routledge, pp. 4–5.

5 Keene, S. 2005. *Fragments of the World: Uses of Museum Collections,* Oxford: Elsevier Butterworth-Heinemann.

6 McLean, K. 2007. "Do museum exhibitions have a future?" *Curator: The Museum Journal* 50(1): 109–121.

7 Phillips, W. 2012. "The Three Agendas," *Management Briefing,* Rex Roundtables for Executives. Available online: RexRoundtable.com.

8 Morgan, G. 1986. *Images of Organization,* Newbury Park, CA: SAGE Publications, pp. 11–17.

9 Steele, K. 2008. "Adjust Your Sails or Be Blown Off Course: Emerging Trends in Canadian PSE." Academica Group. Available online: http://www1.uwindsor.ca/sem/sites/uwindsor.ca.sem/files/adjust-your-sails.pdf, p. 22.

10 Holden, J. 2006. *Cultural Value and the Crisis of Legitimacy: Why Culture Needs a Democratic Mandate,* London: Demos. Available online: http://www.demos.co.uk/files/Cultural valueweb.pdf, pp. 12–13.

11 Delicado, A. 2009. "Scientific Controversies in Museums: Notes from a Semi-Peripheral Country," *Public Understanding of Science* 18(6): 759–767. Available online: http://pus.sagepub.com/content/early/2009/04/07/0963662508098577.abstract.

12 Rifkin, J. 1980. *Entropy: A New World View,* New York: The Viking Press, pp. 217–218.

13 Connor, S. 2009. "Warning: Oil Supplies are Running out Fast." Available online: http://www.independent.co.uk/news/science/warning-oil-supplies-are-running-out-fast-1766585.html.

14 Worts, D. 2008. "Rising to the Challenge: Fostering a Culture of Sustainability" (Guest Editorial), *MUSE* 26 (September/October), p. 6.

15 Ellis, A. 2005. Quoted in Sudjic, D. "Who Now Will Save Our Museums?" *Observer,* 13 February. Available online: <http://www.guardian.co.uk/artanddesign/2005/feb/13/art.museums>

16 Hicks, D.W. "Teaching for a Better World: Learning for Sustainability." Available online: http://www.teaching4abetterworld.co.uk/transition.html.

17 *Merriam-Webster's Collegiate Dictionary, 10th Edn,* Springfield, MA: Merriam-Webster, Incorporated, 2002, p. 993.

18 Homer-Dixon, *The Upside of Down,* pp. 20–21, 283–287.

19 Homer-Dixon, T. 2009. "The Newest Science: Replacing Physics, Ecology Will Be the Master Science of the 21st Century," *Alternatives Journal* 35(4): 10–11, 38–39.

20 Homer-Dixon, *The Upside of Down,* pp. 22–23.

21 Nee, E. 2009. Interview with Judith Rodin, Head of the Rockefeller Foundation. In *Stanford Social Innovation Review,* Summer. Available online: http://www.ssireview.org/articles/entry/q_a_judith_rodin/.

22 Nee, Interview with Judith Rodin.

23 Positive Deviance Initiative. Available online: http://www.positivedeviance.org/.

24 *Nutrition in Vietnam* (1990–2004). Positive Deviance Initiative. Available online: http: http://www.positivedeviance.org/projects/countries.html?id=105.

25 *Water Smart Home – Project Description.* Museum Victoria, Melbourne, Australia. Available online: http://museumvictoria.com.au/collections/themes/2729/water-smart-home-project-description.

26 Heifer Village. Available online: http://www.heifer.org/what-you-can-do/experience-heifer/heifer-village/index.html.

27 Tien, Chieh-Ching 2010. "The Formation and Impact of Museum Clusters: Two Case Studies from Taiwan," *Museum Management and Curatorship* 25(1): 69–85.

28 A full discussion of the singular qualities and capabilities of museums can be found on pp. 178–182 in Janes, R. R. (2009) *Museums in a Troubled World: Renewal, Irrelevance or Collapse?* London and New York: Routledge.

29 See: The International Council of Museums. Available online: http://icom.museum/resources/frequently-asked-questions/.

30 Berry W. 1993. *Sex, Economy, Freedom and Community*, New York and San Francisco: Pantheon Books, p. 24.

31 Berry, *Sex, Economy, Freedom and Community*, pp. 82–83.

32 Wheatley, M.J. See "Turning to One Another (2002)." Available online: http://en.wikiquote.org/wiki/Margaret_Wheatley.

33 Wilson, E.O. 2006. *Creation: An Appeal to Save Life on Earth*, New York: W.W. Norton and Company, Inc., p. 81.

34 Handy, C. 1994. *The Age of Paradox*, Boston: Harvard Business School Press, p. 183.

35 Koestler, A. 1959. *The Sleepwalkers: A History of Man's Changing Vision of the Universe*, London: Hutchison and Co., p. 48.

18

WHAT ARE MUSEUMS FOR?*

Revisiting *Museums in a Troubled World*

Introduction

This chapter aims to do three things. First, it will put recent Nordic museum developments into context, and it will introduce the reader to the thoughts and ideas of Robert R. Janes, as presented in his 2009 book *Museums in a Troubled World: Renewal, Irrelevance or Collapse?* These initial sections are developed by the first author. This is then followed by a themed discussion between the first author and Robert R. Janes, drawing on his perspectives concerning the "troubled museums." Finally, a hands-on perspective is added, as some current challenges in the sector are treated, hopefully adding to a prosperous debate on the future of Nordic museums.[1] It should be stressed that, while aiming for debate, the terms and concepts presented by the authors might seem open ended; this is fully intentional, as the authors are not pressing for any predetermined, fixed model, or solution. Rather, our intention is to encourage a more reflective and self-critical approach to museum development, which might present itself in a variety of ways. In other words, in reading through the text the keyword should be "reflection" and not "fixed solution."

In recent years, museums in the Nordic countries have been under tremendous pressure to perform and act as private companies, rationalizing and focusing on profits over traditional museum activities. This is hardly a surprise, as the international museum scene, at least since the 1990s, has been much influenced by private business and politicians with an unprecedented belief

---

Source: Morten Karnøe Søndergaard and Robert R. Janes, *Nordisk Museologi* 2012 (1): 20–34. Morten Karnøe Søndergaard is Professor, Department of Learning and Philosophy, Aalborg University, Aalborg, Denmark, and Director of INCEVIDA – Interregional Centre for Knowledge and Educational Studies.

in continuous economic growth. For museums, the result has typically been voluminous prestigious buildings – referred to as "vanity architecture" by critics. Oftentimes, the very same museums have committed to investing enormous sums of money into short-term special exhibitions: instant and positive consequences have been a substantial rise in audience attendance. However, the long-term effects include heavy debts, as the initial interest is followed by a decreasing number of visitors, while fixed costs remain high. Currently, this type of development is also identifiable in Nordic countries, although to a lesser extent. Another trend, which has marked the Nordic countries, is a museum sector divided into A and B sectors as a result of some museums rejecting the economic growth paradigm, often choosing entrenchment and sticking with tradition or the "usual" practice which, boldly stated, has hindered any kind of development.[2]

There is certainly a paradox in having a museum sector that at the same time is over and underdeveloped. Sadly, one common feature shared by many museums is that they have increasingly lost their relevance to surrounding society. Too much emphasis on revenue generating has meant that museums have shortened their scope to counting visitor numbers, instead of asking questions about relevancy. Following a path of solid entrenchment is far from doing better, as relevancy is not even put up for debate. While some traditionalists might dispute such remarks, while claiming a self-evident museum relevancy, there is a growing debate in the Nordic countries on what the future of museums should look like. It has become increasingly legitimate to question the purpose of museums. While this debate is rather new in the Nordic context, such questions have been on the agenda of the international museum community for some years.

A participant in provoking and propelling this international debate is the co-author of this chapter, who, in 2009, published the book *Museums in a Troubled World: Renewal, Irrelevance or Collapse?* Despite being an independent work, the book builds on ideas and perspectives which Janes discussed earlier in his 2007 article, "Museums, Corporatism and the Civil Society," and equally so in his book *Museums and the Paradox of Change: A Case Study in Urgent Adaptation* (1995; 1997), as well as in edited volumes such as *Museum Management and Marketing* (with Richard Sandell, 2007) and *Looking Reality in the Eye: Museums and Social Responsibility* (with Gerald T. Conaty, 2005).[3] All these works should be of interest to Nordic museum professionals in the present context, but undoubtedly *Museums in a Troubled World* is the magnum opus. Fortunately, Janes has since remained very much on the same track, which is illustrated by the Q and A between the author and the co-author from a previous article:[4]

> MKS: In your final section [of the article: "Museums, Corporatism and the Civil Society"] you quote Stephen Weil that there is no essence of museums. Museums should simply exist of and by society in an ever-changing process. This also means branding and rebranding. In your perspective, why are museums lagging behind in this area?

RRJ: Museums have led a privileged existence as agenda-free and respected custodians of mainstream cultural values – certainly not beholden to the incessant demands of the so-called real world. There is no doubt that museums enjoy a great deal of trust and respect from society at large, whether or not it is merited. This, in turn, has created a sense of complacency among museum practitioners, causing them to assume that traditional thinking and practices are adequate. This perspective is further exacerbated by the many museums managers and leaders who may have 20 years of experience, but it is the same year repeated 20 times. In other words, there is an unwillingness or inability to learn and grow, in part because of intense work pressures. Complacency, a sense of entitlement, the absence of learning, and the weight of tradition all contribute to the failure to rethink and reinvent the role and responsibilities of museums.

The problem with museum branding is that it has been borrowed uncritically from the private sector and, with few exceptions, most museums do not brand their values, ideas, mission, or substantive contributions. They brand "stuff," using the language of the marketplace, and treat visitors and users as consumers and customers. It is time for museums to move beyond the language of the marketplace to create civic brands around ideas and values that are based on the answers to key questions. These questions should consider why the museum exists, what changes it is trying to effect, and what solutions it will generate. Branding values and ideas is an essential means of heightening museum consciousness and moving beyond the reigning model of economic utility.

The relevancy of bringing Janes to the scene should be evident from the above. Janes takes pride in museum development, and he can easily visualize the ideal museum and, referring to the words of one reviewer of his 2009 book, he manages to put his points in a provocative, yet thoughtful way.[5]

Museums in a Troubled World revisited

Most readers of *Museums in a Troubled World* will admit that it leaves no one unaffected.[6] Janes deliberately provokes thought by addressing themes that are controversial or, at the very least, untested in a museum setting. So, what are the themes and issues which Janes brings to the forefront?

Essentially one question stands before all others with Janes, and that is the role of museums as social institutions. He is curious about why museums are embracing, knowingly or unknowingly, the values of relentless consumption, while at the same time neglecting issues related to the well-being of their communities, including social challenges and environmental issues (these are repeated topics throughout the book). Janes' main argument, or criticism, is that much more could, and should, be expected from museums that are publicly supported, knowledge-based, and trusted civic institutions. Janes builds his work around four basic assumptions. The first of which is the assumption that human beings are the co-creators of their lives and their organizations if they accept the responsibility to do so. Translated into the museum context, the point is that museum boards, staff, and supporters are potentially the real experts on what is needed, but they need to unlock their tacit knowledge and put it to use. Museums also need to include unorthodox and non-museum perspectives, which they have a tendency to neglect, and hence there exists a lot of untapped knowledge.

Janes' second assumption is that museums have the potential to be among the most free and creative workplaces, but will fail to fulfill this potential as long as museum mission statements are focused on *how* the work is done, instead of asking *why* these tasks are relevant. The third assumption is that there is a lack of self-criticism, or an inability to ask difficult and uncomfortable questions among museum workers and their museums. Janes' assumption is that learning is grounded in the idea of self-critical and reflective thought, a task which has become a survival skill for those organizations who wish to learn.[7] Janes' fourth assumption is that the future is not knowable, meaning that instead of all museums doing precisely the same thing i.e., upgrading on technology, there should be more debate and discussions. Museums should, in Janes' words, "question everything," including what tomorrow might bring. From these basic assumptions, Janes dives in.

One of the main topics dealt with is the fact that the world is facing global environmental changes that threaten our public resources, and museums need to react as responsible knowledge institutions to this unfolding. The threats are laid out as interrelated stress factors, putting human and ecological existence under pressure. Factors included by Janes are environmental damage and pollution, climate change, and important in this context, economic instability. The role of museums should be to raise awareness about such issues and exercise stewardship. As pointed out by Janes, stewardship lies at the heart of public museums, making them ideal instruments for engaging in long-term involvements for the future. The call for change is urgent, as more and more museum leaders seem to be keen on doing the same thing over and over again. In Janes' perspective, the unreflective pursuit of economic growth is a destructive practice. Museums need do more on behalf of their communities, but they also need to be reflective, especially concerning their role and potential in society.

The call to become engaged and let go of traditional thinking is becoming even clearer as Janes, in his fourth and fifth chapters of *Museums in a Troubled World*, deals with the marketplace and corporatism. He states that these entities have to be seen for what they are, as they continue to derail museums from focusing on their core values and building their strengths as social institutions. Another argument is that corporatism, and the values embedded in the framework of the free market, are actually obstacles to achieving any kind of long-term sustainability. This is a hint, not just for museum professionals, but also for private entrepreneurs and corporate leadership, that a new and more responsible approach is called for. And, as Janes points out, there are alternative and new ways of collaborating across diverse perspectives, but they are not found in conformity and unthinking consumption.

It is clear to all that there is certainly a clash of values between private businesses and museums. Market ideology and corporatism have failed to demonstrate any real ability to deal with the complexities of a competent museum. Subjecting a museum to market forces is essentially undermining the core of the museum. There is, however, as indicated by Janes, potential in creating shared values and societal responsibilities between business and museums. Truly recognizing this could be the first step in renewing insights and potentially obtaining sustainability. This perspective will guide the following discussion.

Discussion: collaboration between museums and business[8]

After establishing the framework within which the Nordic museums find themselves, and introducing some of the thoughts and ideas put forward by Robert R. Janes, this section is dedicated to a themed discussion between the authors. The pivotal theme will be collaboration between museums and business, a focus that is very much derived from Janes' chapters on corporatism and the marketplace.

MKS: The twenty-first century has been an age of accelerated interdependence. Cross-sectoral collaboration between corporations, nonprofits, networks, governments etc. will intensify. A convergence of political, economic, and social pressures is fostering such collaboration. Part of your focus is on museums meeting private business. Looking at the overall picture, what would you say is the greatest risk which might come from this meeting?

RRJ: I think that the greatest risk is already widespread, with museums increasingly held captive by neo-classical economics and marketplace ideology – the idea that economic growth and consumption are the keys to prosperity and societal well-being. In North America, at least, business leaders and economists are some of the most influential people in society. Yet, they advocate ways of thinking and behavior that are completely outmoded and, in fact, are unintelligent and harmful to our collective well-being. Business leaders, business school academics, economists, and politicians are apparently oblivious to several profound issues, including the depletion of natural resources (including fossil fuels, minerals, and water), the proliferation of negative environmental impacts (including the burning of fossil fuels), and the inability of governments and banks to deal with the enormous government and private debt that has accumulated over the last 20 years.[9]

Economic growth is essentially finished as a result of these issues, and the real question now is how society is going to adapt to a non-growing, equilibrium economy. As the energy expert Richard Heinberg succinctly noted, "Civilization is about to be downsized."[10] This is not apocalyptic thinking, as resource depletion, climate impact, and systemic financial failures (international bank failures, the European debt crisis, house foreclosures in the United States, etc.) are already well underway. The risk for museums in collaborating with business is becoming complicit in this destructive view of the world, which is based on wealth accumulation in the short term with no regard for the future. Not only do the vast majority of corporations and businesses remain committed to growth and profit irrespective of the societal costs, they are also highly tribalistic.

By tribalistic, I mean a particular reference group in which individuals identify with each other through common language, ritual, and legend.[11] Business tribalism has several faces, including the celebrity worship of business leaders; in-group thinking that excludes non-business people; immature and self-serving corporate governance; and narcissistic notions of personal worth as measured by obscenely high salaries for executives in North America and Western Europe. These faces of business are now corroding museum practice, disguised by the imperative that museums must become more like businesses. Museums must consider just how invasive this commercial ideology has become, recognize it for what it is, and change direction. It doesn't make sense for museums to partner with business organizations that are oblivious to the profound issues confronting society and the planet. This culture of business is a dominant factor in blinding museums to a sense of their own worth and well-being, and constitutes the second risk of aligning with business, along with the complicity mentioned above.

MKS: Museums, and cultural institutions at large, work from different optics than private business. However, the search for new alliances is on, as it is becoming obvious that resources and insights might be drawn from this. What are, in your mind, the essential ingredients in casting an alliance between a museum and a private business?

RRJ: There are various stories about museum/private sector partnerships, some of which are happy while others have been disastrous, but all of which contain many hard-won insights and lessons. At the outset, it is best for the museum to choose its own partner and this means developing criteria in advance for what is required in any museum/business alliance. There is no sense in wasting time and energy in reacting to a partner you didn't choose. Avoiding this passive role requires defining what success looks like at the outset, and then selecting your partner accordingly. This, in turn, requires a holistic consideration of the museum's mission, purpose, and values in advance of the alliance, and not fixating on the celebrity building as an easy solution, for example. Sustained rigour in decision making is essential, which means paying attention to content and substance, and not succumbing to the inevitable, commercial dogma that accompanies corporatism, business hype, marketing, and the search for quick fixes.

Museums must continually revisit their mission, and ask *why* they are doing what they're doing, and how will the new business alliance enrich the mission and the results. The momentum and excitement of a corporate courtship can easily sidetrack the key question – "Will our mission and values be advanced by this initiative, or is it a superficial solution to more important concerns?" It is easy to assume the merits of a corporate alliance, and it is necessary for both the governing authority and the staff to truly reflect on the potential advantages and disadvantages. The boards of directors of many museums have an obvious business bias because many of the board members come from business – this can be dangerous. The marketplace has but one master – the bottom line – and to think otherwise is unrealistic and naïve. As the former CEO of the Glenbow Museum in Calgary, Canada noted, "There's no such thing as pure corporate philanthropy – it's all strategic now."[12]

MKS: In your book, you stipulate the meeting between museums and private business as a clash of values. While this perspective undoubtedly holds to be true what, or perhaps who, can facilitate mediation between the two types of values?

RRJ: Values are essential and enduring beliefs that articulate how a museum will conduct itself. Values also serve as guiding beacons by describing how the museum wants to treat others, as well as how it wishes to be treated. It would seem that in the marketplace, there is little time for considering values. Instead, values are replaced by imperatives – more visitors, more earned revenues, more collections, etc. Unthinking adherence to the marketplace by museums has caused a conflict of values, because every museum, in the language of the marketplace, is a mixed portfolio. Some museum work is clearly subject to market forces, such as restaurants, shops and product development, while other activities, such as collections care, scientific research and community engagement, are not. The latter bear no relation to the market economy and, in fact, require a safe distance from marketplace and corporatist influences.

Further, marketplace ideology and corporatism have failed to demonstrate any real ability to deal with the complexities of a competent museum and are, instead, homogenizing the complex portfolio with a stultifying adherence to financial considerations – at the expense of most everything else. The tyranny of quantitative measures, such as attendance numbers and shop revenues, is a clear indication of this reality.

It is obvious that the marketplace is incapable of addressing the collective good, while museums are potentially key agents in doing so. Corporations, both national and multinational, are second only to governments in their influence on public policy and have clearly demonstrated time and again that the common good can be an inexhaustible arena for private gain. Business people believe that markets create communities when, in fact, the opposite is true – marketplace activities actually deplete trust.[13] Communities and their nonprofit organizations create and sustain the trust upon which the marketplace is based. Many museums are apparently unaware of their role and their strengths in this vital responsibility, and are willing to let their unique assets be subsumed under the rhetoric of business imperatives. For all these reasons, I believe that each museum must be the final arbiter of its own best interests, irrespective of any business alliance it might have.

MKS: A different aspect of collaboration between museums and business is the question of life span. In your work you address this topic by noting the fact that the average life expectancy of multinational corporations is between 40 and 50 years, while museums, on the other hand, are more or less intended to exist for an indefinite number of years. Yet, behind this lie very different strategies and understandings. What in your view is the most damaging effect of museums having adopted "the corporation" mentality? And are there any positive effects?

RRJ: Overall, I believe that the preoccupation with money and quantitative measures has diverted museums from fulfilling their potential role as trusted social institutions, aligned with the interests, aspirations, and issues of their communities. It is important to realize that the private ownership of natural resources; the increased centralization of power between governments and corporations; the elimination of biological and human diversity; the irrational belief that science and technology will undo or fix the problems we have created; the refusal to set limits on production and consumption; and the concept of progress at the expense of the biosphere – all of these things are the consequences of marketplace ideology or are in the service of this ideology. Why museums would embrace commercial dogma as a strategy for the future when heightened stewardship is of paramount importance remains a vexing and essential question.

In fact, the toxicity of the corporate/business world has become so pronounced that the *Harvard Business Review* recently published an article which notes that the capitalist system is under siege and that business is increasingly seen as the major cause of social, environmental, and economic problems.[14] How refreshing to see this admission of failure in the world's leading business publication, although the authors maintain that corporations are still superior to government and the social sector in leading social progress. Predictably, business tribalism and arrogance persist, despite the authors' admission that "the legitimacy of business has fallen to levels not seen in recent history."[15] There are certainly positive effects coming from business, however, and perhaps the most important is the introduction of business literacy to the museum community – a topic that is discussed later in this interview.

MKS: A general trend throughout your book is the call for museums to position themselves in a development that will take us from "ego" to "eco." In other words, putting museums at the forefront when it comes to addressing pressing social and environmental issues. What is it specifically about museums that makes them appropriate to perform this task?

RRJ: Museums and galleries are potentially the most free and creative work environments on the planet, and the scope for creativity and initiative should be just about limitless in a well-run museum. There are very few other workplaces that offer more opportunities for thinking and acting in ways that can blend personal satisfaction and growth with organizational and societal goals. These opportunities constitute the true privilege of museum work, and it is up to each museum worker to seize them. Unlike the private sector, museums do not have production or sales quotas, although the imposition of quantitative measures has certainly moved museums in that direction. Nonetheless, they are still relatively immune to the tyranny of production that marks the private sector. In contrast to the public sector, museums are not forced to administer unpopular government policies.

Most importantly, museums are privileged because they are organizations whose purpose is their meaning.[16] This elegant observation by Charles Handy suggests that any activity unaligned with organizational purpose could jeopardize the meaning. The failure of museums to ask *why* they do what they do prevents self-critical reflection, which is a prerequisite to heightened awareness, organizational alignment, and social relevance. Instead, in the absence of *why*, the focus is largely on the *how*, or the clichéd processes of collecting, preserving and earning revenue – the latter being the cause of much of the organizational drifting characteristic of many contemporary museums.

MKS: In the latter decades there has been a tendency, especially among politicians, to treat museums as a mere consumer good. Museums have had to play along, focusing on becoming actors in the so-called experience economy. While this perspective is perhaps fading out in some countries, what are the effects of such "here and now" ideas, which are forced onto the museum sector? And is the call to forge alliances and collaborate with private business just another short-term trend?

RRJ: For museums, one of the most misleading ideas coming from the business world is that of financial self-sufficiency. It is a myth that permits museums and their governing authorities to pursue growth and consumption as the keys to the future, thus avoiding any substantive consideration of what sustainability might look like in the long term. Sustainability could actually mean a smaller core staff or a smaller building; or starting afresh with a new mission and values focused on social responsibility; or merging with like-minded organizations, or even deaccessioning or mothballing a portion of the collection. Forging alliances with private business should be part of this thinking, as there are undoubtedly a variety of innovative opportunities that require risk taking and experimentation.

In seeking long-term sustainability, boards and staff should also ask two essential questions – "If museums did not exist, would we reinvent them and what would they look like?" And, "If the museum were to be reinvented what would be the role of the public in the reinvented institution?" It might also be helpful to bear in mind the observation that "the crucial dimensions of scarcity in human life are not economic, but existential. They are related to our needs for leisure and contemplation, peace of mind, love, community and self-realization."[17]

MKS: Museum professionals are rarely trained business professionals, who have a strong focus on strategies, revenues, and earnings. Rather, museum professionals are trained in having a sharp focus on arts or history. In an era of new and changing times, where does this status of training and experience rank the museum professionals when it comes to the ability to engage in "business practice"? Can museum professionals act and intermediate beyond their professional context; or what is necessary to build this capability?

RRJ: Irrespective of my criticism of business, I want to make it make it perfectly clear that business literacy is essential for any competent museum. By business literacy, I mean the staff's ability, at all levels of the organization, to fully understand the museum in all its complexity.[18] If the staff understands the "big picture," or the larger context within which the museum operates, they will have a greater appreciation and investment in the outcome of the work. Knowledge of the operating and capital budgets, along with the long-term financial outlook for the museum, are critical parts of the "big picture."

Business literacy begins with "open-book" management, whereby the museum staff is given full budget information along with the assistance required to make sense of it. This approach also requires that senior management communicate fully and openly about the museum's strategic priorities, opportunities, and threats. I know of many museums that do none of these things and some directors who withhold financial information from staff in order to maintain power and control.

Business literacy in museums is not only necessary for enhanced sustainability in an era of scarce resources, but it is also essential to individual and organizational accountability. A working knowledge of finances/budgeting, earned revenues, business processes, time management, public service, project management, and so forth are the foundation for enhanced effectiveness and efficiency – the purpose and outcome of business literacy. But it is important to note again that business literacy is about methods and techniques, not values.

MKS: It has been mentioned that tradition is an inherent, key value for many museums. Therefore, it might be questioned whether it is, in fact, realistic to have the museum scene change in a major way – seeking new and supplementary tasks of relevancy. Do you, drawing on your international background, believe that there is a critical mass of willingness to change or is it rather a utopian dream?

RRJ: It is true that museums are conservative institutions and suffer from a variety of self-inflicted challenges and intractable traditions that make innovation, creativity, and experimentation difficult. These self-inflicted challenges and traditions include the lone museum director with too much authority; myopic management that is unwilling or unable to embrace socially relevant missions; unimaginative exhibition methods and techniques that remain unchanged; and the unswerving commitment to the permanent collection – despite the museum's inability to keep pace with the enormous cost of keeping collections forever in accordance with rigorous, professional standards. Until museums fully embrace the need to question, reflect, and innovate, much of the emotion, imagination, and intuition – the best qualities of the people who work in museums and the arts – will remain largely unrecognized and unused.

At the same time, museums have existed for centuries, unlike most business enterprises. Museums have evolved through time, from the elite collections of imperial dominance, to educational institutions for the public, and now to the museum as "mall." The mall is the culmination of marketplace dominance – over-merchandised and devoted to consumption, edutainment, and entertainment.[19] There is an important lesson in this historical trajectory, however, and it is the ability of museums to learn and adapt as circumstances require, however slowly. Although we have no explicit record of museums giving prominence to societal considerations, their development over time mirrors such concerns, as their missions changed to suit the times. Whether or not museums themselves led this change is immaterial. I am not a utopian, but this evolutionary record of museums makes me optimistic about the future.

There are important initiatives and experiments now underway around the world, as museums awaken to their social responsibilities. In addition, new developments are apparently taking place that are redefining how companies and nonprofit organizations interact and learn from one another. These initiatives will hopefully create new opportunities to address some of society's long-standing and complex issues, while strengthening business and nonprofits in the process.[20] The choice for all museums is between more of the same – with an emphasis on business – or embracing a greater awareness of the world in pursuit of societal relevance. Time is of the essence as global issues intensify.

Hands-on perspective

There is hope, possibilities, and meaning for museums as entities in modern-day society. This is basically the positive lesson to be had from the above discussion. A vital note, however, is that turning the tide and finding new perspectives only comes with an effort. This can be seen as common knowledge but, all too often, when focusing on challenges within the museum sector, the practitioners' perspective is neglected. Therefore, in this section some pointers will be given, drawing from the insights and experiences of the authors and previous literature, as to what type of collaborations might be initiated between museums and business; what the value construction might look like; and what drivers and enablers should be considered essential.

Looking at the different types of collaboration that might exist, it is important to perceive these as evolving, rather than as static entities. Some collaboration could and should evolve over time, from one type of collaboration to another. Research findings from the field of strategic collaboration indicate that three types of collaboration are predominant between nonprofit and profits in this context – meaning museums and business.[21] These are: philanthropic, transactional, and integrative. In the philanthropic stage, the nature of collaboration is largely that of charitable donors and recipients. In a Nordic perspective, this type of collaboration is especially well known from the art museum scene, where there is a long tradition of art museums being underpinned by a number of benefactors. Typically, this relationship is quite conservative, as donors and recipients have been involved for many years.

In the transactional stage, there are explicit resource exchanges focused on specific activities. For example, event sponsorship, cause-related marketing, and contractual service arrangements would fall into this category. In recent years, more museums in the Nordic sphere have moved into this type of collaboration. One example is the European Union (EU)-funded IKON-project, which consists of 48 collaborative partners – primarily cultural heritage museums, art museums, and municipalities in Denmark, Norway, and Sweden.

The goal of the network is to have an increased number of visitors coming to the region and visit the museums. A predominant activity within the network has been to arrange events, and the typical set-up has been one museum taking the role as prime organizer, focusing on a given theme. An example is Limfjordsmuseet in Løgstør, Northern Jutland (adjacent to the Limfjord), which is devoted to the life in and around the fiord. In 2009, when the project was initiated, it was natural to organize a seafood festival with the help of local sponsors and partners, including restaurateurs, jazz-bands, port authorities, the fishing industry, and fishermen. The event was co-marketed with the local tourist organization and became a yearly and successful event – backed by both event sponsorship and related marketing.[22]

The third type of collaboration identified is the integrative stage, in which collaborations have progressed, so that partners' missions, people, and activities have begun to merge into more collective action and organizational integration. Few, if any, museums in the Nordic context have managed to move to this stage. However, there are rich possibilities for museums to develop in this direction. Sustainability is a topic of relevance to all, locally, regionally, and globally. Because Denmark is well known and respected for its industry and development work with wind power, it makes sense for a museum to engage in collaboration with the wind power industry, having a mutual mission of creating awareness and anchoring the values in a local and historically conscious setting.

Another idea, again using Denmark as the example, would be for a museum to focus on sustainable catches within the fisheries. Denmark is, and has for number of years been, a leading fisheries nation within the EU. Despite this status, the museums dealing with fisheries history are not prioritizing the responsibility aspect of the fisheries. There might be more reasons for this: political, economic, and strategic. Nevertheless, it could be meaningful to have a much greater outreach and collaboration, which most likely would benefit both the industry and the museums involved, as they are reconnected with the local community and gain a higher profile on the growing sustainability agenda.

One requirement is, of course, identifying the types of collaboration that exist, how they work, and bringing up suggestions on which collaborations might be initiated. Another is to understand how the creation of common values functions. It should be quite clear that the degree of value in any collaboration is related to the nature of the resources involved. Related to the collaboration typology above, value creation includes three categories: generic resource transfer, core competencies exchange, and joint value creation. The first type of value creation equals the classical approach of a company or private patron – giving money to a museum and the museum then supplies good deeds and good feelings. Core competencies exchange is focused on using each partner's distinctive capabilities to generate benefits, as in the example of Limfjordsmuseet. Finally, joint value creation represents benefits that are not bilateral resource exchange, but rather joint products or processes developed from a common pool of resources and understandings.[23]

Having a joint value setting is a particularly high-value source, as it is unique in its nature and therefore nonreplicable. However, the extent to which this type of collaboration can be accessed and deployed is very much dependent on the quality and closeness of the partners' relationship. There also needs to be a value balance in the development of the collaboration, as imbalances eventually will end up being "deal busters."[24] Looking at the Nordic museum landscape, there are certainly possibilities of joint value creation, but it remains to be seen if these can be constructed with the necessary mutual balance.

What should ultimately be understood from the above is that museums certainly have possibilities for collaboration, as well as opportunities for gaining increased relevancy. When everything is said and done, however, it all boils down to personality and skills. Building joint values relies on exactly these skills, plus connections and relationships. Therefore, when trying to renew museum values and regain relevancy, museum leaders should be recruiting individuals who might be able to open up more discourses, while at the same time being able to stand firm when creating balanced relationships. The Nordic museum scene is undergoing changes presently, and hopefully these changes will enable museums to assume the relevant position they could have in society.

Notes

1 To fully inform the reader on the origins of the different sections in this chapter it should be specified that the Introduction (which includes the two initial sections leading up to the discussion) is solely developed by the first author. The discussion section, which is designed as an interview (for details see note 8), is the co-responsibility of both authors, The same applies for the final section entitled "Hands-on perspectives."

2 M. Karnøe, "Museernes non-essense. En dialog med Robert R. Janes," in *Danske Museer* 2011, 24, 6, pp. 14–17.

3 R. R. Janes, *Museums in a Troubled World: Renewal, Irrelevance or Collapse?*, London & New York: Routledge, 2009; R. R. Janes, "Museums, Corporatism and the Civil Society," *Curator: The Museum. Journal*, 2007, 50, 2, pp. 219–237; R. R. Janes, *Museums and the Paradox of Change: A Case Study in Urgent Adaptation*, Glenbow Museum, 1997; R. Sandell and R. R. Janes, *Museum Management and Marketing*, New York: Routledge, 2007; R. R. Janes and G. T. Conaty, *Looking Reality In The Eye: Museums and Social Responsibility*, Alberta: University of Calgary Press, 2005.

4 M. Karnøe, "Museernes non-essense. En dialog med Robert R. Janes," p. 16.

5 S. B. Hafsteinsson, "Robert R. Janes: Museums in a Troubled World: Renewal, Irrelevance or Collapse?" Review in *Nordisk Museologi*, 2010, 1, pp. 149–151.

6 R. R. Janes, *Museums in a Troubled World: Renewal, Irrelevance or Collapse* has been the subject of more reviews. The reader is referred to the following: S. B. Hafsteinsson, "Robert R. Janes: Museums in a Troubled World: Renewal, Irrelevance or Collapse?" Review in *Nordisk Museologi*, 2010, 1, pp. 149–151. Mary Case, "Troubled Waters," in *Museum*, May–June, 2010, pp. 22–23; J. P. Greene: "Museums in a Troubled World: Renewal, Irrelevance or Collapse?" (review) in *Recollections – Journal of the National Museum of Australia*, October 2009, vol. 4, no. 2 (unpaginated.) S. Davies, "Museums in a Troubled World: Renewal, Irrelevance or Collapse?" Review in *Curator*, April 2011, vol. 4, no. 2, pp. 227–223; M. Schwarzer, "Museums in a Troubled World" Review, in *Museum Management and Curatorship*, 2009, vol. 24, no. 4, pp. 389–392.

7 R. F. Nelson, "How Then Shall We Live?" *The Post-Industrial Future Project Working Paper No. 2*, Canmore, Alberta, 1989, p. 45.

8 The discussion in this section was conducted as an e-mail "interview." In a correspondence ranging from November 30, 2011 through January 31, 2012, the first author sent questions to the co-author which, in turn, were replied to. Follow-up questions were then formulated and final replies given.

9 R. Heinberg, *The End of Growth*, Gabriola Island, Canada: New Society Publishers, 2011, pp. 1–4.

10 Heinberg, *The End of Growth*, p. 27.

11 R. B. Lee and I. DeVore (eds.), *Man the Hunter*, Chicago: Aldine Publishing Company, 1968, p. 188.

12 Interviews with Michael P. Robinson: transcript, p. 6, also 30 October 2008 (telephone).

13 J. Rifkin, "The End of Work." Public address on behalf of the Volunteer Centre of Calgary, Palliser Hotel, Calgary, Alberta, Canada, November 13, 1997.

14 M. E. Porter and M. R. Kramer, "Creating Shared Value: How to Reinvent Capitalism and Unleash a Wave of Innovation and Growth," *Harvard Business Review*, January–February, 2011, pp. 62–77.

15 Porter and Kramer, "Creating Shared Value," p. 77.

16 C. Handy, *The Age of Paradox*, Boston: The Harvard Business School Press, 1994, p. 183.

17 Walter Weisskopf quoted in F. Capra, *The Turning Point: Science, Society and the Rising Culture*, New York and Toronto: Bantam Books, 1983, p. 397.

18 M. Morris, "Organizational Health," *NEWStandard* (1)3, The American Association of Museums, Washington, DC, 1998, p. 4.

19 A. Gopnik, "The Mindful Museum," *The Walrus* (4, June), 2007, p. 89. This article is adapted from the 2006 Holtby Lecture at the Royal Ontario Museum in Toronto, Canada.

20 K. Pickus, "The Disappearing Barriers between Business and Nonprofits Are Driving Innovation" In CO.EXIST. Available online at: http://www.fastcoexist.com/1679040/the-disappearing-barriers-between-business-and-nonprofits-are-driving-innovation#comments.

21 J. E. Austin, "Strategic Collaboration Between Nonprofits and Business," *Nonprofit and Voluntary Sector Quarterly* 2000, 29, pp. 69–97; J. E. Austin, *The Collaboration Challenge: How Nonprofits and Business Succeed through Strategic Alliances*, San Francisco: Jossey-Bass, 2000.

22 Further information on the IKON project and Limfjordsmuseet available at: http://www.ikon-eu.org/.

23 Austin, "Strategic Collaboration Between Nonprofits and Business," pp. 78–80.

24 R. M. Kanter, *When Giants Learn to Dance*, New York: Simon & Schuster, 1989, pp. 19–20.

Literature

Austin, J. E., *The Collaboration Challenge: How Nonprofits and Business Succeed Through Strategic Alliances*, San Francisco: Jossey-Bass, 2000.

Austin, J. E., "Strategic Collaboration Between Nonprofits and Business," *Nonprofit and Voluntary Sector Quarterly* 2000, 29, 69–97.

Capra, F., *The Turning Point: Science, Society and the Rising Culture*, New York and Toronto: Bantam Books, 1983.

Case, M., "Troubled Waters," *Museum*, May–June, 2010, 22–23.

Davies, S., "Museums in a Troubled World: Renewal, Irrelevance or Collapse?" *Curator*, April 2011, 2, 227–230.

Gopnik, A., "The Mindful Museum," *The Walrus* (June), 2007, 4, 89.

Greene, J. P., "Museums in a Troubled World: Renewal, Irrelevance or Collapse?" *Recollections – Journal of the National Museum of Australia*, October 2009, 2 (unpaginated).

Hafsteinsson, S. B., "Robert R. Janes, Museums in a Troubled World: Renewal, Irrelevance or Collapse?" *Nordisk Museologi*, 2010, 1, 149–151.

Handy, C., *The Age of Paradox*, Boston: The Harvard Business School Press, 1994.

Heinberg, R., *The End of Growth*, Gabriola Island, Canada: New Society Publishers, 2011.

Janes, R. R., *Museums in a Troubled World: Renewal, Irrelevance or Collapse?*, London and New York: Routledge, 2009.

Janes, R. R., "Museums, Corporatism and the Civil Society," *Curator: The Museum Journal*, 2007, 2, 219–237.

Janes, R. R. and G. T. Conaty, *Looking Reality in the Eye: Museums and Social Responsibility*, Calgary, Alberta: University of Calgary Press, 2005.

Janes, R. R., *Museums and the Paradox of Change: A Case Study in Urgent Adaptation*, Calgary, Alberta: Glenbow Museum, 1997.

Kanter, R. M., *When Giants Learn to Dance*, New York: Simon & Schuster, 1989.

Karnoe, M., "Museernes non-essense. En dialog med Robert R. Janes," *Danske Museer*, 6, 2011, 14–17.

Lee, R. B. and I. DeVore (eds.), *Man the Hunter*, Chicago: Aldine Publishing Company, 1968.

Morris, M., "Organizational health," *NEWStandard* (1)3, The American Association of Museums, Washington, DC, 1998, 4.

Nelson, R. F., "How Then Shall We Live?" *The Post-Industrial Future Project Working Paper No. 2*, Canmore, Alberta, 1989, 45.

Pickus, K., "The Disappearing Barriers between Business and Nonprofits Are Driving Innovation." *CO.EXIST.* Available online at: http://www.fastcoexist.com/1679040/the-disappearing-barriers-between-business-and-nonprofits-are-driving-innovation#comments.

Porter, M. E. and M. R. Kramer, "Creating Shared Value: How to Reinvent Capitalism and Unleash a Wave of Innovation and Growth," *Harvard Business Review*, January–February, 2011, 62–77.

Rifkin, J., "The End of Work." Public address on behalf of the Volunteer Centre of Calgary, PalliserHotel, Calgary, Alberta, Canada, November 13, 1997.

Sandell, R. and R. R. Janes, *Museum Management and Marketing*, New York: Routledge, 2007.

Schwarzer, M., "Museums in a Troubled World," *Museum Management and Curatorship*, 2009, 4, 389–392.

PART 4

Dangerous times
Activism and ethics

I've spent years wondering why it is that so many people seem unable to conceive of any future other than business as usual, on the one hand, and apocalyptic extremism on the other. Whatever the motives that drive this curious fixation, though, it results in a nearly complete blindness to the real risks the future is more likely to hold for us.

(John Michael Greer 2011: 240)

INTRODUCTION

My concern is with the real risks that Greer refers to on the preceding page, and what role museums might play in averting them. I have written and spoken about these concerns for nearly two decades, sometimes using mildly apocalyptic language, although with little or no discernible reaction from the museum community. Perhaps this is because museum workers have grown immune to the sounds of alarm. Many have suffered through innumerable budget crises, well-meaning boards of directors, and self-absorbed senior managers – making stoicism, silence, and equanimity adaptive qualities.

The world has changed dramatically, however, and internal museum concerns have been overtaken by societal threats with staggering consequences – the most notable being climate change and disruption. Our inescapable challenge as global citizens is to now phase out more than half of the global use of fossil fuels by 2050, in order to forestall the worst impacts of climate disruption (Ehrlich and Ehrlich 2013: 3). Yet, our actions continue to ignore the consequences of not doing so – the carbon footprint of excessive and trivial jet travel is a case in point. Aviation has been growing faster than any other source of greenhouse gases. For example, the greenhouse gas emissions from aviation in the European Union increased by 87% between 1990 and 2006 (Wikipedia 2014). With no apparent political will to address the reality of climate disruption globally, it's as if "we're in a car, heading toward a cliff, and we're arguing about which radio station we should be listening to" (Rand 2014: 33). The public conversation about climate change has entered the theatre of the absurd (Rand 2014: 27).

The question is no longer if museums can retain their historical privilege of authoritative neutrality, but whether they will concede that society and its institutions have now collectively entered a dangerous time. One of the biggest factors

FIGURE 9 Asian megacities (Bangkok, Thailand; Manila, Philippines; and Ho Chi Minh City, Vietnam) are at risk of billions of dollars in damage from climate change, due to increases in temperature and flooding. Photo © Reuters/Erik de Castro.

in societal denial is short-term thinking – dominated by short-term, corporate profits and self-serving political agendas. It cannot be overstated that museums are unique institutions, given their larger view of time. I was in the habit of advising Glenbow's Board of Governors that the museum's business plan for collections care was 500 years in duration, in order to emphasize the time depth of this fiduciary responsibility – unbounded by time.

This was always met with polite bemusement by the board members, who had only private sector experience. In a similar vein, Macy and Johnstone (2014: 142) asked, "for how long would we like our family to continue? If the next generation matters to us, and the children born to it do as well, then what about their children, and their children's children?" The narrow timescape that dominates our thinking is a major determinant in the unsustainable consumption that is unraveling the biosphere. Museums are predisposed to exercise their larger view of time as stewards of the biosphere – acknowledging both its material legacy and its intangible memory.

Memory is the vital connection to ancestors – albeit the value of ancestors remains largely unacknowledged in North America by descendants of both the Industrial Age and the Information Age. Museums are a pathway of interconnectedness between our ancestors and future generations, as well as being the custodians of the former's individual and collective wisdom, achievements, and failings. All of these things make up the web of life as we know it today, and constitute the deep sense of time that underpins stewardship. Museums are the only societal institutions whose purpose is the bygone web of life.

If there is any truth in the potential for museums to transform themselves based on mutuality, dialogue, and community engagement, this will require museum staff to think differently about everything – audiences, organizational design, the meaning of collections, the *why* of programs, and so on – nothing less than the purpose and nature of museums. For museum studies departments, museum training programs, and the many leadership seminars, what are the implications of the urgent need for more conscious museum workers grounded in a larger view of time?

The time has come for an international intervention similar to the American Association of Museum's (AAM) "Museum and Community Initiative." The result was *Mastering Civic Engagement: A Challenge to Museums* (American Association of Museums 2002) – a report asking museums to revisit the power of community and consider what assets museums contribute to the shared enterprise of building and strengthening community bonds. This initiative was described as a call to action. There is now an urgent need for another call to action, this time with a focus on the role of museums in addressing the socio-environmental issues confronting the biosphere. Perhaps an intervention by the world's museum associations, such as the one achieved by the AAM in 1992, could shine a light on the civic responsibilities of museums and serve as a much needed call to arms.

There is certainly cause for optimism, as the power of museums to address societal needs and aspirations has been clearly demonstrated. One need only read the report *Museums on Call: How Museums Are Addressing Health Issues* to appreciate the role museums are playing in health care – from autism, to medical training, to visual impairment (American Alliance of Museums 2013). This potential for good is largely untapped, however, considering that there are 55,000 museums in the world and that together they absorb an enormous amount of public and private money. With few exceptions, the multifaceted resources and expertise of museums are lying dormant and unavailable for activism in the public interest.

If museum workers are waiting for a more certain future before taking action, all indications are that they will be waiting for a long time. There is an overwhelming and immediate need for new ideas, new commitments, and new ways of working in order to address our contemporary challenges – using whatever resources are best suited. In the words of John Greer again (2009: 191):

> Culture is memory. An authentic culture roots into the collective experience of a community's past and from this source draws meaning for the present and tools for the future. Thus culture is a constant negotiation between the living and the dead, as new conditions call for reinterpretation of past experience and redefine the meanings that are relevant and the tools that are useful. When a society gives up on these negotiations and abandons the link with its past, what remains is not originality, but stasis . . .

Our collective challenges are now severe enough to require that all museums and their sister institutions redefine their meaning and the "tools that are useful" – using their unique combination of resources and intelligence to ensure the durability of individuals, communities, and the natural world. The writings that follow are devoted to some of the possibilities and challenges in doing so.

The first chapter, "Experimenting with Leadership: *Primus inter Pares*," chronicles an experiment in collective leadership at Glenbow. It demonstrates the vital necessity of trust and integrity among senior staff and the consequences of its absence. The next chapter, "Persistent Paradoxes – 1997 and 2012," examines several fundamental and enduring paradoxes underlying the complexity of museum work. Although paradoxes cannot be eliminated, they can be managed through a healthy scepticism of tradition, risk taking, and redistributing power and privilege within the museum.

In the third chapter, "Debunking the Marketplace," I return to a theme that was first identified in Part 2 – the intrusion of marketplace ideology in museum affairs. My earlier observations were less severe than in this chapter, wherein I assess the current museum preoccupation with the marketplace and its debilitating consequences – ranging from vanity architecture to business tribalism. In short, money is not the measure of worth for a competent museum and it never will be. The next chapter, "Museums and the New Reality," is a manifesto of sorts about the ethical responsibilities of museums in contemporary society. It was described as "insurgent" and "confrontational" when it was first published as a commentary and I will let the reader be the judge.

The penultimate chapter, "Museum Management and the Ethical Imperative," speculates on alternative futures for museums in the light of intensifying socio-environmental pressures. Some of these scenarios are happy; others are not. The core of this chapter is a more detailed elaboration of a museum's ethical responsibilities, followed by a conceptual framework to guide museum management – a marked departure from standard management considerations. The conclusion is decidedly optimistic, recognizing the museum's complex mix of humanism, science, time-depth, and societal respect. The final chapter in this book, "Museums in a Dangerous Time," is appropriately a summary of many things – set in the current age of disruption and mega-uncertainties. I offer questions for museums to ponder, along with a detailed inquiry into how museums can contribute to a brighter and more intelligent future based on six qualities unique to museums.

In closing, global society is in dire need of a wide range of voices and approaches to motivate, empower, and inspire the profound and concerted change that is urgently required (Marshall 2009). The long journey underlying the contents of this book clearly demonstrates that museums are not only key contributors to this need, but that they could also be leading the way.

References

American Association of Museums (2002) *Mastering Civic Engagement: A Challenge to Museums*, Washington DC: American Association of Museums.

American Association of Museums (2013) *Museums On Call: How Museums Are Addressing Health Issues*. Available online: http://www.aam-us.org/docs/default-source/advocacy/museums-on-call.pdf?sfvrsn=8.

Ehrlich, P.R. and Ehrlich, A.H. (2013) "Can a Collapse of Global Civilization Be Avoided?" *Proceedings of the Royal Society* B, 280: 20122845. Available online: http://rspb.royalsociety publishing.org/content/280/1754/20122845.full.pdf+html.

Greer, J.M. (2009) *The Ecotechnic Future: Envisioning a Post-Peak World*, Gabriola Island, Canada: New Society Publishers.

—— (2011) *The Wealth of Nature: Economics as if Survival Mattered*, Gabriola Island, Canada: New Society Publishers.

Macy, J. and Johnstone, C. (2012) *Active Hope: How to Face the Mess We're in without Going Crazy*, Novato, CA: New World Library.

Marshall, G. "Why We Still Don't Believe in Climate Change." *Climate Change Denial*, July 24. Available online: http://climatedenial.org/2009/07/24/why-we-still-dont-believe-in-climate-change/

Rand, T. (2014) *Waking the Frog: Solutions for Our Climate Change Paralysis*, Toronto: ECW Press, pp. 27–33.

Wikipedia – The Free Encyclopaedia (2014) "Environmental Impact of Aviation." Available online: http://en.wikipedia.org/wiki/Environmental_impact_of_aviation.

19

EXPERIMENTING WITH LEADERSHIP*

Primus inter pares

Author's note: In 1995, I experimented with the *primus inter pares* leadership model when I took a leave of absence from Glenbow to prepare the second edition of *Museums and the Paradox of Change* (1997). The result was a painful failure. Three of Glenbow's directors acted as the primus during my absence, but one of them used the opportunity to abuse the position – extending executive authority and influence in a manner that caused widespread disturbance in the organization. I came back to a hotbed of psycho-politics, recriminations, and anxiety. Clearly, one must know and trust one's colleagues if a shared leadership model is to work, and I had been naïve and unsuspecting.

I attempted this experiment again for two months in 1997 when I took a leave of absence to study self-organizing systems at the Banff Centre (Canada). Each of Glenbow's Vice-Presidents acted as *primus* for a two-week period and it worked well this time. An evaluation of this second experiment emphasized the importance of the *primus*'s ability to act without any prior approval from me. To ensure that the authority of the *primus* was not undermined, it was important that staff understood this at the outset.

I believe in the *primus* model despite the first failure, as the all-powerful, lone director or CEO remains a self-inflicted challenge for many museums. What follows is the proposal I prepared for my senior management colleagues at Glenbow in advance of the first *primus inter pares* experiment. I am hopeful that new approaches to leadership will be considered in the dangerous times that lie ahead for museums.

---

*Source: Robert R. Janes, unpublished briefing paper prepared for the Glenbow Museum's Strategy Group (senior management), Glenbow Museum, Calgary, Alberta, Canada, November, 1994.

Introduction

There are basically two organizational traditions with respect to leadership (Greenleaf 1977: 61). The first of these is the hierarchy, which places one person in charge as the lone chief at the top of a pyramidal structure. Nearly all the institutions we are familiar with, from businesses to universities, are organized this way. We apparently see no other course than to hold one person responsible. The second tradition originates in Roman times and is based on the idea that the principal leader is *primus inter pares*, or first among equals (Greenleaf 1977: 61). There is still a "first," a leader, but that leader is not the chief (the most important; the most influential; the most valuable). The *primus* must constantly test and prove that leadership among a group of able peers. In effect, this means a leadership team with a first among equals, where administrative responsibility is assigned by the Board of Governors to a team of equals.

Flaws in the concept of the lone CEO

Robert Greenleaf, in his book *Servant Leadership* (1977: 63–66), is one of the few management writers to address the difficulties inherent in the lone CEO model, and I am indebted to him for the following discussion. In short, to be a lone chief atop the hierarchical pyramid is plagued with difficulties. Here are some examples:

1. *It is abnormal* – a person in this position no longer has colleagues, only subordinates. To a great extent, subordinates do not talk to the boss in the same way they talk with their equals, and normal communication patterns are distorted. The pyramidal structure weakens informal links, and dries up channels of honest reaction and feedback. This is a significant liability, as one's judgement is dependent upon interaction with others who are free to challenge and criticize.
2. *It is lonely* – the lone CEO is often not on the communications grapevine. Most of what they know is what other people choose to tell them.
3. *It reveals the burden of indecisiveness* – when one person is chief, the liability to the organization resulting from indecision can be devastating.
4. *The lone CEO is grossly overburdened* – he or she must often resort to concentrated briefings and ghost writers, because there is simply too much to do. The demands of the office diminish the creativity of the very person who should be the model of growth in awareness, communication, and human sensitivity.
5. *There is major disruption when the lone CEO leaves* – the search then begins for the "person who has everything" and, in the meantime, the single chief is a lame duck and nothing much gets done.

These are some of the disadvantages of the single leader or lone CEO model. Unfortunately, we have very little to compare it to, as the *primus inter pares* model is only now being recognized. I understand that some firms, such as the Mellon Bank and General Electric are experimenting with this approach. In fact, the Royal Bank of Canada has organized a six-member group office, with a Chief Executive Officer as the *primus* (*Financial Post* 1994: 5). The new CEO observed that "there's no such thing as one person running a whole organization. It is a team. You need a flatter organization. You can't do it with a pyramid structure."

I am not aware of any organization in the cultural sector that has adopted the *primus inter pares* model. I now want to review the plan for implementing this management model at Glenbow in my absence.

Implementation

I propose to test the *primus inter pares* model for two months at Glenbow in January and February of 1995, while I am taking a sabbatical leave to begin writing a book on organizational change in museums. The details for implementing this leadership model are as follows:

The model

- The Strategy Group, which consists of the six Directors, and the Manager of Human Resources, will manage Glenbow collectively as the *primus inter pares* leadership group.
- Each of the six Directors of the Work Units will act as *primus*, or the first among equals, for seven working days of the 42-day leave (January 2 through February 28, 1995).
- This will split the responsibility of the *primus* evenly among the Directors.

The role of the primus

- The *primus* will be the first among equals in the leadership team.
- The *primus* will report to the Chairman of the Board of Governors and will attend Board and Board Committee meetings.
- The *primus* will handle any emergencies or controversies that arise and will represent Glenbow as required – internally and externally – in conjunction with the leadership group.
- The duties of the *primus* will be performed over and above the regular duties of the Directors and they will be compensated CAN$350.00 each for taking on these additional duties.
- This money (CAN$2,100.00 total) will come from revenue earned by the Executive Director's consulting services, which is held in a designated account at Glenbow.
- It is expected that the *primus* will use both the office of the Executive Director and his or her own office, depending upon the circumstances.

Executive support

- The *primus* will work as part of the Executive Director's Office (EDO) team, which includes the Executive Assistant and the Executive Secretary – both of whom will provide the *primus* with a broad range of administrative support, including:

  o Sorting and routing of mail
  o Assisting with the preparation of correspondence, speeches, reports and presentations
  o Planning and preparation of daily activities, including daily meetings to review calendar of appointments, mail, follow-up, staff meetings, etc.
  o Preparation and administration of the EDO budget
  o Staff liaison throughout the institution
  o Advice re: protocol
  o Follow-up and research on a variety of issues
  o Secretarial support.

- The *primus* will be expected to meet daily with both the Executive Assistant and the Executive Secretary in the office of the Executive Director – these meetings will be arranged at a mutually convenient time.
- The Executive Assistant serves as an advisor to the Strategy Group and will provide advice and assistance to each *primus*.
- The *primus* is authorized to spend funds from the Executive Director's budget, with the understanding that these expenditures relate to the performance of his or her duties as *primus*.

Evaluation

I will evaluate this model upon my return through personal interviews with the Directors, the Manager of Human Resources, the Executive Assistant, and the Executive Secretary, as well as a follow-up discussion with the Strategy Group and the Board of Governors.

Postscript – 2015

The *primus* model remains a valid leadership alternative, irrespective of the first, failed experiment at Glenbow. In addition to its advantages discussed earlier in this proposal, it also addresses the negative perceptions that many museum staff have of their senior leaders – which stem in part from the power, authority, and privilege granted to the lone CEO. In the *primus inter pares* model, the authority and responsibility of leadership are shared.

Equally important, this leadership model would contribute much to succession planning in the museum community – a growing and dire need – as the retirement of the baby-boomer generation unfolds. We continue to limit the opportunity for leaders to emerge, as our conventional organizational design provides for only one leader at a time. The *primus* model provides a fertile testing ground for aspiring leaders – by providing an opportunity wherein they can demonstrate both their abilities and their interests.

I sense that this leadership model is as radical today as it was when it was described by Robert Greenleaf in 1977. Its value cannot be denied, especially in comparison to the lone CEO model, but it departs so markedly from mainstream organizational thinking that it may never be seriously considered, much less adopted. Hierarchical leadership in museums is a weighty tradition.

References

Financial Post, September 8, 1994, p. 5.

Greenleaf, R. K. (1977) *Servant Leadership: A Journey into the Nature of Legitimate Power and Greatness,* New York/Mahwah, New Jersey: Paulist Press.

Janes, R.R. (1997) *Museums and the Paradox of Change: A Case Study in Urgent Adaptation* (Second Edition), Calgary, Canada: Glenbow Museum and the University of Calgary Press.

20

PERSISTENT PARADOXES*

1997 and 2012

PERSISTENT PARADOXES–1997

Introduction

> It is typically easier to see what should be done which simply requires a judgement than to get it done which requires a more extensive analysis of the situation and the marshalling of support. Despair is thus frequently the shadow to ambition in the museum world, like devils following one in the night.
>
> *(Michael M. Ames[1])*

I am not sure that there is a more incisive statement than this of the effort required to ensure that museums continue to be valued as social institutions in our society. We have good reason to worry about this, or even to despair. Despite the many efforts at change currently underway in museums worldwide, however modest, there remains little or no indication that they will ensure a desirable future for museums as we know them. This is not a matter of being optimistic or pessimistic, but rather a reflection of several persistent questions which may, in fact, not be answerable but which must be acknowledged. These questions are paradoxical, meaning that they are simultaneously contradictory, unbelievable, absurd, true or false in their meaning and implications.

Charles Handy, who has given up his cherished belief in a perfect world and "A Theory of Everything," observes that the more turbulent and complex the world, the more paradoxes there are.[2] He notes that paradoxes are like the weather – "something to be lived with, not solved, the worst aspects mitigated, the best enjoyed and used as clues to the way forward." Coping with paradoxes also means accepting

*Source: Robert R. Janes, pp. 295–323 in Robert R. Janes (2013) *Museums and the Paradox of Change: A Case Study in Urgent Adaptation* (Third Edition), London and New York: Routledge.

the fact that even understanding does not always mean resolution. Indeed, it is perhaps those intellectual and creative problems that we will never resolve which claim the lion's share of our energies.[3] What follows is an attempt to look at a sample of paradoxical questions which continue to dominate the museum landscape, with a view to uncovering any clues to understanding the future that they might contain.

Is the customer always right?

All sectors of society, be it government, industry or arts and culture, are inundated with the dictum to serve the customer. This language of customer service is a relatively new one to museums, and has been met with a predictable amount of hostility – not only because of its newness, but also because of its association with the coarse goings-on of the marketplace. This cool reception must be acknowledged, as even the private sector is now admitting that the customer is not always right, and that superior service is no guarantee of future success.[4] As has been noted on numerous occasions, the customer did not demand the compact disc player or ABS braking systems – these were developed through the creative efforts of highly trained and motivated engineers, working in an environment which allowed the free expression of their abilities.

Furthermore, will museums ever be able to entice an unlimited number of what our culture calls the typical consumer, recognizing that professional museums currently occupy a niche market which appeals primarily to well-educated and well-off people? Can museums ever become broadly popular, recognizing that they are knowledge based and will always require people to read and think in order to derive benefit and pleasure from their visit? These are questions which the customer-service rhetoric in museums ignores.

> The great challenge to our times is to harness research, invention, and professional practice to deliberately embraced human values . . . Experts . . . perform both center stage and in the wings. And all of us speak from the citizens' chorus. The fateful questions are how the specialists will interact with citizens, and whether the performance can be imbued with wisdom, courage and vision.
>
> —*William Lowrance*[5]

Although these are legitimate questions, they are not sufficient cause to dismiss customer service as yet another management fad or popular panacea. Museums, to a greater or lesser extent, have always engaged in some sort of service, from school programs to answering telephone calls about the collections. What the late twentieth century is demanding is a redefinition of what service means. For museums, it will mean going beyond the self-interest that governs much of what museums do, and assuming more accountability for the museum and its relationship to the broader society. This is not meant to imply that this sense of greater responsibility was missing in the past. It was there, albeit unevenly, but most museums were simply not internally aligned to allow its full expression.

Making a commitment to service requires that a museum achieve a balance of power where people can act on their own choices, help to define purpose and meaning, and are rewarded equitably.[6] Many museums are only now beginning to address these issues, which are all about governance and management. How we govern and manage will either inhibit or promote our collective ability to commit to something outside of ourselves, and it is increasingly clear that organizational compliance and control will not get museums to where they need to be.

Herein lie the paradoxes. At a time when museum work is becoming more complex and more time consuming because of multidisciplinary collaboration in the absence of traditional, functional departments, we must insist that there be greater public involvement in our work. At a time when we are told that the customer is "king," we are rediscovering our potential to show leadership as brokers of complex relationships and societal issues, none of which are value free and all of which demand engagement, not passivity. At a time of diminishing resources, we must provide new and creative ways of serving a growing and diverse clientele. At a time when we are placing renewed emphasis on our unique role as knowledge workers, we are advising staff that there may not be time for them to spend an hour answering a curatorial inquiry. There are no lasting solutions to these contradictory tensions. Our only hope is for committed staff who will accept and cope with them, and perhaps even make sense of them over time.

Are museums sustainable without significant contributions of public money?

Although hindsight will be the judge of this, I believe that the answer to this question is possibly yes, but that this path is virtually uncharted. I base this less-than-optimistic response on my limited experience at Glenbow, which continues to be one of Canada's most financially self-sufficient museums. Of the top ten museums in the country, there are none which approach Glenbow's 1994/95 operating budget of 52% self-generated revenues and 48% of provincial and federal revenues. Admittedly, our efforts at self-sufficiency are made much easier because of our relative autonomy from government – an advantage that few of the other museums in the top ten category share.

Earned revenues

Despite this autonomy and unprecedented level of commitment to money-making activities at Glenbow, our revenue projections for 1995/96 reflect only modest increases. These projections are even more modest if you exclude the increased income from our endowment funds. Why only modest revenue increases in an organization with a clear track record of self-sufficiency? To begin with, our private sector fundraising projections are mostly flat. With government providing less money to health and education, the intense competition for funding among non-profits is almost comical. This at a time when there is simply less money to go around, if we believe what we are told by the private sector. Museums must also realize that fundraising is intensely competitive on the personal level, and requires aggressive, sustained action on the part of individual board members. It is easy to lose ground in this work when a board and staff are preoccupied with organizational change, but such neglect cannot be allowed to persist for long.

Another hindrance is the fact that commercial activities, a new and potentially important source of revenue for Glenbow, require a more gradual build-up than we had anticipated. Despite a booming facility rentals business, which hosts weddings and dinner parties in gallery spaces, it takes time to develop a client base. It also takes time to identify commercial partnerships, such as the one we have developed with a long-distance telephone wholesaler. By signing up our members, volunteers, and staff, we are able to share in a percentage of the wholesaler's profits on a monthly basis. Convincing staff that their professional knowledge is saleable has also been difficult, and we are still struggling to normalize this revenue stream within an overall attempt to levy fees for a variety of museum services which have always been free.

In short, despite a diversified revenue base and numerous innovative initiatives to further diversify this base, the idea of complete self-sufficiency with no public money is currently unachievable for Glenbow, given our current sense of self-reference (the skills, traditions, values, and aspirations that guide the museum). It may be possible, however, given the following two strategies. The first strategy would be to cut back all operations to a point where public monies are no longer required. The risk here is the beginning of a vicious cycle, whereby less money means diminished visibility, which in turn leads to greater indifference among the museum's constituencies, followed by less financial support, and so on. It might also be possible to reduce the scope of operations as part of this strategy, without risking the vicious cycle described above, by rethinking what is actually required to fulfil the purpose of a museum. We must pose the question – if we did not exist, would we reinvent ourselves and what would we look like?[7] All medium and large museums in Canada have tremendous overhead costs, due in large part to the tradition of employing a wide variety of specialists and technicians on a year-round basis, coupled with the tradition of working in virtual isolation from even closely related institutions.

Perhaps it's time to disassemble some of the country's larger museums, and reduce them to a core of say 25 to 75 knowledge specialists, who would then purchase all the additional services they require from a host of professional and technical people outside of the organization. This is the true meaning of the shamrock organization, and might possibly enhance effectiveness and reduce expenditures simultaneously. In addition, museums could position themselves to benefit from more support and interaction with like-minded organizations – universities for example. The Museum of Anthropology (MOA) at the University of British Columbia in Vancouver

(Canada) is a noteworthy example of this model in North America. This museum currently has a core of about 18 professional museum staff, several of whom have academic cross-appointments. They, in turn, are supported by up to 80 students who work for MOA in a variety of capacities as they pursue their undergraduate and graduate degrees.

The second strategy for achieving economic self-sufficiency represents a pronounced departure from the core business of museums. It would require becoming very aggressive about generating revenue, and creating opportunities that have little or nothing to do with the core activities as we know them. It might mean purchasing a high-profile fast-food franchise or assuming a partnership in an oil and gas venture. Sending tax money to Revenue Canada might be the kind of problem museums would like to have. There are plenty of opportunities for making money, if one is willing to set aside a commitment to self-reference. Juggling these two extremes may be quite possible, although there is plenty of evidence from the business world that engaging in alien business ventures can result in costly failure. Museums may be forced to consider such unholy alliances if public funding continues to evaporate, and it is not as unusual as it may appear at first glance.

The growing presence of IMAX and OmniMax theatres at museums and science centres is a relevant example of broadening the revenue base in a more familiar manner than opening a McDonald's restaurant on the other side of town. If one is serious about reconciling opposites, and avoiding either–or thinking, museums must remain open to the possibility of balancing the core purpose of a knowledge-based organization with one or more businesses that might be considered completely unrelated from a traditional perspective. Doing this would require a firm sense of purpose, the necessary expertise to operate the commercial activities, and unswerving commitment to the notion that the business ventures exist to serve the museum and its needs, not the other way around. There would have to be a clear separation of church and state, so to speak.

Research and development

The real difficulty at this point in time is that most, if not all, museums have virtually no discretionary money with which to experiment with new approaches to sustainability. At Glenbow, for example, our operating budget is so tight that nearly all revenues must go to fund operating costs. There is no money to set aside for the research and development that is required to identify, pilot, and assess new ways of achieving financial stability. I am not referring to blockbuster exhibitions here, as they are mostly more of the same with greater and greater costs and risks. Strategic partnerships with business are obviously one alternative, and numerous discussions are underway across the country between museums and agents of the Information Highway (such as the Digital Corporation in Canada), to determine if alliances are feasible.

The thinking is that museums would supply the content in the form of images and artifacts, and the corporations would supply the technology – all for the purpose of making money. But whose money, how much, and what are people paying for? Herein lies the paradox. At a time when a concerted effort must be made to identify new ways of enhancing the sustainability of museums, it is all most museums can do to keep the "wolf from the door." Experimenting, improvising, designing, testing, and implementing new forms of sustainability all cost money, which underscores the adage that it takes money to make money. Partnerships with the private sector are a real possibility.

Many museums have not yet confronted this paradox of having to learn and grow without additional resources, but it is only a matter of time. This paradox, too, will also have to be managed by reconciling opposites, if we are to continue to shape the "second curve." Charles Handy, the philosopher and management thinker, uses the sigmoid curve to illustrate how organizations start slowly, wax, and wane.[8] A new future, rather than demise, is achievable if a second or new curve is started before the first one dies out. Starting the new curve means challenging all assumptions and devising alternatives, including everything from new ways of operating to meaningful public service. This is difficult to achieve because so many museum people want to prolong the old ways indefinitely, yet enhancing sustainability in the face of decreasing public money is part of the second curve that all museums must acknowledge.

My only fear is that we might have left it too late, because of the current lack of resources to test, evaluate, and implement new approaches to sustainability. We are fortunate, however, that asking questions and generating new possibilities do not cost money. It is essential that this questioning become an urgent task for all museums, if we are to find a path through this paradox of sustainability before events overtake us. There is some comfort in knowing that there will never be any flawless solutions to any of this. For the traditionalists who decry the entrepreneurial museum, I am afraid there will be little solace in the years to come.

Are there too many museums?

In short, yes there are. I have already referred to an overbuilt situation in Alberta (Canada) but this condition extends far beyond this province. Perhaps it is not that there are too many museums in the country, but that there are too many museums with undifferentiated resources.[9] That is, the public may not see the difference between one museum or another as being all that critical, because they have neither the inclination nor the knowledge to differentiate on the basis of the breadth and depth of the collections – in the way that museum professionals do. If museum collections are largely undifferentiated in the mind of the public, then I suppose that to a great extent all museums are in competition with each other. We know that we are competing for both people's time and their disposable income, but it is not all that clear what competitive business we actually see ourselves in. Is it heritage, education, preservation, leisure, tourism, entertainment, or knowledge production?[10] Is it all of these? Although few museums are explicit about this, it appears that nearly two-thirds of Glenbow's annual expenditures are spent directly or indirectly on the care of the permanent collections. Does this mean that we are basically in the warehouse business? If so, do we need an unknown number of museums spending a great deal of time and money warehousing the same objects? We always tell ourselves that it is our collections which make us unique, but are they sufficient to give us an advantage in the race for people's leisure time and attention? There are many more related questions, none of which has received sufficient attention as museums pursue the status quo with ever-increasing fervour.

One solution, albeit a painful one, may lie in reducing the number of museums. As Weil has observed, "Museum people have a gut sense that all museums are not of equal quality, that some museums are better than others."[11] Through the application of performance measures, assessment, and accreditation, decisions could be made about which museums merit public support. Such assessments would have to recognize the extraordinary variability among museums in terms of origin, funding, governance, and collections, and herein lies the difficulty. The application of some universal accreditation scheme would undoubtedly ride roughshod over the concept of local autonomy – that all manner of work should be done at the most local level where it can be done well. If museums, however small or undifferentiated, can successfully compete for grants, function with a volunteer staff, or close their doors on a seasonal basis to conserve resources, then so be it. Their adaptive skills would appear to be in order.

The difficulties and the potential solutions are more the purview of the larger, so-called professional museums and galleries. I use the word professional primarily to indicate the presence of trained staff who adhere to a recognized body of museological method and theory, have advanced education, and share common values. These institutions have it in their power to rethink their interrelationships, especially within a geographical or political jurisdiction, with a view to finding the right mix of critical resources among themselves. This could be the basis of defining competitive advantages among museums, which up until now appear to be largely undifferentiated in the public's view as noted earlier. Any attempt to challenge the insularity and fierce independence characteristic of museums would have to be a gradual process.

It must begin in Canada, however, with both the federal and provincial governments agreeing to a moratorium on the construction of any new museum or gallery facilities for at least the next five to ten years, as the Canadian Museums Association recently recommended. The only exceptions would be those new initiatives which can demonstrate absolutely no need for public money. This may sound harsh, but the consequences of not doing so are worse. It is no longer reasonable for museums to be built on political whim, as highways and hospitals have been. In Alberta in 1995, there is yet another multi-million-dollar heritage facility under construction, funded in large part by public money. The ongoing operating costs have not been publicly discussed, except to observe that admission revenues will carry the day. This notion of self-sufficiency through gate receipts is one of the newest red herrings to appear on the Alberta museum scene, and in other places as well. It diverts attention from the real issue of sustainability, as I know of no professional museum in Canada where admission fees even come close to paying the operating costs. This is simply not feasible at this time, no matter how fervently we wish it to be so.

The next step, after a construction moratorium, requires assessing the feasibility of consolidating collections, with a view to eliminating redundancy and enhancing quality. Why does Glenbow need to keep one of the best mineralogical collections in North America, when we are a human history museum and have no curator of mineralogy? It once made sense, when we operated a mineralogy department. Now, we rationalize keeping the collection on the basis that the minerals continue to draw visitors. There is obvious truth in this, but perhaps this valuable exhibition space might be more effectively used in other ways more germane to our mandate. The double standard which emanates from the force of tradition is intriguing. It is professionally acceptable to retain and exhibit collections for which there is no in-house curatorial expertise, but it is still largely unacceptable in Canadian museums to present exhibitions, often of a topical nature, which have no basis in the permanent collections. It is more sensible to send the minerals to the Provincial Museum of Alberta in Edmonton, which, as a human and natural history museum, already has an outstanding mineralogical collection. The addition of our material would make their collection superlative.

In the interests of further differentiating our resources, I suggest that, in return, the Provincial Museum augment our internationally renowned Northern Plains ethnology collections by making available through gift, loan, or trade, the relevant material in their collections. This transaction, subject to whatever conditions are mutually acceptable, would assist each of our institutions in strengthening what we are already doing well. It means making a choice between having a little bit of everything, or consolidating and refining our unique strengths to the point where they are critical masses of highly visible resources.

The light bulb may appear over your head . . . but it may be a while before it actually goes on.

—*Frank Conroy*[12]
©*1988 Harper's Magazine. All Rights reserved.*
Reproduced from the November issue by special permission.

There is an excellent example of critical resources in the Royal Tyrrell Museum, located in the small town of Drumheller in southeastern Alberta, Canada. There you will find a palaeontology museum, second to none in the world, that draws hundreds of thousands of visitors from all over the world. Admittedly, dinosaurs rank right up there with mummies and shrunken heads for their popular appeal, but the Royal Tyrrell has raised this appeal to new heights with its single-minded focus. The Royal Tyrrell's approach may, in fact, represent a new form of elitism, something which Michael Ames advises that museums should never abandon. The task, in his view, is to retain quality and make that more accessible, rather than making museum presentations more "popular," simply to attract crowds.[13] Ames points to holy shrines as elite in a religious sense, and yet thoroughly popular in terms of attendance. Similarly, the Royal Tyrrell combines first-rate public presentation with leading-edge research.

Autonomy and cooperation

Perhaps the single, largest obstacle to this idea of strategic sharing and consolidation comes from the highly developed proprietary interests so characteristic of museums. By proprietary, I mean the strong sense of ownership that museums claim over everything they do and have. This proprietary sense is still sufficiently strong to prevent or discourage any real collaboration, as exemplified by my failure to launch a collaborative arts and heritage magazine among a group of museums in western Canada. All of them wished to continue to publish separate periodicals. Julian Spalding, Director of Glasgow Museums and Art Galleries, lamented these proprietary instincts in another form, when he observed that the curator must be removed from the possession of the object.[14] In his view, curators must be encouraged to love and study objects but not possess them, as it is this possession which creates so much undue worry and conflict. It is curious that one thing we have in common with the business world is proprietorship, and it is rapidly becoming a liability. Overcoming the resistance it engenders will require a new conceptual model and a great deal of will.

The question, then, in considering the number and variety of museums within a particular province or region, is how to combine autonomy with cooperation. There needs to be some model or mechanism with which to overcome the tyranny of institutional and individual territoriality, although tyranny may be too strong a word. There is presumably no malice in the persuasive tendency for most specialists, including senior government officials, to insulate themselves from broader concerns. Nevertheless, the result has been less than adequate communication between museums as organizations which, in turn, contributes to a seeming inability to devise fresh, lateral perspectives on a variety of issues and concerns.

The federal organization

Perhaps it is time to consider the concept of a federal organization and whether or not it would be useful in the conduct of museum affairs, whether locally, provincially, or nationally. Federalism implies a variety of individual groups allied together under a common flag with some shared identity.[15] Federalism seeks "to make it big by keeping it small," or at least independent, combining autonomy with cooperation. Federalism is an old idea, but an appropriate one at this time, because it matches paradox with paradox. The potential of this federal model of organization for addressing the paradoxes confronting museums is sufficiently impressive to merit a more detailed look at its characteristics. In doing so, I once again call on the ideas of Charles Handy for the following discussion.[16]

Federalism is not the same as decentralization, as the latter implies that the centre delegates certain tasks while remaining in overall control. The centre still initiates, delegates, and directs. In federalism, the centre's powers are given to it by the outlying groups. As a result, the centre coordinates, advises, suggests, and influences, with the initiative, drive, and the energy coming mostly from the parts. Nor is federalism the same thing as confederation, which is an alliance of interested parties who agree to do some things together. They are organizations of expediency, not of common purpose, and hence are not going anywhere because there is no structure or mechanism to decide what direction to take.[17] Other salient characteristics of federalism include: being big in some things and small in others; centralized in some respects, and decentralized in others. The individual parts or members turn over some of their powers to the centre, because they believe that the centre can do some things better collectively. The powers of the centre are negotiated jointly and independence is maximized while ensuring interdependence. Difference is encouraged while maintaining a strong centre – led from the centre but managed by its parts.

The role of the centre, more specifically, is to be responsible for developing and orchestrating the strategic vision, as well as developing the shared administrative and organizational infrastructure. This infrastructure might include everything from legal services to human resources to communications. Although those in the centre have a view of the whole, it should be sufficiently small not to allow them to run the organization. The Information Age has now made federalism possible, in Handy's view, because the centre can be well informed, small and strong, but dispersed.[18] In summary, the federal idea is a recurring theme throughout my museum writing. No individual, executive group, or single organization in the museum world is sufficiently all-knowing and competent to balance all the opposites and manage all the paradoxes.

The concept of federalism is equally as applicable to a group of like-minded organizations as it is to the internal workings of a single organization. Consider, for example, the possibility of a federal model linking a number of major institutions in western Canada, ranging from the Royal British Columbia Museum [Royal BC Museum] to the Manitoba Museum of Man and Nature [The Manitoba Museum]. A joint purpose could be developed, with common standards and common aspirations, followed by negotiations leading to a formal constitution. The constitution would specify the power of the centre. The centre would then have to be designed and staffed with the appropriate executives, who would be largely concerned with the future – plans, possibilities, scenarios, and options.

The principle would be to leave power as close to the action as possible, while at the same time forging these local and separate institutions into one whole, served by a common centre. Federalism is about managing the paradox, and there would be some restriction on local independence, if it helps the larger whole. This will only work if there is confidence in the central function, coupled with a sense of belonging to the larger whole. A federation with sufficient critical mass might also foster the development of professional and technical service companies, staffed by former museum employees who have lost their permanent jobs. A federation of museums could provide a sufficient level of work to these companies to justify their start-up, and to ensure their continuance.

Clearly this flies in the face of Canadian museum tradition, with its emphasis on government-controlled museums which operate singularly and mostly in isolation, whether on a national, provincial, or local level. In a time of scarce resources, museums continue to increase their costs and dissipate their declining funds, *ad nauseam*, by publishing separate periodicals, developing their own information systems, purchasing materials and supplies separately, and so on. As a result, museums have few, if any, resources to invest in the research and development that is required to ensure that they remain sceptical, curious, and inventive. Perhaps the federal model would permit some creative efforts in this direction, as it is clear that nearly all museums, perhaps with the exception of the largest ones in Canada (the National Museums, the Royal Ontario Museum, and the Art Gallery of Ontario), are increasingly incapable of doing this work on their own.

I am not proposing the rebirth of the defunct National Museums Corporation (NMC) in a provincial or regional setting, under the guise of a federal model. The NMC was a command and control bureaucracy in the traditional sense, which failed to negotiate a mutual understanding of the power of the centre and the autonomy of the parts. Achieving workable federalism is not magic, but rather the hard work of forging a common purpose which holds the parts together. This is the leadership of ideas and consensus, not personalities.[19]

The weight of tradition will not be the only obstacle to experimenting with the federal model. A more formidable obstacle will be the whole notion of power, as federalism is an exercise in the balancing of power. The hard truth is that we are always reluctant to give up power unless we have to, especially to an idea whose outcome is unpredictable, very different, undoubtedly messy, and a far cry from what we are doing today.[20] In the final analysis, the best reason for considering the federal idea is simply because the status quo is losing ground to the mounting complexities in contemporary museum work. If there are alternatives, they should considered.

Yes, there are more paradoxes. At a time when the public money available for museums diminishes annually, various governments continue to build heritage facilities in the name of economic development or political expediency. At a time when far too many museums are preoccupied with their survival, it is imperative that they accomplish their purpose. In a not-for-profit organization, survival does not necessarily equate with success.[21] At a time when expansive organizational networks are vital to renewal, we stumble under the twin burdens of insularity and myopic, professional pride in our own achievements. At a time when the future is rife with possibilities such as federalism, we are constrained by government domination of the museum sector in Canada, which is based on the belief that if you want to control it, own it.[22] Or conversely, if you want to own it, control it. Either way, will provincial cultural ministries embrace the notion of federalism, with all its implications for the loss of power in the centre? Perhaps not, especially when one considers that various people in positions of power have been there for a long time.

Occupying one's museum position for a long period of time also tends to foster contempt, or at least discomfort, with reframing one's understanding of things. This is part of the sense of infallibility that inevitably develops from past success. All of the obstacles and paradoxes noted above, however onerous they may appear, should not dissuade museum workers from pursuing new ways of working. This effort of will must be accompanied by a genuine effort to change the way we think about what is possible. The current need for cooperation, group expertise, and diversity represents such a major psychological and philosophical change in how we do things, that one writer has called it a shift in human consciousness.[23] Federalism is obviously not the only answer to the challenges confronting museums, but it might very well help to cope with this new reality in unprecedented and creative ways.

Can museums fulfil their potential?

Put another way, is an adaptive museum an oxymoron? If adaptability means the ability to adjust to new or changed circumstances, the answer to this question requires some serious reflection. There are many hindrances to adaptation in the museum world, some self-imposed and others not, beginning with the very purpose of a competent museum. There is more to achieving purpose in museums, however, than answering the question – "what does it mean to be a human being?" As noted in one of the epigraphs of this book, a good museum must also be an argument with its society, and direct attention to what is difficult and even painful to think about.[24] Fulfilling this purpose, and hence remaining adaptive, must therefore proceed without any assurances that what is being done will be appreciated.

Many boards of directors and many more colleagues are quick to judge and cast doubts on different, and perhaps untested, ways of achieving purpose and meaning under changing circumstances. In the end, the only escape from this inherent conservatism is through conviction and tenacity. There will certainly be mistakes in charting new directions and some, hopefully not too many, will go nowhere. Better this than the paralysis that comes from fear of disapproval. Although working individually or organizationally with minimal reinforcement under stressful conditions is no one's idea of rewarding work, this might also be viewed as the peculiar fate of competent museums who admit to never being certain and never being done.

The museum stereotype

We must also contend with a societal stereotype that seems as firmly planted in people's minds as eating turkey on Thanksgiving Day in Canada and the United States. Museums, in this stereotypical view, are dusty, stodgy, and essentially frozen in time in both content and approach. There is a story from Vancouver which is a priceless confirmation of this stereotypical image of museums.[25] A production company working in Vancouver (Canada) was in need of a curator's office for a film they were shooting. They were shown a curatorial office at the Museum of Anthropology, which they rejected because it was of contemporary design, clean and well-lit, had no jumble of books, papers and artifacts and, furthermore, was equipped with a computer and all the associated hardware. The film company decided to create their own curator's office, instead, which conformed to their stereotype of the curatorial inner sanctum. My imagination sees it as cluttered, eccentric, old-fashioned, and tacitly irrelevant to the demands of everyday life.

We in the museum business must assume some ownership for this stereotype, because where there's smoke there is bound to be something burning. We have much to do to enhance our appeal, from ensuring that there is a full range of visitor amenities in our buildings, to overcoming the urge to keep the light levels in galleries so low that visitors become angry and alienated. None of these admonishments is new, but all of them require constant attention. It is simply not acceptable to indicate that an artifact on exhibition was removed for treatment in 1981, when the year is 1994. Nor is it necessary to go through the agony of creating the definitive, scholarly text panel which leaves most readers with information so dense that little, if any, communication occurs. Museums must abandon their self-imposed task of being the authority, and replace this stubborn tradition with alternative views and rigorous insights which are designed to promote thought and feeling, not compliance. Many museums are making significant progress in this respect, but the potential for museums to serve as brokers of societal complexity remains largely unfilled.

Maybe the inherent difficulty in addressing the future is in the museum's bones. Perhaps the museum's very preoccupation with things that have survived the long passage of time creates scepticism about the undefined future. After all, what is the impact of the next three to five years, if one is absorbed with objects and knowledge that are centuries and millennia old? It is not surprising that scepticism should greet the arrival of yet another prognostication about where we are headed as individuals and as organizations. As social institutions, however, museums cannot permit themselves this intellectual isolation, no matter how sensible it may seem from a long-term perspective.

Exclusive commitment to the past, present or future – all are maladaptive. All of these perspectives must exist simultaneously in our thinking and in our work. I cannot help but think of the world-renowned thinker and futurist, Buckminster Fuller. Although he was the inventor of the geodesic dome and the dymaxion car, as well as the author of the *Operating Manual for Spaceship Earth*, he apparently spent a good deal of time on an island off the coast of Maine living in a rustic house with no electricity or running water.[26] Just thinking about this sort of contradiction is useful, as it parallels the oppositional forces with which museums must contend.

Beyond the stereotype

One can actually view this paradox of old and new from a different perspective, and conclude that museums are the only contemporary institutions with the privilege of bringing to bear the perspective of time on the elucidation of old and new societal issues. Government embodies the short-term perspective, as a consequence of both unquestioned tradition and obvious self-interest. Industry is also a master of this, with its preoccupation on next quarter's financial performance to appease increasingly militant shareholders – or so the corporations say. In fairness, this is not universally true, as some corporations are increasingly aware of the need to invest in knowledge building for the long term. Nevertheless, the private sector as we know it has little interest or capability in addressing the questions which confound us as a species. Overall, their concern is with consumption and profit making.

Nor are institutions of advanced education particularly suited to this task, as they exist to convey knowledge, meaning, and increasingly training to a limited audience – their students. Although major efforts are underway through cooperative programs and continuing education to forge new relationships between colleges, universities, and the broader community, this still requires a formal commitment on the part of each participant to enroll, pay a fee, and dedicate their time. The museum, in contrast, exists as an institution of learning in that ambiguous realm which straddles education and entertainment, and is in a position to provide knowledge and meaning as a so-called leisure activity in a manner far more accessible than universities will ever be able to do.

It is not only a matter of museums adapting as organizations, but also whether they will fulfil their potential to enrich the evolution of our collective consciousness. Groundbreaking work in this direction is currently underway, such as museums loaning or returning sacred objects from their collections to First Nations, but this is only the beginning. There are powerful urges for museums to keep their distance as social institutions, however, whether because of their sensitivity to the fullness of time (accompanied by a puzzling rejection of topical issues), so-called professional standards, or the comfortable insularity of the museum community and its institutions. None of these are insurmountable barriers to adaptation, if we are first willing to admit to them.

The tyranny of tradition

How does effective adaptation express itself in a business as idiosyncratic as that of museums? In museums which are conscious of their future, adaptation requires at least two related types of behaviour – freeing one's self from tradition and redistributing power and privilege. I will comment on each of these in turn. The idea of freedom from tradition often engenders hostility in the museum community, because of the assumption that it means the erosion of professional standards and practice. Although professional practice is certainly part of this, freedom from tradition must also be seen more broadly.

Rethinking exhibitions

The tyranny of museum traditions takes many forms from the mundane to the significant, and I will provide several examples of both to underscore the need for change. The permanent or semi-permanent exhibition, as it is euphemistically called, is the most pervasive expression of what a particular museum represents. These exhibitions are the most time-intensive and capital-intensive work museums do, and they can remain in place from 15 years to a half-century or more, despite the fact that they become dated, lifeless, and shabby. The one defence they have is the legitimate claim that museums have certain concepts and facts that they wish to convey to all visitors, and permanent exhibitions are an effective way to do this. Implicit in this view is that such information is more or less timeless, an assumption which is easily challenged. More importantly, the linear inertia which characterizes 99% of these installations has lost its appeal for many people, including most of today's youth. I am not suggesting that permanent exhibitions be replaced by instant gratification through multi-media technology – that's too easy and devoid of substance. Instead, we must completely rethink the permanent exhibition concept.

Why not look at what works in people's private and social lives? Within the domestic dwellings common to the Western world, there is normally a defined space known as a living room, family room, or great room. Meaning and enjoyment in these spaces comes from a variety of sources, including conversations and discussions grounded in memory and experience; the presence of numerous material objects that are valued for their personal, family, or social history; a variety of technological devices from televisions, to VCRs (videocassette recorder), to computers, [to an array of handheld devices], as well as an eclectic selection of printed materials including books, magazines, and photographs. All these things are arranged formally or informally, and are used intermittently or constantly, depending upon the changing needs and interests of the users.

If this summary description of how people build and sustain some of the meaning and pleasure in their lives is even partially accurate, how can museums assume that a brightly (or dully) painted construction of wood and glass, incorporating 20,000 words of two-dimensional text in conjunction with objects that can only be visually examined, is necessarily effective in providing meaning and enjoyment? Further, how can we assume that a dazzling array of multi-media hardware is any more effective than the three-dimensional books we build called exhibitions? Interactivity notwithstanding, there is still the fact that this approach easily becomes unbalanced and is too much of a good thing. Again, it is time to fundamentally rethink the exhibition.

I suggest that the next semi-permanent exhibition be a series of family rooms, modules, or activity areas, call them what you wish – with each devoted to a theme or topic based on sound research and topicality. There the visitor would be free to engage in the variety of behaviours outlined earlier, whether it is reading, watching, and talking, or just sitting in a unique environment. The contents of these activity areas could change as required, without prohibitively expensive capital renovations. How well this would work is admittedly unknown. The point is that we must begin to truly experiment with exhibitions, at the expense of what has become an enslavement to an increasingly ineffective exhibition tradition.

Responding rapidly

Another area which requires rethinking is the museum's inability to respond to issues, topics, or crises of broad societal interest, which present themselves with little or no lead time. Committed to the grindstones of habit and control, museums rarely, if ever, are able to respond to these events, much less play a leadership role in initiating and creating such opportunities. The time has come to designate a team among staff who are ready and able to initiate and respond to broader issues and concerns that are unanticipated in the typical museum planning process. This team must have a budget, be multidisciplinary, and have a rotating membership in order to distribute the stress and the experience among the staff. An organizational capability to respond or initiate in a timely fashion could do much to enhance the museum's adaptability and relevance, and perhaps diminish the view that doing something new in a museum is like "turning a ship around."

Obsessive conservation

A third consideration in enhancing the museum's adaptive abilities also requires a re-examination of tradition. In short, museums must stop being so compulsive about the collections, especially with respect to conservation. It is erroneous to simply blame this behaviour on individual conservators, however, as they are responding to the requirements of their professional training. Access versus preservation is an age-old tension in museums, and the problem is that it continues despite the best efforts of many conservators to reach daily compromises in the course of their work. The problem is obviously deeper than this and requires much closer communication between those who train conservators and those who are responsible for delivering public services. Museums are increasingly in need of generalist conservators, who are devoted to making objects "safely accessible," in Julian Spalding's words, not securing them for all time.[27]

The hapless victim of this lack of communication appears to be the contemporary conservator, who is tempted to fight rearguard actions or leave in frustration because professional training is not aligned with organizational imperatives. I know that the awareness of this difficulty is increasing but it does not seem to be happening fast enough.[28] The internal struggles caused by this lack of alignment are responsible for a considerable waste of organizational time and energy, not to mention ill-will among staff.

The importance of learning

Related to rethinking professional training among conservators is the general need for continually raising the professional standards among museum knowledge workers in general. Advanced training and continual learning are key ingredients in effective adaptation, both individually and organizationally, and a review of the educational profile of Glenbow staff reveals some interesting information. Nearly

50% of the roughly 100 staff have undergraduate university degrees, with only four of the staff having no high-school diploma. Of those with the university degrees, a dozen or so have advanced degrees such as a master's or doctorate. This is not a simplistic plea for advanced degrees as the solution to enhancing our effectiveness, but rather recognition of the fact this trend is already established.

It is now virtually impossible to obtain an entry-level position in any professional museum without an undergraduate degree or some form of advanced training. Training on the job will continue to be essential, but it is no longer sufficient for a career in a professional museum. Educational standards are rising substantially throughout North America, and museums cannot be exempted if they are to maintain their credibility. Learning must be continuous if we are to adapt effectively, especially for those who might have joined a museum staff before the trend for advanced degrees was well established. It is no longer possible to ignore this trend as being a requirement of the ivory tower, and hence irrelevant to the "real" world of museums. Museums deal in knowledge, so anything that enhances the collection, creation, or dissemination of this knowledge is adaptive. It wasn't that long ago when the director of a major Canadian museum prided himself on having only a high-school diploma. I'm afraid that nowadays that director would be out of a job.

Arguing with society

The last consideration in freeing ourselves from tradition is less tangible than the preceding discussion, and has more to do with attitude and perspective. Simply put, museums must grasp the fact that they need not tell people what they already know. For example, we do not need museums that dazzle us with electronic and digital technology, and we do not need museums that celebrate this. North American culture is already providing us with a surfeit of this.[29] If museums can start substantive discussions with society and keep them going, by providing alternative views of complex things with frankness and integrity, museums will be able to adapt and reinvent themselves for a new century. It is up to museums to do this, however, because society and museum supporters will not demand this.

If museums elect not to, society's disinterest will probably increase and, without the large injection of public money that museums are accustomed to, museums may finally suffer the fate of the unsuccessful in the marketplace. They will be put out of their misery because not enough people will wish to buy museum programs and services. This is not an economic argument based on the almighty bottom line, but a surmise which hinges on whether or not museums are able to consistently offer some sense of reality that differs from current political, corporatist, and advertising agency dogma. If museums can do this, the support will be there.

Redistributing power and privilege

In addition to the adaptive value of always casting a critical eye on museum traditions and assumptions, the redistribution of power and privilege within museums is another pathway to the future. This redistribution encompasses everything from reducing the number of managers to eliminating the absoluteness of functional departments. There are many other ways to achieve this redistribution, but the intent remains the same. That is, to make each staff member responsible for the organization's culture; responsible for delivering meaning and value to visitors and supporters, and responsible for the quality of their own experiences.[30]

Redistributing privilege is considerably more provocative for the executive director of a large museum than is defying professional traditions. In effect, we perpetuate work structures and management practices, born of our own societal traditions, that reinforce a class system. These practices keep ownership and responsibility focused at the top.[31] The executive class has privileges that the other staff do not have, and we argue that such prerogatives come with the greater responsibility inherent in these positions. There is much truth in this, but there is still the nagging doubt that there might be a better way to do things. Does this mean that we have to reintegrate the managing and doing of work? As I look around Glenbow, this trend is established or underway throughout the organization. Does this also mean that all executives should be doing their own typing and making their own travel arrangements, as one writer suggests?[32]

At first glance, this seems nonsensical – is this a wise use of an executive's time? Nonetheless, one cannot deny that the typical museum governance structure (board, executives, and managers) is not necessarily a consistent route to an authentic partnership with staff. There is still something missing. Are we talking about rank without privilege? What does this mean for museum executives who are already underpaid compared to positions of similar complexity in other sectors, not to mention the long hours? Is reducing the limited privileges among museum executives more palatable than it is in other sectors, because museum executives don't generate wealth and they don't save lives? Yet, many of society's most distinguished citizens flock to museums for the status and prestige they confer, often simply by association. We are inundated by paradox.

I know of at least one instance where these unanswered questions have not prevented a redistribution of power and privilege. This occurred recently in Glenbow's Library and Archives, as part of an arrangement whereby the staff now elect their own director from among themselves for a two-year term. Election to this position is normally accompanied by a substantial, albeit temporary, increase in salary. The staff of this work unit recently agreed, at their own initiative, to substantially reduce this salary increase and to use the surplus to fund additional temporary staff within the Library and Archives to address a variety of priorities. This was a quiet, but signal, rethinking of current practices about power and privilege that cannot be ignored. The implications of this decision are far from clear but, intentional or not, it has become a new template for considering power and privilege at Glenbow.

Such considerations are more than philosophical, as they also have implications for the design of adaptive organizations.[33] Research indicates that those organizations that have fewer distinctions in power and rewards, i.e., are more egalitarian, give people fewer things to lose. This apparently makes people more willing to accept the changes that inevitably occur as the work changes. Ultimately, the redistribution of power and privilege must be seen far beyond the organization – in the communities where museums work. There is no doubt in my mind that meaningful community involvement in a museum's work is a direct reflection of the museum's management style. Simply put, patriarchy, hierarchy, and control foster isolation; while individual responsibility, self-organization, and stewardship nurture the web of community relationships.

The future is unknown

Typically, paradoxes abound in this consideration of our ability to adapt to the future. Although seldom discussed, all competent museums have an obligation to the dead and the unborn, as well as to visitors and users. Yet, neither the dead nor the unborn vote or buy. This is apparently a conundrum that has defied the imaginations of politicians and funders, as museums are increasingly judged by the number of people through the door. Another aspect of this paradox has to do with what one does to keep those numbers up. Can you compare a museum that rents a blockbuster exhibition and thus serves as impresario, to a museum that serves the needs of internationally acclaimed researchers and writers? Of course not, because the same things are not being compared. But funding agencies and politicians everywhere have yet to concede that there is a qualitative difference in this example that cannot be judged by visitor statistics alone.

Another profound paradox lies in the fact that, despite all the work devoted to designing for the future, no one will be able to assess the efficacy of this work until it is over. By then, it is too late, or just in time to start over. There are no answers and there are no guarantees. While this doesn't mean that organizational change and adaptation are a game of chance, it does mean that one will never know the outcome until it happens. This, in turn, means that the demand for prescient knowledge cannot be met and hence cannot be used as an excuse for inaction. Intimately related to this is the fact that leaders are liable for what happens in the future, in addition to what is happening day to day.[34] The duties and performance of all museum leaders and managers must also include the future, and much of this performance cannot be reviewed until after the fact. Success or failure may only be apparent in the months or years to come.

Finally, organizations, including museums, are many things at once and no one will ever know them completely.[35] Irrespective of all the details I recount in *Museums and the Paradox of Change*, I can claim only a partial understanding of Glenbow.[36] We can only know organizations through our experience of them, which means there can be a huge difference between the rich reality of an organization and the knowledge an individual is able to gain about that organization. This continuous learning may help to explain the rollercoaster ride which best describes organizational life in the 1990s.

Ideally, what is learned from all these highs and lows will contribute to new mental maps, as museum staff must continually guide and shape their perceptions, and then translate these changing perceptions into action.[37] If not, and if museums continue to listen to the silent promptings of comfortable self-interest; if they continue to defer to culture critics whose main interest is the sanctity of their own opinions, and if they are seduced by the promise of government support in exchange for adherence to the lowest common denominator, then all museums workers must ask themselves, as Peggy Lee did in her famous song, "Is that all there is?"

PERSISTENT PARADOXES – 2012

In reviewing this discussion of paradoxes 15 years later, I find that all of them persist with increasing complexity, and that Handy's earlier comment on paradoxes being like the weather – "something to be lived with, not solved, the worst aspects mitigated, the best enjoyed and used as clues to the way forward" – still rings true.[38] In the remainder of this chapter, I will update several of the paradoxes identified in 1997 and assess their changing meaning and relevance.

Is the customer always right?

Customer service was the dictum in the 1990s, but I now prefer to use the traditional names "visitor" and "user." Irrespective of what they are called, the public has a greater presence than ever before, thanks in large part to the advent of social media. Museums are scrambling to address this global phenomenon through the use of Facebook, Twitter, mobile applications, Internet forums, weblogs, podcasts, photographs, video, and so forth. There is good reason to believe, however, that a more measured response is in order, as museums are in danger of confusing the means with the end. According to Paul Marty, a museum informatics specialist:

> On a basic level, there's the simple fact that platforms like Facebook or Twitter require a significant investment – you can't just throw up a Facebook page and then forget about it. People can be very quick to jump on the latest bandwagon, only to find out that they simply don't have the resources to keep it up or engage with it at the necessary level.[39]

As early as 2007, Marty also stressed that museums need to understand whether new technology will contribute to, or detract from, their core mission, and to avoid the dangerous possibility of adopting technology for technology's sake. Put another way, "The core competency of a museum is not the management of complex technology, it's the creative use of it."[40] Recent research reveals that using social media to encourage two-way communication to involve visitors as active participants in the co-construction of new knowledge is, in fact, very difficult.[41] Using Twitter, for example, as a marketing tool is distinctly different than building and sustaining meaningful relationships with an online community. Museums have yet to truly understand and capitalize on the latter.

Museums would be wise to think critically before they rush to incorporate the newest technologies, as they also must do in borrowing any method or practice from the private sector, be it corporate hierarchy or the branding of stuff. It makes perfect sense for some museums, at least, to consider themselves as antidotes and refuges from the increasingly frenetic and superficial digital world. Marjorie Schwarzer, the museum educator and author, has described this role for museums as "a respite for deep thought and slowness . . . There just aren't many institutions left that do this – at least secular ones."[42] Herein lies a core strength of museums that is easily overshadowed by technology's loud and incessant seduction.

One other development concerning visitors and users merits comment, as it was only emerging in the late 1990s when Glenbow adopted public service as one of its six essential strategies for renewal. Gail Anderson, in the second edition of her invaluable compendium on the function and purpose of modern museums, writes: "The collection holdings are no longer viewed as the sole measure of value for a museum; rather, the relevant and effective role of the museum in service to its public has become the central measure of value."[43] As much as I would like to believe that this shift from the collections to the visitor has occurred, there is still much evidence to the contrary.

For example, the 2012 future forecasting exercise by US museums professionals belies the purported shift away from the preoccupation with collections, and reveals that concerns about the collections are the main undercurrent in thinking about the future of museums.[44] This report provides the most current and informed view of the future by one of the largest museum professional organizations in the world and it is indeed revelatory – and also disheartening. The results of this inquiry unequivocally demonstrate that internal museum concerns are still the most pressing. Yes, there are important insights in this report about the need to curtail collecting and share collections; the need to respond to growing cultural diversity, and the need to create more transparent organizations.

Overall, however, there is little or no sense of the museum's connectedness to the broader world. This notion of a shift away from the collections must also accommodate a much broader view of what public service actually means in the twenty-first century, as museum education and entertainment are conventional and limiting. Public service can no longer be separated from the many issues impinging upon communities, and opportunities for enlarging the meaning of museum public service and the visitor experience must become a priority.

Are museums sustainable without significant contributions of public money?

I wrote in 1997 that it might be possible for museums to exist without the benefit of significant public funding. I now recant that optimistic speculation and note again that an intelligent balance between earned revenue and public funding for museums is required, not complete financial self-sufficiency. Determining what this balance should be requires a concerted professional discussion, and the balance will vary depending upon the museum and the jurisdiction. These guidelines are essential for various reasons – not only to end the tyranny of quantitative measures, but also to suspend the persistent pressure from governing authorities and museum executives to extract more and more earned revenues from their museums.

Museums in Canada and the US have actually done exceedingly well at augmenting their earned revenues over the past two decades, but there are limits.[45] This overall success has led to the mistaken belief that increasing earned income is the solution to budgetary difficulties. Museums are not businesses, although they are duty bound to be business literate. I also wrote in 1997 that museums should consider incorporating revenue streams unrelated to their core missions, such as an oil and gas venture, to enhance their financial self-sufficiency. This, too, was ill-considered in retrospect, both because of the potential for diluting the core mission and the threat it could pose for the nonprofit status of museums. Governments have tighter budgets now, and are increasingly less tolerant of the taxation privileges granted to nonprofit organizations.

One of the major obstacles to enhanced sustainability remains the lack of research and development money to allow museums to experiment with new ways of thinking and working. There is cause for optimism, however, as at least one UK charitable foundation is committed to a process of development and organizational change within museums and galleries that are committed to active partnership with their communities. The purpose of the Paul Hamlyn Foundation's initiative, *Our Museum*, is "to support and develop museums and galleries to place community needs, values, aspirations and active collaboration at the core of their work."[46] The Foundation's ambition is to affect the museum sector more widely, and it is essential to note that this initiative is seeking long-term sustainability through effective community engagement, and not by underwriting traditional museum practices such as blockbuster exhibitions. With their spiralling costs and the high risk of failure, blockbusters are becoming increasingly problematic. Overall, the matter of museum sustainability is intensifying, which only a substantive change in attitude and practice will rectify.

In exploring the long-term sustainability of museums as social organizations, it is also necessary to consider the new landscape of organizations that seek to produce social benefits by using private resources, or the new social economy.[47] The key distinction of the new social economy is the blurring of what are still considered to be distinct sectors – nonprofit, public, and profit. Herein lies an unprecedented opportunity for museums to reduce their insularity and seek opportunities and solutions built on the collective potential of the new social economy. I am not suggesting a greater emphasis on marketplace activities, however, as catering to cultural consumption has already driven many museums to a high level of distraction and aimlessness.

Rather, a new integrated vision will require that museum boards and practitioners reject the conventional dichotomy that for-profit organizations generate growth and well-being, and nonprofit organizations do the humane work of society. This work is now underway with the rise of the hybrid organization – one that combines aspects of nonprofit and for-profit organizations.[48] Social missions are pursued but rely significantly on commercial revenue to sustain operations. Museums would do well to investigate this possibility.

Are there too many museums?

The number of museums continues to grow, despite all their challenges, and very few have actually closed their doors in the recent past. Although there are roughly 55,000 museums in 202 countries, there aren't any statistics on the failure rate of museums, nationally or internationally.[49] It is safe to say that museum closures do not even come close to the number of business failures and bankruptcy. In Canada alone, 3,500 firms declared bankruptcy during the first 10 months of 2010 – 26% below the rate seen in 2009, and less than half of the average seen over the past 20 years.[50] I suggested a moratorium on new museum development in 1997, as had the Canadian Museums Association. Instead, the mid-1990s marked the beginning of one of the most concerted building booms in museum history, which has only recently subsided.

The museum world now has a new legacy of vanity buildings and renovations, an unknown number of which have sacrificed function and accessibility for architectural conceit, while accompanied by capital debt, operating deficits, and staff and program reductions to pay the increased building costs. There is now some recognition of the trap of substituting architecture for substance, with the discovery that museum health does not mean growth.[51] This revelation was a long time coming and much damage to organizational health and stability must now be rectified. In the meantime, all museums continue to have the challenge of differentiating themselves in the minds of their visitors, as discussed earlier. This requires that museums highlight their particular strengths and assets – the basis of all intelligent strategic planning, as well as branding. This will also require a much more thoughtful approach to branding – moving away from consumption in all its forms – and focusing on the intellectual, civic, and learning resources that make the museum unique.

As discussed in 1997, this rethinking must also include rationalizing and sharing collections, with a view to reducing wasteful redundancy and building on existing strengths within each museum. This is a radical challenge for mainstream museums, but the need to do so has not abated. The concept of the museum federation, discussed earlier, is still a viable one although it, too, is a fundamental departure from the comfortable insularity and unacknowledged competiveness among museums. As a consultant, I presented the federation concept to a small political jurisdiction with over two dozen museums. The federal organization was potentially an ideal model for coalescing the strengths and resources of these small museums, with its emphasis on individual museums allied together under a common flag with some shared identity. The idea was rejected without discussion.

Too many museums inevitably means reduced funding for all, and an unconventional alternative that could relieve this pressure recently emerged in Corpus Christi, Texas (US). In 2012, the City Council approved a two-year, private management agreement with a private company for the Corpus Christi Museum of Science and History.[52] The company is run by a local family who owns several entertainment venues in the area. The Corpus Christi Joint Venture agreement requires this private company to bring in the same amount of revenue the city has provided through rentals and museum tickets. Additional revenue first would go toward facility improvements that meet city approval. The Joint Venture will include another entertainment company and an investment manager who will work together to develop a long-term strategy for the museum, including making the exhibitions more interactive for children.

Although taxpayers have funded the museum's operations since it opened in 1957, the museum has been in decline during the past decade because of budget cuts and a steady decline in attendance. This is a bold and important experiment that will test the robustness of a museum mission completely immersed in the marketplace. Will the museum endure and intelligently adapt, or collapse? The museum community will not learn or grow in the absence of initiatives such as this one, and it is important that this project be revisited and evaluated.

Museum potential and the tyranny of tradition

I noted in 1997 that museums, if they were to adapt and prosper, had to confront a variety of obstacles, including some that were self-imposed. As I continued working in and around museums, these self-imposed obstacles loomed larger and larger in my thinking. I have expanded this list of self-inflicted challenges and beliefs and they are discussed in "Museum Management Revisited" in this book (Chapter 12). They are diagnosed there with the hope of strengthening museum management.

In 1997, I also wrote of the potential of museums to be "brokers of societal complexity," and this is even more imperative now. As noted elsewhere, tradition is a mixed blessing – while maintaining the integrity of method and theory, it conspires against new thinking. Promising developments are underway, nonetheless, with one of the most surprising sources being the Canadian Conservation Institute (CCI, Ottawa, Canada). The CCI, one of the world's distinguished conservation laboratories and service centres, notes that certain types of artifacts are much more sensitive to relative humidity fluctuation than others, and it is neither economical nor environmentally acceptable to have tightly controlled conditions if they are not necessary. Further details on CCI's challenge to conventional museum thinking are discussed in "The Mindful Museum" (Chapter 11). It is now most important that this reinterpretation be disseminated throughout the museum world so that practitioners and their museums can escape the tyranny of absolute environmental controls.

To conclude, all of the persistent paradoxes of 1997 and 2012 are alive and well, and now take their place alongside a new array of harbingers and hazards to add yet more complexity to museum management. Some of these are discussed in the chapters that follow, and all of them signal new and profound changes for museums. Most of these were not apparent or unacknowledged 18 years ago when I prepared the first iteration of "Persistent Paradoxes."

> Strong leadership does not have within itself the capability to create the fundamental changes our organizations require. It is not the fault of the people in these positions, it is the fault of the way we all have framed the role. Our search for strong leadership in others expresses a desire for others to assume the ownership and responsibility for our group, our organization, our society.
>
> —*Peter Block*[53]

References

1 M. Ames, *Cannibal Tours and Glass Boxes: The Anthropology of Museums*, Vancouver, Canada: UBC Press, 1992, p. 5.

2 Handy, C. (1994) *The Age of Paradox*, Boston, MA: Harvard Business School Press, pp. 12–13.

3 F. Conroy, "Think About It – Ways We Know and Don't," *Harper's* (277/1662), 1988, 70.

4 D. Evans, "The Myth of Customer Service," *Canadian Business*, March, 1991, 34–39; E. Shapiro, "Fad Surfing in the Board Room," *The Globe and Mail Report on Business Magazine*, July, 1995, 35–42.

5 Lowrance, W. (1986). *Modern Science and Human Values*, London: Oxford University Press, 1986, p. 209.

6 Block, P. (1993) *Stewardship*, San Francisco: Berrett-Koehler Publishers, pp. xx–xxi.

7 Handy, *The Age of Paradox*, p. 58.

8 Handy, *The Age of Paradox*, pp. 50–67.

9 Hatton, A. "Museum Planning and Museum Plans," *Museum Development*, January, 1992, 32–35.

10 Hatton, "Museum Planning and Museum Plans," 34–35.

11 S.E. Weil, "Organization-Wide Quality Assessments of Museums: An Immodest Proposal." Paper presented at the International Council of Museums' International Committee on Management Meeting, London, September, 1994: 2.

12 Conroy, "Think About It – Ways We Know and Don't," 68.

13 M. Ames, M. Personal communication, January 10, 1992.

14 Spalding, J. "Interpretation? No, Communication." Keynote address to the Annual Conference of the Canadian Museums Association, Regina, Saskatchewan, 1993.

15 Handy, C. *The Age of Unreason*, Boston, MA: Harvard Business School Press, 1989, p. 117.

16 Handy, *The Age of Unreason*, pp. 117–140; Handy, *The Age of Paradox*, pp. 109–113, 135–139.

17 Handy, *The Age of Paradox*, p. 112.

18 Handy, *The Age of Paradox*, p. 137.

19 Handy, *The Age of Unreason*, p. 124.

20 Handy, *The Age of Paradox*, p. 111.

21 Weil, "Organization-Wide Quality Assessments of Museums," 4.

22 Handy, *The Age of Unreason*, p. 239.

23 von Sass, P., "The Virtual Corporation," *Business in Calgary*, March, 1993, 25.

24 Postman, N. "Museum as Dialogue," *Museum News* (69/5), 1990, 58.

25 Ames, M. Personal communication, January 10, 1992.

26 Fuller, B. *Operating Manual for Spaceship Earth*, New York: Pocket Books, 1969.

27 Spalding, "Interpretation? No, Communication."

28 Clavir, M. "Conceptual Integrity of Conservation in Museums." Per Guldbeck Memorial Lecture at the 19th Annual International Institute of Conservation – Canadian Group Conference, Halifax, Canada, 1993.

29 Postman, "Museum as Dialogue," 58.

30 Block, *Stewardship*, p. 50.

31 Block, *Stewardship*, p. 51.

32 Block, *Stewardship*, p. 47.

33 Beer, M.A. "Leading Change," *Harvard Business School Note* 9-488-03, Cambridge, MA, 1988, 7.

34 De Pree, M. *Leadership Is an Art*, New York: Bantam Doubleday Dell Publishing Group, 1989, p. 114.

35 Morgan, G. *Images of Organization*, Newbury Park, CA: Sage Publications, 1986, pp. 340–341.

36 Janes, R.R. *Museums and the Paradox of Change: A Case Study in Urgent Adaptation* (Third edition), London and New York: Routledge, 2013.

37 Senge, P. *The Fifth Discipline*, New York: Bantam Doubleday Dell Publishing Group, 1990, pp. 239–240.

38 Handy, *The Age of Paradox*, pp. 12–13.

39 Marty, P.F. Email, July 29, 2012.

40 Marty, P.F. "The Changing Nature of Information Work in Museums," *Journal of the American Society for Information Science and Technology* (58/1), 2007, p. 8. Preprint available online at: http://marty.cci.fsu.edu/preprints/marty_jasist_2007.pdf .

41 Russo, A. and Peacock, D. "Great Expectations: Sustaining Participation in Social Media Spaces," in Trant, J. and Bearman, D. (eds), *Museums and the Web 2009: Proceedings*, Toronto: Archives & Museum Informatics, March 31, 2009. Available online at: http://www.archimuse.com/mw2009/papers/russo/russo.html

42 Schwarzer, M. Email, July 23, 2012.

43 Anderson, G. (ed.), *Reinventing the Museum: The Evolving Conversation and Paradigm Shift* (Second edition), Lanham, MD: AltaMira Press, 2012, p. 5.

44 American Association of Museums – Center for the Future of Museums, "Forecasting the Future of Museum Ethics," 2011/2012. Available online at: http://futureofmuseums. org/thinking/loader.cfm?csModule=security/getfile&pageid=2387, pp. 1–2.

45 Janes, *Museums and the Paradox of Change*, pp. 351–352.

46 Paul Hamlyn Foundation, "Our Museum: Communities and Museums as Active Partners," Paul Hamlyn Foundation, 2012. Available online at: http://ourmuseum. ning. com/page/6436099, p. 603.

47 Bergeron, L. "Honour the Stanford Mission, Be of Value to Society" (commencement address by Professor Rob Reich), *Stanford University News*, June 11, 2011. Available online at: http://news.stanford.edu/news/2011/june/classday-talk-reich-061111.html.

48 Battilana, J., Lee, J.M., Walker, J. and Dorsey, C. "In Search of the Hybrid Ideal," *Stanford Social Innovation Review*, Summer, 2012, pp. 51–55. Available online at: http://www.ssireview.org/pdf/Summer_2012_In_Search_of_the_Hybrid_Ideal.pdf.

49 International Council of Museums, "Frequently Asked Questions," September 20, 2012. Available online at: http://icom.museum/resources/frequently-asked-questions/.

50 CBC News – Business, "Bankruptcy Rate at Record Low: CIBC," February 3, 2011. Available online at: http://www.cbc.ca/news/business/story/2011/02/03/cibc-bankruptcy-data.html.

51 Badger, E. "We Built Way Too Many Cultural Institutions during the Good Years," *The Atlantic Cities*, July 5, 2012. Available online at: http://www.theatlanticcities.com/arts-and-lifestyle/2012/07/we-built-way-too-many-cultural-institutions-during-good-years/2456/.

52 Savage, J. "Corpus Christi Museum of Science and History to Be Run by Private Company," *Caller.com*, August 21, 2012. Available online at: http://www.caller.com/news/2012/aug/21/corpus-christi-museum-science-and-history-be-run-p/.

53 Block, *Stewardship*, p. 13.

21

DEBUNKING THE MARKETPLACE*

Introduction

There is no doubt that museums and galleries worldwide are struggling to maintain their stability in response to the complex challenges facing the non-profit world. These challenges range from declining attendance for most and over-attendance for some, to finding the appropriate balance between public funding and earned revenues, and none of them is easily overcome. Many of these challenges are inescapably economic, and originate in the belief that unlimited economic growth and unconstrained consumption are essential to our well-being. Indeed, capitalism and the lure of the marketplace have become inescapable for all of us, including organizations.

As philosopher Mark Kingwell notes, "every moment of waking and sleeping life is shot through with commitment to the goods and services of the global economy. We are capitalism made flesh."[1] The dominant ideology of capitalism and the decline of public funding for museums have coupled to produce a harmful offspring – a preoccupation with the marketplace and commerce, characterized by the primacy of economic interests in institutional decision making.

Many museums now see no other way but to consume their way to survival or prosperity, failing to recognize that this is increasing their vulnerability as social institutions. The purpose of this chapter is to consider some alternatives. The other face of marketplace ideology is corporatism – based on "our adoration of self-interest and our denial of public good," to quote the Canadian essayist John Ralston Saul.[2] He notes that corporatism also results in individual passivity, conformity, and silence, because the corporatist system depends upon the citizen's

---

*Source: Robert R. Janes, pp. 94–120 in Robert R. Janes (2009) *Museums in a Troubled World: Renewal, Irrelevance or Collapse?* London and New York: Routledge.

desire for inner comfort. Instead, John Ralston Saul argues that our individual and collective responsibilities in a democracy hinge upon participation and the psychic discomfort which inevitably accompanies active engagement in the public sphere. In his view, "the acceptance of psychic discomfort is the acceptance of consciousness."[3]

Corporatism has arrived

Like many individuals in our complacent society, many museums are in the grip of passivity and conformity, tacitly rejecting the discomfort that accompanies the uncertain search for relevance. The growing influence of corporatist values in museums is puzzling, however, considering the critical thinking that should accompany the self-proclaimed role of museums as knowledge-based institutions. The marketplace and corporatism are admittedly potent forces, as governments are now "imbued with a theological belief in the supremacy of free markets," to quote the historian Eric Hobsbawm.[4]

This trend, in combination with the free-market worship of the consumer's supreme power, has made things quite difficult for museums. This is all the more reason why museum boards, directors, senior managers, and staff must exercise both reflection and caution, and seriously ponder a critically important distinction. That is, while we can acknowledge that the market is the key element in economics and in wealth creation, we are not bound to accept a free-market society, where everything is to be achieved through the pursuit of private interest.[5] It is patently obvious that the marketplace is incapable of addressing the collective good, while museums are potentially key agents in doing so. Corporations, both national and multinational, are second only to governments in their influence on public policy and, as noted earlier, have clearly demonstrated time and again that the common good can be an inexhaustible arena for private gain. It is essential that museums become more conscious of the market forces they are embracing, in an effort to avoid the consequences described in this chapter.

Understandably, criticism of the reigning economic model is considered to be gratuitous by museum boards and executives, who are responsible for the fiscal health of their museums in the face of declining or stagnant public funding, apathetic audiences, competitive fundraising, and the abundance of entertaining distractions for the populace at large. Some museum directors point out that they would not be pursuing a marketplace agenda if they were not forced to by financial circumstances. Recognizing the very real fiscal pressures confronting museums, this chapter is devoted to a critique of the marketplace and corporatism, and their deleterious effects on museums. Both the marketplace and corporatism must be seen for what they are, as they continue to enfeeble otherwise competent museums and divert them from their core values and strengths as social institutions. Moreover, it will be argued that corporatism, the values implicit in the free market, and the strict application of business models are actually obstacles to achieving accountability and long-term sustainability. There are alternatives, but they are not to be found in conformity and unthinking consumption.

Back to the beginning

As the reader might well question my qualifications for undertaking this critique of corporatism and the free market, I must begin by relating some formative experiences that have led me to my current perspective, and which are also the foundation of my current bias against the preoccupation with money as the measure of worth. When I took my first museum job as the founding director of the Prince of Wales Northern Heritage Centre (PWNHC) in Canada's remote Northwest Territories in 1976, there were no concerns about money. It was a 100% government-funded project, complete with both capital and operating budgets. Unpredictable budget reductions and increases were common, and we never received all the funding that we requested, but admission was free, fundraising was not required, and there was no need to generate earned revenues. In fact, fundraising and earned revenues were never discussed during my 10-year tenure as Director, because the government and the taxpayer assumed the full responsibility. Furthermore, as a line department of government, the PWNHC had an advisory council rather than a board of directors. The museum was accountable to a government minister only.

Our mission was to serve 65 remote communities in the region by providing professional services – ranging from travelling exhibitions to archaeological research. This experience was the antithesis of the corporatist imperative and, in retrospect, lacked the discipline and appreciation that come from a greater sensitivity to audience needs and aspirations. Actually, I was so naïve and presumptuous that I refused to allow the wife of the government leader to host a tea for dignitaries in our public lounge, claiming that social functions were not the museum's responsibility. She accepted my refusal, as did the government, a tribute to their tolerance of my self-serving lack of imagination.

My perspective matured when I left that position and became the founding director of the Science Institute of the Northwest Territories (SINT) in 1986, an arm's-length agency devoted to bridging the gap between mainstream scientific work and the needs and aspirations of northern residents. Beginning a century earlier, the peoples of the Northwest Territories, who include Euro-Canadians, Dene, Inuit and Metis, were the subjects of countless scientific investigations conducted by an international cadre of academics and graduate students (see Note 1). Few, if any, of these researchers ever shared the results or the implications of their work with their research subjects. This was particularly exasperating for the Northwest Territories' Indigenous peoples (the Dene, Inuit and Metis), who constituted two-thirds of the population at that time. They were not opposed to research; they simply wanted to know how they could benefit, individually or collectively, from the ongoing generation of knowledge in their homeland. Although not labeled as such, this was an early call for science in the public interest. Northerners have always had a practical bent – it's a survival skill in a severe land. A group of citizens and scientists eventually decided that this intellectual colonialism must cease, and they envisioned the SINT as the mechanism for democratization.

With a culturally diverse board of northern citizens and barely sufficient core funding from the government, the SINT was obliged to reach out and define its relevance amidst the volatile politics of remote northern communities, as well as to establish its credibility in the world of mainstream science and grantsmanship. This was done, with programs ranging from the licensing of researchers (to ensure follow-up), to youth programs based on traditional knowledge, to the operation of remote research facilities to assist mainstream scientists and resident researchers in their investigations. The learning was clear – service and accountability to both northern communities and the scientific establishment required grassroots support stemming from real and perceived relevance. In retrospect, this was the best fiscal model of all – a governing body of diverse citizens, reliable (albeit modest) core funding, external monetary support from diverse sources for innovation and growth, and the autonomy to act in the best interests of organizational and community aspirations. With my next position, the balance between public funding and earned revenues was destined to change, with the fiscal pendulum careening into the marketplace.

Shortly after I became the CEO of the Glenbow Museum in 1989, I was advised by the Chair of the Board of Governors that the museum's funding agreement with the province of Alberta had expired and no new arrangements had been negotiated. None of this had been discussed during the interviews and selection process, an unfortunate or intentional oversight familiar to many new museum directors. This oversight was the harbinger of a fateful future, as Glenbow had been receiving between 80% and 90% of its annual operating budget from the province until I arrived. The year was 1992 and a conservative estimate of income and expenditures revealed a shocking projection – a cumulative deficit of CAN\$7.7 million by 1997. In short, if we continued at our current rate of expenditures, in the face of declining government support, we would be bankrupt and closed within five years. Thus began a massive organizational change process which led to the redesign and renewal of the museum based on six strategies, all of which has been chronicled in Part 2 of this book and elsewhere.[6]

One of these strategies was devoted to developing commercial alliances and business ventures for the sole purpose of increasing earned revenues, and thus began my immersion in the marketplace. We designed and developed Glenbow Enterprises, a for-profit business unit, and engaged in a variety of commercial activities including consulting services, art rentals, facility rentals, and the design and construction of collection storage facilities and exhibitions for corporate offices in Calgary. All of these earned revenues were allocated to Glenbow's operating expenses. Federal tax officials had no problem with this initiative, as long as we engaged in activities that were directly related to our mandate as a non-profit organization. As the CEO, I was also given a revenue line in the annual operating budget and was expected to meet it with consulting and public speaking fees. This I did.

To shorten a long and arduous story, when I left my position in 2000 after 10 weary years of relentless budget balancing (deficit spending was a cause for dismissal), Glenbow was getting 23% of its funding from the province and 10% from the City of Calgary. The remainder of the CAN$11 million budget, or 67%, came from investment income (an endowment invested in stocks, bonds, and cash), fundraising, commercial activities, admissions, and memberships.[7]

This degree of financial self-sufficiency continued with my successor, with Glenbow reporting a budget of CAN$13 million for 2006–2007, made up of 37% of public funding and 63% coming from fundraising, investment income, commercial activities, admissions, and membership.[8] Although Glenbow has been the most self-sufficient of Canada's 10 largest museums for well over a decade, this distinction has come with a significant cost, and has meant a preoccupation with attendance numbers, borrowed blockbuster exhibitions, and fundraising. To what extent this has hindered more innovative community engagement is difficult to say, but a preoccupation with the bottom line is precisely that. This has also prompted the Glenbow's board to chase the allure of corporate partnerships, a cautionary tale which will be discussed later in this chapter.

The circle is now complete, and my thinking has returned to where I began as a novice director, only this time with an understanding of what is required. With the benefit of having engaged in the three most typical operating models used by museums, I can only conclude that the domination of the earned-income imperative is debilitating, inappropriate, and unnecessary. The totally dependent PWNHC is also unacceptable, as the introversion afforded by complete government funding impairs or prevents true accountability. This model is a twentieth-century relic – nice if you can get it, but ultimately untenable. In short, over-reliance on public funding can be as insidious as the market model. Nor is the severe economic self-sufficiency of Glenbow realistic, as it is oblivious to the purpose and values of museums, as well as being dangerously consumptive of staff energy and commitment. Long-term sustainability lies in a diversified and reasonable balance of public money and earned income, similar to that of the SINT.

As noted earlier, however, there has never been any concerted discussion within the museum community about what the mixture of public funding and earned revenues should be. Unfortunately, in this age of hyper-capitalism, maximum self-sufficiency based on earned income has become the grail of many museum boards, subjecting all concerned to myriad complexities and pressures that have nothing to do with the inherent purpose of museums. But if health care, prisons, public transportation, the quality of food, the availability of water, media concentration, and so on, are all subjected to the profit motives of the marketplace, why should museums be exempt from the imposition of marketplace ideology, especially when public funding is inadequate to keep them afloat?

Museums are not immune to the marketplace, nor should they be, as business literacy and efficiency are essential in a competent museum. More on this later. For museums, however, financial self-sufficiency is a myth that permits museums and their boards to pursue growth and consumption as the keys to the future, thus avoiding any substantive consideration of what sustainability might look like in the long term. Sustainability could actually mean a smaller core staff, or a smaller building, or starting afresh with a new mission and values, or merging with like-minded organizations, or even deaccessioning or mothballing a portion of the collection. Boards and staff might begin by asking two essential questions – "If museums did not exist, would we reinvent them and what would they look like?" And, "If the museum were to be reinvented, what would be the public's role in the reinvented institution?" These are the conversations that are actually required, because to ignore them is both illusory and dangerous, as global issues mount and the unique world of museums inevitably chills. It is helpful to recall the observation from Chapter 9 – "the crucial dimensions of scarcity in human life are not economic, but existential. They are related to our needs for leisure and contemplation, peace of mind, love, community and self-realization."[9]

A clash of values

The marketplace is now the "elephant in the room" for a host of museums, and the danger lies in both the size and the nature of the beast. This elephant can no longer be ignored because it has created a conflict in values, which has nothing to do with the use of sound business practices in museums. The inappropriateness of unthinking adherence to the marketplace lies in the complexity of museums as institutions, because every museum, in the language of the marketplace, is a mixed portfolio. Some museum work is clearly subject to market forces, such as restaurants, shops, and product development, while other activities such as collections care, scientific research, and community engagement are not. The latter bear no relation to the market economy and, in fact, require a safe distance from the marketplace and its corporatist fallout.

Market ideology and corporatism have failed to demonstrate any real ability to deal with the complexities of a competent museum and are, instead, homogenizing the complex portfolio with a stultifying adherence to financial considerations – at the expense of almost everything else. The tyranny of quantitative measures, such as attendance numbers and shop revenues, is a clear indication of this reality. I am curious about how a bottom-line mentality would cope with the complexities inherent in the following fictionalized glimpse of a museum director's meeting schedule, the details of which are all based in fact.

The museum director's datebook

Tuesday, 4 January
Meeting with conservation and curatorial staff concerning the storage of a sacred medicine bundle.

Reality check – It has come to the attention of the curatorial staff that the elders of the First Nation who borrowed this medicine bundle for ceremonial use consider it to be the equivalent of a living child. Professional conservation standards require that the bundle be placed in a freezer to prevent any infestation of the existing collections when the bundle is returned to storage after the loan.

Thursday, 11 January
Meeting with the Director of Development concerning the raffle results at the annual fundraising event.

Reality check – A donated motorcycle was raffled off at the annual signature fundraising event, but the winner, a prominent citizen, does not want the motorcycle and wishes to donate it back to the museum for a tax receipt.

Tuesday, 15 January
Meeting with the Investment Oversight Committee of the Board of Directors concerning the underperformance of the endowment fund.

Reality check – The endowment is currently managed by two investment firms that have different investment philosophies to ensure a balanced approach. Both firms have underperformed for three consecutive quarters and a change in approach has been recommended by a board member who owns a wealth management company.

Friday, 4 February
Meeting with government protocol staff concerning the upcoming visit of senior elected leaders.

Reality check – The government wishes to host a large reception for foreign delegates to an international trade meeting, which will require the closure of several public galleries for a full day. The reception happens to be on a Saturday, which is a free admission day to encourage attendance by underprivileged families, the costs of which are underwritten by a family foundation.

Monday, 14 February
Meeting with the Senior Vice-President of Community Affairs for a multinational corporation

Reality check – Three years ago this corporation signed a five year funding agreement to underwrite 75% of the costs of an innovative education program devoted to children with learning disabilities. Senior personnel have changed, along with corporate interests and priorities, and the corporation now wants to reduce their financial commitment by half within 30 days.

Tuesday, 22 February
Special meeting of the Senior Management Group and the Executive of the employees union.

Reality check – At the request of the Senior Ethnologist, the Senior Management Group and the Manager of Personnel agreed to recognize the traditional knowledge of several First Nations staff as equivalent to a master's degree for the purposes of job classification and the rate of pay. The union executive and the majority of curators are challenging this decision.

Monday, 28 February
Emergency meeting of the full Board of Directors.

Reality check – The Gay/Lesbian Alliance of People of Colour were given permission by a junior staff person to host a sexuality film festival in the museum's theatre. All of the films will have to be rated by the film classification board before being approved and no one under 18 will be admitted. One half of the Board wants the film festival cancelled immediately. The Alliance has threatened court action for censorship, along with a large demonstration, if they are not allowed to hold the event.

In light of the competing values and interests noted above, making a profit in the business world is likely to be much easier. It is the complexity of museums – these interminable shades of grey – that makes the marketplace not only less than useful as a source of guidance but also an obstacle to the trust and understanding of the broader community. Contrary to the received wisdom of the marketplace, the marketplace and its activities actually deplete trust.[10] It is the so-called third sector or civil society, occupying the space between business and government, which contains the organizations upon which the marketplace depends – these third sector organizations are neither business nor government. There is no stability without the third sector, because the markets build upon the strength of this sector. All the organizations in the third sector, including museums, generate the social capital – the networks, norms, trust, and shared values – which is transferred into the social sphere and not only helps to hold society together but is also instrumental in facilitating an understanding of the interconnectedness of society and the interests within it. Social capital is born of long-term associations that are not explicitly self-interested or coerced, and it typically diminishes if it is not regularly renewed or replaced.[11]

Corporatists and marketplace ideologues believe, as do business people in general, that markets create communities when, in fact, the opposite is true. Communities create and sustain the trust upon which the marketplace is based. Museums are apparently unaware of their role and their strengths in this vital responsibility, willing to let their unique assets be subsumed under the rhetoric that would have them become businesses. This may be appealing theoretically, but it is impossible in reality, as the imperative of the marketplace cannot accommodate the real-life complexities when the final arbiter is the bottom line.

The insatiable motive of the bottom line is ultimately monetary gain, in whatever guise, not collective well-being. It wasn't that long ago when the third sector was seen as a much-needed antidote to the materialism that dominated twentieth-century thinking, recognizing the third sector's emphasis on service, relationships, and a sense of grounding in the larger community.[12] It is now the twenty-first century and it appears that museums are oblivious to this unfulfilled potential, while continuing to lose their way under the influence of heightened commercialism.

The anatomy of failure

The failed relationship between museums and the marketplace goes beyond the clash of values to include a litany of embarrassing and injurious contradictions and consequences, as museums drift onto the shoals of unthinking conformity. These afflictions include short-term thinking, money as the measure of worth, conspicuous consumption, and business tribalism, each of which is discussed below. It is time for some independence of thought; even some well-considered rebellion to the influence of hyper-capitalism.

The 500-year business plan

The most obvious clash of values is apparent in how museums have traditionally viewed time, as compared to the marketplace. Museums are about time and are time machines in a sense, although their bias has always been for the past, not the future – unlike the classic time machine. This commitment to the continuum of time is vitally important, as the writer and philosopher Robert Grudin notes, "We usually fail to understand that the present achieves full reality only when seen by those who retain the perspectives of past and future, that indeed no aspect of time is really available to us except in terms of the continuum."[13] Depending upon the museum and its collection, be it paleontological or contemporary art, this continuum can be longer or shorter, but all museums share a long-term commitment to the objects in their care.

As a museum director, I often noted that collections management required a 500-year business plan, much to the bemusement of our corporate board members – all in an effort to operationalize the sentiment that museums keep collections "forever." Humankind is in dire need of a long-term perspective to counteract the short-term thinking which drives the marketplace – be it the focus on quarterly results, shareholder value, or the immediate gratification of consumerism. This is the time continuum at play, and is the special realm of museums. The commitment to the long term is an irreplaceable contribution that only museums can make, yet it is eroding under an ideology that is oblivious to its value.

The short-lived corporation

Recognizing that short-term thinking is the foundation of marketplace ideology, it is appropriate to note that the average life expectancy of multinational corporations is between 40 and 50 years, a discovery that provoked such alarm that an inquiry was undertaken to determine why.[14] The author of this work, Arie DeGeus, a senior planner at Royal Dutch Shell, concluded that the exclusive focus on the production of goods and services has doomed the vast majority of companies to rapid extinction. DeGeus also identified four traits that characterized 30 companies which have existed for 100 to 700 years. These traits are conservative financing (governing growth and evolution both effectively and frugally); sensitivity to the world around them (the ability to learn and adapt); cohesion and identity (the ability to build a community of employees who feel they belong, as well as a persona for the organization); and last, considerable tolerance, encouragement, and decentralization for experiments and learning which promote change.[15]

Most importantly for this discussion, DeGeus concludes that,

> The twin policies of managing for profit and maximizing shareholder value, at the expense of all other goals, are vestigial management traditions. They no longer reflect the imperatives of the world we live in today. They are suboptimal, even destructive – not just to the rest of society, but to the companies that adopt them.[16]

Yet, these twin policies continue to grow in status and influence, and have now entered the museum boardroom in the guise of quantitative measures, earned revenues, excess consumption, hollow imitation of others' successes, and "the customer is always right" mantra. On the contrary, DeGeus sees companies as living organisms, existing for their own improvement, to fulfil their potential, and become as great as they can be – just as human beings exist to survive and thrive. Why should museums be any different? DeGeus' book, now a business classic, has apparently escaped the attention of both the for-profit and nonprofit sectors, and much tension and conflict can now be expected to accompany the rearguard action to rid museums of their burgeoning, yet outmoded, belief in the marketplace.

Money as the measure of worth

Underlying the pervasive power of short-term thinking is the new orthodoxy of money as the measure of worth, and herein lies another significant clash in values. This orthodoxy has so imbued our everyday lives that we seem oblivious to it, and it is no wonder that it now pervades the museum world. Psychologist Mihaly Csikszentmihalyi notes that:

> The most important functions of society, which used to be relatively independent of the market, have now become servants of Wall Street. From managed health care to agribusiness, from the media to genetic research, from education to music and entertainment, the intrinsic value of these institutions has been overshadowed by their valuation on the market.[17]

Indeed, even warfare has once again been privatized, and mercenaries are now employed from Iraq to Africa, including the provision of logistical support for government armies.[18]

In the museum world, the extent to which money has cast its spell is visible in recent remarks delivered at the Midwinter Meeting of the Association of Art Museum Directors in January of 2008.[19] John Wetenhall, an art museum director, introduced a panel discussion on the performance of art galleries by referring to the three means of competition as taught by management schools – price, quality, or differentiation. He added speed and flexibility to the holy trinity and noted "how quickly we can deliver results affects how many accomplishments we may pursue."[20] He rightly questioned the need for continuous institutional growth, and noted that a mature art gallery can be likened to a "mature industry," otherwise known as "a cash cow, valued for spinning off quarterly dividends to shareholders – the stuff of so-called widow and orphan stocks."[21]

A curious and telling choice of language, to be sure. Art galleries do, indeed, have "dividends," including the quality of the art shown, the richness of cultural programming, and the associated learning and personal experiences. But why entomb these qualities in the vacuous language of commerce? Is this meant to legitimize the work of art galleries in the competitive marketplace, or to satisfy colleagues and trustees who are already immersed? I would hope that art gallery directors are capable of using language that is more natural and more appropriate than commercial dogma. Perhaps it is more difficult now, with the marketplace elephant in the room.

This juggernaut of market forces cannot be blamed on the business community alone, although it is definitely the prime mover. Society as a whole must also assume responsibility, for intentionally or not, we have all developed a taste for comfort, excess, and the highest possible return on investment in the shortest amount of time. As difficult as it may be to concede, the marketplace now provides much of our ostensible happiness and sense of worth, and museums are not immune. This has not gone unnoticed, and there is obvious concern in the museum community about the advent of money as the measure of worth. Veteran museum executive Tom Freudenheim writes that "The money worm has burrowed into museum foundations in the last five decades, weakening structures already challenged by power politics, relevancy issues, and contemporary anxieties."[22] He further notes that "the idea of a museum . . . as a money-making machine is frighteningly pervasive."

Similar anxieties are also emerging from the UK, where the Museums Association (MA) notes that more and more museums are adopting the short-term, money focus characteristic of business. The MA's landmark report questions the sustainability of museums that occupy energy-hungry buildings, have expanding collections, and continually destroy old exhibitions with little reuse or recycling, while also promoting international tourism that involves energy-consuming travel.[23] All in the service of the marketplace, of course.

Fighting fog with fog

Alas, even the debilitating effects of marketplace ideology have been insufficient to mobilize the museum community to rise to its own defense. The result has been the insidious imposition of quantitative performance measures based on money as the measure of worth (attendance, number of exhibitions, earned revenues, cost per visitor, and so forth), in the absence of any substantive evaluation or comment by the museum community itself. There was, however, a flurry of interest in performance measures throughout the 1990s, but none of the ensuing published papers, conference sessions, or actual strategic plans led to any consensus (local, national, or international) on which types of measures are appropriate – including the appropriate mix of the quantitative and the qualitative.

Without such dialogue and evaluation, museums have once again chosen passivity and isolation, bereft of any influence to counteract the dominance of simplistic, commercial indicators. To relinquish the definition of performance measures is dangerous, as these measures are, in effect, professional standards. For museums to claim professional status and then decline the setting of standards has created a debilitating trajectory governed by external forces. One can only assume a tacit belief on the part of museums that they would remain immune to the societal demand for accountability.

The need to involve the museum community in its own performance assessment has not gone away, however, and it will continue to grow, as performance measurement systems are themselves problematic and require intelligence and discipline to design and monitor. This is underscored by research in Austria where, in 2002, the eight national museums became responsible for their own budgets.[24] The ministry retained ownership of the collections, but the museums assumed operational control and are required to report a number of key figures to measure their performance. Based on interviews with museum managers, curators, artists, and government officials about their experiences, the researchers concluded that:

> Neither museum managers nor ministerial agencies are satisfied with the existing reporting system. They are all aware that the performance measurement systems actually can be compared to shooting clay pigeons in the fog. Both groups try to find the solution in a continuous elaboration of the key figures in use, which results in an inflation of numbers. As numbers lack the capability to provide full transparency, it is the attempt to fight "fog" with more "fog".[25]

"Shooting clay pigeons in the fog," and "fighting fog with fog," are not exactly bold inducements to forging an intelligent performance management system for museums. In the absence of a deliberate approach to measurement in North America, however, the imposition of money as the measure of worth will continue, until museums either confront its essential meaninglessness, or the marketplace collapses from its own excesses. Based on museum inertia to date, my money is on the latter.

Culture as consumption

Both short-term thinking and money as the measure of worth are key ingredients in another contemporary museum phenomenon – culture as consumption. Again, it is helpful to look at what museum directors are saying to each other, and to their constituencies, for an indication of how deeply consumption has pervaded the museum scene. In a 2007 address to the Empire Club of Canada (which includes some of Canada's most influential professional, business, labour, and government leaders), William Thorsell, Director and CEO of Toronto's Royal Ontario Museum (ROM), spoke of the museum as the new agora. He noted that architecture is the most public of arts and "cultural institutions have a responsibility to be vigorous patrons of architecture, pushing boundaries and empowering genius."[26] Thorsell is committed to this sentiment and recently opened their newly renovated museum, complete with a Daniel Libeskind's architectural "Crystal." Thorsell sees the museum as the new meeting place, or agora, replacing the town hall and the church, and "providing an opportunity to meet new people in an elegant setting that includes restaurants, lounges and distinctive retail."[27]

Herein lies the other agenda, as the ROM was short CAN$50 million at the time of writing to complete the CAN$303 million project, as well as requiring an increase to its operating budget. Earned revenues are essential and consumers are increasingly the source, or are at least hoped to be. Thorsell concludes his address with the request "please don't be shy about ordering that ROMtini (signature martini) in Crystal Five – Toronto's amazing new rooftop restaurant and bar. What Agora would be complete without one?"[28] Although eating and drinking have always been part of public life, this is certainly a new take on the agora of old.

What's interesting is the prominent role that consumption, in a variety of forms, now plays in defining the ostensible uniqueness of museums, usually eclipsing any reference to purpose, values, or the world of the non-elite. The argument is well known by now – economic necessity – born of diminishing budgets, rising costs, and the need to get people's attention. Surprisingly, museum excess has begun to annoy even the financial sector. In an investment commentary entitled "Enough is Enough," William Gross, Managing Director of Pacific Investment Management Company (one of the largest fixed-income managers in the world), takes issue with the growing disparity between the rich, the middle, and the lower classes. Art museums emerge as one of his bellwethers, as Gross notes:

> Trust funds for the kids, inheritances for the grandkids, multiple vacation homes, private planes, multi-million dollar birthday bashes and ego-rich donations to local art museums and concert halls are but a few of the ways that rich people waste money . . . When millions of people are dying from AIDS and malaria in Africa, it is hard to justify the umpteenth society gala held for the benefit of a performing arts center or an art museum. A thirty million dollar gift for a concert hall is not philanthropy, it is a Napoleonic coronation.[29]

Irrespective of the rich, consumer spending on culture, including museums, has reached deeper into society, with Canadian consumers spending over CAN$25 billion on cultural goods and services in 2005.[30] This spending was 5% higher than the combined consumer spending on household furniture, appliances, and tools. Consumer spending on cultural goods and services is also over three times larger than the CAN$7.7 billion spent on culture in Canada by all levels of government in 2003/04, and grew by 48% between 1997 and 2005 – much higher than the 18% rise in the Consumer Price Index during the same period. This is but one example from Canada. It appears that the so-called cultural industries, including museums, are enjoying unprecedented acceptance in our mercantile world, while the biosphere buckles under the strain. Actually, bigger is no longer better – it is becoming culpable.

This heightened level of consumption has assumed even greater import in the broader economy, as evidenced by the 2008 International Forum on the Creative Economy devoted to "Measuring Arts and Culture as an Economic and Social Engine of a Country's Wealth."[31] One of the conference themes invited research on the measurement of the contribution of the arts and cultural sector to a country's economy. A second theme, "Consumption Dynamics: Consumers Driving Change," was devoted to research that focuses on the profile of Canadian and international consumers of cultural goods and services, including trends in consumption and new roles for consumers in artistic and cultural activities. With initiatives such as these, there is little doubt that museums and their sister disciplines (the literary and performing arts) are competing for recognition as the new frontier for generating wealth.

From whom remains a mystery, however, judging by the precarious balance sheets of even the most senior museums. Museums, in fact, have grown fond of debt as the marketplace euphoria unfolds, and have turned once again to bond offerings to finance various initiatives.[32] Bond sales are not new, as the Art Institute of Chicago was doing this as far back as 1978, but the technique has now spread to smaller institutions. For example, the Holocaust Memorial Foundation of Illinois raised US$28.5 million in 2006 through a bond offering to build a museum and education centre. The Please Touch Museum in Philadelphia, where children are encouraged to handle the displays, sold US$60 million in bonds in 2006 to help expand and move to a historic site. That same year, the Telfair Museum of Art in Savannah, Georgia, raised US$8 million through bonds to help pay for new facilities. With due regard for this entrepreneurial spirit, the fact remains that bonds require the museum to pay back the interest, as well as the principal – a significant obligation as compared to donations, grants, and earned revenues. Debt, consumption, and growth have always been bedfellows in the world of commerce; they are now becoming familiar companions among museums.

Vanity architecture

Nowhere is culture as consumption more visible than in the realm of celebrity, vanity, conceit, or simply new architecture – a widespread phenomenon throughout the museum world. China, for example, is planning to build 1,000 new museums by 2015, so that every city with a population of 100,000 or more has at least one. The newly renovated Capital Museum in Beijing is 60,000 square metres (645,000 square feet) and as large as the Louvre Museum in Paris.[33] Celebrity architects are not a prerequisite, however, as museums are also building and renovating without necessarily employing high-profile personalities. Although often likened to a renaissance, this architectural boom doesn't merit this praise, lacking as it commonly does any vigorous intellectual or creative resurgence within the museum itself. In fact, the opposite prevails, as the "If you build it, he will come" syndrome readily diverts attention away from a consideration of purpose, values, and the requirements for long-term sustainability. If this seems unduly harsh, I will now consider some implications and consequences of this contemporary bandwagon.

In pursuit of both stability and prosperity, various museums have chosen to increase their profile, popularity, and earned revenues through architectural renewal, which usually strives to include some expression of sensationalism.[34] Various museums have adopted this approach, especially larger ones, although its contribution to the museum's long-term sustainability is decidedly in doubt, as well as being controversial.[35] In a research paper commissioned by the Getty Leadership Institute, museum consultant Adrian Ellis concluded that this approach is not sustainable.[36] The problem with the expansion plan, or the "galvanizing building initiative," as the context to raise funds, refinance, and move forward, is cogently summarized by Ellis:

> This strategy . . . is a form of pyramid selling or Ponzi scheme. Eventually, after the noise has died down and the new building is completed, the logic of the weakening balance sheet kicks in again. Unless the scheme was so successful that it has generated a whole new set of contributed funding opportunities, then the systemic underfinancing reappears, and in a heightened form, given the larger facility and the more ambitious programming on which the facility is premised. The museum stands faced, again, with the three options of crisis appeal, more populist programming, or obfuscatory expansion.[37]

Ellis draws several valuable and sobering conclusions, which he offers as recommendations to museum directors. He suggests that they analyze and articulate the full cost, rather than the marginal cost of program growth, in a format that allows this to be done and communicated effectively to the outside world. In addition, he suggests that museum directors think about, and articulate, the requirements for institutional growth in parallel with program growth, as well as including goals for capital structure and investment as part of their strategic planning. Ellis also asks museum leaders to "Remember that the reason they [museums] are nonprofit organizations is not just because they are mission driven. It's not just because their mission is valued by society. It's also because the pursuit of mission is an axiomatically unprofitable activity."[38] This is essential advice, indeed, recognizing the ubiquity of commercial dogma, and Ellis is to be acknowledged for his candor.

Similar concerns have also emerged from Western Europe, where James M. Bradburne has been writing for over a decade about museums, sustainability, and the tyranny of museum architecture, or the "edifice complex," as I prefer to call it. In a frank and highly readable article entitled "The Museum Time Bomb: Overbuilt, Overtraded and Overdrawn," Bradburne articulates the path to potential ruin by noting that operating costs are the heart of the museum time bomb for old museums as well as new ones, as inflation continues unabated. Large buildings require larger staff and incur substantially higher operating costs – costs which are rarely, if ever, recognized by private or public funders.[39] Bradburne follows this progression to its logical conclusion – museums are required to increase earned revenues to pay the increased costs, mostly by arguing that increased visitation to the new or renovated building will generate the additional revenue. He concludes by noting that:

After the initial burst of popularity, visitor numbers inevitably decline, leaving the new institution starved for the cash desperately needed to renew facilities and attract new revenue. At best, the institution can limp along for a few years. At worst, the institution faces bankruptcy. In both cases the state is faced with the prospect of either refinancing the institution, or letting it go bust . . . In reality, the course commonly adopted is to provide an additional injection of one-time funds conditional on becoming self-sufficient in a given time frame. All this does, however, is to emasculate the institution further, and push it further away from its initial mission. In either case, what remains is a building; another monument to short-sighted planning.[40]

The so-called "Bilbao Effect"

It remains a mystery why the thoughtful work of Ellis and Bradburne is not more widely known and discussed in the museum community. One might conclude that there is a complicit ban on challenging the underpinnings of the "If you build it, he will come" syndrome. Or, it may be that the museum community is in a state of denial although, in fairness, this infatuation with growth and numbers is backed by a seductive poster child known as the "Bilbao Effect." The "Bilbao Effect" refers to the Guggenheim Museum Bilbao (GMB), the architectural monument designed by Frank Gehry and rumoured to be the transformative agent in revitalizing the depressed industrial economy of the Basque region of Spain. In short, for urban planners, politicians, consultants, museum directors, and trustees, the "Bilbao Effect" means "the transformation of a city by a new museum or cultural facility into a vibrant and attractive place for residents, visitors and inward investment."[41] Alas, the "Bilbao Effect" might well be an illusion, now that the boosterism is being replaced by evaluation and reflection.

In a recent article by Beatriz Plaza, an economist in the Faculty of Economics at the University of the Basque Country (Bilbao, Spain), we learn that the "Bilbao Effect" is definitely not the silver bullet so fervently hoped for by those museums and their consultants in search of painless renewal. Contrary to the ardent believers who credit the GMB with transformative powers, Plaza writes that the GMB was part of a much larger economic redevelopment strategy, which included, among many other things, a new subway line, new drainage and water systems, an airport, residential and business complexes, a seaport, and industrial and technology parks. In Plaza's words, "The icing on the cake was the construction of the GMB and additional cultural investments, such as a concert hall and a centre for young artists to promote art and cultural tourism as a means of diversifying the economy and reducing unemployment."[42]

Plaza's quantitative and qualitative analysis is in blunt contrast to the simplistic coronation of the "Bilbao Effect" – much heralded by directors, trustees, governments, and consultants, as well as the celebrity architects themselves, as the solution to irrelevant museums, urban blight, and economic renewal.[43] In summing up her analysis, Plaza could not be more explicit:

Last, but not least . . . it is inaccurate to define the Bilbao case as a cultur-ally led regeneration process. On the contrary, Bilbao is an integral part of a larger coherent public policy targeted at productivity and diversity, with a strong cultural component. The Basque Country was industrial in the past, and remains industrial at present, although some '*Made in the Basque Country*' goods are now heavily branded by the innovative image of the GMB.[44]

Whither jet travel?

It would be unfair to reduce the "Bilbao Effect" to branded goods, but Plaza's conclusion does bring the marketplace rhetoric into proper perspective. In addition to requiring concerted and committed civic action from all levels of government, a herculean task in any jurisdiction, the "Bilbao Effect" embodies another nasty surprise – its undisguised dependence on tourism, especially international tourism. In fact, GMB attracts an average of 800,000 non-Basque visitors a year, compared with less than 100,000 before the GMB opened.[45] In an article entitled, "The War on Travel," Chris Lorway points out that travel is becoming notably difficult and unpleasant as a result of post-9/11 (the terrorist attacks on New York City) security restrictions and unprofitable airlines. He quotes a cultural tourism expert who notes "that cultural tourism as we know it has peaked and that we are moving towards a more localized cultural sector which will focus on regional artists and audiences as opposed to national and international ones."[46] For those museums counting on the "Bilbao Effect" to work its magic, this is a brisk touch with reality.

For example, as a result of the new requirement that all travelers to and from the Americas must carry a passport to enter or re-enter the USA, there will be 7.7 million fewer US visits to Canada between 2005 and 2008, representing a loss of CAN\$1.8 billion in Canadian tourism revenue. Over the same period, Canadian outbound visits to the US are projected to drop by 3.5 million, representing a loss of US\$785 million in US tourism revenue.[47] Furthermore, these scenarios do not even acknowledge the rising costs of jet fuel and gasoline – the prolonged crisis that is already well under way. What are the implications for the traveling public if oil rises to US\$200 or US\$300 a barrel? The answer is obvious – the democratization of jet travel will unravel and flying will once again become an elite activity. What will this mean for museums dependent upon national and international tourism?

There is no doubt that bold and creative buildings attract visitors and can provide meaningful visitor experiences, but these inducements are increasingly irrelevant, perhaps irresponsible, in a world beset by a litany of social and environ-mental pressures ranging from climate change to global poverty. The superficial truisms of the marketplace have proven to be not only inadequate as solutions, but also the source of many of our present difficulties. Are museums destined to achieve their sought-after legitimacy in the mercantile structure, just in time to witness the inevitable rejection of marketplace values by thinking people? How ironic and how unnecessary, especially when practitioners and consultants, like

Ellis and Bradburne, have been waving the red flag for years. What is the meaning of this myopia? Where does it originate? Is it arrogance, introversion, or a combination of both?

Business tribalism

In addition to short-term thinking, money as the measure of worth, and culture as consumption, there is another feature of the marketplace that imbues it with considerable control and influence, and is best described as the culture of business. This culture underscores the clash of values discussed here, and is a dominant factor in blinding museums to a sense of their own worth and well-being. For those museums that have no edifice complex and may be feeling smug at this point in the discussion, I note that the culture of business (irrespective of its useful methods and techniques) possesses an influence that not only outstrips its usefulness, but also discourages the analysis and reflection required for museums to choose a different path. The cause of much of this difficulty lies in the tribal nature of business.

By tribal, I mean a particular reference group in which individuals identify with each other through common language, ritual, and legend.[48] The business tribe itself is not centralized or hierarchical in its organization and, to a great extent, is culturally and linguistically homogeneous – with English as the *lingua franca* and grounded in capitalist values. This tribalism sets values that orient the behaviour of individuals around common interests. There are various manifestations of this business culture, and I will focus on several that are diminishing the role of museums as social institutions. Clearly, the culture of business contributes much that is essential to our collective well-being, but that is not my concern here.

Much of the current strength and profile of the global business culture derives from the contemporary worship of business people, along with scientists, as the wise leaders and icons of our material success. The pairing of business leaders and scientists is interesting in itself, as much of science is now in the service of business, and not in the production of knowledge for its own sake. Business leaders and scientists have now replaced nobility and the clergy as the focus of our acclaim, presumably because production and consumption are now the benchmarks of our well-being.[49] Our societal veneration of business leaders has seeded their influence far and wide – throughout every sector of society and at the highest levels of leadership, including the governance of museums. Many museums have come to resemble corporate entities, with revenues and attendance being the predominant measures of worth. Many of their boards are increasingly indistinguishable from their corporate counterparts, with too many directors being chosen for their business, legal, or accounting experience.

Although such qualifications are essential, the danger lies in the growing tendency for these boards to self-select on the basis of these criteria alone, to the exclusion of other attributes such as cultural diversity, community connectedness, and broader socio-environmental awareness. This self-selection is particularly obvious when potential board members are bypassed because they are seen to lack the necessary social or business connections, or are not wealthy in their own right. My personal experience, as well as that of colleagues, confirms that neither position nor social standing is any indication of an individual's ability or willingness to raise money. On the contrary, the more elevated the individual, the greater the chance that he or she will be reluctant to use up their "credit" (professional/social reputation and the attendant connections) except in the most exceptional circumstances. As well, professionals, such as lawyers, are generally averse to fundraising for fear of alienating existing or potential clients. There is nothing wrong with these personal constraints, as long as they are made explicit by board members at the outset – a rarity in the museum world. The danger lies in the tribalistic groupthink that excludes non-business people from museum boards, based on the myth that they cannot add value to governance.

A lethal mix of business tribalism and loose governance led to the recent scandals that swept through a number of corporations and businesses, including Enron and WorldCom.[50] This, in turn, provoked an unprecedented concern about ethics and accountability, and the corporate and financial reformation is still under way. Suffice it to say that museum boards have always consisted of 100% independent directors, except in those uncommon situations where the museum director is also a board member. In addition, the role of chief executive and board chair has always been separated in museums, thus removing another conflict of interest. Museums are also not embroiled in controversies about corporate political contributions. Why, then, is corporate governance celebrated in the business literature and extolled as something the non-profit sector should emulate? Business tribalism is alive, well, and teeming with hubris – there is no other explanation.

Business tribalism also has its lighter moments, if one is able to recognize it for what it is. I recall attending the opening of a centre for non-profit management, designed to impart the wisdom and techniques of the business world to the wayward and uninitiated. The CEO of a multinational oil company began his remarks by noting that non-profit management was an oxymoron, and that the business world could fix that. "We know how to manage; you don't" – tribalism at its best. The management centre often struggled with its non-profit clients, as the latter were subjected to business solutions from business people, who knew little or nothing of the complexities of competing values and interests in the non-profit world. As for the CEO's comment that non-profit management is oxymoronic, I am delighted to have such a fine example of business groupthink.

Me first

In addition to the narrow-mindedness of business governance, there is a darker side of business tribalism that is essentially narcissistic – the excessive and preposterous salaries that boards, CEOs, and executives pay themselves, all in the name of enhancing shareholder value. In 2006, the average pay of chief executives at Standard and Poor's 500 (an index of publicly traded companies) was US$10.5 million.[51] In 2007, chief executives of the 500 biggest companies in the US earned an average of US$12.8 million apiece.[52] Money is the obvious measure of worth for these business leaders, and their excessive salaries are conveniently maintained by a self-perpetuating system. Consultants advise their clients on salary levels while executive search firms push up the salary levels, and many of them sit on each other's pay review boards. Not surprisingly, the average chief executive's pay in the US in 2006 was 369 times larger than an ordinary worker's salary.[53] Is the CEO really this disproportionately responsible for the results of the business? The pay levels imply this, but nothing could be more ludicrous.

This corporate love affair with high salaries and abundant privileges marred the museum world recently, in the person of Lawrence Small, who headed up the Smithsonian Institution from 2000 to 2007.[54] Mr. Small was hired to operate the Smithsonian in "a businesslike manner, in keeping with his nonscientific background as an executive at Citibank and Fannie Mae." He left under the cloud of an internal audit that showed he was paid for inappropriate and lavish expenses. In addition to being paid a salary of US$915,698 in 2007 (two and a half times more than his predecessor), Small collected an additional US$5.7 million by serving on several corporate boards while directing the Smithsonian.[55] It appears that the Board of Regents failed to exercise due diligence and, in combination with the naïve belief that Small's background as a corporate executive would make him a better manager, created an unhappy outcome for the Smithsonian. Although this is an isolated incident (only the Smithsonian could afford Mr. Small), Mr. Small's tenure is an object lesson in the clash of values. It is also a stark reminder of the danger in assuming that the business community has any monopoly on competence or virtue.

Cause-related hypocrisy?

Probing more deeply into the dark side of corporate tribalism reveals another disturbing trend – the patina of philanthropy.[56] In short, various business leaders continue their pursuit of profits while employing strategies that mask their true intentions. Over the past decades, in both Canada and the USA, independent corporate foundations have been collapsed and merged with in-house marketing and communication departments to serve corporate interests – not necessarily those of local communities or the larger society. Cause-related marketing, one of the newest corporate strategies, is now revealing its real meaning. Cause-related marketing ties consumers' desires to see a social good with the corporations' desires to see higher profits. For example, "The Product (RED)" campaign tells us that if we buy a (RED) product a portion of the purchase price goes to help Africa cope with HIV/AIDS.

In reality, this is just one more example of the business tribe aligning its operations with its central purpose of increasing profits, except it is dressed up as philanthropy.[57] In fact, business profits are up, in part because of their association with charities. Studies show that people are more likely to buy from companies with cause-related arrangements, and that's why corporations spent more than US$100 million advertising their association with (RED), while raising under

US$18 million for charity.[58] How can one avoid being cynical when these facts are revealed? Not only are these businesses boosting their profits with a ruse, they are doing it by encouraging even more mindless consumption of unnecessary stuff, which happens to be red in colour. Where is the corporate transparency and accountability? Can we really consume our way to a better world? How do corporations view the consuming public – as dupes? It's highly likely, because it appears that we are. In defense of our collective unconsciousness, I recommend that "corporate social responsibility" be the newest oxymoron, replacing the oil executive's reference to non-profit management as an oxymoron.

Corrosive ideology

To sum up, business tribalism has several faces, including the celebrity worship of business leaders; in-group thinking that excludes non-business people; immature/self-serving corporate governance; narcissistic notions of personal worth as measured by obscene salaries; and profiteering (HIV/AIDS is an emergency, by the way) disguised as the public good. We know about these liabilities and falsehoods in our minds, if not our hearts, and they permeate our everyday lives – albeit largely unacknowledged for the damage they are doing. These faces of business are now corroding museum practice, wrapped up in the service of marketplace ideology. Museums can elect to look the other way, which seems to be the strategy of choice, or they can consider just how invasive the commercial ideology has become and change direction.

The trouble with ideology, of any kind, is that it is a vehicle for laziness and self-deceit. Robert Grudin has aptly described its characteristics as follows:

> Ideology enables us to pass judgments on a variety of issues while lacking adequate information or analytic skill or commitment to discovering the truth. And ideology not only substitutes for information, analysis, and commitment, but also for conscience. The fact that a given action or lack of action conforms to our ideology absolves us from having to worry about it or take responsibility for it. With ideology we may appear to be well-informed, analytically skillful, inquisitive, conscientious, and morally responsible without really being so.[59]

The market values and tribalistic traits discussed above are ideological, and remain alarmingly unexamined and assumed by the museum community. Museums cannot consciously evolve without analyzing their assumptions, no matter how deep and well protected these beliefs may be. Organizational self-knowledge requires that the ideology that governs purpose and values, both individually and organizationally, be made explicit.[60] It is imperative that museums embark on this journey of self-knowledge, not only to make practical sense of a beleaguered world, but also to define a meaningful contribution to society. Although the marketplace has narrowed the scope of museum action, they still have a choice – will museums be stewards or spectators?

Courting the corporatists: a cautionary tale

What follows is a cautionary tale about what can happen when a corporation and a large museum decide to collaborate for what was thought to be mutual gain. I am indebted to Michael P. Robinson, the former CEO of the Glenbow Museum (2000–2008), for his candid description of these events.[61] As discussed earlier, the Glenbow Museum had adopted an entrepreneurial approach to its work, as a result of a rapid and drastic reduction in its provincial government funding. Although these initiatives began in the early 1990s, innovation and new ways of working continued with my successor, in part because provincial government funding remained modest, with only minor inflationary increases.

In the midst of studying various alternatives for renewal, Glenbow was approached by a representative of the UK celebrity architect Norman Foster, with the idea of becoming the cultural component of a major corporate office slated for Calgary. In October of 2006, EnCana Corporation, one of the largest oil and gas companies in the world, unveiled plans to build a new 158,000 square metre (1.7 million sq. ft.), 58-story office headquarters in downtown Calgary, Canada. EnCana's CEO, along with the architects, had embraced the "creative city" concept, and wished to promote the synergy between culture, retail, and the corporation – what Robinson calls the "cultural adjacency" model. He coined this term to describe the benefits that accrue from the presence of a major cultural facility and its various amenities. EnCana needed a prestigious, non-profit partner, while Glenbow wished to renew and expand their entrepreneurialism by moving out of their government-owned building into a new and high-profile facility. The museum had outgrown its building, which had always been devoid of architectural appeal. The partners were willing and the courtship began.

For the next year and a half, Glenbow's CEO, senior staff, and Board of Governors spent the lion's share of their collective time preparing a space and program plan for EnCana, which included travel to the UK to meet with the architects, employing a consultant to assist with the planning, meetings with provincial cabinet ministers and federal members of Parliament, as well as the preparation of a case for support to test the prospects of a private sector fundraising campaign to support this initiative. There were countless board meetings and special committee meetings to analyze the facts and issues surrounding the proposed move to EnCana's EnCentre project. A special team of advisors was also assembled with legal, financial, corporate real estate, and architectural expertise, to fill in where the Glenbow staff and board lacked experience and knowledge. In Robinson's words, "I spent two years of my life on this project."[62] By all accounts, it was indeed a thorough and well-orchestrated exercise in responsible decision making, and the board voted unanimously to negotiate their inclusion in the EnCana project. But the suitor fled before consummation, much to the surprise of the bride.

What happened? The unraveling began with the retirement of EnCana's CEO who had the vision of profit and non-profit synergy. He was replaced by a CEO whose concerns were more pragmatic. With the change in CEOs came a renewed focus on share price and shareholder value and, as noted by Robinson, "great experiments in culture and civility do not enter this equation in quite the same way."[63] Glenbow's original proposal required 75,000 square metres (250,000 sq. ft.) of museum space, and Glenbow was prepared to raise CAN$170 million to cover these capital costs. The CAN$170 million included a suggested gift of CAN$25 million from the corporate partner, in recognition of the value which would accrue to the building as a result of Glenbow's visitors parking, eating, and shopping in the complex. Based on their previous experience with EnCana, the Glenbow's Board and staff believed that these were reasonable negotiating points. Instead, EnCana countered with an offer of 15,000 square metres (50,000 square feet – an 80% reduction) and no philanthropic gift. Glenbow also wanted a condominium tenancy, whereby they would own their own space.

Unknown to Glenbow, the rules of this marketplace game had changed dramatically, with EnCana announcing its plan to sell the building and lease it back from the new owner. *Ipso facto*, Glenbow need not contribute the CAN$170 million, but they would not have ownership of their space and would be required to pay CAN$2.8 million annually in commercial rent for one-fifth of the space they required. In addition, EnCana wanted CAN$40 million in tenant improvements for the leased space. In short, EnCana was seeking a tenant, not creative philanthropy, but unfortunately failed to advise their so-called partner of this. Nor did they compensate Glenbow for the enormous effort it made to plan the prospective marriage. Glenbow's Board of Governors declined EnCana's offer.

This story, both tortuous and salutary, contains many hard-won insights and lessons, not the least of which is that when the "elephant in the room" changes position, one has to be astute enough to avoid being crushed – this Glenbow did. Can you imagine what the new building owners might think when they discover that one of their tenants is a museum? How long would that lease last? Robinson offered several other summary observations, beginning with the counsel that it is best to choose your own partner.[64] In this instance, the suitor came to Glenbow and, in retrospect, Glenbow did not develop any criteria for the match. Instead, Glenbow spent its time and energy reacting to a partner they didn't choose.

Avoiding this passive role requires defining what success looks like at the outset, and then selecting your partner accordingly. This, in turn, requires a holistic consideration of the museum's mission, purpose, and values, and not fixating on the celebrity building as the solution. Sustained rigour in decision making is essential, which means paying attention to content and substance, and not succumbing to the inevitable commercial dogma that accompanies corporatism, celebrity architecture, and the search for quick fixes.

Robinson concedes that the momentum and excitement of the courtship sidetracked the key question – "Will our mission and values be advanced by this initiative, or is it a facile solution to deeper concerns?" For Glenbow, the merits of the corporate marriage were assumed, not discussed, which was in part a reflection of the Glenbow Board's business bias. One can only hope that more museum directors, with similar accounts of corporate encounters, will be as forthcoming as Robinson. The marketplace has but one master – the bottom line – and to think otherwise is unrealistic and naïve, despite our well-disposed hopes to the contrary. Robinson's final words on the subject – "There's no such thing as pure corporate philanthropy – it's all strategic now."[65]

Business literacy

Having catalogued some of the real and potential consequences of marketplace ideology and commercial dogma, it is important to note that their counterpart, business literacy, is essential for any competent museum. In brief, business literacy means the staff's ability, at all levels of the organization, to fully understand the museum in all its complexity.[66] If staff understand the "big picture," or the larger context within which the museum operates, they will have a greater appreciation of and, hopefully, a greater investment in the outcome of the work. Business literacy begins with "open-book" management, whereby museum workers are given full budget information along with the assistance in making sense of it. This approach also requires that senior management communicate fully and openly about the museum's strategic priorities, opportunities, and threats.

Business literacy is not only necessary for enhanced self-sufficiency in an era of scarce resources, but it is also essential to individual and organizational account-ability. A working knowledge of finances/budgeting, business processes, time management, public service, project management, and so forth are the foundation for enhanced effectiveness and efficiency – the purpose and outcome of business literacy. Business processes are a case in point. As the new director of Glenbow, I was challenged to reduce our operating costs and chose as one of our strategies to closely examine our procedural bureaucracy – the culmination of 25 years of cumulative processes in a top-down organization.

By using a business process-mapping technique obtained from a business consultant, we closely analyzed how we actually did our work – challenging our assumptions and our habits. Our artifact loan procedure, for example, required over 20 separate steps and several different staff positions to complete. By identify-ing these time-honoured, bureaucratic intricacies and habits, and then carefully scrutinizing them, we reduced the number of steps by nearly two-thirds and freed up valuable time and energy for useful work. This is business literacy at its best – but it is about methods and techniques, not values.

Methods aren't values

The distinction between methods and values recalls the earlier discussion of the characteristics of long-lived companies – sensitivity to the environment, cohesion and identity, tolerance and decentralization, and conservative financing.[67] None of these defining factors has anything to do with commercial dogma or business literacy – they are values. Values are essential and enduring beliefs that articulate how an organization will conduct itself. Values also serve as guiding beacons by describing how the museum wants to treat others, as well as how it wishes to be treated. It would seem that in the pressure cooker called the marketplace, there is little time for or attention to values. Instead, values are replaced by imperatives – more visitors, more earned revenues, more collections, etc. Museums cannot claim victimhood for these quantitative measures, however, as I previously noted the museum community's collective failure to define what constitutes effective museum performance, above and beyond the bottom line.

I suggest that DeGeus' characteristics of long-lived companies might well serve as a useful departure for the consideration of qualitative, value-based, performance measures for museums. I can't help but wonder how many museums can claim to model any or all of DeGeus' traits – such an assessment would be highly revealing. Except for perhaps cohesion and identity, many museums are failing to learn and adapt, while decentralization and collaboration remain unrecognized or undeveloped. When it comes to conservative financing, museums are volatile at best, as the economic imperative of unmindful growth assumes increasing influence in the museum community at large.

Stewards or spectators?

Furthermore, classical economic theory and commercial dogma do not allow for the needs of future generations, because marketplace decisions are based on the relative abundance or scarcity of things as they affect us, now. In Jeremy Rifkin's words, "No one speaks for future generations at the marketplace, and for this reason, everyone who comes after us starts off much poorer than we did in terms of nature's remaining endowment."[68] The marketplace notion that "the present is all there is" is antithetical to the very nature of museums, whose existence is predicated on the stewardship of posterity. It is now imperative that this sense of the future assume greater influence in all aspects of museum work, aided and abetted by business literacy, but not beholden to the values of the marketplace. The marketplace pendulum, once the instrument of increased accountability for museums, has now swung too far.

As described earlier, museums are mixed portfolios and must continue to maintain this dynamic and seamless complexity if they are to operate effectively in the service of the public good. This means that adequate public support, whether from government, foundations or individuals, is essential to counterbalance the increasing emphasis on earned revenues. This is assuming, of course, that museums add sufficient societal value to merit this support. The simplicity of the marketplace, with its selling, buying, and profit making, simply cannot manage the complexities of a mixed portfolio – it's the bottom line at the expense of all else, including employees and the environment. As an example, the US$17,530 earned by the average Wal-Mart employee last year was US$1,820 below the poverty line for a family of four, while five of America's 10 richest people are Wal-Mart heirs.[69]

What's wrong with this picture? If the marketplace could address the complexities of a mixed portfolio, museums would be rich, which they plainly are not.

The opposite is true, in fact, and the situation continues to worsen. As the author and scholar Bill McKibben notes, "it's extremely important to bear in mind that we're *not*, despite the insistence of our leaders, growing wealthier; that is one of several stubborn and counterintuitive facts about the world – growth simply isn't enriching most of us."[70] For example, the wealthiest 20% of households in 1973 accounted for 44% of total US income, according to the Census Bureau. Their share jumped to 50% in 2002, while everyone else's fell. For the bottom fifth, the share dropped from 4.2% to 3.5%.[71] Wealth inequality has worsened considerably since this chapter was originally published in 2009, with the richest 1% of the world's population now owning more than 48% of global wealth.[72]

Museums have a profound choice to make about their role as social institutions. Will they honour their communities as stewards of the highest order, or become agents of marketplace dysfunction? Happily, a variety of museums have chosen to move well beyond the marketplace, and various examples are recounted throughout this book.

Note

1 Inuit are the Aboriginal people of Arctic Canada; the Dene people (DEN-ay) are an aboriginal group of First Nations who live in the northern boreal and subarctic regions of Canada, and the Metis are descendants of people born of relations between First Nations (formerly Indian) women and European men.

References

1 M. Kingwell, *The World We Want: Virtue, Vice, and the Good Citizen*, Toronto: Viking, 2000, p. 184.
2 J. Ralston Saul, *The Unconscious Civilization*, Concord, Canada: House of Anansi Press, 1995, p. 2.
3 Ralston Saul, *The Unconscious Civilization*, p. 190.
4 E. Hobsbawm, *On the Edge of the New Century*, New York: The New Press, 2000, p. 35.
5 Hobsbawm, *On the Edge of the New Century*, p. 106.
6 R.R. Janes, *Museums and the Paradox of Change: A Case Study in Urgent Adaptation*, London and New York: Routledge, 2013 (Third edition); Calgary, Canada: Glenbow Museum and the University of Calgary Press, 1997 (Second edition).
7 *Glenbow Annual Report 2000*, Calgary, Canada: Glenbow Museum, 2000, p. 7.
8 *Glenbow Museum Annual Report, 2006–2007*, Calgary, Canada: Glenbow Museum, p. 23. Available online at <http://www.glenbow.org/media/AR2007-Glenbow.pdf> (accessed 26 June 2008).
9 F. Capra, *The Turning Point: Science, Society and the Rising Culture*, New York and Toronto: Bantam Books, 1983, p. 397.
10 J. Rifkin, "The end of work." Public address on behalf of the Volunteer Centre of Calgary, Palliser Hotel, Calgary, Alberta, Canada, 13 November 1997.
11 A. Bullock and S. Trombley (eds), *The New Fontana Dictionary of Modern Thought*, London: HarperCollins, 1999, p. 798.
12 J. Rifkin, *The End of Work*, New York: G.P. Putnam's Sons, 1996, p. 246.
13 R. Grudin, *Time and the Art of Living*, New York: Houghton Mifflin Company, 1982, p. 18.

14 A. DeGeus, *The Living Company: Habits for Survival in a Turbulent Business Environment*, Boston: Harvard Business School Press, 1997, p. 1.

15 DeGeus, *The Living Company*, pp. 5–9.

16 DeGeus, *The Living Company*, pp. 15–16.

17 M. Csikszentmihalyi, *Good Business: Leadership, Flow and the Making of Meaning*, New York: Viking Penguin, 2003, p. 189.

18 Hobsbawm, *On the Edge of the New Century*, pp. 12–15.

19 J. Wetenhall, "Impossible job: The changing role of the museum director." Available online at <http://www.getty.edu/leadership/compleat_leader/downloads/aamd08 wetenhall.pdf> (accessed 2 July 2008).

20 Wetenhall, "Impossible job," pp. 3–4.

21 Wetenhall, "Impossible job," p. 5.

22 T. Freudenheim, "Fifty museum years, and then some," *Curator: The Museum Journal* (50/1), 2007, 55–62, 55, 60.

23 M. Davies and H. Wilkinson, *Sustainability and Museums: Your Chance to Make a Difference*, London: Museums Association, 2008. Available online at <http://www.museums association.org/asset_arena/text/al/sustainability_web_final.pdf> (accessed 2 July 2008).

24 T. Gstraunthaler and M. Piber, "Performance measurement and accounting: Museums in Austria," *Museum Management and Curatorship* (22/4), 2007, 361–75.

25 Gstraunthaler and Piber, "Performance measurement and accounting," 373.

26 W. Thorsell, "The museum as the new agora" (2007), p. 3. Available online at <http:// www.rom. on.ca/about/pdf/agoraspeech.pdf> (accessed 3 July 2008).

27 Thorsell, "The museum as the new agora," p. 5.

28 Thorsell, "The museum as the new agora," p. 5. In fairness, I note that the Royal Ontario Museum recently hosted a forum on "International Intervention in Genocidal Situations," which was subsequently aired in December 2008 on the "Ideas" radio program (Canadian Broadcasting Corporation). This kind of substantive discussion lies at the heart of the true agora.

29 W. Gross, "Enough is enough" (2007), p. 1. Available online at <http://www.pimco.com/ LeftNav/Featured+Market+Commentary/IO/2007/IO+August+2007.htm> (accessed 3 July 2008).

30 *Consumer Spending on Culture in Canada the Provinces and 15 Metropolitan Areas in 2005*, pp. 1–8. Ottawa: Hill Strategies Inc., 2007. Available online at <http://www.hillstrategies. com/docs/Consumer_spending2005.pdf> (accessed 3 July 2008).

31 *International Forum on the Creative Economy*, 17–18 March 2008. Ottawa, Canada: The Conference Board of Canada. Available online at <http://www.conferenceboard.ca/ documents. asp?rnext=2567> (accessed 3 July 2008).

32 S. Beatty, "Museums learn to love debt," *The Wall Street Journal Online*, 30 March 2007. Online. Available online at <http://online.wsj.com/article_email/SB117521262951653880-lMyQjAxMDE3NzM1MDIzMTAyWj.html> (accessed 3 July 2008).

33 A. Ellis, "The impact of globalization on the cultural sector." Arts Administration Graduate Student Association, Drexel University, 22 May 2007, p. 16. Available online at <http://www.drexel.edu/westphal/pdf/aadm/TheImpactofGlobalization.pdf> (accessed 30 September 2008). See also V. Dickenson, Commentary: "A trip to China: Observations and reflections," *Museum Management and Curatorship* (22/3), 2007, 237–45.

34 N. Grattan, (ed.), "New museums," *MUSE* (XXIV/3), 2006, 10–11; and C. Hume, "Arts story: Cultural vacuum," *The Toronto Star* (26 August 2000), pp. 1–5; and C. Hume, "A fragile renaissance: Toronto's big-name architecture is rising against perilous landscape. Once the fever subsides, how we will afford our culture?" *The Toronto Star* (9 October 2005), p. H1.

35 A. Hudson, "New! Improved! The rhetoric of relevancy in a construction boom," *MUSE* (XXIV/3), 2006, 38–41.

36 A. Ellis,"Planning in a cold climate," research paper prepared for the Directors' seminar: "Leading retrenchment." Los Angeles, California: The Getty Leadership Institute, 2002. Available online at <http://www.getty.edu/leadership/compleat_leader/down loads/ellis.pdf> (accessed 7 July 2008).

37 Ellis, "Planning in a cold climate," p. 21.

38 Ellis, "Planning in a cold climate," pp. 22–3.

39 J.M. Bradburne, "The museum time bomb: Overbuilt, overtraded, overdrawn," *The Informal Learning Review*, 65, 2004, 4–13. Available online at <http://www.bradburne. org/downloads/museums/InstitutioninCrisisWEB.pdf> (accessed 7 July 2008).

40 Bradburne, "The museum time bomb," 34.

41 G. Lord and M. Sabau, "The Bilbao effect: From poor port to must-see city," *The Art Newspaper* 184, 2007, pp. 32–3. Available online at <http://www.lord.ca/Media/ TheArtNewspaper32-33Museums.pdf> (accessed 7 July 2008).

42 B. Plaza, "On some challenges and conditions for the Guggenheim Museum Bilbao to be an effective economic re-activator," *International Journal of Urban and Regional Research* (32/2), 2008, 506–16, 507.

43 Lord and Sabau, "The Bilbao effect: From poor port to must-see city," pp. 32–3.

44 Plaza, "On some challenges and conditions for the Guggenheim Museum," p. 514.

45 Plaza, "On some challenges and conditions for the Guggenheim Museum," p. 506.

46 C. Lorway, "The war on travel," *Platform*/AEA Consulting 5(3), 2007, pp. 7–8. Available online at <http://www.aeaconsulting.com/sites/aea/images/1815/aea_1815.pdf> (accessed 21 October 2008).

47 Lorway, "The war on travel," p. 7.

48 R.B. Lee and I. DeVore (eds), *Man the Hunter*, Chicago: Aldine Publishing Company, 1968, p. 188.

49 M. Csikszentmihalyi, *Good Business: Leadership, Flow and the Making of Meaning*, pp. 6–10.

50 *Wall Street Reform*, Online NewsHour. Available online at <http://www.pbs.org/news hour/ forum/july02/b_ethics4.html> (accessed 8 July 2008). See also Joe Knight's "Lessons from the orgy of corporate greed," The Business Literacy Institute. Available online at <http://www.business-literacy.com/joeknight/corporategreed.html> (accessed 10 July 2008).

51 S. Stern, "Fat-cat pay rate shows no signs of moderation," *National Post*, 1 November 2006, p. WK 5.

52 S. DeCarlo, "Top paid US CEOs," *Forbes*, 7 May 2007. Available online at <http:// www.cbc.ca/ money/story/2008/05/06/fforbes-toppaidceos.html> (accessed 8 July 2008).

53 Stern, "Fat-cat pay rate shows no signs of moderation," p. WK 5.

54 Editorial, "The Smithsonian Challenge," *The New York Times*, 28 March 2007. Available online at <http://www.nytimes.com/2007/03/28/opinion/28wed3.html?_r=1& ex=1175745600&en=84ad07fa9de6b7b5&ei=5070&emc=eta1&oref=slogin> (accessed 8 July 2008).

55 R. Pogrebin, "Smithsonian ex-chief criticized in report," *The New York Times*, 21 June 2007, pp. 1–2. Available online at <http://www.nytimes.com/2007/06/21/arts/ design/21smit.html> (accessed 8 July 2008).

56 M. Rosenman, "Blog: The patina of philanthropy," *Stanford Social Innovation Review*, 11 April 2007, 1. Available online at <http://www.ssireview.org/opinion/entry/the_ patina_of_ philanthropy/> (accessed 8 July 2008).

57 Rosenman, "Blog: The patina of philanthropy," 1.

58 Rosenman, "Blog: The patina of philanthropy," 1.

59 R. Grudin, *The Grace of Great Things: Creativity and Innovation*, New York: Houghton Mifflin Company, 1990, p. 220.

60 Grudin, *The Grace of Great Things*, pp. 220–1.

61 Interview with Michael P. Robinson, 3 December 2007, Canmore, Alberta, Canada: transcript, pp. 1–9.

62 Interview with Michael P. Robinson: transcript, p. 4.

63 Michael P. Robinson, *President's Report, November 22, 2007*, Calgary, Alberta, Canada: Glenbow Museum, p. 5.

64 Interview with Michael P. Robinson: transcript, p. 7.

65 Interviews with Michael P. Robinson: transcript, p. 6, also 30 October 2008 (telephone).

66 M. Morris, "Organizational health," *NEWStandard* (1)3, The American Association of Museums, Washington, DC, 1998, p. 4.

67 DeGeus, *The Living Company*, p. 9.

68 J. Rifkin, *Entropy: A New World View*, New York: The Viking Press, 1980, p. 134.

69 C. Jeffrey, "A look at the numbers: How the rich get richer," *Mother Jones*, May/June, 2006, p. 1. Available online at <http://www.motherjones.com/news/exhibit/2006/05/perks_of_privilege. html> (accessed 10 July 2008).

70 B. McKibben, *Deep Economy: The Wealth of Communities and the Durable Future*, New York: Henry Holt and Company, LLC, 2007, p. 14.

71 P. Nyhan and S. Skolnik, "America's income gap grows; Rich get richer," *Seattle-Post Intelligencer*, 17 August 2004, p. 1. Available online at <http://seattlepi.nwsource.com/local/186625_incomegap17.html> (accessed 10 July 2008).

72 Treanor, J. "Richest 1% of People Own Nearly Half of Global Wealth," *Guardian*, Tuesday 14 October 2014, 07.00 BST. Available online: http://www.theguardian.com/business/2014/oct/14/richest-1percent-half-global-wealth-credit-suisse-report.

22

MUSEUMS AND THE NEW REALITY*

The myth of economic growth

Museums are rarely acknowledged in the global discussion of climate change, environmental degradation, the inevitability of depleted fossil fuels, and the myriad local issues concerning the well-being of particular communities – suggesting the irrelevance of museums as social institutions. The world's issues and challenges have intensified dramatically since I published *Museums in a Troubled World* (Janes 2009), and they now include blatant corporate malfeasance along with the litany of social-environmental issues noted above.

There is no doubt that the United States, Canada, and Western Europe, including museums, are held captive by neo-classical economics and marketplace ideology – the idea that economic growth and consumption are the keys to prosperity and societal well-being. Business leaders and economists are among the most influential people in these countries. Yet, they advocate ways of thinking and behavior that are completely outmoded and, in fact, are frankly stupid and patently harmful to our collective well-being. The private ownership of natural resources; the increased centralization of power between governments and corporations; the elimination of biological and human diversity; the irrational belief that science and technology will undo or fix the problems we have created; the refusal to set limits on production and consumption; and the concept of progress at the expense of the biosphere – all of these things are the consequences of marketplace ideology and the overarching commitment to economic growth. Why museums would embrace this commercial dogma as a strategy for the future is a vexing and essential question, especially when heightened stewardship is of paramount importance.

Source: Robert R. Janes, *Museums & Social Issues: A Journal of Reflective Discourse*, Vol. 6, No. 2, Fall, (2011): 137–146.

Business leaders, business schools, economists, and our so-called political leaders refuse to admit the truth or existence of several profound realities, including the depletion of natural resources (including fossil fuels, minerals, and water), the proliferation of negative environmental impacts (including the burning of fossil fuels), and the inability of governments and banks to deal with the enormous government and private debt that has accumulated over the last 20 years (Heinberg 2011: 1–4).

Economic growth is essentially finished because of these realities, and the real question now is how society, including museums, is going to adapt to a non-growing, equilibrium economy. As the energy expert Richard Heinberg succinctly noted, "Civilization is about to be downsized" (Heinberg 2011: 27). This is the harbinger of a new societal context for museums, because the implications for change and continued prosperity are profound and immensely challenging. This is not apocalyptic thinking, however, as resource depletion, climate impact, and systemic financial failures (including bank failures, the European debt crisis, and house foreclosures in the United States) are well underway. The risk for museums in collaborating with business is becoming complicit in this destructive view of the world, which is based on wealth accumulation in the short term with little or no regard for the future.

The toxicity of corporatism

The toxicity of corporate business has become so pronounced that even the *Harvard Business Review* published an article which stated that the capitalist system is under siege and that business is increasingly seen as the major cause of social, environmental, and economic problems (Porter and Kramer 2011). How refreshing to see this admission of failure in the world's leading business publication, although the authors maintain that corporations are still superior to government and the social sector in leading social progress. Predictably, business tribalism and arrogance persist, despite the authors' admission that "the legitimacy of business has fallen to levels not seen in recent history" (Porter and Kramer 2011: 77).

All museum boards and staff should be concerned with the unprecedented concentration of power in transnational corporations that owe no allegiance to any nation or place, undermine democracy, distort economic priorities, and concentrate wealth in socially destructive ways (Korten 2009: 164). Ruben Nelson, one of Canada's few professional futurists, noted that the future of politics will not be about the Right, the Centrists or the Left – it will be about individuals and communities versus corporations (Nelson, personal communication, October 1, 2010). The time has come for museums of all sizes and shapes to take their place in this critical debate.

Questioning the corporatists

Interestingly, the corporate support of museums and galleries is now being questioned, but not by the museum community. Several of the United Kingdom's biggest museums and galleries, including the British Museum, the National Portrait Gallery, and the Tate, announced in 2011 that they will renew their sponsorship agreements with British Petroleum (BP), despite opposition from the public (Brown 2011). These agreements are worth nearly CAN$16 million. In a refreshingly critical article about these sponsorships, Robert Newman (2011) of the *Guardian* newspaper wrote:

> What nobody seems to think worth mentioning is how corporate sponsorship changes the very meaning of these palaces of culture. The British Museum and the National Portrait Gallery, in particular, are meant to stand for who we are as a people, as a democracy. They are the cathedrals of democracy. Corporations are not democratic institutions. They are vast blocs of unaccountable private power; and the more they advance into the central areas of public life, the more they stultify the ways in which we talk to each other and think about our place in the world.

Are museum governing authorities, staff, and their professional associations considering their roles in this critical and formative discussion? Clearly, these UK museum and gallery directors are pleased with their renewed stream of cash, but it is disconcerting that the protests emerged from outside of the museum field. I suggest that all museum directors exercise their critical thinking and assess the implications of their corporate sponsorships. The economic argument, i.e., "we need money from wherever," is no longer good enough in this era of corporate malfeasance. Why should museums and galleries allow corporations like BP, with its track record of environmental catastrophes and gross incompetence, "to buy visibility and respectability in the mainstream of British cultural life?" (Newman 2011). If fundraising norms are starting to unravel as exemplified above, are museums preparing for changing public perceptions of corporate largesse?

Museums and the plutocracy

Related to the rethinking of self-serving corporate support is the changing relationship between museums and their elite benefactors, all members of the plutocracy (government by the wealthy). In the wake of reduced public funding over the past several decades, many museums have successfully diversified and strengthened their operating budgets through individual donations from wealthy supporters, in addition to earned revenues and corporate support. To assume that this funding support will continue to offset declining admissions and tight government funding may be ill-founded, however, as noted by Erik Ledbetter (2011). He is a special advisor to the "Forecasting the Future of Museum Ethics," a joint project initiated in 2011 by the American Association of Museums and Seton Hall University's Institute for Museum Ethics (US).

Ledbetter questions if the wealthy will continue to fund existing museums and concludes that history and present trends suggest not. He writes that the plutocracy will likely prefer to establish its own museums, as it did in the late nineteenth century in the United States. That was a time, similar to today, marked by a vast increase in the concentration of wealth in the top 1% of society and a deep gap between the top and the rest of society.

Ledbetter's observations are more than speculation, as the development of private museums is well underway and is causing a great deal of consternation, according to Elizabeth Ellis, an art consultant (Schuker 2008). Ellis notes that "the rise of private museums is causing a lot of fear and anxiety" and that museum directors are reacting in a number of ways. These include expanding their exhibition space to display more works to appease donors who don't want their gifts sitting in storage, as well as appointing collectors to their boards with the hope of eventually getting important art pieces for their collections.

Ellis also discusses another shock to museums, as more collectors start foundations to serve as lending libraries for their collections, rather than donating their collections to museums. One example is Los Angeles-based collector Eli Broad, who started his own foundation because the lending model allows the artworks to get more exposure. He noted that "we created the lending library to show art that would otherwise be in storage" (Schuker 2008). It should also be noted that the advent of private museums is not restricted to art museums, and Ledbetter discusses a new private railroad museum in the United States which will be superior to the majority of public railroad museums in the country.

For the vast majority of museums that operate without million-dollar budgets, these concerns are likely improbable. Although private museums will never replace public ones, this is a trend worth noting for the simple reason that museums have always relied on the well-to-do, both as visitors and for financial support. In fact, it is common knowledge that the well-off and well-educated are the mainstays of museum support throughout the world. The museum community should take note as wealthy citizens privatize their interests, because this means the amount of available funding will continue to diminish. Perhaps more ominously, there may well be ethical implications as museums compete for funds and attention from the new plutocracy. Erik Ledbetter (2011) has also considered this:

> Some of our current fussiness about curatorial independence will go discreetly overboard. Current AAM ethical guidance places a premium on maintaining an arm's-length relationship between museums and donors to avoid even the appearance of conflict of interest. But how can an existing museum compete when the donor could as easily found her own museum, and become effectively curator in chief, director, and chair of the acquisitions committee all in one?

It is in the best interests of museums to note these trends and ensure that the implications of "government by the wealthy" are monitored and managed, along with the increasing inroads of corporatism. As the corporatists continue to become the elite and join the plutocracy, the need for museums to pay attention and act responsibly is essential. Although universities around the world are now hand-maidens to corporate interests embedded in the plutocracy, museums need not follow. In fact, museums are still in a position to model a newfound sense of purpose and integrity.

Museums and their tacit silence

Museums, unwittingly or not, have embraced the values of relentless consumption that underlie our planetary difficulties. I argued in *Museums in a Troubled World* (2009) that much more can be expected of museums as publicly supported and knowledge-based institutions. By disregarding environmental and social issues which, in effect, are ethical issues, museums have opted to serve the prevailing corporate structure. Underlying all of these issues and concerns is the need to break the tacit silence that surrounds the role of contemporary museums as keepers of the status quo, at a time when the façade of democracy disguises the extent to which big business, transnational corporations, and the financial sector rule our lives and our governments.

A healthy economy is not the property of private capital and private interests. It is "an aggregation of contributions by private capital, government, and the civil society, each in proper balance" (Korten 2009: 100). I question the role of museums, galleries, and science centres, as agents of the civil society, in legitimizing this façade through their unquestioning silence or complicity, not to mention their collective passivity as a litany of economic, social, and environmental issues continues to erode societal well-being.

This concern far transcends whether or not museums ponder the ethical behavior of their own institutions, or that of their corporate sponsors or partners. The heart of the matter is actually the widespread corporate violation of public interest, and the corresponding erosion of individual and community sovereignty as a result of hyper-capitalism and corporate malfeasance. At the same time, governments are facilitating the consolidation of corporate power. I wish to cast museums once again onto the societal stage, as I did in *Museums in a Troubled World*, to bring attention to the critical role of museums, galleries, and science centres in generating social capital – the networks, norms, trust, and shared values that are not self-interested and that hold society together (Janes 2007).

The six responsibilities

In considering a renewed mandate for museums, there is one foundational question which must guide this exploration – how can museums, as publicly supported, social institutions, improve the quality of life for individuals and communities? As a foundation for a renewed mandate, and building on the work of Jeffrey Sachs (2008: 291–292), the economist and sustainability advocate, I suggest that museums have six overarching, ethical responsibilities in the twenty-first century. These include:

1. Public advocacy – on issues where the museum can add perspective, expertise, and value;
2. Problem solving – on issues where the museum can provide advice, assistance, and expertise;
3. Collaborating on the funding of solutions – where these solutions relate to community interests, concerns, and aspirations;
4. Insisting on the accountability of government and the private sector – irrespective of the museum's funding sources: this is the courage to say "no";
5. Scientific and humanities research – both basic and applied;
6. Maintaining collections as knowledge data banks – the record of material diversity is akin to biodiversity, as adaptive solutions are sought in an increasingly maladapted and brittle world.

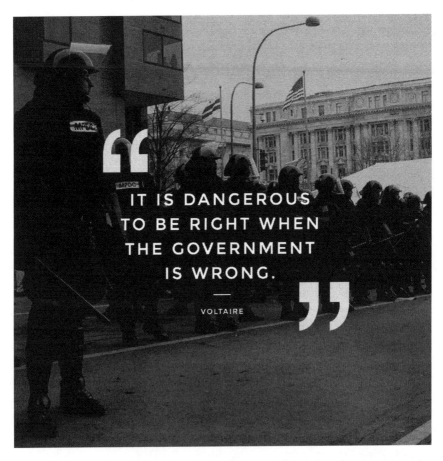

FIGURE 10 The Voltaire poster – It is dangerous to be right when the government is wrong. Design by http://livelearnevolve.com.

Complexity is the new reality for museums

As discussed in the recent report of the World Economic Forum (2011), current organizational models no longer work. New and different forms of organizations (including networks of experts and citizens) must now be developed to determine what we don't know, including how to move ahead intelligently and with foresight. This is particularly true for museums, because of their unique position in society and the respect and the status they enjoy. No one would disagree that museums exist to tell our stories about people, communities, nations, and civilizations. Who is telling the story of the early twenty-first century, with all of its global issues and their threatening consequences? With few exceptions, museums are not. Corporations and governments at all levels are, but it is the story of ceaseless economic growth designed to reinforce their power and privilege within the status quo.

Relevant, aware, and competent museums can provide their communities with the means of intellectual self-defense and the resourcefulness necessary to reduce the corrosive dominance of corporations, government complicity, and the vacuous consumer society. Museums of all kinds are untapped and untested sources of ideas, knowledge, and information, and are ideally placed to foster individual and community participation in the quest for greater awareness and workable solutions to our worsening global problems. In short, museums have the opportunity and obligation to both resist the status quo and question the way in which society is governed.

We need museums of cultural frameworks (Ruben Nelson, personal communication, October 1, 2010) to identify and explore the myths, perceptions, and misperceptions that now threaten our very existence – such as the assumption that unlimited economic growth is essential to our well-being. How is it that museums, as historically conscious and knowledge-based institutions in the public sphere, may remain aloof from the litany of social and environmental issues that confront us when many of these issues are intimately related to the missions and capabilities of museums as we know them? This is the new reality for museums.

References

Brown, M. (2011). Galleries renew £10m BP deal despite environmental protests. Retrieved from www.guardian.co.uk/culture/2011/dec/19/galleries-renew-bp-deal-protests.

Heinberg, R. (2011). *The end of growth*. Gabriola Island, Canada: New Society.

Janes, R.R. (2007). Museums, corporatism and the civil society. *Curator 50*(2), 219–237.

Janes, R.R. (2009). *Museums in a troubled world: Renewal, irrelevance or collapse?* London and New York: Routledge.

Korten, D.C. (2009). *Agenda for a new economy*, San Francisco: Berrett-Koehler.

Ledbetter, E. (2011). Museum ethics in a gilded age. Tuesday, August 23, 2011. Retrieved from http://futureofmuseums.blogspot.ca/2011/08/museum-ethics-in-gilded-age.html.

Newman, R. (2011). Why are Britain's great art houses in bed with Big Oil? Retrieved from www.guardian.co.uk/commentisfree/2011/dec/20/britains-great-art-houses-big-oil.

Porter, M.E., and Kramer, M.R. (2011). Creating shared value: How to reinvent capitalism and unleash a wave of innovation and growth. *Harvard Business Review*, January–February, 62–77.

Sachs, J.D. (2008). *Common wealth: Economics for a crowded planet*, New York: Penguin Press.

Schuker, L.A.E. (2008). The firestorm over private museums. Retrieved from online.wsj.com/article/SB120727433942088537.html.

World Economic Forum. (2011). *Global risks 2011 sixth edition: An initiative of the risk response network*. Retrieved from riskreport.wefo-rum.org/.

23

MUSEUM MANAGEMENT AND THE ETHICAL IMPERATIVE*

Introduction

The long-term consequences of museum inertia, marked by its preoccupation with the status quo, continue to unfold. Now is the opportune time for intelligent management, which requires being skeptical, curious, and inventive before the situation demands it. My purpose here is to speculate on the future role and responsibilities of museums in light of the intensifying socio-environmental pressures – locally and globally. This examination will be part cautionary tale, coupled with some alarmism and a hint of the apocalyptic, all for the purpose of emphasizing the centrality of mindfulness to responsible museum management. An acute awareness of alternative futures for museums need not be distressing or debilitating – it can actually be liberating. I will make this case within an ethical framework, as I also believe that there are right and wrong choices to be made, irrespective of the so-called neutrality that so many museums are ardent to retain.

Four scenarios to contemplate

I am indebted to the work of Bridget McKenzie and her blog, "The Learning Planet," for her assistance in thinking about possible futures for the biosphere, including museums.[1] McKenzie has adopted scenario planning in her work, an approach I discussed at length in *Museums in a Troubled World*.[2] In short, scenario planning is a technique to assist with the creation of new mental models that result in powerful stories about how the future might unfold.[3] It is not about predicting the future, but rather about exploring the future. McKenzie has identified four

*Source: Robert R. Janes, pp. 371–398 in Robert R. Janes (2013) *Museums and the Paradox of Change: A Case Study in Urgent Adaptation* (Third Edition), London and New York: Routledge.

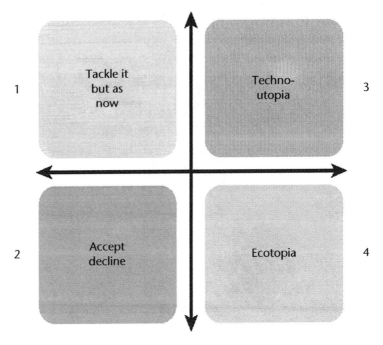

FIGURE 11 The four scenarios. Courtesy of Bridget McKenzie.

scenarios, taking into account global ecological and economic issues. I summarize each scenario below (from the future looking back) with the intention of reminding museum workers that the world is going to be a very different place several decades from now, irrespective of how optimistic or pessimistic one might be. Further, museums are equipped and positioned to contribute to the shaping of the future, not only in terms of the scenarios below, but also by creating new ones. Scenario planning is the antidote to the widespread denial that underpins societal inaction, and is a cogent reminder that no institution can ignore the vagaries of the future, not even museums.

1 The Red Global Scenario: tackle it but as now

In this scenario, there were serious efforts to address the environmental and resource crisis globally, but they were dominated by technology and the marketplace, without sufficient attention paid to regulating the ensuing damage to the biosphere, coupled with insufficient efforts to restore ecosystems. Inequality and conflict over resources persisted.[4]

2 The Black Global Scenario: accept decline

This is the darkest scenario, as efforts to address the environmental and resource crises were ineffective and too late, lacking both purpose and enthusiasm. The consequences were varied, with some communities accepting the decline, some choosing crime and conflict, and still other communities becoming nomadic. McKenzie notes that "Others might form protective spiritual clans that 'live for now' while aspiring to morality."[5]

3 The Silver Global Scenario: techno-utopia

In the second decade of the twenty-first century, there was a redoubled effort, supported by all of the biggest corporations and countries, to replace fossil fuels with alternative energy sources and to engineer new sources of food and water. The effects of climate change increased, however, and the oceans continued to acidify and deserts spread. The reduction in greenhouse gas emissions enabled some cities to persevere and bring back climate stability over the next 1,000 years.[6] There were some remarkable technological advances.

4 The Green Global Scenario: ecotopia

In the second decade of the twenty-first century, the inherent value of the biosphere was finally recognized and efforts to restore and "rewild" the forests and oceans intensified. Urban gardens became commonplace. All of these efforts failed to prevent the tipping point of climate change feedback, however. It was hoped that wilderness could be restored in some regions to allow for biodiversity to recover. Humans and nature are thriving in some areas, but not globally.[7]

Assessing the scenarios

Because all of McKenzie's scenarios are plausible, aligning with one or another is a matter of personal choice and will undoubtedly reflect one's life experiences and anxieties. Grandparents will undoubtedly feel greater distress, for example, when considering the implications of the Red and Black Global Scenarios for their grandchildren. The Red Global Scenario is an apt description of the status quo, which is failing and will continue to do so. It is only the temporary abundance of inexpensive fossil fuels and myopic politicians that provide a sense of normalcy. The Red Global Scenario is also not new, and we have the catastrophic events of the distant past to ponder, such as the disappearance of the Mayan civilization and the demise of ancient Egypt. The stories of these collapsed societies are popular analogues for the present, and their meaning and implications for contemporary challenges have been examined by various writers.[8]

Two Canadian writers, Ronald Wright and Thomas Homer-Dixon, provide the backdrop for what will be seen as one of the greatest fallacies of our time – the idea that we can get along without natural resources, an idea that is now apparently widespread in wealthy countries.[9] We now have the benefit of archaeology and ecology, which neither the ancient Maya nor the Egyptians had, to teach us how and why those ancient societies failed and how ecological diversity is essential to the health of the biosphere.[10] With a heightened historical consciousness, fostered and assisted by museums, society could take advantage of this knowledge and do much to avoid the mistakes that led to the catastrophic collapses of the past.

The Red Global Scenario is the precursor to the Black Global Scenario and the latter is indeed "black" – marked by tragedy, disaster, and despair. This is the apocalyptic scenario made popular in films and books – where chaos and lawlessness are the order of the day. Environmental collapse is assumed in this scenario and the irrelevance of museums is complete, except for those survivors who discover museums as seed banks of older and adaptive technologies. More on this later. There is not much to write about the Black Scenario – it is too dismal and devoid of hope.

If the Black Global Scenario comes to pass, it must be noted that we brought it on knowingly. Our collective denial and passivity will have created what E.O. Wilson, the Pulitzer Prize-winning naturalist, calls the Eremozoic Era – the Age of Loneliness. This will mark the sixth mass extinction on earth, following the meteoric demise of the dinosaurs 65 million years ago. Unlike any of the earth's previous five great disturbances and the loss of biodiversity, "we will have done it all on our own, and conscious of what was happening," writes Wilson.[11] Museums are not exempt from this collective responsibility.

The third scenario, "Techno-utopia" is what the corporatist/government complex would like us to believe, and many intelligent and responsible people have joined the chorus. Apparently it is difficult to be heretical in light of all the technological benefits our civilization has enjoyed. In fact, governments (especially Canada and the United States) continue to jeopardize the future with the simple-minded belief that technology will fix everything. At the very least, all of society, including our so-called political leaders, should be exercising the precautionary principle in light of what is currently unfolding in society and the environment. The precautionary principle means that if an action or policy has a suspected risk of causing harm to the public or to the environment (in the absence of scientific consensus that the action or policy is harmful), the burden of proof that it is *not* harmful falls on those taking the action.[12]

The hubris underlying the "technological fix" is the result of both willful ignorance and the plutocracy's self-interest, both of which are driven by neo-classical economics and the belief that economic growth is the dominant benchmark of societal well-being. To reiterate, this school of economics (and its public policies) has been called a form of brain damage, and for good reason.[13] "Techno-utopia" is too little and too late, a common theme throughout history where privatized interests are in control – why change if you are reaping all the benefits?

Although the "Techno-utopia" is theoretically probable, it will fail because it is predicated on the denial of the current and unfolding damage to the biosphere's systems. Our species will become irrelevant, because the natural world will have decoupled and prevailed, as it always has. For a truly sobering account of how irrelevant our species really is when natural processes take over, I recommend

The World Without Us.[14] Technology, and its newest iteration, "Techno-utopia," remains the uncritical, money-driven, and partial solution it has always been.

This leaves "Ecotopia" as a fourth possibility and it will not unfold as described without the unequivocal collaboration of public and private institutions, including museums. An unprecedented sensitivity to the integrity of the biosphere will be required, as well as a commitment to individual and community self-reliance not seen since the Second World War. All of this is possible and is, in fact, underway in a variety of local, regional, and national initiatives that remain largely unacknowledged by the corporatist/government complex. Nonetheless, these initiatives are the door and the key to the future, and will be discussed shortly.

Six ethical responsibilities for museum management

Clearly, there are many possible scenarios, but the four discussed above are sufficient to demonstrate the degree of change that museums must consider in this time of radical disruption and profound socio-environmental change. Personally, I align with "Ecotopia" because it is a metaphor for the transcendence that society and its institutions must achieve. Irrespective of any particular scenario, it is essential to examine the role and responsibilities of museums in assisting with the emergence of a viable future. The other three scenarios lead nowhere, as they assume that what our species has accomplished will largely unravel and disappear. This may come to pass, but legitimizing this outcome only maintains collective passivity. How, then, can museums contribute to constructive outcomes *now*, when now is of the essence? There are clearly ways and means, but it will require moving beyond traditional museum practices and assumptions.

In considering the role of museums as active agents of cultural change, I have three expectations of them as public institutions: (1) to be open to influence and impact from outside interests; (2) to be responsive to citizens' interests and concerns; and (3) to be fully transparent in fulfilling the first two expectations. Fulfilling these expectations will require that museums expand their understanding of their mandate and purpose at this point in history. Such rethinking and reinvention are already underway in other sectors of society and I am indebted to the economist Jeffrey Sachs (yes, an economist) for his assessment of the environmental degradation, rapid population growth, and extreme poverty that threaten global peace and prosperity.

Sachs argues forcefully that these so-called "soft issues" will become the hard issues of geopolitics in the coming years.[15] He writes that dealing with these issues will require the energies and talents of all parts of society, and he notes that the public sector, the private sector, and the nonprofit sector (including foundations and academia) have always played interlocking roles in global problem solving, although the success of this collaboration is certainly debatable. He then goes on to specify the core responsibilities of each sector, with the proviso that only clearly stated and shared goals can orient the multitude of individual actions that are necessary to confront these challenges.[16]

Although museums are never mentioned in Sachs' book, I submit that they are potential sources of relevant science and entrepreneurship. Mobilizing science, entrepreneurship, and applying solutions are the key components of Sach's blue-print for change, and museums are potentially capable of all three. Building on Sachs' description of the nonprofit sector's key roles in global problem solving, I submit that museums have six ethical responsibilities in a troubled world.[17] In using the word "ethical," I am referring to such things as justice, right conduct, and duty. I agree with Janet Marstine's observation that "the new museum ethics stresses the agency to do good with museum resources."[18]

Public advocacy

As commonly understood among museum practitioners, advocacy means lobby-ing governments for greater recognition of museums and more funding. It means letting legislators, policy makers, and other stakeholders know what museums are, what they do in their communities, and why they are valuable. Lately, it also includes a concerted effort to get politicians to visit the museums in their constitu-encies, as recent research reveals that constituent visits have more influence than any other strategy.[19] The American Association of Museums (AAM) organized an initiative in the summer of 2012 for this purpose, with an emphasis on showing the US Congress how essential museums are. It is interesting to note in this regard that the US House of Representatives declared museums to be luxuries for the wealthy in their 2012 budget deliberations, thus giving a new and urgent meaning to museum advocacy work in that country. This situation prompted the AAM in 2012 to change its name to the Alliance of American Museums "to support our goal of uniting all US museums in an alliance that will amplify our influence and give us the collective clout to be a powerful driver of change."[20]

However, museum workers advocating for museums is not the meaning of public advocacy as an ethical responsibility. As an ethical responsibility, public advocacy is concerned with broader societal issues and concerns where the museum can add perspective, expertise, and value. It means moving beyond the many internal agendas devoted to the museum's well-being, and using the museum's resources to enhance individual and community well-being. In doing so, it is inevitable that a museum will broaden its constituency and strengthen its role as a recognized com-munity organization. As noted elsewhere in this book, the only real obstacle to this is the conventional museum thinking that praises neutrality over all things.

A museum need not sacrifice its traditional activities to advocate publicly, and an excellent example of this accommodation is the Museo Pambata, a children's museum in Manila, Philippines.[21] As global warming continues to threaten the biosphere, Nina Lim-Yuson, President of Museo Pambata, said that "children have been underutilized in the campaign against climate change and they should no longer be left behind in this advocacy." Yuson made this statement during the opening of the three-day "Children and Climate Change – 2nd Asian Children's Museum Conference" in Manila in 2012. Yuson noted that even if children have limited experience, they are one of the sectors most vulnerable to the effects of climate change. Over a hundred participants from different fields came together for the conference to discuss climate change awareness and how to teach children about the role they play in facing the effects of climate change.

Problem solving

Problem solving as an ethical responsibility is closely related to public advocacy, as one may serve the other. They can be seamless or, depending on the project, be separate in thought and execution – in part because problem solving may not require advocacy. Or the advocacy requires no problem solving – just bringing attention to a particular issue. Again, the focus of problem solving as an ethical responsibility is on societal issues and concerns where the museum can provide advice, assistance, and expertise. Because problem solving in a public context is not commonly done in museums, some discussion is in order. With the pervasive litany of socio-environmental issues, problem solving is unlimited in scope and must, therefore, mirror the museum's particular resources and expertise. Problem solving will also require a greater degree of engagement than advocacy, as it will require both the examination of what needs to be done and the marshalling of support in order to follow through. The latter will also require collaboration, as no museum is sufficient in expertise and resources to act alone. Clearly stated goals will also have to be developed, but the initial work can take the form of a pilot project, where the new thinking and initiatives can be seen as a proving ground.

Museums have a distinct advantage in adopting this experimental approach because they are relatively free of the biases that constrain both public and private institutions, although they certainly have their own liabilities and limitations as discussed throughout this book. Museums do not represent commercial interests and, with the exception of national museums, are not agents of national policy. Nonetheless, most museums still have much to do to test their autonomy internally with staff and governing authorities, in order to determine their appetite for taking action.

An excellent example of problem solving is the American Museum of Natural History (AMNH) in New York, which introduced its first Master of Arts in Teaching Program in 2012.[22] Students with a background in science can spend 15 months at the museum learning to become earth science teachers. The goal is to produce 50 new science teachers over two years for the state's high-needs schools, which have long coped with a critical shortage of math and science instructors. The AMNH is making an essential contribution of expertise to society at large, as science literacy will be the foundation of the resilience required to cope with the profound social-environmental changes underway. This is the first urban teacher residency program offered by a museum, and offers coursework at a world-renowned museum with the opportunity to work alongside scientists/curators and urban teachers. Candidates who complete the AMNH program will be awarded a Master of Arts in Teaching degree, with a Specialization in Earth Science for grades 7–12. The program description has a clearly activist tone: "Play your part in the intellectual, cultural, and social community of New York City. Apply now to start your new life inspiring the next generation with science. Change lives. Teach science."[23]

Assisting with societal problem solving is only limited by the nature and scope of the problems themselves, and will depend upon the particular circumstances of a particular museum. There is no formulaic approach, as evidenced by a dramatic example from Africa. Jack Lohman, former Director of the Museum of London and now the CEO of the Royal British Columbia Museum [Royal BC Museum], Canada, recently joined the International Advisory Board of the National Institute of Museums in Rwanda. He was interested to learn that they were running an orphanage as part of their core business, presumably in the wake of the horrendous 1994 genocide in that country.[24]

Collaborating on the funding of solutions

Collaborating on the funding of solutions is perhaps one of the more potentially contentious responsibilities for museums, recognizing the severe financial pressures they contend with daily. How could one conceive of parting with scarce funds, even for a related interest? This is where courage and imagination are required, as collaborating on the funding of solutions can take various forms. Depending on the issue or concern, there could be a direct connection between public advocacy, problem solving, and funding, with one leading sequentially to the other. Or the museum's financial support might be in kind – through collection loans, staff expertise, or exhibition production, for example. In deciding to share a museum's funding with outside agencies, it is important to note that there are a great many nonprofit organizations, working in all sectors of society, that have far more meager finances than many museums. Even a thousand dollars, spent collaboratively, could have a significant impact.

A fine example of sharing money is the Chicago Botanic Garden's Green Youth Farm, a one-acre farm in suburban North Chicago that offers high-school students the opportunity to learn all aspects of organic farming.[25] Activities include planting seeds and starts, managing a hive of bees, cooking with the food grown, and selling it at farm stands, markets, and the Garden Café – where the chef incorporates the fresh organic produce into menu items available to Chicago Botanic Garden visitors. Students work at the farm for four hours per week in the spring and fall, and 20 hours per week in the summer – all paid labour. With mounting concern over the ill-effects of industrial food, this is vital work and the Botanic Garden pays the wages. Everyone benefits, although the Botanic Garden could easily have supported the industrial food business as nearly all museums do. Instead, the Botanic Garden chose to commit to change and to provide financial support to students in the process. There is another related possibility that arises from this example. Why not engage other kinds of businesses that also want to be part of societal change? They could benefit enormously by the support, insight, and motivation that are characteristic of many museum workers.

Insisting on the accountability of government and the private sector

For two decades or more, the watchword has been improving the accountability of museums. Governments, foundations, and the private sector variously concluded that museums needed to be more open, more fiscally responsible, and more accountable to the visitor. Performance indicators and quantitative measures were also introduced (albeit unsystematically and with no consensus in the sector), and there was a move to reduce the authority of self-interested, professional groups – notably curators. This, in turn, led to the unconfirmed "death of the curator" – a rumour which is still alive and well, but essentially untrue. It is now generally believed that museums spend more time on their visitors than on their collections, although this has yet to be substantiated. Much good has been accomplished as a result of this insistence on greater accountability and much remains to be done.

In light of what has been accomplished in the maturation of museums, it is now appropriate to consider a reversal of accountability, wherein museums exercise their right as social institutions to insist on the accountability of government (at any level) and the private sector. It is clear that both government and the private sector require a much greater degree of accountability, as both persist with decisions, actions, and inactions that threaten the well-being of individuals, communities, and the biosphere. The most obvious reason for not doing so lies in the risk of "biting the hand that feeds," recognizing that government and business are key funders of museums.

In 2012, for example, the Canadian government enacted legislation that will bring more scrutiny to foreign funding for charities, including how charities use money for political purposes. The government targeted environmental organizations with this legislation because many of them are actively opposed to major resource extraction projects that the federal government is promoting.[26] Similar consequences could befall activist museums, but this possibility is not a sufficient justification for inaction. Some courageous risk taking is in order. At the same time, I recognize that there are countries throughout the world where insisting upon the accountability of government could risk one's life. Any challenges to the system originating in the museum sector in these countries will have to be more subtle and appropriate than what is being recommended here.

Admittedly, insisting on government and private sector accountability as an ethical responsibility borders on the theoretical, as finding examples in the world of museums is nearly impossible. Of necessity, I must rely on an example about private sector accountability that I have been using since 2005 – the Liberty Science Center (LSC) in Jersey City, US.[27] The LSC took on the role of social activist when they learned that the use of tobacco was the number-one adolescent health problem in the United States. As a result, the LSC collaborated with the New Jersey Department of Health to inform fourth- to twelfth-grade students about the realities of youth smoking. A key part of their hard-hitting, anti-tobacco program was called "Live From . . . The Cardiac Classroom," which used two-way videoconferencing technology to connect students to a cardiac surgical suite in a major hospital. Students were immersed in open heart surgery, which typically began with a message from the chief surgeon about the lifetime smoker on the operating table.

In short, the LSC "provides experiences that seek to make a difference in young lives by making science and technology understandable."[28] Challenging the tobacco industry required a remarkable degree of courage and organizational self-possession, and the LSC has never looked back. They went on to contract their innovative educational programs to the state government and thereby enhance the LSC's long-term, financial sustainability. Who would have guessed that activism would have this result?

Confronting climate change

I also want to recognize the work of Australian Research Fellow Fiona Cameron, whose current work on museums and climate change constitutes an important contribution to fostering the accountability of government and the private sector.[29] She presents the research findings pertaining to the current and potential roles of natural history museums, science museums, and science centres in climate change in Australia and the United States. Overall, her findings showed a greater emphasis on networks, collective action, and political advocacy in Australia. Her research also challenges museums and science centres to bring the past, present, and future together as a focus for concern, including new forums for formulating creative thought and action.

In terms of creative thought and action, Cameron's work is timely in light of a valuable revelation about the nature of the climate change debate. In a recent article entitled "Climate Science as Culture War," the author Andrew Hoffman, Professor of Sustainable Enterprise at the University of Michigan (US), notes that the public debate around climate change in the United States is no longer about science but about values, culture, and ideology.[30] Although there is a scientific consensus on the issue of climate change, there is not a social consensus. Hoffman notes that upwards of two-thirds of Americans do not clearly understand science or the scientific process and fewer are able to pass even a basic scientific literacy test. As a result, people's opinions on this and other complex scientific issues are "based on their prior ideological preferences, personal experience, and values – all of which are heavily influenced by their referent groups and their individual psychology."[31] Acceptance of the scientific consensus is now seen as an alignment with liberal views consistent with other "cultural" issues that divide the United States, including abortion, gun control, health care, and evolution.

In summary, climate change is now part of the so-called culture wars in the United States and in Canada, as well as in other countries, I suspect. Hoffman suggests a consensus-based approach to resolve this clash of ideologies. This will require thoughtful societal debate, focused on the full range of the technical and social dimensions of climate change, including the feasibility and desirability of developing multiple solutions. This is really about the need for a broker or a facilitator to integrate scientific knowledge with public concerns, in order to explore possible courses of action. There are no organizations better equipped and positioned than museums to initiate and host this dialogue between individuals, communities, and scientists. Museums are grounded in a sense of place, committed to stewardship, and widely respected – they can readily serve as the vital bridge between science and the public interest.

Fostering scientific, humanities and social science research

Research has long been a core function of competent museums, although its importance has declined over the past several decades, at least in North America and the UK.[32] It has suffered from decreased public funding to museums and the need to allocate limited resources to enhance fund raising and increase earned revenues. Most museum research is devoted to the collections, however, and its societal relevance may not be readily apparent to the non-expert. My concern with scientific and humanities research as an ethical responsibility is directed at increasing our knowledge and understanding of pressing social and environmental issues – not only by championing practical approaches, but also by engaging in local problem solving. This will not only serve the cause of science in the public interest, but would also raise the profile and value of museum-based research.

Physical and life sciences

An excellent example of both a practical approach and local problem solving comes from the Canadian Museum of Nature in Ottawa, Canada, which established the Canadian Centre for Biodiversity (CCB).[33] The CCB determined that environmental change is an issue of widespread concern to Canadians, while recognizing that changes in biodiversity are key correlates of potential environmental change. The CCB, in conjunction with the Museum's earth sciences, life sciences, and systematics divisions, undertakes research about biodiversity, as well as developing policies and practices for the conservation and wise use of biodiversity in the context of human impact and environmental change. This requires collaboration in a variety of networks, as well as education and training. Of particular note are their efforts to foster stewardship of native plant diversity and best practices at the community level, by encouraging communication and collaboration among stakeholders and the general public. A charitable foundation supports them in their efforts to integrate pure and applied science in the service of key global issues. The CCB embodies a commitment to ethical science in the public interest and paves the way for a more responsible future. This work is also closely aligned with the museum as seed bank, with museum taxonomy and biodiversity studies as key ingredients. More on this shortly.

Another example, from the Royal Saskatchewan Museum (RSM) in Regina, Canada, is based on the museum's taxonomic strengths. Using a state-of-the-art digital imaging system, museum scientists are studying bees to determine how some of Saskatchewan's 200 native species of bees can be best managed to help pollinate Saskatchewan's crops.[34] The new technology allows the most accurate taxonomic research possible, through the detailed examination and identification of different bee species. The provincial government is an ardent proponent of this work, and sees it as the means of better understanding and managing wild bee pollination in an environmentally friendly and cost-efficient way. The government wishes to enhance Saskatchewan's agricultural crops and "continue as a leader in world food security." The RSM's expertise is thus highly relevant in this collaboration to address a growing global issue.

Humanities and social science research

Although humanities and social science research in museums is seemingly less developed and visible than the physical and life sciences discussed above, this research is also underway. A prominent contributor is the School of Museum Studies at the University of Leicester, UK, which operates the Research Centre for Museums and Galleries (RCMG). The RCMG is concerned with nurturing critical thinking and developing new approaches that equip museums to take up socially purposeful roles, as exemplified by their investigation into the social role of botanic gardens in the UK. This research was commissioned by Botanic Gardens Conservation International (BGCI) to challenge traditional thought patterns in botanic gardens. The purpose was to support these gardens in examining their philosophies, values, and practices so that they can make more effective contributions to social and environmental awareness and change. The RCMG examined the current situation and concluded that there is the potential for these gardens to do much more to be socially relevant.[35]

I must also acknowledge Richard Sandell and Jocelyn Dodd, also at Leicester's School of Museum Studies, for their pioneering work on rethinking the representation of disability in museums and galleries.[36] This was another experimental project initiated by the RCMG, designed to develop new approaches to the interpretation of disability and the representation of disabled people's lives in UK museums and galleries. The RCMG worked with nine museums as partners to develop politically aware approaches to interpretation, drawing on the social model of disability. This collaboration resulted in exhibitions and educational programs that offered visitors alternative (non-prejudiced) ways of thinking about disability. This project demonstrates both the value and necessity of collaboration between museums academics and practitioners, and sets the standard for enhancing the method and theory of progressive museum practice.

As an ethical responsibility, humanities and social science research in museums is that which studies the human condition in analytical and critical ways, in an effort to enhance our understanding of modern social, cultural, technological, environmental, and economic issues. Similar to the physical and life sciences discussed above, humanities and social science research is also an attempt to determine what we need to know and do in order to meet the many challenges confronting global society. At the time of writing, I could not determine how much humanities and social science research was actually being done in museums, thus making this a topic for future inquiry. The collaborations between academics and practitioners described above are full of promise.

Maintaining and sharing collections as knowledge seed banks

The role of museums as knowledge seed banks is perhaps the most obvious, and the most easily achieved of the six ethical responsibilities, recognizing that all museums have permanent collections by definition. Museum collections are a time capsule of material diversity (albeit biased and selective) and distinguish museums as the only social institution with a three-dimensional, cultural memory bank. In this respect, museums are as valuable as seed banks. If seed banks are gene banks, then museums are tool, technology, history, and art banks – curating the most distinctive trait of our species – the ability to make tools and things of beauty.[37]

Recalling McKenzie's four scenarios discussed earlier, museums will be a fundamental source of technological memory, as solutions are sought for failed technology. The need to revisit this cumulative knowledge and adaptive genius from the past is necessary now, as industrial technology becomes increasingly maladaptive. Modernity has also led to the loss of knowledge of sustainable living practices that have guided our species for millennia, making the record of material diversity contained in museums as valuable as biodiversity – as adaptive solutions are sought in an increasingly fragile world. Moreover, museums contain our civilization's most comprehensive catalogue of *both* cultural and natural diversity.

Should the worst come to pass and the world plunges into some variant of an apocalyptic or post-apocalyptic scenario, and if some museums survive, they will play a stewardship role that finally justifies the keeping of collections for posterity. As author James Kunstler asks:

> If the social and economic platform fails, how long before the knowledge base dissolves? Two hundred years from now, will anyone know how to build or even repair a 1962 Chrysler slant-six engine? Not to mention a Nordex 1500 kW wind turbine?[38]

As implied above, the concept of museums as seed banks also transcends the objects themselves, to include the local and traditional knowledge that resides not only in the objects, but also in the written and oral testimony that accompanies them. Both these forms of knowledge are currently under siege, for "as knowledge expands globally, it is being lost locally," writes Wendell Berry.[39] Berry notes further that "modern humans typically are using places whose nature they have never known and whose history they have forgotten; thus ignorant, they almost necessarily abuse what they use." Museologist and author Marjorie Schwarzer noted that exterminating the plains bison was acceptable at the time as part of building the railroad across the United States.[40] This is another indication that even our ways of thinking are bound by time. The thinking that led to this extermination is now an artifact of its time, but is also an invaluable lesson for future decision making.

Museums are the custodians of our collective material culture and its associated knowledge, in addition to the knowledge and memories that reside in individuals and communities, and there need not be an apocalypse to reap the benefits of the museum's unique form of stewardship. All museums are positioned to share their collections as knowledge banks, and some have already made this connection. The Western Development Museum in Saskatchewan, Canada, not only installed wind turbines to offset their utility costs, but also created an exhibition that publicly monitors the performance of the wind turbines while featuring the pioneering innovations of early prairie farmers to capture the wind.[41] The result is the museum's historical consciousness at play with the present, based on the collections and a pressing environmental issue.

Climate change and the museum seed bank

Every museum, irrespective of size and subject, can make this connection between the collections and knowledge they hold, and the issues and challenges that confront society now. To do so, museums must move beyond the museum conventions of entertainment and ancillary education, and start examining the compelling, societal questions that are shaping the future. One of these compelling questions is how our civilization will respond to climate change, and it is now recognized that natural history collections in museums and research institutions are a valuable resource for climate change research.

In a recent article entitled "Climate Change and Biosphere Response: Unlocking the Collections Vault," the authors noted that "natural history collections hold billions of specimens collected over the past two centuries, each potentially witness to past ecological conditions and irrefutable evidence of historical biogeographic distributions."[42] The multiple authors of this article, most of whom work in museums, call for a strategic realignment among holders of natural history collections to expand their existing focus on taxonomy and systematics – with climate change as a priority. They also note that setting these new priorities will require strong partnerships between collection holders and global change biologists.[43] This is a fine example of conscious museum workers who are rethinking their role and responsibilities because of the value of their collections as seed banks. Inevitably, they will have to broaden their collaboration to include consumers, media, business, government, and educational organizations if this work is to have a substantive impact.

Forces for good

There is no doubt that these six ethical responsibilities represent a new order of business for museum management, staff, and their governing authorities. I can hear the distant sound of protest and dismay, as museum practitioners weigh the implications of this seemingly radical agenda against the demands of business as usual. There is a source of pragmatic comfort, however, for those who recoil at the thought of museums adopting an ethical agenda. It comes from the nonprofit world, where the ethical responsibility to "advocate and serve" has been identified as one of the six powerful practices of high-impact, nonprofit organizations. This finding was the result of several years of research on 12 of the most successful nonprofits in recent US history – selected for study because they have achieved significant levels of impact. Interestingly, one of the 12 is the Exploratorium, The Museum of Science, Art and Human Perception.[44]

The practice of "advocating and serving" is of particular interest here, because the research revealed that these successful nonprofit organizations started out providing excellent programs, but eventually realized that they could not achieve systemic change through service delivery alone. So they added policy advocacy, along with providing services.[45] Underlying this commitment to advocacy is the critical requirement that these organizations and their leaders want to solve many of the issues besetting the world – climate change, failing education, poverty, etc. In short, they want to change the world.[46] To what extent this desire for change can be found in the museum community is unknown, but it is obviously essential in adopting advocacy as both a strategy and an ethical responsibility.

The intersection of the two – a desire for social change coupled with new and better solutions and initiatives – is now called social entrepreneurship, a concept that is slowly taking shape in the museum world. Noteworthy examples include the Happy Museum Project (to be discussed shortly), the Federation of International Human Rights Museums, and the International Coalition of Sites of Conscience. As discussed earlier, there are also individual museums engaged in such work, such as Museo Pambata and the Liberty Science Center, but social entrepreneurship is the exception and not mainstream museum practice.

Leadership is the foundational requirement in social entrepreneurship and, in deference to the typical museum hierarchy, adopting an ethical agenda remains dependent on the interests, courage, and will of the individual museum director. Ideally, the museum leader will serve as a catalyst who will then galvanize the governing authority. In the absence of senior management and board leadership, the status quo will prevail.

Irrespective of the moral imperative inherent in advocacy, the study of high-impact nonprofits identified several other practices that are immediately relevant to museum management in general, as well as to some of the other ethical responsibilities discussed above. Briefly, these effective practices include creating meaningful ways to emotionally engage individuals in the organization's mission, as well as building networks of related nonprofits to advance the field.[47] This latter practice is of particular importance, as most museums still pay lip-service to collaboration and mostly see other museums as competitors for scarce resources. The high-impact nonprofits actually help the competition succeed by sharing money, talent, expertise, and power with their peers. This commitment to building and nurturing nonprofit networks relates directly to the second and third of the ethical responsibilities – problem solving and collaborating on the funding of solutions.

In addition, the research into effective nonprofits also identified the importance of continuous adaptation and responding to change with new thinking, experimentation, and an endless series of innovations – including mistakes and failures.[48] This means listening, learning, and then modifying one's work as a result – the definition of a learning organization. Finally, the 12 most successful nonprofits distributed leadership throughout the organization and built enduring executive teams, knowing that they had to share power to be effective.[49] The lone and beleaguered CEO was discussed earlier and bears repeating here. To wit, the lone CEO with the oversized ego was absent in these effective nonprofits.

In concluding this discussion of ethical responsibilities and their relationship to highly effective nonprofit organizations, there is one counter-intuitive revelation of considerable value. That is, none of the traditional characteristics of excellent nonprofit management had anything to do with organizational effectiveness or impact.[50] The authors of the study assumed at the outset that excellence in non-profit management consisted of time-tested practices such as marketing, brand awareness, strategic planning, large budgets, systems, work processes, and so forth. Surprisingly, they discovered that "greatness has more to do with how nonprofits work outside the boundaries of their organizations than how they manage their own internal operations."[51]

One need only look at museum annual reports to see the distance between this revelation and mainstream museum practice, where the preoccupation with internal concerns is still paramount – be it funding, collections, or buildings. Annual reports continue to be promotional pieces celebrating the accomplishments of the museum from the museum's perspective. If challenges are mentioned, they relate to the museum's agenda, and not the broader concerns of the community it serves. Although institutional promotion is necessary and important, how refreshing to one day see an annual report that contextualizes a museum beyond its own self-indulgence.

From thinking to doing

Moving the six ethical responsibilities beyond the realm of reflection requires revisiting the earlier discussions on the myth of economic growth. The reader will recall that the so-called developed world, including museums, is held captive by neo-classical economics and marketplace ideology – the idea that economic growth and consumption are the keys to prosperity and societal well-being. The real question, however, is how society is going to adapt to a non-growing, equilibrium economy. The six ethical responsibilities discussed above are possible courses of action for museums to consider, as exemplified by the following initiatives that are already underway.

Transition Towns

There are widespread opportunities for museums to fulfill one or more of the six ethical responsibilities, as the reality of a no-growth economy becomes more apparent.

One of the most cogent expressions of this potential is the Transition Initiative, or Transition Towns.[52] The "transition" refers to moving away from a growth-based, fossil-fuel economy to one that is sustainable and resilient – resilience being the ability of individuals and communities to "hold together and maintain their ability to function in the face of change and shocks from the outside."[53] Reducing, as well as restricting or eliminating fossil-fuel consumption, go hand in hand with building or rebuilding resilience. Our ancestors were decidedly resilient and their cumulative resilience has ironically resulted in the current technological complexity that is decreasingly resilient.

Transition Towns are a massive economic, cultural, and spiritual experiment which will require unprecedented individual and community action. Transition Initiatives currently exist or are underway in England (by far the most), Scotland, Ireland, Wales, Australia, New Zealand, Chile, Japan, Italy, the Netherlands, the United States, and Canada.[54] I do not know of any museums involved in the Transition Town movement; nor are they mentioned in the literature as possible participants. In fact, the Transition Initiatives are largely invisible, even to the people in the towns and cities where they are flourishing.[55]

It has been suggested that what is needed is a storefront approach, to make the concept of a no-growth economy visible and understandable to the community at large. As mentioned earlier, the museum is now commonly referred to as the new agora, and many museum leaders have embraced this rhetoric and the profile – if not the socially responsible agenda to accompany it. The museum as agora has largely come to mean restaurants, shops, and abundant, often empty, architectural space. The Transition Movement is an unprecedented opportunity for museums and galleries to substantiate the agora rhetoric, as they are ideally positioned to provide sound knowledge and safe, illustrative space to foster awareness of the Transition Initiatives.

By so doing, museums and galleries could assist their communities in becoming intelligently informed, beyond the superficiality of mainstream media, including the identification of sustainable alternatives to confront the difficulties arising from the ongoing breakdown of the growth economy. Museums could well be the comfortable facilitators of the Transition Initiative, recognizing their civil orientation, their knowledge-based legacy, their historical consciousness, and the trust and respect they are afforded by their communities. The missing ingredients continue to be the imagination and courage of leaders, managers, and governing authorities.

The Community Economic Laboratory

There is one approach to nurturing a no-growth economy that integrates public advocacy, problem solving, collaboration, accountability, and the museum seed bank – in a coalition of nonprofit organizations and businesses called a Community Economic Laboratory, or CEL.[56] This model would provide a variety of services, ranging from individual learning to community involvement, and could include a food cooperative, a community garden, a tool library, a work centre to match people's skills with community needs, a recycling centre, and a community education centre, as well as a museum or gallery with all of their unique resources and services.

Of particular importance here is the museum as seed bank, as the reader will recall that the growth-based economy has led to the loss of knowledge about sustainable living practices that have guided our species for millennia. Museums are the repositories of the evidence of our adaptive failures and successes, not to mention the chroniclers of our creativity and pathos. As noted earlier, museums are akin to the biological seed banks that store seeds as a source for planting, in case seed reserves elsewhere are destroyed. In this role alone, museums would provide invaluable perspective and knowledge to a Community Economic Laboratory, including the benefit of real objects for study and learning.

The idea of museums as seed banks is perhaps the strongest endorsement for museums to participate in defining a future divorced from economic growth – both as stewards and as disseminators of a historical consciousness in support of rethinking contemporary assumptions and misperceptions. Museums are uniquely endowed to do so, as they care for a body of material evidence, as well as the knowledge, stories, and oral histories that will become increasingly vital to understanding and coping with contemporary challenges. If historical consciousness can be defined "as a form of resourcefulness in using historical data as 'material' to make sense of our world," then museums are the embodiment of that consciousness.[57] This is such an obvious role for museums in a troubled world that I remain bewildered why the value of museums continues to be defined by participation in exhibitions, programs, and events that ignore contemporary, socio-environmental issues. This unquestioned treadmill is perpetually recast by every new museum director, with museums getting better and better at what they are already doing well.

A large dose of objectivity is urgently needed, and it would be salutary for museum workers to suspend, for the sake of reflection, all the professional and conventional opinions about what meaningful museum work is and, instead, consider what the work of museums should be in the early twenty-first century. Culture is not only about leisure, distraction, gadgets, and entertainment, contrary to the overwhelming intrusion of social media – much of which is simply corporatism in new clothes. Culture is actually about how we lead our lives and not what we do in our leisure time.[58] Culture is also about organizations and individuals thinking critically and assuming responsibility, as there are acute issues confronting our species that require concerted public involvement with the aid of intelligent social organizations like museums.

Instead, museums continue to ask "How many people will attend?"; "Will there be a catalogue?"; "What will we sell in our shop?"; and "Are people having fun?" Although these are valid questions from a traditional perspective, they are insufficient. None of these questions is creating an authentic future for museums or the communities they ostensibly serve. In summary, and at the risk of reiterating the obvious, museums must play a role in creating a meaningful future for humans on this planet. The six ethical responsibilities are intended to push museums toward this larger purpose, beyond the survival and prosperity of their own institutions. The opportunities for embracing even one of these six ethical responsibilities are legion.

The Happy Museum Project

Fortunately, there are museum practitioners and funders who are thinking beyond exhibitions, consumption, and visitor studies, in pursuit of meaningful engagement with their communities. A noteworthy example is the Happy Museum Project, a moniker that was initially disconcerting to me with its implication that museums could or should be "happy" – what does happiness have to do with the social responsibilities of museums? My reaction could not have been more uninformed, as the Happy Museum Project is "seeking to create a community of practice in UK museums committed to supporting the transition to a high well-being, sustainable society."[59] The Happy Museum Project is led by Tony Butler, the Director of the Museum of East Anglian Life, and funded through the Paul Hamlyn Foundation's Breakthrough Fund. Once again, the innovative Hamlyn Foundation is challenging the museum community. The Happy Museum Project would be an ideal participant in the Community Economic Laboratory discussed above.

The project began with the launch of a paper, *The Happy Museum*, the purpose of which was to begin an inquiry into re-imagining the purpose of museums. Of particular interest are eight principles to help guide museums through the transition to a low-carbon world:[60]

1. *Make people happy* – seek to understand the importance of well-being.
2. *Pursue mutual relationships* – find ways to have more mutual relationships with communities, supporters, and visitors.
3. *Value the environment* – past, present, and future.
4. *Measure what matters* – counting visitors tells nothing about the quality of their experience or the contribution to their well-being.
5. *Lead on innovation to transition* – museums don't have to be only storehouses of the past, but can also be hubs of innovation.
6. *Think global, be networked* – "think global, act local" should be a guide for museums in transition.
7. *Support learning for resilience* – the future will need resilient, creative, resourceful, and empathetic people who think in terms of systems, exactly the kind of capacities museum learning can support.
8. *Find your niche* – build on all your assets (collections, buildings, knowledge, skills, communities, and audiences) to identify your distinct role.

The Happy Museum Project translated these principles into action in 2011 by awarding funding to six UK museums to explore a variety of topics, including a connection to the natural world; mental "wellness" (rather than illness); museums as a place of healing; museums as a place of story and play; working with the homeless;

the stewardship of local communities; and strong local partnerships.[61] This Project has assumed a leadership role by combining the sentiments in this book with both funding and strategies – to chart practical opportunities for learning and change. The Paul Hamlyn Foundation is also clearly a leader, with its commitment to supporting and developing museums and galleries to place community needs, values, aspirations, and active collaboration at the core of their work. All of this is cause for much optimism.

The biggest elephant in the room

These opportunities and examples, from Transition Towns to the Happy Museum Project, are clear indications that mindfulness is increasing, significant change is afoot, and there is a vital role for museums in rethinking the future. As is the case with all professions, however, museum practitioners must contend with both inertia and conservatism, both of which protect the method, theory, and practice of any profession. At the same time, they also make it difficult to embrace new ways of thinking and working. There is nothing to be gained in arguing whether or not museum work is a profession, as it demonstrates all of the characteristics of a profession, save one.[62] Museum work is full time; it has its own training schools and university schools; it has local, national, and international associations; and there are codes of professional ethics and conduct. The only missing factor is the requirement to be licensed in order to work. It is both obvious and crucial that one of the most significant barriers to change in museums resides in the rubric of professionalism – a double-edged sword with various blessings and liabilities.

To highlight the dialectical tension in museum professionalism, I refer to a project on museum ethics undertaken by the Center for the Future of Museums (CFM) and the Institute of Museum Ethics' (IME) in 2011/2012.[63] This study involved nearly two hundred museum professionals, as well as professionals from related fields including librarians, archivists, attorneys, futurists, journalists, and ethicists. Seventy-nine individuals agreed to participate in a forecasting exercise that would take place on the Internet. In addition, over one hundred members of the general public provided comments on various aspects of the project. The work resulted in "Forecasting the Future of Museum Ethics," a report which identified "six issues likely to be of profound importance to museums in the next ten to twenty-five years." These issues are (in alphabetical order):[64]

- *Accessibility* – balancing accessibility to collections and institutions with preservation.
- *Collecting and deaccessioning* – responding to ethical challenges regarding collecting and deaccessioning.
- *Conflict of interest* – responding to ethical challenges related to conflicts of interest, with particular reference to collections.
- *Control of content* – responding to challenges concerning the control of content by staff and academic experts versus community curation; public participation in content creation (e.g., crowd sourcing, participatory design); and censorship.

- *Diversity* – responding to practical concerns related to cultural and demographic diversity.
- *Transparency and accountability* – responding to ethical challenges related to transparency and accountability in governance, operations, and finance, as well as providing metrics that reflect a museum's performance (including financial information, visitation, membership, energy use, etc.).

This report provides the most current and informed view of the future by one of the largest professional museum organizations in the world (second only to the International Council of Museums), and is indeed revelatory – and also disheartening. The results of this inquiry unequivocally demonstrate that internal museum concerns are still the most pressing. Yes, there are important insights in this report about the need to curtail collecting and share collections; the need to respond to growing cultural diversity, and the need to create more transparent organizations. Overall, however, there is little or no sense of the museum's connectedness to the broader world. It's as if museums can persevere in isolation, by attending to their internal agendas and "responding" to the external world when the pressures demand. There is a strange passivity in this world view, which fails to recognize that museums are societal players, and not empty vessels waiting to be filled.

I could not find the words "innovate" or "rethink" anywhere in the CFM/IME report, while "experiment" appeared once. Climate change was identified as a threat to the preservation of collections; not to the individuals and communities who make possible the museum. The report also noted that "economic challenges and changing public attitudes about environmental issues will raise more issues about the amount of resources (of all kinds) that we spend on collections in the name of preservation."[65] This observation is not about mobilizing the collections to inform broader societal issues, but rather a concern that museums may emerge as a lower funding priority. This supposed eventuality is already crystal clear and will remain so until such time as museums reconsider what their new work should be.

As a museum practitioner for 39 years with varied experiences, I concede that the issues identified in "Forecasting the Future of Museum Ethics" are well considered and legitimate. Taken together, however, they are a myopic and insufficient response to any sober assessment of the world in which museums currently operate. This forecast indicates that the profound issues of the future are to be defined in terms of the museum's preoccupations, and not with respect to the socio-environmental complexities that are already undermining the status quo. In short, the six issues which summarize the challenges confronting the museums are startlingly self-serving.

Put another way, the collective perspective of the museum community is dangerously narrow at this point in history. The world and all its complexities continue to be seen through a myopic museum lens, and I cannot help but think of the metaphor which refers to a pedantic preoccupation with irrelevant concerns, or "how many angels can dance on the head of a pin?" With no intention of denying the veracity of the issues identified in the forecast, I submit that there are topics of far greater immediate and practical value to museums and the communities they serve.

A framework for ethical management

In concluding this discussion of the need for museum management to be guided by ethical considerations, above and beyond the standard professional ones, I offer the following framework. It consists of three interrelated considerations which serve as both a rationale and framework for adopting an ethical approach to museum management. The first component is the meaning of management itself, which, despite the teachings of most business schools, is far more than a bundle of techniques and procedures. Rather, in the words of the self-described social ecologist, Peter Drucker, "The essence of management is to make knowledge productive. Management, in other words, is a social function. In its practice, management is truly a 'liberal art'."[66]

Following directly from Drucker's idea of management as a liberal art is the practice of "intellectual activism." This is defined in *The Independent Scholar's Handbook* as activities which do not necessarily create new knowledge, but make existing knowledge more accessible, understandable, and useful to others.[67] Most importantly, intellectual activism creates the conditions for fresh discoveries through "the conjunction of challenging ideas, or stimulates others to discover." These activities can range from speaking to audiences other than one's peers, to bringing scholarly work to a wider public, to creatively managing organizations such as museums.

The third consideration in building a framework for ethical management is the pressing need for museums to "become reality-based."[68] Recognizing the profusion of different "realities" that define our humanness, I refer to the epigraph by Neil Postman in this book wherein he notes that a museum must be an argument with its society, and that "a good museum always will direct attention to what is difficult and even painful to contemplate." This is what I mean by pressing for museums to become reality-based – to become more visionary, to become more involved in the broader world, and to confront the socio-environmental issues that museums are equipped to address, recognizing their individual perspective, resources, strengths, and limitations.

Again, there is no formulaic approach in doing this, as the earlier examples of responsible practice demonstrate. It is up to the creative predilections of each museum to determine where they can add value. Becoming reality-based means recognizing that business as usual, i.e., internal agendas driven internally, is not an entitlement. Becoming reality-based also means embracing a sense of urgency – the need to see things as they really are in terms of the challenges to our collective well-being, including what role museums can play in civic cooperation and support. These three considerations – making knowledge productive, intellectual activism, and becoming reality based – constitute the building blocks for an ethical approach to museum management in a troubled world.

These three considerations may also be thought of as three agendas to guide museum management in the twenty-first century. In summary, the first agenda is "what" – to make knowledge productive; the second agenda is "how" – through intellectual activism, and the third agenda is "why" – to become reality-based in order to unlock the potential of museums as responsible community organizations. The last component of this ethical management framework is the question of "for whom," and the answer to that is "for everyone." If the value of a museum lies in "freeing society from the tyranny of the present," to paraphrase Neil Postman, this framework for ethical management is intended to assist with that task.[69] If nothing else, this framework can assist museums in freeing themselves from their own self-imposed tyranny.

Concluding thoughts

Overall, there is a significant solitude between the ethical responsibilities proposed above and the issues identified as being of profound importance to museums in the next 10–25 years. "Forecasting the Future of Museum Ethics" does provide a brief glimpse of the importance of fostering museum research and maintaining collections as knowledge seed banks, but there is not enough substantive discussion to conclude that they are important concerns. The result is an inadvertent tension between the "professional" museum perspective, as expressed in the Forecast, and the work that *really* needs to be done. The latter call to action is undoubtedly improbable to the museum boards and directors who are committed to the status quo. Hence, the ethical management agenda set out here is clearly not for every museum.

Furthermore, the future is not knowable because the links between cause and effect in organizations are complex, and mostly lost in the detail of what actually happens in between.[70] If museum staff and boards cannot know where their museums are going because the future is unknowable, then they should not all believe in the same things. They should question everything, and generate new perspectives through discussion, debate, and dialogue. The survival and prosperity of our species require this diversity in outlook and action.

Even the founder of the World Economic Forum, Klaus Schwab, asked what has become of our culture and heritage in the face of rampant economic growth.[71] Although the past, with its focus on economic growth, is no longer a reliable guide to the future, the knowledge of the past – its successes and failures – will be essential in moving beyond the political and economic ideologies that threaten the survival of individuals, communities, and the biosphere. The potential for museums to foster a public understanding of the past, as influencing and acting upon the present, remains vast, uncharted, and absolutely necessary.

At what point do museums, as historically conscious and knowledge-based institutions in the public sphere, acknowledge their civic responsibilities? This is a pointed question for museums, especially because of their unique position in society and the respect and status they enjoy. As the discussion of the six ethical responsibilities confirms, competent museums can provide their communities with the means of intellectual self-defense and resourcefulness to move beyond the increasing dominance of corporations, government complicity, and the consumer society. Museums have the opportunity and obligation to both resist the status quo and question the way in which society is governed.

As discussed earlier in this book, we are in urgent need of museums to provide cultural frameworks to identify, explore, and challenge the myths, perceptions, and misperceptions that govern (and threaten) daily life. We are also in need of a new alliance of environmental organizations, farmers, gardeners, social agencies, local businesses, universities, and museums of all kinds, in order to "re-imagine human culture from the ground up, using our intelligence and passion for the welfare of the next generations, and the integrity of nature's web, as our primary guides."[72]

There is no doubt that for-profit organizations are also as capable as nonprofits to "re-imagine human culture from the ground up . . ." Fulfilling this potential will require not only new cultural frameworks, but also practical, collaborative mechanisms involving museums and the for-profit sector, such as the hybrid organization discussed earlier in "Persistent Paradoxes" [Chapter 20]. It will also require that museums acknowledge the unknown, including "what we don't know that we don't know," or the unknown–unknowns.[73] This will be difficult for most museums, recognizing their inherent discomfort with uncertainty and their wish to be in control. There are no ready answers to re-imagining the future – this book and all others like it notwithstanding. The future of all organizations lies in exploration, experimentation, risk, and resilience.

Long live the museum

Had museums been more mindful of their unique attributes, they might well have served as distant early warning systems as global socio-environmental issues came into sight decades ago. Museums are uniquely positioned to do so, with their complex mix of humanism, science, time–depth, and societal respect. But many of the warning signs have now become crises, and all public institutions must adapt and evolve to both serve and prosper. Paradoxically, and despite their inherent conservatism, museums have existed for thousands of years, unlike the vast majority of commercial enterprises. Museums have always had some kind of adaptive intuition – to reinvent and transform, however slowly and unconsciously. I do not know what else to call this special quality of adaptive intuition and I know of no explanation to account for it. Nonetheless, museums have evolved through time, from the elite collections of imperial dominance, to educational institutions for the public, and now to the museum as "mall" and appendage of consumer society.[74]

There is an important lesson in this historical trajectory and it resides in the ability of museums to learn and adapt as circumstances require. This ability is one of the characteristics of the long-lived companies discussed in "Debunking the Marketplace" in this book [Chapter 21], and can be described as organizations remaining "in harmony with the world around them" and reacting in a "timely fashion to the conditions of society around them."[75] Socio-environmental conditions are changing rapidly and the museum as mall is the current and latest chapter in this enduring trajectory.

The museum's next iteration awaits articulation and will hinge upon enlarging the context of museum work to provide sustained public benefit. There are numerous examples in this book, and in the museum community at large, that foreshadow this new and enlightened era for museums, and therein lies the key to the elusive notion of sustainability. The challenge of sustainability for every museum – be it large or small, volunteer or paid – is to redefine the ultimate purpose and standards of museum work. Professionalism and the yearning for popularity must make room for a commitment to the durability and well-being of individuals, communities and the natural world.[76]

Notes

1 Bridget McKenzie, "Seeing Museums in 2060," *The Learning Planet Blog*, May 8, 2012. Available online at: http://thelearningplanet.wordpress.com/tag/museums/.

2 R.R. Janes, *Museums in a Troubled World: Renewal, Irrelevance or Collapse?*, London and New York: Routledge, 2009, pp. 156–158.

3 For an overview of scenario planning, see P. Schwartz, *The Art of the Long View*, New York: Currency Doubleday, 1996; and A. de Geus, *The Living Company: Habits for Survival in a Turbulent Business Environment*, Boston: Harvard Business School Press, 1997, pp. 38–54.

4 McKenzie, "Seeing Museums in 2060."

5 McKenzie, "Seeing Museums in 2060."

6 McKenzie, "Seeing Museums in 2060."

7 McKenzie, "Seeing Museums in 2060."

8 T. Homer-Dixon, *The Upside of Down: Catastrophe, Creativity, and the Renewal of Civilization*, Toronto: Alfred A. Knopf, 2006; R. Wright, *A Short History of Progress*, Toronto: House of Anansi Press, 2004.

9 T. Homer-Dixon, *The Ingenuity Gap*, Toronto: Vintage Canada Edition, 2001, pp. 31, 241.

10 R. Heinberg, *The End of Growth*, Gabriola Island, Canada: New Society Publishers, 2011, p. 53.

11 E.O. Wilson, *Creation: An Appeal to Save Life on Earth*, New York: W.W. Norton & Co, 2006, p. 91.

12 *Wikipedia*. Available online at: http://en.wikipedia.org/wiki/Precautionary_principle.

13 H. Henderson, "Making a Living Without Making Money," *East West Journal*, March, 1980, 22–27.

14 A. Weisman, *The World Without Us*, New York: Thomas Dunne Books, 2007.

15 J.D. Sachs, *Common Wealth: Economics for a Crowded Planet*, New York: Penguin, 2008.

16 Sachs, *Common Wealth*, pp. 291–293.

17 Sachs, *Common Wealth*, p. 292.

18 J. Marstine, "The Contingent Nature of the New Museum Ethics," in J. Marstine (ed.), *The Routledge Companion to Museum Ethics*, London and New York: Routledge, 2011, p. 8.

19 F.W. Bell, "AAM Announces 'Invite Congress to Visit Your Museum' Week – Museums Need to Show Congress How Essential They Are," American Association of Museums, American Association of Museums, Washington, DC. Available online at: http://www.speakupformuseums.org/invitecongresstovisitaugust.htm.

20 F.W. Bell, "The Future of Museums, and of AAM," blog post, September 6, 2012. The Center for the Future of Museums, American Alliance of Museums. Available online at: http://futureofmuseums.blogspot.ca/2012/09/the-future-of-museums-and-of-aam. html.

21 Museo Pambata, 2nd Asian Children's Museum Conference, "Children and Climate Change." Available online at: http://www.museopambata.org/acmc/.

22 American Museum of Natural History, "Master of Arts in Teaching Program." Available online at: http://www.amnh.org/education/mat.

23 American Museum of Natural History, "Master of Arts in Teaching Program."

24 J. Lohman, personal communication, August 16, 2012.

25 Chicago Botanic Garden, "North Chicago Green Youth Farm." Available online at: http://www.chicagobotanic.org/urbanagriculture/youthfarm. See also the Garden Café at: http:// www.chicagobotanic.org/cafe/index.php.

26 G. Hoekstra, "Groups Fight Back After Conservatives Try to Dilute Environmental Laws," *Vancouver Sun*, June 8, 2012. Available online at: http://www.driving.ca/news/ Groups+fight+back+after+Conservatives+dilute+environmental+laws/6747634/ story.html.

27 E.H. Koster and S.H. Baumann, "Liberty Science Center in the United States: A Mission Focused on External Relevance," in R.R. Janes and G.T. Conaty (eds), *Looking Reality in the Eye: Museums and Social Responsibility*, Calgary, Canada: University of Calgary Press and the Museums Association of Saskatchewan, 2005, pp. 85–111.

28 Koster and Baumann, "Liberty Science Center in the United States," p. 100.

29 F.R. Cameron, "Climate Change, Agencies and the Museum and Science Centre Sector," *Museum Management and Curatorship* (27/4), 2012, 317–339.

30 A.J. Hoffman, "Climate Science as Culture War," *Stanford Social Innovation Review*, Fall, 2012. Available online at: http://www.ssireview.org/articles/entry/climate_science_ as_culture_war?utm_source=Enews&utm_medium=email&utm_content=1&utm_ campaign=Hoffman.

31 Hoffman, "Climate Science as Culture War."

32 "Assessing priorities: research at museums" (M.S. Graham, Guest Editor), *Museum Management and Curatorship* (20/4), December, 2005, 287–371.

33 Canadian Museum of Nature, "The Canadian Centre for Biodiversity – Mission and Method." Available online at: http://nature.ca/pdf/ann02-03nature_e.pdf, p.13.

34 Government of Saskatchewan News Release, "Royal Saskatchewan Museum Poised to Lead Bee Research in Canada," July 31, 2012. Available online at: http://www.gov. sk.ca/ news?newsId=ab5c0e2f-91ad-4146-b57e-a40d8e510d9e.

35 J. Dodd and C. Jones, *Towards a New Social Purpose: Redefining the Role of Botanic Gardens*, Richmond, Surrey, UK: Botanic Gardens Conservation International, November, 2010, p. 2. Available online at: http://www2.le.ac.uk/departments/museumstudies/ rcmg/projects/redefining-the-role-of-botanic-gardens/Towards%20a%20new%20 social%20 purpose%20summary.pdf.

36 J. Dodd, R. Sandell, D. Jolly and C. Jones (eds), *Rethinking Disability Representation in Museums and Galleries*, Leicester, UK: Research Centre for Museums and Galleries (RCMG), Department of Museum Studies, 2008. Available online at: http://www2. le.ac.uk/departments/museumstudies/rcmg/projects/rethinking-disability-representation- 1/rdrsmallest.pdf.

37 Janes, *Museums in a Troubled World*, p. 179.

38 J.H. Kunstler, *The Long Emergency: Surviving the End of Oil, Climate Change, and Other Converging Catastrophes of the Twenty-First Century*, New York: Grove Press, 2005, p. 130.

39 W. Berry, *Life Is a Miracle*, Berkeley, CA: Counterpoint, 2000, pp. 90–91.

40 M. Schwarzer, personal communication, July 23, 2012.

41 R.R. Janes, "It's a Jungle in Here: Museums and Their Self-Inflicted Challenges," *MUSE* (27/5), 2009, 30–33.

42 K.G. Johnson, S.J. Brooks, P.B. Fenberg, A.G. Glover, K.E. James, A.M. Lister, E. Michel, M. Spencer, J.A. Todd, E. Valsami-Jones, J.R. Young, and J.R. Stewart, "Climate Change and Biosphere Response: Unlocking the Collections Vault," *BioScience* (61/2), February, 2011, 147–153.

43 Johnson et al., "Climate Change and Biosphere Response," 147.

44 L.R. Crutchfield and H.M. Grant, *Forces for Good: The Six Practices of High-Impact Nonprofits*, San Francisco: Jossey-Bass, A Wiley Imprint, 2008, p. 11.

45 Crutchfield and Grant, *Forces for Good*, p. 21.

46 Crutchfield and Grant, *Forces for Good*, p. 24.

47 Crutchfield and Grant, *Forces for Good*, p. 22.

48 Crutchfield and Grant, *Forces for Good*, p. 22.

49 Crutchfield and Grant, *Forces for Good*, p. 22.

50 Crutchfield and Grant, *Forces for Good*, pp. 14–19.

51 Crutchfield and Grant, *Forces for Good*, p. 19

52 R. Heinberg, *The End of Growth*, Gabriola Island, Canada: New Society Publishers, 2011, pp. 270–273.

53 R. Hopkins, *The Transition Handbook: From Oil Dependency to Local Resilience*, White River Junction, VT: Chelsea Green Publishing Company, 2008, p. 12.

54 Hopkins, *The Transition Handbook*, pp. 134–137.

55 Heinberg, *The End of Growth*, p. 275.

56 Heinberg, *The End of Growth*, pp. 276–277.

57 V. Gosselin, personal communication – email, February 12, 2012.

58 D. Worts, "Rising to the Challenge: Fostering a Culture of Sustainability" (Guest Editorial), *MUSE* (26, September/October), 2008, p. 6.

59 "About Us," The Happy Museum. Available online at: http://www.happymuseum project.org/about-us.

60 *The Happy Museum Paper*, The Happy Museum. Available online at: http://www. happy museumproject.org/the-happy-museum-paper-and-manifesto/the-happy-museum-paper.

61 "Happy Museum Funded Commission Announced," The Happy Museum. Available online at: http://www.happymuseumproject.org/news/happy-museum-funded-commis sions-announced.

62 *Wikipedia*, "What Is a Profession?" Available online at: http://en.wikipedia.org/wiki/ Profession.

63 American Association of Museums – Center for the Future of Museums, "Forecasting the Future of Museum Ethics." Available online at: http://futureofmuseums.org/thinking/ loader.cfm?csModule=security/getfile&pageid=2387, pp. 1–2.

64 American Association of Museums, "Forecasting the Future of Museum Ethics," p. 4.

65 American Association of Museums, "Forecasting the Future of Museum Ethics," p. 7.

66 P.F. Drucker, *Managing in a Time of Great Change*, New York: Truman Talley Books/ Plume, 1998, p. 250.

67 R. Gross, *The Independent Scholar's Handbook*, Berkeley, CA: Ten Speed Press, 1993, pp. 164–70. Available online at: http://www.sfu.ca/independentscholars/ISbook.pdf.

68 J.H. Kunstler, *The Long Emergency: Surviving the End of Oil, Climate Change, and Other Converging Catastrophes of the Twenty-First Century*, New York: Grove Press, 2005, p. 324.

69 N. Postman, "Museum as Dialogue," *Museum News* (69/5), 58.

70 R.D. Stacey, *Managing the Unknowable: Strategic Boundaries Between Order and Chaos in Organizations*, San Francisco: Jossey-Bass, 1992, p. 11.

71 T. Milewski, "Occupy Davos? Leaders Greeted by Doubts About Capitalism," 2012, p. 1. Available online at: http://www.cbc.ca/news/politics/story/2012/01/25/pol-vp-milewski-davos-harper.html.

72 R. Heinberg, *Peak Everything: Waking Up to the Century of Declines*, Gabriola Island, Canada: New Society Publishers, 2010, p. 65.

73 Homer-Dixon, T. 2001. *The Ingenuity Gap: Can We Solve the Problems of the Future?* Toronto: Vintage Canada.

74 A. Gopnik, "The Mindful Museum," *The Walrus* (4), June, 2007, 89. This article is adapted from the 2006 Holtby Lecture at the Royal Ontario Museum in Toronto, Canada.

75 A. de Geus, *The Living Company: Habits for Survival in a Turbulent Business Environment*, Boston, MA: Harvard Business School Press, 1997, p. 6.

76 Berry, *Life Is a Miracle*, p. 134.

24

MUSEUMS IN A DANGEROUS TIME*

Introduction

I am honoured to be giving the Fellows Lecture for the Canadian Museums Association and I am very conscious of this privileged opportunity to speak to you today. Keynote addresses are intended to reinforce the conference theme – in this instance "Intention, Innovation and Invention." I will address these themes, but I will not concern myself with what museums are already doing well – things like collections management, school programs, and retailing. I want to explain at the outset why I'm presenting this particular keynote, including the rather ominous title "Museums in a Dangerous Time."

I have spent 39 years working in and around museums and my personal mission has always been to encourage museums to creatively answer the question – "what does it mean to be a human being?"[1] This question has now become immeasurably more important because each of us must figure out what it means to be a human being now – at a time when every living system is declining – and the rate of decline is accelerating.[2] I regret to note that this question should be the central preoccupation of our lives – it certainly will be for our children. As for our grandchildren, who knows? The year 2050 will undoubtedly be markedly different from the privileged lives we lead today.

I must note, however, that I am still optimistic about the future, as compared to being hopeful. Holding on to hope can rob one of the present moment and divert attention from what needs to be done.[3] In keeping with the conference theme, I am more interested in *intention*, and I think relentlessly about what role museums might play in addressing the challenges we face. As a result, I do not feel particularly

---

*Source: Robert R. Janes, the Fellows Lecture, Annual Conference of the Canadian Museums Association, Toronto, Canada, April 10, 2014.

calm and contented. But I do remain optimistic for a variety of reasons that I intend to make clear.

I will attempt to connect the seemingly unconnected, with the intention of describing a broader vision of museum practice in an increasingly troubled world. My approach in doing so is not analytical – as analysis means taking something apart to understand it. I will use a systems perspective instead, which means putting museums into the context of the larger whole – that is the world in which we live and work.[4] I'll use the word "museum," but I include art galleries, science centres, historic sites, and all other sister institutions.

The age of disruption

We are reminded daily that we are living in an Age of Disruption.[5] The problems and uncertainties we face are unprecedented, yet the possibilities and opportunities for change and renewal have never been greater. My presentation will be part cautionary tale, coupled with some alarmism and a hint of the apocalyptic, all for the purpose of asking you to consider an alternative future for museums as participants and problem solvers in this Age of Disruption. I firmly believe that there is a role for museums as agents of change and forces for good, and I have some modest thoughts on how museums might contribute to a brighter and more intelligent future. As a prelude to that discussion, however, I want to set the stage with an overview of some of the challenges we face.

Environmental problems

It is now commonplace to hear people refer to a global collapse – thoughts that were rare or unheard of a decade ago. The biologists Paul and Anne Ehrlich recently wrote "the odds of avoiding collapse seem small, because the risks are clearly not obvious to most people and the classic signs of impending collapse . . . are everywhere."[6] The United Kingdom's Chief Scientific Advisor, John Beddington, has called our current predicament a "perfect storm" of environmental problems.[7] Our highly technological, interconnected, global civilization is now threatened with collapse by an array of environmental problems, including the following:[8]

1. Climate change and disruption – more on this shortly.
2. The accelerating extinction of animal and plant populations which are essential for human survival. For example, more than 85% of the world's fisheries have been pushed to, or beyond, their biological limits, and the planet has already lost 80% of its forest cover to deforestation.[9] Food prices are expected to double by 2030.[10]
3. The spread of toxic compounds, such as flame-retardant chemicals. They have been widely used for decades in everything from furniture to sleepwear, but they are now a serious threat to human health.[11]
4. The unnecessary use of environmentally damaging technologies to service our unbridled consumption. Fracking for oil and gas comes to mind.

FIGURE 12 A polar bear jumps between ice floes. Climate change is more severe
in the Arctic than in most of the rest of the world, and the Arctic is
warming at a rate nearly twice the global average © Vladimir Melnik/
Shutterstock.

This is only a glimpse of the environmental challenges, and climate change merits
further discussion because of its growing impact on our lives. We have now passed
the milestone level of 400 parts per million (ppm) of climate-warming carbon in
the atmosphere for the first time in human existence – without even a national
discussion or an outcry by the citizenry or the press, much less the intelligentsia.[12]
The 400 ppm threshold is a dire wake-up call for all of us to support clean energy
technology and reduce the emission of greenhouse gases. Time is of the essence,
as our profound challenge is to now phase out more than half of the global use of
fossil fuels by 2050, in order to forestall the worst impacts of climate disruption.[13]

Yet, Canada's Federal Government has approved the expansion of the Alberta
tar sands without any plan to curb climate-warming emissions. The earth simply
cannot handle the consequences of increased fossil-fuel use and, sadly, Canada
doesn't even rank in the top 10 of those countries investing in renewable energy.[14]
Have you considered solar panels for your museum?

Mega-uncertainties

In addition to these environmental problems, there are various mega-uncertainties,
or "key issues where little is known and forecasts are impossible." Mega-uncertainties
are also characterized by disconnected and disputed facts, and opinions.[15] What are
some of these uncertainties?[16]

1. *Will we run out of essential resources?* Renewable resources (notably water) and many non-renewable resources (such as oil, arable land, and earth elements) are becoming more difficult to acquire. For example, a rare-earth metal called Indium (essential for touch screens) will apparently be exhausted in 10 years.[17]

2. *How many people in 2050?* Global population projections indicate more than 9 billion people by 2050, compared to today's population of 7.1 billion. Can the earth sustain this number of human beings?

3. *Will everyone have employment that meets basic needs?* This is currently a serious, long-term problem, especially for younger generations, that is decidedly aggravated by digital technology and robotics. Predictions indicate that by 2030 more than 2 billion jobs will disappear as a result of disruptive technologies – roughly 50% of all the jobs on the planet.[18]

4. *Will financial inequality and plutocracy continue to increase?* Global trends in increasing inequality are a matter of record, including the parallel trend to governance by the very rich. Although there is no definition when a "democracy" becomes overtaken by "plutocracy," the prognosis is bleak. Experts note that "the developed world is on a path toward a degree of inequality that will likely reach levels that cause severe social disruption."[19]

5. *Can effective global governance and law emerge?* We have created a global economy and global problems such as climate change, but there are no effective institutions of global governance and global law to address these issues.

We cannot, as museum practitioners, simply dismiss these issues as someone else's problems, as they are about our individual and collective well-being. For museums to claim intellectual neutrality for fear of espousing values is nonsense. To sit on the sidelines is to embrace the status quo, and the status quo is increasingly perilous. A summary point is in order here. All of these issues and mega-uncertainties are not separate problems, despite our fondness for reductionism, as all of them "interact within two gigantic, complex, adaptive systems: the biosphere and the human socio-economic system." Embedded in this complexity lies what has been called "the human predicament."[20]

Sleepwalking into the future

John Greer, an ecological historian, summed up the human predicament this way:

> Most ordinary people in the industrial world . . . are sleepwalking through one of history's great transitions. The issues that concern them are still defined entirely by the calculus of *abundance* . . . It has not yet entered their darkest dreams that they need to worry about access to such basic necessities as food . . . or the fate of local economies and communities shredded by decades of malign neglect, or the rise of serious threats to the survival of constitutional government and the rule of law.[21]

Museums

Greer's description of "sleepwalking" is provocative, and the museum community is no exception. In a 2013 article for *Muse* magazine, John Grimes, a veteran museum practitioner, surveyed 55 executive directors of Canadian museums about what changes could dramatically reconfigure the sector. The major external threats are believed to be the reduction or elimination of government funding; competition for private sector donations; competition for audiences; and an insufficient or decreasing level of public interest in arts and culture.[22] Must we accept that these are truly the priorities of Canadian museums at this point in history – more money and bigger audiences? Doesn't the contrast between the demand for more money and the declining public interest signal the need to rethink the status quo?

There is another example of sleepwalking from the US that was described "as a convening of the gods" to discuss the "Future of the Museum," and it involved the heads of the Metropolitan Museum of Art, the Getty Trust, and the Boston Museum of Fine Arts.[23] I watched the webcast of this event where the discussion of collections predominated, with some attention paid to exhibitions and building expansions. There was no mention of any of the issues discussed here, and I can only say that the lack of foresight among these museum directors was astounding – not to mention their privileged insularity. If these are the "gods" of the museum world, we mortal museum workers are indeed in trouble.

The museum community cannot be singled out for blame, however, as the majority of government, corporate, and university leaders are also sleepwalking into the future – refusing to admit the existence of the problems and uncertainties mentioned earlier. Nor are the many boards governing the business community open to such inconvenient truths. According to a survey by McKinsey & Company, only about 30% of executives say their companies are actively managing sustainability and embedding it in their business practices.[24] What do you suppose that number would be for museums?

How might museums contribute to a brighter future?

Museums may not be able to contribute to the resolution of many of our global problems, but museums are in a position to invent a new future for themselves and their communities. Museums could at least help create an image of a desirable future – the essential first step in its realization. I cannot emphasize enough that the sustainability of museums cannot be separated from the sustainability of the biosphere. By biosphere I mean the global ecological system integrating all living beings and their relationships. An ecological metaphor is useful here, as ecology is about the relationships between organisms and their environments – dependent, independent, and interdependent relationships. I suggest that in the process of overlooking the meaning of interdependence, museums continue to contribute to their own marginalization. Forging an ecology of museums is long overdue – an ecology that recognizes that a broad web of societal relationships is the only way for museums to sustain themselves.

This is the harbinger of a new future for museums. Museums of all kinds are untapped and untested sources of ideas and knowledge, and are ideally placed to foster individual and community participation in the quest for greater awareness and workable solutions to our global problems. As deeply trusted, social institutions in civil society, museums are essential in fostering public support of decisive and timely action to address our human predicament.

Making choices

How, then, might museums make meaningful choices and contributions in light of these global challenges? We must first begin by dealing with our denial, and there are at least three kinds, including existential denial – as in "there's no problem, it's not happening." Or consequential denial, as in "it doesn't really matter – there are more important concerns." Or third, fatalistic denial, as in "there's nothing I can do about it anyway."[25] Or perhaps most of us are simply sleepwalking into the future, in the unthinking "me and now" mode. None of these reactions, however, will contribute to learning and adapting.

Fundamental institutional change is also required in all other organizations, especially those institutions that educate, yet fail to inform people how the world actually works – thereby perpetuating a variety of misperceptions.[26] Education is a core mission of museums, but what sort of education is it? What the world needs are museums that provide cultural frameworks to identify, explore, and challenge the myths, perceptions, and misperceptions that threaten all of us – such as the myth that unlimited economic growth is essential to our well-being.[27]

Taking action

In considering what museums might actually do to become agents of change, I will describe six defining characteristics of museums, along with some ideas for taking action.[28] I am hoping that these suggestions will expand conventional museum practice and contribute to a greater museum presence in the world.

Museums are seed banks

My first defining characteristic of museums is that their collections are a time capsule of material diversity and, in this respect, museums are as valuable as seed banks. If seed banks are gene banks for the world's flora, then museums are tool, technology, and art banks – curating the most distinctive trait of our species – the ability to make tools and things of beauty. The record of material diversity contained in museum collections has a value akin to biodiversity, as destructive industrial technology is replaced with more adaptive solutions.

My suggestion for taking action is to embrace the idea that museums are unparalleled repositories of our material legacy. Museums could work together, for example, to inventory pre-fossil-fuel technology to assess what is adaptive and relevant to today's challenges. As the price of oil continues its inevitable rise, it will be essential to access this dormant knowledge and consider ways of reducing consumption with other forms of technology. Modernity has led to the loss of knowledge of culturally diverse, sustainable living practices that have guided our species for millennia, and museums curate that material record and the knowledge base.

I note that the American Museum of Natural History and the National Museum of Australia recently hosted a workshop called "Collecting the Future," and now a website, to address the question – "How can museums move beyond science education to address the physical, social, cultural and emotional dimensions of climate change – to help people re-imagine and reshape their lives in a profoundly altered world?"[29]

Museums embody diversity

My second defining characteristic of museums is that they embody diversity. Globalization is creating a stultifying degree of sameness throughout the world, and is undoing the natural and cultural diversity that underlies the resilience of our species. There are over 55,000 museums in the world and each one of them is unique, making the inherent diversity of museums a significant antidote to global homogenization.

My suggestion for taking action here is to protect and grow all aspects of your museum's diversity, as it is under threat. The current approach to museum governance is one example, with its emphasis on selecting corporate people as board members – hence the overwhelming museum preoccupation with finances and the marketplace.[30] Instead, reach farther and wider into your community and seek out those people with different and diverse values, perspectives, and local knowledge – including new networks of community relationships that are not marketplace driven.

Museums are the keepers of locality

My third defining characteristic of museums is that they are keepers of locality. Most citizens and experts who worry about ecological collapse see local communities as the key to intelligent adaptation. Wendell Berry, the poet/farmer, writes that "the real work of planet-saving will be small, humble and humbling," and that problem solving will require individuals, families, and communities.[31] There is no doubt that most of the world's museums are expressions of locality, and the familiarity and trust that museums enjoy are the building blocks of an intelligent future, especially as the need increases to seek ingenuity and solutions in communities.

My suggestion for taking action here is to meet with social and environmental organizations in your community and find out what these community leaders consider to be important. Be curious and expand your understanding of their issues and aspirations. I predict that you will encounter a vast solitude when you meet, waiting to be filled with creative and collaborative work. The trust that museums enjoy, and their relative wealth compared to many other non-profits, will go a long way in building group action and collective impact.

In a recent survey of 12 of the most successful non-profits in US history, the researchers concluded that "greatness has more to do with how nonprofits work *outside* the boundaries of their organizations than how they manage their own internal operations."[32] For example, consider hosting an exhibition or a fundraiser for an unrelated organization, such as Doctors Without Borders. In a manner which defies Western logic, giving will engender receiving, and receiving will engender giving.[33]

I note that the Children's Museum Pittsburgh has five non-profit partners housed in their museum, ranging from a child's advocacy group, to a radio production company devoted to youth literacy. All of them pay below market rents, and serve or interact with the museum's visitors.[34]

Museums are the bridge between the two cultures

My fourth defining characteristic of museums is that they are the bridge between the so-called two cultures – the sciences and the humanities.[35] Museums are one of few institutions equipped to bridge the divide between these two ways of looking at the world – a divide that continues to befuddle our understanding of human presence on the earth. The purpose here is to explore the possibility of museums becoming the meeting place for the two cultures that is currently lacking.

My suggestion for taking action here is for all museums to link nature and culture in their work, whether or not they are natural history or science museums. Why can't museums focus on critical scientific and cultural issues which are "engaging and relevant to the public's daily lives and civic responsibilities?"[36] The Manitoba Museum is breaking new ground in this respect with their exhibition *Lake Winnipeg: Shared Solutions*. With Lake Winnipeg thought to be the most threatened lake in the world, this museum has partnered with 10 organizations to create a simulation that allows visitors to explore the tough questions that affect the Lake's health, make choices, and see the results of their actions.[37] Society is crying out for this sort of leadership from its public institutions.

Museums bear witness

My fifth defining characteristic of museums is that they bear witness. All museums specialize in assembling evidence based on knowledge, experience, and belief, and in making things known – the meaning of bearing witness. It is puzzling that so fundamental a museum trait is languishing, obscured by the pressures of the marketplace and the apparent timidity of museums.

My suggestion for taking action here is for museums to become intellectual activists and begin to address the vexing issues of our time. Intellectual activism means activities which do not necessarily create new knowledge, but make existing knowledge more accessible, understandable, and useful to others.[38] You already know that one of the most vexing issues is climate change. It has been noted that the public debate around climate change in the US is no longer about science, but about values, culture, and ideology.[39] Climate change is now part of the so-called culture wars in the US, along with other "cultural" issues such as abortion and evolution.

I suggest that this may also be true in Canada – note the federal government's single-minded emphasis on tar sands development. If you oppose it, you are against Canada's well-being. What we actually need, rather than conservative economic ideology, is a thoughtful societal debate focused on the full range of the technical and social dimensions of climate change. Museums are grounded in a sense of place, committed to stewardship, and universally respected, and can readily serve as the vital bridge between science and the public interest by initiating and hosting this dialogue.

Because of these characteristics – sense of place, stewardship, and societal respect, museums are also ideally placed to address many other issues of intense public concern. I note that Touchstones Nelson, the Museum of Art and History in Nelson, British Columbia (Canada), developed *Good Medicine* – an exhibition that explores both the development and the decline of health services in their community, including a public forum on the "Social Determinants of Health."[40]

Museums are free to choose and act

The sixth and last defining characteristic of museums is that they are potentially one of the most free work environments on the planet, and the scope for creativity and initiative should be just about limitless in a well-run museum. There are very few other workplaces which offer more opportunities for thinking and acting in ways that can blend personal satisfaction and growth with organizational goals.

My suggestion for taking action is to cultivate your personal agency. By personal agency, I mean the capacity of individual museum workers, not just their leaders and managers, to take action in the world.[41] I trust that each of you is insightful and motivated by concerns beyond the museum, and possess personal values that guide your everyday life. Yet, many people shy away from expressing their values and assuming their personal agency – for fear of losing their job or their friends. I think that this fear is exaggerated. So rock the boat, fly under the radar, and do what you need to do if you feel that something is important and needs to be addressed. In doing so, it will be better to ask for forgiveness, not approval. I note the recent formation of the Social Justice Alliance for Museums in the UK, whose hope is that members of the Alliance will find ways to work together in the pursuit of social justice, and to support each other's efforts.[42]

These six defining characteristics are opportunities for museums to become forces for good. What actions you decide to pursue can be as modest and pragmatic as you wish. The question is this – can museums finally subordinate themselves to concerns that are larger than their own? If they do, museums will, of necessity, become more "reality-based," and by this I mean becoming more involved in the broader world, embracing a sense of urgency, and seeing things as they *really* are in terms of the challenges to our well-being.[43]

Conclusions

"There is no justification for the permanent destruction of the world," noted Wendell Berry, and yet that is exactly what we are doing.[44] A fundamental question, as the destruction proceeds, is the fate of our social and cultural enterprise – will it diminish or wither away along with "every last lump of coal; every last tree, and every last ton of tar sands?"[45] Furthermore, what is the role of museums in charting a path to sustainability that will preserve and use our irreplaceable cultural legacy? Like it or not, this question lies at the heart of contemporary museum governance and management.

In considering the role of museums in charting a path to sustainability, I want to leave you with three questions to ponder:

1. Why do we believe that museums may abstain from addressing societal needs and aspirations and be absolved of greater accountability, especially at this time of extraordinary societal upheaval?
2. What is your museum's higher calling – meaning the public value you wish to contribute to your community and the world?
3. When you think about your own museum, where does it sit on the continuum from internally focused to externally mindful?

Despite all that I have said, I remain enduringly optimistic about museums as vital social institutions. I am still optimistic because museums have existed for centuries, unlike the vast majority of corporations. Museums have always had some sort of "adaptive intuition" (I don't know what else to call it) – to reinvent and transform themselves, however slowly and unconsciously. Museums have evolved through time, from the elite collections of imperial dominance, to educational institutions for the public, and now to the museum as "mall" and appendage of consumer society.[46]

This historical trajectory is the source of my optimism – that is, the ability of museums to learn and adapt as circumstances require. The museum as mall is the latest chapter in this long trajectory and embodies the dead end of materialism – overly concerned with consumption and leisure entertainment. The museum's next iteration must now be defined, and I submit that the agenda is crystal clear and must be grounded in providing substantive and sustained public benefit.

In conclusion, museums are essential, because they are organizations "whose purpose is their meaning."[47] The meaning and purpose of museums are now in need of urgent redefinition, based on deep listening and responding to the issues and challenges that confront our world. This is the work that *really* needs to be done.

Acknowledgements

I am grateful to a number of colleagues who generously read earlier drafts of this keynote address and provided invaluable comments and guidance, including Kevin Coffee, Joanne DiCosimo, Des Griffin, Bruce Keith, Emlyn Koster, Bart Robinson,

Richard Sandell, and Marjorie Schwarzer. I also want to thank the Fellows of the Canadian Museums Association, particularly Joanne DiCosimo and Sharilyn Ingram, for their interest, support, and the invitation to speak.

Notes

1 N. Postman, "Museum as Dialogue," *Museum News* (69/5), 1990, 55–58.
2 P. Hawken, Commencement Address, University of Portland, Portland, Oregon USA May 3, 2009.
3 E. Steinberg (ed.), *The Pocket Pema Chodron*, Boston and London: Shambala Publications, Inc., 2008, p. 136.
4 F. Capra, *The Web of Life*, New York: Anchor Doubleday, 1997, pp. 29–30.
5 O. Scharmer and K. Kaufer, *Leading from the Emerging Future: From Ego-System to Eco-System Economies*, San Francisco: Berrett-Koehler Publishers, Inc., 2013, p.1.
6 P.R. Ehrlich and A.H. Ehrlich. "Can a Collapse of Global Civilization Be Avoided?" *Proceedings of the Royal Society* B, 280: 20122845, 2013, p. 6. Available online: http://rspb. royalsocietypublishing.org/content/280/1754/20122845.full.pdf+html. See also Nafeez Ahmed, "NASA-funded study: industrial civilisation headed for 'irreversible collapse'?" March, 2014. Available online: http://www.theguardian.com/environment/earth-insight/ 2014/mar/14/nasa-civilisation-irreversible-collapse-study-scientists.
7 Ehrlich and Ehrlich, "Can a Collapse of Global Civilization Be Avoided?" p. 1.
8 Ehrlich and Ehrlich, "Can a Collapse of Global Civilization Be Avoided?" p. 1.
9 For fisheries, see World Wildlife Fund – Threats/Overfishing. Available online: http:// worldwildlife.org/threats/overfishing. For deforestation, see World Preservation Foun dation – Deforestation Statistics. Available online: http://www.worldpreservation foundation.org/blog/news/deforestation-statistics/#.UxZH67mYZKo.
10 Scharmer and Kaufer, *Leading from the Emerging Future*, p. 4.
11 "Tree Bark Shows Global Spread of Toxic Chemicals." Available online: http://www. voanews.com/content/tree_bark_shows_global_spread_of_toxic_chemicals/1622579. html.
12 J. Romm, "Into the Valley of Death Rode the 600, Into the Valley of 400 PPM Rode the 7 Billion." May 5, 2013 at 12:34 pm. Available online: http://thinkprogress.org/author/joe/.
13 Ehrlich and Ehrlich, "Can a collapse of global civilization be avoided?," p. 3.
14 E. May. "Canada is Missing Out on Global Clean-Tech Revolution." Monday, August 12, 2013, in *Articles by Elizabeth*. Available online at HTTP: http://elizabethmaymp.ca/ news/publications/articles/2013/08/12/canada-is-missing-out-on-global-clean-tech-revolution/.
15 M. Marien, "12 Mega-Uncertainties for the Decades Ahead," January 16, 2013. Revised and expanded version for GlobalForesightBooks Update (initial draft, 6/4/12), p. 1. Available online: http://www.globalforesightbooks.org/gfb-updates.html.
16 Marien, "12 Mega-Uncertainties for the Decades Ahead," pp. 1–4.
17 J. Confino, "Business Leaders in Davos Keen to Mainstream Circular Economy," *Guardian Professional*, Monday 27 January 2014 14.36 GMT. Available online: http://www. theguardian.com/sustainable-business/business-leaders-circular-economy-mainstream-.
18 T. Frey, "Two Billion Jobs to Disappear by 2030," The Futurist, World Future Society. Available online: http://www.wfs.org/futurist/2013-issues-futurist/september-october-2013-vol- 47-no-5/top-10-disappearing-futures/disap-2.
19 T.B. Edsall, "Capitalism vs. Democracy," *The Opinion Pages*, Contributing Op-Ed Writer, JAN. 28, 2014. Available online at HTTP: http://www.nytimes.com/2014/01/29/opinion/ capitalism-vs-democracy.html?_r=0.
20 Ehrlich and Ehrlich, "Can a Collapse of Global Civilization Be Avoided?," p. 2.
21 J.M. Greer, *The Wealth of Nature*, Gabriola Island, Canada: New Society Publishers, 2011, p. 239.

22 J.R. Grimes, "Emerging Trends in the Canadian Arts and Culture Sector," *Muse*, May/June, 2013, p. 36.

23 Boston Athenaeum, "The Future of the Museum – The Public." Available online: http://tv.hbgroupinc.com/boston_athenaeum_live?sid=37970. See also http://wgbhnews.org/post/state-arts-museum-heads-discuss-future.

24 McKinsey & Company, "How Companies Manage Sustainability: McKinsey Global Survey Results," March, 2010. Available online: http://www.mckinsey.com/insights/sustainability/how_companies_manage_sustainability_mckinsey_global_survey_results.

25 Ken Steele, "Adjust Your Sails or be Blown Off Course: Emerging Trends in Canadian PSE," 2008. Available online: http://www1.uwindsor.ca/sem/sites/www.uwindsor.ca.sem/files/adjust-your-sails.pdf, p. 22.

26 Ehrlich and Ehrlich, "Can a Collapse of Global Civilization Be Avoided?," p. 5.

27 R. Nelson, personal communication, October 1, 2010.

28 Janes, *Museums in a Troubled World: Renewal, Irrelevance or Collapse?* London and New York: Routledge, pp. 178–182.

29 "Collecting the Future: Museums, Communities and Climate Change." Available online: http://www.amnh.org/our-research/anthropology/news-events/collecting-the-future. See also the website – http://www.amnh.org/our-research/anthropology/projects/museums-and-climate-change-network.

30 Janes, *Museums in a Troubled World: Renewal Irrelevance or Collapse?*, pp. 94–120.

31 W. Berry, *Sex, Economy, Freedom and Community*, New York and San Francisco: Pantheon Books, 1992, p. 24.

32 L.R. Crutchfield and H.M. Grant, *Forces for Good: The Six Practices of High-Impact Nonprofits*, San Francisco: Jossey-Bass, 2008, p. 19.

33 Deepak Chopra, *The Seven Laws of Spiritual Success*, San Rafael, CA: Amber-Allen Publishing, 1994, p. 29.

34 A. Bergeron and B. Tuttle, *Magnetic: The Art and Science of Engagement*, Washington D.C.: The AAM Press, 2013, p. 128.

35 C.P. Snow, *The Two Cultures: And a Second Look*, New York: Cambridge University Press, 1959 and 1963.

36 Mission Statement of the Field Museum. Available online at <http://www.fieldmuseum.org/museum_info/mission_statement.htm> (accessed 17 July 2008).

37 The Manitoba Museum. Lake Winnipeg: Shared Solutions. Available online: http://www.manitobamuseum.ca/main/science-gallery/lake-winnipeg-shared-solutions/.

38 R. Gross, *The Independent Scholar's Handbook*, Berkeley: Ten Speed Press, 1993, pp. 164–170. Available online at http://www.sfu.ca/independentscholars/ISbook.pdf.

39 A.J. Hoffman, "Climate Science as Culture War," *Stanford Social Innovation Review*, Fall, 2012. Available online: http://www.ssireview.org/articles/entry/climate_science_as_culture_war?utm_source=Enews&utm_medium=email&utm_content=1&utm_campaign=hoffman>.

40 Touchstones Nelson – Museum of Art and History. *Good Medicine: Nelson's Healthcare History.* Available online: http://www.touchstonesnelson.ca/exhibitions/index.php#galleryB.

41 J.A. Davis, "Putting Museum Studies to Work," *Museum Management and Curatorship*, (26) 5, December, 2011, pp. 459–479.

42 Social Justice Alliance for Museums. See: http://sjam.org/.

43 J. H. Kunstler, *The Long Emergency: Surviving the End of Oil, Climate Change, and Other Converging Catastrophes of the Twenty-First Century*, New York: Grove Press, 2005, p. 324.

44 Moyers and Company, "Wendell Berry on his Hopes for Humanity." Interview with Wendell Berry, October 4, 2013. Available online at: billmoyers.com/segment/wendell-berry-on-his-hopes-for-humanity.

45 Heinberg, *The End of Growth*, p. 282.

46 A. Gopnik, "The Mindful Museum," *The Walrus* (4, June), 2007, p. 89. This article is adapted from the 2006 Holtby Lecture at the Royal Ontario Museum in Toronto, Canada.

47 C. Handy, *The Age of Paradox*, Boston: Harvard Business School Press, 1994, p. 183.

EPILOGUE

In reflecting on the writing assembled here, I wish to be seen as a defender of the natural world and all who are vulnerable in this changing world – notably grandchildren, their children's children, and Indigenous peoples. The four parts in this book – "Other Voices," "Creative Destruction," "Museums without Borders," and "Dangerous Times" – reflect the cumulative thought and action that underlie this aspiration. The various themes reflected in my writing are also characteristic of the natural world and its original inhabitants, including diversity, complexity, autonomy, paradox, interconnectedness, self-organization, non-linearity, and sustainability. As part of this perspective, I acknowledge my "ecological self" – the wider sense of identity that emerges when one's self-interest includes the natural world (Macy and Johnstone 2012: 94).

These themes have emerged throughout my museum work and have inspired my efforts to understand the meaning and purpose of museum work within the web of life. My personal involvement in wilderness living and farming has also been a source of inspiration. Fritjof Capra, the physicist and ecologist, noted that "Reconnecting with the web of life means building and nurturing sustainable communities in which we can satisfy our needs and aspirations without diminishing the chances of future generations" (Capra 1996: 297). In the words of my friend and colleague, Joy Davis (2011: 459–479), I have also been "cultivating my personal agency" – my capacity to take action in the world motivated by concerns beyond museum work *per se*, including the personal values that guide my life.

It is now imperative that global society, including all museum workers, reconnect with the web of life by exercising their personal and organizational agency. As Neil Postman (1990: 58) wrote, and is quoted in the Epigraph of this book, "a museum must be an argument with its society . . . a good museum always will direct attention to what is difficult and even painful to contemplate." My growing concern over the

FIGURE 13 The Phipps Conservatory and Botanical Garden (Pittsburgh, US) is one of the "greenest" facilities in the world. The Phipps' mission is . . . to advance sustainability and promote human and environmental well-being through action and research. Courtesy of the Phipps Conservatory and Botanical Garden.

past decade originates in the absence of any substantive arguments by the museum community, as no amount of sophisticated audience research, marketing prowess, or the search for popularity will mitigate the positive feedback loops of climate change or the consequences of other critical issues. In the absence of persuasive arguments confronting our distracted and self-absorbed society, it is difficult to be optimistic about successfully adapting to our socio-environmental challenges.

The unavoidable future

The writings selected for this book are an attempt to encourage museum workers to argue with their colleagues and society, be it in support of Indigenous peoples and the environment, or in opposition to corporate malfeasance in all its guises – the issues and opportunities are legion. The museum's "argument with society" is now imperative, as global crises are writ large and civilization must confront the greatest threat in the history of our species – climate disruption and change. The questions remain: Why aren't more museums actively engaged in promoting dialogue, awareness, and solutions to the consequences of climate change, above and beyond the "neutral" stance of providing expert information? Why are museums, knowledge-based in purpose and practice, accepting funding from the corporations and individuals who deny climate change and are thus compounding its consequences? Admittedly, taking action is laden with difficulties, as at least seven categories of psychological barriers, or "dragons of inaction" have been identified (Gifford 2011: 290). Nevertheless, museum workers have a vital role in working with scientists, technical experts, and policy makers to overcome these barriers.

It appears, however, that the majority of museums require rethinking their purpose and values in order to acknowledge the reality of climate change, as well as many other global issues. To wit, climate change is not ideological – it is science-based and catastrophic consequences are now unfolding that require immediate and collective attention. To hide behind the notion of a museum's so-called neutrality is tantamount to climate change denial, besides being myopic and unethical (Janes 2009: 59).

Perhaps the museum's pretence of neutrality is why corporations and plutocrats are increasingly turning to museums to "green wash" their malfeasance. Happily, society's passivity about the threat of climate change, as well as other pressing issues, is moving beyond denial into collective action. One need only observe the growing opposition to oil and gas pipeline construction in Canada and the US to see that the ground is now shifting (Dirty Oil Sands 2014). But if the ground is shifting for mainstream museum practitioners, consultants, and academics, it is barely perceptible.

Instead, collective action is emerging from outside the museum community, as exemplified by the Natural History Museum (NHM) in New York (US) – an initiative of the arts collective Not An Alternative (Natural History Museum 2015a). The NHM is a new museum that offers exhibitions, educational workshops, and public programming that highlight the social and political forces that shape nature – unlike mainstream natural history museums (Katz 2014). The NHM was a major exhibitor at the 2015 American Alliance of Museums Conference in Atlanta, Georgia (US). In the words of Beka Economopoulos (2014), an NHM spokesperson:

> This is a great opportunity for wide exposure to present a critique of the increasing corporatization of museums, the embedding of the fossil-fuel industry in spaces that communicate science, and the greenwashing museums provide to oil moguls and funders of junk science like David Koch.

Lest museums claim the moral high ground of authoritative neutrality, the NHM notes that climate change denier billionaire David H. Koch is a trustee of the American Museum of Natural History (New York) and on the advisory board of the Smithsonian National Museum of Natural History (Washington, DC). Mr. Koch is alleged to be exerting influence on programming at these public institutions, causing omissions or misrepresentations of climate science and global warming (Natural History Museum 2015b). This is tragic – that the integrity of

FIGURE 14 The Natural History Museum's mobile museum – a 15-passenger tour, expedition, and action bus. Courtesy of the Natural History Museum.

these venerable institutions and their science could be jeopardized in this allegedly venal manner. Surely museums are thoughtful enough to avoid these ethical fire-storms, and not risk squandering the public trust that they have been gifted. What will it take for museums to embrace this realization? What will be required to move the corporatist elephant out of the museum board room?

Economopoulos' phrase (above) concerning "the increasing corporatization of museums" is indeed familiar. As I have noted throughout this book, museums of all sizes are suffering from this affliction, not just the big institutions. But why aren't museum boards and staff pushing back? This persistent silence makes the prognosis for significant and thoughtful change in the global museum community uncertain, as the majority of museum workers persist in their preoccupation with popularity, money, and internal fiddling.

Some museum associations are attuned to the need for their members to become more socially responsible, most notably the United Kingdom's Museums Association (Museums Association 2009) and the American Alliance of Museums (American Alliance of Museums 2015a, 2015b). In practice, however, the museum profession (practitioners, academics, consultants, students, and their associations) continues to play at the margins of authentic engagement in societal issues and aspirations. Museums and their workers remain transfixed with fear, wonder, or apathy (perhaps all three), apparently hoping that government and business will mitigate or resolve the consequences of climate disruption and other pressing issues – leaving them above the fray to pursue their internal agendas while apparently unconscious of their obligations to intergenerational equity.[1]

Change the story

I noted earlier that museums exist to tell stories – about people, communities, nations, and civilizations – but who is telling the story of the early twenty-first century with all of its global issues and their threatening consequences? Corporations and governments are, but it is the story of ceaseless economic growth. Their rhetoric is agonizingly familiar and destructive – time is money; consumption means happiness; corporations create wealth and governments consume it; economic inequality is unavoidable; rampant environmental damage is regrettable, and humans are individualistic competitors (Korten 2014: 2–3). Even though many of us are acutely aware that this story is corrupt, false, and lethal, it is the predominant story in our public lives and it defines our common future. It is the only story we hear and all of us have accepted it in one way or another.

Humanity needs a new story; museums need a new story – a completely new story (Korten 2014). Joanna Macy, a Buddhist scholar and activist, calls this story the Great Turning – "the transition from a doomed economy of industrial growth to a life-sustaining society committed to the recovery of our world" (Macy and Johnstone 2012: 26). It is incumbent on all museums to help envision and create this new narrative in tandem with their communities, and then deliver this story using their unique skills and perspectives. This new story must be grounded in the web of life and boldly committed to building sustainable communities – recognizing that the connection between individuals, communities, and nature is the key to our collective well-being. This new narrative must also recognize that the purpose of human institutions, including museums, is "to provide all people with the opportunity to make a healthy, meaningful living in a balanced, co-productive relationship with Earth's community of life" (Korten 2014: 4).

The responsibility of individual museum workers to foster this new narrative is so plainly obvious that their reluctance to do so eludes me. I am hoping that some of the experiences recounted in this book will be helpful, as the challenges and opportunities for progressive museum practice are limited only by one's imagination. For example, First Nations are still seeking the repatriation of their patrimony in the face of museum intransigence; museum leadership remains grounded in unimaginative hierarchy; corporatism continues its amoral march into museum board rooms; museums remain blissfully impervious or in denial of their self-inflicted challenges; and the gulf between museum studies and practice is still dangerously wide. This separation between academics and practitioners is particularly vexing, as museum studies are a ready source of ideas and approaches for fostering progressive museums – ranging from research into improving organizational dynamics, to research confirming that objects and memories create well-being.

It would seem that our collective reluctance to move beyond the familiar has something to do with the psychic discomfort that it creates. Allowing this discomfort to limit the vision and purpose of museums at this point in history is potentially disastrous – perhaps spelling the decline or collapse of museums in a world that can no longer afford irrelevance. The Western world's citizen-based democracy is dependent upon participation, and to participate is to be permanently uncomfortable – psychically (Saul 1995: 190). Museums must embrace this discomfort and the uncertainty and nonconformity that it requires, in order to become the authentic participants they are equipped to be, and to make good on their singular combination of historical consciousness, sense of place, and public accessibility.

In the absence of the psychic discomfort that accompanies increased mindfulness and participation, there is only the imprisonment of tradition, inner comfort, and delusion. Museums are long-lived organizations and they have yet to succumb to these temptations in their millennia of existence; nor should they now. There is no doubt that museums are key intellectual and civic resources in this time of profound social and environmental change, and that their participation is now vital. Urgency, however, has the upper hand.

Note

1 Intergenerational equity is the concept that humans hold the Earth in common with other members of the present generation, as well as with other generations both past and future. It means that we inherit the Earth from previous generations and have an obligation to pass it on in reasonable condition to future generations. See: "Intergenerational Equity." Available online: http://www.uow.edu.au/~sharonb/STS300/equity/meaning/integen.html.

References

American Alliance of Museums (2015a) "Addressing Human and Social Needs through Museum Programs and Operations." Annual Meeting of the American Alliance of Museums, Georgia World Congress, April 26, 2015. Available online: http://www.aam-us.org/events/annual-meeting/program/sessions-and-events?ID=2793&utm_source=Magnet Mail&utm_medium=Email&utm_campaign=Time%20is%20Running%20Out%20on%20the%20Lowest%20Rate%20for%20Annual%20Meeting%21

American Alliance of Museums (2015b) "The Social Value of Museums: Inspiring Change." American Alliance of Museums 2015 Annual Meeting Theme. Available online: http://www.aam-us.org/events/annual-meeting/2015-annual-meeting-theme.

Capra, F. (1996) *The Web of Life: A New Scientific Understanding of Living Systems*. New York: Anchor Books.

Davis, J.A. (2011) "Putting Museum Studies to Work." *Museum Management and Curatorship*, (26) 5, 459–479.

Dirty Oil Sands (2014) Dirty Oil Sands is a network of over 50 non-profit environmental organizations, First Nations, community groups, and landowners working to stop the expansion of the tar sands and promote the transition to a clean energy economy. Available online: http://www.dirtyoilsands.org/about-2/. See also: http://environmentaldefence.ca/blog/ugly-truth-about-energy-east-%E2%80%93-north-america%E2%80%99s-largest-proposed-tar-sands-pipeline.

Economopoulos, B. (2014) "The Natural History Museum." Email communication (26 February).

Gifford, R. (2011) "The Dragons of Inaction: Psychological Barriers that Limit Climate Change Mitigation and Adaptation." *American Psychologist*, 66 (4), May–June, 290–302.

Janes, R.R. (2009) *Museums in a Troubled World: Renewal, Irrelevance or Collapse?* London and New York: Routledge.

Katz, M.M. (2014) "Artists Take on Corporate Influence in Natural History Museums." *Creative Time Reports*, 2 September. Available online: http://creativetimereports.org/2014/09/02/not-an-alternative-natural-history-museum/.

Korten, D. (2014) "Change the Story, Change the Future: A Living Economy for a Living Earth." Presentation at the Praxis Peace Institute Conference, San Francisco, California, 7 October 7. Available online: http://livingeconomiesforum.org/sites/files/pdfs/David%20Korten%20Praxis%20Peace%20Oct%207%202014%20for%20distribution.pdf.

Macy, J. and Johnstone, C. (2012) *Active Hope: How to Face the Mess We're in without Going Crazy*. Novato, CA: New World Library.

Museums Association (2009) *Sustainability and Museums: Report on Consultation*. London: Museums Association. Available online: http://www.museumsassociation.org/download?id=17944. See also the "Sustainability Campaign," Museums Association. Available online: http://www.museumsassociation.org/campaigns/sustainability/sustainability-report.

Natural History Museum (2015a) "An Open Letter to Museums from Members of the Scientific Community." Available online: http://thenaturalhistorymuseum.org/open-letter-to-museums-from-scientists/.

Natural History Museum (2015b) "Mission, Advisory Board, and About the Natural History Museum." Available online: http://thenaturalhistorymuseum.org/about/.

Postman, N. (1990) "Museum as Dialogue." *Museum News*, (69), 5, September/October, 58.

Saul, J.R. (1995) *The Unconscious Civilization*. Concord, Canada: House of Anansi Press.

BIBLIOGRAPHY OF
ROBERT R. JANES

Books

1974 *The Archaeology of Fort Alexander, NWT.* Report of the Environmental-Social Committee, Northern Pipelines, Task Force on Northern Development, Ottawa. Report No. 74-34, 108 pp.

1983 *Archaeological Ethnography among Mackenzie Basin Dene.* The Arctic Institute of North America Technical Paper No. 28, Calgary, 124 pp.

1991 *Preserving Diversity: Ethnoarchaeological Perspectives on Culture Change in the Western Canadian Subarctic.* New York: Garland Publishing Inc., 224 pp.

1995 *Museums and the Paradox of Change.* Calgary: Glenbow Museum Publishing, 193 pp.

1997 *Museums and the Paradox of Change* (2nd edition). Calgary: Glenbow Museum and the University of Calgary Press, 280 pp.

2009 *Museums in a Troubled World: Renewal, Irrelevance or Collapse?* London and New York: Routledge, 208 pp. (2nd printing).

2012 *Museums in a Troubled World: Renewal, Irrelevance or Collapse?* Taipei, Taiwan: Farterng Culture Co. Ltd. (translated into Traditional Chinese Characters), 208 pp.

2012 *Museums in a Troubled World: Renewal, Irrelevance or Collapse?* Taipei, Taiwan: Farterng Culture Co. Ltd. (translated into Simplified Chinese Characters), 204 pp.

2013 *Museums and the Paradox of Change* (3rd edition). London and New York: Routledge, 412 pp.

2016 *Museums without Borders: Selected Writings of Robert R. Janes.* London and New York: Routledge.

Edited books, collections and occasional papers

1983 Janes, Robert R. and Charles D. Arnold (Co-editors). Selected Papers of the Symposium on Northern Archaeology, Canadian Archaeological Association. *Musk-ox,* No. 33, Winter, 93 pp.

1985 Patterson, Margaret J., Charles D. Arnold and Robert R. Janes (Co-editors). Collected Papers on the Human History of the Northwest Territories. *Occasional Papers of the Prince of Wales Northern Heritage Centre,* No. 1, Yellowknife, NWT, 167 pp.

1986 Bielawski, Ellen, Carolyn Kobelka and Robert R. Janes (Co-editors). Thule Pioneers, by C.D. Arnold. *Occasional Papers of the Prince of Wales Northern Heritage Centre*, No. 2, Yellowknife, NWT, 110 pp.

1996 Janes, Robert R. (Editor for Anthropology). *Sir John Franklin's Journals and Correspondence: The First Arctic Land Expedition, 1819–1822*. Edited by Richard C. Davis. Toronto: The Champlain Society, 463 pp.

2005 Janes, Robert R. and Gerald T. Conaty (Co-editors). *Looking Reality in the Eye: Museums and Social Responsibility*. Calgary: The Museums Association of Saskatchewan and the University of Calgary Press, 196 pp. (3rd printing).

2007 Sandell, Richard and Robert R. Janes (Co-editors). *Museum Management and Marketing*. London and New York: Routledge, 420 pp. (4th printing).

Chapters in books

1977 Janes, R.R. and J.H. Kelley. Observations on Crisis Cult Activities in the Mackenzie Basin. In *Prehistory of the North American Sub-Arctic, The Athapaskan Question*. Proceedings of the Ninth Annual Chacmool Conference, Archaeological Association of the University of Calgary, Calgary, pp. 153–164.

1983 Museums in the North. In *Planning Our Museums*, edited by Barry Lord and Gail Dexter Lord, Museums Assistance Programme, National Museums of Canada, Ottawa, pp. 277–284.

1989 The Organization of Household Activities at a Contemporary Dene Hunting Camp – Ten Years in Retrospect. In *Households and Communities: Proceedings of the 21st Annual Chacmool Conference*, Calgary: Archaeological Association of the University of Calgary, pp. 517–524.

1996 Concevoir pour l'avenir: les changements, en matière d'organisation et de formation, au Glenbow Museum. In *Musées Gérer Autrement: Un Regard International*, edited by Jean-Michel Tobelem, Paris: La Documentation Française, pp. 161–170.

1997 Don't Lose Your Nerve: Museums and Organizational Change. In *Museums for the New Millennium*: Washington, DC: Center for Museum Studies, Smithsonian Institution in association with The American Association of Museums, pp. 81–96.

1998 Seven Years of Change and No End in Sight: Reflections from the Glenbow Museum. In *Cultural Organizations of the Future*, Colloquium Proceedings, edited by François Colbert, École des Hautes Etudes Commerciales de Montreal, Montreal, pp. 185–192.

1999 Embracing Organizational Change in Museums: A Work in Progress. In *Management in Museums*, edited by Kevin Moore, London and New Brunswick, NJ: The Athlone Press, pp. 7–27.

1999 Museums and Change: Don't Lose Your Nerve. In *Thinking about Museums*, Addresses from the Annual Meetings of the Association of Midwest Museums 1996–1998, St Louis, Missouri, pp. 7–27.

2004 Persistent Paradoxes. In *Reinventing the Museum: Historical and Contemporary Perspectives on the Paradigm Shift,* edited by Gail Anderson, Walnut Creek, CA: Altamira Press, pp. 375–394.

2007 Museums, Social Responsibility and the Future We Desire. In *Museum Revolutions*, edited by S. Knell, S. MacLeod and S. Watson, London and New York: Routledge, pp. 134–146.

2011 Museums and the End of Materialism. In *Redefining Ethics for the Twenty-First Century Museum*, edited by Janet Marstine, London and New York: Routledge, pp. 54–69.

2012 Museums, Corporatism and the Civil Society. In *Museum Studies: An Anthology of Texts,* edited by Bettina M. Carbonell, New York: John Wiley and Sons, pp. 549–561.

2012 The Mindful Museum. In *Reinventing the Museum: The Evolving Conversation on the Paradigm Shift* (2nd edition), edited by Gail Anderson, Lanham, MD: AltaMira Press, a division of Rowman & Littlefield. Publishers, pp. 508–520.

2015 Prologue. In *We Are Coming Home! Repatriation and the Restoration of Blackfoot Cultural Confidence*, edited by Gerald T. Conaty. Edmonton, Alberta, Canada: Athabasca University Press, pp. 3–20.

2015 The Blackfoot Repatriation: A Personal Epilogue. In *We Are Coming Home! Repatriation and the Restoration of Blackfoot Cultural Confidence*, edited by Gerald T. Conaty. Edmonton, Alberta, Canada: Athabasca University Press, pp. 241–262.

In press Museums and the Responsibility Gap. In *Museums as Sites of Historical Consciousness: Perspectives on Museum Theory and Practice in Canada*, edited by Viviane Gosselin and Phaedra Livingstone, Vancouver, British Columbia, Canada: University of British Columbia Press.

Refereed publications

1973 Indian and Eskimo Contact in Southern Keewatin: An Ethnohistorical Approach. *Ethnohistory*, Vol. 29, No. 1, pp. 39–54.

1974 Ethnoarchaeology and Contemporary Subarctic Hunters and Trappers: A Preliminary Proposal. *Napao*, Vol. 4, No. 2, pp. 7–11.

1974 Janes, R.R. and T.C. Losey. Recent Discoveries in Fur Trade Archaeology of Upper and Central Mackenzie River Regions. *Canadian Archaeological Association Bulletin*, No. 6, pp. 93–120.

1975 The Athapaskan and the Fur Trade: Observations from Archaeology and Ethnohistory. *The Western Canadian Journal of Anthropology*, Vol. V, Nos 3–4, pp. 159–186.

1982 Archaeology in the Northwest Territories: The Social Context. *Northern Perspectives*, Vol. 10, No. 6, pp. 5–10.

1982 The Preservation and Ethnohistory of a Frozen Historic Site in the Canadian Arctic. *Arctic*, Vol. 35, No. 3, pp. 358–385.

1983 Ethnoarchaeological Observations among the Willow Lake Dene, Northwest Territories, Canada. *Musk-ox*, No. 33, Winter, pp. 56–67.

1983 Janes, R.R. and C.D. Arnold. Public Archaeology in the Northwest Territories. *Musk-ox*, No. 33, Winter, pp. 42–48.

1989 An Ethnoarchaeological Model for the Identification of Prehistoric Tipi Remains in the Boreal Forest. *Arctic*, Vol. 42, No. 2, pp. 128–138.

1994 Beyond Strategic Planning: The Glenbow Example. *History News* (American Association for State and Local History), Vol. 49, No. 4, July/August, pp. 19–24.

1994 Solicited Dialogue on a Never Ending Story: Historical Developments in Canadian Archaeology and the Quest for Federal Heritage Legislation. *Canadian Journal of Archaeology*, Vol. 18, pp. 120–122.

1994 Personal, Academic and Institutional Perspectives on Museums and First Nations. *The Canadian Journal of Native Studies*, Vol. XIV, No. 1, pp. 147–156.

1995 Janes, R.R. and C.J. Simpson. Designing for the Future: Organizational Change at the Glenbow, Canada. *Midwest Museums Conference Annual Review, 1993–94*, Midwest Museums Conference, St Louis, Missouri, pp. 7–27.

1996 No pierda la serenidad: Los museos y el cambio organizativo. *Revista de Museologia*, No. 9, Madrid, Spain, pp. 10–17.

1997 Conaty, G.T. and R.R. Janes. Issues of Repatriation: A Canadian View. *European Review of Native American Studies* Vol. 11, no. 2, pp. 31–37.

1999 Seven Years of Change and No End in Sight: Reflections from the Glenbow Museum. *International Journal of Arts Management*, Vol. 1, No. 2, Winter, pp. 48–53.

2007 Museums, Corporatism and the Civil Society. *Curator*, Vol. 50, No. 2, pp. 219–237.

2010 The Mindful Museum. *Curator*, Vol. 53, No. 3, pp. 325–338.

2010 Museums and the Biosphere. *Tetradia Mouseiologias (Cahiers de Museologie)*, Vol. 7, pp. 4–13. (Translated into Greek).

2011 Museum Directors and Curators: Managers or Spectators? *Theoretical and Practical Issues of Management*, No. 2, February, pp. 93–103 (official journal of the International Scientific and Research Institute for Management Issues, Russian Federation – Translated into Russian).

2011 Museums and the Biosphere. *Museology Quarterly* (National Museum of Natural Science, Taiwan), Vol. 25, No. 4, pp. 5–15 (Translated into Chinese).

2012 Søndergaard, M.K. and R.R. Janes. What Are Museums For? – Revisiting 'Museums in a Troubled World', *Nordisk Museologi*, Vol. 1, pp. 20–34.

Notes and commentaries in referred journals

1976 Culture Contact in the 19th Century Mackenzie Basin, Canada. *Current Anthropology*, Vol. 17, No. 2, pp. 344–345.

1977 More on Culture Contact in the Mackenzie Basin, Canada. *Current Anthropology*, Vol. 18, No. 3, pp. 554–556.

1980 Comment on Archaeology and Development, by Daniel Miller. *Current Anthropology*, Vol. 10, No. 6, pp. 719–720.

1984 Remarks on the 1984 Presentation of the Smith-Wintemberg Award. *Canadian Journal of Archaeology*, Vol. 8, No. 1, pp. 1–2.

1985 Comment on Demographic Estimates in Archaeology: Contributions from Ethnoarchaeology on Mesoamerican Peasants, by Charles C. Kolb. *Current Anthropology*, Vol. 26, No. 5, pp. 593–594.

1989 Comment on Microdebitage Analyses and Cultural Site Formation Processes among Tipi Dwellers. *American Antiquity*, Vol. 54, No. 4, pp. 851–855.

1996 Comment on Power, Objects and a Voice for Anthropology, by Jonathan Haas. *Current Anthropology*, Vol. 37, Supplement, February, pp. 514–515.

2011 The Non-essence of Museums: A Conversation with Robert R. Janes. By Morten Karnøe Søndergaard. *Danske Museer*, Vol. 24, No. 6, December, pp. 14–15.

2011 Museums and the New Reality. *Museums and Social Issues*, Vol. 6, No. 2, Fall, pp. 137–146.

2014 Museums for All Seasons. *Museum Management and Curatorship*, Vol. 29, No. 5, pp. 403–411.

Book reviews

1982 Review of *Athapaskan Clothing and Related Objects in the Collections of Field Museum of Natural History*, by James W. Van Stone. *Fieldiana*, Anthropology, New Series, No. 4, 1981. In *Arctic*, Vol. 35, No. 2, pp. 340–341.

1983 Review of *Indians, Animals and the Fur Trade*, edited by Shepard Krech III. The University of Georgia Press, 1981. In *Arctic*, Vol. 36, No. 4, pp. 388–389.

1985 Review of *Tahltan Ethnoarchaeology*, by Sylvia Albright. Publication No. 15 of the Department of Archaeology, Simon Fraser University, 1984. In *The Canadian Journal of Archaeology*, Vol. 8, No. 2, pp. 164–166.

1986 Review of *The Franklin Era in Canadian Arctic History, 1845–1859*, by Patricia D. Sutherland. *National Museum of Man Mercury Series*, Archaeological Survey of Canada Paper No. 131, 1985. In *Arctic*, Vol. 39, No. 4, pp. 374–375.

1988 Review of *The Subarctic Indians and the Fur Trade*, by Colin C. Yerbury. The University of British Columbia Press, 1986. In *Ethnohistory*, Vol. 35, No. 2, pp. 204–206.

1989 Review of *The Report of the Chipp-Ikpikpuk River and Upper Meade River Oral History Project*, by Wendy H. Arundale and William S. Schneider. In *Arctic*, Vol. 42, No. 3, pp. 294–295.

1990 Review of *Ethnoarchaeological and Cultural Frontiers: Athapaskan, Algonquin and European Adaptations in the Central Subarctic*, by Hetty Jo Brumbach and Robert Jarvenpa. Peter Lang Publishing. Inc., 1989. In *Arctic Anthropology*, Vol. 27, No. 2, pp. 126–127.

2014 Review of *Magnetic: The Art and Science of Engagement*, by Anne Bergeron and Beth Tuttle. Washington, DC: American Alliance of Museums Press, 2013. In *Curator, The Museum Journal*, Vol. 57, No. 3, pp. 375–379.

Non-refereed publications

1975 Fort Alexander. *The Society for Historical Archaeology Newsletter*, Vol. 8, No. 2, pp. 39–40.

1977 An Introduction to the Territorial Central Museum. *Echoes*, No. 308, Autumn, pp. 25–32.

1978 The Dealy Island Archaeological Project – 1978. *The Calgary Archaeologist*, No. 6/7, pp. 15–17.

1979 Our Northern Heritage. Introduction to *Our Northern Heritage*. Department of Information, Government of the Northwest Territories Annual Report, Yellowknife, pp. 8–21.

1979 Fur Trading in the Mackenzie. *Northern Nights*, 10 October, p. 17.

1979 The Prince of Wales Northern Heritage Centre: The North's Newest Museum. *About Arts and Crafts*, Winter, pp. 2–5.

1982 Northern Museum Development: A View from the North. *Gazette* (former journal of the Canadian Museums Association), Vol. 15, No. 1, pp. 14–23.

1984 The Need for Arms-Length Heritage Councils. In *On Cultural Needs*, by Rene Lamothe, pp. 35–37. Department of Information, Government of the Northwest Territories, Yellowknife.

1984 Preserving the Northern Legacy: A Report from the Prince of Wales Northern Heritage Centre. *Fram: The Journal of Polar Studies*, Vol. 1, No. 2, pp. 695–706.

1985 Foreword. *Occasional Papers of the Prince of Wales Northern Heritage Centre*, No. 1, pp. 3–6.

1985 Janes, R.R. and J.D. Stewart. A Frozen Glimpse of British Exploration in the High Arctic. *Occasional Papers of the Prince of Wales Northern Heritage Centre*, No. 1, pp. 34–49.

1985 Harper, L. and R.R. Janes. An Enduring Legacy. *The Canadian Collector*, Vol. 20, No. 5, pp. 16–21.

1986 An Introduction to the Science Institute of the Northwest Territories. In *Education, Research: Information Systems and the North*. Proceedings of the 1986 Annual Meeting of the Association of Canadian Universities for Northern Studies, the Association of Canadian Universities for Northern Studies, Ottawa, pp. 72–75.

1987 Museum Ideology and Practice in Canada's Third World. *MUSE* (Journal of the Canadian Museums Association), Vol. IV, No. 4, pp. 33–39.

1988 Introduction to the *Occasional Papers of the Prince of Wales Northern Heritage Centre*, No. 3, Yellowknife, NWT, pp. 8–10.

1988 Vernacular Architecture at a Contemporary Dene Hunting Camp. *Society for the Study of Architecture in Canada Bulletin*, Vol. 13, No. 2, pp. 4–13.

1990 Foreword (with Martha A. Peever). In *Ron Moppett – Painting Nature with a Mirror* by Katharine Ylitalo. Glenbow Museum, Calgary, Alberta, p. i.

1990 Foreword (with Martha A. Peever) In *The Face of Dance – Yup'ik Eskimo Masks from Alaska* by Lynn Ager Wallen. Glenbow Museum, Calgary, Alberta, p. 4.

1991 Foreword (with Martha A. Peever). In *The Embodied Viewer* by Vera Lemecha. Glenbow Museum, Calgary, Alberta, p. 6.

1991 Foreword. In *Correspondences: Jack Shadbolt* by Patricia Ainslie. Glenbow Museum, Calgary, Alberta, p. 7.

1991 Introduction. In *Treasures of the Glenbow Museum* by Hugh A. Dempsey. Glenbow Museum, Calgary, Alberta, pp. 11–12.

1991 Janes, R.R. and M.A. Peever. Partnerships: Museums and Native Living Cultures. *Alberta Museums Review*, Vol. 17, No. 2, pp 14–16.

1993 Foreword. In *Reclaiming History – Ledger Drawings by the Assiniboine Artist Hongeeyeesa* by Valerie Robertson. Glenbow Museum, Calgary, Alberta, p. 7.

1993 We Must Make Some Major Changes. *Glenbow*, Vol. 12, No. 4, p. 3.

1993 Janes, R.R. and P. Ainslie. Glenbow Deaccessioning. *MUSE*, Vol. XI, No. 3, p. 4

1994 Beyond Strategic Planning – The Glenbow Example. *MUSE*, Vol. XI, No. 4, pp. 12–16.

1995 Museums and the Paradox of Change. *Western Museums Association Newsletter*, No. 4, pp. 1–3.

1995 Moore, J.S. and R.R. Janes. Pas de Deux: The Intricate Relationship between Business and the Arts – Comments and Criticism. *Business Quarterly*, Vol. 59, No. 4, pp. 18–20.

1996 Don't Lose Your Nerve: Museums and Organizational Change. *Museum Store*. Winter, Denver, Colorado, pp. 52–56, 76–77, 80.

1996 Museum Workers are the Alberta Advantage: Acceptance Speech at the Alberta Museums Association's Awards Presentation, Banff, Alberta. *Alberta Museums Review*, Vol. 22, No. 4, pp. 61–62.

1997 Opening Remarks. In *The Challenges of Exhibit Design for Diverse Audiences*. Proceedings of a Design Forum, 7 February. Calgary, Alberta, Canada: The Glenbow Museum, pp. 4–6.

1997 Don't Lose Your Nerve: Museums and Organizational Change. In *ACE Management Matters*, Newsletter of the Association of Cultural Executives, Waterloo, Ontario, April, pp. 1–5.

1998 Non-Profits Can Manage Too. *Alberta Museums Review*, Vol. 24, No. 2, September, pp. 22–25.

1998 Non-Profits Can Manage Too (Acceptance speech for the Association of Cultural Executive's 1998 ACE Award). In *ACE NEWS*, Annual General Meeting Issue II, December. Association of Cultural Executives, Waterloo, Ontario, pp. 1–6.

1998 Comment in "Mentoring Strategies for Museums and Museum Workers" by Dan Thorburn. *MUSE*, Vol. XVI, No. 4, p. 34.

1999 Museums and Change: Some Thoughts on Creativity, Destruction and Self-Organization. *Museum International*, Vol. 51, No. 2, pp. 4–11 (translated into French, Spanish and Russian).

1999 Repatriation Could Help Reshape Museums. *Museum Trusteeship* (Quarterly Publication of the Museum Trustee Association), Vol. 13, No. 1, Spring, p. 5.

1999 Non-Profits Can Manage, Too, *Arts Reach*, Vol. VII, No. 5, March, pp. 1, 19–22.

1999 Seeking Various Views of the Challenges, Opportunities, Choices and Trends in Museums in the New Century. *Alberta Museums Review*, Vol. 25, No. 2, Fall/Winter September, p. 6.

2000 Repatriation. *Alberta Views*, Vol. 3, No. 4, July/August, p. 18.

2001 Exploring Stewardship. *MUSE*, Vol. 19, No. 2, pp. 16–21.

2003 A Conversation with Robert Janes. Edited by Ken Tingley, *Alberta Museums Review*, Vol. 29, No. 1, Fall, pp. 11–28.

2004 Janes, R.R. and J. Kanigan-Fairen. Social Responsibility: A Saskatchewan Perspective. *MUSE*, Vol. 22, No. 5, pp. 42–45.

2008 Museums in a Troubled World: Making the Case for Socially Responsible Museums. *MUSE*, Vol. 26, No. 5, pp. 20–25.

2009 It's a Jungle in Here: Museums and Their Self-Inflicted Challenges. *MUSE*, Vol. 27, No. 5, pp. 30–33.

2013 Mission-Driven Performance Measurement: An Interview with Robert R. Janes. Edited by Dan Holbrow, *Museums and Sustainability*, Museums Association of Saskatchewan, pp. 14–15.

New media

2009 *Museums in a Troubled World* – video. Future of Museums, Center for the Future of Museums, American Alliance of Museums. Available online: http://www.youtube.com/watch?v=OSdvEtOxavs.

2010 *It's a Jungle in Here: Museums and Their Self-Inflicted Challenges*. The European Museum Academy Article of the Month. Available online: http://www.europeanmuseumacademy.eu/pdf/JungleInHere.pdf and http://www.europeanmuseumacademy.eu/pdf/NotesOn Contributor.pdf.

2011 *Songs of the Tvicho Drum Dance*. New Year's Eve 1982, Behchokǫ, Northwest Territories. CD Recording. Prince of Wales Northern Heritage Centre, Tvicho Government, the Dene Nation and CBC North, Yelloknife, Northwest Territories. Available online: http://www.nwtarchives.ca/item_display.asp?Accession_Number=N-1998-030& Item_Number=0115.

2012 *Museums and the Responsibility Gap* – video. Museums as Sites of Historical Consciousness Unconference, Museum of Vancouver, Canada. Available online: http://vimeo.com/46392120.

2012 *Do Something for Tomorrow* – video. Convocation Address. Western University, London, Ontario. Available online: http://www.youtube.com/watch?v=DL- 4caG0U20&list= PLbZM4TW_GWGS4evnQJkiyidlo4AjQxyeR&index=4.

2013 *What Are Museums For? – Revisiting "Museums in a Troubled World."* (with Morten Karnøe Søndergaard). The European Museum Academy Article of the Month. Available online: http://www.europeanmuseumacademy.eu/4/articles_of_the_month_406182.htm.

2013 *The Mindful Museum: Challenges and Opportunities in the 21st Century* – video. School of Museum Studies, The University of Leicester, United Kingdom. Available online: http://www.youtube.com/watch?v=mkXcm2ImwqQ.

2014 *Museums and Climate Change* – video. Future of Museums. Center for the Future of Museums, American Alliance of Museums. Available online: http://www.youtube.com/watch?v=d7PT_Ew0hhE&list=UUJ-kwlcPuvyC- T70DQC58tw&feature=share.

2014 *Museums in a Dangerous Time*. Center for the Future of Museums Blog, American Alliance of Museums. Available online: http://futureofmuseums.blogspot.ca/2014/06/museums-in-dangerous-time.

2014 *Museums in a Time of Change*. The Museum Life with Carol Bossert. VoiceAmerica Variety Channel (radio), 14 November 14. Available online: http://www.voiceamerica.com/episode/81428/museums-in-a-time-of- change?Refrerr=Pdf.

2015 We Are Coming Home: Repatriation and the Restoration of Blackfoot Cultural Confidence, August 25, 2015. Federation for the Humanities and Social Sciences. Available online: http://www.ideas-idees.ca/blog/we-are-coming-home-repatriation-and-restoration-blackfoot-cultural-confidence.

INDEX

AAM *see* American Association of
  Museums
Abbey, E. vi
Aboriginal Material Operating Policy
  (AMOP) 228
Abraham, M. 234
Abramovitz, J.N. 200
accountability: of government/private
  sector 355–7; of museums 218, 355
action learning cycle 177
Active Hope 188
activism 6–7, 20, 168, 212, 275, 354,
  355–6, 368–9, 382
admission fees 172, 289–90
AFN (Assembly of First Nations) 69n2
ambiguity 152
American Alliance of Museums (*formerly*
  American Association of Museums) 275,
  352, 389, 390
American Association of Museums (AAM)
  166, 170, 181, 275, 303(n44), 341, 352,
  366(n63)
American Federation of the Arts (AFA) 91
American Museum of Natural History
  (AMNH) 353–4, 381, 389–90
Ames, M.M. 59, 109, 211, 283, 290–1,
  294(n25)
AMOP (Aboriginal Material Operating
  Policy) 228
Anderson, G. 222, 303
Anderson, J.Q. 169
Anoee, E. 15

anthropology 32–3, 46, 55, 60
archaeology 49–51, 203–4
architecture 172, 305, 321–2, 323–5
Argyris, C. 68, 127
The Arts Business Exchange 219
Assembly of First Nations (AFN) 69n2
Assembly of First Nations/Canadian
  Museums Association 44; Task Force on
  Museums and First Peoples 41, 44–5,
  46n2, 52, 54, 58
Association of Art Museum Directors 319
Association of Science and Technology
  Centers 181
assumptions 8–10
Athapaskan *see* Dene people
Austin, J.E. 265(n21), 266(n2)
autonomous museums 233–4, 291–4
Avolio, B.J. 179

Baby Boomer generation 214–15, 281–2
bad museum behaviours 170–1
Badger, E. 305(n51)
Banff National Park 200
Barkley, B. 216
Barnhill, D.L. 17
Battilana, J. 305(n48)
Baumann, S.H. 233, 355(n27)
Beatty, S. 323(n32)
Beddington, J. 376
Beer, M.A. 108, 300(n33)
Bell, F.W. 352
Bennett, T. 211

Bergeron, A. 382(n34)
Bergeron, L. 304(n47)
Bernstein, B. 58
Berry, W. 4–5, 13n5, 164, 185, 187, 250, 359, 381, 384
BGCI (Botanic Gardens Conservation International) 358
"Bilbao Effect" 325–6
bioregionalism 230–1
biosphere 5, 6, 7, 8, 357, 360, 379
Blackfoot Confederacy 19, 20n2, 42, 47n5; Brave Dog Society 69; Kainai Nation 47n, 228, 238n2; sacred bundles 56n4, 62–4, 113, 122n2; universe 63
Block, P. 73, 145, 210, 216, 217, 218, 285(n6), 300(n30)
boards of directors 165–6, 167, 205
Boas, F. 69n3
Bohm, D. 138–9, 180
borders 2
Boston Museum of Fine Arts 379
Botanic Gardens Conservation International (BGCI) 358
Boyd, W.L. 109
Bradburne, J.M. 324–5, 327
branding 155, 195–6, 234–5
Bridges, W. 102
Brink, J. 58
British Museum 211, 341
Broad, E. 342
Brooks, D. 188
Brown, A.K. 144
Brown, J.E. 198, 206, 207, 212
Brown, M. 341
built environment 200
Bullock, A. 143, 213, 225, 226, 317(n11)
Burggraf, B. 104n2
Burton, C. 135, 213, 231
business literacy 194–5, 263–4, 333
business tribalism 260, 327–30
business–museum collaboration 259–67, 331–3
Butler, T. 365
Byrne, B. 45

California Association of Museums 180–1
CAM (Commonwealth Association of Museums) 156
Cameron, D.F. 211, 217
Cameron, F.R. 356
Canada: Federal Government 20n1; museum development 21
Canada Science and Technology Museum 173

Canadian Centre for Biodiversity (CCB) 357
Canadian Conservation Institute (CCI) 27, 156–7, 306
Canadian Council on Social Devleopment 232
Canadian Museum of History 27, 69n8
Canadian Museum of Nature, Ottawa 357
Canadian Museums Association (CMA) 29, 69n2, 169, 170, 181, 232, 305; see also Assembly of First Nations/Canadian Museums Association
Canadian War Museum 173
Canizzo, J. 29, 30, 31, 32, 33, 34
Capital Museum, Beijing 323
Capra, F. 131, 315(9), 376(n4), 387
Carding, J. 172–3
Carpenter, E. 58
Carter, B. 139
Carter, J.C. 90, 115
Case, M. 2, 106, 120
catagenesis 247
CCB (Canadian Centre for Biodiversity) 357
CCI see Canadian Conservation Institute
CEL (Community Economic Laboratory) 363–5
Center for the Future of Museums (CFM) 366–7
Centre for Civil Society, London School of Economics 225
change management see Glenbow Museum: organizational change
Chapin, H. 112
Charlton, J. 202–3
Cheney, T. 136, 231
Chicago Botanic Garden: Green Youth Farm 354
Children's Museum Pittsburgh 382
Chopra, D. 382(n33)
Christensen, L. 104n2
civil society 225–6; see also social capital; branding the civil society 234–5; Colorado River Project 230–1; definition 225; and museums 6, 7, 10, 226–7
Clavir, M. 60
Clifford, J. 60
climate change 273, 274f, 352–3, 356–7, 360, 377, 382–3, 389
Clore Leadership Programme (UK) 136
CMA see Canadian Museums Association
collaboration: autonomy and cooperation 291–4; co-management of collections 54–5; federal organization 291–4, 305;

on funding of solutions 354; museum clusters 157, 249; museum–business collaboration 259–67, 331–3; union–management collaboration 100–1
collections: access 61, 62, 227; costs 155, 204; as knowledge seed banks 250, 359–60, 364, 380–1; management of 54–5, 204, 243, 290, 303; sanctity of 164–5; and social capital 228–9
Colorado River Project 230–1
Commonwealth Association of Museums (CAM) 156
communication 176, 216–17, 222–3, 231–2
community 25–6, 35–6, 191, 193, 379–80
community centres 26
Community Economic Laboratory (CEL) 363–5
complexity 6, 134–5, 137–43, 152–3, 345
Conaty, G.T. 54, 57, 58, 60, 65, 69n6, 139, 144, 145, 155, 189–90, 207, 235
Confino, J. 378(n17)
conflict 132
Connor, S. 246(n13)
Conroy, F. 7–8, 146, 187, 196, 284(n3), 290
conservation 60, 298
corporatism 258–9, 311–12, 391; accommodating corporatism 232–5; beyond corporatism 224–5, 340; lifespan of corporations 261, 318–19; museum corporatism 223–4, 243, 340–1, 389, 390; philanthropy 329–30, 331–3
Corpus Christi Museum of Science and History, Texas 306
Cranmer Webster, G. 45
creativity 145
Crew, S.R. 105–6, 119, 121
Crowshoe, R. 55
Cruikshank, J. 60
Crutchfield, L.R. 361(n44), 382(n32)
Csikszentmihalyi, M. 319, 327(n49)
Cultural Creatives 192–3
cultural diversity xi, 17, 55, 242
cultural tourism 325, 326–7
culture 275, 321–3, 364, 382
customer service 284–5

Dahrendorf, R. 226, 227
Dallet, N. 230
Dana, J.C. 217
David, N. 56n3
Davies, M. 320
Davis, J.A. 8, 174, 383(n41), 387

de Geus, A. 140, 143, 205, 225, 318–19, 333–4, 347(n3), 370(n75)
de Pree, M. 103, 106, 131, 301(n34)
deaccessioning 83, 109, 121, 126, 164
DeCarlo, S. 329(n52)
Declaration of the Importance and Value of Universal Museums 20
Delicado, A. 245
DeMallie, R. 60, 61
Demos 137, 235, 245
Dempsey, H. 41
Dene people 3, 12n1, 18, 22, 28n1, 38n1; culture 49, 51; history and language 36, 56n2; material culture 25–6, 34, 38, 204
Denmark 265–6
Detroit Institute of Arts (DIA) 172
DeVore, I. 260(n11), 327(n48)
Dewees, S. 232
DiCosimo, J. 83, 207
Dirty Oil Sands 389
disability in museums 358
divisible vs indivisible benefits 202
Dodd, J. 1, 358
double-loop thinking 127
Drucker, P.F. 127, 128, 137–8, 145, 149, 368
dualism 17, 201
Dumka, H. 60

earned revenues 166–7
ecology 17, 159, 189, 349–50, 379–80, 387
economic growth 192, 223, 339–40, 350
economics 5, 202–3
The Economist 110
Economopoulos, B. 389, 390
Edsall, T.B. 378(n19)
educational resource centres 26
Ehrlich, A.H. 273, 376, 377(n13), 378(n20), 380(n26)
Ehrlich, P.R. 273, 376, 377(n13), 378(n20), 380(n26)
Eisler, R. 207
Elgin, D. 218
Ellis, A. 224, 236, 246, 323(n33), 324, 327
Ellis, E. 342
emotional intelligence 193–4
EnCana Corporation 331–3
environmental controls 18, 24–5, 45–6, 157, 262, 360
environmental problems 153–4, 258, 273, 376–7
Eskimo see Inuit
ethical responsibilities for museum management 343–4, 347, 351–2, 369–71; see also social responsibility;

accountability of government/private sector 355–7; collaborating on funding of solutions 354; Community Economic Laboratory 363–5; forces for good 360–2; framework 368–9; the future 366–8, 369–71; Happy Museum Project 361, 365–6; maintaining and sharing collections 359–60; museums and the plutocracy 341–3; museums and their tacit silence 343; problem solving 353–4; public advocacy 352–3, 361; research 357–9; scenario planning 347–51, 348f; Transition Towns 362–3
ethnoarchaeology 51, 56n3
Evans, D. 284(n4)
exhibitions 26, 33–4, 60, 112, 119, 128, 173, 243, 296–7
Exploratorium 361

Fairtlough, G. 139
Falk, J.H. 236
Farson, R. 138, 205
federal organization 291–4, 305
Federation of International Human Rights Museums 361
Feest, C.F. 57–8, 64–5, 66–7
Ferguson, R. 235
fiduciary trust 52
Field Museum 382(n36)
finances 236; *see also* Glenbow Museum: organizational change; admission fees 172, 289–90; collaborating on funding of solutions 354; earned revenues 166–7; executive salaries 328–9; money as measure of worth 319–21; personal agency 176
Financial Post 280
financial sustainability 181, 263, 285–7, 303–5, 314–15
First Nations 48–9, 205–6; *see also* Blackfoot Confederacy; Dene people; First Nations and museums; Glenbow Museum, Calgary; Nis'gaa First Nation; in Alberta 19; an academic view 51; and Christianity 64, 66; Great Council of Animals 207–8, 212; and human rights 19–20; in NWT 18, 19; a personal view 49–51; repatriation 40–1, 64–6; sacred objects 54–5, 62–4
First Nations and museums 59–61; fiduciary trust 52; issues 51–2; professional standards 53–4; prospects 54–5; trust 53
Flower, J. 107, 117
Fontana, D. 150

Ford Excursion 199
Fortmann, L.P. 162
Foster, N. 331
Franklin, U.M. 201, 202, 203, 207
Freudenheim, T. 320
Frey, T. 378(n18)
Friedman, A.J. 181–2
Fritz, R. 68, 103
Fuller, B. 295
Fulton, K. 140
the future 9, 189, 191–2, 244, 301–2, 388–92; age of disruption 376–8; branding, knowledge, and consumption 195–6; business literacy 194–5; Cultural Creatives 192–3; executive leadership 193–4; museum and the community 191, 193, 379–80; quality of life vs economic growth 192; sleepwalking into the future 378–9; taking action 380–4

Gait, V. 138, 140
Galbraith, J.K. 93, 107
Garnier, A. 104n2
Garvin, D.A. 67
Gehry, F. 325
Getty Leadership Institute (USA) 136
Getty Trust 379
Gifford, R. 389
Glasgow Museum Resource Centre [Scotland] (GMRC) 228–9
Glenbow Alberta Institute Act (1966) 121
Glenbow Enterprises 84, 99, 110, 116, 120–1, 126
Glenbow Library and Archives 62, 75, 82, 85, 99, 107, 125, 300
Glenbow Magazine 82
Glenbow Museum, Calgary 6–7, 107–8; access to collections 61, 62; environmental controls 45–6; First Nations Advisory Council 45, 52, 53, 54, 61–2; *First Nations Policy* 61–2; future possibilities 44–5; issues 19, 51–5; MOU with Mookaakin Society 228; Native Affairs Group 54; policy and practice 41–2, 61–2; professional standards 53–4; prospects 54–5; repatriation 42–3; *Sacred Loans Policy* 62; sacred objects 62–4, 65, 113; "Spirit Sings" exhibition 41, 47n3; trust 52, 53
Glenbow Museum: organizational change 10, 75–8, 80–92, 93–104, 105–22, 124–6, 313–14; Board of Governors 82, 84, 205; business processes 109, 125; commercial activities 109–10,

126, 313; considerations, speculation, advice 90–1; corporate and strategic plans 94, 331; deaccessioning 83, 109, 121, 126; a difficult apprenticeship 103; exhibitions 112, 119, 128; finance and funding 75, 80, 82, 83, 94–5, 103, 111, 125, 285–6, 289–90, 313–14; issues and concerns 89; knowledge and self-organization 113–14; layoffs 98, 100–1, 110–11, 119–20; leadership 114–15, 119, 120, 121–2, 278–82; learning 118–19; managing change 87–9, 100; the marketplace 117; neutral zone 102; new organization 96–9, 109, 125; opportunities and prospects 112–15; paradoxes and hazards 115–18; power sharing 113, 119; projects, activities, innovations 81–4; public service 109, 125; reflection 81; self-reference 116; senior management 83–4; six strategies 95, 108–10, 125–6; staff 82–3; staff perspectives 84–7; survivor's syndrome 101–2; union–management collaboration 100–1, 119–20; volunteers 83; discussion 119–22

Glenbow Museum School 112, 128–9
Glenbow Society 82
GMB (Guggenheim Museum Bilbao) 325–6
GMRC (Glasgow Museum Resource Centre [Scotland]) 228–9
Goler, R. 120
Gopnik, A. 150, 264(n19), 370(n74), 384(n45)
Gosselin, V. 364(n57)
governance 165–6, 175, 204–5
government 173, 355–7
Graham, M.S. 357(n32)
Grant, H.M. 361(n44), 382(n32)
Grasset, C.D. 211
Grattan, N. 223, 224, 324(n334)
Gray, C. 4
Green Museum Accord 180–1
Green Museum Initiative 180
Greenleaf, R.K. 114, 115, 137, 141, 142, 279
Greenspan, A. 202–3
Greer, J. M. 271, 273, 275, 378
Griffin, D.J.G. 107, 234
Grimes, J.R. 379
Gross, R. 368, 382(n38)
Gross, W. 322
Grove, R. 217
Grudin, R. 318, 330
Gstraunthaler, T. 321(n24)

Guggenheim Museum Bilbao (GMB) 325–6
Gulf Canada 121
Gurian, E.H. 2
Guthe, C.E. 23

Haas, J. 68
habitat loss 200
Hafsteinsson, S.B. 257(n5)
Handy, C. 10, 67, 97, 115–16, 126, 130, 131, 137, 140, 191, 201, 218, 219, 252, 262, 283, 286(n7), 288, 291–3, 302, 384(n46)
Happy Museum Project 361, 365–6
Hardin, G. 52, 81
Harrison, J. et al. 4, 58, 76
Hart, S. 90
Hart, T. 90
Harvard Business Review 262
Hatton, A. 288(n9)
Hawken, P. et al. 153, 154, 206, 375(n2)
Hayward, A. 99, 104n2, 227
health care 138, 275, 355–6, 383
Heath, J. 233, 234
Hegel, G.W.F. 225
Heifer Village Museum and Foundation, Little Rock 249
Heinberg, R. 259, 340, 350(n10), 363(n52), 370(n72), 384(n44)
Henderson, H. 202, 350(n13)
Heye Foundation 40
Hicks, D.W. 246(n16)
hierarchy and hierarchical structures 96, 114, 138–9, 158, 174, 179, 243, 391; at Glenbow 75, 76, 86, 95, 125; the lone CEO 114, 120, 136, 167, 279–80, 361
Hill Strategies Research Inc. 231
Hill, T. 44, 45, 52
Hill, Y. 58
Hinshaw, R. 28, 46
Hobsbawm, E. 311, 319
Hoekstra, G. 355(n26)
Hoffer, E. 198
Hoffman, A.J. 356, 383(n39)
Holden, J. 245(n10)
Holocaust Memorial Foundation of Illinois 323
home economics 5
Homer-Dixon, T. 160n1, 242(n3), 247, 349, 370(n73)
Honda Motor Company 129
Hooper-Greenhill, E. 158, 237
Hopkins, R. 363(n53)
Hout, T.M. 90, 115
Hudson, A. 224, 324(n335)

human rights 19–20
humanness 9
Hume, C. 212, 223, 224
Hutcheon, L. 61
hybrid organizations 305, 370
hypocrisy 329–30

ICI *see* Inuit Cultural Institute
identity 132
IHT *see* Inuit Heritage Trust
IKON-project 265
individualism 214
InnoCentive 248
Institute for Media, Policy and Civil
    Society 235
Institute of Museum and Library Services
    (US) 248
Institute of Museum Ethics (IME) 341,
    366–7
intellectual activism 368, 382–3
intellectual sustainability 181–2
interconnectedness 217
International Coalition of Sites of
    Conscience 361
International Council of Museums
    305(n49)
International Forum on the Creative
    Economy 323
Inuit 18, 19–20, 22, 26, 28n1, 38n1,
    41, 46n1
Inuit Cultural Institute (ICI) 26, 36
Inuit Heritage Trust (IHT) 36, 39n4

Jacknis, I. 69n3
Jackson, T. 111
Jacobsen, L. 41
James, W. 188
Janes, R.R. xi, 3, 10, 34, 50f, 51, 58,
    104n2, 105–6, 144, 145, 154, 155, 188,
    205, 226, 234, 235, 255, 256, 389
Jantsch, E. 109, 125
Jaworski, J. 138–9
Jeffrey, C. 334(n69)
Johnson K.G. et al. 360(n42)
Johnson, S.S. 127, 156
Johnstone, C. 188, 274, 387, 391
Joiner, W.B. 102
Jones, C. 358(n35)

Kabat-Zinn, J. 142, 150–1, 217, 237
Kainai Nation 47n5, 228, 238n2
Kane, H. 200
Kanter, R.M. 140, 266(n24)
Kaplan, A. 4
Karnøe, M. 256(n2), 256(n4)

Katz, M.M. 389
Katz, P. 166
Kaufer, K. 376(n5)
Kaye, F. 108
Keating, C. et al. 132
Keene, S. 227, 232, 243(n5)
Kellner-Rogers, M. 196
Kimmelman, M. 223
Kingwell, M. 214, 223, 310
Kirchberg, V. 231
knowledge: and power 67–9; seed
    banks 250, 359–60, 364, 380–1; and
    self-organization 113–14; sharing 145–6
Knustler, J. 246
Koch, D.H. 389–90
Koestler, A. 252
Korten, D.C. 340, 343, 391
Koster, E.H. 233, 355(n27)
Kotler, N. 234
Kotler, N.G. et al. 155
Kotler, P. 234
Kotter, J.P. 139, 141
Kramer, C. 56n3
Kramer, M.R. 262(n14), 340
Krug, K. et al 139
Kuhn, T.S. 162
Kunstler, J.H. 359, 368(n68), 383(n43)
Kusel, J. 162

languages 30, 56n2, 200
Lapierre, L. 145
Lasch, C. 203
layoffs 98, 100–1, 110–11, 119–20
leadership 129, 136–7, 146, 204, 279;
    executive leadership 193–4; the lone
    CEO 114, 120, 136, 167, 279–80, 361;
    and management 141–2, 175, 299–301;
    primus inter pares 114–15, 119, 167, 278,
    280–2; Principle of Systematic Neglect
    141–2; training 136
leading up 179
learning 8–9, 67–8, 132, 298–9
learning organizations 67–8, 118–19
Ledbetter, E. 341–2
Lee, R.B. 260(n11), 327(n48)
Leka, S. et al. 138
Lenzner, R. 127
Leonard, G. 217, 219
Leone, M. et al. 61
Levit, R. 223
Levy, E. 223
Lezner, R. 156
Liberty Science Center (LSC), Jersey City
    355–6, 361
Libeskind, D. 322

Lim-Yuson, N. 352
Limfjordsmuseet, Løgstør 265–6
Locke, C. 139
Lohman, J. 354
Lopez, B. 206, 220
Lord, G. 325(n41)
Lorway, C. 326
Louvre Museum, Paris 323
Lowrance, W.W. 48, 284
LSC *see* Liberty Science Center

McArthur, K. 199
McCall, V. 4
McDonald, J. et al. 60
McGhee, R. 61
McKenzie, B. 170, 347–9, 359
Mackenzie River survey 49–51, 50f, 56n1
McKeough, R. 89
McKibben, B. 160n1, 212, 214, 215, 335
McKinsey & Company 379
McLean, K. 173, 243(n6)
McMaster, G. 45
McMullen Art Gallery, Edmonton 230
Macy, J. 28, 188, 274, 387, 391
Makah Cultural Centre Ozette,
    Washington 60
management *see* museum management
Manitoba Museum 54, 382
Marien, M. 377
marketing: anatomy of failure 317–30;
    debunking the marketplace 130–1,
    310–35; museum attendance 135–6;
    reforming the marketplace 117, 233
Marshall, G. 275
Marstine, J. 352
Martin, A. 135, 231
Marty, P.F. 302
Matanovic, M. 193
material culture: conservation research
    60; Dene people 25–6, 34, 38, 204;
    Northwest Territories, Canada
    (NWT) 25–6
May, E. 377(n14)
Médecins Sans Frontières (MSF) 2
memory 274, 275
Merrill, W.J. et al. 58
Metis 18, 19–20, 22, 28n1, 38n1
Metropoolitan Museum of Art 379
Milewski, T. 369(n71)
Millar, J. 3
mindfulness 5, 149–60; ambiguity 152;
    becoming more mindful 152–3; chaotic
    cascades 150–1; characteristics of
    153–4; consequences of inaction 158–9;
    ecological metaphor 159; exemplars of

2, 3, 156–7, 366; museum chatter 151,
    153; museum clusters 157; negative
    people 151–2; opportunities 155–6;
    post-museums 158
Minister's Round Table 200
Mintzberg, H. 127, 140, 191, 204
Mish, F.C. 198
mission statements 257–8
MMC (Museum Management and Curatorship)
    177–8
MOA *see* Museum of Anthropology,
    Vancouver
Mookaakin Society 228
Moore, K. 77
More, Sir Thomas 189
Morgan, G. 98, 126, 127, 244, 301(n35)
Morris, M. 107, 165, 194, 263(n18), 333
MSF (Médecins Sans Frontières) 2
multidisciplinary teams 54, 80, 84, 98, 114,
    139, 229, 298
Murphy, M. 217, 219
MUSE 29
Museo Pambata, Manila 352, 361
museum chatter 151, 153
museum clusters 157, 249
museum conferences 168–70
Museum Directors' Group (*later* Museums
    Anonymous) 80, 91, 92n2
museum management 134–47; *see also*
    ethical responsibilities for museum
    management; Glenbow Museum:
    organizational change; leadership;
    social responsibility; admission fees
    172, 289–90; bad museum behaviours
    170–1; complexity 134–5, 137–43,
    344–5; conferences 168–70; creativity
    145; directors 165–6, 167, 205;
    earned revenues 166–7; government
    intervention 173; honouring the
    practitioner/scholar 3, 177–9; insularity,
    diffidence, arrogance 170; limits to
    growth 143–4; marketing issues 135–6;
    meditations on magical beliefs 163–4;
    miscellaneous impositions 171–3;
    neutrality 164; "No People" 179–80;
    personal agency 8, 174–7; reflexive
    management 139–40; sanctity of
    collections 164–5; second curve thinking
    140–1; self-organization 113–14,
    129–30, 138–9; self-reference 116, 144;
    strengthening management 173–82;
    sustainability 180–2; towards a new
    paradigm 162–3; workers 8, 165, 174–7
Museum Management and Curatorship (MMC)
    177–8

Museum of Anthropology, Vancouver
(MOA) 139, 286–7
Museum of East Anglian Life (UK) 365
Museum of London 354
Museum Planning (blog) 172
museum studies departments 136, 167, 178
Museum Victoria, Melbourne 248
museum workers 8, 165, 174–7
MuseumLink 172
museums: bearing witness 250–1, 382–3;
    as brains 127; bridging cultures 382; in
    the community 193; as creators of social
    capital 194, 227; defining characteristics
    of 380–3; diversity 250, 381; freedom to
    choose and act 383; as keepers of locality
    250, 381–2; as machines 127; number
    of 288–94, 305–6; and the plutocracy
    341–3; as political systems 127; private
    museums 342–3; as seed banks 250,
    359–60, 364, 380–1; stereotypes 294–5;
    three agendas 243–4; vital signs 132
Museums Anonymous *see* Museum
    Directors' Group
Museums Association (UK) 164, 181, 320,
    390
Museums in a Troubled World 255–9;
    hands-on perspective 265–7; discussion:
    museum–business collaboration 259–65

National Film Board of Canada 106
National Institute of Museums, Rwanda
    354
National Museum of American History 107
National Museum of Australia 381
National Museum of the American Indian
    40–1
National Museums Corporation (NMC)
    27, 293
National Portrait Gallery (England) 341
Native American Graves Protection and
    Repatriation Act (NAGPRA) 58, 65
Native Americans 40–1, 46n1, 206, 220
Natural History Museum (NHM), New
    York 389, 390*f*
Nee, E. 247(n21)
negative people 151–2, 179–80
Nelson, R. 241–2, 340, 345, 380(n27)
Nelson, R.F. 258(n7)
neutrality 164
New Museology 4
Newman, R. 341
Nicks, T. 44, 45, 52, 58
Nis'gaa First Nation 69n8
NMC *see* National Museums Corporation
Nordic museums 255–6, 265–7

Northwest Territories, Canada (NWT)
    17–28, 29–30; *see also* Prince of
    Wales Northern Heritage Centre;
    archaeological fieldwork 49–51;
    community centres 26; community
    participation 25–6; cultural awareness 28,
    37–8; educational resource centres 26;
    environmental controls 24–5; exhibitions
    26; land and people 22–3, 22*f*, 30;
    languages 30, 56n2; material culture
    25–6; Native museums 26–7; political
    setting 23, 30, 37; research 27
Not An Alternative 389
Nunavut 38n3, 39n4
Nyhan, P. 335(n71)

Ohmae, K. 144
O'Neill, M. 238n3
organization 6–7, 204–5; adaptive
    organizations 300–1; federal organization
    291–4, 305; hybrid organizations 305,
    370; and mindfulness 154
organizational change; *see also* Glenbow
    Museum: organizational change:
    current realities 126; the marketplace
    as cautionary tale 130–1; organization
    as metaphor 126–8; the past is not the
    future 128–9; self-organization and
    shared responsibility 129–30, 131
orthogonal thinking 237
Owen, H. 114

paradoxes and hazards 115–16, 283–4, 302;
    customer service 284–5, 302–3; fulfilling
    potential 294–6, 306; the future 301–2;
    Glenbow Museum 115–18; number of
    museums 288–94, 305–6; power and
    privilege 299–301; sustainability 285–7,
    303–5; tyranny of tradition 296–9, 306
Pascale, R. et al. 132
Paul Hamlyn Foundation 304, 365–6
PD (Positive Deviance) 248
Peacock, D. 2, 6, 76, 168–9, 302(41)
Peers, L. 144
performance measures 320–1
performers and learners 68
Perl, J. 223
personal agency 8, 174–7, 383, 387–8
Pew Research Centre 167
Phillips, W. 107, 129, 243(n7)
Phipps Conservatory and Botanical Garden,
    Pittsburgh 388*f*
Piber, M. 321(n24)
Pickus, K. 265(n20)
The Pinky Show 163

Plaza, B. 325–6
Please Touch Museum, Philadelphia 323
Pogrebin, R. 329(n55)
Pointe, S. 230, 233
Porter, M. 157, 249
Porter, M.E. 262(n14), 340
Positive Deviance (PD) 248
post-museums 158, 237
Postman, N. vi, 9, 112, 188, 198, 203, 219, 294(n24), 299(n29), 368, 369, 375(n1), 387
postmodernism 207, 214–15
Potter, A. 233, 234
power and privilege 67–8, 132, 299–301
Powers, W.K. 65
primus inter pares 114–15, 119, 167, 278, 280–2
Prince of Wales Northern Heritage Centre (PWNHC) 3–4, 6, 17–19, 21–2, 31–8, 31f, 314; collection 18, 23; community participation 35–6; empowerment 36–7; environmental controls 18, 24–5, 45–6; exhibitions 33–4; Heritage Advisory Services 35–6; history and role 31–2, 312; ideology 32–3; Indigenous representation 34–7
private museums 342–3
problem solving 353–4
professional standards 53–4, 366
proprietorship 291
public advocacy 352–3, 361
public programming 155–6
Putnam, R.D. 227

quality of life vs economic growth 192
Quinn, J.B. et al. 113, 114
Quinn, R. 90

Rainie, L. 169
Rand, T. 273
rapid response groups 154, 298
Ray, P.H. 192
RBCM *see* Royal British Columbia Museum
reductionism 201
repatriation 219; Canadian view 58; European view 57–8; and First Nations 40–1, 64–6; Glenbow Museum 42–3; and restitution 64–5; discussion 66–8
research and development 27, 60, 77, 243, 287–8, 357–8, 358–9
Research Centre for Museums and Galleries (RCMG) 358
resilience 246–7, 363
restitution 64–5

Ridington, R. 60
Ridley, M. 146f
Rifkin, J. 131, 159, 213, 246, 261(n13), 317(n10), 317(n12), 334
Roberts, P. 199
Robinson, L. 192
Robinson, M.P. 261(n12), 331–3
roles and responsibilities of museums 5, 6, 7, 10; *see also* ethical responsibilities for museum management; social responsibility; stewardship
Romm, J. 377(n12)
Rosenman, M. 329(n56)
Roshi, S. 139
Royal British Columbia Museum (RBCM) 69n8, 228, 354
Royal Ontario Museum (ROM) 172, 321–2
Royal Saskatchewan Museum (RSM) 54, 357–8
Royal Tyrrell Museum, Drumheller 290–1
Russo, A. 302(41)

Sabau, M. 325(n41)
Sachs, J.D. 343, 351–2
sacred bundles 54–5, 56n4, 62–4, 65–7, 113, 122n2
Said, E. 67
Sandell, R. x–xii, 1, 144, 243(n4), 358
Saul, J.R. 116, 117, 177, 310–11, 392
Savage, J. 306(n52)
Scearce, D. 140
scenario planning 140, 347–51, 348f
Scharmer, O. 376(n5)
scholar-practitioners 3, 177–9
School of Museum Studies, University of Leicester, UK 358
Schuker, L.A.E. 342
Schwab, K. 369
Schwartz, P. 140, 347(n3)
Schwarzer, M. 303, 359
Science Institute of the Northwest Territories (SINT) 312–13, 314
Scott, C. 135, 213, 231, 234
Scott, K. 232
second curve thinking 140–1
self-actualization 126
self-criticism 258
self-organization 6, 138–9; and knowledge 113–14; and shared responsibility 129–30, 131
self-reference 116, 144
Semmel, M.L. 177
Senge, P. 302(n37)
Seton Hall University 341

shamrock organization 97, 286
Sheppard, B.K. 236
Simon, N. 75, 78
SINT *see* Science Institute of the
   Northwest Territories
Skolnik, S. 335(n71)
Small, L. 329
Smithsonian Institution 40–1, 105, 106,
   144, 329, 389–90
Snow, C.P. 382(n35)
social capital 213–14, 226; art and healing
   230; and collections 228–9; defined 227;
   museums and bioregionalism 230–1;
   museums as creators of 194, 227–8
social ecology 17, 189
social entrepreneurship 361
social justice 18
Social Justice Alliance for Museums (UK)
   383
social responsibility 6, 144–6, 168, 187–90,
   251*f*, 257–8, 304–5; *see also* ethical
   responsibilities for museum management;
   assumptions and biases 219–20; the
   future 191–6; history 210–11; insularity
   170; museum conferences 168–70;
   purpose and sustainability 145, 211–15;
   values 145, 216–19
social sustainability 182
Søndergaard, M.K. 190, 255, 256–7,
   259–64
Soros, G. 130
Spalding, J. 168, 291, 298
Stacey, R.D. 9, 127, 128, 129, 138, 139,
   140, 369(n70)
Starnes, R. 106
stasis/change 9–10
Statistics Canada 166, 231
Steele K. 245(n9), 380(n25)
Steinberg, E. 188, 375(n3)
Stern, S. 328(n51), 329(n53)
stewards or spectators? 241–2; beyond
   tradition 248–9; consequences of
   inattentiveness 245–6; the future 244;
   myopia 244–5; new thinking for new
   vision 247–8; in praise of museums
   249–51; resilience 246–7; stresses 242–3;
   three agendas 243–4
stewardship 5, 6, 198–9, 258; *see also*
   stewards or spectators?; assault on
   stewardship 199–203; building on
   strengths 203–6; definition 198;
   sharpening our skills 206–7
Stocking, G.W., Jr. 59
strategic planning *see* Glenbow Museum:
   organizational change

Sturtevant, W.C. 58
Suchy, S. 193–4
survivor's syndrome 101–2
sustainability 211–15, 266, 363, 379,
   384; beyond green 181–2; financial
   sustainability 181, 263, 285–7, 303–5,
   314–15; greening the museum 180–1;
   research and development 287–8; social
   sustainability 182

Tate (England) 188*f*, 341
Tax, S. 28, 46
Te Papa (Museum of New Zealand) 229
Telfair Museum of Art, Savannah 323
Territorial Museum Policy 31
Terry, R.W. 127, 131
themes 6–8
Thomas, D.H. 58
Thorsell, W. 321–2
Tien, C. 157, 249
Toepler, S. 231, 232
Touchstones Nelson 383
Tough, P. 110
tourism 325, 326–7
Toynbee, A.J. 222
tradition 5, 6, 9, 296, 306; beyond tradition
   248–9, 264, 296–9
Transition Towns 362–3
Traub, J. 106
Treanor, J. 335(n72)
Trombley, S. 143, 213, 225, 226,
   317(n11)
trust 52, 53
Tuttle, B. 382(n34)
Tuxill, J. 200
Tyler B. 92n2

values 145, 154, 216–19, 261, 315–17;
   brands 234–5; and methods 333–4
Van Mensch, P. 222
Vogel, M.L.V. 58

Walmsley, A. 118
Water Smart Home 248
Weil, S.E. vi, 2, 115, 147, 158, 162, 163,
   174, 222, 223, 231, 232, 237, 238, 256,
   289, 293(n21)
Weisman, A. 351(n14)
Weisskopf, T.E. 131
Weisskopf, W. 263(n17)
West, W.R., Jr. 58
Western Development Museum,
   Saskatchewan 360
Wetenhall, J. 319
Whalley, G. 217

Wheatley, M.J. 116, 117, 118, 129–30, 137, 144, 152–3, 158, 160, 196, 251(n32)
White, E.B. 118
Wilber, K. 214, 218
Wilkinson, H. 320
Wilson, E.O. 150, 160n1, 201, 202, 207, 252, 350
Wilson, T.H. et al. 58
Wood, E. 5
Woodhouse, M.B. 198, 201, 207, 215
Woodhurst (2005) 138
work design 176

work environment 175
World Economic Forum 344–5, 369
Worts, D. 246, 364(n58)
Wright, R. 349

Yakaleya, E. 50f
Yakaleya, J. 50f
Yellowknife *see* Northwest Territories; Prince of Wales Northern Heritage Centre

Zernan, J. 207, 215

eBooks
from Taylor & Francis

Helping you to choose the right eBooks for your Library

Add to your library's digital collection today with Taylor & Francis eBooks. We have over 50,000 eBooks in the Humanities, Social Sciences, Behavioural Sciences, Built Environment and Law, from leading imprints, including Routledge, Focal Press and Psychology Press.

Choose from a range of subject packages or create your own!

Benefits for you

- Free MARC records
- COUNTER-compliant usage statistics
- Flexible purchase and pricing options
- All titles DRM-free.

Benefits for your user

- Off-site, anytime access via Athens or referring URL
- Print or copy pages or chapters
- Full content search
- Bookmark, highlight and annotate text
- Access to thousands of pages of quality research at the click of a button.

Free Trials Available
We offer free trials to qualifying academic, corporate and government customers.

eCollections

Choose from over 30 subject eCollections, including:

Archaeology	Language Learning
Architecture	Law
Asian Studies	Literature
Business & Management	Media & Communication
Classical Studies	Middle East Studies
Construction	Music
Creative & Media Arts	Philosophy
Criminology & Criminal Justice	Planning
Economics	Politics
Education	Psychology & Mental Health
Energy	Religion
Engineering	Security
English Language & Linguistics	Social Work
Environment & Sustainability	Sociology
Geography	Sport
Health Studies	Theatre & Performance
History	Tourism, Hospitality & Events

For more information, pricing enquiries or to order a free trial, please contact your local sales team:
www.tandfebooks.com/page/sales

www.tandfebooks.com